IBM® PC ASSEMBLY LANGUAGE AND PROGRAMMING

Fourth Edition

Peter Abel

Professor Emeritus
British Columbia
Institute of Technology

PRENTICE HALL, Upper Saddle River, New Jersey 07458

Library of Congress Cataloging-in-Publication Data

Abel, Peter. 1932-
IBM PC assembly language and programming / by Peter Abel. — 4th ed.
p. cm.
Includes index.
ISBN 0-13-756610-7
1. IBM Personal Computer—Programming. 2. Assembler language (Computer program language) I. Title. II. Title: IBM PC assembly language and programming.
QA76.8.I2594A236 1998
005.265—DC21 97-8688
CIP

Associate editor: Alice Dworkin
Editor in Chief: Marcia Horton
Production editor: Ann Marie Longobardo
Copy editor: Marjorie Shustak
Director of production and manufacturing: David W. Riccardi
Managing editor: Bayani Mendoza de Leon
Cover designer: Bruce Kenselaar
Manufacturing buyer: Donna Sullivan
Editorial assistant: Dolores Mars

Printed in the United States of America

10 9 8 7 6 5 4 3 2

ISBN 0-13-756610-7

Prentice-Hall International (UK) Limited, London
Prentice-Hall of Australia Pty. Limited, Sydney
Prentice-Hall Canada Inc., Toronto
Prentice-Hall Hispanoamericana, S.A., Mexico
Prentice-Hall of India Private Limited, New Delhi
Prentice-Hall of Japan, Inc., Tokyo
Simon & Schuster Asia Pte. Ltd., Singapore
Editora Prentice-Hall do Brasil, Ltda., Rio de Janeiro\

Contents

PREFACE *xiii*

Part A Fundamentals of PC Hardware and Software **1**

1 BASIC FEATURES OF PC HARDWARE *1*

Introduction 1
Bits and Bytes 1
Binary Numbers 3
Hexadecimal Representation 6
ASCII Code 7
The Processor 7
Internal Memory 9
Segments and Addressing 11
Registers 13
Key Points 17
Questions 18

2 REQUIREMENTS FOR USING PC SOFTWARE *20*

Introduction 20
Features of the Operating System 20
The Boot Process 21
Input-Output Interface 22
The System Program Loader 22

The Stack 23
Addressing of Instructions and Data 25
Instruction Operands 27
Key Points 27
Questions 28

3 *EXECUTING COMPUTER INSTRUCTIONS* 29

Introduction 29
Using the DEBUG Program 30
Viewing Memory Locations 31
Machine Language Example I: Immediate Data 34
Machine Language Example II: Defined Data 38
An Assembly Language Example 41
Using the INT Instruction 42
Saving a Program from Within DEBUG 45
Using the PTR Operator 45
Key Points 46
Questions 47

Part B Fundamentals of Assembly Language **49**

4 *REQUIREMENTS FOR CODING IN ASSEMBLY LANGUAGE* 49

Introduction 49
Assemblers and Compilers 50
Program Comments 50
Reserved Words 51
Identifiers 51
Statements 52
Directives 53
Instructions for Initializing a Program 57
Instructions for Ending Program Execution 59
Example of a Source Program 59
Initializing for Protected Mode 60
Simplified Segment Directives 61
Data Definition 62
Directives for Defining Data 65
The EQU Directive 69
Key Points 70
Questions 71

5 *ASSEMBLING, LINKING, AND EXECUTING A PROGRAM* 73

Introduction 73
Preparing a Program for Execution 73

Assembling a Source Program 74
Using Conventional Segment Definitions 76
Using Simplified Segment Directives 81
Two-Pass Assembler 83
Linking an Object Program 83
Executing a Program 86
Cross-Reference Listing 86
Error Diagnostics 87
The Assembler Location Counter 89
Key Points 89
Questions 89

6 *SYMBOLIC INSTRUCTIONS AND ADDRESSING* 91

Introduction 91
The Symbolic Instruction Set 91
Instruction Operands 94
The MOV Instruction 97
Move-and-Fill Instructions 98
Immediate Operands 99
The XCHG Instruction 100
The LEA Instruction 101
The INC and DEC Instructions 101
Extended Move Operations 101
The INT Instruction 103
Aligning Data Addresses 104
Near and Far Addresses 104
The Segment Override Prefix 105
Key Points 105
Questions 106

7 *WRITING .COM PROGRAMS* 108

Introduction 108
Differences Between an .EXE and a .COM Program 108
Converting into .COM Format 109
Example of a .COM Program 110
The .COM Stack 111
Debugging Tips 112
Key Points 112
Questions 113

8 *PROGRAMMING REQUIREMENTS FOR LOGIC AND CONTROL* 114

Introduction 114
Short, Near, and Far Addresses 115

Instruction Labels 115
The JMP Instruction 116
The LOOP Instruction 118
The Flags Register 119
The CMP Instruction 120
Conditional Jump Instructions 121
Calling Procedures 123
Effect of Program Execution on the Stack 126
Boolean Operations 127
Program: Changing Uppercase to Lowercase 129
Shifting Bits 130
Rotating Bits 132
Jump Tables 134
Organizing a Program 136
Key Points 137
Questions 137

Part C Screen and Keyboard Operations 139

9 INTRODUCTION TO SCREEN AND KEYBOARD PROCESSING 139

Introduction 139
The Screen 140
Setting the Cursor 140
Clearing the Screen 141
INT 21H Function 09H for Screen Display 142
INT 21H Function 0AH for Keyboard Input 144
Program: Accepting and Displaying Names 145
Using Control Characters in a Screen Display 149
INT 21H Function 02H for Screen Display 150
File Handles 150
INT 21H Function 40H for Screen Display 151
INT 21H Function 3FH for Keyboard Input 152
Key Points 154
Questions 154

10 ADVANCED FEATURES OF SCREEN PROCESSING 156

Introduction 156
Video Adapters 157
Setting the Video Mode 157
Using Text Mode 158
Screen Pages 161
Using INT 10H for Text Mode 161

Program: Displaying the ASCII Character Set 167
ASCII Characters for Boxes and Menus 170
Program: Blinking, Reverse Video, and Scrolling 171
Direct Video Display 173
Using Graphics Mode 175
INT 10H for Graphics 177
Program: Setting and Displaying Graphics Mode 180
Determining the Type of Video Adapter 182
Key Points 182
Questions 183

11 ADVANCED FEATURES OF KEYBOARD PROCESSING 185

Introduction 185
The Keyboard 186
Keyboard Shift Status 186
The Keyboard Buffer 187
Using INT 21H for Keyboard Input 188
Using INT 16H for Keyboard Input 189
Extended Function Keys and Scan Codes 191
Program: Selecting from a Menu 193
BIOS INT 09H and the Keyboard Buffer 197
Keying in the Full ASCII Character Set 201
Key Points 201
Questions 202

Part D Data Manipulation 203

12 PROCESSING STRING DATA 203

Introduction 203
Features of String Operations 204
REP: Repeat String Prefix 204
MOVS: Move String Instruction 205
LODS: Load String Instruction 207
STOS: Store String Instruction 208
Program: Using LODS and STOS to Transfer Data 209
CMPS: Compare String Instruction 211
SCAS: Scan String Instruction 213
Example: Using Scan and Replace 214
Alternative Coding for String Instructions 214
Duplicating a Pattern 215
Program: Right Adjusting a Screen Display 215
Key Points 218
Questions 218

13 *ARITHMETIC: I—PROCESSING BINARY DATA* 220

Introduction 220
Processing Unsigned and Signed Data 221
Addition and Subtraction 222
Extending Values in a Register 224
Performing Arithmetic on Doubleword Values 225
Multiplication 227
Performing Doubleword Multiplication 231
Special Multiplication Instructions 234
Multiplication by Shifting 235
Division 235
Division by Shifting 239
Reversing the Sign 240
The Numeric Data Processor 240
Key Points 242
Questions 243

14 *ARITHMETIC: II—PROCESSING ASCII AND BCD DATA* 244

Introduction 244
Data in Decimal Format 245
Processing ASCII Data 246
Processing Unpacked BCD Data 249
Processing Packed BCD Data 251
Converting ASCII Data to Binary Format 253
Converting Binary Data to ASCII Format 255
Shifting and Rounding a Product 257
Program: Converting ASCII Data 257
Key Points 263
Questions 264

15 *DEFINING AND PROCESSING TABLES* 265

Introduction 265
Defining Tables 265
Direct Addressing of Table Entries 267
Searching a Table 271
The XLAT (Translate) Instruction 277
Program: Displaying Hex and ASCII Characters 278
Sorting Table Entries 280
Linked Lists 281
The TYPE, LENGTH, and SIZE Operators 286
Key Points 286
Questions 287

Part E Advanced Input/Output 289

16 DISK STORAGE I: ORGANIZATION 289

Introduction 289
Disk Characteristics 289
The Disk System Area and Data Area 292
The Boot Record 294
The Directory 294
The File Allocation Table 296
Exercise: Examining the FAT 299
Processing Files on Disk 302
Key Points 302
Questions 302

17 DISK STORAGE II: WRITING AND READING FILES 304

Introduction 304
ASCIIZ Strings 305
File Handles 305
Error Return Codes 305
File Pointers 306
Using File Handles to Create Disk Files 306
Using File Handles to Read Disk Files 311
Using File Handles for Random Processing 313
Program: Processing an ASCII File 320
Absolute Disk I/O 324
Disk Services Using File Control Blocks 325
Key Points 330
Questions 330

18 DISK STORAGE III: INT 21H FUNCTIONS FOR SUPPORTING DISKS AND FILES 332

Introduction 332
Operations Handling Disk Drives 333
Program: Reading Data from Sectors 342
Operations Handling the Directory and the FAT 345
Program: Displaying the Directory 346
Operations Handling Disk Files 348
Program: Selectively Deleting Files 353
Key Points 356
Questions 356

19 DISK STORAGE IV: INT 13H DISK FUNCTIONS *357*

Introduction 357
BIOS Status Byte 358
Basic INT 13H Disk Operations 358
Program: Using INT 13H to Read Sectors 360
Other INT 13H Disk Operations 363
Key Points 368
Questions 368

20 FACILITIES FOR PRINTING *369*

Introduction 369
Common Printer Control Characters 370
INT 21H Function 40H: Print Characters 370
Program: Printing With Page Overflow and Headings 371
Program: Printing ASCII Files and Handling Tabs 374
INT 21H Function 05H: Print Character 378
Special Printer Control Characters 379
INT 17H Functions for Printing 380
Key Points 381
Questions 381

21 OTHER INPUT/OUTPUT FACILITIES *383*

Introduction 383
Mouse Features 383
Mouse Functions 384
Common INT 33H Operations 385
Program: Using the Mouse 391
Ports 394
String Input/Output 395
Generating Sound 397
Key Points 397
Questions 398

Part F Advanced Programming **400**

22 DEFINING AND USING MACROS *400*

Introduction 400
Two Simple Macro Definitions 401
Using Parameters in Macros 402
Macro Comments 403

Using a Macro Within a Macro Definition 405
The LOCAL Directive 407
Including Macros from a Library 407
Concatenation 410
Repetition Directives 410
Conditional Directives 412
Key Points 416
Questions 417

23 LINKING TO SUBPROGRAMS ***419***

Introduction 419
The SEGMENT Directive 420
Intrasegment Calls 421
Intersegment Calls 422
The EXTRN and PUBLIC Attributes 423
Using EXTRN and PUBLIC for an Entry Point 425
Defining the Code Segment as PUBLIC 427
Using Simplified Segment Directives 429
Defining Common Data as PUBLIC 430
Defining Data in Both Programs 431
Passing Parameters to a Subprogram 433
Linking Pascal with an Assembly Language Program 436
Linking C with an Assembly Language Program 440
Key Points 442
Questions 444

24 MEMORY MANAGEMENT ***445***

Introduction 445
The Main DOS Programs 445
The High-Memory Area 446
The Program Segment Prefix 447
Memory Blocks 452
Memory Allocation Strategy 455
The Program Loader 456
Allocating and Freeing Memory 462
Loading or Executing a Program Function 463
Program Overlays 464
Resident Programs 470
Key Points 475
Questions 476

Part G Reference Chapters **478**

25 BIOS DATA AREAS AND PROGRAM INTERRUPTS *478*

Introduction 478
The Boot Process 478
The BIOS Data Area 479
Interrupt Services 482
BIOS Interrupts 483
BIOS:DOS Interface 487
DOS Interrupts 487
INT 21H Services 488
Key Points 494
Questions 495

26 OPERATORS AND DIRECTIVES *497*

Introduction 497
Type Specifiers 497
Operators 498
Directives 504

27 THE PC INSTRUCTION SET *525*

Introduction 525
Register Notation 526
The Addressing Mode Byte 526
Two-Byte Instructions 527
Three-Byte Instructions 528
Four-Byte Instructions 528
Instruction Set 529

APPENDIXES

A Conversion Between Hexadecimal and Decimal Numbers 557
B ASCII Character Codes 560
C Reserved Words 562
D Assembler and Link Options 564
E The DEBUG Program 572
F Keyboard Scan Codes and ASCII Codes 579

ANSWERS TO SELECTED QUESTIONS *583*

INDEX *595*

PREFACE

The heart of a personal computer is a microprocessor, which handles the computer's requirements for arithmetic, logic, and control. The microprocessor had its origin in the 1960s, when research designers devised the integrated circuit (IC) by combining various electronic components into a single component on a silicon "chip." The manufacturers set this tiny chip into a device resembling a centipede and connected it into a functioning system. In the early 1970s, Intel introduced the 8008 chip, which ushered in the first generation of microprocessors.

By 1974, the 8008 had evolved into the 8080, a popular second-generation microprocessor with general-purpose use. In 1978, Intel produced the third-generation 8086 processor, which provided some compatibility with the 8080 and represented a significant advance on its design. Next, Intel developed the 8088, a variation of the 8086 that provided a slightly simpler design and compatibility with then-current input/output devices. The 8088 was selected by IBM in 1981 for its forthcoming personal computer. An enhanced version of the 8088 is the 80188, and enhanced versions of the 8086 are the 80186, 80286, 80386, 80486, Pentium (or 586), PentiumPro (or 6x86) each of which provides additional operations and processing power.

Each family of processors has its own unique set of instructions that are used to direct its operations, such as accept input from a keyboard, display data on a screen, and perform arithmetic. This set of instructions is known as the system's machine language, which (as you will soon discover) is too complex and obscure for developing programs. Software suppliers provide an assembly language for the processor family that represents the various instructions in a more understandable symbolic code.

High-level languages such as C and BASIC were designed to eliminate the technicalities of a particular computer, whereas a low-level assembly language is designed for a specific family of processors.

The use of assembly language provides a number of advantages:

- A program written in assembly language requires considerably less memory and execution time than a program written in a high-level language.
- Assembly language gives a programmer the ability to perform highly technical tasks that would be difficult, if not impossible, in a high-level language.
- A knowledge of assembly language provides an understanding of machine architecture that no high-level language can ever provide.
- Although most software specialists develop new applications in high-level languages, which are easier to write and maintain, a common practice is to recode in assembly language those routines that have caused processing bottlenecks.
- Resident programs (that reside in memory while other programs execute) and interrupt service routines (that handle input and output) are almost always developed in assembly language.

The following material is required for learning PC assembly language:

- Access to an IBM personal computer (any model) or equivalent compatible.
- A copy of the DOS operating system (preferably a recent version) and familiarity with its use.
- A copy of an assembler translator program (preferably a recent version). Common suppliers include Microsoft, Borland, and SLR systems.

The following are *not* required for learning assembly language:

- Prior knowledge of a programming language, although such knowledge may help you grasp some programming concepts more readily.
- Prior knowledge of electronics or circuitry. This book provides all the information about the PC's architecture that you require for programming in assembly language.

OPERATING SYSTEMS

The major purposes of an operating system are (1) to allow users to instruct a computer regarding actions it is to take (such as executing a particular program) and (2) to provide means of storing (cataloging) information on disk and of accessing it.

The basic operating system for the PC and its compatibles is MS-DOS from Microsoft, known as PC-DOS on the IBM PC. Each version of DOS has provided additional features that have extended the capability of the PC. It is much easier to learn the intricacies of assembly language while within a relatively simple operating system like DOS rather than attempt it from within the OS/2 or Windows environment. Within DOS, you can freely experiment and can later step up to more advanced systems.

FOCUS OF THIS BOOK

The primary aim of this book is to assist readers in learning assembly programming. To this end, the book first covers the simpler aspects of the hardware and the language and then introduces instructions as they are needed. As well, the text emphasizes clarity in program examples. Thus the examples use those instructions and approaches that are the easiest to understand, even though a professional programmer would often solve similar problems with more sophisticated—but less clear—code.

The programs also omit macro instructions (explained in Chapter 22); although professional programmers use macros extensively, their appearance in a book of this nature would interfere with learning the principles of the language. Once you have learned these principles, you can then adopt the clever techniques of the professional.

THE APPROACH TO TAKE

This book can act as both a tutorial and a permanent reference. To make the most effective use of your investment in a PC and software, work through each chapter carefully, and reread any material that is not immediately clear. Key the program examples into your computer, convert them into executable "modules," and get them to execute (or "run"). Also, be sure to work through the exercises at the end of each chapter.

The first nine chapters furnish the foundation material for the book and for assembly language. After studying these chapters, you can proceed with Chapters 12, 13, 15, 16, 20, 21, or 22. Chapters 25, 26, and 27 are intended as references. Chapters related to each other are:

- 9 through 11 (on screen and keyboard operations)
- 13 and 14 (on arithmetic operations)
- 16 through 19 (on disk processing)
- 23 and 24 (on subprograms and memory management)

On completing this book, you will be able to:

- Understand the hardware of the personal computer.
- Understand machine-language code and hexadecimal format.
- Understand the steps involved in assembling, linking, and executing programs.
- Write programs in assembly language to handle the keyboard and screen, perform arithmetic, convert between ASCII and binary formats, perform table searches and sorts, and handle disk input and output.
- Trace machine execution as an aid in program debugging.
- Write your own macro instructions to facilitate faster coding.
- Link separately assembled programs into one executable program.

Learning assembly language and getting your programs to work is an exciting and challenging experience. For the time and effort invested, the rewards are sure to be great.

NOTES ON THE FOURTH EDITION

This fourth edition reflects a considerable number of enhancements to the previous edition, including the following:

- More features of the Intel 80486 and later processors
- More program examples and exercises
- Earlier introduction to interrupt operations
- Inclusion of material on more recent assembler versions
- Considerable reorganization and revision of explanations throughout the text
- Revised and additional questions at the end of each chapter.

Users of the third edition should note that the contents of Chapters 25 and 26 have been combined in this edition. Also, the conditional jump instructions described in Chapter 27 ("The PC Instruction Set") are now organized and summarized in a table.

ACKNOWLEDGMENTS

The author is grateful for the assistance and cooperation of all those who contributed suggestions for, reviews of, and corrections to earlier editions.

PART A—Fundamentals of PC Hardware and Software

1 BASIC FEATURES OF PC HARDWARE

Objective: To explain the basic features of microcomputer hardware and program organization.

INTRODUCTION

Writing a program in assembly language requires knowledge of the computer's hardware (or architecture) and the details of its instruction set. An explanation of the basic hardware—bits, bytes, registers, memory, processor, and data bus—is provided in this chapter. The instruction set and its use are developed throughout the rest of this book.

The main internal *hardware* features of a computer are the microprocessor, memory, and registers; external hardware features are the computer's input/output devices such as the keyboard, monitor, and disk. *Software* consists of the various programs and data files (including the operating system) stored on the disk. To execute (or run) a program, the system copies it from disk into internal memory. (Internal memory is what people mean when they claim that their computer has, for example, 16 megabytes of memory.) The microprocessor executes the program instructions, and the registers handle the requested arithmetic, data movement, and addressing.

BITS AND BYTES

The fundamental building block of computer storage is the *bit*. A bit may be *off*, so that its value is considered 0, or it may be *on*, so that its value is considered 1. A single bit doesn't provide much information, but it is surprising what a bunch of them can do.

Bytes

A group of nine related bits is called a *byte,* which represents storage locations both internally in memory and externally on disk. Each byte consists of 8 bits for data and 1 bit for parity:

0	0	0	0	0	0	0	0	1

```
|—————————————— data bits ——————————————| parity |
```

The 8 data bits provide the basis for binary arithmetic and for representing such characters as the letter A and the asterisk symbol (*). Eight bits allow 256 (2^8) different combinations of on-off conditions, from all bits off (00000000) through all bits on (11111111). For example, a representation of the bits for the letter A is 01000001 and for the asterisk is 00101010, although you don't have to memorize such facts.

According to the rule of parity, the number of bits in each byte that are on is always odd. Because the letter A contains two bits that are on, the processor forces odd parity by automatically setting the parity bit on (01000001-1). Similarly, since the asterisk contains three bits that are on, the processor maintains odd parity by turning the parity bit off (00101010-0). When an instruction references a byte in internal storage, the processor checks its bits for parity. If parity is even, the system assumes that a bit is "lost" and displays an error message. A parity error may be a result of a hardware fault or an electrical disturbance; either way, it is a rare event.

How does a computer "know" that bit value 01000001 represents the letter A? When you key in A on the keyboard, the system delivers a signal from that particular key into memory and sets a byte (in an internal location) to the bit value 01000001. You can move the contents of this byte about in memory as you will, and you can even print it or display it on the screen as the letter A.

The bits in a byte are numbered 0 to 7 from right to left, as shown here for the letter A (for purposes of programming, we no longer need be concerned with the parity bit):

```
Bit contents (A): 0 1 0 0 0 0 0 1
Bit number:       7 6 5 4 3 2 1 0
```

Related Bytes

A program can treat a group of one or more related bytes as a unit of data, such as time or distance. A group of bytes that defines a particular value is commonly known as a *data item* or *field.* The PC also supports certain data sizes that are natural to it:

- *Word.* A 2-byte (16-bit) data item.
- *Doubleword.* A 4-byte (32-bit) data item.
- *Quadword.* An 8-byte (64-bit) data item.
- *Paragraph.* A 16-byte (128-bit) area.
- *Kilobyte (KB).* The number 2^{10} equals 1,024, which happens to be the value K, for kilobyte. Thus 640K of memory is $640 \times 1{,}024 = 655{,}360$ bytes.
- *Megabyte (MB).* The number 2^{20} equals 1,048,576, or 1 megabyte.

Bits in a word are numbered 0 through 15 from right to left, as shown here for the letters 'PC', with the 'P' (01010000) in the leftmost byte and the 'C' (01000011) in the rightmost byte:

Bit contents (PC):	0	1	0	1	0	0	0	0	0	1	0	0	0	0	1	1
Bit number:	15	14	13	12	11	10	9	8	7	6	5	4	3	2	1	0

Each byte in memory has a unique *address.* The first byte in the lowest memory location is numbered 0, the second is numbered 1, and so forth.

BINARY NUMBERS

Because a computer can distinguish only between 0 and 1 bits, it works in a base-2 numbering system known as binary. In fact, the word "bit" is a contraction of "Binary digIT."

A collection of bits can represent any numeric value. The value of a binary number is based on the presence of 1-bits and their relative positions. Just as in decimal numbers, the positions represent ascending powers (but of 2, not 10) from right to left. In the following 8-bit number, all bits are set to 1 (on):

Bit value:	1	1	1	1	1	1	1	1
Position value:	128	64	32	16	8	4	2	1
Bit number:	7	6	5	4	3	2	1	0

The rightmost bit assumes the value 1 (2^0), the next bit to the left assumes the value 2 (2^1), the next bit the value 4 (2^2), and so forth. The value of the binary number in this case is $1 + 2 + 4 + \ldots + 128 = 255$ (or $2^8 - 1$).

In a similar manner, the value of the binary number 01000001 is calculated as 1 plus 64, or 65:

Bit value:	0	1	0	0	0	0	0	1
Position value:	128	64	32	16	8	4	2	1

But wait—isn't 01000001 the letter A? Indeed, it is. The bits 01000001 can represent either the number 65 or the letter A, as follows:

- If your program defines and uses the data for arithmetic purposes, then the bit value 01000001 represents a binary number equivalent to the decimal number 65.
- If your program defines and uses the data for descriptive purposes, such as a heading, then 01000001 represents an alphabetic character.

When you start programming, you will see this distinction more clearly, because you define and use each data item for a specific purpose, that is, arithmetic data for arithmetic purposes and descriptive data for displayed output. In practice, the two uses are seldom a source of confusion.

A binary number is not limited to 8 bits. A processor that uses 16-bit (or 32-bit) architecture handles 16-bit (or 32-bit) numbers automatically. For 16 bits, $2^{16}-1$ provides values up to 65,535 and, for 32 bits, $2^{32}-1$ provides values up to 4,294,967,295.

Binary Arithmetic

Because a microcomputer performs arithmetic only in binary format, an assembly language programmer has to be familiar with binary format and binary addition. The following four examples illustrate simple binary addition:

```
 0       0      1      1
+0      +1     +1     +1
--      --     --     +1
 0       1     10     --
                      11
```

Note the carry of the 1-bit in the last two examples. Now, let's add the bit values 01000001 and 00101010. Are we adding the letter A and an asterisk? No, this time they represent the decimal values 65 and 42:

```
Decimal       Binary
  65         01000001
 +42        +00101010
 ---        ---------
 107         01101011
```

To check that the binary sum 01101011 is actually 107, add the values of the 1-bits. As another example, let's add the decimal values 60 and 53 and their binary equivalents:

```
Decimal       Binary
  60         00111100
 +53        +00110101
 ---        ---------
 113         01110001
```

Again, be sure to check that the binary sum really equals 113.

Negative Binary Numbers

A signed binary number is considered to be positive if its leftmost bit is a 0, whereas a signed negative binary number contains a 1-bit in its leftmost position. However, representing a binary number as negative is not as simple as setting the leftmost bit to 1, such as converting 01000001 (+65) to 11000001. Instead, a negative binary value is expressed in *two's complement notation;* that is, the rule to represent a binary number as negative is: ***Reverse the bit values and add 1.*** As an example, let's use this rule to find the two's complement of 01000001 (or 65):

```
Number +65:            01000001
Reverse the bits:      10111110
Add 1:                        1
                       --------
Number -65:            10111111
```

A signed binary number is negative if its leftmost bit is 1, but if you add the 1-bit values to determine the decimal value of the binary number 10111111, you won't get 65. To determine the absolute value of a negative binary number, simply apply the two's complement rule; that is, reverse the bits and add 1:

```
Number -65:              10111111
Reverse the bits:        01000000
Add 1:                          1
                         --------
Number +65:              01000001
```

To illustrate that this procedure works properly, the sum of +65 and −65 should be zero. Let's try it:

```
 +65      01000001
 -65     +10111111
 ---     ---------
  00   (1)00000000
```

In the sum, the 8-bit value is all zeros, and the carry of the 1-bit on the left is lost. But because there is a carry into the sign bit and a carry out, the result is considered to be correct.

To handle binary subtraction, simply convert the number being subtracted to two's complement format, and add the numbers. For example, let's subtract 42 from 65. The binary representation for 42 is 00101010, and its two's complement is 11010110. Simply add −42 to 65, like this:

```
    65      01000001
+(-42)     +11010110
------     ---------
    23   (1)00010111
```

The result, 23, is correct. Note that, once again, there is a valid carry into and out of the sign bit.

If the justification for two's complement notation isn't immediately clear, consider the following question: What value would you have to add to binary 00000001 to make it equal to 00000000? In terms of decimal numbers, the answer would be −1. The two's complement of 00000001 is 11111111. So we add +1 and −1 as follows:

```
      1      00000001
  +(-1)      11111111
             --------
Result:   (1)00000000
```

Ignoring the carry of 1, you can see that the binary number 11111111 is equivalent to decimal −1. You can also see a pattern form as the binary numbers decrease in value:

```
+3    00000011
+2    00000010
+1    00000001
 0    00000000
-1    11111111
-2    11111110
-3    11111101
```

In fact, the 0-bits in a negative binary number indicate its (absolute) value: Treat the positional value of each 0-bit as if it were a 1-bit, sum the values, and add 1.

You'll find this material on binary arithmetic and negative numbers particularly relevant when you get to Chapters 12 and 13 on arithmetic.

HEXADECIMAL REPRESENTATION

Although a byte may contain any of the 256 bit combinations, there is no way to display or print many of them as standard ASCII characters. (Examples of such characters include the bit configurations for such operations as Tab, Enter, Form Feed, and Escape.) Consequently, computer designers developed a shorthand method of representing binary data that divides each byte in half and expresses the value of each half-byte.

Imagine that you want to view the contents of a binary value in 4 adjacent bytes (a doubleword) in memory. Consider the following 4 bytes, shown in both binary and decimal formats:

Binary:	0101	1001	0011	0101	1011	1001	1100	1110
Decimal:	5	9	3	5	11	9	12	14

Because the decimal numbers 11, 12, and 14 each require two digits, let's extend the numbering system so that 10 = A, 11 = B, 12 = C, 13 = D, 14 = E, and 15 = F. In this way, the numbering system involves the "digits" 0 through F and, since there are 16 such digits, the system is known as *hexadecimal* (or *hex*) representation. Here's the revised shorthand number that represents the contents of the bytes just given:

Binary:	0101	1001	0011	0101	1011	1001	1100	1110
Hexadecimal:	5	9	3	5	B	9	C	E

Figure 1-1 shows the decimal numbers 0 through 15 along with their equivalent binary and hexadecimal values.

Binary	Decimal	Hexadecimal	Binary	Decimal	Hexadecimal
0000	0	0	1000	8	8
0001	1	1	1001	9	9
0010	2	2	1010	10	A
0011	3	3	1011	11	B
0100	4	4	1100	12	C
0101	5	5	1101	13	D
0110	6	6	1110	14	E
0111	7	7	1111	15	F

Figure 1-1 Binary, Decimal, and Hexadecimal Representation

Assembly language makes considerable use of hexadecimal format. A listing of an assembled program shows, in hexadecimal, all addresses, machine-code instructions, and the contents of data constants. For debugging your programs, you can use the DOS DEBUG program, which also displays the addresses and contents of bytes in hexadecimal format.

You'll soon get used to working in hexadecimal format. Keep in mind that the hex number immediately following hex F is hex 10, which is decimal value 16. Following are some simple examples of hex arithmetic:

```
  7     6     F     F    10    38    FF
 +3    +7    +1    +F   +30   +18   + 1
 --    --    --    --   ---   ---   ---
  A     D    10    1E    40    50   100
```

Note also that hex 40 equals decimal 64, hex 100 is decimal 256, and hex 1000 is decimal 4,096. For the example 38 + 18 = 50, note that hex 8 + 8 equals 10.

To indicate a hex number in a program, you code an "H" immediately after the number, such as 25H (decimal 37). An assembly language requirement is that a hex number always begins with a decimal digit 0–9, so you should code B8H as 0B8H. In this book, we indicate a hexadecimal value with the word "hex" or an "H" following the number (such as hex 4C or 4CH); a binary value with the word binary or a "B" following the number (such as binary 01001100 or 01001100B); and a decimal value simply by a number (such as 76). An occasional exception occurs where the base is obvious from its context.

Appendix A gives an explanation of how to convert hex numbers to decimal format and vice versa.

ASCII CODE

To standardize the representation of data, microcomputer manufacturers have adopted the ASCII (American National Standard Code for Information Interchange) code, which facilitates the transfer of data between different computer devices. The 8-bit ASCII code that the PC uses provides 256 characters, including symbols for foreign alphabets. For example, we have already seen that the combination of bits 01000001 (hex 41) indicates the letter A. Appendix B provides a convenient list of the 256 ASCII characters, and Chapter 8 shows how to display most of them on the screen.

THE PROCESSOR

An important hardware element of the PC is the system unit, which contains a system board, power supply, and expansion slots for optional boards. Features of the system board are an Intel (or equivalent) microprocessor, read-only memory (ROM), and random access memory (RAM).

The brain of the PC is a microprocessor based on the Intel 8086 family that performs all executing of instructions and processing of data. Processors vary in their speed and capacity of memory, registers, and data bus. A data bus transfers data between the processor, memory, and external devices, in effect managing the data traffic. Following is a brief description of various Intel processors:

8088/80188. These processors have 16-bit registers and an 8-bit data bus and can address up to 1 million bytes of internal memory. Although the registers can process 2 bytes at a time, the data bus can transfer only 1 byte at a time. The 80188 is a souped-up 8088 with a few additional instructions. These processors run in what is known as *real mode,* that is, one program at a time.

8086/80186. These processors are similar to the 8088/80188, but have a 16-bit data bus and can run faster. The 80186 is a souped-up 8086 with a few additional instructions.

80286. This processor runs faster than the preceding processors and can address up to 16 million bytes. It can operate in real mode or in *protected mode* for multitasking (running more than one job at a time).

80386. This processor has 32-bit registers and a 32-bit data bus and can address up to 4 billion bytes of memory. It can operate in real mode or in protected mode for multitasking.

80486. This processor also has 32-bit registers and a 32-bit data bus (although some clones have a 16-bit data bus) and is designed for enhanced performance. It can run in real mode or in protected mode for multitasking.

Pentium (or 80586). This processor has 32-bit registers and a 64-bit data bus and can execute more than one instruction per clock cycle. (Intel adopted the name "Pentium" because, in contrast to numbers, names can be copyrighted.)

PentiumPro (or 6x86). This processor further advances the capacity of registers and the data bus. For example, where the previous processors' connection to a storage cache on the system board caused delays, this processor is connected to a built-in storage cache by a 64-bit wide bus.

Execution Unit and Bus Interface Unit

As illustrated in Figure 1-2, the processor is partitioned into two logical units: an execution unit (EU) and a bus interface unit (BIU). The role of the EU is to execute instructions, whereas the BIU delivers instructions and data to the EU. The EU contains an arithmetic and logic unit (ALU), a control unit (CU), and a number of registers. These features provide for execution of instructions and arithmetic and logical operations.

The most important function of the BIU is to manage the bus control unit, segment registers, and instruction queue. The BIU controls the buses that transfer data to the EU, to memory, and to external input/output devices, whereas the segment registers control memory addressing.

Another function of the BIU is to provide access to instructions. Because the instructions for a program that is executing are in memory, the BIU must access instructions from memory and place them in an *instruction queue,* which varies in size depending on the processor. This feature enables the BIU to look ahead and prefetch instructions so that there is always a queue of instructions ready to execute.

The EU and BIU work in parallel, with the BIU keeping one step ahead. The EU notifies the BIU when it needs access to data in memory or an I/O device. Also, the EU requests machine instructions from the BIU instruction queue. The top instruction is the currently ex-

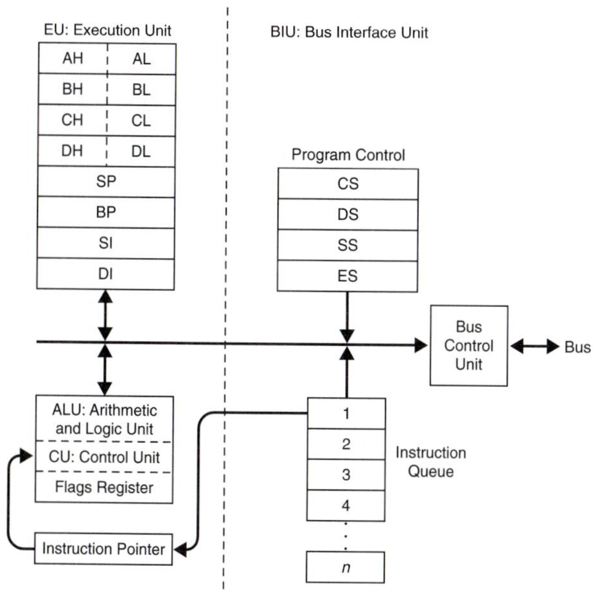

Figure 1-2 Execution Unit and Bus Interface Unit

ecutable one and, while the EU is occupied executing an instruction, the BIU fetches another instruction from memory. This fetching overlaps with execution and speeds up processing.

Processors up through the 80486 have what is known as a *single-stage pipeline,* which restricts them to completing one instruction before starting the next. Pipelining involves the way a processor divides an instruction into sequential steps using different resources. The Pentium has a five-stage pipelined structure, and the PentiumPro has a 12-stage superpipelined structure. This feature enables them to run many operations in parallel.

A problem faced by designers is that because the processor runs considerably faster than does memory, it has to wait for memory to deliver instructions. To handle this problem, each advanced processor in turn has more capability in *dynamic execution,* which consists of three elements:

1. Multiple branch prediction, whereby the processor looks ahead a number of steps to predict what to process next;
2. Dataflow analysis, which involves analyzing dependencies between instructions; and
3. Speculative execution, which uses the results of the first two elements to speculatively execute instructions.

As a programmer, you are not able to access any of these features of the processor.

INTERNAL MEMORY

The two types of internal memory on the PC are *random access memory* (*RAM*) and *read-only memory* (*ROM*). Bytes in memory are numbered consecutively, beginning with 00, so that each location has a uniquely numbered address.

Figure 1-3 shows a physical memory map of an 8086-type PC. Of the first megabyte of memory, the first 640K is base RAM, most of which is available for your own use.

ROM. ROM consists of special memory chips that (as the full name suggests) can only be read. Because instructions and data are permanently "burned into" the chips, they cannot be altered. The ROM Basic Input/Output System (BIOS) begins at address 768K and handles input/output devices, such as a hard disk controller. ROM beginning at 960K controls the computer's basic functions, such as the power-on self-test, dot patterns for graphics, and the disk self-loader. When you switch on the power, ROM performs various check-outs and loads special system data from disk into RAM.

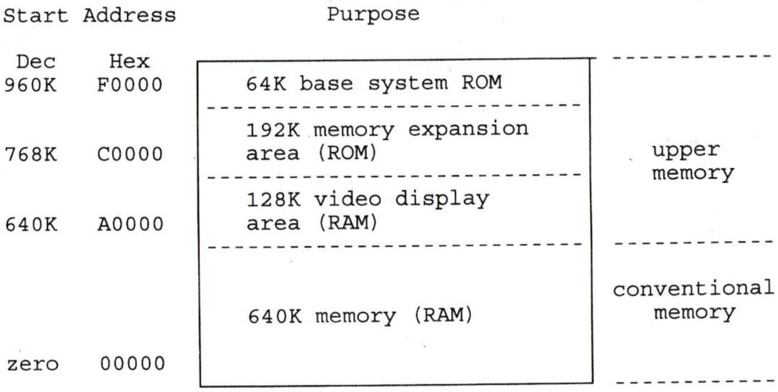

```
Start Address            Purpose

 Dec     Hex     ----------------------------  ------------
960K    F0000   | 64K base system ROM        |
                |----------------------------|
                | 192K memory expansion      |
768K    C0000   | area (ROM)                 |    upper
                |----------------------------|    memory
                | 128K video display         |
640K    A0000   | area (RAM)                 |
                |----------------------------|  ------------
                |                            |
                |                            | conventional
                | 640K memory (RAM)          |    memory
                |                            |
zero    00000   |                            |
                 ----------------------------  ------------
```

Figure 1-3 Map of Base Memory

RAM. A programmer is mainly concerned with RAM, which would be better named "read-write memory." RAM is available as a "worksheet" for temporary storage and execution of programs.

Because the contents of RAM are lost when you turn off the power, you need separate, external storage for keeping programs and data. When you turn on the power, the ROM boot-up procedure loads a portion of the operating system into RAM. You then request it to perform actions, such as loading a program from a disk into RAM. Your program executes in RAM and normally produces output on the screen, printer, or disk. When finished, you may ask the system to load another program into RAM, an action that overwrites the previous program. All further discussions of RAM use the general term "memory."

Addressing Data in Memory

Depending on model, the processor can access one or more bytes of memory at a time. Consider the decimal number 1,315. The hex representation of this value, 0529H, requires 2 bytes, or 1 word, of memory. It consists of a high-order (most significant) byte, 05, and a low-order (least significant) byte, 29. The system stores the data in memory in *reverse-byte sequence:* the low-order byte in the low memory address and the high-order byte in the high memory address. For example, the processor transfers 0529H from a register (a special processor component) into memory addresses 7612 and 7613 like this:

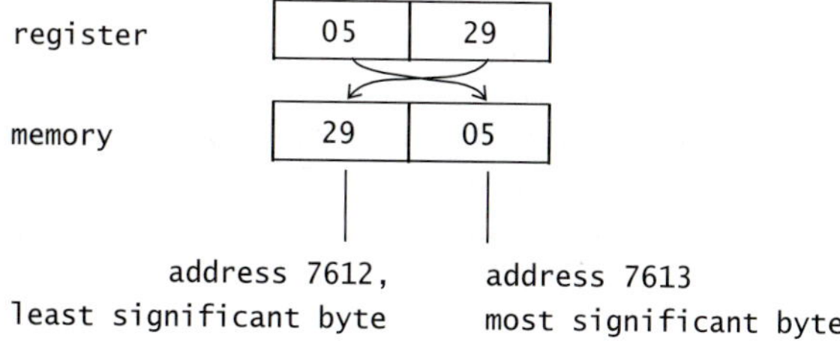

The processor expects numeric data in memory to be in reverse-byte sequence and processes the data accordingly. When the processor retrieves the word from memory, it again reverses the bytes, restoring them correctly in the register as hex 05 29. Although this feature is entirely automatic, you have to be alert to it when programming and debugging assembly language programs.

An assembly language programmer has to distinguish clearly between the *address* of a memory location and its *contents.* In the preceding example, the contents of address 7612 is 29, and the contents of address 7613 is 05.

SEGMENTS AND ADDRESSING

A *segment* is a special area defined in a program that begins on a *paragraph boundary,* that is, at a location evenly divisible by 16, or hex 10. Although a segment may be located almost anywhere in memory and in real mode may be up to 64K bytes, it requires only as much space as the program requires for its execution.

There may be any number of segments; to address a particular segment, it is necessary only to change the address in an appropriate segment register. The three main segments are the *code, data,* and *stack* segments.

Code Segment

The *code segment* contains the machine instructions that are to execute. Typically, the first executable instruction is at the start of this segment, and the operating system links to that location to begin program execution. As the name implies, the code segment (CS) register addresses the code segment. If your code area requires more than 64K, your program may need to define more than one code segment.

Data Segment

The *data segment* contains a program's defined data, constants, and work areas. The data segment (DS) register addresses the data segment. If your data area requires more than 64K, your program may need to define more than one data segment.

Stack Segment

In simple terms, the *stack* contains any data and addresses that you need to save temporarily or for use by your own "called" subroutines. The stack segment (SS) register addresses the stack segment.

Segment Boundaries

A segment register contains the starting address of a segment. Figure 1-4 presents a graphic view of the SS, DS, and CS registers and their relationships to the stack, data, and code segments. (The registers and segments are not necessarily in the order shown.) Other segment registers are the ES (extra segment) and, on the 80386 and later processors, the FS and GS registers, which have specialized uses.

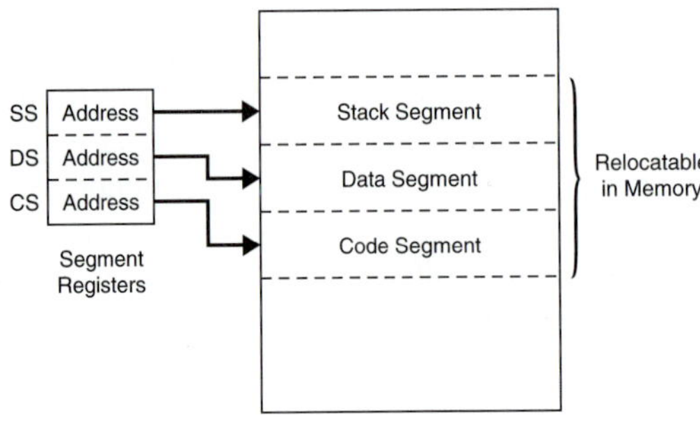

Figure 1-4 Segments and Registers

As mentioned earlier, a segment begins on a paragraph boundary, which is an address evenly divisible by decimal 16, or hex 10. Consider a data segment that begins at memory location 038E0H. Because in this and all other cases the rightmost hex digit is zero, the computer designers decided that it would be unnecessary to store the zero digit in the segment register. Thus 038E0H is stored as 038E, with the rightmost zero understood. Where appropriate, this text uses square brackets to refer to the rightmost zero, such as 038E[0].

Segment Offsets

Within a program, all memory locations are relative to a segment's starting address. The distance in bytes from the segment address to another location within the segment is expressed as an *offset* (or displacement). A 2-byte (16-bit) offset can range from 0000H through FFFFH, or zero through 65,535. Thus the first byte of the code segment is at offset 00, the second byte is at offset 01, and so forth, through to offset 65,535. To reference any memory location in a segment, the processor combines the segment address in a segment register with an offset value.

Consider a data segment that begins at location 038E0H. The DS register contains the segment address of the data segment, 038E[0]H, and an instruction references a location with an offset of 0032H bytes within the data segment:

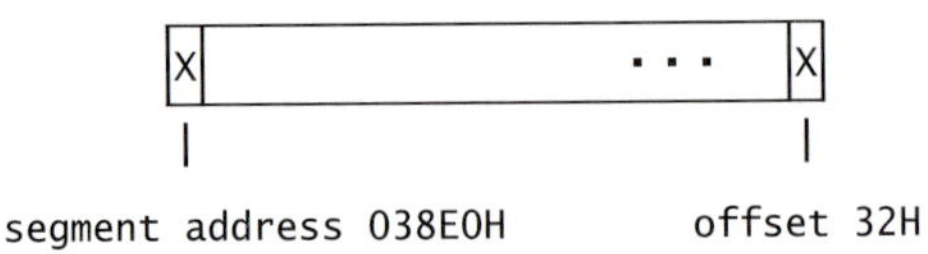

The actual memory location of the byte referenced by the instruction is therefore 03912H:

```
DS segment address:      038E0H
Offset:                 + 0032H
                        -------
Actual address:          03912H
```

Note that a program contains one or more segments, which may begin almost anywhere in memory, may vary in size, and may be in any sequence.

Addressing Capacity

The various Intel processors used by the PC series provide different addressing capabilities.

8086/8088 Addressing. The registers of the 8086/8088 processors provide 16 bits. Because a segment address is on a paragraph boundary (evenly divisible by 16, or hex 10), the rightmost 4 bits of its address are zero. As discussed earlier, a segment address is stored in a segment register, and the processor assumes 4 rightmost 0-bits, as hex nnnn[0]. Now, FFFF[0]H allows addressing up to 1,048,560 bytes. If you are uncertain, decode each hex F as binary 1111, allow for the 4 rightmost 0-bits, and add the values of the 1-bits.

80286 Addressing. In real mode, the 80286 processor handles addressing the same as an 8086 does. In protected mode, the processor uses 24 bits for addressing, so that FFFFF[0] allows addressing up to 16 million bytes. The segment registers act as selectors for accessing a 24-bit segment address from memory and add this value to a 16-bit offset address:

```
Segment register:     | 16 bits [0000] |
Segment address:    |      24 bits     |
```

80386/486/Pentium Addressing. In real mode, these processors also handle addressing much the same as an 8086 does. In protected mode, the processors use 48 bits for addressing, which allows addressing segments up to 4 billion bytes. The 16-bit segment registers act as selectors for accessing a 32-bit segment address from memory and add this value to a 32-bit offset address:

```
Segment register:     | 16 bits [0000] |
Segment address:    |      32 bits     |
```

REGISTERS

The processor's *registers* are used to control instructions being executed, to handle addressing of memory, and to provide arithmetic capability. The registers are addressable by name, such as CS, DS, and SS. Bits in a register are conventionally numbered from right to left, beginning with 0, as

```
. . .15  14  13  12  11  10  9  8  7  6  5  4  3  2  1  0
```

Segment Registers

A *segment register* is 16 bits long and provides for addressing an area of memory known as the current segment. Because a segment aligns on a paragraph boundary, its address in a segment register assumes 4 0-bits to its right.

CS register. Contains the starting address of a program's code segment. This segment address, plus an offset value in the instruction pointer (IP) register, indicates the address of an instruction to be fetched for execution. For normal programming purposes, you need not reference the CS register.

DS register. Contains the starting address of a program's data segment. Instructions use this address to locate data: This address, plus an offset value in an instruction, causes a reference to a specific byte location in the data segment.

SS register. Permits the implementation of a stack in memory, which a program uses for temporary storage of addresses and data. The system stores the starting address of a program's stack segment in the SS register. This segment address, plus an offset value in the stack pointer (SP) register, indicates the current word in the stack being addressed. For normal programming purposes, you need not directly reference the SS register.

ES register. Used by some string (character data) operations to handle memory addressing. In this context, the ES (extra segment) register is associated with the DI (index) register. A program that requires the use of the ES may initialize it with an appropriate segment address.

FS and GS registers. Additional extra segment registers on the 80386 and later processors.

Pointer Registers

The three pointer registers are the IP, SP, and BP.

Instruction Pointer (IP) register. The 16-bit IP register contains the offset address of the next instruction that is to execute. The IP is associated with the CS register in that the IP indicates the current instruction within the currently executing code segment. You do not normally reference the IP register in a program, but you can change its value when using the DEBUG program to test a program. The 80386 and later processors have an extended 32-bit IP called the EIP.

In the following example, the CS register contains 39B4[0]H and the IP contains 514H. To find the next instruction to be executed, the processor combines the address in the CS and with the offset in the IP:

```
Segment address in CS              39B40H
Plus offset address in IP         + 514H
                                  ------
Address of next instruction        3A054H
```

The SP (stack pointer) and BP (base pointer) registers are associated with the SS register and permit the system to access data in the stack segment.

Stack Pointer (SP) register. The 16-bit SP register provides an offset value, which, when associated with the SS register, refers to the current word being processed in the stack. The 80386 and later processors have an extended 32-bit stack pointer, the ESP register. The system automatically handles these registers.

In the following example, the SS register contains segment address 4BB3[0]H and the SP contains offset 412H. To find the current word being processed in the stack, the processor combines the address in the SS with the offset in the SP:

```
Segment address in SS        4BB30H
Plus offset in SP            + 412H
                             ------
Address in stack             4BF42H
```

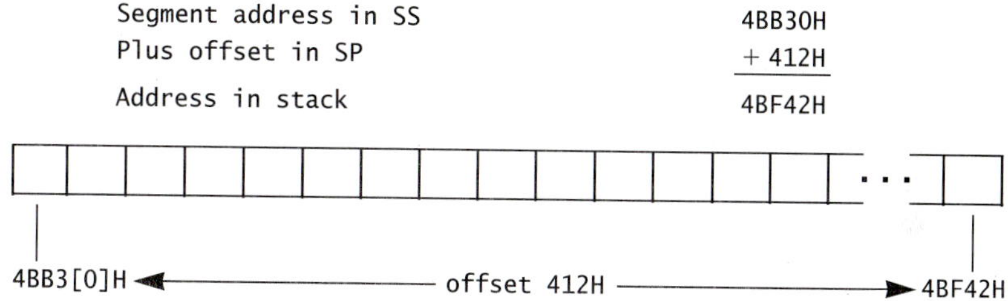

Base Pointer (BP) register. The 16-bit BP facilitates referencing parameters, which are data and addresses that a program passes via the stack. The processor combines the address in the SS with the offset in the BP. The 80386 and later processors have an extended 32-bit BP called the EBP register.

General-Purpose Registers

The AX, BX, CX, and DX general-purpose registers are the workhorses of the system. They are unique in that you can address them as one word or as a 1-byte portion. The leftmost byte is the "high" portion and the rightmost byte is the "low" portion. For example, the AX register consists of an AH (high) and an AL (low) portion, and you can reference any portion by its name. The 80386 and later processors support all the general-purpose registers, plus 32-bit extended versions of them: the EAX, EBX, ECX, and EDX.

The following assembler instructions move zeros to the AX, BH, and ECX registers, respectively:

```
MOV   AX,00
MOV   BH,00
MOV   ECX,00
```

AX register. The AX register, the primary accumulator, is used for operations involving input/output and most arithmetic. For example, the multiply, divide, and translate instructions assume the use of the AX. Also, some instructions generate more efficient code if they reference the AX rather than another register.

```
                 AX: |   AH   |   AL   |
EAX: |                                 |
```

BX register. The BX is known as the base register since it is the only general-purpose register that can be used as an index to extend addressing. Another common purpose of the BX is for computations.

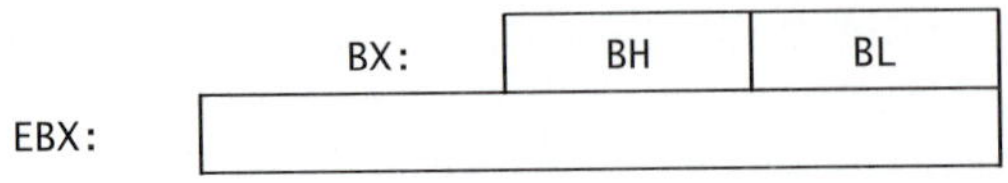

BX: | BH | BL
EBX:

CX register. The CX is known as the count register. It may contain a value to control the number of times a loop is repeated or a value to shift bits left or right. The CX may also be used for many computations.

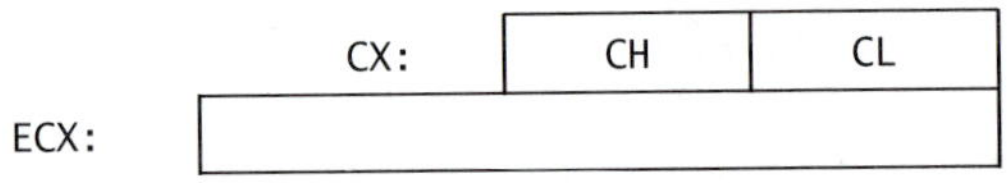

CX: | CH | CL
ECX:

DX register. The DX is known as the data register. Some input/output operations require its use, and multiply and divide operations that involve large values assume the use of the DX and AX together as a pair.

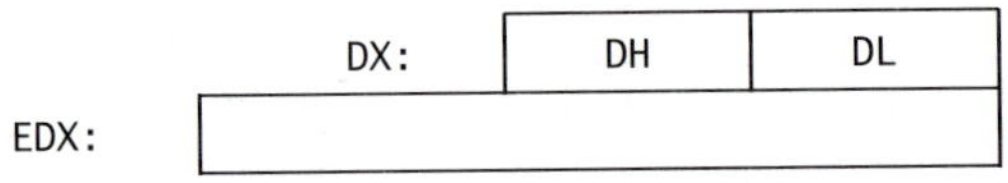

DX: | DH | DL
EDX:

You may use any of these general-purpose registers for addition and subtraction of 8-bit, 16-bit, or 32-bit values.

Index Registers

The SI and DI registers are available for indexed addressing and for use in addition and subtraction.

SI register. The 16-bit source index register is required for some string (character) operations. In this context, the SI is associated with the DS register. The 80386 and later processors support a 32-bit extended register, the ESI.

DI register. The 16-bit destination index register is also required for some string operations. In this context, the DI is associated with the ES register. The 80386 and later processors support a 32-bit extended register, the EDI.

Flags Register

Nine of the 16 bits of the flags register are common to all 8086-family processors to indicate the current status of the computer and the results of processing. Many instructions involving comparisons and arithmetic change the status of the flags, which some instructions may test to determine subsequent action.

The following briefly describes the common flag bits:

- OF (overflow). Indicates overflow of a high-order (leftmost) bit following arithmetic.
- DF (direction). Determines left or right direction for moving or comparing string (character) data.
- IF (interrupt). Indicates that all external interrupts, such as keyboard entry, are to be processed or ignored.
- TF (trap). Permits operation of the processor in single-step mode. Debugger programs such as DEBUG set the trap flag so that you can step through execution a single instruction at a time to examine the effect on registers and memory.
- SF (sign). Contains the resulting sign of an arithmetic operation (0 = positive and 1 = negative).
- ZF (zero). Indicates the result of an arithmetic or comparison operation (0 = nonzero and 1 = zero result).
- AF (auxiliary carry). Contains a carry out of bit 3 on 8-bit data, for specialized arithmetic.
- PF (parity). Indicates even or odd parity of a low-order (rightmost) 8-bit data operation.
- CF (carry). Contains carries from a high-order (leftmost) bit following an arithmetic operation; also, contains the contents of the last bit of a shift or rotate operation.

The flags are in the flags register in the following locations (which you need not memorize):

Flag:					O	D	I	T	S	Z		A		P		C
Bit no.:	15	14	13	12	11	10	9	8	7	6	5	4	3	2	1	0

The flags most relevant to assembly programming are OF, SF, ZF, and CF for comparisons and arithmetic operations, and DF for the direction of string operations. The 80286 and later processors have some flags used for internal purposes, concerned primarily with protected mode. The 80386 and later processors have a 32-bit extended flags register known as Eflags. Chapter 8 contains more details about the flags register.

KEY POINTS

- The processor distinguishes only between bits that are 0 (off) and 1 (on) and performs arithmetic only in binary format.
- The value of a binary number is determined by the placement of its bits. For example, the binary value 1101 equals (from right to left) $2^0 + 0^1 + 2^2 + 2^3$, or 13.
- A negative binary number is represented in two's complement notation: Reverse the bits of its positive representation and add 1.
- A single location of memory is a byte, comprised of 8 data bits and 1 parity bit. Two adjacent bytes comprise a word, and 4 adjacent bytes comprise a doubleword.
- The value K equals 2^{10}, or 1,024 bytes.

- Hexadecimal format is a shorthand notation for representing groups of 4 bits. Hex digits 0–9 and A–F represent the binary values 0000 through 1111.
- The representation of character data is done in ASCII format.
- The heart of the PC is a microprocessor. The processor stores numeric data in words in memory in reverse-byte sequence.
- The two types of internal memory are ROM and RAM.
- An assembly language program consists of one or more segments: a stack segment for maintaining return addresses, a data segment for defined data and work areas, and a code segment for executable instructions. Addresses within a segment are expressed as an offset relative to the segment's starting address.
- The CS, DS, and SS registers provide for addressing the code, data, and stack segments, respectively.
- The IP register contains the offset address of the next instruction that is to execute.
- The SP and BP pointer registers are associated with the SS register and permit the system to access data in the stack segment.
- The AX, BX, CX, and DX general-purpose registers are the system's workhorses. The leftmost byte is the "high" portion, and the rightmost byte is the "low" portion. The AX (primary accumulator) is used for input/output and most arithmetic. The BX (base register) can be used as an index to extend addressing. The CX is known as the count register, and the DX is known as the data register.
- The SI and DI index registers are available for extended addressing and for use in addition and subtraction. These registers are also required for some string (character) operations.
- The flags register indicates the current status of the processor and the results of executing instructions.

QUESTIONS

1-1. (a) What is the basic building block of computer storage? (b) What are its two conditions?

1-2. (a) A collection of nine elements mentioned in Question 1-1 is known as what? (b) Eight of the elements are used for what purpose, and what is the purpose of the ninth element?

1-3. Provide the length of the following data items: (a) word; (b) doubleword; (c) paragraph; (d) kilobyte.

1-4. Convert the following decimal numbers into binary format: (a) 5; (b) 13; (c) 23; (d) 29; (e) 31.

1-5. Add the following binary numbers:

```
(a) 00011101     (b) 00101110     (c) 00011111     (d) 01010101
    00000101         00111001         00000001         00111111
    --------         --------         --------         --------
```

1-6. Provide the two's complement of the following binary numbers: (a) 00100110; (b) 00111011; (c) 01111000; (d) 00000000.

1-7. Convert the following negative binary numbers into positive binary values: (a) 11000100; (b) 10111011; (c) 11111100; (d) 11111111.

1-8. Provide the hex representation of the following values: (a) ASCII letter W; (b) ASCII number 9; (c) binary 01010111; (d) binary 01101111.

1-9. Add the following hex numbers:

```
(a) 24A5   (b) 62FC  (c) 7889   (d) DBCD   (e) FCBB
  + 0033     + 0004    + 0777     + 35B5     + 0BAF
```

1-10. Determine the hex representation of the following decimal numbers. Refer to Appendix A for the conversion method. You could also check your result by converting the hex to binary and adding the 1-bits. (a) 18; (b) 34; (c) 87; (d) 255; (e) 4,095; (f) 62,472.

1-11. Provide the bit configuration for the following 1-byte ASCII characters. Use Appendix B as a guide: (a) Q; (b) q; (c) ?; (d) 8; (e) $; (f) comma.

1-12. What are the main functions of the processor?

1-13. Identify the two main kinds of memory on the PC and give their main purposes.

1-14. Show how the processor stores the following as values in memory: (a) hex 1234; (b) hex 01C3B5.

1-15. Explain each of the following terms: (a) segment; (b) offset; (c) address boundary.

1-16. What are (a) the three kinds of segments, (b) their maximum size, and (c) the address boundary on which they begin?

1-17. What is the purpose of each of the four segment registers?

1-18. Explain which registers are used for the following purposes: (a) addressing segments; (b) offset address of an instruction that is to execute; (c) addition and subtraction; (d) multiplication and division; (e) counting for looping; (f) indication of a zero result.

1-19. Show the EDX register and the size and position of the DH, DL, and DX within it.

1-20. Code the assembler instructions to move (MOV) the value 36 to each of the following registers: (a) BX; (b) BH; (c) BL; (d) EBX.

1-21. Code the assembler instructions to add (ADD) the value 36 to each of the following registers: (a) DX; (b) DH; (c) DL; (d) EDX.

2 REQUIREMENTS FOR USING PC SOFTWARE

Objective: To explain the general software environment of the PC.

INTRODUCTION

In this chapter, we describe the PC software environment: the functions of the operating system and its main components. We examine the boot process (how the system loads itself when you power up the computer), and consider how the system loads a program for execution, how the system uses the stack, and how an instruction in the code segment addresses data in the data segment.

The chapter completes the basic explanations of the PC's hardware and software and enables you to proceed to Chapter 3, where you can begin keying simple programs into memory and executing them step by step.

FEATURES OF THE OPERATING SYSTEM

The operating system provides general, device-independent access to the resources of a computer for such devices as keyboards, screens, and disk drives. "Device independence" means that you don't have to address devices specifically, because the system can handle input/output (I/O) operations at the device level, independent of the program that requested the operation.

Among the DOS functions that concern us in this book are the following:

- File management. DOS maintains the directories and files on the system's disks. Programs create and update files, but the system is responsible for managing their location on disk.
- Input/output. Programs request input data from the system or deliver such data to the system by means of interrupts. The programmer is relieved of coding at the low I/O level.
- Program loading. When a user or program requests execution of a program, the program loader handles the steps involved in accessing the program from disk, placing it in memory, and initializing it for execution.
- Memory management. When the program loader loads a program from disk into memory for execution, it allocates a large enough space in memory for the program code and its data. Programs can process data within their memory area, can release unwanted memory, and can request additional memory.
- Interrupt handling. The system allows users to install resident programs that attach themselves to the interrupt system to perform special functions.

Organization of the Operating System

The three major components of MS-DOS are IO.SYS, MSDOS.SYS, and COMMAND.COM.

IO.SYS performs initialization functions at bootup time and also contains important input/output functions and device drivers that supplement the primitive I/O support in ROM BIOS. This component is stored on disk as a hidden system file and is known under PC-DOS as IBMBIO.COM.

MSDOS.SYS acts as the system kernel and is concerned with file management, memory management, and input/output. This component is stored on disk as a hidden system file and is known under PC-DOS as IBMDOS.COM.

COMMAND.COM is a command processor or shell that acts as the interface between the user and the operating system. It displays the user prompt, monitors the keyboard, and processes user commands such as deleting a file or loading a program for execution.

THE BOOT PROCESS

Turning on the computer's power causes a "cold boot." The processor enters a reset state, clears all memory locations to zero, performs a parity check of memory, and sets the CS register to segment address FFFF[0]H and the IP register to offset zero. The first instruction to execute, therefore, is at the address formed by the CS:IP pair, which is FFFF0H, the entry point to BIOS in ROM.

The BIOS routine beginning at location FFFF0H checks the various ports to identify and initialize devices that are attached to the computer. BIOS then establishes two data areas:

1. An *interrupt vector table,* which begins in low memory at location 0 and contains addresses for interrupts that occur.
2. A *BIOS data area* beginning at location 40[0], largely concerned with attached devices.

BIOS next determines whether a disk containing the system files is present and, if so, it accesses the bootstrap loader from the disk. This program loads system files IO.SYS and MSDOS.SYS from the disk into memory and transfers control to the entry point of IO.SYS, which contains device drivers and other hardware-specific code. IO.SYS relocates itself in memory and transfers control in its turn to MSDOS.SYS. This module initializes internal DOS tables and the DOS portion of the interrupt table. It also reads the CONFIG.SYS file and executes its commands. Finally, MSDOS.SYS passes control to COMMAND.COM, which processes the AUTOEXEC.BAT file, displays its prompt, and monitors the keyboard for input.

At this point, conventional memory up to 640K appears as shown in Figure 2-1. Under memory management, part of the system may be relocated into high memory.

```
640K
     COMMAND.COM transient portion
     (executing programs may erase it)
     ----------------------------------------------
     Available for programs' use
     ----------------------------------------------
     COMMAND.COM resident portion (resides permanently)
     ----------------------------------------------
     System files IO.SYS and MSDOS.SYS
     ----------------------------------------------
     BIOS data area
     ----------------------------------------------
0K   Interrupt vector table
```

Figure 2-1 Map of Conventional Memory

INPUT-OUTPUT INTERFACE

BIOS contains a set of routines in ROM to provide device support. BIOS tests and initializes attached devices and provides services that are used for reading to and for writing from the devices. One task of DOS is to interface with BIOS when there is a need to access its facilities.

When a user program requests an I/O service of the operating system, it transfers the request to BIOS, which in its turn accesses the requested device. Sometimes, however, a program makes requests directly to BIOS, especially for keyboard and screen services. At other times—although rarely and not recommended—a program can bypass both DOS and BIOS to access a device directly. Figure 2-2 shows these alternative paths.

THE SYSTEM PROGRAM LOADER

The two types of executable programs are .COM and .EXE. A *.COM program* consists of one segment that contains code, data, and the stack. A .COM program is useful as a small utility program or as a resident program (one that is installed in memory and is available while other programs run). An *.EXE program* consists of separate code, data, and stack seg-

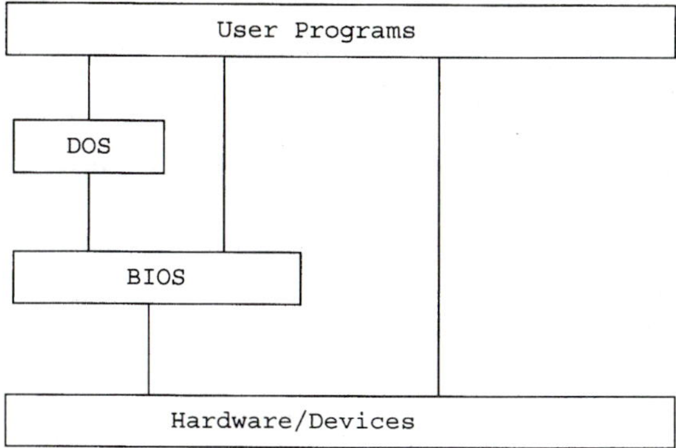

Figure 2-2 Input-Output Interface

ments and is the method used for more serious programs. This book makes use of both types of programs.

When you request the system to load an .EXE program from disk into memory for execution, the loader performs the following steps:

1. Accesses the .EXE program from disk.
2. Constructs a 256-byte (100H) program segment prefix (PSP) on a paragraph boundary in available internal memory.
3. Stores the program in memory immediately following the PSP.
4. Loads the address of the PSP in the DS and ES registers.
5. Loads the address of the code segment in the CS register and sets the IP register to the offset of the first instruction (usually zero) in the code segment.
6. Loads the address of the stack in the SS register and sets the SP register to the size of the stack.
7. Transfers control to the program for execution, beginning (usually) with the first instruction in the code segment.

In the foregoing way, the program loader correctly initializes the CS:IP and SS:SP registers. But note that the program loader stores the address of the PSP in both the DS and ES registers, although your program normally needs the address of the data segment in these registers. As a consequence, your .EXE programs have to initialize the DS with the address of the data segment, as you'll see in Chapter 4.

We'll now examine the stack and the code and data segments.

THE STACK

Both .COM and .EXE programs require an area in the program reserved as a *stack.* The purpose of the stack is to provide a space for the temporary storage of addresses and data items.

The program loader automatically defines the stack for a .COM program, whereas you must explicitly define a stack for an .EXE program. Each data item in the stack is 1 word (2 bytes). The SS register, as initialized by the loader, contains the address of the beginning of the stack. Initially, the SP register contains the size of the stack, a value that points to the byte past the end of the stack. The stack differs from other segments in its method of storing data: It begins storing data at the highest location in the segment and stores data downward through memory.

The PUSH and POP instructions are two of a number of instructions that modify the contents of the SP register and are used for storing data on the stack and retrieving it. PUSH executes by decrementing the SP by 2 to the next lower storage word in the stack and storing (or pushing) a value there. POP executes by returning a value from the stack and incrementing the SP by 2 to the next higher storage word.

The following example illustrates pushing the contents of the AX and BX registers onto the stack and then subsequently popping the data from the stack back to the registers. Assume that the AX contains hex 026B, the BX contains 04E3, and the SP contains 36. (The segment address in the SS does not concern us here.)

1. Initially, the stack is empty and looks like this:

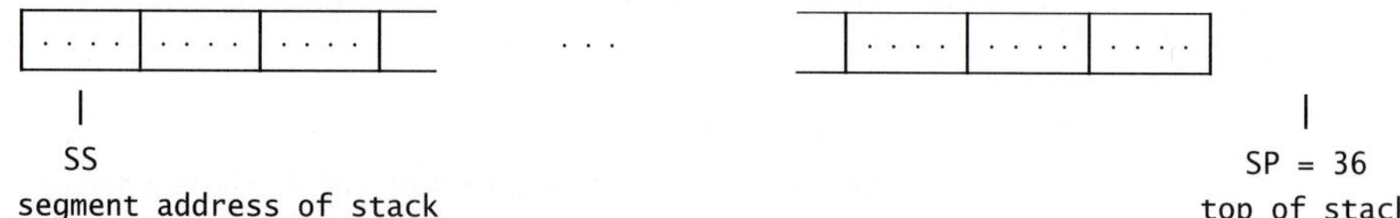

2. PUSH AX: Decrements the SP by 2 (to 34) and stores the contents of the AX, 026B, in the stack. Note that the operation reverses the sequence of the stored bytes, so that 026B becomes 6B02:

3. PUSH BX: Decrements the SP by 2 (to 32) and stores the contents of the BX, 04E3, in the stack as E304:

4. POP BX: Restores the word from where the SP points in the stack (E304) to the BX register and increments the SP by 2 (to 34). The BX now contains 04E3, with the bytes correctly restored. The stack now appears as:

5. POP AX: Restores the word from where the SP points in the stack (6B02) to the AX register and increments the SP by 2 (to 36). The AX now contains 026B, with the bytes correctly restored. The stack now appears as:

Note that POP instructions are coded in reverse sequence from PUSH instructions; the example pushed the AX and BX registers, but popped the BX and AX, in that order. Also, the values pushed onto the stack are still there, although the SP no longer points to them.

You should always ensure that your program coordinates pushing values onto the stack with popping them off of it. Although this is a fairly straightforward requirement, an error can result in a program crash. Also, for an .EXE program the stack you define must be large enough to contain all values that could be pushed onto it.

Other related instructions that push values onto the stack and pop them off are:

- PUSHF and POPF: Save and restore the status of the flags.
- PUSHA and POPA (for the 80286 and later): Save and restore the contents of all the general-purpose registers.

ADDRESSING OF INSTRUCTIONS AND DATA

An assembly language programmer writes a program in symbolic code and uses the assembler to translate it into machine code. For program execution, the system loads only the machine code into memory. Every instruction consists of at least an operation, such as move, add, or return. Depending on the operation, an instruction may also have one or more operands that reference the data the operation is to process.

As already discussed, for an .EXE program the CS register provides the address of the beginning of a program's code segment, and the DS register provides the address of the beginning of the data segment. The code segment contains instructions that are to be executed, whereas the data segment contains data that the instructions reference. The IP register indicates the offset address of the current instruction in the code segment that is to be executed. An instruction operand indicates an offset address in the data segment to be referenced.

Consider an example in which the program loader has determined that it is to load an .EXE program into memory, beginning at location 05BE0H. The loader accordingly sets the CS register with segment address 05BE[0]H. The program has already begun executing, and the IP currently contains the offset 0023H. The CS:IP together determine the address of the next instruction to execute, as follows:

```
CS segment address:     5BE0H
IP offset:             +0023H
                       ------
Instruction address:    5C03H
```

Let's say that the instruction beginning at 05C03H copies the contents of a byte in memory into the AL register; the byte is at offset 0016H in the data segment. Here are both the machine code and the symbolic code for this operation:

```
            A01600     MOV    AL,[0016]
            |
Location 05C03H
```

Memory address 05C03H contains the first byte (A0) of the instruction the processor is to access. The second and third bytes contain the offset value, in reversed-byte sequence (0016 has become 1600).

Let's say that the loader has initialized the DS register with segment address 05D1[0]H. To access the data item, the processor determines its location from the segment address in the DS register plus the offset (0016H) in the instruction operand. Because the DS contains 05D1[0]H, the actual location of the referenced data item is

```
DS segment address:        5D10H
Segment offset:          + 0016H
                         -------
Address of data item:      5D26H
```

Let's say that address 05D26H contains 4AH. The processor now extracts the 4AH at address 05D26H and copies it into the AL register, as shown in Figure 2-3.

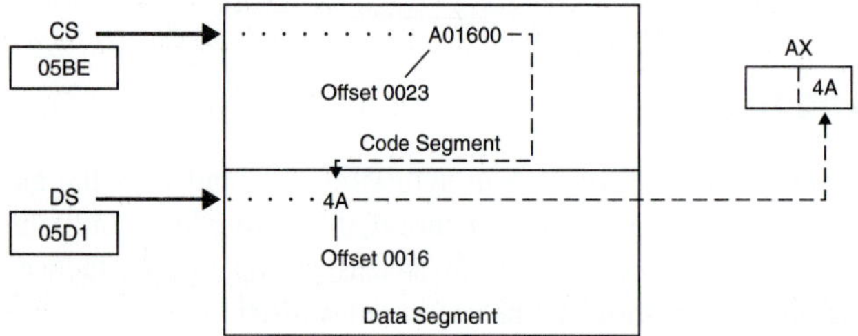

Figure 2-3 Segments and offsets

As the processor fetches each byte of the instruction, it increments the IP register by 1. Because the IP originally was 23H and the executed machine code was 3 bytes, the IP now contains 0026H, which is the offset for the next instruction. The processor is now ready to execute the next instruction, which it derives once again from the segment address in the CS (05BE0H) plus the current offset in the IP (0026H), in effect, 05C06H.

An instruction may also access more than one byte at a time. For example, suppose an instruction is to store the contents of the AX register (0248H) in two adjacent bytes in the data segment beginning at offset 0016H. The symbolic code is MOV [0016],AX. The operand [0016] in square brackets (an index operator) indicates a memory location, to distinguish it from simply the number 16. The processor loads the two bytes in the AX in reversed-byte sequence as

```
Contents of bytes:          48    02
                            |     |
Offset in data segment:   0016  0017
```

Another instruction, MOV AX, [0016], subsequently could retrieve these bytes by copying them from memory back into the AX. The operation reverses (and corrects) the bytes in the AX as 02 48.

INSTRUCTION OPERANDS

One feature about instruction operands to get clear is the use of normal names, of names in square brackets, and of numbers. In the following example, a DW defines WORDX as a word (2 bytes):

```
WORDX  DW     0            ;Define WORDX as word
       ...
       MOV    CX,WORDX     ;Move contents of WORDX to CX
       MOV    CX,25        ;Move value 25 to CX
       MOV    CX,DX        ;Move contents of DX to CX
       MOV    CX,[DX]      ;Move contents of location addressed by DX
```

- The first MOV transfers data between memory and a register.
- The second MOV transfers immediate data to a register.
- The third MOV transfers data between registers.
- The square brackets in the fourth MOV define an *index operator* that means: Use the offset address in the DX (combined with the segment address in the DS, as DS:DX) to locate a word in memory, and move its contents to the CX. Compare the effect of this instruction with that of the third MOV, which simply moves the contents of the DX to the CX.

KEY POINTS

- The three major components of the operating system are IO.SYS, MSDOS.SYS, and COMMAND.COM.
- Turning on the computer's power causes a "cold boot." The processor enters a reset state, clears all memory locations to zero, performs a parity check of memory, and sets the CS register and the IP register to the entry point of BIOS in ROM.
- The two types of programs are .COM and .EXE.
- When you request the system to load an .EXE program for execution, the program loader constructs a 256-byte (100H) PSP on a paragraph boundary in memory and stores the program immediately following the PSP. It then loads the address of the PSP in the DS and ES registers, loads the address of the code segment in the CS, sets the IP to the offset of the first instruction in the code segment, loads the address of the stack in the SS, and sets the SP to the size of the stack. Finally, the loader transfers control to the program for execution.
- The purpose of the stack is to provide a space for the temporary storage of addresses and data items. Each data item in the stack is one word (2 bytes).
- The program loader defines the stack for a .COM program, whereas you must explicitly define a stack for an .EXE program.
- As the processor fetches each byte of an instruction, it increments the IP register so that the IP contains the offset for the next instruction.

QUESTIONS

2-1. Identify the five main functions of the operating system.

2-2. Give the three main components of the operating system and explain the purpose of each.

2-3. Give the steps that the system takes on a "cold boot."

2-4. The program loader constructs and stores a data area in front of an executable module when it loads the module for execution. (a) What is the name of this data area? (b) What is its size?

2-5. The program loader performs certain operations when it loads an .EXE program for execution. What values does the loader initialize (a) in the DS and ES registers? (b) in the CS and IP registers? (c) in the SS and SP registers?

2-6. Explain the purpose of the stack.

2-7. Explain how the stack is defined for (a) a .COM program and (b) an .EXE program. (That is, who or what defines the stack?)

2-8. (a) Where initially is the top of the stack, and how is it addressed? (b) What is the size of each entry in the stack?

2-9. During execution of a program, the CS contains 6C3A[0], the SS contains 6C62[0], the IP contains 42H, and the SP contains 36H. (Values are shown in normal, not reversed-byte, sequence.) Calculate the addresses of (a) the instruction to execute and (b) the top (current location) of the stack.

2-10. During execution of a program, the CS contains 74A5[0], the SS contains 752B[0], the IP contains 54H, and the SP contains 24H. (Values are shown in normal, not reversed-byte, sequence.) Calculate the addresses of (a) the instruction to execute and (b) the top (current location) of the stack.

2-11. Calculate the memory address of the referenced data for the following. (a) The DS contains 4D34[0], and an instruction that moves data from memory to the AL is A02B04 (where A0 means "move"). (b) The DS contains 5B24[0], and an instruction that moves data from memory to the AL is A03A01.

3 EXECUTING COMPUTER INSTRUCTIONS

Objective: To introduce the entering and executing of programs in memory.

INTRODUCTION

This chapter uses a DOS program named DEBUG that allows you to view memory, to enter programs in memory, and to trace their execution. The text describes how you can enter these programs directly into memory in a code segment and provides an explanation of each execution step. Although there are more sophisticated debuggers such as CODEVIEW and TurboDebugger, we'll use DEBUG because it is simple to use and universally available.

In the initial exercises, you get to inspect the contents of particular areas of memory. The first program example uses "immediate" data defined within the instructions for loading data into registers and performing arithmetic. The second program example uses data defined separately from the executable instructions. Tracing these instructions as they execute provides insight into the operation of a processor and the role of the registers.

You can start right away with no prior knowledge of assembly language or even of programming. All you need is an Intel-based PC and a disk containing the DOS operating system. We do assume, however, that you are familiar with keying in system commands and selecting disk drives and files.

USING THE DEBUG PROGRAM

The DOS system comes with a program named DEBUG that is used for testing and debugging executable programs. A feature of DEBUG is that it displays all program code and data in hexadecimal format, and any data that you enter into memory must also be in hex format. DEBUG also provides a single-step mode, which allows you to execute a program one instruction at a time, so that you can view the effect of each instruction on memory locations and registers.

DEBUG Commands

DEBUG's set of commands lets you perform a number of useful operations. The commands of interest at this point are the following:

A Assemble symbolic instructions into machine code
D Display the contents of an area of memory
E Enter data into memory, beginning at a specific location
G Run the executable program in memory (G means "go")
N Name a program
P Proceed, or execute a set of related instructions
Q Quit the DEBUG session
R Display the contents of one or more registers
T Trace the execution of one instruction
U Unassemble (really, disassemble) machine code into symbolic code
W Write a program onto disk.

Appendix E provides a full description of all the DEBUG commands.

Rules of DEBUG Commands

Here are some basic rules for using DEBUG:

- For its own purposes, DEBUG does not distinguish between lowercase and uppercase letters, so you may enter commands either way.
- You enter a space only where it is needed to separate parameters in a command.
- You specify segments and offsets with a colon, in the form segment:offset.
- DEBUG assumes that all numbers are in hexadecimal format.

The following three examples use DEBUG's D command to display the same area of memory, beginning at offset 200H in the data segment (DS):

```
D DS:200     (D command in uppercase, space following)
DDS:200      (D command in uppercase, no space following)
dds:200      (d command in lowercase, no space following)
```

The DEBUG Display

The D command displays the contents of a requested data area on the screen. The display consists of three parts:

1. To the left is the hex address of the leftmost displayed byte, in segment:offset format.
2. The wide area in the center is the hex representation of the displayed area.
3. To the right is the ASCII representation of bytes that contain displayable characters, which can help you interpret the hex area.

The operation displays 8 lines of data, each containing 16 bytes (32 hex digits), for 128 bytes in all, beginning with the address that you specify in the D command. Diagrammatically, we have:

```
Address     |<-------- Hexadecimal representation -------->|<--ASCII-->|

xxxx:xx10   xx ................ xx-xx ................ xx x.........x
xxxx:xx20   xx ................ xx-xx ................ xx x.........x
xxxx:xx30   xx ................ xx-xx ................ xx x.........x
...
xxxx:xx80   xx ................ xx-xx ................ xx x.........x
```

The address to the left refers only to the leftmost (beginning) byte, in segment:offset format; you can count across the line to determine the position of each other byte. The hex representation area shows two hex characters for each byte, followed by a space for readability. Also, a hyphen separates the second 8 bytes from the first 8, again for readability. Thus if you want to locate the byte at offset xx13H, start with xx10H, and count three bytes successively to the right.

This book makes considerable use of DEBUG and explains details of its commands as they are needed.

Starting DEBUG

To start DEBUG, set the system to the directory on hard disk containing DEBUG, or insert in the default drive a diskette containing DEBUG. To initiate the program, key in the word DEBUG and press <Enter>. DEBUG should load from disk into memory. When DEBUG's prompt, a hyphen (-), appears on the screen, DEBUG is ready to accept your commands. (That is a hyphen, although it resembles the cursor.) Let's now use DEBUG to snoop about in memory.

VIEWING MEMORY LOCATIONS

In the first five exercises, you use DEBUG to view the contents of selected memory locations. The only command with which this exercise is concerned is D (Display), which lists 8 lines of 16 bytes each and shows both the hex and ASCII representations of data.

Checking System Equipment

Let's first see what BIOS has determined is your installed equipment. An equipment status word in the BIOS data area provides a primitive indication of installed devices. This word is at locations 410H-411H, which you can view from DEBUG by means of a two-part address: 40 for the segment address (the last zero is assumed) and 10 for the offset from the segment address. Interpret the address 40:10 as segment 40[0]H plus offset 10H. Key in the following exactly as you see it:

```
D 40:10 (and press <Enter>)
```

The display should begin like this:

```
0040:0010 xx xx .. .. ..
```

Let's say that the 2 bytes in the equipment status word contain the hex values 63 and 44. To interpret them, you have to reverse the bytes (to 44 63) and convert them to binary format:

```
Bit:    15 14 13 12 11 10 9 8 7 6 5 4 3 2 1 0
Binary: 0  1  0  0  0  1 0 0 0 1 1 0 0 0 1 1
```

Here's an explanation of the bits, from left to right:

BITS	DEVICE
15,14	Number of parallel printer ports attached = 1 (binary 01)
11–9	Number of serial ports attached = 2 (binary 010)
7,6	Number of diskette devices = 2 (where 00 = 1, 01 = 2, 10 = 3, and 11 = 4)
5,4	Initial video mode = 10 (where 01 = 40 × 25 color, 10 = 80 × 25 color, and 11 = 80 × 25 monochrome)
1	1 = math coprocessor is present
0	1 = diskette drive is present

Unreferenced bits are not used. You can stay in DEBUG for the next exercise or press Q to quit.

Checking Memory Size

The next step is to examine the amount of base memory that BIOS "thinks" you have installed. Depending on the computer model, the value may be based on switches set internally and may indicate less memory than is actually installed. The value is in the BIOS data area at locations 413H and 414H, which you can interpret as segment 40[0]H plus offsets 13H and 14H. Key in the following exactly as you see it:

```
D 40:13 (and press <Enter>)
```

The display should begin like this:

```
0040:0013 .. .. .. xx xx . . .
```

The first two bytes displayed at offset 0013H are kilobytes of memory size in hexadecimal, with the bytes in reverse sequence. For example, if the data area contains 8002H, its corrected value is 0280H, which indicates base memory of 640K.

The first two exercises examined the contents of the BIOS data area in low memory. The system initializes these values when the computer power is turned on. The next three exercises examine data in ROM BIOS in high memory.

Checking Serial Number and Copyright Notice

The computer's serial number is embedded in ROM BIOS at location FE000H. To view segment FE00[0] and offset 0, type

```
D FE00:0 (and press <Enter>)
```

The operation should display a 7-digit serial number followed, on conventional machines, by a copyright notice. The serial number is viewable as hex numbers, whereas the copyright notice is more recognizable from the characters in the ASCII area to the right. The copyright notice may continue past what is already displayed; to view it, simply press D again followed by <Enter>.

Checking ROM BIOS Date

The date of manufacture of your ROM BIOS, recorded as mm/dd/yy, begins at location FFFF5H. To request segment FFFF[0] and offset 5, type

```
D FFFF:5 (and press <Enter>)
```

Knowing this date could be useful for determining a computer's age and model.

Checking Model ID

Immediately following the ROM BIOS manufacture date is a 1-byte model ID at location FFFFEH, or FFFF:E. Here are a number of model IDs:

CODE	MODEL
F8	PS/2 models 70 and 80
FA	PS/2 model 30
FB	PC-XT (1986)
FC	PC-AT (1984), PC-XT model 286, PS/2 models 50 and 60, etc.
FE	PC-XT (1982), portable (1982)
FF	Original IBM PC

Now that you know how to use the display command, you can view the contents of any storage location. You can also step through memory simply by pressing D repeatedly—DEBUG displays 8 lines successively, continuing from the last D operation.

When you've completed probing about, key in Q (for quit) to exit from DEBUG, or continue with the next exercise.

MACHINE LANGUAGE EXAMPLE I: IMMEDIATE DATA

Let's now use DEBUG to enter the first of two programs directly into memory and trace their execution. Both programs illustrate simple machine language instructions as they appear in main storage and the effect of their execution. For this purpose, we'll begin with the DEBUG E (Enter) command. Be especially careful in its use, since entering data at a wrong location or entering incorrect data may cause unpredictable results. You are not likely to cause any damage, but you may get a bit of a surprise and may lose data that you entered during the DEBUG session.

The first program uses *immediate data*—data defined as part of an instruction. We show both the machine language in hexadecimal format and, for readability, the symbolic code, along with an explanation. For the first instruction, the symbolic code is MOV AX,0123, which moves (or copies) the value 0123H to the AX register. (You don't have to define an immediate value in reverse-byte sequence.) MOV is the instruction, the AX register is the first operand, and the immediate value 0123H is the second operand.

MACHINE INSTRUCTION	SYMBOLIC CODE	EXPLANATION
B82301	MOV AX,0123	Move value 0123H to AX.
052500	ADD AX,0025	Add value 0025H to AX.
8BD8	MOV BX,AX	Move contents of AX to BX.
03D8	ADD BX,AX	Add contents of AX to BX.
8BCB	MOV CX,BX	Move contents of BX to CX.
2BC8	SUB CX,AX	Subtract contents of AX from CX.
2BC0	SUB AX,AX	Subtract AX from AX (clear AX).
90	NOP	No operation (do nothing).

Note that machine instructions may be one, two, or three bytes in length. The first byte is the actual operation, and any other bytes that are present are *operands*—references to an immediate value, a register, or a memory location. Program execution begins with the first machine instruction and steps through each instruction, one after another sequentially. At this point do not expect to make much sense of the machine code; for example, in one case the machine code (the first byte) for move is hex B8 and in another case the code for move is hex 8B.

Keying in Program Instructions

Begin this exercise just as you did the preceding one: Key in the command DEBUG and press <Enter>. When DEBUG is fully loaded, it displays its prompt (-). To key this program directly into memory, just type in the machine language portion, but *not* the symbolic code or explanation. Key in the following E (Enter) command, including the blanks, where indicated:

```
E CS:100 B8 23 01 05 25 00 (and press <Enter>)
```

CS:100 indicates the starting memory address at which the data is to be stored—100H (256) bytes following the start of the code segment (the normal starting address for machine code under DEBUG). The E command causes DEBUG to store each pair of hexadecimal digits into a byte in memory, from CS:100 through CS:105.

The next E command stores 6 bytes, starting at CS:106 through 107, 108, 109, 10A, and 10B:

```
E CS:106 8B D8 03 D8 8B CB (followed by <Enter>)
```

The last E command stores 5 bytes, starting at CS:10C through 10D, 10E, 10F, and 110:

```
E CS:10C 2B C8 2B C0 90 (followed by <Enter>)
```

If you key in an incorrect command, simply repeat it with the correct values.

Executing Program Instructions

Now it's a simple matter to execute the preceding instructions one at a time. Figure 3-1 shows all the steps, including the E commands used to key in the machine code. Your screen should display similar results as you enter each DEBUG command. You can also view the contents of the registers after executing each instruction. The DEBUG commands that concern us here are R (Register) and T (Trace).

To view the initial contents of the registers and flags, key in the R command, followed by <Enter>, as shown in line 4 of Figure 3-1. DEBUG displays the contents of the registers in hexadecimal format as

```
AX = 0000 BX = 0000 . . .
```

Because of differences in computer configurations, some register contents on your screen may differ from those shown in Figure 3-1. The IP register should display IP = 0100, indicating that instruction execution is to begin 100H bytes past the start of the code segment. (That is why you used E CS:100 to enter the start of the program.)

The flags register in Figure 3-1 shows the following settings for the overflow, direction, interrupt, sign, zero, auxiliary carry, parity, and carry flags:

```
NV UP EI PL NZ NA PO NC
```

These settings mean no overflow, up (or right) direction, enable interrupt, plus sign, nonzero, no auxiliary carry, parity odd, and no carry, respectively. At this time, none of these settings is important to us.

Immediately following the registers and also displayed by the R command is the first instruction to be executed. Note that in the figure the CS register contains 21C1. Because your CS segment address is sure to differ from this, we'll show it as xxxx for the instructions:

```
xxxx:0100 B82301  MOV AX,0123
```

- xxxx indicates the start of the code segment as xxxx[0]. The value xxxx:0100 means offset 100H bytes following the CS segment address xxxx[0].
- B82301 is the machine code that you entered at CS:100.

```
-E CS:100 B8 23 01 05 25 00
-E CS:106 8B D8 03 D8 8B CB
-E CS:10C 2B C8 2B C0 90
-R
AX=0000  BX=0000  CX=0000  DX=0000  SP=FFEE  BP=0000  SI=0000  DI=0000
DS=21C1  ES=21C1  SS=21C1  CS=21C1  IP=0100   NV UP EI PL NZ NA PO NC
21C1:0100 B82301        MOV     AX,0123
-T

AX=0123  BX=0000  CX=0000  DX=0000  SP=FFEE  BP=0000  SI=0000  DI=0000
DS=21C1  ES=21C1  SS=21C1  CS=21C1  IP=0103   NV UP EI PL NZ NA PO NC
21C1:0103 052500        ADD     AX,0025
-T

AX=0148  BX=0000  CX=0000  DX=0000  SP=FFEE  BP=0000  SI=0000  DI=0000
DS=21C1  ES=21C1  SS=21C1  CS=21C1  IP=0106   NV UP EI PL NZ NA PE NC
21C1:0106 8BD8          MOV     BX,AX
-T

AX=0148  BX=0148  CX=0000  DX=0000  SP=FFEE  BP=0000  SI=0000  DI=0000
DS=21C1  ES=21C1  SS=21C1  CS=21C1  IP=0108   NV UP EI PL NZ NA PE NC
21C1:0108 03D8          ADD     BX,AX
-T

AX=0148  BX=0290  CX=0000  DX=0000  SP=FFEE  BP=0000  SI=0000  DI=0000
DS=21C1  ES=21C1  SS=21C1  CS=21C1  IP=010A   NV UP EI PL NZ AC PE NC
21C1:010A 8BCB          MOV     CX,BX
-T

AX=0148  BX=0290  CX=0290  DX=0000  SP=FFEE  BP=0000  SI=0000  DI=0000
DS=21C1  ES=21C1  SS=21C1  CS=21C1  IP=010C   NV UP EI PL NZ AC PE NC
21C1:010C 2BC8          SUB     CX,AX
-T

AX=0148  BX=0290  CX=0148  DX=0000  SP=FFEE  BP=0000  SI=0000  DI=0000
DS=21C1  ES=21C1  SS=21C1  CS=21C1  IP=010E   NV UP EI PL NZ AC PE NC
21C1:010E 2BC0          SUB     AX,AX
-T

AX=0000  BX=0290  CX=0148  DX=0000  SP=FFEE  BP=0000  SI=0000  DI=0000
DS=21C1  ES=21C1  SS=21C1  CS=21C1  IP=0110   NV UP EI PL ZR NA PE NC
21C1:0110 90            NOP
-
```

Figure 3-1 Tracing Machine Instructions

- MOV AX,0123 is the symbolic assembly instruction that DEBUG determined from the machine code. This instruction means, in effect, move the immediate value 0123H into the AX register. DEBUG has "unassembled" the machine instructions so that you may interpret them more easily. After this chapter, you will code symbolic assembly instructions exclusively.

At this point, the MOV instruction has not executed. For that purpose, key in T (Trace) and press <Enter>. The machine code is B8 (move to AX register) followed by 2301. The operation moves the 23 to the low half (AL) of the AX register and the 01 to the high half (AH) of the AX register:

	AH	AL
AX:	01	23

DEBUG displays the effect of the operation on the registers. The IP register now contains 0103H (the original 0100H plus 3 bytes for the first machine code instruction). The value indicates the offset location in the code segment of the next instruction to be executed, namely:

```
xxxx:0103 052500 ADD AX,0025
```

To execute this ADD instruction, enter another T. The instruction adds 25H to the low half (AL) of the AX register and 00H to the high half (AH), in effect adding 0025H to the AX. AX now contains 0148H, and IP contains 0106H for the next instruction to be executed:

```
xxxx:0106 8BD8 MOV BX,AX
```

Key in another T command. The MOV instruction moves the contents of the AX register to the BX register. Note that after the move the BX contains 0148H. The AX still contains 0148H because MOV *copies* rather than actually moves the data from one location to another.

Now key in successive T commands to step through the remaining instructions. The ADD instruction adds the contents of AX to BX, giving 0290H in BX. Then the program moves (copies) the contents of BX into CX, subtracts AX from CX, and subtracts AX from itself. After this last operation, the zero flag is changed from NZ (nonzero) to ZR (zero), to indicate that the result of the last operation was zero. (Subtracting AX from itself cleared it to zero.)

If you want to reexecute these instructions, you have to reset the IP register to 100H. In fact, you'll do this quite often, so here is the procedure:

1. Key in R IP to display the contents of the IP, and
2. Type in the value 100 followed by <Enter>.

This procedure takes you to the start of the program, where you can now repeat the previous steps: Key in R and the required number of T commands, all followed by <Enter>.

Displaying Memory Contents

Although you can also press T for the last instruction, NOP (no-operation), this instruction doesn't perform anything. Instead, to view the machine language program in the code segment, request a display as follows:

```
D CS:100
```

Figure 3-2 shows the results of this command, with 16 bytes (32 hex digits) of data displayed on each line. To the right is the ASCII representation (if a standard character) of each byte. In the case of machine code, the ASCII representation is meaningless and may be ignored. Later sections discuss the right side of the display in more detail.

The first line of the display begins at offset 100H of the code segment and represents the contents of locations CS:100 through CS:10F. The second line represents the contents of CS:110 through CS:11F. Although the program actually ends at CS:110, the D command automatically displays 8 lines from CS:100 through CS:170. For our purposes, any data following CS:110 is "garbage."

Expect only the machine code from CS:100 through 110 to be identical to that of your own display; the bytes that follow could contain anything. Also, Figure 3-2 shows that the

```
-D CS:100
21C1:0100  B8 23 01 05 25 00 8B D8-03 D8 8B CB 2B C8 2B C0   .#..%.......+.+.
21C1:0110  90 C3 8D 46 14 50 51 52-FF 76 28 E8 74 00 8B E5   ...F.PQR.v(.t...
21C1:0120  B8 01 00 50 FF 76 32 FF-76 30 FF 76 2E FF 76 28   ...P.v2.v0.v..v(
21C1:0130  E8 88 15 8B E5 FF 36 18-12 FF 36 16 12 8B 76 28   ......6...6...v(
21C1:0140  FF 74 3A 89 46 06 E8 22-CE 8B E5 30 E4 3D 0A 00   .t:.F.."...0.=..
21C1:0150  75 32 A1 16 12 2D 01 00-8B 1E 18 12 83 DB 00 53   u2...-.........S
21C1:0160  50 8B 76 28 FF 74 3A A3-16 12 89 1E 18 12 E8 FA   P.v(.t:.........
21C1:0170  CD 8B E5 30 E4 3D 0D 00-74 0A 83 06 16 12 01 83   ...0.=..t.......
-
```

Figure 3-2 Dump of the Code Segment

DS, ES, SS, and CS registers all contain the same address. This is because DEBUG happens to treat the area as a .COM program, with code and data (if any) in the same segment, although you must keep them separated within the segment.

Enter Q (Quit) to end the DEBUG session or continue with the next exercise.

Correcting an Entry

If you enter an incorrect value into the program, simply reenter the E command to correct it. Also, to resume execution at the first instruction, reset the IP register to 0100—follow the procedure described earlier: Type in R IP and enter the value 100. Next, key in an R command (without the IP). DEBUG displays the registers, flags, and first instruction to be executed. You can now use T to retrace the instruction steps. If your program accumulates totals, you may have to clear some memory locations and registers. But be sure not to change the contents of the CS, DS, SP, and SS registers, all of which have specific purposes.

MACHINE LANGUAGE EXAMPLE II: DEFINED DATA

The preceding example used immediate values defined directly within MOV and ADD instructions. We next illustrate a similar example that defines the values (or constants) 0123H and 0025H as separate data items within the program. The program is to access the memory locations that contain these values.

Working through this example should give you an insight into how a computer accesses data by means of an address in the DS register and offset addresses. The example defines the following data items and contents beginning at offset 0200H, which is clearly separate from the instructions at 0100H:

DS OFFSET	HEX CONTENTS
0200H	2301H
0202H	2500H
0204H	0000H
0206H	2A2A2AH

Remember that a hex digit occupies a half-byte, so that, for example, 23H is stored in offset 0200H (the first byte) of the data area, and 01H is stored in offset 0201H (the second byte). Here are the machine instructions that process these data items. The values are entered in reverse-byte sequence, for example, 0200 as 0002:

INSTRUCTION	EXPLANATION
A10002	Move the word (2 bytes) beginning at DS offset 0200H into the AX register.
03060202	Add the contents of the word (2 bytes) beginning at DS offset 0202H into the AX register.
A30402	Move the contents of the AX register to the word beginning at DS offset 0204H.
90	No operation.

You may have noticed that the two move instructions have different machine codes: A1 and A3. The actual machine code is dependent on the registers that are referenced, the size of data (byte or word), the direction of data transfer (from or to a register), and the reference to immediate data, memory, or register.

Keying in Program Instructions and Data

Again, you can use DEBUG to key in the program and to watch its execution. First, use the E command to key in the instructions, beginning at CS:0100:

```
E  CS:100  A1  00  02  03  06  02  02  (press <Enter>)
E  CS:107  A3  04  02  90   (press <Enter>)
```

Now use E (Enter) commands for defining data, beginning arbitrarily at DS:0200:

```
E  DS:0200  23  01  25  00  00  00  (press <Enter>)
E  DS:0206  2A  2A  2A   (press <Enter>)
```

The first E command stores the 3 words (6 bytes) at the start of the data area at offset 0200. You have to key in each of these words with the bytes reversed, so that 0123 is 2301 and 0025 is 2500. When a MOV instruction subsequently accesses these words and loads them into a register, it "unreverses" the bytes, so that 2301 becomes 0123 and 2500 becomes 0025.

The second E command stores three asterisks (***), defined as 2A2A2A so that you can view them later using the D (Display) command. Otherwise, these asterisks serve no particular purpose in the data area.

Figure 3-3 shows all the steps in the program, including the E commands. Your screen should display similar results, although addresses in the CS and DS probably differ. To examine the stored data (at DS:200H through 208H) and the instructions (at CS:100H through 10AH), key in the following D commands:

To view the code:	`D  CS:100,10A  <Enter>`
To view the data:	`D  DS:200,208  <Enter>`

Check that the contents of both areas are identical to what is shown in Figure 3-3.

```
-E DS:200 23 01 25 00 00 00
-E DS:206 2A 2A 2A
-E CS:100 A1 00 02 03 06 02 02
-E CS:107 A3 04 02 90
-D DS:200,208
21C1:0200   23 01 25 00 00 00 2A 2A-2A                          #.%...***
-D CS:100,10A
21C1:0100   A1 00 02 03 06 02 02 A3-04 02 90                    ...........
-R
AX=0000  BX=0000  CX=0000  DX=0000  SP=FFEE  BP=0000  SI=0000  DI=0000
DS=21C1  ES=21C1  SS=21C1  CS=21C1  IP=0100   NV UP EI PL NZ NA PO NC
21C1:0100 A10002        MOV    AX,[0200]                    DS:0200=0123
-T

AX=0123  BX=0000  CX=0000  DX=0000  SP=FFEE  BP=0000  SI=0000  DI=0000
DS=21C1  ES=21C1  SS=21C1  CS=21C1  IP=0103   NV UP EI PL NZ NA PO NC
21C1:0103 03060202      ADD    AX,[0202]                    DS:0202=0025
-T

AX=0148  BX=0000  CX=0000  DX=0000  SP=FFEE  BP=0000  SI=0000  DI=0000
DS=21C1  ES=21C1  SS=21C1  CS=21C1  IP=0107   NV UP EI PL NZ NA PE NC
21C1:0107 A30402        MOV    [0204],AX                    DS:0204=0000
-T

AX=0148  BX=0000  CX=0000  DX=0000  SP=FFEE  BP=0000  SI=0000  DI=0000
DS=21C1  ES=21C1  SS=21C1  CS=21C1  IP=010A   NV UP EI PL NZ NA PE NC
21C1:010A 90            NOP
-D DS:0200,0208
21C1:0000   23 01 25 00 48 01 2A 2A-2A                          #.%.H.***
-Q
```

Figure 3-3 Tracing Machine Instructions

Executing the Program Instructions

Having keyed in the instructions, you can now execute them just as you did earlier. First make sure that the IP contains 100H. Then press R to view the contents of the registers and flags and to display the first instruction. Although the AX register may still contain a value from the previous exercise, you'll replace it shortly. The first displayed instruction is

```
xxxx:0100 A10002 MOV AX,[0200]
```

CS:0100 references your first instruction, A10002. DEBUG interprets this instruction as a MOV and has determined that the reference is to the first location [0200H] in the data area. The square brackets tell you that this reference is to a memory address and not an immediate value. (An immediate value for moving 0200H to the AX register would appear as MOV AX,0200.)

Now key in the T (Trace) command. The instruction MOV AX,[0200] moves the contents of the word at offset 0200H to the AX register. The contents are 2301H, which the operation reverses in the AX as 0123H and replaces any previous contents in the AX.

Key in another T command to cause execution of the next instruction, ADD. The operation adds the contents of the word in memory at DS offset 0202 to the AX register. The result in the AX is now the sum of 0123H and 0025H, or 0148H.

The next instruction is MOV [0204],AX. Key in a T command for it to execute. The instruction moves the contents of the AX register (0148H) to the data area at DS offsets 204H and 205H and is reversed as 4801H. To view the changed contents of the data from 200H through 208H, key in

```
D DS:200,208 <Enter>
```

The displayed values should be:

Value in data area:	23	01	25	00	48	01	2A	2A	2A
	|	|	|	|	|	|	|	|	|
Offset :	200	201	202	203	204	205	206	207	208

The left side of the display shows the actual machine code as it appears in memory. The right side simply helps you locate character data more easily. Note that these hex values are represented on the right of the screen by their ASCII equivalents. Thus 23H generates a number (#) symbol, and 25H generates a percent (%) symbol, while the three 2AH bytes generate asterisks (*).

Because there are no more instructions to execute, enter Q (Quit) to end the DEBUG session, or continue with the next exercise (and remember to reset the IP to 100).

AN ASSEMBLY LANGUAGE EXAMPLE

Although to this point the program examples have been in machine language format, you can also use DEBUG to key in assembly language statements. You may find occasions to use both methods. Let's now examine DEBUG's A and U commands used to enter assembler statements into the computer.

The A (Assemble) Command

The A command tells DEBUG to begin accepting symbolic assembly instructions and to convert them into machine language. Initialize the starting address for your instructions in the code segment at offset 100H as

```
A 100 <Enter>
```

DEBUG displays the address of the code segment and the offset (0100) as xxxx:0100. Type in the following instructions, each followed by <Enter>:

```
MOV   CL,42    <Enter>
MOV   DL,2A    <Enter>
ADD   CL,DL    <Enter>
NOP            <Enter>, <Enter>
```

When you've keyed in the program, press <Enter> again to exit from the A command. That's one extra <Enter>, which tells DEBUG you have no more symbolic instructions to enter. On completion, DEBUG should display the following:

```
xxxx:0100      MOV    CL,42
xxxx:0102      MOV    DL,2A
xxxx:0104      ADD    CL,DL
xxxx:0106      NOP
```

You can see that DEBUG has determined the starting location of each instruction. But before executing the program, let's use DEBUG's U (Unassemble) command to examine the generated machine language.

The U (Unassemble) Command

DEBUG's U command displays the machine code for your assembly language instructions. You can use this command to tell DEBUG the locations of the first and last instructions that you want to see, in this case, 100H and 106H. Key in

```
U 100,106 <Enter>
```

The screen displays columns for the location, machine code, and symbolic code like this:

```
xxxx:0100  B142     MOV  CL,42
xxxx:0102  B22A     MOV  DL,2A
xxxx:0104  00D1     ADD  CL,DL
xxxx:0106  90       NOP
```

Now trace the execution of the program—the machine code is what actually executes. Begin by keying in R to display the registers and the first instruction, and then successive T commands to trace subsequent instructions. When you get to the NOP at location 106H, the IP should contain 106H and the CL should contain 6CH. Continue with the next exercise or press Q to quit execution.

You have now seen how to key in a program in machine language and in assembly language. However, DEBUG is really intended for what its name implies—debugging programs—and most of your efforts will involve the use of conventional assembly language, which is not associated with DEBUG.

USING THE INT INSTRUCTION

The following four examples show how to request information about the system. To this end, you use the INT (interrupt) instruction, which exits from your program, enters a DOS or BIOS routine, performs the requested function, and returns to your program. There are different types of INT operations, some of which require a *function code* in the AH register to request a specific action. Rather than using the T command for single-stepping, we'll use the P (Proceed) command to execute through the whole interrupt routine. Be sure to reset the IP to 100H.

Getting the Current Date

The instruction to access the current date is INT 21H function code 2AH. Once again, type in the DEBUG command A 100 and then the following assembler instructions:

```
MOV   AH,2A
INT   21
NOP
```

Type in R to display the registers and T to execute the MOV. Then type in P to proceed through the interrupt routine; the operation stops at the NOP instruction. The registers contain this information in hex format:

```
AL:    Day of the week, where 0 = Sunday
CX:    Year (for example, 07D0H = 2000)
DH:    Month (01H through 0CH)
DL:    Day of the month (01H through 1FH)
```

Press Q to quit, or continue with the next exercise (and reset the IP to 100).

Determining the Size of Memory

In an early exercise in this chapter, you checked locations 413H and 414H for the amount of base memory that your computer contains. BIOS also provides an interrupt routine, INT 12H, that delivers the size of memory. Type in the DEBUG command A 100 and then these instructions:

```
INT   12
NOP
```

Key in R to display the registers and the first instruction. The instruction, INT 12H, passes control to a routine in BIOS that delivers the size of base memory to the AX. Press T and <Enter> repeatedly to see each BIOS instruction execute. (Yes, we are violating a rule against tracing through an interrupt, but this operation works all right.)

The actual instructions in your BIOS may differ somewhat from these, depending on the version installed (the comments to the right are the author's):

```
STI                   ;Set interrupt
PUSH  DS              ;Save DS address in stack
MOV   AX,0040         ;Retrieve memory size at
MOV   DS,AX           ; segment 40[0]H plus
MOV   AX,[0013]       ; offset 0013H
POP   DS              ;Restore address in DS
IRET                  ;Return from interrupt
```

If you survived this adventure into BIOS, the AX now contains the size of base memory, in 1K bytes. The last T command exits from BIOS and returns to DEBUG. The displayed instruction is now the NOP that you entered. Press Q to quit or continue with the next exercise (and reset the IP to 100).

Using INT to Display

This exercise, which displays data on the screen, introduces a few new features. Type in the DEBUG command A 100 and then these assembler instructions:

```
100     MOV AH,09
102     MOV DX,108
105     INT 21
107     NOP
108     DB  'your name', '$'
```

The two MOV instructions tell INT 21H to display (AH = 09) and from what starting address (DX = 108). Note that offset 108 begins the definition of your name. The DB means "define byte" and the characters are contained in single quotes. Following your name is a dollar sign, also in quotes, which tells the INT to end the display.

Key in R to display the registers and the first instruction and key in T commands for the two MOVs. Key in P to execute the INT and you'll see your name displayed. Press Q to quit or continue with the next exercise (and reset the IP to 100).

Using INT for Keyboard Input

This exercise, which accepts characters from the keyboard, also introduces a few new features. Type in the DEBUG command A 100 and then these assembler instructions:

```
100 MOV AH,10
102 INT 16
104 JMP 100
106 NOP
```

The first instruction, MOV, is to tell INT 16H to accept data from the keyboard (AH = 10); the operation delivers the character from the keyboard to the AL register. The JMP instruction causes the processor to replace the value in the IP with 100, so that the next instruction to execute is the MOV back at 100H. By this means, you can execute one or more instructions repeatedly.

Key in R to display the registers and the first instruction and key in a T command for the MOV. When you type in P for the INT, the system waits for you to press a key. If you press '1,' you'll see that the operation delivers 31H (hex for ASCII '1') to the AL. Key in T to execute the JMP, and you're back at the MOV at 100. Use T to execute the MOV. When you key in P for the INT, the system again waits for you to press a key. If you press '2,' you'll see that the operation delivers 32H to the AL. You can continue like this indefinitely. Press Q to quit or continue with the next exercise (and reset the IP to 100).

SAVING A PROGRAM FROM WITHIN DEBUG

You may use DEBUG to save a program on disk under two circumstances:

1. To retrieve an existing program from disk, modify it, and then save it, follow these steps:
   - Read the program under its name: DEBUG n:filename.
   - Use the D command to view the machine language program and E to enter changes.
   - Use the W (Write) command to write the revised program.
2. To use DEBUG to create a very small machine language program that you now want to save, follow these steps:
   - Request the DEBUG program.
   - Use the A (Assemble) and E commands to key in the source program.
   - Type N filename.COM to name the program. The program extension must be .COM. (See Chapter 7 for details of .COM files.)
   - Because only you know where the program really ends, insert in the BX:CX pair the size of the program in bytes. Consider this example:

     ```
     xxxx:0100  MOV CL,42
     xxxx:0102  MOV DL,2A
     xxxx:0104  ADD CL,DL
     xxxx:0106  NOP
     ```

   Note that although you key in symbolic code, DEBUG generates machine code, and that is what you are going to save. Because the last instruction, NOP, is 1 byte, the program size is 100H through 106H inclusive, or 7.
   - First use R BX to display the BX (the high portion of the size), and enter 0 to clear it.
   - Next use R CX to display the CX register. DEBUG replies with CX nnnn (whatever value it contains), and you replace it with the program size, 7.
   - Key in W <Enter> to write the revised program on disk.

DEBUG displays a message, "Writing 7 bytes." If the number is zero, you have failed to enter the program length; try again. Watch out for the size of the program, because the last instruction could be longer than 1 byte.

USING THE PTR OPERATOR

Let's now examine another program that introduces some new features. In this example, you move and add data between registers and memory locations. Here are the assembler instructions for that purpose:

```
100    MOV    AX,[11A]
103    ADD    AX,[11C]
107    ADD    AX,25
10A    MOV    [11E],AX
10D    MOV    WORD PTR [120],25
```

```
113     MOV     BYTE PTR [122],30
118     NOP
119     NOP
11A     DB      14 23
11C     DB      05 00
11E     DB      00 00
120     DB      00 00 00
```

An explanation of the instructions is as follows:

100: Move the contents of memory locations 11AH–11BH to the AX. The square brackets indicate a memory address rather than an immediate value.

103: Add the contents of memory locations 11CH-11DH to the AX.

107: Add the immediate value 25H to the AX.

10A: Move the contents of the AX to memory locations 11EH–11FH.

10D: Move the immediate value 25H to memory locations 120H–121H. Note the use of the WORD PTR operator, which tells DEBUG that the 25H is to move into a word in memory. If you were to code the instruction as MOV [120],25, DEBUG would have no way of determining what length is intended and would display an ERROR message. Although you will seldom need to use the PTR operator, it's vital to know when it is needed.

113: Move the immediate value 30H to memory location 122H. This time, we want to move a byte, and the BYTE PTR operator indicates this length.

11A: Define the byte values 14H and 23H. DB here means "define byte(s)" and allows you to define data items that your instructions (such as the one at 100) are to reference.

11C, 11E, and 120: Define other byte values for use in the program.

To key in this program, first type A 100 <Enter>, and then key in each symbolic instruction (but not the location). At the end, key in an additional <Enter> to exit from the A command. To execute the program, begin by entering R to display the registers and the first instruction; then type in successive T commands. Quit execution when you get to the NOP at 118. Key in D 110 to view the changed contents of the AX (233E) and of locations 11EH-11FH (3E23), 120H-121H (2500), and 122H (30).

You've covered a lot of material in this chapter that will become clearer through repetition.

KEY POINTS

- The DEBUG program is useful for testing and debugging machine language and assembly language programs.
- DEBUG provides a set of commands that lets you perform a number of useful operations, such as display, enter, and trace.
- Because DEBUG does not distinguish between lowercase and uppercase letters, you may enter commands either way.

- DEBUG assumes that all numbers are in hexadecimal format.
- If you enter an incorrect value in the data segment or code segment, reenter the E command to correct it.
- To resume execution at the first instruction, set the instruction pointer (IP) register to 0100. Key in the R (Register) command, followed by the designated register, as R IP <Enter>. DEBUG displays the contents of the IP and waits for an entry. Key in the value 0100, followed by <Enter>.

QUESTIONS

3-1. Explain the purpose of each of the following DEBUG commands:
(a) D; (b) E; (c) R; (d) Q; (e) T; (f) A; (g) U; (h) P.

3-2. Provide the DEBUG commands for the following unrelated requirements.
(a) Display the memory beginning at offset 1A5H in the data segment.
(b) Display the memory beginning at location B40H. (Note: Separate this address into its segment and offset values.)
(c) Key in the hex value 444E41 into the data segment beginning at location 18AH.
(d) Display the contents of all registers.
(e) Display the contents of the IP register only.
(f) Unassemble the symbolic code in locations 100H through 11AH.

3-3. Provide the machine code instructions for the following operations: (a) Move the hex value 324B to the AX register; (b) add the immediate hex value 024B to the AX.

3-4. Assume that you have used DEBUG to enter the following E command:

```
E CS:100 B8 36 01 05 25 00
```

The hex value 36 was supposed to be 54. Code another E command to correct only the one byte that is incorrect; that is, change the 36 to 54 directly.

3-5. Assume that you have used DEBUG to enter the following E command:

```
E CS:100 B8 06 20 05 00 30 90
```

(a) What are the three symbolic instructions represented here? (The first program in this chapter gives a clue.)
(b) On executing this program, you discover that the AX register ends up with 5006 instead of the expected 0650. What is the error, and how would you correct it?
(c) Having corrected the instructions, you now want to reexecute the program from the first instruction. What DEBUG commands are required?

3-6. Consider the machine language instructions

```
B0 2A D0 E0 B3 12 F6 E3 90
```

This program performs the following:

- Moves the hex value 2A to the AL register.
- Shifts the contents of the AL one bit to the left. (The result is 54.)
- Moves the hex value 12 to the BL register.
- Multiplies the AL by the BL.

Use DEBUG's E command to enter the program beginning at CS:100. Remember that these are hexadecimal values. After entering the program, key in D CS:100 to view it. Then key in R and enough successive T commands to step through the program until reaching the NOP. What is the final product in the AX register?

3-7. Use DEBUG's E command to enter the following machine language program: Machine code (at 100H): `A0 00 02 D0 E0 F6 26 01 02 A3 02 02 90`

Data (at 200H): `2A 12 00 00`

This program performs the following:

- Moves the contents of the one byte at DS:0200 (2A) to the AL register.
- Shifts the AL contents one bit to the left. (The result is 54.)
- Multiplies the AL by the one-byte contents at DS:0201 (12).
- Moves the product from the AX to the word beginning at DS:0202.

After keying in the program, type in D commands to view the code and the data. Then key in R and enough successive T commands to step through the program until reaching the NOP. At this point, the AX should contain the product as 05E8H. Key in another D DS:0200, and note that the product at DS:0202 is stored as E805H.

3-8. For Question 3-7, code the commands that write the program on disk under the name HEXMULT.COM.

3-9. Use DEBUG's A command to enter the following instructions:

```
MOV    CX,3B
ADD    CX,1C
SHL    CX,01
SUB    CX,36
NOP
```

Unassemble the instructions and trace their execution through to the NOP, and check the value in the BX after each instruction.

3-10. What is the purpose of the INT instruction?

3-11. Use DEBUG to create and run a program that displays the phrase "Out to Lunch." Start with A 100 for entering the instructions and use A 110 for the phrase (and remember the $ delimiter). Hint: See the example in the section "Using INT to Display."

3-12. Use DEBUG to create and run a program that accepts three characters from the keyboard and displays them. (a) Start with A 100. (b) Use INT 16 to accept a character into the AL and move the character to location [120]. (c) Use a second INT 16 to accept a character into the AL and move the character to location [121]. (d) Use another INT 16 to accept a third character into the AL and move the character to location [122]. (e) Now use INT 21 to display the characters. (f) Finally, use an E 123 '$' command to define a '$' at the end of the three stored characters. Hint: See the example in the section "Using INT for Keyboard Input" (but you don't need the JMP instruction for this exercise).

4 REQUIREMENTS FOR CODING IN ASSEMBLY LANGUAGE

Objective: To cover the basic requirements for coding an assembly language program and defining data items.

INTRODUCTION

In Chapter 3, you learned how to use DEBUG for keying in and executing machine language programs. No doubt you were very much aware of the difficulty in deciphering the machine code, even for a small program. Probably no one seriously codes in machine language other than for the tiniest programs. You also used DEBUG's A command for keying in a small assembly source program, and no doubt you noticed that it was much easier to understand than machine code. The use of DEBUG's A command is a mere convenience, because as of this chapter you'll start developing larger programs and you'll need far more capability in documenting and revising them.

You write an assembly program according to a strict set of rules, use an editor or word processor for keying it into the computer as a file, and then use the assembler translator program to read the file and to convert it into machine code.

In this chapter, we explain the basic requirements for developing an assembly program: the use of comments, the general coding format, the directives for controlling the assembled program listing, and the requirements for defining segments and procedures. We also cover the general organization of a program, including initializing the program and ending its execution. Finally, we cover the requirements for defining data items.

ASSEMBLERS AND COMPILERS

The two main classes of programming languages are *high level* and *low level.* Programmers writing in a high-level language such as C and BASIC use powerful commands, each of which may generate many machine language instructions. Programmers writing in a low-level assembly language, on the other hand, code symbolic instructions, each of which generates one machine instruction. Despite the fact that coding in a high-level language is more productive, some advantages to coding in assembly language are that it:

- Provides more control over handling particular hardware requirements.
- May generate smaller, more compact executable modules.
- Often results in faster execution.

A common practice is to combine the benefits of both programming levels: Code the bulk of a project in a high-level language, and code critical modules (those that cause noticeable delays) in assembly language.

Regardless of the programming language you use, it is still a symbolic language that has to be translated into a form the computer can execute. A high-level language uses a *compiler* program to translate the source code into machine code (technically, object code). A low-level language uses an *assembler* program to perform the translation. A *linker* program for both high and low levels completes the process by converting the object code into executable machine language.

PROGRAM COMMENTS

The use of comments throughout a program can improve its clarity, especially in assembly language, where the purpose of a set of instructions is often unclear. For example, it is obvious that the instruction MOV AH,10H moves 10H to the AH register, but the reason for doing this may be unclear. A comment begins with a semicolon (;), and wherever you code it, the assembler assumes that all characters on the line to its right are comments. A comment may contain any printable character, including a blank.

A comment may appear on a line by itself, like this:

```
;Calculate productivity ratio
```

or on the same line following an instruction, like this:

```
ADD AX,BX ;Accumulate total quantity
```

Because a comment appears only on a listing of an assembled source program and generates no machine code, you may include any number of comments without affecting the assembled program's size or execution. In this book, all assembly instructions are in uppercase letters and all comments are in lowercase, only as a convention and to make the programs more readable. Technically, you can freely use either uppercase or lowercase for instructions and comments.

Another way to provide comments is by means of the COMMENT directive, described in Chapter 27.

RESERVED WORDS

Certain names in assembly language are *reserved* for their own purposes, to be used only under special conditions. By category, reserved words include

- *instructions,* such as MOV and ADD, which are operations that the computer can execute;
- *directives,* such as END or SEGMENT, which you use to provide information to the assembler;
- *operators,* such as FAR and SIZE, which you use in expressions; and
- *predefined symbols,* such as @Data and @Model, which return information to your program.

Using a reserved word for a wrong purpose causes the assembler to generate an error message. See Appendix C for a list of reserved words.

IDENTIFIERS

An *identifier* (or symbol) is a name that you apply to an item in your program that you expect to reference. The two types of identifier are name and label:

1. *Name* refers to the address of a data item, such as COUNTER in
   ```
   COUNTER DB 0
   ```
2. *Label* refers to the address of an instruction, procedure, or segment, such as MAIN in the statement
   ```
   MAIN PROC FAR
   ```

The same rules apply to both names and labels. An identifier can use the following characters:

CATEGORY	ALLOWABLE CHARACTERS
Alphabetic letters:	A through Z and a through z
Digits:	0 through 9 (may not be the first character)
Special characters:	question mark (?)
	underline (_)
	dollar ($)
	at (@)
	period (.) (may not be the first character)

The first character of an identifier must be an alphabetic letter or a special character, except for the period. Because the assembler uses some special words that begin with the @ symbol, you should avoid using it for your own definitions.

By default, the assembler treats uppercase and lowercase letters the same. (See Appendix D for a command line that forces the assembler to be case sensitive.) The maximum length of an identifier is 31 characters (247 since MASM 6.0). Examples of valid names are TOTAL, QTY250, and $P50. Descriptive, meaningful names are recommended. The names of registers, such as AH, BX, and DS, are reserved for referencing those registers. Consequently, in an instruction such as

```
ADD CX,BX
```

the assembler automatically knows that CX and BX refer to registers. However, in an instruction such as

```
MOV REGSAVE,CX
```

the assembler can recognize the name REGSAVE only if you define it as a data item in the program.

STATEMENTS

An assembly program consists of a set of *statements*. The two types of statements are:

1. *instructions* such as MOV and ADD, which the assembler translates to object code; and
2. *directives,* which tell the assembler to perform a specific action, such as define a data item.

Here is the general format for a statement, where square brackets indicate an optional entry:

[identifier]	operation	[operand(s)]	[;comment]

An identifier (if any), operation, and operand (if any) are separated by at least one blank or tab character. There is a maximum of 132 characters on a line (512 since MASM 6.0), although most programmers prefer to stay within 80 characters because that is the maximum number most screens can accommodate. Two examples of statements are the following:

	IDENTIFIER	OPERATION	OPERAND	COMMENT
Directive:	COUNT	DB	1	;Name, operation, operand
Instruction:	P30	MOV	AX,0	;Operation, two operands

The identifier, operation, and operand may begin in any column. However, consistently starting at the same column for these entries makes a more readable program. Also, most editor programs provide useful tab stops every eight positions to facilitate spacing the fields.

As described earlier under the heading "Identifiers," the term *name* applies to the name of a defined item or directive, whereas the term *label* applies to the name of an instruction; we'll use these terms from now on.

The *operation,* which must be coded, is most commonly used for defining data areas and coding instructions. For a data item, an operation such as DB or DW defines a field, work area, or constant. For an instruction, an operation such as MOV or ADD indicates an action to perform.

The *operand* (if any) provides information for the operation to act on. For a data item, the operand defines its initial value. For example, in the following definition of a data item named COUNTER, the operation DB means "define byte," and the operand initializes its contents with a zero value:

NAME	OPERATION	OPERAND	COMMENT
COUNTER	DB	0	;Define byte (DB) with 0 value

For an instruction, an operand indicates where to perform the action. An instruction's operand may contain one, two, or even no entries. Here are three examples:

OPERANDS	OPERATION	OPERAND	COMMENT
None	RET		;Return
One	INC	BX	;Increment BX register by 1
Two	ADD	CX, 25	;Add 25 to CX register

DIRECTIVES

Assembly language supports a number of statements that enable you to control the way in which a program assembles and lists. These statements, called directives, act only during the assembly of a program and generate no machine-executable code. The most common directives are explained in the next few sections. Chapter 27 covers all of the directives in detail; you may use that chapter as a reference any time.

The PAGE and TITLE Listing Directives

The PAGE and TITLE directives help to control the format of a listing of an assembled program. This is their only purpose, and they have no effect on subsequent execution of the program.

PAGE. At the start of a program, the PAGE directive designates the maximum number of lines to list on a page and the maximum number of characters on a line. Its general format is

```
PAGE [length][,width]
```

For example, the directive PAGE 60,132 provides 60 lines per page and 132 characters per line.

Under a typical assembler, the number of lines per page may range from 10 through 255, and the number of characters per line may range from 60 through 132. Omission of a PAGE statement causes the assembler to default to PAGE 50,80.

Suppose that a program defines the maximum line count for PAGE as 60. When the assembler is printing the assembled program and has listed 60 lines, it automatically advances to the top of the next page and increments the page count.

You may also want to force a page to eject at a specific line in the program listing, such as the end of a segment. At the required line, simply code PAGE with no operand. On encountering PAGE, the assembler advances to the top of the next page where it resumes the listing.

TITLE. You can use the TITLE directive to cause a title for a program to print on line 2 of each page of the program listing. You may code TITLE once, at the start of the program. Its general format is

```
TITLE text [comment]
```

For the text operand, a recommended technique is to use the name of the program, as cataloged on disk. For example, if you named the program ASMSORT, code that name plus an optional descriptive comment (a leading ';' is not required), all up to 60 characters in length, like this:

```
TITLE ASMSORT Assembly program to sort customer names
```

SEGMENT Directive

As described in Chapter 2, an assembly program in .EXE format consists of one or more segments. A stack segment defines stack storage, a data segment defines data items, and a code segment provides for executable code. The directives for defining a segment, SEGMENT and ENDS, have the following format:

```
NAME    OPERATION   OPERAND     COMMENT
name    SEGMENT     [options]   ;Begin segment
          .
          .
          .
name    ENDS                    ;End segment
```

The SEGMENT statement defines the start of a segment. The segment name must be present, must be unique, and must follow assembler naming conventions. The ENDS statement indicates the end of the segment and contains the same name as the SEGMENT statement. The maximum size of a segment in real mode is 64K. The operand of a SEGMENT statement may contain three types of options: alignment, combine, and class, coded in this format:

```
name  SEGMENT  align  combine  'class'
```

Alignment type. The *align* entry indicates the boundary on which the segment is to begin. For the typical requirement, PARA, the segment aligns on a paragraph boundary, so that the starting address is evenly divisible by 16, or 10H. Omission of the align operand causes the assembler to default to PARA.

Combine type. The *combine* entry indicates whether to combine the segment with other segments when they are linked after assembly (explained later under "Linking the Program"). Combine types are STACK, COMMON, PUBLIC, and AT expression. For example, the stack segment is commonly defined as

```
name SEGMENT PARA STACK
```

You may use PUBLIC and COMMON where you intend to combine separately assembled programs when linking them. Otherwise, where a program is not to be combined with other programs, you may omit this option or code NONE.

Class type. The *class* entry, enclosed in apostrophes, is used to group related segments when linking. This book uses the classes 'code' for the code segment (recommended by Microsoft), 'data' for the data segment, and 'stack' for the stack segment.

The following example defines a stack segment with alignment (PARA), combine (STACK), and class ('Stack') types:

```
name SEGMENT PARA STACK 'Stack'
```

The partial program in Figure 4-1 illustrates SEGMENT statements with various options.

```
         page    60,132
TITLE    A04ASM1 Skeleton of an .EXE Program
; -------------------------------------------
STACKSG  SEGMENT PARA STACK 'Stack'
         ...
STACKSG  ENDS
; -----------------------------------------------
DATASG  SEGMENT PARA 'Data'
        ...
DATASG  ENDS
; -----------------------------------------------
CODESG  SEGMENT PARA 'Code'
MAIN    PROC    FAR
        ASSUME  SS:STACKSG,DS:DATASG,CS:CODESG
        MOV     AX,DATASG         ;Set address of data
        MOV     DS,AX             ;  segment in DS
        ...
        MOV     AX,4C00H          ;End processing
        INT     21H
MAIN    ENDP                      ;End of procedure
CODESG  ENDS                      ;End of segment
        END     MAIN              ;End of program
```

Figure 4-1 Skeleton of an .EXE Program

PROC Directive

The code segment contains the executable code for a program, which consists of one or more *procedures,* defined with the PROC directive. A segment that contains only one procedure would appear as follows:

NAME	OPERATION	OPERAND	COMMENT
segname	SEGMENT	PARA	
procname	PROC	FAR	;One
	.		;procedure
	.		;within
	.		;the code
procname	ENDP		;segment
segname	ENDS		

The procedure name must be present, must be unique, and must follow assembler naming conventions. The operand FAR in this case is related to program execution. When you request execution of a program, the program loader uses this procedure as the entry point for the first instruction to execute.

The ENDP directive indicates the end of a procedure and contains the same name as the PROC statement to enable the assembler to relate the end to the start. Because a procedure must be fully contained within a segment, ENDP defines the end of the procedure before ENDS defines the end of the segment.

The code segment may contain any number of procedures used as subroutines, each with its own set of PROC and ENDP statements. Each additional PROC is usually coded with (or defaults to) the NEAR operand, as covered in Chapter 7.

ASSUME Directive

An .EXE program uses the SS register to address the stack, the DS register to address the data segment, and the CS register to address the code segment. To this end, you have to tell the assembler the purpose of each segment in the program. The required directive is ASSUME, coded in the code segment as follows:

OPERATION	OPERAND
ASSUME	SS:stackname,DS:datasegname,CS:codesegname, . . .

SS:stackname means that the assembler is to associate the name of the stack segment with the SS register, and similarly for the other operands shown. The operands may appear in any sequence. ASSUME may also contain an entry for the ES, such as ES:datasegname; if your program does not use the ES register, you may omit its reference or code ES:NOTHING. (Since MASM 6.0, the assembler automatically generates an ASSUME for the code segment.)

Like other directives, ASSUME is just a message to help the assembler convert symbolic code to machine code; you may still have to code instructions that physically load addresses in segment registers at execute time.

END Directive

As already mentioned, the ENDS directive ends a segment, and the ENDP directive ends a procedure. An END directive ends the entire program and appears as the last statement. Its general format is:

OPERATION	OPERAND
END	[procname]

The operand may be blank if the program is not to execute; for example, you may want to assemble only data definitions, or you may want to link the program with another module. In most programs, the operand contains the name of the first or only PROC designated as FAR, where program execution is to begin.

INSTRUCTIONS FOR INITIALIZING A PROGRAM

The two basic types of executable programs are .EXE and .COM. We'll develop the requirements for .EXE programs first and leave .COM programs for Chapter 7. Figure 4-1 provides a skeleton of an .EXE program showing the stack, data, and code segments. Let's examine the program statements by line number:

LINE	EXPLANATION
1	The PAGE directive for this listing establishes 60 lines and 132 columns per page.
2	The TITLE directive identifies the program's name as A04ASM1.
3	Lines 3, 7, and 11 are comments that clearly set out the three defined segments.
4–6	These statements define the stack segment, STACKSG (but not its contents in this example).
8–10	These statements define the data segment, DATASG (but not its contents).
12–21	These statements define the code segment, CODESG.
13–20	These statements define the code segment's only procedure, named MAIN in this example. This procedure illustrates common initialization and exit requirements for an .EXE program. The two requirements for initializing are (1) notify the assembler which segments to associate with segment registers and (2) load the DS with the address of the data segment.

14 The ASSUME directive notifies the assembler to associate certain segments with certain segment registers in this case, STACKSG with the SS, DATASG with the DS, and CODESG with the CS:

```
ASSUME  SS:STACKSG,DS:DATASG,CS:CODESG
```

By associating segments with segment registers, the assembler can determine offset addresses for items in the stack, for data items in the data segment, and for instructions in the code segment. For example, each machine instruction in the code segment is a specific length. The first instruction in machine language would be at offset 0 and, if it is 2 bytes long, the second instruction would be at offset 2, and so forth.

15, 16 Two instructions initialize the address of the data segment in the DS register:

```
MOV  AX,DATASG       ;Get address of data segment
MOV  DS,AX           ;Store address in DS
```

The first MOV loads the address of the data segment into the AX register and the second MOV copies the address from the AX into the DS. Two MOVs are required because no instruction can move data directly from memory to a segment register; you have to move the address from another register to the segment register. Thus the statement MOV DS,DATASG would be illegal. Chapter 5 discusses initializing segment registers in more detail.

18, 19 These two instructions request an end to program execution and a return to the operating system. A later section discusses them in more detail.

22 The END statement tells the assembler that this is the end of the program, and the MAIN operand provides the entry point for subsequent program execution. MAIN could be any other name acceptable to the assembler.

The sequence in which you define segments is usually unimportant. Figure 4-1 defines them as follows:

```
STACKSG  SEGMENT  PARA  STACK  'Stack'
DATASG   SEGMENT  PARA  'Data'
CODESG   SEGMENT  PARA  'Code'
```

Note that the program in the figure is coded in *symbolic language.* To execute it, you have to use an assembler and a linker to translate it into executable machine code as an .EXE program.

As described in Chapter 2, when the program loader reads an .EXE program from disk into memory for execution, it constructs a 256-byte (100H) PSP on a paragraph boundary in available internal memory and stores the program immediately following the boundary. The loader then

- loads the address of the code segment in the CS;
- loads the address of the stack in the SS; and
- loads the address of the PSP in the DS and ES registers.

The loader initializes the CS:IP and SS:SP registers, but not the DS and ES registers. However, your program normally needs the address of the data segment in the DS (and often in the ES as well). As a consequence, you have to initialize the DS with the address of the data segment, as shown by the two MOV instructions in Figure 4-1.

Now, even if this initialization is not clear at this point, take heart: Every .EXE program has virtually identical initialization steps that you can duplicate each time you code an assembly program.

INSTRUCTIONS FOR ENDING PROGRAM EXECUTION

INT 21H is a common DOS interrupt that uses a function code in the AH register to specify an action to be performed. The many functions of INT 21H include keyboard input, screen handling, disk I/O, and printer output. The function that concerns us here is 4CH, which INT 21H recognizes as a request to end program execution. You can also use this operation to pass a return code in the AL for subsequent testing in a batch file (via the IF ERRORLEVEL statement), as follows:

```
MOV AH,4CH          ;Request end processing
MOV AL,retcode      ;Optional return code
INT 21H             ;Call interrupt service
```

The return code for normal completion of a program is usually 0 (zero). You may also code the two MOVs as one statement (as shown in Figure 4-1):

```
MOV AX,4C00H ;Request normal exit
```

INT 21H function 4CH has superseded operations INT 20H and INT 21H function 00H originally used to end processing.

EXAMPLE OF A SOURCE PROGRAM

Figure 4-2 combines the preceding information into a simple but complete assembly source program that adds two data items in the AX register. The segments are defined in this way:

- STACKSG contains one entry, DW (Define Word), that defines 32 words initialized to zero, an adequate size for small programs.
- DATASG defines three words named FLDD (initialized with 175), FLDE (initialized with 150), and FLDF (uninitialized).
- CODESG contains the executable instructions for the program, although the first statement, ASSUME, generates no executable code.

The ASSUME directive performs these operations:

- Assigns STACKSG to the SS register, so that the system uses the address in the SS register for addressing STACKSG.

```
          page    60,132
TITLE     A04ASM1 (EXE)  Move and add operations
; ---------------------------------------------------
STACKSG   SEGMENT PARA STACK 'Stack'
          DW      32 DUP(0)
STACKSG   ENDS
; ---------------------------------------------------
DATASG    SEGMENT PARA 'Data'
FLDD      DW      175
FLDE      DW      150
FLDF      DW      ?
DATASG    ENDS
; ---------------------------------------------------
CODESG    SEGMENT PARA 'Code'
MAIN      PROC    FAR
          ASSUME  SS:STACKSG,DS:DATASG,CS:CODESG
          MOV     AX,DATASG      ;Set address of data
          MOV     DS,AX          ;  segment in DS

          MOV     AX,FLDD        ;Move 0175 to AX
          ADD     AX,FLDE        ;Add  0150 to AX
          MOV     FLDF,AX        ;Store sum in FLDF
          MOV     AX,4C00H       ;End processing
          INT     21H
MAIN      ENDP                   ;End of procedure
CODESG    ENDS                   ;End of segment
          END     MAIN           ;End of program
```

Figure 4-2 .EXE Program with Conventional Segments

- Assigns DATASG to the DS register, so that the system uses the address in the DS register for addressing DATASG.
- Assigns CODESG to the CS register, so that the system uses the address in the CS register for addressing CODESG.

When loading a program from disk into memory for execution, the program loader sets the actual addresses in the SS and CS registers, but, as shown by the first two MOV instructions, you have to initialize the DS (and possibly the ES) register.

We'll trace the assembly, linkage, and execution of this program in Chapter 5.

INITIALIZING FOR PROTECTED MODE

In protected mode under the 80386 and later processors, a program may address up to 16 megabytes of memory. The use of DWORD to align segments on a doubleword address speeds up accessing memory for a 32-bit data bus. In the following example, the .386 directive tells the assembler to accept instructions that are unique to the 80386 and later; the USE32 use type tells the assembler to generate code appropriate to 32-bit protected mode:

```
.386
segname SEGMENT  DWORD USE32
```

Initialization of the data segment register could look like this, since on these processors the DS register is still 16 bits in size:

```
MOV   EAX,DATASG      ;Get address of data segment
MOV   DS,AX           ;Load 16-bit portion
```

The STI, CLI, IN, and OUT instructions, available in real mode, are not allowed in protected mode.

SIMPLIFIED SEGMENT DIRECTIVES

The assembler provides some shortcuts in defining segments. To use them, you have to initialize the memory model before defining any segment. The general format (including the leading period) is

```
.MODEL memory-model
```

The memory model may be TINY, SMALL, MEDIUM, COMPACT, or LARGE. (Another model, HUGE, need not concern us here.) The requirements for each model are:

MODEL	NUMBER OF CODE SEGMENTS	NUMBER OF DATA SEGMENTS
TINY	*	*
SMALL	1	1
MEDIUM	More than 1	1
COMPACT	1	More than 1
LARGE	More than 1	More than 1

You may use any of these models for a stand-alone program (that is, a program that is not linked to another program). As of MASM 6.0 and TASM 4.0, the TINY model is intended for the use of .COM programs, which have their data, code, and stack in one 64K segment. The SMALL model requires that code fits within a 64K segment and data fits within another 64K segment; this model is suitable for most of the examples in the book. The .MODEL directive automatically generates the required ASSUME statement.

The general formats (including the leading period) for the directives that define the stack, data, and code segments are

```
.STACK   [size]
.DATA
.CODE    [name]
```

Each of these directives causes the assembler to generate the required SEGMENT statement and its matching ENDS. The default segment names (which you don't have to define) are STACK, _DATA, and _TEXT (for the code segment). The underline (or break) character at the beginning of _DATA and _TEXT is intended. As the coding format indicates, you may override the default name for the code segment. The default stack size is 1,024 bytes, which you may also override. You use these directives to identify where in the program the three segments are to be located. Note, however, that the instructions you now use to initialize the address of a data segment in the DS are:

```
MOV  AX,@data
MOV  DS,AX
```

Figure 4-2 gave an example of a program using conventionally defined segments. Figure 4-3 provides the same example, but this time using the simplified segment directives .STACK, .DATA, and .CODE. The memory model is specified as SMALL in the fourth line. The stack is defined as 64 bytes (32 words). Note that the assembler does not generate conventional SEGMENT and ENDS statements, and you also don't code an ASSUME statement.

```
        page   60,132
TITLE   A04ASM2 (EXE)   Move and add operations
;-----------------------------------------------------------
        .MODEL  SMALL
        .STACK  64                   ;Define stack
        .DATA                        ;Define data
FLDD    DW      175
FLDE    DW      150
FLDF    DW      ?
;-----------------------------------------------------------
        .CODE                        ;Define code segment
MAIN    PROC    FAR
        MOV     AX,@data             ;Set address of data
        MOV     DS,AX                ;   segment in DS

        MOV     AX,FLDD              ;Move 0175 to AX
        ADD     AX,FLDE              ;Add  0150 to AX
        MOV     FLDF,AX              ;Store sum in FLDF

        MOV     AX,4C00H             ;End processing
        INT     21H
MAIN    ENDP                         ;End of procedure
        END     MAIN                 ;End of program
```

Figure 4-3 .EXE Source Program with Simplified Segment Directives

As you'll see in the next chapter, the assembler handles programs coded with simplified segment directives slightly differently from those using conventional segment directives.

The .STARTUP and .EXIT Directives

MASM 6.0 introduced the .STARTUP and .EXIT directives to simplify program initialization and termination. .STARTUP generates the instructions to initialize the segment registers, whereas .EXIT generates the INT 21H function 4CH instructions for exiting the program. TASM Ideal mode uses the terms STARTUPCODE and EXITCODE. For purposes of learning assembly language, examples in this use the full sets of instructions and leave shortcuts to more experienced programmers.

DATA DEFINITION

As already discussed, the purpose of the data segment in an .EXE program is to define constants, work areas, and input/output areas. The assembler permits definitions of items in various lengths according to a set of directives that define data; for example, DB defines a byte and DW defines a word. A data item may contain an *undefined* (that is, uninitialized) value, or it may contain a *constant*, defined either as a character string or as a numeric value. Here is the general format for data definition:

[name]	Dn	expression

Name. A program that references a data item does so by means of a name. The name of an item is otherwise optional, as indicated by the square brackets. The earlier section "Statements" provides the rules for names.

Directive (Dn). The directives that define data items are DB (byte), DW (word), DD (doubleword), DF (farword), DQ (quadword), and DT (tenbytes), each of which explicitly indicates the length of the defined item. MASM 6.0 introduced the terms BYTE, WORD, DWORD, FWORD, QWORD, and TWORD, respectively, for these directives.

Expression. The expression in an operand may define an uninitialized value or an initial constant. To indicate an uninitialized item, define the operand with a question mark, such as

```
FLDA DB ? ;Uninitialized item
```

In this case, when your program begins execution, the initial value of FLDA is unknown to you. The normal practice before using this item is to move some value into it, but it must fit the defined size.

You can use the operand to define a constant, such as

```
FLDB DB/BYTE 25 ;Initialized item
```

You can freely use this initialized value 25 throughout your program and can even change the value.

An expression may contain multiple constants separated by commas and limited only by the length of the line, as follows:

```
FLDC DB/BYTE 21, 22, 23, 24, 25, 26, . . .
```

The assembler defines these constants in adjacent bytes. A reference to FLDC is to the first 1-byte constant, 21 (you could think of the first byte as FLDC+0), and a reference to FLDC+1 is to the second constant, 22. For example, the instruction

```
MOV AL,FLDC+3
```

loads the value 24 (18H) into the AL register. The expression also permits duplication of constants in a statement of the general form

[name]	Dn	repeat-count DUP(expression) ...

The following examples illustrate duplication:

```
DW/WORD  10 DUP(?)           ;Ten words, uninitialized
DB/BYTE  5 DUP(12)           ;Five bytes containing hex 0C0C0C0C0C
DB/BYTE  3 DUP(5 DUP(4))     ;Fifteen 4s
```

The third example generates five copies of the digit 4 (44444) and duplicates that value three times, giving 15 4s in all.

An expression may define and initialize a character string or a numeric constant.

Character Strings

Character strings are used for descriptive data such as people's names and product descriptions. The string is defined within single quotes, such as 'PC', or within double quotes, such as "PC". The assembler stores character strings as object code in normal ASCII format, without the apostrophes.

Under MASM, DB (or BYTE) is the only format that defines a character string exceeding two characters with the characters stored as left adjusted and in normal left-to-right sequence (like names and addresses). Consequently, DB (or BYTE) is the conventional format for defining character data of any length. An example is

```
DB 'Strawberry Jam'
```

If a string must contain a single or double quote, you can define it in one of these ways:

```
DB  "Crazy Sam's CD Emporium"    ;Double quotes for string,
                                 single quote for apostrophe
DB  'Crazy Sam''s CD Emporium'     ;Single quotes for string, two
                                 single quotes for apostrophe
```

Numeric Constants

Numeric constants are used to define arithmetic values and memory addresses. The constant is not defined within quotes, but is followed by an optional *radix specifier,* such as H in the hexadecimal value 12H. For most of the data definition directives, the assembler converts defined numeric constants to hexadecimal and stores the generated bytes in object code in reverse sequence, from right to left. Following are the various numeric formats.

Binary. Binary format permits defining the binary digits 0 and 1, followed by the radix specifier B. A common use for binary format is to distinguish values for the bit-handling instructions AND, OR, XOR, and TEST.

Decimal. Decimal format permits defining the decimal digits 0 through 9, optionally followed by the radix specifier D, such as 125 or 125D. Although the assembler allows you to define values in decimal format as a coding convenience, it converts your decimal values to binary object code and represents them in hex. For example, a definition of decimal 125 becomes hex 7D.

Hexadecimal. Hex format permits defining the hex digits 0 through F, followed by the radix specifier H. Because the assembler expects that a reference beginning with a letter is a symbolic name, the first digit of a hex constant must be 0 to 9. Examples are 3DH and 0DE8H, which the assembler stores as 3D and E80D, respectively. Note that the bytes in the second example are stored in reverse sequence.

Because the assembler converts all numeric values to binary (and represents them in hex), definitions of decimal 12, hex C, and binary 1100 all generate the same value: binary 00001100 or hex 0C, depending on how you view the contents of the byte.

Because the letters D and B act as both radix specifiers and hex digits, they could conceivably cause some confusion. As a solution, MASM 6.0 introduced the use of T (as in ten) and Y (as in binary) as radix specifiers for decimal and binary, respectively.

Real. The assembler converts a given real value (a decimal or hex constant followed by the radix specifier R) into floating-point format for use with a numeric coprocessor.

Be sure to distinguish between the use of character and numeric constants. For example, a character constant defined as DB '24' generates two ASCII characters, represented as hex 3234. A numeric constant defined as DB 24 generates a binary number, represented as hex 18.

DIRECTIVES FOR DEFINING DATA

The conventional directives used to define data, along with the names introduced by MASM 6.0, are:

DESCRIPTION	CONVENTIONAL DIRECTIVES	MASM 6.0 DIRECTIVES
Byte	DB	BYTE
Word	DW	WORD
Doubleword	DD	DWORD
Farword	DF	FWORD
Quadword	DQ	QWORD
Tenbytes	DT	TBYTE

This text uses the conventional directives because of their still-common usage.

The assembled program in Figure 4-4 provides examples of directives that define character strings and numeric constants. The generated object code, which you are urged to examine, is listed on the left. Note that the object code for uninitialized values appears as hex zeros. Because this program consists of only a data segment, it is not suitable for execution.

DB or BYTE: Define Byte

Of the directives that define data items, one of the most useful is DB (Define Byte). A DB (or BYTE) numeric expression may define one or more 1-byte constants. The maximum of one byte means two hex digits. The largest unsigned 1-byte number is hex FF, or 255. With the leftmost bit acting as the sign, the largest positive 1-byte hex number is 7F; all "higher" num-

```
                                      Page 60,132
                              TITLE   A04DEFIN (EXE)  Define data directives
                                      .MODEL  SMALL
                                      .DATA
                              ;       DB - Define Byte:
                              ;       ----------------
0000 00                       BYTE1   DB   ?             ;Uninitialized
0001 30                       BYTE2   DB   48            ;Decimal constant
0002 30                       BYTE3   DB   30H           ;Hex constant
0003 7A                       BYTE4   DB   01111010B     ;Binary constant
0004 000C[ 00 ]               BYTE5   DB   12 DUP(0)     ;Twelve zeros
0010 43 6F 6D 70 75 74        BYTE6   DB   'Computer Processors'
     65 72 20 50 72 6F                                   ;Character string
     63 65 73 73 6F 72
     73
0023 34 37 38 33 35           BYTE7   DB   '47835'       ;Numbers as chars
0028 01 4A 61 6E 02 46        BYTE8   DB   01,'Jan',02,'Feb',03,'Mar'
     65 62 03 4D 61 72
                                                         ;Table of months

                              ;       DW - Define Word:
                              ;       ----------------
0034 FFF0                     WORD1   DW   0FFF0H        ;Hex constant
0036 007A                     WORD2   DW   01111010B     ;Binary constant
0038 0023 R                   WORD3   DW   BYTE7         ;Address constant
003A 0002 0004 0006 0007 WORD4        DW   2,4,6,7,9     ;Table of five
     0009                                                ;  constants
0044 0006[ 0000 ]             WORD5   DW   6 DUP(0)      ;Six zeros

                              ;       DD - Define Doubleword:
                              ;       ----------------------
0050 00000000                 DWORD1  DD   ?             ;Uninitialized
0054 00007457                 DWORD2  DD   29783         ;Decimal value
0058 0000001B 00000038        DWORD3  DD   27, 56        ;Two constants
0060 00000001                 DWORD4  DD   BYTE3 - BYTE2  ;Diff betw addresses
0064 00005043                 DWORD5  DD   'PC'          ;Character string

                              ;       DQ - Define Quadword:
                              ;       --------------------
0068 0000000000000000         QWORD1  DQ   ?             ;Uninitialized
0070 395E000000000000         QWORD2  DQ   05E39H        ;Hex constant
0078 5774000000000000         QWORD3  DQ   29783         ;Decimal constant

                              ;       DT - Define Tenbytes:
                              ;       --------------------
0080 000000000000000000       TENB1   DT   ?             ;Uninitialized
     00
008A 307829000000000000       TENB2   DT   297830        ;Decimal constant
     00
0094 435000000000000000       TENB3   DT   'PC'          ;Character string
     00
                                      END
```

Figure 4-4 Definitions of Character Strings and Numeric Values

bers, 80 through FF (where the sign bit is 1), represent negative values. In terms of decimal numbers, these limits are +127 and –128. The assembler converts numeric constants to binary object code (represented in hex). In Figure 4-4, numeric DB constants are BYTE2, BYTE3, BYTE4, and BYTE5.

A DB character expression may contain a string of any length up to the end of the line. For examples, see BYTE6 and BYTE7 in the figure. The object code shows the ASCII character for each byte in normal left-to-right sequence, where 20H represents a blank character.

BYTE8 shows a mixture of numeric and string constants suitable for defining a table.

DW or WORD: Define Word

The DW (or WORD) directive defines items that are 1 word (2 bytes) in length. A DW numeric expression may define one or more 1-word constants. The largest *positive* (signed) 1-word hex number is 7FFF; all "higher" numbers, 8000 through FFFF (where the sign bit is 1), represent negative values. In terms of decimal numbers, the limits are +32,767 and −32,768.

The assembler converts DW numeric constants to binary object code (represented in hex), but stores the bytes in reverse sequence. Consequently, a decimal value defined as 12345 converts to hex 3039, but is stored as 3930.

In Figure 4-4, WORD1 and WORD2 define DW numeric constants. WORD3 defines the operand as an address—in this case, the offset address of BYTE7. The generated object code is 0023 (the R to the right means *relocatable*), and a check of the figure shows that the offset address of BYTE7 (the leftmost column) is indeed 0023.

A DW character expression under MASM is limited to two characters. You can see that DW is of limited use for defining character strings.

WORD4 defines a table of five numeric constants. Note that the length of each constant is 1 word (2 bytes). WORD5 defines a table initialized with 6 zeros.

DD or DWORD: Define Doubleword

The DD (or DWORD) directive defines items that are a doubleword (4 bytes) in length. A DD numeric expression may define one or more constants, each with a maximum of 4 bytes (8 hex digits). The largest positive doubleword hex number is 7FFFFFFF; all "higher" numbers, 80000000 through FFFFFFFF (where the sign bit is 1), represent negative values. In terms of decimal numbers, these maximums are +2,147,483,647 and −2,147,483,648.

The assembler converts DD numeric constants to binary object code (represented in hex), but stores the bytes in *reverse sequence*. Consequently, the assembler converts a decimal value defined as 12345678 to 00BC614EH and stores it as 4E61BC00H.

In Figure 4-4, DWORD2 defines a DD numeric constant, and DWORD3 defines two numeric constants. DWORD4 generates the numeric difference between two defined addresses; in this case, the result is the length of BYTE2.

A DD character expression under MASM is limited to two characters and is as trivial as those for DW. The assembler right-adjusts the characters in the 4-byte doubleword, as shown in the object code for DWORD5.

DF or FWORD: Define Farword

The DF (or FWORD) directive defines a farword as 6 bytes. Its normal use is for the 80386 and later processors.

DQ or QWORD: Define Quadword

The DQ (or QWORD) directive defines items that are 4 words (8 bytes) in length. A DQ numeric expression may define one or more constants, each with a maximum of 8 bytes, or 16 hex digits. The largest positive quadword hex number is 7 followed by 15 Fs. As an indication of the magnitude of this number, hex 1 followed by 15 0s equals the decimal number 1,152,921,504,606,846,976.

The assembler handles DQ numeric values and character strings just as it does DD and DW numeric values. In Figure 4-4, QWORD2 and QWORD3 illustrate numeric values.

DT or TBYTE: Define Tenbytes

The DT (or TBYTE) directive defines data items that are 10 bytes long. Its purpose is to define packed BCD (binary-coded decimal) numeric values, which are more useful for numeric coprocessors than for standard arithmetic operations. A BCD number is packed with two decimal digits per byte. Note that DT, unlike the other data directives, stores numeric constants as decimal rather than as hexadecimal values. For a constant defined as 12345678, MASM stores the bytes in reverse sequence as 78 56 34 12 00 00 00 00 00 00, although TASM stores it as right-adjusted in normal sequence.

Figure 4-4 illustrates DT for an uninitialized item, a numeric value, and a two-character constant.

Display of the Data Segment

The partial program in Figure 4-4 contains only a data segment. Although the assembler generated no error messages, the link map displayed "Warning: No STACK Segment," and the linker displayed "There were 1 errors detected." Despite the warning, you can still use DEBUG to view the object code, which is shown in Figure 4-5.

```
-d ds:100
0CA3:0100  00 30 30 7A 00 00 00 00-00 00 00 00 00 00 00 00   .00z............
0CA3:0110  43 6F 6D 70 75 74 65 72-20 50 72 6F 63 65 73 73   Computer Process
0CA3:0120  6F 72 73 34 37 38 33 35-01 4A 61 6E 02 46 65 62   ors47835.Jan.Feb
0CA3:0130  03 4D 61 72 F0 FF 7A 00-23 00 02 00 04 00 06 00   .Mar..z.#.......
0CA3:0140  07 00 09 00 00 00 00 00-00 00 00 00 00 00 00 00   ................
0CA3:0150  00 00 00 00 57 74 00 00-1B 00 00 00 38 00 00 00   ....Wt......8...
0CA3:0160  01 00 00 00 43 50 00 00-00 00 00 00 00 00 00 00   ....CP..........
0CA3:0170  39 5E 00 00 00 00 00 00-57 74 00 00 00 00 00 00   9^......Wt......
-d
0CA3:0180  00 00 00 00 00 00 00 00-00 00 30 78 29 00 00 00   ..........0x)...
0CA3:0190  00 00 00 00 43 50 00 00-00 00 00 00 00 00 21 DE   ....CP........!.
0CA3:01A0  42 D9 21 DE 42 D9 21 23-41 D9 21 23 41 D9 21 23   B.!.B.!#A.!#A.!#
0CA3:01B0  41 D9 21 23 41 D9 21 23-41 D9 21 23 41 D9 21 23   A.!#A.!#A.!#A.!#
0CA3:01C0  41 D9 21 23 41 D9 21 E2-43 D9 21 E2 43 D9 21 E2   A.!#A.!.C.!.C.!.
0CA3:01D0  43 D9 21 E2 43 D9 21 E2-43 D9 21 E2 43 D9 21 E2   C.!.C.!.C.!.C.!.
0CA3:01E0  43 D9 21 E2 43 D9 21 D8-43 D9 21 D8 43 D9 21 D8   C.!.C.!.C.!.C.!.
0CA3:01F0  43 D9 21 D8 43 D9 21 D8-43 D9 21 D8 43 D9 21 D8   C.!.C.!.C.!.C.!.

           <——— hexadecimal representation ———>              <—— ASCII ——>
```

Figure 4-5 Displaying the Data Segment

Assemble and link the program, use DEBUG to load the .EXE file, and key in D DS:100 for a display of the data. The right side of the display shows the ASCII representation, such as "Computer Processors," whereas the hexadecimal values on the left indicate the actual stored contents. Your display should be identical to Figure 4-5 for offsets 0100 through 019D. Expect your segment address (0CA3 in the figure) and data following offset 019D to differ.

The reason you issue DS:100 for the display is because the loader set the DS with the address of the PSP, but the data segment for this program begins 100 bytes after that address. Later, when you use DEBUG for .EXE programs that initialize the DS to the address of the data segment, you can use DS:0 to display it.

THE EQU DIRECTIVE

The EQU directive does not define a data item; instead, it defines a value that the assembler can use to substitute in other instructions. Consider the following EQU statement coded in the data segment:

```
FACTOR EQU 12
```

The name, in this case FACTOR, may be any name acceptable to the assembler. Now, whenever the word FACTOR appears in an instruction or another directive, the assembler substitutes the value 12. For example, the assembler converts the directive

```
TABLEX DB FACTOR DUP(?)
```

to its equivalent value

```
TABLEX DB 12 DUP(?)
```

An instruction may also contain an equated operand, as in the following:

```
LIMITX  EQU  25
        ...
        MOV  CX,LIMITX
```

The assembler replaces LIMITX in the MOV operand with the value 25, making the operand an immediate value, as if it were coded

```
MOV CX,25 ;Assembler substitutes 25
```

The advantage of EQU is that many statements may use the value defined by LIMITX. If the value has to be changed, you need change only the EQU statement. Needless to say, you can use an equated value only where a substitution makes sense to the assembler. You can also equate symbolic names, as in the following code:

```
TOTSALES DW    0
...
TS         EQU  TOTSALES
MPY        EQU  MUL
```

The first EQU equates the nickname TS to the defined item TOTSALES. For any instruction that contains the operand TS, the assembler replaces it with the address of TOTSALES. The second EQU enables a program to use the word MPY in place of the regular symbolic instruction MUL.

MASM 6.0 introduced a TEXTEQU directive for text data with the format

```
name TEXTEQU <text>
```

KEY POINTS

- A semicolon precedes a comment on a line.
- Reserved words in assembly language are used for their own purposes, only under special conditions.
- An identifier is a name that you apply to items in your program. The two types of identifiers are name, which refers to the address of a data item, and label, which refers to the address of an instruction.
- An operation is commonly used for defining data areas and coding instructions. An operand provides information for the operation to act on.
- A program consists of one or more segments, each of which begins on a paragraph boundary.
- The ENDS directive ends each segment, ENDP ends each procedure, and END ends the program.
- The ASSUME directive associates segment registers CS, DS, and SS with their appropriate segment names.
- An .EXE program should define at least 32 words for the stack.
- For an .EXE program, you normally initialize the DS register with the address of the data segment.
- For the simplified segment directives, you initialize the memory model before defining any segment. Options are SMALL (one code segment and one data segment), MEDIUM (any number of code segments and one data segment), COMPACT (one code segment and any number of data segments), and LARGE (any number of code segments and data segments).
- INT 21H function 4CH is the standard instruction for exiting a program.
- Names of data items should be unique and descriptive. For example, an item for an employee's wage could be named EMPWAGE.
- DB is the preferred format for defining character strings, since it permits strings longer than two bytes and converts them to normal left-to-right sequence.
- Decimal and binary (hex) constants generate different values. Consider the effect of adding decimal 25 versus that of adding hex 25:

  ```
  ADD  CX,25      ;Add 25
  ADD  CX,25H     ;Add 37
  ```
- DW, DD, and DQ store numeric values in object code with the bytes in reverse sequence.

- DB items are used for processing half registers (AL, BL, etc.), DW for full registers (AX, BX, etc.), and DD for extended registers (EAX, EBX, etc.). Longer numeric items require special handling.

QUESTIONS

4-1. Distinguish between a compiler and an assembler.

4-2. What is a reserved word in assembler language? Give two examples.

4-3. What are the two types of identifiers?

4-4. Determine which of the following names are valid: (a) CX; (b) 25C4; (c) @$_X; (d) $25; (e) AT&T. If invalid, explain.

4-5. Explain the difference between a directive and an instruction and give two examples of each.

4-6. Give the commands that cause the assembler when listing a program (a) to advance to a new page and (b) to print a heading at the top of a page.

4-7. Explain the purpose of each of the three segments described in this chapter.

4-8. The format for the SEGMENT directive is

```
name SEGMENT align combine 'class'
```

What is the purpose of (a) align; (b) combine; (c)'class'?

4-9. (a) Explain the purpose of a procedure. (b) How do you define the beginning and the end of a procedure? (c) When do you define a procedure as FAR? (d) When do you define a procedure as NEAR?

4-10. What particular END statements are concerned with ending (a) a procedure; (b) a segment; (c) a program?

4-11. Distinguish between the statement that ends an assembly and the statements that end execution.

4-12. Given the names STKSEG, DATSEG, and CDSEG for the stack, data segment, and code segment, respectively, code the required ASSUME statement.

4-13. Consider the instruction MOV AX,4C00H used with INT 21H. (a) Explain what the instruction performs. (b) Explain the purpose of the 4C00H.

4-14. For the simplified segment directives, the .MODEL directive provides for TINY, SMALL, MEDIUM, COMPACT, and LARGE models. Under what circumstances would you use each model?

4-15. Give the lengths in bytes generated by the following data directives: (a) DB; (b) DQ; (c) DT; (d) DW; (e) DD.

4-16. Define a character string named CONAME containing "Computer Services" as a constant.

4-17. Define the following numeric values in data items named AREA1 through AREA5, respectively:

(a) A 1-byte item containing the binary equivalent to decimal 35.
(b) A DW containing the consecutive values 12, 14, 22, 28, 33, and 41.
(c) A 2-byte item containing an undefined value.
(d) A 1-byte item containing the hex equivalent to decimal 58.
(e) A 4-byte item containing the hex equivalent to decimal 436.

4-18. Show the generated hex object code for (a) DB 34; (b) DB '34'; (c) DB 4 DUP(0).

4-19. Determine the assembled hex object code for (a) DD 4A25B2H; (b) DQ 3BA53DH; (c) DB 35H; (d) DW 3728H.

5 ASSEMBLING, LINKING, AND EXECUTING A PROGRAM

Objective: To cover the steps in assembling, linking, and executing an assembly language program.

INTRODUCTION

This chapter explains the procedure for keying in an assembly language program and for assembling, linking, and executing it. The symbolic instructions that you code in assembly language are known as the *source program.* You use an assembler program to translate the source program into machine code, known as the *object program.* Finally, you use a linker program to complete the machine addressing for the object program, generating an *executable module.*

The sections on assembling explain how to request execution of the assembler program, which provides diagnostics (including any error messages) and generates the object program. Also explained are details of the assembler listing and, in general terms, how the assembler processes a source program.

The sections on linking explain how to request execution of the linker program so that you can generate an executable module. Also explained are details of the generated link map, as well as the linker's diagnostics. Finally, a section explains how to request execution of the executable module.

PREPARING A PROGRAM FOR EXECUTION

Figure 4-2 illustrated only the source code for a program not yet in executable format. For keying in this program, you could use any editor or word processing program that produces a standard ASCII file. In the following examples of commands, substitute the appropriate drive for your system. You can also gain a lot of productivity by loading your programs and files into a RAM disk. Call up your editor program, key in the statements for the program in Figure 4-2, and name the resulting file A05ASM1.ASM.

Although spacing is not important to the assembler, a program is more readable if you keep the name, operation, operand, and comments consistently aligned on columns. Most editors have tab stops every eight positions to facilitate aligning columns.

Once you have keyed in all the statements for the program, examine the code for accuracy. Although most editors have a print facility, you may also request the DOS PRINT program:

```
PRINT n:A05ASM1.ASM <Enter>
```

As it stands, this source program is just a text file that cannot execute—you must first assemble and link it.

1. The *assembly step* involves translating the source code into object code and generating an intermediate .OBJ (object) file, or module. (You have already seen examples of machine code and source code in earlier chapters.) One of the assembler's tasks is to calculate the offset for every data item in the data segment and for every instruction in the code segment. The assembler also creates a *header* immediately in front of the generated .OBJ module; part of the header contains information about incomplete addresses. The .OBJ module is not quite in executable form.
2. The *link step* involves converting the .OBJ module to an .EXE (executable) machine code module. The linker's tasks include completing any addresses left open by the assembler and combining separately assembled programs into one executable module.
3. The last step is to *load* the program for execution. Because the loader knows where the program is about to load, it is able to resolve any remaining addresses still left incomplete in the header. The loader drops the header and creates a program segment prefix (PSP) immediately before the program loaded in memory.

Figure 5-1 provides a chart of the steps involved in assembling, linking, and executing a program.

ASSEMBLING A SOURCE PROGRAM

The Microsoft assembler program (up to version 5.x) is MASM.EXE, whereas the Borland Turbo program is TASM.EXE. As of version 6.0, the Microsoft assembler normally uses the ML command, but also accepts MASM for compatibility with earlier versions.

You can key in the command to run MASM or TASM with a command line or by means of prompts. This section shows how to use the command line; see Appendix D for the prompt method. The general format for a command line to assemble a program is

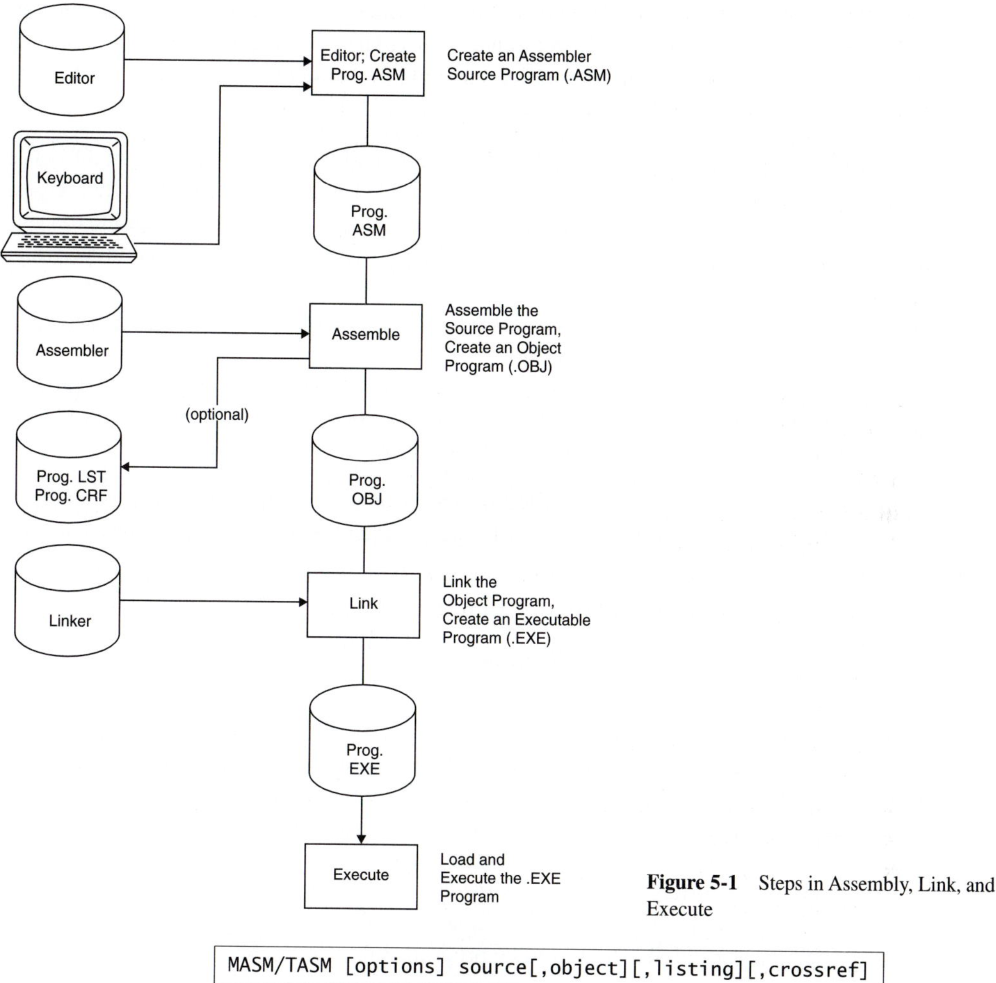

Figure 5-1 Steps in Assembly, Link, and Execute

```
MASM/TASM [options] source[,object][,listing][,crossref]
```

- *Options* provides for such features as setting levels of warning messages and is explained in Appendix D. The assembler's defaults are adequate for our purposes at this time.
- *Source* identifies the name of the source program, such as A05ASM1. The assembler assumes the extension .ASM, so you need not enter it. You can also type in a disk drive number if you don't want to accept the current default drive.
- *Object* provides for a generated .OBJ file. The drive, subdirectory, and filename may be the same as or different from those in the source.
- *Listing* provides for a generated .LST file that contains both the source and object code. The drive, subdirectory, and filename may be the same as or different from those in the source.

- *Crossref* generates a cross-reference file containing the symbols used in the program, which you can use for a cross-reference listing. The extension is .CRF for MASM and .XRF for TASM. The drive, subdirectory, and filename may be the same as or different from those in the source.

You always key in the name of the source file, and you usually request an .OBJ file, which is required for linking a program into executable form. You'll probably often request an .LST file, especially when it contains error diagnostics or you want to examine the generated machine code. A .CRF file is useful for a large program where you want to see which instructions reference which data items. Also, requesting a .CRF file causes the assembler to generate statement numbers for in the .LST file to which the .CRF file refers. Later sections cover .LST and .CRF files in detail.

Following are two examples of assembling A05ASM1. Note that if the filename for .OBJ, .LST, or .CRF is to be the same as the source, you need not repeat it; a reference to drive number is sufficient to indicate a request for the file.

Example 1. Specify source file A05ASM1 on drive D and generate only an object file. In this case, you omit the reference to the .LST and .CRF files and simply enter the command

```
MASM/TASM D:A05ASM1,D:
```

Example 2. Generate object, listing, and cross-reference files:

```
MASM/TASM D:A05ASM1,D:,D:,D:
```

The assembler converts your source statements into machine code and displays any error messages on the screen. Typical errors include a name that violates naming conventions, an operation that is spelled incorrectly (such as MOVE instead of MOV), and an operand containing a name that is not defined. Because there are many possible errors (100 or more) and many different assembler versions, you may refer to your assembler manual for a list. The assembler attempts to correct some errors but, in any event, you should reload your editor, correct the .ASM source program, and reassemble it.

USING CONVENTIONAL SEGMENT DEFINITIONS

Figure 5-2 provides the listing that the MASM assembler produced under the name A05ASM1.LST. The line width is 132 positions as specified by the PAGE entry. You can also print this listing if your printer can compress the print line. Many impact printers have a switch that will force compressed printing, or you could request your editor or word processor to print in compressed mode. Another way is to use the DOS MODE command; for 132 characters per inch and 6 lines per inch, turn on the printer, key in the command MODE LPT1:132,6, and request the PRINT program.

Note at the top of the listing how the assembler has acted on the PAGE and TITLE directives. None of the directives, including SEGMENT, PROC, ASSUME, and END,

```
A05ASM1 (EXE)  Move and add operations                         Page   1-1
                                page     60,132
                         TITLE  A05ASM1  (EXE)  Move and add operations
                         ; -----------------------------------------------
 0000                    STACKSG  SEGMENT PARA STACK 'Stack'
 0000    0020[                    DW      32 DUP(0)
         0000
             ]

 0040                    STACKSG  ENDS
                         ; -----------------------------------------------
 0000                    DATASG   SEGMENT PARA 'Data'
 0000    00AF            FLDD     DW      175
 0002    0096            FLDE     DW      150
 0004    0000            FLDF     DW      ?
 0006                    DATASG   ENDS
                         ; -----------------------------------------------
 0000                    CODESG   SEGMENT PARA 'Code'
 0000                    MAIN     PROC    FAR
                                  ASSUME  SS:STACKSG,DS:DATASG,CS:CODESG
 0000    B8 ---- R                MOV     AX,DATASG      ;Set address of data
 0003    8E D8                    MOV     DS,AX          ;  segment in DS

 0005    A1 0000 R                MOV     AX,FLDD        ;Move 0175 to AX
 0008    03 06 0002 R             ADD     AX,FLDE        ;Add  0150 to AX
 000C    A3 0004 R                MOV     FLDF,AX        ;Store sum in FLDF
 000F    B8 4C00                  MOV     AX,4C00H       ;End processing
 0012    CD 21                    INT     21H
 0014                    MAIN     ENDP                   ;End of procedure
 0014                    CODESG   ENDS                   ;End of segment
                                  END     MAIN           ;End of program
```

```
Segments and Groups:
          N a m e          Length   Align    Combine    Class
CODESG . . . . . . . . . . 0014     PARA     NONE       'CODE'
DATASG . . . . . . . . . . 0006     PARA     NONE       'DATA'
STACKSG  . . . . . . . . . 0040     PARA     STACK      'STACK'

Symbols:
          N a m e            Type    Value    Attr
MAIN   . . . . . . . . . . . F PROC  0000     CODESG  Length = 0014

FLDD . . . . . . . . . . . . L WORD  0000     DATASG
FLDE . . . . . . . . . . . . L WORD  0002     DATASG
FLDF . . . . . . . . . . . . L WORD  0004     DATASG

@CPU . . . . . . . . . . . . TEXT  0101h
@FILENAME  . . . . . . . . . TEXT  a05asm1
@VERSION . . . . . . . . . . TEXT  x10

          27 Source Lines
          27 Total  Lines
          15 Symbols
0 Warning Errors
0 Severe  Errors
```

Figure 5-2 Assembled Program with Conventional Segments

generates machine code, since they are just messages to the assembler. The listing is arranged vertically according to these sections:

1. At the extreme left is the number for each line.
2. The second section shows the hex addresses of data fields and instructions.
3. The third section shows the translated machine code in hexadecimal format.
4. The section to the right is your original source code.

The program is organized into three segments. Each segment contains a SEGMENT directive that notifies the assembler to align the segment on an address that is evenly divisible by hex 10—the SEGMENT statement itself generates no machine code. The program loader stores the contents of each segment in memory and initializes its address in a segment register. The beginning of the segment is offset zero bytes from that address.

Note that each segment is a separate area, with its own offset value for data or instructions.

Stack Segment

The stack segment contains a DW (Define Word) directive that defines 32 words, each generating a zero value designated by (0). This definition of 32 words is a realistic size for a stack because a large program may require many interrupts for input/output and calls to subprograms, all involving use of the stack. The stack segment ends at offset 0040H, which is equivalent to decimal value 64 (32 words $\times$ 2 bytes). The assembler shows the generated constant to the left as 0020[0000]; that is, 20H (32) zero words.

If the stack is too small to contain all the items pushed onto it, neither the assembler nor the linker warns you, and the executing program may crash in an unpredictable way.

Data Segment

The program defines a data segment, DATASG, containing three defined values, all in DW (Define Word) format:

1. FLDD defines a word (2 bytes) initialized with decimal value 175, which the assembler has translated to 00AFH (shown on the left).
2. FLDE defines a word initialized with decimal value 150, assembled as 0096H. The actual storage values of these two constants are, respectively, AF00 and 9600, which you can check with DEBUG.
3. FLDF is coded as a DW with ? in the operand to define a word with an uninitialized constant. The listing shows its contents as 0000.

The offset addresses of FLDD, FLDE, and FLDF are, respectively, 0000, 0002, and 0004, which relate to their field sizes.

Code Segment

The program defines a code segment, CODESG, which contains the program's executable code, all in one procedure (PROC).

Three statements establish the addressability of the data segment:

```
                   ASSUME SS:STACKSG,DS:DATASG,CS;CODESG
0000  B8 ---- R    MOV  AX,DATASG
0003  8E D8        MOV  DS,AX
```

1. The ASSUME directive relates DATASG to the DS register. Note that the program does not require the ES register, although some programmers initialize it as a standard practice. ASSUME simply provides information to the assembler, which generates no machine code for it.
2. The first MOV instruction "stores" DATASG in the AX register. Now, an instruction cannot actually store a segment in a register—the assembler simply recognizes an attempt to load the address of DATASG. Note the machine code to the left: B8----R. The four hyphens mean that at this point the assembler cannot determine the address of DATASG; the system determines this address only when the object program is linked and loaded for execution. Because the loader may locate a program anywhere in memory, the assembler leaves the address open and indicates the fact with an R; the loader is to replace (or relocate) the incomplete address with the actual one.
3. The second MOV instruction moves the contents of the AX register to the DS register. Because there is no valid instruction for a direct move from memory to the DS register, you have to code two instructions to initialize the DS.

Although the loader automatically initializes the SS and CS when it loads a program for execution, it is your responsibility to initialize the DS, and the ES if required.

While all this business may seem unduly involved, at this point you really don't have to understand it. All programs in this book use a standard definition and initialization, and you simply have to reproduce this code for each of your programs. To this end, store a skeleton assembly program on disk, and for each new program that you want to create, copy the skeleton program into a file with its correct name, and use your editor to complete the additional instructions.

The first instruction after initializing the DS register is MOV AX,FLDD, which begins at offset location 0005 and generates machine code A1 0000. The space in the listing between A1 (the operation) and 0000 (the operand) is only for readability. The next instruction, ADD AX,FLDE, begins at offset location 0008 and generates 4 bytes of machine code. The instruction, MOV FLDF,AC, copies the sum in the AX to FLDF at offset 0004 in the data segment. In this example, machine instructions are 2, 3, or 4 bytes in length.

The last statement in the program, END, contains the operand MAIN, which relates to the name of the PROC at offset 0000. This is the location in the code segment where the program loader is to transfer control for execution.

Following the program listing are a Segments and Groups table and a Symbols table.

Segments and Groups Table

The first table at the end of the assembled listing shows any defined segments and groups. Note that segments are not listed in the same sequence as they are coded; the assembler used for this example lists them in alphabetic sequence by name. (This program contains no groups, which is a later topic.) The table provides the length in bytes of each segment, the alignment (all are paragraphs), the combine type, and the class. The assembler has converted the class names to uppercase.

Symbols Table

The second table provides the names of data fields in the data segment (FLDD, FLDE, and FLDF) and the labels applied to instructions in the code segment. For MAIN (the only entry in the example), Type F PROC means far procedure (far because as the entry-point for execution MAIN must be known outside this program). The Value column gives the offset for the beginning of the segment for names, labels, and procedures. The column headed Attr (for attribute) provides the segment in which the item is defined.

Appendix D explains all the options for these tables. To cause the assembler to omit the tables, code a /N option following the MASM/TASM command.

For the last three entries:

@CPU identifies the processor at the time of assembly according to bit number set on:

0	8086	7	privileged instructions
1	80186	8	8087 numeric processor
2	80286	10	80287 numeric processor
4	80486	11	80387 numeric processor
5	80586 (Pentium)		

@FILENAME gives the name of the program

@VERSION shows the assembler version in the form n.nn

Turbo Assembler Listing

Figure 5-3 provides a listing of the same program, this time run under TASM. Differences in the generated code to the left of the listing are the following, by statement number:

	SOURCE	OBJECT CODE	MEANING
3	DW 32 DUP(0)	20*(0000)	20 copies of zero words
9	DW ?	????	An undefined value
15	MOV AX,DATASG	B8 0000s	0000 = incomplete operand and s = segment address
18	MOV AX,FLDD	A1 0000r	0000 = offset address of FLDD and r = relocatable value.

```
A05ASM1 (EXE)  Move and add operations
                     ; -------------------------------------------
    0000             STACKSG SEGMENT PARA STACK    'Stack'
    0000  20*(0000)          DW     32 DUP(0)
    0040             STACKSG ENDS
                     ; -------------------------------------------
    0000             DATASG  SEGMENT PARA 'Data'
    0000  00AF       FLDD    DW     175
    0002  0096       FLDE    DW     150
    0004  ????       FLDF    DW     ?
    0006             DATASG  ENDS
                     ; -------------------------------------------
    0000             CODESG  SEGMENT PARA 'Code'
    0000             MAIN    PROC   FAR
                             ASSUME SS:STACKSG,DS:DATASG,CS:CODESG
    0000  B8 0000s           MOV    AX,DATASG       ;Set address of data
    0003  8E D8              MOV    DS,AX           ;  segment in DS

    0005  A1 0000r           MOV    AX,FLDD         ;Move 0175 to AX
    0008  03 06 0002r        ADD    AX,FLDE         ;Add  0150 to AX
    000C  A3 0004r           MOV    FLDF,AX         ;Move to FLDF
    000F  B8 4C00            MOV    AX,4C00H        ;End processing
    0012  CD 21              INT    21H
    0014             MAIN    ENDP                   ;End of procedure
    0014             CODESG  ENDS                   ;End of segment
                             END    MAIN            ;End of program

Symbol Name              Type      Value

??DATE                   Text      "05/17/xx"
??FILENAME               Text      "a05asm1  "
??TIME                   Text      "16:06:45"
??VERSION                Number    040A
@CPU                     Text      0101H
@CURSEG                  Text      CODESG
@FILENAME                Text      A05ASM1
@WORDSIZE                Text      2
MAIN                     Far       CODESG:0000
FLDD                     Word      DATASG:0000
FLDE                     Word      DATASG:0002
FLDF                     Word      DATASG:0004

Groups & Segments        Bit Size  Align  Combine Class

CODESG                   16  0014  Para   none    CODE
DATASG                   16  0006  Para   none    DATA
STACKSG                  16  0040  Para   Stack   STACK
```

Figure 5-3 Turbo Assembler Listing

Aside from the conventions in the listings, the MASM and TASM assembled programs contain the same generated code.

USING SIMPLIFIED SEGMENT DIRECTIVES

Figure 4-3 showed how to code a program using the simplified segment directives. Figure 5-4 provides the assembled listing of that program. For the simplified segment directives, you initialize the DS like this:

```
 A05ASM2 (EXE)   Move and add operations                     Page   1-1
                                 page  60,132
                       TITLE     A05ASM2 (EXE)  Move and add operations
                       ;------------------------------------------------
                                 .MODEL  SMALL
                                 .STACK  64              ;Define stack
                                 .DATA                   ;Define data
 0000    00AF          FLDD      DW      175
 0002    0096          FLDE      DW      150
 0004    0000          FLDF      DW      ?
                       ;------------------------------------------------
                                 .CODE                   ;Define code segment
 0000                  MAIN      PROC    FAR
 0000    B8 ---- R               MOV     AX,@data        ;Set address of data
 0003    8E D8                   MOV     DS,AX           ;   segment in DS

 0005    A1 0000 R               MOV     AX,FLDD         ;Move 0175 to AX
 0008    03 06 0002 R            ADD     AX,FLDE         ;Add  0150 to AX
 000C    A3 0004 R               MOV     FLDF,AX         ;Store sum in FLDF

 000F    B8 4C00                 MOV     AX,4C00H        ;End processing
 0012    CD 21                   INT     21H
 0014                  MAIN      ENDP                    ;End of procedure
                                 END     MAIN            ;End of program
```

```
Segments and Groups:
          N a m e                Length    Align     Combine   Class
DGROUP . . . . . . . . . . . . . GROUP
  _DATA  . . . . . . . . . . . . 0006      WORD      PUBLIC    'DATA'
  STACK  . . . . . . . . . . . . 0040      PARA      STACK     'STACK'
_TEXT  . . . . . . . . . . . . . 0014      WORD      PUBLIC    'CODE'

Symbols:
          N a m e                Type      Value     Attr
MAIN   . . . . . . . . . . . . . F PROC    0000      _TEXT   Length = 0014

FLDD . . . . . . . . . . . . . . L WORD    0000      _DATA
FLDE . . . . . . . . . . . . . . L WORD    0002      _DATA
FLDF . . . . . . . . . . . . . . L WORD    0004      _DATA

@CODE  . . . . . . . . . . . . . TEXT      _TEXT
@CODESIZE  . . . . . . . . . . . TEXT      0
@CPU . . . . . . . . . . . . . . TEXT      0101h
@DATASIZE  . . . . . . . . . . . TEXT      0
@FILENAME  . . . . . . . . . . . TEXT      a05asm2

     0 Warning Errors
     0 Severe  Errors
```

Figure 5-4 Assembled Program with Simplified Segment Directions

```
MOV  AX,@data
MOV  DS,AX
```

The first part of the symbol table under "Segments and Groups" shows the three segments renamed by the assembler and listed alphabetically:

- _DATA, with a length of 6 bytes
- STACK, with a length of 40H (64 bytes)
- _TEXT, for the code segment, with a length of 14H (20 bytes)

Listed under the heading "Symbols" are names defined in the program or default names. The simplified segment directives provide a number of predefined equates, which begin with an @ symbol and which you are free to reference in a program. As well as @data, they are:

@CODE	Equated to the name of the code segment, _TEXT
@CODESIZE	Set to zero for the small and medium models
@CPU	Model of processor
@DATASIZE	Set to zero for the small and medium models
@FILENAME	Name of the program
@VERSION	Version of assembler (n.nn)

You may use @code and @data in ASSUME and executable statements, such as MOV AX,@data.

TWO-PASS ASSEMBLER

Many assemblers make two or more passes through a source program in order to resolve forward references to addresses not yet encountered in the program. During pass 1, the assembler reads the entire source program and constructs a symbol table of names and labels used in the program, that is, names of data fields and program labels and their relative locations (offsets) within the segment. You can see such a symbol table immediately following the assembled program in Figure 5-3, where the offsets for FLDD, FLDE, and FLDF are 0000, 0002, and 0004 bytes, respectively. Although the program defines no instruction labels, they would appear in the code segment with their own offsets. Pass 1 determines the amount of code to be generated for each instruction. MASM starts generating object code in pass 1, whereas TASM does it in pass 2.

During pass 2, the assembler uses the symbol table that it constructed in pass 1. Now that it knows the length and relative position of each data field and instruction, it can complete the object code for each instruction. It then produces, if requested, the various object (.OBJ), list (.LST), and cross-reference (.REF) files.

A potential problem in pass 1 is a *forward reference:* Certain types of instructions in the code segment may reference a label, but the assembler has not yet encountered its definition. MASM constructs object code based on what it supposes is the length of each generated machine language instruction. If there are any differences between pass 1 and pass 2 concerning instruction lengths, MASM issues an error message "Phase error between passes." Such errors are relatively rare, and, if one appears, you'll have to trace its cause and correct it.

Since version 6.0, MASM handles instruction lengths more effectively, taking as many passes through the file as necessary. TASM can assemble a program in one pass, but you may request that it take more than one if it is having difficulty with forward references (see Appendix D).

LINKING AN OBJECT PROGRAM

When your program is free of error messages, your next step is to link the object module, A05ASM1.OBJ, that was produced by the assembler and that contains only machine code. The linker performs the following functions:

- Combines, if requested, more than one separately assembled module into one executable program, such as two or more assembly programs or an assembly program with a C program.
- Generates an .EXE module and initializes it with special instructions to facilitate its subsequent loading for execution.

Once you have linked one or more .OBJ modules into an .EXE module, you may execute the .EXE module any number of times. But whenever you need to make a change in the program, you must correct the source program, assemble again into an .OBJ module, and link the .OBJ module into an .EXE module. Even if initially these steps are not entirely clear, you will find that with only a little experience, they become automatic.

You may convert some .EXE programs to .COM programs. See Chapter 7 for details.

The linker version for Microsoft is LINK, whereas the Borland version is TLINK. You can key in LINK or TLINK with a command line or by means of prompts. (Since MASM 6.0, the ML command provides for both assembling and linking.) This section shows how to link using a command line; see Appendix D for using prompts. The command line for linking is

```
LINK/TLINK objfile,exefile[,mapfile][,libraryfile]
```

- *Objfile* identifies the object file generated by the assembler. The linker assumes the extension .OBJ, so you need not enter it. The drive, subdirectory, and filename may be the same as or different from those in the source.
- *Exefile* provides for generating an .EXE file. The drive, subdirectory, and filename may be the same as or different from those in the source.
- *Mapfile* provides for generating a file with an extension .MAP that indicates the relative location and size of each segment and any errors that LINK has found. A typical error is the failure to define a stack segment. Entering CON (for console) tells the linker to display the map on the screen (instead of writing it on disk) so that you can view it immediately for errors.
- *Libraryfile* provides for the libraries option, which you don't need at this early stage of assembly programming.

This example links the object file A05ASM1.OBJ that was generated by the earlier assembly. The linker is to write the .EXE file on drive D, display the map (CON), and ignore the library option:

```
LINK D:A05ASM1,D:,CON
```

If the filename is to be the same as that of the source, you need not repeat it: The reference to drive number is sufficient to indicate a request for the file. Appendix D supplies other options.

Link Map for the First Program

For the program A05ASM1, LINK and TLINK both produce this link map:

START	STOP	LENGTH	NAME	CLASS
00000H	0003FH	0040H	STACKSG	STACK
00040H	00045H	0006H	DATASG	DATA
00050H	00063H	0014H	CODESG	CODE
Program entry point at 0005:0000				

- The stack is the first segment and begins at offset 0 bytes from the start of the program. Because it is defined as 32 words, it is 64 bytes long, as its length (40H) indicates.
- The data segment begins at the next paragraph boundary, offset 40H.
- The code segment begins at the next paragraph boundary, offset 50H. (Some assemblers rearrange the segments into alphabetical order.)
- Program entry point 0005:0000, which is in the form "relative (not absolute) segment:offset," refers to the address of the first executable instruction. In effect, the relative starting address is at segment 5[0], offset 0 bytes, which corresponds to the code segment boundary at 50H. The program loader uses this value when it loads the program into memory for execution.

At this stage, the only error that you are likely to encounter is entering wrong filenames. The solution is to restart with the link command.

Link Map for the Second Program

The link map for the second program (A05ASM2), which uses simplified segment directives, shows a somewhat different setup from that of the previous program. First, the assembler has physically rearranged the segments into alphabetical order; second, succeeding segments are aligned on *word* (not paragraph) boundaries, as shown by the link map:

START	STOP	LENGTH	NAME	CLASS
00000H	00013H	0014H	_TEXT	CODE
00014H	00019H	0006H	_DATA	DATA
00020H	0005FH	0040H	STACK	STACK
Program entry point at 0000:0000				

- The code segment is now the first segment and begins at offset 0 bytes from the start of the program.
- The data segment begins at the next word boundary, offset 14H.
- The stack begins at the next word boundary, offset 20H.
- The program entry point is now 0000:0000, which means that the relative location of the code segment begins at segment 0, offset 0.

EXECUTING A PROGRAM

Having assembled and linked a program, you can now (at last!) execute it. If the .EXE file is in the default drive, you could cause the loader to read it into memory for execution by typing

```
A05ASM1.EXE or A05ASM1 (without the .EXE extension)
```

If you omit typing the file extension, the loader assumes it is .EXE (or .COM). However, since this program produces no visible output, it is suggested that you run it under DEBUG and use trace commands to step through its execution. Key in the following, including the .EXE extension:

```
DEBUG D:A05ASM1.EXE
```

DEBUG loads the .EXE program module and displays its hyphen prompt.

To view the stack segment, key in D SS:0. The stack contains all zeros because it was initialized that way.

To view the code segment, key in D CS:0. Compare the displayed machine code with that of the code segment in the assembled listing:

```
B8----8ED8A10000 . . .
```

In this case, the assembled listing does not accurately show the machine code, since the assembler did not know the address for the operand of the first instruction. You can now determine this address by examining the displayed code.

To view the contents of the registers, press R followed by <Enter>. The SP (Stack Pointer) should contain 0040H, which is the size of the stack (32 words = 64 bytes = 40H). The IP (Instruction Pointer) should be 0000H. The SS and CS are properly initialized for execution; their values depend on where in memory your program is loaded.

The first instruction MOV AX,xxxx is ready to execute—it and the following MOV are about to initialize the DS register. To execute the first MOV, press T (for Trace) followed by <Enter> and note the effect on the IP. To execute the second MOV, again press T followed by <Enter>. Check the DS, which is now initialized with a segment address.

The third MOV loads the contents of FLDD into the AX. Press T again and note that the AX now contains 00AF. Now press T to execute the ADD instruction and note that the AX contains 0145. Press T to store the AX in offset 0004 of the data segment.

To check the contents of the data segment, key in D DS:0. The operation displays the three data items as AF 00 96 00 45 01, with the bytes for each word in reverse sequence.

At this point, you can use L to reload and rerun the program or press Q to quit the DEBUG session.

CROSS-REFERENCE LISTING

The assembler generates an optional .CRF or .XRF file that you can use to produce a *cross-reference listing* of a program's identifiers, or symbols. However, you still have to convert the .CRF file to a properly sorted cross-reference file. A program on the assembler disk performs this function: CREF for Microsoft or TCREF for Borland. You can key in CREF or

TCREF with a command line or by means of prompts. This section uses a command line; see Appendix D for using prompts. The command to convert the cross-reference file is

```
CREF/TCREF xreffile,reffile
```

- *xreffile* identifies the cross-reference file generated by the assembler. The program assumes the extension, so you need not enter it. You can also specify a disk drive number.
- *reffile* provides for generating a .REF file. The drive, subdirectory, and filename may be the same as or different from those in the source.

Figure 5-5 shows the cross-reference listing produced by CREF for the program in Figure 5-2. The symbols in the first column are in alphabetic order. The numbers in the second column, shown as n#, indicate the line in the .LST file where each symbol is defined. Numbers to the right of this column are line numbers showing where the symbol is referenced. For example, CODESG is defined in line 17 and is referenced in lines 19 and 29. FLDF is defined in line 14 and referenced in line 25+, where the " + " means its value is modified during program execution (by MOV FLDF,AX).

Assembling a number of programs generates a lot of unnecessary files. You can safely delete .OBJ, .CRF, and .LST files. Keep the .ASM source programs in case of further changes and the .EXE files for executing the programs.

ERROR DIAGNOSTICS

The assembler provides diagnostics for any programming errors that violate its rules. The program in Figure 5-6 is the same as the one in Figure 5-2, except that it has a number of

```
A05ASM1 (EXE)   Move and add operations

Symbol Cross-Reference   (# definition, + modification)

@CPU . . . . . . . . . . . . .    1#
@VERSION . . . . . . . . . . .    1#

MAIN . . . . . . . . . . . . .   18#    28     30

CODE . . . . . . . . . . . . .   17
CODESG . . . . . . . . . . . .   17#    19     29

DATA . . . . . . . . . . . . .   11
DATASG . . . . . . . . . . . .   11#    15     19     20

FLDD . . . . . . . . . . . . .   12#    23
FLDE . . . . . . . . . . . . .   13#    24
FLDF . . . . . . . . . . . . .   14#    25+

STACK. . . . . . . . . . . . .    4
STACKSG. . . . . . . . . . . .    4#     9     19

 12 Symbols
```

Figure 5-5 Cross-Reference Table

```
1                           page 60,132
2               TITLE       A05ASM3 (EXE)  Illustrate assembly errors
3               ; ---------------------------------------------------
4 0000          STACKSG     SEGMENT PARA STACK 'Stack'
5 0000 0020[                DW      32 DUP(0)
6      0000
7           ]
8
9 0040          STACKSG     ENDS
10              ; ---------------------------------------------------
11 0000         DATASG      SEGMENT PARA 'Data'
12 0000 00AF    FLDD        DW      175
13 0002 0096    FLDE        DW      150
14 0004         FLDF        DW
a05asm3.ASM(11): error A2027: Operand expected
15 0004         DATASG      ENDS
16              ; ---------------------------------------------------
17 0000         CODESG      SEGMENT PARA 'Code'
18 0000         BEGIN       PROC    FAR
19                          ASSUME  CS:CODESG,DS:DATASG
20 0000 A1 0000 U           MOV     AX,DATSEG         ;Address of data
a05asm3.ASM(17): error A2009: Symbol not defined: DATSEG
21 0003 8B D0               MOV     DX,AX             ;   segment in DS
22
23                          MOV     AS,FLDD           ;Move 0175 to AX
a05asm3.ASM(20): error A2009: Symbol not defined: AS
24 0005 03 06 0002 R        ADD     AX,FLDE           ;Add  0150 to AX
25 0009 A3 0000 U           MOV     FLDQ,AX           ;Store sum in FLDF
a05asm3.ASM(22): error A2009: Symbol not defined: FLDQ
26 000C B8 4C00             MOV     AX,4C00H          ;End processing
27 000F CD 21               INT     21H
28 0011         BEGIN       ENDP
a05asm3.ASM(25): error A2006: Phase error between passes
29 0011         CODESG  ENDS
30                          END     BEGIN

     0 Warning Errors
     5 Severe  Errors
```

Figure 5-6 Assembler Diagnostics

intentional errors inserted for illustrative purposes. The program was run under MASM; TASM generates a similar error listing. Here are the errors:

LINE	EXPLANATION
14	The definition of FLDF requires an operand.
19	ASSUME does not relate the SS to STACKSG, although the assembler has not detected this omission.
20	DATSEG should be spelled DATASG.
21	DX should be coded as DS, although the assembler does not know that this is an error.
23	AS should be coded as AX.
25	FLDQ should be coded as FLDF.
28	Correcting the other errors will cause this diagnostic to disappear.

The last error message, "Phase error between passes," occurs when addresses generated in pass 1 of a two-pass assembler differ from those of pass 2. To isolate an obscure error under MASM (prior to version 6.0), use the /D option to list both the pass 1 and the pass 2 files, and compare the offset addresses.

THE ASSEMBLER LOCATION COUNTER

The assembler maintains a *location counter* that it uses to account for each defined item in the data segment. Figures 5-3 and 5-5 illustrate its effect by means of the three defined data items:

```
0000 . . . FLDD DW
0002 . . . FLDE DW
0004 . . . FLDF DW
```

Initially, the location counter is set at 0, where the assembler establishes the first data item, FLDD. Because FLDD is defined as a word, the assembler advances the location counter by 2, to 0002, where it establishes FLDE. Because FLDE is also defined as a word, the assembler again advances its location counter by 2, to 0004, for the next data item, FLDE, also a word. The location counter is again advanced by 2, to 0006, but there are no further data items.

The assembler provides a number of ways to change the current value in the location counter. For example, you can use the EVEN or the ALIGN directive to facilitate aligning an address on an even-numbered boundary (Chapter 6), or use the ORG directive to begin a program at a particular offset (Chapter 7) or to redefine data items with different names (Chapter 26).

KEY POINTS

- Both MASM and TASM provide a command line for assembling, including (at least) the name of the source program. MASM also provides prompts for entering options.
- The assembler converts a source program to an .OBJ file and generates an optional listing and cross-reference file.
- The Segments and Groups table following an assembler listing shows any segments and groups defined in the program. The Symbols table shows all symbols (data names and instruction labels).
- The linker (LINK or TLINK) converts an .OBJ file to an executable .EXE file.
- The simplified segment directives generate the names _DATA for the data segment, STACK for the stack segment, and _TEXT for the code segment, as well as a number of predefined equates.
- The CREF (or TCREF) program produces a useful cross-reference listing.

QUESTIONS

5-1. Code the command line to assemble a source program named SQUEEZE.ASM with files .LST, .OBJ, and .CRF. Assume that the source program and assembler are in drive E.

5-2. Code the LINK or TLINK command line to link SQUEEZE.OBJ from Question 5-1.

5-3. Code the commands for SQUEEZE.EXE from Question 5-2 for the following: (a) direct execution from DOS; (b) execution through DEBUG.

5-4. Explain the purpose of each of the following files: (a) file.EXE; (b) file.OBJ; (c) file.MAP; (d) file.ASM; (e) file.CRF; (f) file.LST.

5-5. Assuming conventional segment definitions and DATSEGM as the name of the data segment, code the two MOV instructions to initialize the DS register.

5-6. Write an assembly program using conventional segment definitions for the following: (a) Move the immediate value hex 50 to the AL register; (b) shift the AL contents one bit left (SHL AL,1); (c) move immediate value hex 18 to the CL; (d) multiply AL by CL (MUL CL). Remember the instructions required to end program execution. The program does not need to define or initialize the data segment. Copy a skeleton program and use your editor to develop the program. Assemble, link, and use DEBUG to trace and to check the code segment and registers.

5-7. Revise the program in Question 5-6 for simplified segment directives. Assemble and link it, and compare the object code, symbol tables, and link map with those of the original program.

5-8. Add a data segment to the program in Question 5-6 for the following requirements:

- Define a 1-byte item (DB) named FIELDX containing hex 50 and another named FIELDY containing hex 18.
- Define a 2-byte item (DW) named FIELDZ with no constant.
- Move the contents of FIELDX to the AL register and shift left one bit.
- Multiply the AL by FIELDY (MUL FIELDY).
- Move the product in the AX to FIELDZ.

Assemble, link, and use DEBUG to test the program.

5-9. Revise the program in Question 5-8 for simplified segment directives. Assemble and link it, and compare the object code, symbol tables, and link map with those of the original program. Use DEBUG to test the program.

5-10. For each of the following data items, show the contents of the assembler's location counter:

```
0000  WORDA DW  0
....  WORDB DW  0
....  BYTEA DB  0
            EVEN
....  WORDC DW  0
....  BYTEB DB  0
```

6 SYMBOLIC INSTRUCTIONS AND ADDRESSING

Objective: To provide the basics of the assembly language instruction set and the requirements for addressing data.

INTRODUCTION

This chapter introduces the categories of the processor's instruction set, and then describes the basic addressing formats that are used throughout the rest of the book. The instructions formally covered in this chapter are MOV, MOVSX, MOVZX, XCHNG, LEA, INC, DEC, and INT, as well as the use of constants in instruction operands as immediate values. Finally, the chapter explains address alignment and the segment override prefix.

THE SYMBOLIC INSTRUCTION SET

The following is a list of the symbolic instructions for the 80x86 processor family, arranged by category. Although the list seems formidable, many of the instructions are rarely needed.

Arithmetic

ADC: Add with Carry
ADD: Add Binary Numbers
DEC: Decrement by 1
DIV: Unsigned Divide
IDIV: Signed (Integer) Divide
IMUL: Signed (Integer) Multiply
INC: Increment by 1
MUL: Unsigned Multiply
NEG: Negate
SBB: Subtract with Borrow
SUB: Subtract Binary Values
XADD: Exchange and Add

ASCII-BCD Conversion

AAA: ASCII Adjust After Addition
AAD: ASCII Adjust Before Division
AAM: ASCII Adjust After Multiplication
AAS: ASCII Adjust After Subtraction
DAA: Decimal Adjust After Addition
DAS: Decimal Adjust After Subtraction

Bit Shifting

RCL: Rotate Left Through Carry
RCR: Rotate Right Through Carry
ROL: Rotate Left
ROR: Rotate Right
SAL: Shift Algebraic Left
SAR: Shift Algebraic Right
SHL: Shift Logical Left
SHR: Shift Logical Right
SHLD: Shift Left Double (80386+)
SHRD: Shift Right Double (80386+)

Comparison

BSF/BSR: Bit Scan (80386+)
BT/BTC/BTR/BTS: Bit Test (80386+)
CMP: Compare
CMPSn: Compare String
CMPXCHG: Compare and Exchange (486+)
CMPXCHG8B: Compare and Exchange (586+)
TEST: Test Bits

Data Transfer

LDS: Load Data Segment Register
LEA: Load Effective Address
LES: Load Extra Segment Register
LODS: Load String
LSS: Load Stack Segment Register
MOV: Move Data
MOVS: Move String
MOVSX: Move with Sign-Extend
MOVZX: Move with Zero-Extend
STOS: Store String
XCHG: Exchange
XLAT: Translate

Flag Operations

CLC: Clear Carry Flag
CLD: Clear Direction Flag
CLI: Clear Interrupt Flag
PUSHF: Push Flags onto Stack
SAHF: Store AH in Flags
STC: Set Carry Flag

CMC: Complement Carry Flag
LAHF: Load AH from Flags
POPF: Pop Flags off Stack
STD: Set Direction Flag
STI: Set Interrupt Flag

Input/Output

IN: Input Byte or Word
INSn: Input String (80286+)
OUT: Output Byte or Word
OUTSn: Output String (80286+)

Logical Operations

AND: Logical AND
NOT: Logical NOT
OR: Logical OR
XOR: Exclusive OR

Looping

LOOP: Loop Until Complete
LOOPE: Loop While Equal
LOOPZ: Loop While Zero
LOOPNE: Loop While Not Equal
LOOPNZ: Loop While Not Zero
LOOPNEW: Loop While Not Equal (80386+)
LOOPNZW: Loop While Not Zero (80386+)

Processor Control

ESC: Escape
HLT: Enter Halt State
LOCK: Lock Bus
NOP: No Operation
WAIT: Put Processor in Wait State

Stack Operations

POP: Pop Word off Stack
POPA: Pop All General Registers (80286+)
PUSH: Push Word onto Stack
PUSHA: Push All General Registers (80286+)

String Operations

CMPS: Compare String
LODS: Load String
MOVS: Move String
REP: Repeat String
REPE: Repeat While Equal
REPZ: Repeat While Zero
REPNE: Repeat While Not Equal
REPNZ: Repeat While Not Zero
SCAS: Scan String
STOS: Store String

Transfer (Conditional)

INTO: Interrupt on Overflow
JA: Jump If Above
JAE: Jump If Above/Equal
JB: Jump If Below
JBE: Jump If Below/Equal
JC: Jump If Carry
JCXZ: Jump If CX Is Zero
JE: Jump If Equal
JG: Jump If Greater
JGE: Jump If Greater/Equal
JL: Jump If Less
JLE: Jump If Less/Equal
JNA: Jump If Not Above
JNAE: Jump If Not Above/Equal
JNB: Jump If Not Below
JNBE: Jump If Not Below/Equal
JNC: Jump If No Carry
JNE: Jump If Not Equal
JNG: Jump If Not Greater
JNGE: Jump If Not Greater/Equal
JNL: Jump If Not Less
JNLE: Jump If Not Less/Equal
JNO: Jump If No Overflow
JNP: Jump If No Parity
JNS: Jump If No Sign
JNZ: Jump If Not Zero
JO: Jump If Overflow
JP: Jump If Parity Odd
JPE: Jump If Parity Even
JPO: Jump If Parity Odd
JS: Jump If Sign
JZ: Jump If Zero

Transfer (Unconditional)

CALL: Call a Procedure
INT: Interrupt
IRET: Interrupt Return
JMP: Unconditional Jump
RET: Return
RETN/RETF: Return Near/Return Far

Type Conversion

CBW: Convert Byte to Word
CDQ: Convert Doubleword to Quadword (80386+)
CWD: Convert Word to Doubleword
CWDE: Convert Word to Extended Doubleword (80386+)

INSTRUCTION OPERANDS

An operand provides a source of data for an instruction to process. Some instructions, such as CLC and RET, do not require an operand, whereas other instructions may have one or two operands. Where there are two operands, the second operand is the *source,* which contains either the data to be delivered (immediate) or the address (of a register or in memory) of the data. The source data is unchanged by the operation. The first operand is the *desti-*

nation, which contains data in a register or in memory and which is to be processed. Here is the instruction format:

[label:]	operation	operand1,operand2

Let's now examine how the operand can affect the addressing of data.

Register Operands

For this type, the register provides the name of any one of the 8-, 16-, or 32-bit registers. Depending on the instruction, the register may appear in the first operand, the second operand, or both, as the following examples illustrate:

```
WORDA  DW   ?            ;Define a word
       ...
       MOV  DX,WORDA     ;Register in first operand
       MOV  WORDA,CX     ;Register in second operand
       MOV  EDX,EBX      ;Registers in both operands
```

Because processing data between registers involves no reference to memory, it is the fastest type of operation.

Immediate Operands

In immediate format, the second operand contains a constant value or an expression. (The first operand is never an immediate value.) The destination field in the first operand defines the length of the data and may be a register or a memory location. Here are some examples:

```
COUNT  DB    ?           ;Define a byte
       ...
       ADD   BX,25       ;Add 25 to BX
       MOV   COUNT,50    ;Move 50 to COUNT
```

A later section discusses immediate operands in more detail.

Direct Memory Operands

In this format, one of the operands references a memory location and the other operand references a register. (The only instructions that allow both operands to address memory directly are MOVS and CMPS.) The DS register is the default segment register for addressing data in memory. Here are some examples:

```
WORDA  DW   0            ;Define a word
BYTEA  DB   0            ;Define a byte
       ...
       MOV  BX,WORDA     ;Load WORDA into BX
       ADD  BYTEA,DL     ;Add DL to BYTEA
```

```
MOV  CX,DS:[38B0H]      ;Move word from memory at offset 38B0H
INC  BYTE PTR [1B0H]    ;Increment byte at offset 1B0H
```

The last two examples use square brackets as *index specifiers* to indicate a reference to memory. (An offset value like 38B0H is combined with the address in the DS.) The omission of square brackets, as in MOV CX,38B0H, indicates an immediate value—note the significant difference.

The last example increments the byte in memory at offset 1B0H (the offset combined with the DS address). Because the operand [1B0H] indicates only a starting memory location, you need the BYTE PTR modifier here to define the length.

In the following examples, a data item named CODETBL acts as an offset address in an instruction operand:

```
CODETBL  DB   20 DUP(?)       ;Define a table of bytes
         ...
         MOV  CL,CODETBL[3]   ;Get byte from CODETBL
         MOV  CL,CODETBL+3    ;Same operation
```

The first MOV uses an index specifier to access the fourth byte from CODETBL. (Because CODETBL[0] is the first byte, CODETBL[3] is the fourth.) The second MOV uses a plus (+) operator for exactly the same effect.

Indirect Memory Operands

Indirect addressing is a sophisticated technique that takes advantage of the computer's capability for segment:offset addressing. The registers used for this purpose are BX, DI, SI, and BP, coded within square brackets as an index operator. The BX, DI, and SI are associated with the DS register as DS:BX, DS:DI, and DS:SI, for processing data in the data segment. The BP is associated with the SS register as SS:BP, for handling data in the stack, which we'll do in Chapter 23 when calling subprograms and passing parameters.

When the first operand contains an indirect address, the second operand references a register or immediate value; when the second operand contains an indirect address, the first operand references a register. An indirect address such as [DI] tells the assembler that the memory address to use will be in the DI register when the program subsequently executes.

In the following example, the first MOV initializes the BX with the offset address of DATAVAL. The second MOV uses the address now in the BX to store zero in the memory location to which it points, in this case, DATAVAL:

```
DATAVAL  DB   50                  ;Define a byte
         ...
         MOV  BX,OFFSET DATAVAL   ;Load BX with offset
         MOV  [BX],25             ;Move 25 to DATAVAL
```

The effect of the two MOVs is the same as coding MOV DATAVAL,25, although the uses for indexed addressing are usually not so trivial. The following related instruction moves zero to a location two bytes immediately following DATAVAL:

```
MOV   [BX+2],0          ;Move 0 to DATAVAL+2
```

You may also combine registers in an indirect address; for example, [BX+DI] means the address in BX plus the address in the DI.

Note that a reference in square brackets to the BP, BX, DI, or SI register implies an indirect operand, and the processor treats the contents of the register as an offset address when the program is executing. Here are a few more examples of indirect operands:

```
ADD  CL,[BX]              ;2nd operand = DS:BX
MOV  BYTE PTR [DI],25     ;1st operand = DS:DI
ADD  [BP],CL              ;1st operand = SS:BP
```

Address displacement. This method uses an address displacement for an operand. The following MOV transfers the contents of the BL to DATATAB (a 40-byte table); exactly where in DATATAB is determined by the contents of the DI when the program is executing:

```
DATATAB  DB   40 DUP(?)          ;Define table
         ...
         MOV  DATATAB[DI],BL     ;Move BL to table
```

Indexing on 80386 and later processors. These processors allow an address to be generated from any combination of one or more general registers, an offset, and a scaling factor (1, 2, 4, or 8) associated with the contents of one of the registers. For example, the instruction

```
MOV EBX,[ECX*2+ESP+4]
```

moves a value into the EBX that consists of the contents of (the ECX times 2) plus the contents of (the ESP plus 4).

THE MOV INSTRUCTION

The MOV instruction transfers (that is, copies) data referenced by address of the second operand to the address of the first operand. The sending field is unchanged. The operands that reference memory or registers must agree in size (e.g., both must be bytes, both must be words, or both must be doublewords). The general format for MOV is

[label:]	MOV	register/memory,register/memory/immediate

Here are four examples of valid MOV operations by category, given the following data items:

```
BYTEFLD DB  ?    ;Define a byte
WORDFLD DW  ?    ;Define a word
```

1. Register Moves

```
MOV  EDX,ECX        ;Register-to-register
MOV  DS,BX          ;Register-to-segment register
```

```
MOV  BYTEFLD,DH      ;Register-to-memory, direct
MOV  [DI],BX         ;Register-to-memory, indirect
```

2. Immediate Moves

```
MOV  CX,40              ;Immediate-to-register
MOV  BYTEFLD,40         ;Immediate-to-memory, direct
MOV  WORDFLD[BX],40     ;Immediate-to-memory, indirect
```

3. Direct Memory Moves

```
MOV  CH,BYTEFLD         ;Memory-to-register, direct
MOV  CX,WORDFLD[BX]     ;Memory-to-register, indirect
```

4. Segment Register Moves

```
MOV  CX,DS           ;Segment register-to-register
MOV  WORDFLD,DS      ;Segment register-to-memory
```

You can move to a register a byte (MOV CH,BYTEFLD), a word (MOV CX, WORDFLD), or a doubleword (MOV ECX,DWORDFLD). The operand affects only the portion of the referenced register; for example, moving a byte to the CH does not affect the CL.

Invalid MOV operations are memory-to-memory (keep that one in mind), immediate-to-segment register, and segment register-to-segment register. Performing these operations requires more than one instruction.

MOVE-AND-FILL INSTRUCTIONS

For the MOV instruction, the destination must be the same length as the source, such as byte-to-byte and word-to-word. On the 80386 and later, the MOVSX and MOVZX (move and fill) instructions facilitate transferring data from a byte or word source to a word or doubleword destination. Here is the general format for MOVSX and MOVZX:

[label:]	MOVSX/MOVZX	register/memory,register/memory/immediate

MOVSX, for use with signed arithmetic values, moves a byte or word to a word or doubleword destination and fills the *sign bit* (the leftmost bit of the source) into leftmost bits of the destination. MOVZX, for use with unsigned numeric values, moves a byte or word to a word or doubleword destination and fills *zero bits* into leftmost bits of the destination. As an example, consider moving a byte containing 1011 0000 to a word; the result in the destination word depends on the choice of instruction:

```
MOVSX  CX,10110000B     ;CX = 11111111 10110000
MOVZX  CX,10110000B     ;CX = 00000000 10110000
```

Here are some other examples of using MOVSX and MOVZX:

```
BYTE1   DB     25            ;Byte
WORD1   DW     40            ;Word
DWORD1  DD     160           ;Doubleword
```

```
...
MOVSX  CX,BYTE1      ;Byte to word
MOVZX  WORD1,BH      ;Byte to word
MOVSX  EBX,WORD1     ;Word to doubleword
MOVZX  DWORD1,CX     ;Word to doubleword
```

Chapters 8 and 13 cover signed and unsigned data in detail.

IMMEDIATE OPERANDS

In the following example of an immediate operand, the instruction

```
MOV AX,0245H
```

moves the immediate constant 0245H to the AX register. The 3-byte object code for this instruction is B84502, where B8 means "move an immediate value to the AX register" and the following two bytes contain the value itself (4502H, in reverse-byte sequence). Many instructions provide for two operands; the first operand may be a register or memory location, and the second operand may be an immediate constant.

The use of an immediate operand provides faster processing than defining a numeric constant in the data segment and referencing it in the operand of the MOV, as, for example, in the following:

```
Data segment:  AMTC  DW   0245H      ;Define AMTC as word
                     ...
Code segment:        MOV  AX,AMTC    ;Move AMTC to AX
```

Immediate Formats

Here are some examples of valid immediate constants:

Hexadecimal: 0148H
Decimal: 328 (which the assembler converts to 0148H)
Binary: 101001000B (which converts to 0148H)

Length of Immediate Operands

The length of an immediate constant cannot exceed the length defined by the first operand. In the following invalid example, the immediate operand is 2 bytes, but the AL register is only 1 byte:

```
MOV CL,0245H    ;Invalid immediate length
```

However, if an immediate operand is shorter than a receiving operand, as in

```
ADD CX,48H    ;Valid length
```

the assembler expands the immediate operand to 2 bytes, 0048H, and stores the object code as 4800H.

The 80386 and later processors permit 4-byte (doubleword) immediate operands, such as

```
MOV ECX,12345678H    ;Move doubleword
```

Figure 6-1 gives examples of MOV, ADD, and SUB, which are three of many instructions that allow immediate operands. The .386 directive allows the assembler to recognize the reference to the EDX register. You don't need an 80386 or later processor to assemble this statement, but you would need one to execute it.

```
         page   60,132
TITLE    A06IMMED (EXE)  Example of immediate operands
         .MODEL  SMALL
         .STACK  64              ;Define stack
         .DATA                   ;Define data segment
FLDX     DB      150
FLDY     DW      300
.386
         .CODE
MAIN     PROC    FAR
         MOV     AX,@data        ;Set address of data
         MOV     DS,AX           ;   segment in DS
         MOV     CX,325          ;Move immediate
         ADD     CX,150          ;Add immediate
         MOV     EDX,0           ;Move immediate (80386+)
         ADD     DX,20H          ;Add immediate (hex)
         SUB     FLDX,250        ;Subtract immediate
         MOV     FLDY,40H        ;Move immediate
         MOV     AX,4C00H        ;End processing
         INT     21H
MAIN     ENDP
         END     MAIN
```

Figure 6-1 Using Immediate Operands

Processing data items that exceed the capacity of a register involves additional coding, covered in later chapters.

THE XCHG INSTRUCTION

The XCHG instruction performs another type of data transfer, but rather than simply copy the data from one location to another, XCHG *swaps* the two data items. The general format for XCHG is

[label:]	XCHG	register/memory,register/memory

Valid XCHG operations involve exchanging data between two registers and between a register and memory. Here are two examples:

```
WORDQ  DW  ?           ;Define word
       ...
       XCHG CL,BH      ;Exchange contents of two registers
       XCHG CX,WORDQ   ;Exchange contents of register and memory
```

THE LEA INSTRUCTION

The LEA instruction is useful for initializing a register with an offset address. The general format for LEA is

[label:]	LEA	register,memory

A common use for LEA is to initialize an offset in the BX, DI, or SI register for indexing an address in memory, which is done a lot throughout this book. Here's an example:

```
DATATBL  DB  25 DUP (?)       ;Define a table
BYTEFLD  DB  ?                ;Define a byte
         ...
         LEA  BX,DATATBL      ;Load offset address
         MOV  BYTEFLD,[BX]    ;Move first byte of DATATBL
```

An equivalent operation to LEA is MOV with the OFFSET operator, which generates slightly shorter machine code and is used like this:

```
MOV BX,OFFSET DATATBL, ;Load offset address
```

THE INC AND DEC INSTRUCTIONS

INC and DEC are convenient instructions for incrementing and decrementing the contents of registers and memory locations by 1. The general format for INC and DEC is

[label:]	INC/DEC	register/memory

Note that INC and DEC require only one operand. Depending on the result, the operations clear or set the OF, SF, and ZF flags, which conditional jump instructions may test for minus, zero, or plus.

EXTENDED MOVE OPERATIONS

The programs to this point involved moving immediate data into a register, moving data from defined memory to a register, moving register contents to memory, and moving the contents of one register to another. In all cases, the length of the data was limited to one or two bytes, and no operation moved data from one memory area directly to another memory area. This section explains how to move data that exceeds 2 bytes. Another method, the use of string instructions, is covered in Chapter 12.

In the program in Figure 6-2, the data segment contains two 9-byte fields defined as HEADG1 and HEADG2. The object of the program is to move the contents of HEADG1 to HEADG2:

```
HEADG1: I n t e r T e c h
        ↓ ↓ ↓ ↓ ↓ ↓ ↓ ↓ ↓
HEADG2: L a s e r C o r p
```

```
         page  60,132
TITLE    A06MOVE (EXE)  Extended move operations
;-----------------------------------------------------------
         .MODEL  SMALL
         .STACK  64
;-----------------------------------------------------------
         .DATA
HEADG1   DB      'InterTech'
HEADG2   DB      'LaserCorp', '$'
;-----------------------------------------------------------
         .CODE
A10MAIN  PROC    FAR
         MOV     AX,@data          ;Initialize segment
         MOV     DS,AX             ;  registers
         MOV     ES,AX

         MOV     CX,09             ;Initialize to move 9 chars
         LEA     SI,HEADG1         ;Initialize address of HEADG1
         LEA     DI,HEADG2         ;   and HEADG2
A20:
         MOV     AL,[SI]           ;Get character from HEADG1,
         MOV     [DI],AL           ;  move it to HEADG2
         INC     SI                ;Incr next char in HEADG1
         INC     DI                ;Incr next pos'n in HEADG2
         DEC     CX                ;Decrement count for loop
         JNZ     A20               ;Count not zero? Yes, loop
                                   ;Finished
         MOV     AH,09H            ;Request display
         LEA     DX,HEADG2         ;  of HEADG2
         INT     21H

         MOV     AX,4C00H          ;End processing
         INT     21H
A10MAIN  ENDP
         END     A10MAIN
```

Figure 6-2 Extended Move Operations

Because these fields are each 9 bytes long, more than a simple MOV instruction is required. The program contains a number of new features.

In order to step through HEADG1 and HEADG2, the program initializes the CX register to 9 (the length of both fields) and uses the SI and DI registers for indexing. Two LEA instructions load the offset addresses of HEADG1 and HEADG2 into the SI and DI as follows:

```
LEA SI,HEADG1    ;Load offset addresses
LEA DI,HEADG2    ; of HEADG1 and HEADG2
```

The program uses the addresses in the SI and DI registers to move the first byte of HEADG1 to the first byte of HEADG2. The square brackets around SI and DI in the MOV operands mean that the instructions are to use the offset address in the given register for accessing the memory location. Thus

```
MOV AL,[SI]
```

means "Use the offset address in SI (HEADG1+0) to move the referenced byte to the AL register." And the instruction

```
MOV [DI],AL
```

means "Move the contents of the AL to the offset address referenced by DI (HEADG2+0)." The program has to repeat these two MOV instructions nine times, once for each character in the respective fields. To this end, it uses a conditional jump instruction that we have not yet explained: JNZ (Jump if Not Zero).

Two INC instructions increment the SI and DI by 1 and DEC decrements the CX by 1. DEC also sets or clears the Zero flag, depending on the result in the CX; if the result is not zero, there are still more characters to move, and JNZ jumps back to the label A20 to repeat the move instructions. And because the SI and DI have been incremented by 1, the next MOVs reference HEADG1+1 and HEADG2+1. The loop continues in this fashion until it has moved nine characters in all, up to HEADG2+8.

As well, the program introduces the instructions needed to display the contents of HEADG2 at the end of processing. The required instructions are:

1. Initialize function 09H in the AH register to request a display.
2. Initialize the address of HEADG2 in the DX.
3. Execute the instruction INT 21H.

The INT operation displays all the characters beginning with the first byte of HEADG2 up to the terminating '$' sign, which is defined immediately following HEADG2. Chapter 9 covers this operation in detail.

You may want to key in this program, assemble and link it, and use DEBUG to trace it. Note the effect on the stack, the registers, and the IP (particularly after JNZ executes). Use D DS:0 to view the changes to HEADG2.

THE INT INSTRUCTION

On execution, an INT instruction interrupts processing and accesses the *interrupt vector table* in low memory to determine the address of the requested routine. The operation then transfers to DOS or to BIOS for specified action and returns to your program to resume processing. Most often, the interrupt has to perform the complex steps of an input or output operation. Interrupts require a trail that facilitates exiting a program and, on successful completion, returning to it. For this purpose, INT performs the following:

- Pushes the contents of the flags register onto the stack. (Push first decrements the stack pointer by 2.)
- Clears the interrupt and trap flags.
- Pushes the CS register onto the stack.
- Pushes the instruction pointer (containing the address of the next instruction) onto the stack.
- Causes the required operation to be performed.

To return from an interrupt, the routine issues an IRET (Interrupt Return), which pops the registers off the stack and thus causes a return to the instruction immediately following the INT.

Because the preceding process is entirely automatic, your only concerns are to define a stack large enough for the necessary pushing and popping and to use the appropriate INT operations.

ALIGNING DATA ADDRESSES

Because the 8086 and 80286 have a 16-bit (word) data bus, they execute faster if accessed words begin on an even-numbered (word) address. Consider a situation in which offsets 0012H and 0013H contain the word 63 A7H. The processor can access the full word at offset 0012H directly into a register. But the word could begin on an odd-numbered address, such as 0013H:

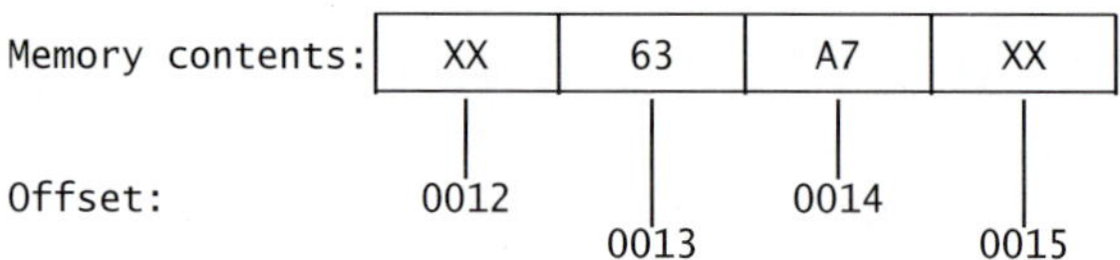

In this case, the processor has to perform two accesses. First, it accesses the bytes at 0012H and 0013H and delivers the byte from 0013H (63) to the AL register. Then, it accesses the bytes at 0014H and 0015H and delivers the byte from 0014H (A7) to the AH register. The AX now contains A763H.

You don't have to perform any special programming for even or odd locations, nor do you have to know whether an address is even or odd. The accessing operation automatically reverses a word from memory into a register so that it resumes its correct sequence.

The 80386 and later processors have a 32-bit data bus and, accordingly, prefer alignment of referenced items on addresses evenly divisible by four (a doubleword address). (Technically, the 486 and later processors prefer alignment on a 16-byte (paragraph) boundary.)

You can use the ALIGN or EVEN directive to force alignment of items on boundaries. For example, either ALIGN 2 or EVEN aligns on a word boundary, and ALIGN 4 aligns on a doubleword boundary. When the assembler adjusts the address of an item according to a boundary, it also advances its location counter accordingly.

Because the data segment when defined with PARA begins on a paragraph boundary, you could organize your data first with doubleword values, then with word values, and, finally, with byte values. However, modern processors execute at such rapid speed that you'll probably never notice the effects of forcing alignment.

NEAR AND FAR ADDRESSES

An address in a program may be near or far. A *near address* consists of only the offset portion of an address. An instruction that references a near address assumes the current segment—namely, the DS for the data segment and the CS for the code segment.

A *far address* consists of both the segment and offset portions, in the form segment:offset. An instruction may reference a far address from within the current segment or in another segment.

Almost all assembly programming makes use of near addresses, which the assembler generates unless instructed otherwise. Larger programs that consist of many segments would require far addresses.

THE SEGMENT OVERRIDE PREFIX

For most purposes, a reference to a data area in a program is to locations in the data segment, handled via the DS register. There are occasions, however—especially for large programs—when you may have to handle data that is subject to another segment register, such as the ES or, on the 386 and later, the FS or GS. An example would be a large table of data loaded from disk into a separate segment in memory.

You can use any instruction to process the data in the other segment, but you must identify the appropriate segment register. Let's say that the address of the other segment is in the ES register, and the BX contains an offset address within that segment. Suppose the requirement is to move 2 bytes (a word) from that location to the DX register:

```
MOV DX,ES:[BX]     ;Move to DX from ES:[BX]
```

The coding of "ES:" indicates an override operator that means "Replace the normal use of the DS segment register with that of the ES." The next example moves a byte value from the CL into this other segment, at an offset formed by the value in the SI plus 36:

```
MOV ES:[SI+36],CL     ;Move to ES:[SI+36] from CL
```

The assembler generates the machine language code with the override operator inserted as a 1-byte prefix (26H) immediately preceding the instruction, just as if you had coded the instructions as

```
ES: MOV DX,[BX]      ;Move to DX from ES:[BX]
ES: MOV [SI+36],CL    ;Move to ES:[SI+36] from CL
```

KEY POINTS

- An operand provides a source of data for an instruction. An instruction may have one, two, or no operands.
- Where there are two operands, the second operand is the source, which references either immediate data or the address (of a register or of memory) of the data. The first operand is the destination, which references data to be processed in a register or in memory.
- In immediate format, the second operand contains a constant value or an expression. Immediate operands should match the size of the destination, that is, both byte, word, or doubleword.

- In direct memory format, one of the operands references a memory location, and the other operand references a register.
- Indirect addressing takes advantage of the processor's capability for segment:offset addressing. The registers used are BP, BX, DI, and SI, coded within square brackets as an index operator. The BP is associated with the SS as SS:BP, for handling data in the stack. The BX, DI, and SI are associated with the DS as DS:BX, DS:DI, and DS:SI, respectively, for processing data in the data segment.
- You may combine registers in an indirect address as [BX+DI], which means the address in BX plus the address in the DI.
- The MOV instruction transfers (or copies) data referenced by the address in the second operand to the address in the first operand.
- The LEA instruction is useful for initializing a register with an offset address.
- INC and DEC are convenient instructions for incrementing and decrementing by 1 the contents of registers and memory locations.
- The INT instruction interrupts processing of your program, transfers to DOS or BIOS for specified action, and IRET returns to your program to resume processing.

QUESTIONS

6-1. For an instruction with two operands, which operand is the source and which is the destination?

6-2. (a) In what significant way do the following instructions differ in execution?

```
ADD   CX,2548H
ADD   CX,[2548H]
```

(b) For the second ADD, one operand is in square brackets. What is the name of this feature?

6-3. (a) In what significant way do the following ADD instructions differ in execution?

```
ADD   BX,25
ADD   [BX],25
```

(b) For the second ADD, what sort of addressing is involved with the first operand?

6-4. Explain the operation of the instruction

```
ADD   DX,[BX+SI+8]
```

6-5. Consider the following statement, which contains an error:

```
ADD   [BX],[DI]
```

(a) Identify the error; (b) explain how to correct the error.

6-6. Given the following data definitions, find the errors in the statements, and code the instructions necessary to correct them:

```
BYTEX    DB   56
BYTEY    DB   27
WORDZ    DW   148
(a)          ADD BYTEX,BYTEY
(b)          ADD AL,WORDZ       ;Operand 2 is correct
(c)          SUB BL,047BH       ;Operand 2 is correct
```

6-7. Code the following as instructions with immediate operands: (a) Add hex 48 to CX; (b) subtract hex 48 from DX; (c) shift the DH one bit to the right; (d) shift BYTEX one bit to the left; (e) store 248 in the CX; (f) compare BYTEX to zero.

6-8. Code one instruction that swaps the contents of a word named WORDZ with the BX.

6-9. Code the instruction to set the BX with the (offset) address of an item named CODETBL.

6-10. Explain in general terms the purpose of the INT instruction.

6-11. Explain how (a) the INT instruction affects the stack, and (b) the IRET instruction affects the stack.

6-12. Code, assemble, link, and use DEBUG to test the following program:

- Define byte items named BYTEX and BYTEY (containing any values) and a word item named WORDZ (containing zero).
- Move the contents of BYTEX to the AL.
- Add the contents of BYTEY to the AL.
- Move the immediate value 34H to the CL.
- Exchange the contents of the AL and CL.
- Multiply the contents of the AL by the CL (MUL CL).
- Transfer the product from the AX to WORDZ.

7 WRITING .COM PROGRAMS

> Objective: To explain the purpose and uses of .COM programs and how to prepare an assembly language program for .COM format.

INTRODUCTION

Up to this chapter, we have written, assembled, and executed only .EXE programs. For an .EXE program, the linker automatically generates a particular format and, when storing it on disk, precedes it with a special header block that is 512 bytes or more long. (Chapter 24 provides details of header blocks.)

You can also write .COM programs for execution. One example of a commonly used .COM program is COMMAND.COM. The advantages of .COM programs are that they are smaller than comparable .EXE programs and are more easily adapted to act as resident programs. The .COM format has its roots in earlier days of microcomputers, when program size was limited to 64K.

DIFFERENCES BETWEEN AN .EXE AND A .COM PROGRAM

Significant differences between a program that is to execute as .EXE and one that is to execute as .COM involve the program's size, segmentation, and initialization.

Program Size

An .EXE program may be virtually any size, whereas a .COM program is restricted to one segment and a maximum of 64K, including the PSP. The PSP is a 256-byte (100H) block that the program loader inserts immediately preceding .COM and .EXE programs when it loads them from disk into memory. The 64K limit for a .COM program is a general rule; you may get around it by coding additional SEGMENT AT statements, a feature that is outside the scope of this chapter.

A .COM program is always smaller than its counterpart .EXE program; one reason is that a 512-byte header record that precedes an .EXE program on disk does not precede a .COM program. (Don't confuse the header record, covered in Chapter 24, with the PSP.) A .COM program is an absolute image of the executable program, with no relocatable address information.

Segments

The use of segments for .COM programs is significantly different (and easier) than for .EXE programs.

Stack segment. You define a stack segment for an .EXE program, whereas the assembler automatically generates a stack for a .COM program. Thus, when you write an assembly program that is to be converted to .COM format, you omit defining the stack. If the 64K program size is not large enough, the assembler establishes the stack after the program, in higher memory.

Data segment. For an .EXE program, you usually define a data segment and initialize the DS register with the address of that segment. For a .COM program, you don't define a data segment; instead, you define the data within the code segment. As you'll see, there are simple ways to handle this situation.

Code segment. A full .COM program combines the PSP, stack, data segment, and code segment into one code segment, in a maximum of 64K bytes.

Initialization

When the program loader loads a .COM program for execution, it automatically initializes all four segment registers with the address of the PSP. Because the CS and DS registers now contain the correct initial segment address at execution time, your program does not have to initialize them.

Because addressing begins at an offset of 100H bytes from the beginning of the PSP, you have to code a directive, ORG 100H, immediately following the code segment's SEGMENT or .CODE statement. The ORG directive tells the assembler to set its location counter at 100H. The assembler then begins generating the object code at an offset of 100H bytes past the start of the PSP, where your coding for the .COM program begins.

CONVERTING INTO .COM FORMAT

If your source program is already written in .EXE format, you can use an editor to convert the instructions into .COM format. MASM and TASM coding formats for .COM programs are identical, although their methods for conversion differ.

Microsoft Conversion

For both .EXE and .COM programs under Microsoft MASM, you assemble and produce an .OBJ file and then link the .OBJ file to produce an .EXE program. If you wrote the program to run as an .EXE program, you can now execute it. If you wrote the program to run as a .COM program, the linker produces a message: **Warning: No STACK Segment.** You may ignore this warning, because there is supposed to be no defined stack. You use a program named EXE2BIN to convert the Microsoft .EXE program to a .COM program. (Actually, it converts .EXE programs to a .BIN (binary) file; the program name means "convert EXE-to-BIN," but you should name your output file extension .COM.) Assuming that EXE2BIN is in the default drive, and that a linked file named SENTINEL.EXE is in drive D, type

```
EXE2BIN D:SENTINEL,D:SENTINEL.COM <Enter>
```

The first operand of the command always references an .EXE file, so do not code the .EXE extension. The second operand may be any valid filename with a .COM extension. If you omit the .COM extension, EXE2BIN assumes .BIN, which you have to rename subsequently as .COM in order to execute the program. (Someone, somewhere, must have thought this was a good idea.)

Borland Conversion

As long as your TASM source program is coded according to .COM requirements, you can convert your object program directly into a .COM program. Use the /T option for TLINK:

```
TLINK /T D:SENTINEL
```

When conversion to .COM format is complete, you may delete the generated .OBJ and .EXE files.

EXAMPLE OF A .COM PROGRAM

The program in Figure 7-1, named A07COM1, is similar to the one in Figure 5-2, but now revised to conform to .COM requirements. Note the following changes from Figure 5-2:

- There is no defined stack or data segment.
- The ASSUME statement tells the assembler to expect that all segment registers will contain the starting address of the code segment (where the PSP begins) when the program is loaded for execution.
- The directive ORG 100H tells the assembler to advance its location counter 100H bytes from the beginning of the PSP. The program loader stores the 100H in the instruction pointer (IP) register when it loads the .COM program.
- A JMP instruction transfers control of execution around the defined data. Some programmers code data items following the instructions, so that no initial JMP instruction is required. Coding data items first may speed up the assembly process slightly,

```
        page 60,132
TITLE   A07COM1 COM program to move and add
CODESG  SEGMENT PARA 'Code'
        ASSUME  CS:CODESG,DS:CODESG,SS:CODESG,ES:CODESG
        ORG     100H             ;Start at end of PSP
BEGIN:  JMP     A10MAIN          ;Jump past data
; ---------------------------------------------------
FLDD    DW      175              ;Data definitions
FLDE    DW      150
FLDF    DW      ?
; ---------------------------------------------------
A10MAIN PROC    NEAR
        MOV     AX,FLDD          ;Move 0175 to AX
        ADD     AX,FLDE          ;Add  0150 to AX
        MOV     FLDF,AX          ;Store sum in FLDF
        MOV     AX,4C00H         ;End processing
        INT     21H
A10MAIN ENDP
CODESG  ENDS
        END     BEGIN
```

Figure 7-1 .COM Source Program with Conventional Segments

but provides no other advantage. Examples in this book define the data first only as a programming convention.

- The names BEGIN and A10MAIN are merely descriptive and are not otherwise meaningful to the assembler. You can use any valid names for these labels.
- The conventional INT 21H function 4CH ends processing and exits to the operating system. You may also use the RET instruction to exit from a .COM program. (It transfers to an INT 20H, an old exit, in byte 01 of the PSP.)

Here are the steps for MASM and TASM to convert the program to .COM format:

MASM	TASM
MASM D:A07COM1,D:	TASM D:A07COM1,D:
LINK D:A07COM1,D:	TLINK /T D:A07COM1,D:
EXE2BIN D:A07COM1,D:A07COM1.COM	

The .EXE and .COM programs are 792 bytes and 24 bytes in size, respectively. The difference is largely caused by the 512-byte header block stored at the beginning of .EXE modules. Type DEBUG D:A07COM1.COM and trace execution of the .COM program up to (but not including) the last instruction.

You may also use simplified segment directives when coding a .COM program, as shown in Figure 7-2. Once again, define only a code segment, not a stack or data segment.

THE .COM STACK

For a .COM program, the system automatically defines the stack and sets the same segment address in all four segment registers. If the 64K segment for the program is large enough, the program loader sets the stack at the end of the segment and sets the SP register with the address of the top of the stack.

```
        page 60,132
TITLE   A07COM2  COM program to move and add data
        .MODEL  SMALL
        .CODE
        ORG     100H            ;Start at end of PSP
BEGIN:  JMP     A10MAIN         ;Jump past data
; ----------------------------------------------------
FLDD    DW      175             ;Data definitions
FLDE    DW      150
FLDF    DW      ?
; ----------------------------------------------------
A10MAIN PROC    NEAR
        MOV     AX,FLDD         ;Move 0175 to AX
        ADD     AX,FLDE         ;Add  0150 to AX
        MOV     FLDF,AX         ;Store sum in FLDF
        MOV     AX,4C00H        ;End processing
        INT     21H
A10MAIN ENDP
        END     BEGIN
```

Figure 7-2 .COM Source Program with Simplified Segment Directives

If the 64K segment does not contain enough space for a stack, the loader sets the stack at the end of memory. In either case, the loader then pushes a zero word onto the stack, which acts as an offset for the IP if you use RET to end execution of a .COM program.

If your program is large, or if memory is restricted, you may have to take care pushing words onto the stack. The DIR command indicates the size of a file and gives you an idea as to the space available for a stack. Many of the smaller programs in this book are in .COM format, and are easily distinguished from .EXE format.

DEBUGGING TIPS

The omission of only one .COM requirement may cause a program to fail. If EXE2BIN finds an error, it simply notifies you that it cannot convert the file, but does not provide a reason. Check the SEGMENT, ASSUME, and END statements. If you omit ORG 100H, the executing program incorrectly references data in the PSP, with unpredictable results.

If you run a .COM program under DEBUG, use D CS:100 to view the data and instructions. Do not follow the program through its termination; instead, use DEBUG's Q command.

An attempt to execute the .EXE module of a program written as .COM will fail; be sure to delete this file.

KEY POINTS

- A .COM program is restricted to one 64K segment and is smaller than its counterpart .EXE program.
- A program written as .COM does not define a stack or data segment, nor does it initialize the DS register.

- A program written as .COM requires ORG 100H immediately following the code segment's SEGMENT statement. The statement sets the offset address to the beginning of execution following the PSP.
- For Microsoft MASM, the EXE2BIN program converts an .EXE file to .COM format. Borland's TLINK can convert an object program directly into .COM format.
- The system installs the stack for a .COM program at the end of the program.

QUESTIONS

7-1. What is the maximum size of a .COM program?

7-2. For a source program to be converted to .COM format, what segment(s) can you define?

7-3. Explain why you code ORG 100H at the beginning of a program to be converted to .COM format.

7-4. Why is it not necessary to define a stack for a .COM program?

7-5. A source program is named PRESSURE.ASM. Provide the commands to convert it to .COM format under (a) MASM; (b) TASM.

7-6. Revise the program in Question 6-12 for .COM format. Assemble, link, convert it to .COM, and execute it under DEBUG.

8 PROGRAMMING REQUIREMENTS FOR LOGIC AND CONTROL

Objectives: To cover the requirements for program control (looping and jumping), for logical comparisons, for logical bit operations, and for program organization.

INTRODUCTION

Up to this chapter, most of our programs have executed in a straight line, with one instruction sequentially following another. Seldom, however, is a programmable problem that simple. Instead, most programs consist of various tests to determine which of several actions to take and a number of loops in which a series of steps repeats until a specific requirement is reached. A common practice, for example, is to test whether a program is to end execution.

Requirements such as these involve a transfer of control to the address of an instruction that does not immediately follow the one currently executing. A transfer of control may be *forward,* to execute a new series of steps, or *backward,* to reexecute the same steps. Instructions that can transfer control outside the normal sequential flow do so by adding an offset value to the IP.

Following are the instructions introduced in this chapter, by category:

Compare Operations	Transfer Operations	Logical Operations	Shift and Rotate
CMP	CALL	AND	SAR/SHR
TEST	JMP	NOT	SAL/SHL
	Jnnn*	OR	RCR/ROR
	LOOP	XOR	RCL/ROL

*Jnnn means all conditional jump instructions such as JNE and JL.

SHORT, NEAR, AND FAR ADDRESSES

The assembler supports three types of addresses that are distinguished by their distance from the currently executing address:

1. A *short* address, limited to a distance of −128 to 127 bytes.
2. A *near* address, limited to a distance of −32,768 to 32,767 bytes within the same segment.
3. A *far* address, which may be at a distance over 32K or in another segment.

A jump operation reaches a short address by a 1-byte offset and reaches a near address by a 1- or 2-word offset. A far address is reached by a segment address and an offset; CALL is the normal instruction for this purpose because it facilitates linking to the requested address and the subsequent return.

The following table lists the rules on distances for JMP, LOOP, and CALL operations. There is little need to memorize these rules, because normal use of these instructions rarely causes problems.

	Short	Near	Far
Instructions	−128 to 127 Same segment	−32,768 to 32,767 Same segment	Over 32K or in another segment
JMP	yes	yes	yes
Jnnn	yes	yes (80386+)	no
LOOP	yes	no	no
CALL	N/A	yes	yes

INSTRUCTION LABELS

The operand of the JMP, Jnnn (conditional jump), and LOOP instructions refer to the label of another instruction. The following example jumps to P50, which is the label of an INC instruction:

```
        JMP     P50
        ...
P50:    INC     CX
        ...
```

The label of an instruction such as P50: is terminated by a colon, which gives it the near attribute—that is, the label is inside a procedure in the same code segment. Watch out: Omission of the colon is a common error, which the assembler signals. Note that an address label in an instruction operand (such as JMP P50) does not have a colon.

You can also code a label on a separate line as

```
P50:
        INC     CX
```

In both cases, the address of P50 references the first byte of the INC instruction.

THE JMP INSTRUCTION

A commonly used instruction for transferring control is the JMP (Jump) instruction. A jump is unconditional, because the operation transfers control under all circumstances. JMP also flushes the processor's prefetch instruction queue; thus a program with many jump operations may lose some processing speed. The general format for JMP is

[label:]	JMP	short, near, or far address

Short and Near Jumps

A JMP operation within the same segment may be short or near (or even far if the destination is a procedure with the FAR attribute). On its first pass through a source program, the assembler generates the length of each instruction. However, a JMP instruction may be two, three, or four bytes long. A JMP operation to a label within −128 to +127 bytes is a *short jump.* The assembler generates one byte for the operation (EB) and one byte for the operand. The operand acts as an offset value that the processor adds to the IP register when executing the program. The limits are 00H to FFH, or −128 to +127.

A JMP that exceeds −128 to +127 bytes becomes a *near jump* (within 32K), for which the assembler generates different machine code (E9) and a 2-byte operand (8086/80286) or 4-byte operand (80386 and later). For now, we'll pass on the far jump.

Backward and Forward Jumps

A jump may be backward or forward. The assembler may have already encountered the designated operand (a *backward jump*) within −128 bytes, as in

```
P50:
        ...
        JMP   P50
```

In this case, the assembler generates a 2-byte machine instruction. In a *forward jump,* the assembler has not yet encountered the designated operand:

```
        JMP   P90
        ...
P90:
```

Because the assembler doesn't know at this point whether the forward jump is short or near, some versions assume near and generate a 3-byte instruction. However, provided that the jump really is short, you can use the SHORT operator to force a short jump and a 2-byte instruction by coding

```
        JMP   SHORT P90
        ...
P90:
```

Program: Using the JMP Instruction

The .COM program in Figure 8-1 illustrates the use of the JMP instruction. The program initializes the AX, BX, and CX registers to the value of 1, and a loop performs the following:

```
                        page 60,132
              TITLE     A08JUMP (COM)   Using JMP for looping
                        .MODEL SMALL
                        .CODE
0100                    ORG     100H
0100          A10MAIN   PROC    NEAR
0100  B8 0001           MOV     AX,01        ;Initialize AX,
0103  BB 0001           MOV     BX,01        ;  BX, and
0106  B9 0001           MOV     CX,01        ;  CX to 01
0109          A20:
0109  05 0001           ADD     AX,01        ;Add 01 to AX
010C  03 D8             ADD     BX,AX        ;Add AX to BX
010E  D1 E1             SHL     CX,1         ;Double CX
0110  EB F7             JMP     A20          ;Jump to A20 label
0112          A10MAIN   ENDP
                        END     A10MAIN
```

Figure 8-1 Using the JMP Instruction

- Add 1 to the AX
- Add the AX to the BX
- Double the value in the CX

At the end of the loop (after the SHL), the instruction JMP A20 transfers control to the instruction labeled A20. The effect of repeating the loop causes the AX to increase as 1, 2, 3, 4, . . . ; the BX to increase according to the sum of the digits as 1, 3, 6, 10, . . . ; and the CX to double as 1, 2, 4, 8, ... Because this loop has no exit, processing is endless—usually not a desirable practice.

In the program, A20 is −9 bytes from the JMP. You can confirm this distance by examining the object code for the JMP: EBF7. EB is the machine code for a near JMP and hex F7 is the two's complement notation for −9. At this point, the IP contains the offset (0112H) of the next instruction to execute. Because this is a backward jump, the operand F7 is negative. The JMP operation adds the F7 (technically, FFF7, because the IP is a word in size) to the IP, which contains the offset 0112H of the instruction following the JMP:

	DECIMAL	HEX	
Instruction register:	274	0112	
JMP operand:	−9	FFF7	(two's complement)
Jump address:	265	(1)0109	

The assembler calculates the jump address as 0109H, where the carry out of 1 is ignored (as a check of the program listing for the offset address of A20 shows). The operation changes the offset value in the IP and flushes the instruction queue.

As a useful practice, key in the program, assemble it, link it, and convert it to .COM format. No data is defined, because immediate operands generate all the required data. Use DEBUG to trace the .COM module for a number of iterations and observe the effect of execution on the AX, BX, CX, and IP. Once the AX contains 08, the BX and CX will be incremented to 24H (decimal 36) and 80H (decimal 128), respectively. Key in Q to quit DEBUG.

THE LOOP INSTRUCTION

As used in Figure 8-1, the JMP instruction causes an endless loop. But a standard practice is to code a routine that loops a specified number of times or until it reaches a particular condition. The LOOP instruction, which serves this purpose, requires an initial value in the CX register. For each iteration, LOOP automatically deducts 1 from the CX. Once the value in the CX reaches zero, control drops through to the following instruction; if the value in the CX is nonzero, control jumps to the operand address. The distance to the operand must be a short jump, within −128 to +127 bytes. For an operation that exceeds this limit, the assembler issues a message such as "relative jump out of range." The general format for LOOP is

[label:]	LOOP	short-address

The program in Figure 8-2 illustrates the use of LOOP. It performs the same operation as the program in Figure 8-1, except that this one uses a MOV instruction to initialize the CX with the value 10 and ends after 10 loops. Because LOOP requires use of the CX, this program now uses the DX in place of CX for doubling the initial value 1. The LOOP instruction replaces JMP A20 and, for faster processing, INC AX (increment the AX by 1) replaces ADD AX,01.

```
                                 page 60,132
                       TITLE     A08LOOP (COM)   Illustration of LOOP
                                 .MODEL SMALL
                                 .CODE
0100                             ORG     100H
0100                   A10MAIN   PROC    NEAR
0100   B8 0001                   MOV     AX,01       ;Initialize AX,
0103   BB 0001                   MOV     BX,01       ;  BX, and
0106   BA 0001                   MOV     DX,01       ;  DX to 01
0109   B9 000A                   MOV     CX,10       ;Initialize for
010C                   A20:                          ;  ten loops
010C   40                        INC     AX          ;Add 01 to AX
010D   03 D8                     ADD     BX,AX       ;Add AX to BX
010F   D1 E2                     SHL     DX,1        ;Double DX
0111   E2 F9                     LOOP    A20         ;Decrement CX,
                                                     ;  loop if nonzero
0113   B8 4C00                   MOV     AX,4C00H    ;End processing
0116   CD 21                     INT     21H
0118                   A10MAIN   ENDP
                                 END     A10MAIN
```

Figure 8-2 Using the LOOP instruction

Just as for JMP, the machine code operand for LOOP contains the distance from the end of the instruction to the address of A20, which the operation adds to the IP when the program executes.

As a useful exercise, modify your copy of Figure 8-1 for these changes, and assemble, link, and convert the program to .COM. Use DEBUG to trace through the entire 10 loops and observe the effect of execution on the AX, BX, CX, DX, and IP. Once the CX is reduced to zero, the contents of AX, BX, and DX are, respectively, 000BH, 0042H, and 0400H. Press Q to quit DEBUG.

There are two variations on the LOOP instruction, both of which also decrement the CX by 1. LOOPE/LOOPZ (loop while equal or loop while zero) continues looping as long as the value in the CX is zero or the zero condition is set. LOOPNE/LOOPNZ (loop while not equal or loop while not zero) continues looping as long as the value in the CX is not zero or the zero condition is not set.

Neither LOOP nor its LOOPxx variations changes the setting of any flags in the flags register. However, because other instructions within the loop routine do change flags, the program in Figure 8-2 uses LOOP, and not its LOOPxx variations.

THE FLAGS REGISTER

The remaining material in this chapter requires a more detailed knowledge of the flags register. This register contains 16 bits, which various instructions set to indicate the status of an operation. In all cases, a flag remains set until another instruction changes it. The flags register for real mode contains the following commonly used bits, described here from right to left:

Bit no.:	15	14	13	12	11	10	9	8	7	6	5	4	3	2	1	0
Flag:					O	D	I	T	S	Z		A		P		C

CF (Carry flag). Contains a carry (0 or 1) from the high-order (leftmost) bit following arithmetic operations and some shift and rotate operations. JC and JNC test this flag.

PF (Parity flag). Contains a check of the low-order 8 bits of data operations. The parity flag is not to be confused with the parity bit described in Chapter 1 and is seldom of concern in conventional programming. An odd number of 1-bits clears the flag to 0, and an even number of 1-bits sets it to 1. JP and JPO test this flag.

AF (Auxiliary carry flag). Concerned with arithmetic on ASCII and BCD packed fields. This flag is set when a 1-byte arithmetic operation causes a carry out of bit 3 (the fourth bit from the right) of a register.

ZF (Zero flag). Cleared or set as a result of an arithmetic or compare operation. Unexpectedly, a nonzero result clears the flag to 0, and a zero result sets it to 1. However, the setting, if not apparently correct, is logically correct: 0 means no (the result is not equal to zero), and 1 means yes (the result equals zero). JE and JZ (among other instructions) test this flag.

SF (Sign flag). Set according to the sign (high-order or leftmost bit) generated by an arithmetic operation: A positive value clears the flag to 0, and negative sets it to 1. JG and JL (among other instructions) test this flag.

TF (Trap flag). When set, causes the processor to execute in single-step mode, that is, one instruction at a time under user control. DEBUG sets this flag when you type in the T command, and that's about the only place where you'd expect to use it.

IF (Interrupt flag). Disables interrupts when 0, and enables interrupts when 1. This flag is rarely used in conventional programming.

DF (Direction flag). Used by string operations to determine the direction of data transfer. When the flag is 0, the string operation performs left-to-right data transfer; when the flag is 1, the string operation performs right-to-left data transfer.

OF (Overflow flag). Indicates a carry into and out of the high-order (leftmost) sign bit following a signed arithmetic operation. JO and JNO test this flag.

THE CMP INSTRUCTION

The CMP instruction is used to compare two numeric data fields, one or both of which are contained in a register. Its general format is

[label:]	CMP	register/memory,register/memory/immediate

Technically, you may use CMP to compare string (character) data, but CMPS (covered in Chapter 12) is the appropriate instruction for this purpose. The result of a CMP operation affects the AF, CF, OF, PF, SF, and ZF flags, although you do not have to test these flags individually. The following code tests the DX register for a zero value:

```
        CMP  DX,00              ;Compare DX to zero
        JE   P50                ;If equal, jump to B50
        .    (action if nonzero)
        .
P50:    ...                     ;Jump point if DX is zero
```

If the DX contains zero, CMP sets the ZF to 1 and may or may not change the settings of other flags. The JE (Jump if Equal) instruction tests only the ZF flag. Because ZF contains 1 (meaning a zero condition), JE transfers control (jumps) to the address indicated by operand P50.

In effect, the CMP operation compares the first to the second operand; for example, is the value of the first operand higher than, equal to, or lower than the value of the second operand? (CMP acts like SUB without the storage cycle.) The next section provides the various ways of transferring control based on tested conditions.

CONDITIONAL JUMP INSTRUCTIONS

The processor supports a variety of conditional jump instructions that transfer control depending on settings in the flags register. For example, you can compare two fields and then jump conditionally according to flag values that the compare sets. The general format for the conditional jump is

[label:]	Jnnn	short-address

As explained earlier, the LOOP instruction decrements the CX register; if it is nonzero, control transfers to the operand address. You could replace the LOOP A20 statement in Figure 8-2 with two statements—one that decrements the CX and another that performs a conditional jump:

```
DEC  CX         ;Equivalent to LOOP
JNZ  A20        ;
...
```

DEC decrements the CX by 1 and sets or clears the zero flag in the flags register. JNZ then tests the setting of the zero flag; if the CX is nonzero, control jumps to A20, and if the CX is zero, control drops through to the next instruction. (A jump operation that branches also flushes the processor's prefetch instruction queue.) Although LOOP has limited uses, in this example it executes faster and uses fewer bytes than does the use of the DEC and JNZ instructions.

Just as for JMP and LOOP, the machine code operand for JNZ contains the distance from the end of the instruction to the address of A20, which the operation adds to the IP register. For the 8086/286, the distance for a conditional jump must be a short, within −128 to +127 bytes. If the operation exceeds this limit, the assembler issues a message "relative jump out of range." The 80386 and later processors also provide for 32-bit (near) offsets that allow reaching any address within 32K.

Signed and Unsigned Data

Distinguishing the purpose of conditional jumps should clarify their use. The type of data (unsigned or signed) on which you are performing comparisons or arithmetic can determine which instruction to use. An *unsigned* numeric item (logical data) treats all bits as data bits; typical examples are numeric values such as customer numbers and phone numbers. A *signed* numeric item (arithmetic data) treats the leftmost bit as a sign, where 0 is positive and 1 is negative; typical examples are quantity, discount, and distance, which may be either positive or negative.

In the next example, assume that the CX contains 11000110 and the DX contains 00010110. The instruction

```
CMP CX,DX
```

compares the contents of the CX to the contents of the DX. If you treat the data as unsigned, the CX value is larger; if you treat the data as signed, however, the CX value is smaller because of the negative sign. The use here of CMP is valid, and you have to select the appropriate conditional jump instruction, such as JB (Jump Below) for unsigned data or JL (Jump Low) for signed data.

Jumps Based on Unsigned (Logical) Data

Use the following conditional jump instructions for unsigned data:

SYMBOL	DESCRIPTION	FLAGS TESTED
JE/JZ	Jump Equal or Jump Zero	ZF
JNE/JNZ	Jump Not Equal or Jump Not Zero	ZF
JA/JNBE	Jump Above or Jump Not Below or Equal	CF, ZF
JAE/JNB	Jump Above or Equal or Jump Not Below	CF
JB/JNAE	Jump Below or Jump Not Above or Equal	CF
JBE/JNA	Jump Below or Equal or Jump Not Above	AF, CF

You can express each of these conditional jumps in one of the two symbolic operations; choose the one that is clearest and most descriptive.

Jumps Based on Signed (Arithmetic) Data

Use the following conditional jump instructions for signed data:

SYMBOL	DESCRIPTION	FLAGS TESTED
JE/JZ	Jump Equal or Jump Zero	ZF
JNE/JNZ	Jump Not Equal or Jump Not Zero	ZF
JG/JNLE	Jump Greater or Jump Not Less or Equal	OF, SF, ZF
JGE/JNL	Jump Greater or Equal or Jump Not Less	OF, SF
JL/JNGE	Jump Less or Jump Not Greater or Equal	OF, SF
JLE/JNG	Jump Less or Equal or Jump Not Greater	OF, SF, ZF

The jumps for testing equal or zero (JE/JZ) and for testing not equal or zero (JNE/JNZ) are included in the lists for both unsigned and signed data, because an equal or zero condition exists regardless of the absence or presence of a sign.

Special Arithmetic Tests

The following conditional jump instructions have special uses:

SYMBOL	DESCRIPTION	FLAGS TESTED
JCXZ	Jump if CX is Zero	none
JC	Jump Carry (same as JB)	CF
JNC	Jump No Carry	CF
JO	Jump Overflow	OF
JNO	Jump No Overflow	OF
JP/JPE	Jump Parity or Jump Parity Even	PF
JNP/JPO	Jump No Parity or Jump Parity Odd	PF
JS	Jump Sign (negative)	SF
JNS	Jump No Sign (positive)	SF

JCXZ tests the contents of the CX register for zero. This instruction need not be placed immediately following an arithmetic or compare operation. One use for JCXZ could be at the start of a loop, to ensure that the routine is bypassed if the CX is initially zero. JC and JNC are often used to test the success of disk operations.

Now, don't expect to memorize all of these instructions. As a reminder, however, note that a jump for *unsigned* data is equal, above, or below, whereas a jump for *signed* data is equal, greater, or less. The jumps for testing the carry, overflow, and parity flags have unique purposes. The assembler translates symbolic to object code, regardless of which instruction you use but, for example, JAE and JGE, although apparently similar, do not test the same flags (because JAE assumes unsigned data and JGE assumes signed data).

The 80386 and later processors permit far conditional jumps. You can specify a short or far jump, for example, as

```
JNB  SHORT address
JBE  FAR address
```

CALLING PROCEDURES

The code segments in our examples to now have consisted of only one procedure, coded as

```
proc-name  PROC  FAR
        .
        .
        .
proc-name  ENDP
```

The FAR operand in this case informs the assembler and linker that the indicated procedure name is the entry point for program execution, whereas the ENDP directive defines the end of the procedure. A code segment, however, may contain any number of procedures, each distinguished by its own PROC and ENDP directives. A called procedure (or subroutine) is a section of code that performs a clearly defined task (such as set cursor or get keyboard input). Organizing a program into procedures provides the following benefits:

- Reduces the amount of code, because a common procedure can be called from any number of places in the code segment.
- Encourages better program organization.
- Facilitates debugging of a program, because defects can be more clearly isolated.
- Helps in the ongoing maintenance of programs, because procedures are readily identified for modification.

CALL and RET Operations

The purpose of the CALL instruction is to transfer control to a called procedure. (The only examples in this book that *jump* to a procedure are at the beginning of .COM programs.) The RET instruction, effectively the counterpart of CALL, returns from the called procedure to the original calling procedure. RET should be the last instruction in the called procedure.

The general formats for CALL and RET are:

[label:]	CALL	proc-name
[label:]	RET	[pop-value]

MASM 5.0 introduced RETN for near returns and RETF for far returns. The particular object code that CALL and RET generate depends on whether the operation involves a NEAR or FAR procedure.

Near call and return. A CALL to a procedure within the same segment is near and performs the following:

- By means of a push, decrements the SP by 2 (1 word) and transfers the IP (containing the offset of the instruction following the CALL) onto the stack.
- Inserts the offset address of the called procedure into the IP. (This operation also flushes the processor's prefetch instruction queue.)

A RET (or RETN) that returns from a near procedure basically reverses the CALL's steps by means of a pop operation:

- Transfers the old IP value from the stack into the IP (which also flushes the processor's prefetch instruction queue).
- Increments the SP by 2.

The CS:IP now points to the instruction following the original CALL in the calling procedure, where execution resumes.

Far call and return. A far CALL calls a procedure labeled FAR, possibly in another code segment. A far CALL pushes both the CS and IP onto the stack, and RET (or RETF) pops them both from the stack. Far calls and returns are the subject of Chapter 23.

Example of a Near Call and Return

A typical organization of near calls and returns appears in Figure 8-3. Note the following features:

- The program is divided into a far procedure, A10MAIN, and two near procedures, B10 and C10. Each procedure has a unique name and contains its own ENDP for ending its definition.
- The PROC directive for A10MAIN has the FAR attribute because it is the entry point from outside this program.
- The PROC directives for B10 and C10 have the attribute NEAR to indicate that these procedures are within the current code segment. Because omission of the attribute causes the assembler to default to NEAR, many subsequent examples omit it.

```
                        page 60,132
               TITLE    A08CALLP (EXE)  Calling procedures
                        .MODEL SMALL
                        .STACK 64
                        .DATA
               ;----------------------------------------------
                        .CODE
0000           A10MAIN  PROC    FAR
0000  E8 0008 R         CALL    B10             ;Call B10
               ;        ...
0003  B8 4C00           MOV     AX,4C00H        ;End processing
0006  CD 21             INT     21H
0008           A10MAIN  ENDP
               ;----------------------------------------------
0008           B10      PROC    NEAR
0008  E8 000C R         CALL    C10             ;Call C10
               ;        ...
000B  C3                RET                     ;Return to
000C           B10      ENDP                    ;  caller
               ;----------------------------------------------
000C           C10      PROC    NEAR
               ;        ...
000C  C3                RET                     ;Return to
000D           C10      ENDP                    ;  caller
               ;----------------------------------------------
                        END     A10MAIN
```

Figure 8-3 Calling Procedures

- In procedure A10MAIN, the CALL instruction transfers program control to the procedure B10 and begins its execution.
- In procedure B10, the CALL instruction transfers control to the procedure C10 and begins its execution.
- In procedure C10, the RET instruction causes control to return to the instruction immediately following CALL C10.
- In procedure B10, the RET instruction causes control to return to the instruction immediately following CALL B10.
- Procedure A10MAIN then resumes processing from that point.
- RET always returns to the calling routine. If B10 did not end with a RET instruction, processing would continue through B10 and drop directly into C10. In fact, if C10 did not contain a RET, the program would execute past the end of C10 into whatever instructions (if any) happen to be there, with unpredictable results.

Note that each procedure begins on a paragraph boundary: A10MAIN on offset 0000, B10 on 0008, and C10 on 000C (12).

As explained earlier, you can transfer control to a near procedure by normal in-line code, and you can also enter a near procedure by means of a jump instruction. However, for clarity and consistency, use CALL to transfer control to a procedure, and use RET/RETN to end the execution of the procedure.

EFFECT OF PROGRAM EXECUTION ON THE STACK

Up to this point, our programs have had little need to push data onto the stack and, consequently, had to define only a very small stack. However, as illustrated in Figure 8-3, a called procedure can CALL another procedure, which in turn can CALL yet another procedure, so that the stack must be large enough to contain all the pushed addresses. All this turns out to be easier than it first appears, and a stack definition of 32 words is ample for most of our purposes.

CALL and PUSH both store a 1-word address or value onto the stack. RET and POP pop the stack and access the previously pushed word. All of these operations increment or decrement the offset address in the SP register for the next word. Because of this feature, RET and POP operations must match their original CALL and PUSH operations.

As a reminder, on loading an .EXE program for execution, the program loader initializes the following register values:

- DS and ES: Address of the PSP, a 256-byte (100H) area that precedes an executable program module in memory.
- CS: Address of the code segment—the entry point to your program.
- IP: Zero, if the first executable instruction is at the beginning of the code segment.
- SS: Address of the stack segment.
- SP: Offset to the top of the stack. For example, for a stack defined as .STACK 64 (64 bytes or 32 words), the SP initially contains 64, or 40H.

Let's trace the simple program in Figure 8-3 through its execution. In practice, called procedures would contain any number of instructions.

The current available location for pushing or popping is the top of the stack. For this example, the program loader would have set the SP to the size of the stack, 64 bytes (40H). Words in memory contain bytes in reverse sequence; for example, 0003 becomes 0300. The program performs the following operations:

- CALL B10 decrements the SP by 2, from 40H to 3EH. It then pushes the IP (containing 0003, the location of the next instruction) onto the top of the stack at offset 3EH. The processor uses the address formed by CS:IP to transfer control to B10.

```
CALL B10 (push 0003): XXXX   XXXX   XXXX   XXXX   0300   SP = 3E00H
                       |      |      |      |      |
Stack offset:         0036   0038   003A   003C   003E
```

- In procedure B10, CALL C10 decrements the SP by 2, to 3CH. It then pushes the IP (containing 000B) onto the top of the stack at offset 3CH. The processor uses the CS:IP addresses to transfer control to C10.

```
CALL C10 (push 000B): XXXX   XXXX   XXXX   0B00   0300   SP = 3C00H
                       |      |      |      |      |
Stack offset:         0036   0038   003A   003C   003E
```

- To return from C10, the RET instruction pops the offset (000B) from the top of the stack at 3CH, inserts it in the IP, and increments the SP by 2 to 3EH. The offset in the IP causes an automatic return to offset 000BH in procedure B10.

```
RET (pop 000B):    XXXX   XXXX   XXXX   0B00   0300   SP = 3E00H
                    |      |      |      |      |
Stack offset:      0036   0038   003A   003C   003E
```

- The RET at the end of procedure B10 pops the address (0003) from the top of the stack at 3EH into the IP and increments the SP by 2 to 40H. The offset in the IP causes an automatic return to offset 0003H, where the program ends its execution.

```
RET (pop 0003):    XXXX   XXXX   XXXX   0B00   0300   SP = 4000H
                    |      |      |      |      |
Stack offset:      0036   0038   003A   003C   003E
```

If you use DEBUG to view the stack, you may find harmless data left there by a previously executed program.

BOOLEAN OPERATIONS

Boolean logic is important in circuitry design and has a parallel in programming logic. The instructions for Boolean logic are AND, OR, XOR, TEST, and NOT, which can be used to clear and set bits and to handle ASCII data for arithmetic purposes (Chapter 13). The general format for the Boolean operations is

[label:]	operation	register/memory,register/memory/immediate

The first operand references one byte, word, or doubleword (80386 and later) in a register or memory and is the only value that is changed. The second operand references a register or immediate value. The operation matches the bits of the two referenced operands and sets the CF, OF, PF, SF, and ZF flags accordingly (AF is undefined).

- AND: If matched bits are both 1, sets the result to 1. All other conditions result in 0.
- OR: If either (or both) of the matched bits is 1, sets the result to 1. If both bits are 0, the result is 0.
- XOR: If one matched bit is 0 and the other 1, sets the result to 1. If matched bits are the same (both 0 or both 1), the result is 0.
- TEST: Sets the flags as AND does, but does not change the bits referenced in the target operand.

The following AND, OR, and XOR operations illustrate the effect of using the same data bits:

```
                          AND    OR     XOR
Operand 1:                0101   0101   0101
Operand 2:                0011   0011   0011
                          ----   ----   ----
Result in operand 1:      0001   0111   0110
```

Here's a useful to rule to remember: ANDing bits with 0 clears them to 0, whereas ORing bits with 1 sets them to 1.

Examples of Boolean Operations

For the following unrelated examples, assume that the BL contains 0011 1010 and the CH contains 1010 0011:

```
1. AND  BL,0FH      ;Sets BL to 0000 1010
2. AND  BL,00H      ;Sets BL to 0000 0000
3. AND  BL,CH       ;Sets BL to 0010 0010
4. OR   CH,BL       ;Sets CH to 1011 1011
5. OR   CH,CH       ;Sets SF and ZF
6. XOR  BL,0FFH     ;Sets BL to 1100 0101
7. XOR  BL,BL       ;Sets BL to 0000 0000
```

Example 1 zeros the left 4 bits of the AL. Examples 2 and 7 provide ways of clearing a register to zero. Although the use of CMP may be clearer, you can use OR for the following purposes:

```
1. OR   DX,DX    ;Test DX for zero
   JZ   ...      ;Jump if zero
2. OR   DX,DX    ;Test DX for sign
   JS   ...      ;Jump if negative sign
```

TEST acts like AND, but only sets flags. Here are some examples:

```
1. TEST  CX,0FFH          ;Does the CX contain
   JZ    ...              ;  a zero value?
2. TEST  BL,00000001B     ;Does the BL contain
   JNZ   ...              ;  an odd number?
3. TEST  CL,11110000B     ;Are any of the 4 leftmost
   JNZ   ...              ;  bits in CL nonzero?
```

The NOT Instruction

The NOT instruction simply reverses the bits in a byte, word, or doubleword (80386 and later) in a register or memory so that 0s become 1s and 1s become 0s. Its general format is

[label:]	NOT	register/memory

For example, if the BL contains 0011 1010, the instruction NOT BL changes the BL to 1100 0101. (The effect is exactly the same as that of XOR BL,0FFH in Example 6 earlier.) Flags are unaffected. NOT differs from NEG, which changes a binary value from positive to negative and vice versa by reversing the bits and adding 1.

PROGRAM: CHANGING UPPERCASE TO LOWERCASE

There are various reasons for converting between uppercase and lowercase letters. For example, you may have a data file in which all the alphabetic data is in uppercase letters. Or a program has to allow users to enter a value as either uppercase or lowercase (such as "YES" or "yes") and converts it to uppercase to facilitate testing it. Uppercase letters A through Z are represented by ASCII values as 41H through 5AH, and lowercase letters a through z as 61H through 7AH. The only difference is that bit 5 is 0 for uppercase and 1 for lowercase, as the following shows:

UPPERCASE		LOWERCASE	
Letter A:	01**0**00001	Letter a:	01**1**00001
Letter Z:	01**0**11010	Letter z:	01**1**11010
Bit:	76543210	Bit:	76543210

The .COM program in Figure 8-4 converts the contents of a data item, CONAME, from uppercase to lowercase, beginning at CONAME+1. The program initializes the BX with the address of CONAME+1 and uses the address to move each character, starting at CONAME+1, to the AH. If the value is between 41H and 5AH, an XOR instruction clears bit 5 to 0:

```
XOR AH,00100000B
```

All characters other than A through Z remain unchanged. The program then moves the changed character back to CONAME and increments the BX for the next character. The program loops 16 times, once for each character from CONAME+1 on. Used this way, the

```
TITLE      A08CASE (COM)  Change uppercase to lowercase
           .MODEL SMALL
           .CODE
           ORG    100H
BEGIN:     JMP    A10MAIN
; ---------------------------------------------------
CONAME     DB     'INTERTECH SYSTEMS', '$'
; ---------------------------------------------------
A10MAIN    PROC   NEAR
           LEA    BX,CONAME+1       ;1st char to change
           MOV    CX,16             ;No. of chars to change
A20:
           MOV    AH,[BX]           ;Character from CONAME
           CMP    AH,41H            ;Is it
           JB     A30               ;  upper
           CMP    AH,5AH            ;  case
           JA     A30               ;  letter?
           XOR    AH,00100000B      ;Yes, convert
           MOV    [BX],AH           ;Restore in CONAME
A30:
           INC    BX                ;Set for next char
           LOOP   A20               ;Loop 16 times
                                    ;Done,
           MOV    AH,09H            ;  display
           LEA    DX,CONAME         ;  CONAME
           INT    21H
           MOV    AX,4C00H          ;End processing
           INT    21H
A10MAIN    ENDP
           END    BEGIN
```

Figure 8-4 Changing Uppercase Letters to Lowercase

BX register acts as an index register for addressing memory locations. You may also use the SI and DI for the same purpose.

At the end, the program displays the changed contents of CONAME. Once this program is assembled, you can run it as standalone or from within DEBUG.

SHIFTING BITS

The shift instructions, which are part of the computer's logical capability, can perform the following actions:

- Reference a register or memory address.
- Shift bits left or right.
- Shift up to 8 bits in a byte, 16 bits in a word, and 32 bits in a doubleword (80386 and later).
- Shift logically (unsigned) or arithmetically (signed).

The second operand contains the shift value, which is a constant (an immediate value) or a reference to the CL register. For the 8088/8086 processors, the shift value may be only 1; a value greater than 1 must be contained in the CL register, whereas later processors allow shift values up to 31. The general format for shift is

[label:]	shift	register/memory,CL/immediate

Shifting Bits Right

The SHR and SAR operations shift bits in the designated register to the right. Each bit shifted off enters the carry flag. SHR (Shift Logical Right) provides for logical (unsigned) data and SAR (Shift Arithmetic Right) for arithmetic (signed) data:

```
SHR:  [0]→[ | | | | | | | ]→[C]
SAR:     [S→| | | | | | | ]→[C]
```

The following related instructions illustrate using SHR to shift unsigned data:

INSTRUCTION	COMMENT	BINARY	DECIMAL	CF
MOV BH,10110111B	;Initialize BH	10110111	183	-
SHR BH,01	;Shift right 1	01011011	91	1
MOV CL,02	;Set shift value			
SHR BH,CL	;Shift right 2 more	00010110	22	1
SHR BH,02 (80286+)	;Shift right 2 more	00000101	5	1

The first SHR shifts the contents of the BH one bit to the right. The shifted 1-bit now resides in the carry flag, and a 0-bit is filled to the left in the BH. The second SHR shifts the BH two more bits. The carry flag contains successively 1 and 1, and two 0-bits are filled to the left in the BH. The third SHR shifts the BH two more bits.

SAR differs from SHR in one important way: SAR uses the *sign bit* to fill leftmost vacated bits. In this way, positive and negative values retain their signs. The following related instructions illustrate using SAR to shift unsigned data in which the sign is a 1-bit:

INSTRUCTION	COMMENT	BINARY	DECIMAL	CF
MOV BH,10110111B	;Initialize BH	10110111	-73	-
SAR BH,01	;Shift right 1	11011011	-37	1
MOV CL,02	;Set shift value			
SAR BH,CL	;Shift right 2 more	11110110	-10	1
SAR BH,02 (80286+)	;Shift right 2 more	11111101	-3	1

Right shifts are especially useful for *halving* values and execute significantly faster than does a divide operation. In the examples of SHR and SAR, the first right shift of 1 bit effectively divides by 2, and the second and third right shifts of 2 bits each divide by 4.

Halving odd numbers such as 5 and 7 generates 2 and 3, respectively, and sets the carry flag to 1. After the shift operation, you can use the JC (Jump if Carry) instruction to test the bit shifted into the carry flag.

Shifting in 32-Bit Registers

The following example transfers the BX:AX to the ECX, where a shift operation divides the value by 2:

```
MOV CX,BX      ;BX to lower ECX
SHL ECX,16     ;Shift to upper ECX
MOV CX,AX      ;AX to lower ECX
SHR ECX,01     ;Divide ECX by 2
```

For the 80386 and later, SHRD can also be used to shift 16- and 32-bit values.

Shifting Bits Left

The SHL (Shift Logical Left) and SAL (Shift Arithmetic Left) operations shift bits in the designated register to the left. Each bit shifted off enters the carry flag. Both instructions are identical in their operation and both provide for logical (unsigned) and arithmetic (signed) data:

```
SHL and SAL:  [C] <- [ | | | | | | | ] <- [0]
```

The following related instructions illustrate the use of SHL to shift unsigned data:

INSTRUCTION	COMMENT	BINARY	DECIMAL	CF
MOV BH,00000101B	;Initialize BH	00000101	5	-
SHL BH,01	;Shift left 1	00001010	10	0
MOV CL,02	;Set shift value			
SHL BH,CL	;Shift left 2 more	00101000	40	0
SHL BH,02 (80286+)	;Shift left 2 more	10100000	160	0

The first SHL shifts the contents of the BH one bit to the left. The shifted 1-bit now resides in the carry flag, and a 0-bit is filled to the right in the BH. The second SHL shifts the BH two more bits. The carry flag contains successively 0 and 0, and two 0-bits are filled to the right in the BH. The third SHL shifts the BH two more bits

Left shifts always fill 0-bits to the right. As a result, SHL and SAL are identical, so that SAL could be used in the previous example with the same effect. Left shifts are especially useful for doubling values and execute significantly faster than does a multiply operation. In the examples of the shift left operation, the first left shift of 1 bit effectively multiplies by 2, and the second and third left shifts of 3 bits each multiply by 8.

After the shift operation, you can use the JC (Jump if Carry) instruction to test the bit shifted into the carry flag.

Shifting in 32-Bit Registers

The following example transfers the DX:AX to the ECX, where a shift operation doubles the value:

```
MOV CX,DX       ;DX to lower ECX
SHL ECX,16      ;Shift to upper ECX
MOV CX,AX       ;AX to lower ECX
SHL ECX,01      ;Multiply ECX by 2
```

For the 80386 and later, SHLD can be used to shift 16- and 32-bit values.

ROTATING BITS

The rotate instructions, which are part of the computer's logical capability, can perform the following actions:

- Reference a register or memory.
- Rotate right or left. The bit that is shifted off rotates to fill the vacated bit position in the memory or register location and is also copied into the carry flag.
- Rotate up to 8 bits in a byte, 16 bits in a word, and 32 bits in a doubleword (80386 and later).
- Rotate logically (unsigned) or arithmetically (signed).

The second operand contains the rotate value, which is a constant (an immediate value) or a reference to the CL register. For the 8088/8086 processors, the rotate value may be only 1; a value greater than 1 must be contained in the CL register, whereas later processors allow rotate values up to 31. The general format for rotate is

[label:]	rotate	register/memory,CL/immediate

Rotating Bits Right

The ROR and RCR operations rotate the bits in the designated register to the right. Each bit rotated off enters the carry flag. ROR (Rotate Logical Right) provides for logical (unsigned) and RCR (Rotate with Carry Right) for arithmetic (signed) data:

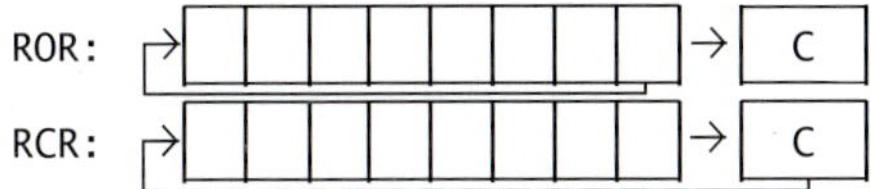

The following related instructions illustrate ROR:

INSTRUCTION	COMMENT	BINARY	CF
MOV BL,10110111B	;Initialize BH	10110111	-
ROR BL,01	;Rotate right 1	11011011	1
MOV CL,03	;Set shift value		
ROR BL,CL	;Rotate right 3 more	01111011	0
ROR BL,03 (80286+)	;Rotate right 3 more	01101111	0

The first ROR rotates the rightmost 1-bit of the BL into the leftmost vacated position and into the CF. The second and third ROR operations rotate the three rightmost bits into the leftmost vacated positions and into the CF.

RCR differs from ROR in this way: Each bit rotated off on the right first moves into the CF, and the CF bit moves into the vacated bit position on the left.

Rotating Bits Left

The ROL and RCL operations rotate the bits in the designated register to the left. Each bit rotated off enters the carry flag. ROL (Rotate Logical Left) provides for logical (unsigned) and RCL (Rotate with Carry Left) for arithmetic (signed) data:

ROL: C

RCL: C

The following related instructions illustrate ROL:

INSTRUCTION	COMMENT	BINARY	CF
MOV BL,10110111B	;Initialize BH	10110111	-
ROL BL,01	;Rotate left 1	01101111	1
MOV CL,03	;Set shift value		
ROL BL,CL	;Rotate left 3 more	01111011	1
ROL BL,03 (80286+)	;Rotate left 3 more	11011011	1

The first ROL rotates the leftmost 1-bit of the BL into the rightmost vacated position and into the carry flag. The second and third ROL operations rotate the three leftmost bits into the rightmost vacated positions and into the carry flag.

RCL differs from ROL in this way: Each bit rotated off on the left moves into the CF, and the CF bit moves into the vacated bit position on the right.

After a rotate operation, you can use the JC (Jump if Carry) instruction to test the bit rotated into the CF.

Doubleword Shift and Rotate

You can also use shift and rotate instructions to multiply and divide doubleword values by multiples of 2. Consider a 32-bit value of which the leftmost 16 bits are in the DX and the rightmost 16 bits are in the AX, as DX:AX. The instructions to "multiply" the value by 2 could be:

```
SHL  AX,1     ;Use left shift to multiply
RCL  DX,1     ; DX:AX pair by 2
```

The SHL operation shifts all bits in the AX to the left, and the leftmost bit shifts into the carry flag. The RCL rotates the DX left and inserts the CF bit into the rightmost vacated bit. To multiply by 4, follow the SHL-RCL pair with an identical SHL-RCL pair.

For division, consider again a 32-bit value in the DX:AX. Instructions to "divide" the value by 2 would be

```
SAR  DX,1     ;Use right shift to divide
RCR  AX,1     ; DX:AX pair by 2
```

To divide by 4, follow the SAR-RCR pair with an identical SAR-RCR pair.

SHRD and SHLD handle double-precision shifts for the 80386 and later processors.

JUMP TABLES

A program may have a routine for testing a number of related conditions, each requiring a jump to another routine. Consider, for example, a system for a company that has established special codes for customers based on their credit rating and sales volume. The codes (named DISCODE) indicate the amount of discount to offer and other special processing that may be required for the customer. Customer codes are 0, 1, 2, 3, and 4.

A conventional way of handling codes is to compare for each customer code successively:

```
CMP  DISCODE,0    ;Code = 0?
JE   D00DSCT
CMP  DISCODE,1    ;Code = 1?
JE   D10DSCT
CMP  DISCODE,2    ;Code = 2?
JE   D20DSCT
CMP  DISCODE,3    ;Code = 3
JE   D30DSCT
CMP  DISCODE,4    ;Code = 4?
JE   D40DSCT
...
```

With this approach, the opportunity for errors is great because of the need for matching the correct codes against their values and jumping to the correct routine.

A more elegant solution involves a table of jump addresses. As shown in the partial program in Figure 8-5, CUSTTAB defines the five addresses successively in words (2 bytes each).

```
                                  TITLE    A08JMPTB (EXE)  Using a jump table
                                           .MODEL SMALL
                                           .STACK 64
                                           .DATA
0000  001E R                      CUSTTAB  DW     B10CDE0    ;Table of addresses
0002  0025 R                               DW     B11CDE1
0004  002C R                               DW     B12CDE2
0006  0033 R                               DW     B13CDE3
0008  003A R                               DW     B14CDE4
000A  43 6F 64 65 20 30  MESSG0   DB     'Code 0 processing', '$'
001C  43 6F 64 65 20 31  MESSG1   DB     'Code 1 processing', '$'
002E  43 6F 64 65 20 32  MESSG2   DB     'Code 2 processing', '$'
0040  43 6F 64 65 20 33  MESSG3   DB     'Code 3 processing', '$'
.       73 73 69 6E 67 24
0052  43 6F 64 65 20 34  MESSG4   DB     'Code 4 processing', '$'
                         ; ----------------------------------------------
                                           .CODE
                         .386
0000                     A10MAIN  PROC   FAR
0000  B8 ---- R                   MOV    AX,@data          ;Initialize
0003  8E D8                       MOV    DS,AX             ;  segment
0005  8E C0                       MOV    ES,AX             ;  registers
0007  E8 000F R                   CALL   B10JUMP
000A  B8 4C00                     MOV    AX,4C00H          ;End processing
000D  CD 21                       INT    21H
000F                     A10MAIN  ENDP
                         ;
000F                     B10JUMP  PROC   NEAR
000F  B4 10                       MOV    AH,10H            ;Get KB char
0011  CD 16                       INT    16H               ;  into AL
0013  24 07                       AND    AL,00000111B      ;Clear left 5 bits
0015  0F B6 D8                    MOVZX  BX,AL             ;Move AL to BX
0018  D1 E3                       SHL    BX,01             ;Double value
001A  FF A7 0000 R                JMP    [CUSTTAB+BX]      ;Jump to cust rtne
001E  8D 16 000A R       B10CDE0: LEA    DX,MESSG0         ;Code 0 routine
0022  EB 1D 90                    JMP    B90
0025  8D 16 001C R       B11CDE1: LEA    DX,MESSG1         ;Code 1 routine
0029  EB 16 90                    JMP    B90
002C  8D 16 002E R       B12CDE2: LEA    DX,MESSG2         ;Code 2 routine
0030  EB 0F 90                    JMP    B90
0033  8D 16 0040 R       B13CDE3: LEA    DX,MESSG3         ;Code 3 routine
0037  EB 08 90                    JMP    B90
003A  8D 16 0052 R       B14CDE4: LEA    DX,MESSG4         ;Code 4 routine
003E  EB 01 90                    JMP    B90
0041                     B90:
0041  B4 09                       MOV    AH,09H            ;Display
0043  CD 21                       INT    21H
0045  C3                          RET
0046                     B10JUMP  ENDP
                                  END    A10MAIN
```

Figure 8-5 Using a Jump Table

The procedure B10JUMP accepts a character from the keyboard in the AL and moves it to the BX. The value is doubled, so that 0 stays 0, 1 becomes 2, 2 becomes 4, and so forth. The doubled value provides an offset into the table: CUSTTAB+0 is the first address, CUSTTAB+2 is the second, CUSTTAB+4 is the third, and so forth. The operand of the

JMP instruction, [CUSTTAB+BX], forms an address based on the start of the table plus an offset into the table. The operation then jumps directly to the appropriate routine.

An important constraint in the program is that the codes may be only the hex values 00–04; any other value would cause dire results, and the program should check for this possibility. If you run this program, key in valid values (0–4) to check the effect of the logic.

The MOVZX instruction used to move the 1-byte keyboard character into the BX works only for the 80386 and later processors. For earlier processors, you could replace it with the following:

```
XOR  BH,BH    ;Clear upper BX
MOV  BL,AL    ;Move discount code
```

ORGANIZING A PROGRAM

The following are recommended steps in writing an assembly program:

1. Have a clear idea of the problem that the program is to solve.
2. Sketch your ideas in general terms, and plan the overall logic. For example, if a problem is to perform multibyte move operations, start by defining the fields to be moved. Then plan the strategy for the instructions: routines for initialization, for using a conditional jump, and for using a loop. The following, which shows the main logic, is pseudocode that many programmers use to plan a program:
   - Initialize segment registers
   - Call the Jump routine
   - Call the Loop routine
   - End processing

   The Jump routine could be planned as
   - Initialize registers for count, addresses of names
     Jump1:
   - Move one character of name
   - Increment for next characters of names
   - Decrement count: If nonzero, Jump1
     If zero, Return

   The Loop routine could be handled in a similar way.
3. Organize the program into logical units such that related routines follow one another. Procedures that are about 25 lines (the size of the screen) are easier to debug than procedures that are longer.
4. Use other programs as guides. Attempts to memorize all the technical material and code "off the top of the head" often result in even more program bugs.
5. Use comments to clarify what a procedure is supposed to accomplish, what arithmetic and comparison operations are performing, and what a seldom-used instruction is doing. (An example of the latter is LOOPNE: Does it loop *while* not equal or *until* not equal?)

6. To facilitate keying in the program, use a saved skeleton program that you can copy into a newly named file.

The remaining programs in this text make considerable use of JMP, LOOP, conditional jumps, CALL, and called procedures. Having covered the basics of assembly language, you are now in a position for more advanced and realistic programming.

KEY POINTS

- A short address is reached by an offset and is limited to a distance of -128 to 127 bytes. A near address is reached by an offset and is limited to a distance of -32,768 to 32,767 bytes within the same segment. A far address in another segment is reached by a segment address and offset.
- An instruction label such as "P50:" requires a colon to indicate that it is a near label.
- Labels for conditional jump and LOOP instructions must be short. The operand generates 1 byte of object code: 01H to 7FH covers the range from decimal +1 to +127, and FFH to 80H covers the range from −1 to −128. Because machine instructions vary in length from 1 to 4 bytes, the range is not obvious, but about two screens full of source code is a practical guide.
- When using LOOP, initialize the CX with a positive value, because LOOP decrements the CX and then checks it for zero.
- When an instruction sets a flag, the flag remains set until another instruction changes it.
- Select the appropriate conditional jump instruction, depending on whether the operation processes signed or unsigned data.
- Use CALL to access a procedure, and include RET/RETN at the end of the procedure for returning. A called procedure may call other procedures, and if you follow the conventions, RET causes the correct address in the stack to pop.
- Use left shift to double a value and right shift to halve a value. Be sure to select the appropriate shift instruction for unsigned and for signed data.

QUESTIONS

8-1. Explain these types of addresses: (a) short; (b) near; (c) far.

8-2. (a) What is the maximum number of bytes that a near JMP, a LOOP, and a conditional jump instruction may jump? (b) What characteristic of the machine code operand causes this limit?

8-3. A JMP instruction begins at offset location 05C8H. Determine the transfer offset address, based on the following object code for the JMP operand: (a) 14H; (b) 7DH; (c) A3H.

8-4. Write a program that calculates the Fibonacci series: 1, 1, 2, 3, 5, 8, 13,. . . . (Except for the first two numbers in the sequence, each number is the sum of the preceding two numbers.) Use LOOP and set the limit for 12 iterations. Assemble, link, and use DEBUG to trace through the routine.

8-5. Assume that AX and BX contain unsigned data and that CX and DX contain signed data. Determine the CMP (where necessary) and conditional jump instructions for the following: (a) Is the AX equal to or smaller than the BX? (b) Is the CX equal to or smaller than the DX? (c) Does the CX value exceed the DX? (d) Does the AX value exceed the BX? (e) Does the DX contain zero? (f) Is there an overflow?

8-6. In the following, what flags are affected, and what would they contain? (a) Processing is in single-step mode; (b) a transfer of string data is to be right to left; (c) a result is negative; (d) a result is zero; (e) an overflow occurred.

8-7. Refer to Figure 8-3 and explain the effect on program execution if the procedure B10 does not contain a RET.

8-8. Explain the difference between defining a PROC operand with NEAR and with FAR.

8-9. Identify three ways in which an executing program can enter a procedure.

8-10. In an .EXE program, F10 calls G10, G10 calls H10, and H10 calls J10. As a result of these calls, how many addresses does the stack now contain?

8-11. Assume that the CH contains 0111 1001 and that an item named TESTVAL contains 1110 0011. Determine the effect on the CH for the following unrelated operations: (a) OR CH,TESTVAL; (b) AND CH,TESTVAL; (c) XOR CH,TESTVAL; (d) AND CH,00000000B; (e) XOR CH,11111111B.

8-12. Revise the program in Figure 8-4 as follows: Define the contents of CONAME as lowercase letters and code the instructions that convert lowercase to uppercase.

8-13. Assume that the BX contains binary 10111001 10111001 and the CL contains 03. Determine the hex contents of the BX after execution of the following unrelated instructions: (a) SHL BL,1; (b) SHL BX,CL; (c) SHR BX,CL; (d) SHR BX,1; (e) SAL BH,1; (f) ROR BX,CL; (g) ROR DL,CL.

8-14. Use shift, move, and add instructions to initialize the CX with 40H and to multiply it by 10.

8-15. An example at the end of the section entitled "Rotating Bits" multiplies the DX:AX by 2. Revise the routine to (a) multiply by 4; (b) divide by 4; (c) multiply the 48 bits in the DX:AX:BX by 2.

8-16. Transfer the contents of the CX:BX to the EAX and use a shift to multiply the EAX by 4.

PART C—SCREEN AND KEYBOARD OPERATIONS

9 INTRODUCTION TO SCREEN AND KEYBOARD PROCESSING

Objective: To introduce the requirements for displaying information on a screen and accepting input from a keyboard.

INTRODUCTION

Up to this chapter, our programs have defined data items either in the data area or as immediate data within an instruction operand. However, most programs require input from a keyboard, disk, mouse, or modem and provide output in a useful format on a screen, printer, or disk. This chapter covers the basic requirements for displaying information on a screen and for accepting input from a keyboard.

The INT (Interrupt) instruction handles input and output for most purposes. The two interrupts covered in this chapter are INT 10H functions for screen handling and INT 21H functions for displaying screen output and accepting keyboard input. These *functions* (or services) request a particular action; you insert a function value in the AH register to identify the type of service the interrupt is to perform.

Low-level BIOS operations such as INT 10H transfer control directly to BIOS. However, to facilitate some of the more complex operations, INT 21H provides an interrupt service that first transfers control to DOS. For example, input from a keyboard may involve a count of characters entered and a check against a maximum number. The INT 21H operation handles much of this additional high-level processing and then transfers control automatically to BIOS, which handles the low-level part of the operation.

As a convention, this book refers to the value 0DH as the Enter character for the keyboard and as Carriage Return for the screen and printer.

Operations introduced in this chapter are:

INT	10H FUNCTIONS	INT	21H FUNCTIONS
02H	Set cursor	02H	Display character on screen
06H	Scroll screen	09H	Display string on screen
		0AH	Input from keyboard
		3FH	Input from keyboard
		40H	Display on screen

Chapters 10 and 11 cover more advanced features for handling the screen and keyboard.

THE SCREEN

A typical video monitor has 25 rows (numbered 0 to 24) and 80 columns (numbered 0 to 79). The rows and columns provide a grid of addressable locations at any one of which the cursor can be set. Here are some examples of cursor locations:

	Decimal Format		Hex Format	
Screen Location	Row	Column	Row	Column
Upper left corner	00	00	00H	00H
Upper right corner	00	79	00H	4FH
Center of screen	12	39/40	0CH	27H/28H
Lower left corner	24	00	18H	00H
Lower right corner	24	79	18H	4FH

The system provides space in memory for a *video display area*, or buffer. The monochrome display area begins at BIOS location B000[0]H and supports 4K bytes of memory, 2K of which are available for characters and 2K for an attribute for each character, such as reverse video, blinking, high intensity, and underlining. The basic color-graphics video display area supports 16K bytes, starting at BIOS location B800[0]H. You can process either in *text mode* for normal character display or in *graphics mode*. For text mode, the display area provides for screen "pages" numbered 0 through 3 for an 80-column screen, with one byte for each character and one for its attribute (such as color). Pages and attributes are covered in detail in Chapter 10; for this chapter, we'll assume page 0.

The interrupts that handle screen displays transfer your data directly to a video display area, depending on the type of video adapter installed, such as VGA or SVGA. Technically, your programs may transfer data directly to the video display area, but there is no assurance that the memory addresses will be the same on all computer models, so writing data directly to a display area, although fast, can be risky. The recommended practice is to use the appropriate INT 10H and INT 21H operations that know the location of the video display area.

SETTING THE CURSOR

Setting the cursor is a common requirement for text mode, because its position determines where the next character is to display. (Graphics mode does not support the cursor.) INT 10H is the BIOS operation for screen handling, and function 02H in the AH tells the operation to set the cursor. Load the required page (or screen) number, normally 0, in the BH register, the row in the DH, and the column in the DL. The contents of the other registers are not important.

The following example sets the cursor to row 08, column 15:

```
MOV     AH,02H      ;Request set cursor
MOV     BH,00       ;Page number 0
MOV     DH,08       ;Row 8
MOV     DL,15       ;Column 15
INT     10H         ;Call interrupt service
```

To set the row and column in the DX, you could also use one MOV instruction with an immediate hex value:

```
MOV DX,080FH    ;Row 08, column 15
```

CLEARING THE SCREEN

INT 10H function 06H handles screen clearing or scrolling. You can clear all or part of a display beginning at any screen location and ending at any higher-numbered location. Load these registers:

- AH = function 06H
- AL = number of lines to scroll, or 00H for the full screen
- BH = attribute value (color, reverse video, blinking)
- CX = starting row:column
- DX = ending row:column

The CX and DX together define the screen area (or window) to be scrolled, and the AL provides the number of lines to be scrolled up. To clear the entire screen, specify the starting row:column in the CX as 00:00H and the ending row:column in the DX as 18:4FH. Attribute 71H in the following example sets the entire screen to white background (attribute 7) with blue foreground (attribute 1):

```
MOV   AX,0600H    ;AH = 06 (scroll), AL = 00 (full screen)
MOV   BH,71H      ;White background (7), blue foreground (1)
MOV   CX,0000H    ;Upper left row:column
MOV   DX,184FH    ;Lower right row:column
INT   10H         ;Call interrupt service
```

For example, to scroll the screen window from row 05, column 00 through row 12, column 79, you load 0500H in the CX and 0C4FH in the DX.

Be careful of mistakenly setting the lower right screen location higher than 184FH. The next chapter describes scrolling in more detail.

A program often has to display messages to a user that requests data or an action the user must take. We'll first examine the methods for the original DOS versions, which are useful for exercises and small programs, and later examine the methods that involve file handles. The original operations work under all versions and in some respects are simpler and easier to use, although use of the newer operations is recommended for software development.

INT 21H FUNCTION 09H FOR SCREEN DISPLAY

The simplicity of the original INT 21H function 09H for displaying still keeps it in common use. It requires definition of a display string in the data area, immediately followed by a dollar sign ($ or 24H) delimiter, which the operation uses to end the display. The following example illustrates:

```
CUSTMSG DB 'Customer name?','$'  ;Display string
```

You can code the dollar sign immediately following the display string as just shown, inside the string as 'Customer name?$', or on the next line as DB '$'. The disadvantage, however, is that you can't use this function to display a $ character on the screen.

Set function 09H in the AH register, use LEA to load the address of the display string in the DX, and issue an INT 21H instruction:

```
MOV   AH,09H        ;Request display
LEA   DX,CUSTMSG    ;Load address of prompt
INT   21H           ;Call interrupt service
```

The INT operation displays the characters from left to right and recognizes the end of data on encountering the dollar sign ($) delimiter. The operation does not change the contents of the registers. A displayed string that exceeds the rightmost screen column automatically continues on the next row and scrolls the screen as necessary. If you omit the dollar sign at the end of the string, the operation continues displaying characters from consecutive memory locations until it encounters one—if there is one.

Using Function 09H to Display ASCII Characters

Most of the 256 ASCII characters are represented by symbols that can be displayed on a video screen. Some values, such as 00H and FFH, have no displayable symbol and appear as blank, although the true ASCII blank character is 20H.

The .COM program in Figure 9-1 displays the entire range of ASCII characters. The procedure A10MAIN calls three procedures:

- B10SCRN uses INT 10H function 06H to clear the screen.
- C10CURS uses INT 10H function 02H to initialize the cursor to 00:00H.
- D10DISP uses INT 21H function 09H to display the contents of ASCHAR, which is initialized to 00H and is successively incremented by 1 to display each character until reaching FFH.

The first displayed line begins with a blank (00H), two "happy faces" (01H and 02H), and then a heart (03H), diamond (04H), and club (05H). Character 06H would have displayed a spade, but is erased by later control characters. Character 07H causes the speaker to sound, 08H causes a backspace, 09H causes a tab, 0AH causes a line feed, and 0DH

```
          page 60,132
TITLE     A09DISAS (COM)  Display ASCII character set
          .MODEL SMALL
          .CODE
          ORG     100H
BEGIN:    JMP     SHORT A10MAIN
ASCHAR    DB      00,'$'             ;Display character

;                 Main procedure:
;                 --------------
A10MAIN   PROC    NEAR
          CALL    B10SCRN            ;Clear screen
          CALL    C10CURS            ;Set cursor
          CALL    D10DISP            ;Display characters
          MOV     AX,4C00H           ;End
          INT     21H                ;  processing
A10MAIN   ENDP
;                 Clear screen:
;                 ------------
B10SCRN   PROC    NEAR
          MOV     AX,0600H           ;Scroll full screen
          MOV     BH,07              ;Attribute: white on black
          MOV     CX,0000            ;Upper left location
          MOV     DX,184FH           ;Lower right location
          INT     10H                ;Call BIOS
          RET                        ;Return to caller
B10SCRN   ENDP
;                 Set cursor to 00,00:
;                 -------------------
C10CURS   PROC    NEAR
          MOV     AH,02H             ;Request set cursor
          MOV     BH,00              ;Page number 0
          MOV     DX,0000            ;Row 0, column 0
          INT     10H                ;Call BIOS
          RET                        ;Return to caller
C10CURS   ENDP
;                 Display ASCII characters:
;                 ------------------------
D10DISP   PROC
          MOV     CX,256             ;Initialize 256 iterations
          LEA     DX,ASCHAR          ;Initialize address of ASCHAR
D20:
          MOV     AH,09H             ;Display ASCII ASCHAR
          INT     21H
          INC     ASCHAR             ;Increment for next character
          LOOP    D20                ;Decrement CX, loop nonzero
          RET                        ;Return to caller
D10DISP   ENDP
          END     BEGIN
```

Figure 9-1 INT 21H to Display the ASCII Character Set

(Enter) causes a "carriage return" to the start of the next line. And, of course, under function 09H, the dollar symbol, 24H, is not displayed at all. (As covered in Chapter 10, you can use BIOS services to display proper symbols for these special characters.) The musical note is 0EH, and 7FH through FFH are extended ASCII characters.

You can revise the program to bypass the attempt to display the control characters. The following instructions bypass all characters between 08H and 0DH; you may want to experiment with bypassing, say, only 08H (Backspace) and 0DH (Carriage Return).

```
D20:
            CMP  ASCHAR,08H      ;Below 08H?
            JB   D30             ;Yes, accept
            CMP  ASCHAR,0DH      ;Below or equal 0DH?
            JBE  D40             ;Yes, bypass
D30:
            MOV  AH,09H          ;Display < 08H and > 0DH
            INT  21H             ;Call interrupt service
D40:
            INC  ASCHAR          ;Increment for next character
            LOOP D20             ;Repeat
```

This exercise bypasses displaying the Backspace, Tab, Line Feed, and Carriage Return characters. Note that displaying them is the normal way to perform these operations.

Suggestion: Reproduce the preceding program, assemble it, link it, and convert it to a .COM file for execution.

INT 21H FUNCTION 0AH FOR KEYBOARD INPUT

INT 21H function 0AH for accepting data from the keyboard is particularly powerful. The input area for keyed-in characters requires a *parameter list* containing specified fields that the INT operation is to process. (If you've worked in a high-level language, you may be used to the term *record* or *structure*.) First, the operation needs to know the maximum length of the input data. The purpose is to prevent users from keying in too many characters; the operation sounds the speaker and does not accept additional characters. Second, the operation delivers to the parameter list the number of bytes actually entered. The parameter list consists of these elements:

1. The first entry provides the name of the parameter list in the form LABEL BYTE. LABEL is a directive with the type attribute of BYTE, which simply causes alignment on a byte boundary. Because that's the normal alignment, the assembler does not advance its location counter. The use of LABEL enables you to assign a name to the parameter list.
2. The first byte of the parameter list contains your limit for the maximum number of input characters. The minimum is 0 and, because this is a 1-byte field, the maximum is FFH, or 255. You decide on the maximum, based on the kind of data you expect users to enter.
3. The second byte is for the operation to store the actual number of characters typed as a binary value.
4. The third byte begins a field that is to contain the typed characters, from left to right.

The following example defines a parameter list for an input area:

```
PARALST LABEL BYTE           ;Start of parameter list
MAXLEN   DB    20            ;Maximum number of input characters
ACTLEN   DB    ?             ;Actual number of input characters
KBDATA   DB    20 DUP(' ')   ;Characters entered from keyboard
```

In the parameter list, the LABEL directive tells the assembler to align on a byte boundary and gives the location the name PARALST. Because LABEL takes no space, PARALST and MAXLEN refer to the same memory location. MAXLEN defines the maximum number of keyboard characters, ACTLEN provides a space for the operation to insert the actual number of characters entered, and KBDATA reserves 20 spaces for the characters. You may use any valid names for these fields.

To request input, set function 0AH in the AH, load the address of the parameter list (PARALST in the example) into the DX, and issue INT 21H:

```
MOV   AH,0AH        ;Request keyboard input
LEA   DX,PARALST    ;Load address of parameter list
INT   21H           ;Call interrupt service
```

The INT operation waits for a user to type characters and checks that they do not exceed the maximum of 20. The operation echoes each typed character onto the screen and advances the cursor. The user presses <Enter> to signal the end of an entry. The operation also transfers the Enter character (0DH) to the input field KBDATA, but does not count its entry in the actual length. If you key in a name such as Porter+<Enter>, the parameter list appears like this:

ASCII:	20	6	P	o	r	t	e	r	#				...
Hex:	14	06	50	6F	72	74	65	72	0D	20	20	20	...

The operation delivers the length of the input name, 06H, into the second byte of the parameter list, named ACTLEN in the example. The Enter character (0DH) is at KBDATA+6. (The # symbol here indicates this character, because 0DH has no printable symbol.) Given that the maximum length of 20 includes the 0DH, the user may type up to only 19 characters.

This operation accepts and acts on the Backspace character, but doesn't add it to the count. Other than Backspace, the operation does not accept more than the maximum number of characters. In the preceding example, if a user keys in 20 characters without pressing <Enter>, the operation causes the speaker to beep; at this point, it accepts only the Enter character.

The operation bypasses extended function keys such as F1, Home, PgUp, and Arrows. If you expect a user to press any of them, use INT 16H or INT 21H function 01H, both covered in Chapter 11.

PROGRAM: ACCEPTING AND DISPLAYING NAMES

The program in Figure 9-2 requests a user to key in a name, and then displays the name at the center of the screen and sounds the speaker. If the user types, for example, the name Dana Porter, the program performs the following:

1. Divides the length 11 by 2: 11/2 = 5, with the remainder ignored.
2. Subtracts this value from 40: 40 − 5 = 35.

```
            page  60,132
TITLE       A09CTRNM (EXE)  Accept names, center on screen
;---------------------------------------------------------
            .MODEL SMALL
            .STACK 64
;---------------------------------------------------------
            .DATA
PARLIST     LABEL  BYTE             ;Name parameter list:
MAXNLEN     DB     20               ;  maximum length of name
ACTULEN     DB     ?                ;  no. of characters entered
KBNAME      DB     21 DUP(' ')      ;  entered name
PROMPT      DB     'Name? ', '$'
;---------------------------------------------------------
            .CODE
            .386
A10MAIN     PROC   FAR
            MOV    AX,@data         ;Initialize segment
            MOV    DS,AX            ;  registers
            MOV    ES,AX
            CALL   Q10CLR           ;Clear screen
A20LOOP:
            MOV    DX,0000          ;Set cursor to 00,00
            CALL   Q20CURS
            CALL   B10PRMPT         ;Display prompt
            CALL   C10INPT          ;Provide for input of name
            CALL   Q10CLR           ;Clear screen
            CMP    ACTULEN,00       ;Name entered?
            JE     A30              ;  no, exit
            CALL   D10CODE          ;Set bell and '$'
            CALL   E10CENT          ;Center, display name
            JMP    A20LOOP
A30:
            MOV    AX,4C00H         ;End processing
            INT    21H
A10MAIN     ENDP
;                  Display prompt:
;                  --------------
B10PRMPT    PROC   NEAR
            MOV    AH,09H           ;Request display
            LEA    DX,PROMPT
            INT    21H
            RET
B10PRMPT    ENDP
;                  Accept input of name:
;                  --------------------
C10INPT     PROC   NEAR
            MOV    AH,0AH           ;Request keyboard
            LEA    DX,PARLIST       ;  input
            INT    21H
            RET
C10INPT     ENDP
```

Figure 9-2a Accepting and Displaying Names

In the procedure E10CENT, the SHR instruction shifts the length 11 one bit to the right, effectively dividing the length by 2: Bits 00001011 become 00000101, or 5. The NEG instruction reverses the sign, changing +5 to −5. ADD adds the value 40, giving the starting position for the column, 35, in the DL register. With the cursor set at row 12, column 35, the name appears on the screen like this:

```
Row 12:   Dana Porter
            |    |
Column:    35   40
```

```
;                 Set bell and '$' delimiter:
;                 --------------------------
D10CODE  PROC     NEAR
         MOVZX    BX,ACTULEN          ;Replace 0DH with 07H
         MOV      KBNAME[BX],07
         MOV      KBNAME[BX+1],'$'    ;Set display delimiter
         RET
D10CODE  ENDP
;                 Center and display name:
;                 ------------------------
E10CENT  PROC     NEAR
         MOV      DL,ACTULEN          ;Locate center column:
         SHR      DL,1                ;  divide length by 2,
         NEG      DL                  ;  reverse sign,
         ADD      DL,40               ;  add 40
         MOV      DH,12               ;Center row
         CALL     Q20CURS             ;Set cursor
         MOV      AH,09H
         LEA      DX,KBNAME           ;Display name
         INT      21H
         RET
E10CENT  ENDP
;                 Clear screen:
;                 ------------
Q10CLR   PROC     NEAR
         MOV      AX,0600H            ;Request scroll screen
         MOV      BH,30               ;Color attribute
         MOV      CX,0000             ;From 00,00
         MOV      DX,184FH            ;To 24,79
         INT      10H
         RET
Q10CLR   ENDP
;                 Set cursor row/column:
;                 ---------------------
Q20CURS  PROC     NEAR                ;DX set on entry
         MOV      AH,02H              ;Request set cursor
         MOV      BH,00               ;Page #0
         INT      10H
         RET
Q20CURS  ENDP
         END      A10MAIN
```

Figure 9-2b Accepting and Displaying Names

Note the instructions in D10CODE that insert the Bell (07H) character in the input area immediately following the name:

```
MOVZX   BX,ACTULEN          ;Replace 0DH with 07H in BX
MOV     KBNAME[BX],07H
```

The MOVSX sets the BX with the number of characters. In the MOV, the index specifier in square brackets means that the BX is to act as a special index register to facilitate extended addressing. The MOV combines the length in the BX with the address of KBNAME and moves the 07H to the calculated address. For a length of 11, the instruction inserts 07H at KBNAME+11 (replacing the Enter character) following the name. The last instruction in D10CODE inserts a '$' delimiter following the 07H so that INT 21H function 09H can display the name and sound the speaker.

Replying with Only the Enter Key

The program continues accepting and displaying names until the user presses only <Enter> as a reply to a prompt. INT 21H function 09H accepts it and inserts a length of 00H in the parameter list, like this:

```
Parameter list (hex): |14|00|0D| ...
```

If the length is zero, the program determines that input is ended, as shown by the instruction CMP ACTLEN,00 in A20LOOP.

Clearing the Enter Character

You can use input characters for various purposes, such as printing on a report, storing in a table, or writing on disk. For these purposes, you may have to replace the Enter character (0DH) wherever it is in KBNAME with a blank (20H). The field containing the actual length of the input data, ACTLEN, provides the relative position of the Enter character. For example, if ACTLEN contains 11, then the Enter character is at KBNAME+11. You can move this length into the BX register for indexing the address of KBNAME as follows:

```
MOVZX   BX,ACTULEN          ;Set BX to 00 0B (11)
MOV     KBNAME[BX],20H      ;Clear Enter character
```

The MOVZX instruction sets the BX with the length 11. The MOV moves a blank (20H) to the address specified in the first operand: the address of KBNAME plus the contents of BX—in effect, KBNAME+11.

Clearing the Input Area

Each character keyed in replaces the previous contents in the input area and remain there until other characters replace them. Consider the following successive input:

```
   Input                     PARLIST (hex)
1. Paine       |14|05|50|61|69|6E|65|0D|20|20|20| ... |20|
2. Franklin    |14|08|46|72|61|6E|6B|6C|69|6E|0D| ... |20|
3. Adams       |14|05|41|64|61|6D|73|0D|69|6E|0D| ... |20|
```

The first name, Paine, requires only 5 bytes. The second name, Franklin, fully replaces the shorter name Paine. But because the third name, Adams, is shorter than Franklin, it replaces only Frank and the Enter character replaces the l. The remaining two letters ("in") still follow Adams. You could also clear KBNAME prior to prompting for a name like this:

```
        MOV  CX,20           ;Initialize for 20 loops
        MOV  SI,0000         ;Start position for name
B30:
```

```
        MOV  KBNAME[SI],20H    ;Move one blank to name
        INC  SI                ;Increment for next character
        LOOP B30               ;Repeat 20 times
```

Instead of the SI register, you could use DI or BX. Also, if the routine moves a word of two blanks, it would require only 10 loops. However, because KBNAME is defined as DB (byte), you would have to override its length with a WORD and PTR (pointer) operand, as the following indicates:

```
        MOV  CX,10                ;Initialize for 10 loops
        LEA  SI,KBNAME            ;Initialize the start of name
B30:
        MOV  WORD PTR[SI],2020H   ;Move two blanks to name
        INC  SI                   ;Increment two positions
        INC  SI                   ; in name
        LOOP B30                  ;Repeat 10 times
```

Interpret the MOV at B30: as "Move a blank word to the memory location where the address in the SI register points." This example uses LEA to initialize the clearing of KBNAME and uses a slightly different method for the MOV at B30 because you cannot code an instruction such as

```
MOV   WORD PTR[KBNAME],2020H    ;First operand is invalid
```

Clearing the input area solves the problem of short names being followed by previous data. For faster processing, you could clear only positions to the right of the most recently entered name.

USING CONTROL CHARACTERS IN A SCREEN DISPLAY

One way to make more effective use of displays is to use the Carriage Return, Line Feed, and Tab control characters. You can code them as ASCII or hex values, like this:

CONTROL CHARACTER	ASCII	HEX	EFFECT ON CURSOR
Carriage return	13	0DH	Resets to left position of screen
Line feed	10	0AH	Advances to next line
Tab	09	09H	Advances to next tab stop

You can use these control characters for handling the cursor whenever you display output or accept input. Here's an example that displays the contents of a character string named REPTITL, followed by Carriage Return (13) and Line Feed (10) to set the cursor on the next line:

```
REPTITL  DB  09, 'Intertech Corp Annual Report', 13, 10, '$'
         ...
```

```
MOV AH,09H          ;Request display
LEA DX,REPTITL      ;Load address of title
INT 21H             ;Call interrupt service
```

Using EQU to redefine the control characters may make a program more readable:

```
CR        EQU  13   (or EQU 0DH)
LF        EQU  10   (or EQU 0AH)
TAB       EQU  09   (or EQU 09H)
REPTITL   DB   TAB, 'Intertech Corp Annual Report', CR, LF, '$'
```

INT 21H FUNCTION 02H FOR SCREEN DISPLAY

You may find INT 21H function 02H useful for displaying single characters. Load in the DL the character that is to display at the current cursor position, and request INT 21H. The Tab, Carriage Return, and Line Feed characters act normally, and the operation automatically advances the cursor. The instructions are:

```
MOV   AH,02H      ;Request display character
MOV   DL,char     ;Character to display
INT   21H         ;Call interrupt service
```

The following example shows how to use this service to display a string of characters. The string to display is defined in COTITLE. The program loads the address of COTITLE in the DI register and its length in the CX. The loop involves incrementing the DI (by INC) for each successive character and decrementing the CX (by LOOP) for the number of characters to display. Here are the instructions:

```
COTITLE DB    'Intertech Corp.', 13, 10
        ...
        MOV   AH,02H         ;Request display character
        MOV   CX,17          ;Length of character string
        LEA   DI,COTITLE     ;Address of character string
C50:    MOV   DL,[DI]        ;Character to display
        INT   21H            ;Call interrupt service
        INC   DI             ;Increment for next character
        LOOP  C50            ;Repeat 17 times
        ...                  ;Finished
```

FILE HANDLES

This section examines the use of *file handles* for screen and keyboard operations, which is more in the UNIX and OS/2 style. A file handle is simply a number that refers to a specific device. Because the following standard file handles are preset, you do not have to define them:

Handle	Device
00	Input, normally keyboard (CON), but may be redirected
01	Output, normally display (CON), but may be redirected
02	Error output, display (CON), may not be redirected
03	Auxiliary device (AUX)
04	Printer (LPT1 or PRN)

As shown, the normal file handles are 00 for keyboard input and 01 for screen display. File handles for disk devices (covered in Chapter 17) have to be set by your program. You can also use these services for redirecting input and output to other devices, although this feature doesn't concern us here.

INT 21H FUNCTION 40H FOR SCREEN DISPLAY

INT 21H function 40H uses file handles to request display operations. To request this service, load the following registers:

AH = Function 40H   CX = Number of characters to display
BX = File handle 01   DX = Address of the display area

A successful INT operation delivers to the AX the number of bytes written and clears the carry flag (which you may test).

An unsuccessful INT operation sets the carry flag and returns an error code in the AX: 05H = access denied (for an invalid or disconnected device) or 06H = invalid handle. Because the AX could contain either a length or an error code, the only way to determine an error condition is to test the carry flag, although display errors are rare:

```
JC error-routine    ;Test for display error
```

The operation acts upon control characters 07H (Beep), 08H (Backspace), 0AH (Line Feed), and 0DH (Carriage Return), just like INT 21H function 09H. The following instructions illustrate function 40H:

```
COTITLE  DB   'Intertech Corp.',  0DH, 0AH    ;Display area
         ...
         MOV  AH,40H          ;Request display
         MOV  BX,01           ;File handle for screen
         MOV  CX,17           ;Display 17 characters
         LEA  DX,COTITLE      ;Display area
         INT  21H             ;Call interrupt service
```

Note that the length of COTITLE includes the 0DH and the 0AH.

Exercise: Displaying on the Screen

Let's use DEBUG to examine the internal effects of using a file handle to display your name. Load DEBUG, and when its prompt appears, type A 100 to begin keying in the following assembler statements (but not the leftmost numbers) at offset location 100H (remember that DEBUG assumes that entered numbers are in hexadecimal format):

```
100    MOV AH,40
102    MOV BX,01
105    MOV CX,xx    (Insert length of your name)
108    MOV DX,10E
10B    INT 21
10D    NOP
10E    DB 'x-------x'  (Insert your name here)
```

The instructions set the AH to request a display and set offset 10EH in the DX—the location of the DB containing your name.

When you have keyed in the instructions, press <Enter> again. To unassemble the program, use the U command (U 100,10D) and, to trace execution, press R and then repeated T commands. On reaching INT 21, use the P (Proceed) command to execute the interrupt through to the NOP instruction; it should display your name on the screen. Use the Q command to quit DEBUG.

INT 21H FUNCTION 3FH FOR KEYBOARD INPUT

INT 21H function 3FH uses file handles to request keyboard input, although it's a somewhat clumsy operation. Load the following registers:

AH = Function 3FH	CX = Maximum number of characters to accept
BX = File handle 00	DX = Address of area for entering characters

A successful INT operation clears the carry flag (which you may test) and sets the AX with the number of characters entered.

An unsuccessful INT operation could occur because of an invalid handle; the operation sets the carry flag and inserts an error code in the AX: 05H = access denied (for an invalid or disconnected device) or 06H = invalid handle. Because the AX could contain either a length or an error code, the only way to determine an error condition is to test the carry flag, although keyboard errors are rare.

Like INT 21H function 0AH, function 3FH also acts on Backspace, but ignores extended function keys such as F1, Home, and PageUp, seriously limiting its usefulness.

The following instructions illustrate the use of function 3FH:

```
KBINPUT  DB   20 DUP(' ')    ;Input area
         ...
         MOV  AH,3FH         ;Request keyboard input
         MOV  BX,00          ;File handle for keyboard
         MOV  CX,20          ;Maximum 20 characters
         LEA  DX,KBINPUT     ;Input area
         INT  21H            ;Call interrupt service
```

The INT operation waits for you to enter characters, but unfortunately does not check whether the number of characters exceeds the maximum in the CX register (20 in the example). Pressing <Enter> (0DH) signals the end of an entry. For example, typing the characters "Intertech Corp" delivers the following to KBINPUT:

```
|Intertech Corp|0DH|0AH|
```

The typed characters are immediately followed by Enter (0DH), which you typed, and Line Feed (0AH), which you did not type. Because of this feature, the maximum number and the length of the input area that you define should provide for an additional two characters. If you type fewer characters than the maximum, the locations in memory following the typed characters still contain the previous contents.

A successful INT operation clears the carry flag and sets the AX with the number of characters delivered. In the preceding example, this number is 14, plus 2 for the Enter and Line Feed characters, or 16. Accordingly, a program can use the value in the AX to determine the actual number of characters typed. Although this feature is trivial for YES and NO type of replies, it is useful for replies with variable length, such as names.

If the number of characters that you key in exceeds the maximum in the CX register, the operation actually accepts all the characters. Consider a situation in which the maximum in the CX is 08 and a user types the characters "PC Exchange". The operation sets the first eight characters in the input area to "PC Excha" with no Enter and Line Feed following and sets the AX with a length of 08. Now, watch this—the next INT operation to execute does not accept a name directly from the keyboard, because it still has the rest of the previous string in its buffer. It delivers "nge" followed by Enter and Line Feed to the input area and sets the AX to 05. Both operations are "normal" and clear the carry flag:

```
 First INT:  PC Excha       AX = 08
Second INT:  nge, 0DH, 0AH  AX = 05
```

A program can tell whether a user has keyed in a "valid" number of characters if (a) the number returned in the AX is less than the number in the CX or (b) the number returned in the AX is equal to that in the CX, and the last two characters in the input area are 0DH and 0AH. If neither condition is true, you'll have to issue additional INTs to accept the remaining characters. After all this, you may well wonder what is the point of specifying a maximum length in the CX at all!

Exercise: Keying in Data

Here's a DEBUG exercise in which you can view the effect of using INT 21H function 3FH for keying in data. The program allows you to key in up to 12 characters, including a character for Enter and one for Line Feed. Load DEBUG, and when the prompt appears, type A 100 to begin entering the following instructions (but not the numbers) at location 100H:

```
100  MOV AH,3F
102  MOV BX,00
```

```
105  MOV CX,0C
108  MOV DX,10F
10B  INT 21
10D  JMP 100
10F  DB 20 20 20 20 20 20 20 20 20 20 20 20
```

When you have keyed in the instructions, press <Enter> again. The program sets the AH and BX to request keyboard input and inserts the maximum length in the CX. It also sets offset 10FH in the DX—the location of the DB, where the entered characters are to begin.

Try the U command (U 100,10E) to unassemble the program. Use R and repeated T commands to trace the execution of the four MOV instructions. At location 10BH, use P (Proceed) to execute through the interrupt; the operation waits for you to key in characters followed by <Enter>. Check the contents of the AX register and the carry flag, and use D DS:10F to display the entered characters in memory. You can continue looping indefinitely. Key in Q to quit DEBUG.

KEY POINTS

- The basic color display supports 16K bytes and can operate in color or monochrome. You can process either in text mode for normal character display or in graphics mode.
- Monochrome display supports 4K bytes of memory, 2K of which are available for characters and 2K for an attribute for each character.
- The INT 10H instruction transfers control to BIOS for display operations. Two common operations are function 02H (set cursor) and 06H (scroll screen).
- INT 21H provides special functions to handle some of the complexity of input/output.
- When using INT 21H function 09H for displaying, define a delimiter ($) immediately following the display area. A missing delimiter can cause spectacular effects on the screen.
- INT 21H function 0AH for keyboard input expects the first byte to contain a maximum value and automatically inserts an actual value in the second byte.
- A file handle is a number that refers to a specific device. The numbers for file handles 00 through 04 are preset, whereas others can be set by your program.
- For INT 21H function 40H to display, use handle 01 in the BX.
- For INT 21H function 3FH for keyboard input, use handle 00 in the BX. The operation inserts Enter and Line Feed following the typed characters in the input area, but does not check for characters that exceed your specified maximum.

QUESTIONS

9-1. On an 80-column screen, what are the locations as hex values for (a) the bottom rightmost location and (b) the top leftmost location?

9-2. Write the instructions to set the cursor to row 16, column 20.

9-3. Write the instructions to clear the screen, beginning at row 06, column 0, with any color attribute.

9-4. Define data items and use INT 21H function 09H to display a message "What is the date (mm/dd/yy)?" Follow the message with a beep.

9-5. Define data items and use INT 21H function 0AH to accept input from the keyboard according to the format in Question 9-4.

9-6. The section titled "Clearing the Input Area" shows how to clear to blank the entire keyboard input area, defined as KBNAME. Change the example so that it clears only the characters immediately to the right of the most recently entered name.

9-7. Key in the program in Figure 9-2 with the following changes: (a) Instead of row 12, set the center at row 09; (b) instead of clearing the entire screen, clear only rows 0 through 08; use attribute 17H in the operation. Assemble, link, and test the program.

9-8. Identify the standard file handles for (a) the printer; (b) keyboard input; (c) normal screen display.

9-9. Define data items and use INT 21H function 40H to display the message "What is the date (mm/dd/yy)?" Follow the message with a beep.

9-10. Define data items and use INT 21H function 3FH to accept input from the keyboard according to the format in Question 9-9.

9-11. Revise Question 9-7 for use with INT 21H, functions 3FH and 40H, for input and display. Assemble, link, and test the revised program.

10 ADVANCED FEATURES OF SCREEN PROCESSING

Objective: To cover advanced features of screen handling, including scrolling, reverse video, blinking, and the use of color graphics.

INTRODUCTION

Chapter 9 introduced the basic features concerned with screen handling and keyboard input. This chapter provides advanced features related to video adapters, setting modes (text or graphics), and other screen handling features.

The first section describes the common video adapters and their associated video display areas. The sections on text mode explain the use of the attribute byte for color, blinking, and high intensity, as well as the instructions to set the cursor size and location, to scroll up or down the screen, and to display characters. The last few sections explain the use of graphics mode, together with the various functions used for displaying graphics.

This chapter covers the following services offered by BIOS INT 10H:

```
00H Set video mode                 0BH Set color palette
01H Set cursor size                0CH Write pixel dot
02H Set cursor position            0DH Read pixel dot
03H Read cursor position           0EH Write teletype
04H Read light pen position        0FH Get current video mode
05H Select active page             11H Character generator
06H Scroll up screen               12H Select alternative routine
07H Scroll down screen             13H Display character string
08H Read attribute/character       1BH Return state information
```

```
09H Display attribute/character   1CH Save/restore video state
0AH Display character
```

VIDEO ADAPTERS

The common (or once-common) video adapters include:

MDA	Monochrome display adapter
CGA	Color graphics adapter
EGA	Enhanced graphics adapter
MCGA	Multicolor graphics array (PS/2 models 25 and 30)
VGA	Video graphics array

The VGA and its superVGA successors replaced the CGA and EGA video adapters. Software written for a CGA or an EGA usually can run on a VGA system, although software written specifically for a VGA doesn't run on a CGA or an EGA.

A video display consists of three basic components: the video controller, video BIOS, and video display area.

1. The *video controller,* the workhorse unit, generates the monitor's scan signals for the selected text or graphics mode. The computer's processor sends instructions to the controller's registers and reads status information from them.
2. The *video BIOS,* which acts as an interface to the video adapter, contains such routines as setting the cursor and displaying characters.
3. The *video display area* in memory contains the information that the monitor is to display. The interrupts that handle screen displays transfer your data directly to this area. The various video modes reside in different areas of the video display area. Following are the beginning segment addresses for major video adapters:
   - A000:[0] Used for font descriptors when in text mode and for high-resolution graphics for VGA, EGA, and MCGA
   - B000:[0] Monochrome text mode for VGA, EGA, and MDA
   - B800:[0] Text and graphics modes for VGA, EGA, MCGA, and CGA.

SETTING THE VIDEO MODE

The *video mode* is determined by such factors as text or graphics, color or monochrome, screen resolution, and the number of colors. You use BIOS INT 10H function 00H to initialize the mode for the currently executing program or to switch between text and graphics. Setting the mode also clears the screen. As an example, mode 03 provides text mode, 25 rows × 80 columns, color, and 720 × 400 screen resolution for a VGA monitor.

To set the mode, request INT 10H with function 00H in the AH register and the mode in the AL. The following example sets the video mode for standard color text on any type of color monitor (it is also a fast way to clear the screen):

```
MOV  AH,00H    ;Request set mode
MOV  AL,03H    ;80 x 25 standard color text
INT  10H       ;Call interrupt service
```

If you write software for unknown video monitors, you can use INT 10H function 0FH (covered later), which returns the current video mode in the AL. Another approach is to use BIOS INT 11H to determine the device attached to the system, although the information delivered is rather primitive. The operation returns a value to the AX, with bits 5 and 4 indicating video mode:

- 01: 40 columns × 25 rows, using a color adapter
- 10: 80 columns × 25 rows, using a color adapter
- 11: 80 columns × 25 rows, using a monochrome adapter

You can test the AX for the type of monitor and then set the mode accordingly.

USING TEXT MODE

Text mode is used for the normal display of the full extended ASCII 256-character set on the screen. Processing is similar for both color and monochrome, except that color does not support the underline attribute. Figure 10-1 shows common text modes, with the mode number on the left.

Mode	Size	Type	Adapter	Resolution	Colors
00	(25 rows, 40 cols)	Mono	CGA	320 x 200	
			EGA	320 x 350	
			MCGA	320 x 400	
			VGA	360 x 400	
01	(25 rows, 40 cols)	Color	CGA	320 x 200	16
			EGA	320 x 350	16 of 64
			MCGA	320 x 400	16 of 262,144
			VGA	360 x 400	16 of 262,144
02	(25 rows, 80 cols)	Mono	CGA	640 x 200	
			EGA	640 x 350	
			MCGA	640 x 400	
			VGA	720 x 400	
03	(25 rows, 80 cols)	Color	CGA	640 x 200	16
			EGA	640 x 350	16 of 64
			MCGA	640 x 400	16 of 262,144
			VGA	720 x 400	16 of 262,144
07	(25 rows, 80 cols)	Mono	MDA	720 x 350	
			EGA	720 x 350	
			VGA	720 x 400	

Note: MDA: Monochrome display adapter
CGA: Color graphics adapter
MCGA: Multicolor graphics array
VGA: Video graphics array

Figure 10-1 Text Modes for Video Displays

- Text modes 00 (mono) and 01 (color). Provide 40-column format; although originally designed for the CGA, also work on VGA and EGA systems.
- Text modes 02 (mono) and 03 (color). Provide conventional 80-column format; although originally designed for the CGA, also work on VGA and EGA systems.
- Text mode 07 (mono). The standard monochrome mode for VGA, EGA, and MDA, with respectable screen resolutions.

Attribute Byte

An *attribute byte* in text (not graphics) mode determines the characteristics of each displayed character. When a program sets an attribute, it remains set; that is, all subsequent displayed characters have the same attribute until another operation changes it. You can use INT 10H functions to generate a screen attribute and perform such actions as scroll up, scroll down, read attribute or character, or display attribute or character. If you use DEBUG to view the video display area of your system, you can see each 1-byte character, immediately followed by its 1-byte attribute.

The attribute byte has the following format, according to bit position:

		Background			Foreground			
Attribute:	BL	R	G	B	I	R	G	B
Bit number:	7	6	5	4	3	2	1	0

The letters R, G, and B indicate bit positions for red, green, and blue, respectively, for each of the three primary additive colors.

- Bit 7 (BL) sets *blinking*
- Bits 6–4 determine the screen *background*
- Bit 3 (I) sets high *intensity*
- Bits 2–0 determine the *foreground* (for the character being displayed).

The common RGB color graphics monitor accepts input signals that are sent to three separate electron guns—red, green, and blue—for each of the primary additive colors. The RGB bits define a color; on both color and monochrome, 000 is black and 111 is white. For example, an attribute set with the value 0000 0111 means black background with white foreground.

Color Display

For most color monitors, the background can display 1 of 8 colors and the foreground characters can display 1 of 16 colors. Blinking and intensity apply only to the foreground. You can also select 1 of 16 colors for the border. Color monitors do not provide underlining; instead, setting bit 0 selects the blue color as foreground.

The three basic colors are red (R), green (G), and blue (B). You can combine these in the attribute byte to form a total of 8 colors (including black and white) and can set high intensity (I in the following chart), for a total of 16 colors:

COLOR	I	R	G	B	COLOR	I	R	G	B
Black	0	0	0	0	Gray	1	0	0	0
Blue	0	0	0	1	Light blue	1	0	0	1
Green	0	0	1	0	Light green	1	0	1	0
Cyan	0	0	1	1	Light cyan	1	0	1	1
Red	0	1	0	0	Light red	1	1	0	0
Magenta	0	1	0	1	Light magenta	1	1	0	1
Brown	0	1	1	0	Yellow	1	1	1	0
White	0	1	1	1	High-intensity white	1	1	1	1

If the background and foreground colors are the same, the displayed character is invisible. You can also use the attribute byte to cause a foreground character to blink. Here are some typical attributes, where BL means blinking:

BACK-GROUND	FORE-GROUND	BACKGROUND BL	R	G	B	FOREGROUND I	R	G	B	HEX
Black	Black	0	0	0	0	0	0	0	0	00
Black	Blue	0	0	0	0	0	0	0	1	01
Blue	Red	0	0	0	1	0	1	0	0	14
Green	Cyan	0	0	1	0	0	0	1	1	23
White	Light magenta	0	1	1	1	1	1	0	1	7D
Green	Gray (blinking)	1	0	1	0	1	0	0	0	A8

Monochrome Display

For a monochrome monitor, the attribute byte is used the same way as was shown for a color monitor, except that bit 0 sets the underline attribute. To specify attributes, you may set combinations of bits as follows:

BACK-GROUND	FORE-GROUND	FEATURE	BACKGROUND BL	R	G	B	FOREGROUND I	R	G	B	HEX
Black	Black	Nondisplay	0	0	0	0	0	0	0	0	00H
Black	White	Normal	0	0	0	0	0	1	1	1	07H
Black	White	Blinking	1	0	0	0	0	1	1	1	87H
Black	White	Intense	0	0	0	0	1	1	1	1	0FH
White	Black	Reverse video	0	1	1	1	0	0	0	0	70H
White	Black	Reverse blinking	1	1	1	1	0	0	0	0	F0H
		Underline	0	0	0	0	0	0	0	1	01H

Setting the Attribute

You can use INT 11H to determine the type of monitor installed. Then, for color, use any of the color combinations described or, for monochrome, use 07H to set the normal attribute (black background, white foreground). The attribute remains set until another operation changes it. Text mode also supports screen pages 0–3, where page 0 is the normal screen.

As an example, the following INT 10H operation (explained later) uses function 09H to display 12 brown, blinking (1110) asterisks on a blue (0001) background:

```
MOV  AH,09H     ;Request display
MOV  AL,'*'     ;Asterisk
MOV  BH,00H     ;Page number 0
MOV  BL,1EH     ;Color attribute (0001 1110)
MOV  CX,12      ;12 successive characters
INT  10H        ;Call interrupt service
```

You can use DEBUG to check out this example, as well as trying other color combinations.

SCREEN PAGES

The various text modes allow you to store data in video memory in *pages*. A page stores a screenful of data and is numbered 0 through 3 for normal 80-column mode (and 0 through 7 for the rarely used 40-column screen). In 80-column mode, page number 0 is the default and begins in the video display area at B800[0], page 1 begins at B900[0], page 2 at BA00[0], and page 3 at BB00[0].

You may format any of the pages in memory, although you can display only one page at a time. Each character to be displayed on the screen requires two bytes of memory—one byte for the character and a second for its attribute. In this way, a full page of characters for 80 columns and 25 rows requires $80 \times 25 \times 2 = 4{,}000$ bytes. The amount of memory actually allocated for each page is 4K, or 4,096 bytes, so that 96 unused bytes immediately follow each page.

USING INT 10H FOR TEXT MODE

Earlier, we used INT 10H function 00H for setting the display mode. INT 10H supports other services (available through function codes in the AH) to facilitate full screen handling. The INT operation preserves the contents of the BX, CX, DX, DI, SI, and BP registers, but not the AX—a point to remember if you use INT 10H in a loop. The following sections describe each function.

INT 10H Function 00H: Set Video Mode

As described earlier, you use this operation by setting the mode in the AL, such as 03 for color or 07 for monochrome. (See Figure 10-1.)

INT 10H Function 01H: Set Cursor Size

The cursor is not part of the ASCII character set and exists only in text mode. The computer maintains its own hardware for cursor control, with special INT operations for its use. The normal cursor symbol is similar to an underline or break character, but you can adjust the cursor size vertically by means of function 01H. Set these registers:

- CH (bits 4–0) = top of cursor ("start scan line")
- CL (bits 4–0) = bottom of cursor ("end scan line")

You can adjust the cursor size between the top and bottom scan lines—0:14 for VGA, 0:13 for monochrome and EGA, and 0:7 for CGA. The following code enlarges the cursor for a VGA to its maximum size:

```
MOV  AH,01H     ;Request set cursor size
MOV  CH,00      ;Start scan line
MOV  CL,14      ;End scan line
INT  10H        ;Call interrupt service
```

The cursor now blinks as a solid rectangle. You can adjust its size anywhere between the stated limits, such as 04:08, 03:10, and so forth. The cursor retains these attributes until another operation changes them. Using 0:14 (VGA), 12:13 (monochrome or EGA), or 6:7 (CGA) resets the cursor to normal. If you are unsure of the cursor's bounds on your monitor, try executing function 03H while in DEBUG.

INT 10H Function 02H: Set Cursor Position

This useful operation sets the cursor anywhere on a screen, according to row:column coordinates. Set these registers:

- BH = Page number, can be 0 (default), 1, 2, or 3 for 80-column text mode
- DH = Row
- DL = Column

The cursor location on each page is independent of its location on the other pages. This example sets row 12, column 30, for page 0:

```
MOV  AH,02H     ;Request set cursor
MOV  BH,00      ;Page number 0
MOV  DH,12      ;Row 12
MOV  DL,30      ;Column 30
INT  10H        ;Call interrupt service
```

INT 10H Function 03H: Read Cursor Position

A program can use function 03H to determine the present row, column, and size of the cursor, particularly in situations where the program has to use the screen temporarily and has to save and reset the original screen. Set the page number in the BH, just as for function 02H:

```
MOV  AH,03H     ;Request cursor location
MOV  BH,00      ;Page number 0 (normal)
INT  10H        ;Call interrupt service
```

The operation returns these values:

AX = Unchanged	CL = Ending scan line
BX = Unchanged	DH = Row
CH = Starting scan line	DL = Column

The following example uses function 03H to read the cursor and determine its location and size; it then uses function 02H to advance the cursor to the next column on the screen:

```
MOV  AH,03H     ;Request cursor position
MOV  BH,00      ;Page 0
INT  10H        ;Returns column in DL
MOV  AH,02H     ;Request set cursor
INC  DL         ; at next column
INT  10H        ;Call interrupt service
```

INT 10H Function 05H: Select Active Page

Function 05H for text modes 0–3 and 13–16 lets you select the page that is to be displayed. You can create different pages and request alternating between pages 0–3 (in 80-column mode). The operation is simply a request that returns no values:

```
MOV  AH,05H       ;Request active page
MOV  AL,page#     ;Page number
INT  10H          ;Call interrupt service
```

INT 10H Function 06H: Scroll Up Screen

If a program displays text down the screen past the bottom, the next line wraps around to start at the top. But even if the INT operation specifies column 0, the new lines are improperly indented, and succeeding lines may be badly skewed. The solution is to scroll the screen, so that displayed lines scroll off at the top and blank lines appear at the bottom.

You already used function 06H in Chapter 9 to clear the screen, where setting a zero value in the AL caused the entire screen to scroll up, effectively clearing it. Setting a nonzero value in the AL causes that number of lines to scroll up. Load the following registers:

AL = Number of rows (00 for full screen)	CX = Starting row:column
BH = Attribute	DX = Ending row:column

The following example sets a color attribute and scrolls the full screen one line:

```
MOV  AX,0601H    ;Request scroll up one line
MOV  BH,61H      ;Brown background, blue foreground
MOV  CX,0000     ;From 00:00 through
```

```
MOV  DX,184FH     ; 24:79 (full screen)
INT  10H          ;Call interrupt service
```

Here's a standard approach to scrolling one line:

1. For setting the row location of the cursor, define an item named, for example, ROW, initialized to zero.
2. Display a line and advance the cursor to the next line.
3. Test to see whether ROW is near the bottom of the screen (CMP ROW,22).
4. If yes, scroll one line, use ROW to set the cursor, and clear ROW to 00.
5. If no, increment ROW (INC ROW).

The CX and DX registers permit scrolling any portion of the screen. Be careful to coordinate the AL value with the distance in the CX:DX, especially when you reference a partial screen. The following instructions create a window (with its own attributes) of 7 rows and 30 columns, with the top left at 12:25, the top right at 12:54, the bottom left at 18:25 and the bottom right at 18:54:

```
MOV  AX,0607H     ;Request scroll 7 lines
MOV  BH,30H       ;Cyan background, black foreground
MOV  CX,0C19H     ;From row 12, column 25 through
MOV  DX,1236H     ; row 18, column 54 (window)
INT  10H          ;Call interrupt service
```

This example specifies scrolling 7 lines, which is the same value as the distance between rows 12 and 18 inclusive, so that only the window is cleared. It's a common practice when creating a window to scroll (and clear) all of its rows, and subsequently, say, one row at a time. Because the attribute for a window remains set until another operation changes it, you may set various windows to different attributes at the same time.

INT 10H Function 07H: Scroll Down Screen

For text mode, scrolling down the screen causes the bottom lines to scroll off and blank lines to appear at the top. Other than the fact that this function scrolls down, it works the same as function 06H, which scrolls up. Load the following registers:

AL = Number of rows (00 for full screen)	CX = Starting row:column
BH = Attribute	DX = Ending row:column

INT 10H Function 08H: Read Attribute or Character at Cursor Position

Function 08H can read both a character and its attribute from the video display area in either text or graphics mode. Set the page number, normally 0, in the BH, as the following example shows:

```
MOV  AH,08H     ;Request read attribute/character
MOV  BH,00      ;Page number 0 (normal)
INT  10H        ;Call interrupt service
```

The operation delivers the character to the AL and its attribute to the AH. In graphics mode, the operation returns 00H for a non-ASCII character. Because the operation reads only one character at a time, you have to code a loop to read successive characters.

INT 10H Function 09H: Display Attribute or Character at Cursor Position

Here's a useful operation that displays a specified number of characters in text or graphics mode according to a given attribute. Set these registers:

AL = ASCII character to be displayed	BL = Attribute
BH = Page number	CX = Count

The count in the CX specifies the number of times the operation is to repetitively display the character in the AL. The following example sets a color attribute and displays 60 "happy faces" (01H):

```
MOV  AH,09H     ;Request display
MOV  AL,01H     ;Happy face for display
MOV  BH,0       ;Page number 0 (normal)
MOV  BL,16H     ;Blue background, brown foreground
MOV  CX,60      ;60 repeated characters
INT  10H        ;Call interrupt service
```

The operation does not advance the cursor or respond to the Bell, Carriage Return, Line Feed, or Tab characters; instead, it attempts to display them as ASCII characters. The following example displays ten blinking hearts with reverse video:

```
MOV  AH,09H     ;Request display
MOV  AL,03H     ;Heart (to be displayed)
MOV  BH,00      ;Page number 0 (normal)
MOV  BL,0F0H    ;Blink and reverse video
MOV  CX,10      ;Ten times
INT  10H        ;Call interrupt service
```

Displaying different characters requires a loop. In text but not graphics mode, when the display exceeds the rightmost column, function 09H automatically continues the display on the next row at column 00. To display a prompt or message, code a routine that sets the CX to 01 and loops to move one character at a time from memory into the AL. (Because the CX is occupied, you can't easily use the LOOP instruction.) Also, after displaying each character, use INT 10H function 02H to advance the cursor to the next column.

INT 10H Function 0AH: Display Character at Cursor Position

This operation displays a character in text or graphics mode. The only difference between functions 0AH and 09H in text mode is that function 0AH uses the current attribute, whereas function 09H sets the attribute. Here is the code for function 0AH:

```
MOV  AH,0AH           ;Request display
MOV  AL,char          ;Character to display
MOV  BH,page#         ;Page number
MOV  CX,repetition    ;Number of repeated characters
INT  10H              ;Call interrupt service
```

INT 21H operations that can display a string of characters and respond to screen control characters are sometimes more convenient to use than INT 10H operations.

INT 10H Function 0EH: Write Teletype

This operation lets you use the monitor as a terminal for simple displays. Set function 0EH in the AH, the character to display in the AL, page number in the BH, and foreground color (graphics mode) in the BL:

```
MOV  AH,0EH      ;Request display
MOV  AL,char     ;Character to display
MOV  BH,page#    ;Active page number (some systems)
MOV  BL,color    ;Foreground color (graphics mode)
INT  10H         ;Call interrupt service
```

The Backspace (08H), Bell (07H), Carriage Return (0DH), and Line Feed (0AH) control characters act as commands for screen formatting. The operation automatically advances the cursor, wraps characters onto the next line, scrolls the screen, and maintains the present screen attributes.

INT 10H Function 0FH: Get Current Video Mode

You can use this function to determine the current video mode. (See also function 00H.) Here's an example:

```
MOV  AH,0FH    ;Request video mode
INT  10H       ;Call interrupt service
CMP  AL,03     ;If mode 3,
JE   ...       ; jump
```

The INT operation returns these values:

AL = Current video mode

AH = Characters per line = 20, 40, or 80 (14H, 28H, or 50H)

BH = Current page number.

INT 10H Function 11H: Character Generator

This complex function for VGA, EGA, and MCGA systems initiates a mode set and resets the video environment. A discussion is outside the scope of this text.

INT 10H Function 12H: Select Alternative Screen Routine

This function supports VGA and EGA monitors. To get information on these monitors, simply load 10H in the BL and use this function; the operation returns:

- BH = 00H for color and 01H for monochrome
- BL = 00H for 64K, 01H for 128K, 02H for 192K, and 03H for 256K
- CH = Adapter bits
- CL = Switch setting

The operation supports a number of elaborate functions, such as 30H (select scan lines), 31H (default palette loading), and 34H (cursor emulation).

INT 10H Function 13H: Display Character String

For VGA and EGA monitors, this operation displays strings of any length with options for setting the attribute and moving the cursor. The ES:BP registers should contain the segment:offset address of the string to display. The operation acts on the Backspace, Bell, Carriage Return, and Line Feed control characters. Here's an example:

```
MOV  AH,13H            ;Request display string
MOV  AL,subfunction    ;00, 01, 02, or 03 (see below)
MOV  BH,page#          ;Page number
MOV  BL,attribute      ;Screen attribute
LEA  BP,address        ;Address of string in ES:BP
MOV  CX,length         ;Length of string
MOV  DX,screen         ;Relative starting location on screen
INT  10H               ;Call interrupt service
```

The four subfunctions that you set in the AL are:

- 00 Display attribute and string; do not advance cursor
- 01 Display attribute and string; advance cursor
- 02 Display character and then attribute; do not advance cursor
- 03 Display character and then attribute; advance cursor

PROGRAM: DISPLAYING THE ASCII CHARACTER SET

The program in Figure 9-1 used INT 21H to display the ASCII character set, but the operation *acted* on the Backspace, Bell, Carriage Return, and Line Feed control characters, rather than *displaying* them. To solve this problem, the revised program in Figure 10-2 uses INT 10H with the following functions:

```
TITLE       A10BIOAS (COM)  INT 10H to display ASCII character set
            .MODEL SMALL
            .CODE
            ORG     100H
BEGIN:      JMP     SHORT A10MAIN
CTR         DB      00              ;Counter for ASCII characters
COL         DB      24              ;Column of screen
ROW         DB      04              ;Row of screen
MODE        DB      ?               ;Video mode
;                   Main procedure:
;                   --------------
A10MAIN     PROC    NEAR
            CALL    B10MODE         ;Get/set video mode
            CALL    C10CLR          ;Clear screen
A20:
            CALL    D10SET          ;Set cursor
            CALL    E10DISP         ;Display characters
            CMP     CTR,0FFH        ;Last character displayed?
            JE      A30             ;  yes, exit
            INC     CTR             ;Increment char. counter
            ADD     COL,02          ;Increment column
            CMP     COL,56          ;At end of column?
            JNE     A20             ;  no, bypass
            INC     ROW             ;  yes, increment row
            MOV     COL,24          ;  and reset column
            JMP     A20
A30:
            CALL    F10READ         ;Get keyboard character
            CALL    G10MODE         ;Restore video mode
            MOV     AX,4C00H        ;End of processing
            INT     21H
A10MAIN     ENDP
;                   Get and set video mode:
;                   ----------------------
B10MODE     PROC    NEAR
            MOV     AH,0FH          ;Request get mode
            INT     10H
            MOV     MODE,AL         ;Save mode
            MOV     AH,00H          ;Request set new mode
            MOV     AL,03           ;Standard color
            INT     10H
            RET
B10MODE     ENDP
;                   Clear screen and create window:
;                   ------------------------------
C10CLR      PROC    NEAR
            MOV     AH,08H          ;Request get current
            INT     10H             ;  attribute in AH
            MOV     BH,AH           ;Move it to BH
            MOV     AX,0600H        ;Scroll whole screen
            MOV     CX,0000         ;Upper left location
            MOV     DX,184FH        ;Lower right location
            INT     10H
            MOV     AX,0610H        ;Create 16-line window
            MOV     BH,16H          ;Blue back, brown foregrd.
            MOV     CX,0418H        ;Upper left corner  04:24
            MOV     DX,1336H        ;Lower right corner 19:54
            INT     10H
            RET
C10CLR      ENDP
```

Figure 10-2 INT 10H to Display the ASCII Character Set

```
;                       Set cursor to row and column:
;                       ----------------------------
D10SET    PROC    NEAR
          MOV     AH,02H          ;Request set cursor
          MOV     BH,00           ;Page 0 (normal)
          MOV     DH,ROW          ;New row
          MOV     DL,COL          ;New column
          INT     10H
          RET
D10SET    ENDP
;                       Display ASCII characters:
;                       ------------------------
E10DISP   PROC    NEAR
          MOV     AH,0AH          ;Request display
          MOV     AL,CTR          ;ASCII char
          MOV     BH,00           ;Page 0
          MOV     CX,01           ;One character
          INT     10H
          RET
E10DISP   ENDP
;                       Force pause, get keyboard character:
;                       -----------------------------------
F10READ   PROC    NEAR
          MOV     AH,10H          ;Request get character
          INT     16H
          RET
F10READ   ENDP
;                       Restore original video mode:
;                       ---------------------------
G10MODE   PROC    NEAR
          MOV     AH,00H          ;Request set mode
          MOV     AL,MODE         ;Original value
          INT     10H
          RET
G10MODE   ENDP
          END     BEGIN
```

Figure 10-2 INT 10H to Display the ASCII Character Set

0FH Get the current video mode and save it.

00H Set video mode 03 for this program, and restore the original mode on exiting.

08H Read the attribute at the current cursor position, for use by function 06H.

06H Scroll up the screen to clear the entire screen, using the attribute just read. Also, create a 16-line window with brown foreground and blue background for the displayed characters.

02H Set the cursor initially, and advance it for each displayed character.

0AH Display each character, including control characters, at the current cursor position.

The characters are displayed in 16 columns and 16 rows. This program, like others in this book, are written for clarity rather than processing speed. You could revise the program to make it run faster, for example, by using registers for the row, column, and ASCII character generator. Also, because INT 10H destroys only the contents of the AX register, the values in the other registers don't have to be reloaded. However, the program won't run noticeably faster and it would lose some clarity.

ASCII CHARACTERS FOR BOXES AND MENUS

Among the extended ASCII characters 128–255 (80H–FFH) are a number of special characters that are useful for displaying prompts, menus, and logos, as shown in Appendix B and Figure 10-3.

The following example uses INT 10H function 09H to draw a solid horizontal line 25 positions long:

```
MOV  AH,09H      ;Request display
MOV  AL,0C4H     ;Solid single line
MOV  BH,00       ;Page number 0
MOV  BL,0FH      ;Black fore, white back, intense
MOV  CX,25       ;25 repetitions
INT  10H         ;Call interrupt service
```

Remember that although function 09H displays a string of characters, it does not advance the cursor.

The simplest way to display a box is to define it in the data segment and display the whole area. This next example defines and displays a menu in a solid single-line box:

```
CR    EQU  0DH                      ;Carriage return
LF    EQU  0AH                      ;Line feed
MENU  DB   0DAH,  17 DUP(0C4H), 0BFH, CR, LF
      DB   0B3H,  ' Add records     ', 0B3H, CR, LF
      DB   0B3H,  ' Delete records  ', 0B3H, CR, LF
      DB   0B3H,  ' Enter orders    ', 0B3H, CR, LF
      DB   0B3H,  ' Print report    ', 0B3H, CR, LF
      DB   0B3H,  ' Update accounts ', 0B3H, CR, LF
      DB   0B3H,  ' View records    ', 0B3H, CR, LF
      DB   0C0H,  17 DUP(0C4H), 0D9H, CR, LF
      ...
      MOV  AH,40H                   ;Request display
      MOV  BX,01                    ;File handle for screen
      MOV  CX,168                   ;Number of characters: 8 rows
      LEA  DX,MENU                  ; x 21 columns
      INT  21H                      ;Call interrupt service
```

In the next chapter, Figures 11-1 and 11-2 illustrate a similar menu in a double-line box, along with "dots on" characters for a drop shadow to the right and bottom of the box. The following lists the various characters:

One-quarter dots on	B0H	Solid shadow, upper half	DFH
One-half dots on	B1H	Solid shadow, left half	DDH
Three-quarter dots on	B2H	Solid shadow, right half	DEH
Solid shadow	DBH	Solid shadow, lower half	DCH

```
                        SINGLE       DOUBLE
CHARACTER                LINE         LINE          MIXED LINES
Straight Lines:
  Horizontal            C4H  ─      CDH  ═
  Vertical              B3H  │      BAH  ║
Corners:
  Top left              DAH  ┌      C9H  ╔      D6H  ╓      D5H  ╒
  Top right             BFH  ┐      BBH  ╗      B7H  ╖      B8H  ╕
  Bottom left           C0H  └      C8H  ╚      D3H  ╙      D4H  ╘
  Bottom right          D9H  ┘      BCH  ╝      BDH  ╜      BEH  ╛
Middle:
  Left                  C3H  ├      CCH  ╠      C7H  ╟      C6H  ╞
  Right                 B4H  ┤      B9H  ╣      B6H  ╢      B5H  ╡
  Top                   C2H  ┬      CBH  ╦      D2H  ╥      D1H  ╤
  Bottom                C1H  ┴      CAH  ╩      D0H  ╨      CFH  ╧
Center Cross            C5H  ┼      CEH  ╬      D7H  ╫      D8H  ╪

Blocks:
  One-quarter dots on        B0H  ░   Solid shadow, upper half   DFH  ▀
  One-half dots on           B1H  ▒   Solid shadow, left half    DDH  ▌
  Three-quarter dots on      B2H  ▓   Solid shadow, right half   DEH  ▐
  Solid shadow               DBH  █   Solid shadow, lower half   DCH  ▄
```

Figure 10-3 ASCII Characters for Boxes and Menus

PROGRAM: BLINKING, REVERSE VIDEO, AND SCROLLING

The program in Figure 10-4 accepts names from the keyboard and displays them on the screen. To make things more interesting, it displays the prompt with reverse video (blue on white), accepts the name normally (white on blue), and displays the name at column 40 in the same row with blinking and reverse video. Here is the format:

```
        Name? Benjamin Franklin   Benjamin Franklin [blinking]
        |                         |
    Column 0                  Column 40
```

To control the placement of the cursor, the program defines and increments ROW for the screen row and COL for advancing the cursor when displaying the prompt and name. (INT 10H function 09H does not automatically advance the cursor.) The program consists of the following procedures:

- A10MAIN provides the main logic for accepting any number of keyboard entries.
- B10PROM displays a prompt for the user to enter a name.
- C10INPT uses INT 21H function 0AH for keyboard input.
- D10NAME displays down the screen until it reaches row 20 and then begins scrolling up one line for each additional prompt.
- E10DISP uses INT 10H function 09H for displaying each name as individual characters.
- Q10SCRN handles scrolling of the screen, and assumes the number in the AX on entry.
- Q20CURS sets the cursor according to the current values in ROW and COL.

```
TITLE     A10NMSCR (EXE) Reverse video, blinking, scrolling
          .MODEL  SMALL
          .STACK  64
; ----------------------------------------------------------
          .DATA
PARLIST   LABEL  BYTE                 ;Name parameter list:
MAXLEN    DB     20                   ;  maximum length of name
ACTLEN    DB     ?                    ;  no. of chars entered
KBNAME    DB     20 DUP(' ')          ;  name

COL       DB     00
COUNT     DB     ?
PROMPT    DB     'Name? '
ROW       DB     00
; ----------------------------------------------------------
          .CODE
A10MAIN   PROC   FAR
          MOV    AX,@data             ;Initialize segment
          MOV    DS,AX                ;  registers
          MOV    ES,AX
          MOV    AX,0600H
          CALL   Q10SCRN              ;Clear screen
A20LOOP:
          MOV    COL,00               ;Set column to 0
          CALL   Q20CURS
          CALL   B10PROM              ;Display prompt
          CALL   C10INPT              ;Provide for input of name
          CMP    ACTLEN,00            ;No name?
          JNE    A30                  ;  if not, bypass
          MOV    AX,0600H             ;If so,
          CALL   Q10SCRN              ;  clear screen,
          MOV    AX,4C00H             ;End of processing
          INT    21H
A30:
          CALL   D10NAME              ;Display name
          JMP    A20LOOP
A10MAIN   ENDP
;                Display prompt:
;                --------------
B10PROM   PROC   NEAR
          LEA    SI,PROMPT            ;Set address of prompt
          MOV    COUNT,05
B20:
          MOV    BL,71H               ;Reverse video
          CALL   E10DISP              ;Display routine
          INC    SI                   ;Next character in name
          INC    COL                  ;Next column
          CALL   Q20CURS              ;Set cursor
          DEC    COUNT                ;Countdown
          JNZ    B20                  ;Loop n times
          RET
B10PROM   ENDP
;                Accept input of name:
;                --------------------
C10INPT   PROC   NEAR
          MOV    AH,0AH               ;Request keyboard
          LEA    DX,PARLIST           ;  input
          INT    21H
          RET
C10INPT   ENDP
```

Figure 10-4a Blinking, Reverse Video, and Scrolling

```
;               Display name with blinking reverse video:
;               ----------------------------------------
D10NAME   PROC  NEAR
          LEA   SI,KBNAME           ;Initialize name
          MOV   COL,40              ;Set screen column
D20:
          CALL  Q20CURS             ;Set cursor
          MOV   BL,0F1H             ;Blink reverse video
          CALL  E10DISP             ;Display routine
          INC   SI                  ;Next character in name
          INC   COL                 ;Next screen column
          DEC   ACTLEN              ;Countdown name length
          JNZ   D20                 ;Loop n times

          CMP   ROW,20              ;Near bottom of screen?
          JAE   D30
          INC   ROW                 ;  no, increment row
          RET
D30:
          MOV   AX,0601H            ;  yes,
          CALL  Q10SCRN             ;  scroll screen
          RET
D10NAME   ENDP
;               Display character:
;               -----------------
E10DISP   PROC  NEAR                ;BL (attribute) set on entry
          MOV   AH,09H              ;Request display
          MOV   AL,[SI]             ;Get name character
          MOV   BH,00               ;Page number
          MOV   CX,01               ;One character
          INT   10H
          RET
E10DISP   ENDP
;               Scroll screen:
;               -------------
Q10SCRN   PROC  NEAR                ;AX set on entry
          MOV   BH,17H              ;White on blue
          MOV   CX,0000
          MOV   DX,184FH            ;Full screen
          INT   10H
          RET
Q10SCRN   ENDP
;               Set cursor row/col:
;               ------------------
Q20CURS   PROC  NEAR
          MOV   AH,02H
          MOV   BH,00               ;Page
          MOV   DH,ROW              ;Row
          MOV   DL,COL              ;Column
          INT   10H
          RET
Q20CURS   ENDP
          END   A10MAIN
```

Figure 10-4b Blinking, Reverse Video, and Scrolling

DIRECT VIDEO DISPLAY

For some applications, the video display is routed through the operating system and BIOS may be noticeably slow. The fastest way to display screen characters (text or graphics) is to transfer them directly to the appropriate video display area. For example, the address of page 0 in the video area for mode 03 (color, text) is B800[0]H. Each screen character requires two bytes of memory—one for the character and one immediately following for its attribute. With a screen size of 80 columns and 25 rows, a page in the video area requires $80 \times 25 \times 2 = 4{,}000$ bytes.

The first two bytes in the video display area represent one screen location, for row 00, column 00, and the bytes at F9EH and F9FH represent the screen location for row 24, column 79. Simply moving a character:attribute into the video area of the active page causes the character to appear immediately on the screen. You can use DEBUG commands to check this feature. First, display the video area at B800[0]H:

```
D B800:00
```

The display shows what was on the screen at the time you typed the command, which is usually a set of bytes containing 20 07H (for blank character, black background, and white foreground). Note that both DEBUG and you are competing for the same display area and screen. Try changing the screen with these commands to display happy faces (01, 02, and 03) with various attributes (25, 36, and 47) on the top and bottom rows:

```
E B800:000 01 25 02 36 03 47
E B800:F90 01 25 02 36 03 47
```

The program in Figure 10-5 gives an example of transferring data directly to the video display area at B900[0]H—that is, page 1, rather than the default page 0. The program uses the SEGMENT AT feature to define the BIOS video display area, in effect as a dummy segment. DSPAREA identifies the location of page 1, at the start of the segment.

The program displays characters in rows 5 through 20 and columns 10 through 69. The first row displays a string of the character A (41H) with an attribute of 01H, the second row displays a string of the character B (42H) with an attribute of 02H, and so forth, with the character and attribute incremented for each row.

The program establishes the starting position of a page in the video display area based on the fact that there are $80 \times 2 = 160$ columns in a row. The starting position, then, for row 05, column 10, is $(160 \times 5 \text{ rows}) + (10 \text{ columns} \times 2) = 820$. After displaying one row, the program advances 40 positions in the display area for the start of the next line and ends on reaching the letter Q (51H).

The video display segment for page 1 is defined as DSPSEG and the page as DSPAREA. The program establishes the ES register as the segment register for DSPSEG. At the start, the program saves the current mode and page and then sets mode 03 and page 01.

In the procedure B10PROC, the starting character and attribute are initialized in the AX and the starting video area offset in the DI. The instruction MOV WORD PTR [DSPAREA+DI], AX moves the contents of the AL (the character) to the first byte of the display area and the AH (the attribute) to the second byte. The LOOP routine executes this instruction 60 times, displaying the character:attribute across the screen. It then increments the character:attribute and adds 40 to the DI—20 for the end of the current row and 20 for indenting the start of the next row (on the screen, 10 columns each). The routine then repeats the display of the next row of characters.

On completion of the display, the procedure C10INPT waits for the user to press a key and then the program restores the original mode and page before ending.

```
TITLE       P10GRAFX (COM)  Graphics display
            .MODEL SMALL
            .CODE
            ORG     100H
BEGIN       PROC    NEAR
            MOV     AH,0FH          ;Preserve
            INT     10H             ;  original
            PUSH    AX              ;  video mode
            CALL    B10MODE         ;Set graphics mode
            CALL    C10DISP         ;Display color graphics
            CALL    D10KEY          ;Get keyboard response
            POP     AX              ;Restore
            MOV     AH,00H          ;  original mode
            INT     10H             ;  (in AL)
            MOV     AX,4C00H        ;Exit to DOS
            INT     21H
BEGIN       ENDP

B10MODE     PROC    NEAR
            MOV     AH,00H          ;Set EGA/VGA graphics mode
            MOV     AL,10H          ;640 cols x 350 rows
            INT     10H
            MOV     AH,0BH          ;Set background palette
            MOV     BH,00           ;Background
            MOV     BL,07H          ;Gray
            INT     10H
            RET
B10MODE     ENDP

C10DISP     PROC    NEAR
            MOV     BX,00           ;Set initial page,
            MOV     CX,64           ;  color, column,
            MOV     DX,70           ;  and row
C20:
            MOV     AH,0CH          ;Write pixel dot
            MOV     AL,BL           ;Set color
            INT     10H             ;BX, CX, & DX are preserved
            INC     CX              ;Increment column
            CMP     CX,576          ;Column at 576?
            JNE     C20             ;  no, loop
            MOV     CX,64           ;  yes, reset column
            INC     BL              ;Change color
            INC     DX              ;Increment row
            CMP     DX,280          ;Row at 280?
            JNE     C20             ;  no, loop
            RET                     ;  yes, terminate
C10DISP     ENDP

D10KEY      PROC    NEAR
            MOV     AH,10H          ;Request keyboard
            INT     16H             ;  input
            RET
D10KEY      ENDP
            END     BEGIN
```

Figure 10-5 Using Direct Video Display

USING GRAPHICS MODE

Graphics adapters have two basic modes of operation: text (the default) and graphics. Use BIOS INT 10H function 00H to set graphics or text mode, as the following two examples show:

Mode	Type	Adapter	Resolution	Colors
04H	Color	CGA,EGA,MCGA,VGA	320 x 200	4
05H	Mono	CGA,EGA,MCGA,VGA	320 x 200	
06H	Mono	CGA,EGA,MCGA,VGA	640 x 200	
0DH	Color	EGA,VGA	320 x 200	16
0EH	Color	EGA,VGA	640 x 200	16
0FH	Mono	EGA,VGA	640 x 350	
10H	Color	EGA,VGA	640 x 350	16
11H	Color	MCGA,VGA	640 x 480	2 of 262,144
12H	Color	VGA	640 x 480	16 of 262,144
13H	Color	MCGA,VGA	320 x 200	256 of 262,144

Figure 10-6 Graphics Modes for Video Displays

1. Set graphics mode for VGA:

```
MOV  AH,00H      ;Request set mode
MOV  AL,0CH      ;Color graphics
INT  10H         ;Call interrupt service
```

2. Set text mode:

```
MOV  AH,00H      ;Request set mode
MOV  AL,03H      ;Color text
INT  10H         ;Call interrupt service
```

Resolutions and modes for graphics adapters as shown in Figure 10-6 are as follows.

- *Graphics modes 04H, 05H, and 06H.* These original CGA modes are also used by the VGA and EGA for upward compatibility, so that many programs written for the CGA can run on a VGA or EGA. The address of the video display area for these modes is B800[0].
- *Graphics modes 0DH, 0EH, 0FH, and 10H.* These original EGA modes are also used by the VGA for upward compatibility, so that many programs written for the EGA can run on a VGA. These modes also support 8, 4, 2, and 2 pages of video display area, respectively, with page 0 the default. The address of the video display area for these modes is A000[0].
- *Graphics modes 11H, 12H, and 13H.* These modes are specifically designed for the VGA (and the now rare MCGA) and are not usable by other video adapters. The address of the video display area for these modes is A000[0].

In graphics mode, ROM contains dot patterns for only the first (bottom) 128 characters. INT 1FH provides access to a 1K area in memory that defines the top 128 characters, 8 bytes per character.

Pixels

Graphics mode uses *pixels* (picture elements or pels) to generate color patterns. For example, mode 04H for standard color graphics provides 200 rows of 320 pixels. Each byte represents 4 pixels (that is, 2 bits per pixel), numbered 0 through 3, as follows:

byte:	C1 C0	C1 C0	C1 C0	C1 C0
pixel:	0	1	2	3

At any given time, there are four available colors, numbered 0 through 3. The limitation of four colors is because a 2-bit pixel provides 4 bit combinations: 00, 01, 10, and 11. You can choose pixel 00 for any one of the 16 available colors for the background:

COLOR		COLOR	
Black	0000	Gray	1000
Blue	0001	Light blue	1001
Green	0010	Light green	1010
Cyan	0011	Light cyan	1011
Red	0100	Light red	1100
Magenta	0101	Light magenta	1101
Brown	0110	Yellow	1110
Light gray	0111	White	1111

And you can choose pixels 01, 10, and 11 for any one of two 3-color palettes:

C1	C0	PALETTE 0	PALETTE 1
0	0	background	background
0	1	green	cyan
1	0	red	magenta
1	1	brown	white

Use INT 10H function 0BH to select a color palette and the background. If you choose background color yellow and palette 0, the available colors are yellow, green, red, and brown. A byte consisting of the pixel value 10101010 would display as all red. If you choose background color blue and palette 1, the available colors are blue, cyan, magenta, and white. A byte consisting of pixel value 00011011 would display blue, cyan, magenta, and white.

INT 10H FOR GRAPHICS

BIOS INT 10H facilitates full screen handling for both graphics and text mode, as described earlier. The operation preserves the contents of the BX, CX, DX, DI, SI, and BP registers, but not the AX. The following sections describe each of the functions of INT 10H that are concerned with graphics.

INT 10H Function 00H: Set Video Mode

Function 00H in the AH and mode 12H in the AL set standard VGA color graphics mode:

```
MOV  AH,00H      ;Request set mode for
MOV  AL,12H      ;  640 x 480 VGA resolution
INT  10H         ;Call interrupt service
```

Setting graphics mode causes the cursor to disappear.

INT 10H Function 04H: Read Light Pen Position

Use this function with graphics to determine the status of a light pen. The operation delivers the following information:

AH	0 if status is not triggered and 1 if triggered.
DX	Row in the DH and column in the DL.
CH:BX	Pixel location, with raster (horizontal) line in the BH and column or dot in the BX.

INT 10H Function 08H: Read Attribute or Character at Cursor Position

This function can read both characters and attributes from the display area in either text or graphics mode. See the earlier section, "Using INT 10H for Text Mode."

INT 10H Function 09H: Display Attribute or Character at Current Cursor Position

For graphics mode, use the BL for defining the foreground color. If bit 7 is 0, the defined color replaces present pixel colors; if bit 7 is 1, the defined color is combined (XORed) with them. For details, see the earlier section, "Using INT 10H for Text Mode."

INT 10H Function 0AH: Display a Character at Cursor Position

See the earlier section "Using INT 10H for Text Mode."

INT 10H Function 0BH: Set Color Palette

Use this function to set the color palette and display a graphics character. The value in the BH (00 or 01) determines the purpose of the BL register:

- BH = 00. Select the background color, where the BL contains the color value in bits 0–3 (any of 16 colors):

```
MOV  AH,0BH     ;Request
MOV  BH,00      ;  background
MOV  BL,04      ;  color red
INT  10H        ;Call interrupt service
```

- BH = 01. Select the palette for graphics, where the BL contains the palette (0 or 1):

```
MOV  AH,0BH    ;Request color
MOV  BH,01     ;Select palette
MOV  BL,00     ;  number 0 (green, red, brown)
INT  10H       ;Call interrupt service
```

Once you set a palette, it remains set, but when you change the palette, the whole screen changes to that color combination. If you use function 0BH while in text mode, the value set for color 0 for the palette determines the color of the border.

INT 10H Function 0CH: Write Pixel Dot

Use function 0CH to display a selected color (background and palette). Set these registers:

AL = Color of the pixel   CX = Column
BH = Page number (VGA/EGA)   DX = Row

The minimum value for the column or row is 0, and the maximum value depends on the video mode. The following example sets a pixel at column 200, row 50:

```
MOV  AH,0CH    ;Request write dot
MOV  AL,03     ;Color of pixel
MOV  BH,0      ;Page number 0
MOV  CX,200    ;Horizontal position (column)
MOV  DX,50     ;Vertical position (row)
INT  10H       ;Call interrupt service
```

VGA/EGA modes 0DH, 0EH, 0FH, and 10H provide 8, 4, 2, and 2 pages of video display area, respectively. The default page is number 0.

INT 10H Function 0DH: Read Pixel Dot

This operation, the opposite of function 0CH, reads a dot to determine its color value. Set the BH for page number (VGA/EGA), the CX for column, and the DX for row. The minimum value for the column or row is 0, and the maximum value depends on the video mode. The operation returns the pixel color in the AL.

INT 10H Function 0EH: Write Teletype

See the earlier section, "Using INT 10H for Text Mode."

INT 10H Function 10H: Set Palette Registers

This function handles VGA/EGA systems. A subfunction code in the AL determines the operation:

- 00 Set a palette register, where the BH contains the value to set and the BL contains the register to set.
- 01 Set the overscan register, where the BH contains the value to set.
- 02 Set all palette registers and overscan. ES:DX points to a 17-byte table, where bytes 0–15 are palette values and byte 16 is the overscan value.
- 03 Toggle the intensity/blinking bit, where 00 in the BL enables intensity and 01 enables blinking.

Other AL subfunction codes for the VGA under function 10H are 07H (read individual palette register), 08H (read overscan register), 09H (read all palette registers and overscan), 10H (set individual color register), 12H (set block of color registers), 13H (select color page), 15H (read individual color register), 17H (read block of color registers), and 1AH (read color page state).

INT 10H Function 1AH: Read/Write Display Combination Code

This operation returns codes that identify the type of display that is in use.

INT 10H Function 1BH: Return Functionality/State Information

This complex operation returns information to a 64-byte buffer identifying the video mode, cursor size, page supported, and so forth.

INT 10H Function 1CH: Save or Restore Video State

This function saves and restores the video state, including the status of color registers, BIOS data area, and video hardware.

PROGRAM: SETTING AND DISPLAYING GRAPHICS MODE

The program in Figure 10-7 includes the following INT 10H functions for a display of graphics:

- 0FH = Preserve the original mode
- 00H = Set graphics mode 12H
- 0BH = Select background color green
- 0CH = Write pixel dots for 640 columns and 480 rows.

The actual window displayed is 210 rows and 512 columns (columns 64 through 576). Note that rows and columns are in terms of dots, not characters.

The program increments the color for each row (so that bits 0000 become 0001, etc.) and, because only the rightmost 4 bits are used, the colors repeat after every 16 rows. The display begins 64 columns from the left of the screen and ends 64 columns from the right.

```
TITLE      A10GRAFX (COM)  Graphics display
           .MODEL SMALL
           .CODE
           ORG    100H
A10MAIN    PROC   NEAR
           MOV    AH,0FH          ;Preserve
           INT    10H             ;  original
           PUSH   AX              ;  video mode
           CALL   B10MODE         ;Set graphics mode
           CALL   C10DISP         ;Display color graphics
           CALL   D10KEYB         ;Get keyboard response
           POP    AX              ;Restore
           MOV    AH,00H          ;  original mode
           INT    10H             ;  (in AL)
           MOV    AX,4C00H        ;End of processing
           INT    21H
A10MAIN    ENDP

;                 Set graphics mode:
B10MODE    PROC   NEAR
           MOV    AH,00H          ;Request VGA graphics mode
           MOV    AL,12H          ;640 cols x 480 rows
           INT    10H
           MOV    AH,0BH          ;Request color palette
           MOV    BH,00           ;Background
           MOV    BL,07H          ;Gray
           INT    10H
           RET
B10MODE    ENDP

;                 Display rows of graphics dots:
C10DISP    PROC   NEAR
           MOV    BX,00           ;Set initial page,
           MOV    CX,64           ;  column,
           MOV    DX,70           ;  and row
C20:
           MOV    AH,0CH          ;Request pixel dot
           MOV    AL,BL           ;Color
           INT    10H             ;BX, CX, & DX are preserved
           INC    CX              ;Increment column
           CMP    CX,576          ;Column at 576?
           JNE    C20             ;  no, loop
           MOV    CX,64           ;  yes, reset column
           INC    BL              ;Change color
           INC    DX              ;Increment row
           CMP    DX,280          ;Row at 280?
           JNE    C20             ;  no, loop
           RET                    ;  yes, ended
C10DISP    ENDP

;                 Delay, wait for keyboard entry:
D10KEYB    PROC   NEAR
           MOV    AH,10H          ;Request keyboard
           INT    16H             ;  input
           RET
D10KEYB    ENDP
           END    A10MAIN
```

Figure 10-7 Color Graphics Display

At the end, the program waits for the user to press a key, and then it resets the display to the original mode. You could modify this program for various graphics modes.

DETERMINING THE TYPE OF VIDEO ADAPTER

Because video graphics adapters support various services, there may be times when you want to know what type of adapter is installed in a system. A recommended way is to check first for VGA, then for EGA, and last for CGA or MDA. Here are the steps:

1. To determine whether a VGA is installed:

```
MOV  AH,1AH      ;Request VGA function
MOV  AL,0        ;  and subfunction 0
INT  10H         ;Call interrupt service
CMP  AL,1AH      ;If AL contains 1AH on return,
JE   VGAFOUND    ;  system contains a VGA
```

2. To determine whether an EGA is installed:

```
MOV  AH,12H      ;Request EGA function
MOV  BL,10H      ;Amount of EGA memory
INT  10H         ;Call interrupt service
CMP  BL,10H      ;If BL no longer contains 10H,
JNE  EGAFOUND    ; system contains an EGA
```

   Because an EGA may be installed along with an MDA or CGA, you may want to determine whether the EGA is active. The BIOS data area at 40:0087 contains an EGA instruction byte. Check bit 3, where 0 means that the EGA is active and 1 means that it is inactive.

3. To determine whether a CGA or MDA is installed, examine the word at location 40:0063, which contains the base address of the memory controller. Note that 3BxH means MDA and 3DxH means CGA.

KEY POINTS

- The attribute byte for text mode provides for blinking, reverse video, and high intensity. For color text, the RGB bits enable you to select colors, but not underlining.
- BIOS INT 10H provides functions for full screen processing, such as setting the video mode, setting the cursor location, scrolling the screen, reading from the keyboard, and writing characters.
- If your program displays lines down the screen, use INT 10H function 06H to scroll up before the display reaches the bottom.
- INT 10H services that display a character do not automatically advance the cursor.
- The 16K memory for color display permits storing additional "pages" or "screens." There are four pages per 80-column screen.
- The fastest way to display screen characters (text or graphics) is to transfer them directly to the appropriate video display area.

- A pixel (picture element) consists of a specified number of bits, depending on the graphics adapter and resolution (low, medium, or high).
- For graphics modes 04 and 05, you can select four colors, of which one is any of the 16 available colors and the other three are from a color palette.

QUESTIONS

10-1. Provide the attribute bytes, in binary, for color monitors for the following: (a) yellow on brown; (b) light cyan on magenta; (c) green on black, blinking.

10-2. Provide the attribute bytes, in binary, for monochrome monitors for the following: (a) underline only; (b) white on black, normal intensity; (c) reverse video, intense.

10-3. Code the following routines: (a) Set the mode for an 80-column monochrome screen; (b) set the cursor size to start at scan line 4 and end at scan line 10; (c) scroll up the screen 14 lines; (d) display 25 blinking "dots" with one-half dots (B1H) on.

10-4. Under text mode 03, how many colors are available for background and for foreground?

10-5. Code the instructions for displaying 6 club (05H) characters in text mode with yellow on blue.

10-6. What modes permit the use of screen pages?

10-7. Write a program that uses INT 21H function 0AH to accept data from the keyboard and function 09H to display the characters. The program will clear the screen, set screen colors (your choice), set the cursor at row 8, column 10, and accept a set of data from the keyboard beginning at the current position of the cursor. The set of data could be four or five lines (say, any length up to 25 characters) entered from the keyboard, with each line followed by <Enter> and stored in fields in the data segment under the names LINE1, LINE2, etc. You could use a variety of colors, reverse video, or beeping as an experiment. Then set the cursor to a row 18 and column 10, and display the entered data on one row for each line of stored data. The program is to accept any number of sets of data and ends when the user presses <Enter> with no data. Write the program with a short main logic routine and a series of called subroutines. Include some concise comments.

10-8. Revise the program in Question 10-7 so that it uses INT 16H for keyboard input and INT 10H function 09H for the display.

10-9. Explain how the common attribute byte limits the number of available colors.

10-10. Write the instructions to set graphics mode for these resolutions: (a) 320 × 200; (b) 640 × 200; (c) 640 × 480.

10-11. Write the instructions for selecting the background color green in graphics mode.

10-12. Write the instructions to read a dot from row 44, column 120, in graphics mode.

10-13. Revise the program in Figure 10-7 so that it provides for the following: (a) background color blue; (b) row beginning at 50 and ending at 400; (c) column beginning at 72 and ending at 568.

10-14. Based on the changes you made in Question 10–13, revise the program to display graphics dots one column (instead of row) at a time. That is, display dots down the screen, then advance to the next column, and so forth.

11 ADVANCED FEATURES OF KEYBOARD PROCESSING

Objectives: To cover all the keyboard operations and advanced features of keyboard input, including the shift status, keyboard buffer, and scan codes.

INTRODUCTION

This chapter describes the many different operations for handling keyboard input, some of which have specialized uses. Of these operations, INT 21H function 0AH (covered in Chapter 9), and INT 16H (covered in this chapter) should provide almost all the keyboard operations you'll require.

Other topics in the chapter include the keyboard shift status bytes, scan codes, and the keyboard buffer area. The *shift status* bytes in the BIOS data area enables a program to determine, for example, whether the <Ctrl>, <Shift>, or <Alt> keys have been pressed. The *scan code* is a unique number assigned to each key on the keyboard that enables the system to identify the source of a pressed key and enables a program to check if the user has pressed an extended function key such as <Home>, <PgUp>, or <Arrow>. And the *keyboard buffer area* provides space in memory for you to type ahead before a program actually requests input.

Operations introduced in this chapter are the following:

INT 21H FUNCTIONS	INT 16H FUNCTIONS
01H Keyboard input with echo	00H Read a character
06H Direct console I/O	01H Determine if character present
07H Direct keyboard input without echo	02H Return current shift status
08H Keyboard input without echo	05H Keyboard write

0AH Buffered keyboard input
0BH Check keyboard status
0CH Clear buffer & invoke function
10H Read keyboard character
11H Determine if character present
12H Return current shift status

THE KEYBOARD

The keyboard provides three basic types of keys:

1. *Standard characters,* which consist of the letters A through Z, numbers 0 through 9, and such characters as %, $, and #.
2. *Extended function keys,* which consist of:
   - Program function keys, such as <F1> and <Shift>+<F1>
   - Numeric keypad keys with NumLock toggled off:<Home>, <End>, <Arrows>, <Del>, <Ins>, <PgUp>, and <PgDn>, and the duplicate keys for them on the extended keyboard
   - <Alt>+alphabetics and <Alt>+program-function keys
3. *Control keys <Alt>, <Ctrl>, and <Shift>,* which work in association with other keys. BIOS does not deliver them as ASCII characters to your program. Instead, BIOS treats these differently from other keys by updating their current state in the shift status bytes in the BIOS data area.

The original PC with its 83 keys suffered from a short-sighted design decision that caused keys on the so-called numeric keypad to perform two actions. Thus numbers shared keys with <Home>, <End>, <Arrows>, <Del>, <Ins>, <PgUp>, and <PgDn>, with the <NumLock> key toggling between them. To overcome problems caused by this layout, designers produced an enhanced keyboard with 101 keys and subsequently 104 keys for Windows. Of the 18 new keys, only <F11> and <F12> provide a new function; the rest duplicate the function of keys on the original keyboard. If your programs allow users to press <F11>, <F12>, or any of the fancy new key combinations, the users must have an enhanced keyboard and a computer with a BIOS that can process them. For most other keyboard operations, your programs need not be concerned with the type of keyboard that is installed.

KEYBOARD SHIFT STATUS

The BIOS data area at segment 40[0]H in low memory contains a number of useful data items. These include the first byte of the current keyboard shift status at 40:17H, where the bits set to 1 indicate the following:

BIT	ACTION	BIT	ACTION
7	Insert active	3	<Alt> pressed
6	CapsLock state active	2	<Ctrl> pressed
5	NumLock state active	1	<Left Shift> pressed
4	Scroll Lock state active	0	<Right Shift> pressed

You may use INT 16H function 02H (covered later), to check these values. Note that "active" means that the user is currently holding down the key; releasing the key causes BIOS to clear the bit value. The 83-key keyboard uses only this shift status byte.

The enhanced keyboards have duplicate (left and right) <Ctrl> and <Alt> keys, so that additional information is needed to test for them. The second byte of the keyboard status needed for the enhanced keyboard is at 40:18H, where a 1-bit indicates the following:

BIT	ACTION	BIT	ACTION
7	Insert pressed	3	Ctrl/NumLock (pause) active
6	CapsLock pressed	2	SysReq pressed
5	NumLock pressed	1	Left Alt pressed
4	Scroll Lock pressed	0	Left Ctrl pressed

Bits 0, 1, and 2 are associated with the enhanced keyboard. You can test, for example, whether either <Ctrl> or <Alt> is pressed, or both.

Another keyboard status byte resides at 40:96H. The item of interest to us here is bit 4; when on, it indicates that an enhanced keyboard is installed.

Exercise: Examining the Shift Status

To see the effect on the shift status bytes of pressing <Ctrl>, <Alt>, and <Shift>, load DEBUG for execution. Type D 40:17 to view the contents of the status bytes. Press <CapsLock>, <NumLock>, and <ScrollLock>, and type D 40:17 again to see the result on both status bytes. The byte at 40:17H should show 70H (0111 0000B), and the byte at 40:18H is probably 00H. The byte at 40:96H should show the presence (or absence) of an enhanced keyboard.

Try changing the contents of the status byte at 40:17H—type E 40:17 00. If your keyboard Lock keys have indicator lights, they should turn off. Now try typing E 40:17 70 to turn them on again.

You could try various combinations, although it's difficult to type a valid DEBUG command while holding down the <Ctrl> and <Alt> keys. Key in Q to quit DEBUG.

THE KEYBOARD BUFFER

An item of interest in the BIOS data area at 40:1EH is the *keyboard buffer.* This feature allows you to type up to 15 characters before a program requests keyboard input. When you press a key, the keyboard's processor generates the key's scan code (its unique assigned number) and automatically requests BIOS INT 09H.

In simple terms, the INT 09H routine gets the scan code from the keyboard, converts it to an ASCII character, and delivers it to the keyboard buffer area. Subsequently, INT 16H (the lowest level keyboard operation) reads the character from the buffer and delivers it to your program. Your program need never request INT 09H, because BIOS performs it automatically when you press a key. A later section covers INT 09H and the keyboard buffer in detail.

USING INT 21H FOR KEYBOARD INPUT

This section covers the INT 21H services that handle keyboard input. For this type of keyboard input, insert the required function code in the AH and request INT 21H. All of these operations except function 0AH accept only one character. (To handle a string of characters, you have to code a loop that accepts a character, checks for Backspace and Enter, echoes the character to the screen if necessary, and advances the cursor.) These operations have been superseded by function 3FH (covered in Chapter 9), but are included here for completeness. In the discussion of the operations that follow, the term "respond to a <Ctrl>+<Break> request" means that the system will terminate the program if the user presses the <Ctrl>+<Break> or <Ctrl>+<C> keys together.

INT 21H Function 01H: Keyboard Input with Echo

This operation accepts a character from the keyboard buffer or, if none is present, waits for keyboard entry. The operation returns one of two status codes:

- AL = a nonzero value means that a standard ASCII character (such as a letter or number) is present, which the operation echoes on the screen
- AL = zero means that the user has pressed an extended function key such as <Home>, <F1>, or <PgUp>, and the AH still contains the original function. The operation handles extended functions clumsily, attempting to echo them on the screen. And to get the scan code for the function key in the AL, you immediately have to repeat the INT 21H operation. The operation also responds to a <Ctrl>+<Break> request.

The following example illustrates this function:

```
MOV  AH,01H    ;Request keyboard input
INT  21H       ;Call interrupt service
CMP  AL,00     ;Extended function key pressed?
JNZ  ...       ;  no, ASCII character
INT  21H       ;  yes, repeat operation
...            ;  for scan code
```

INT 21H Function 06H: Direct Console I/O

This rather bizarre operation can transfer any character or control code with no interference from DOS. There are two versions, for input and for output. For input, load 0FFH into the DL. If no character is in the keyboard buffer, the operation sets the zero flag and does not wait for input. If a character is waiting in the buffer, the operation stores the character in the AL and clears the zero flag. The operation does not echo the character on the screen and does not check for <Ctrl>+<Break> or <Ctrl>+PrtSc. A nonzero value in the AL represents a standard ASCII character, such as a letter or number. Zero in the AL means that the user has pressed an extended function key such as <Home>, <F1>, or <PgUp>. To get its scan code in the AL, immediately repeat the INT 21H operation.

For screen output, load the ASCII character (not 0FFH) into the DL.

INT 21H Function 07H: Direct Keyboard Input Without Echo

This operation works like function 01H, except that the entered character does not echo on the screen and the operation does not respond to a <Ctrl>+<Break> request. You could use the operation to key in a password that is to be invisible or where you don't want to disturb the screen.

INT 21H Function 08H: Keyboard Input Without Echo

This operation works like function 01H, except that the entered character does not echo on the screen.

INT 21H Function 0AH: Buffered Keyboard Input

This useful keyboard operation is covered in detail in Chapter 9. However, its inability to accept extended function keys limits its capability.

INT 21H Function 0BH: Check Keyboard Status

This operation returns FFH in the AL if an input character is available in the keyboard buffer and 00H if no character is available. Note that the operation does not expect the user to press a key; rather, it simply checks the buffer. The function is related to those others that do not wait for keyboard input.

INT 21H Function 0CH: Clear Keyboard Buffer and Invoke Function

You may use this operation in association with function 01H, 06H, 07H, 08H, or 0AH. Load the required function into the AL:

```
MOV   AH,0CH          ;Request keyboard input
MOV   AL,function     ;Required function
MOV   DX,KBAREA       ;Keyboard input area
INT   21H             ;Call interrupt service
```

The operation clears the keyboard buffer, executes the function in the AL, and accepts (or waits for) a character, according to the function request in the AL. You could use this operation for a program that does not allow a user to type ahead.

USING INT 16H FOR KEYBOARD INPUT

INT 16H, the basic BIOS keyboard operation used extensively by software developers, provides the following services according to the function code in the AH.

INT 16H Function 00H: Read a Character

This keyboard operation handles the keys on the 83-key keyboard, but does not accept input from the additional keys on the enhanced keyboard, such as <F11> and <F12>. See function 10H, which is the same as this one but also handles the enhanced keyboard.

INT 16H Function 01H: Determine Whether a Character Is Present

This operation handles the keys on the 83-key keyboard, but does not recognize input from the additional keys on the enhanced keyboard. See function 11H, which is the same as this one but also handles the enhanced keyboard.

INT 16H Function 02H: Return the Current <Shift> Status

This operation returns to the AL the status of the keyboard shift from the BIOS data area at location 417H (40:17H). (See the earlier section, "Keyboard Shift Status.") The following example tests whether the <Left Shift> (bit 1) or <Right Shift> (bit 0) keys are pressed:

```
MOV  AH,02H          ;Request shift status
INT  16H             ;Call interrupt service
OR   AL,00000011B    ;Left or right shift pressed?
JE   xxxx            ; yes ...
```

See function 12H for handling the shift status at location 418H for extended functions from the enhanced keyboard.

INT 16H Function 05H: Keyboard Write

This operation allows your program to insert characters in the keyboard buffer as if a user had pressed a key. Load the ASCII character into the CH and its scan code into the CL. The operation allows you to key characters into the buffer until it is full.

INT 16H Function 10H: Read a Keyboard Character

This operation is the same as function 00H, except that this one accepts the additional extended functions from the enhanced keyboard.

The operation checks the keyboard buffer for an entered character. If none is present, the operation waits for the user to press a key. If a character is present, the operation delivers it to the AL and its scan code to the AH. If the pressed key is an extended function such as <Home> or <F1>, the character in the AL is 00H. On the enhanced keyboard, <F11> and <F12> also return 00H to the AL, but the other new (duplicate) control keys, such as <Home> and <PgUp>, return E0H. Here are the three possibilities:

KEY PRESSED	AH	AL
Regular ASCII character	Scan code	ASCII character
Extended function key	Scan code	00H
Extended duplicate control key	Scan code	E0H

You can test the AL for 00H or E0H to determine whether the user has pressed an extended function key:

```
MOV  AH,10H      ;Request BIOS keyboard input
INT  16H         ;Call interrupt service
CMP  AL,00H      ;Extended function key?
JE   K10         ;  yes, exit
CMP  AL,0E0H     ;Extended function key?
JE   K10         ;  yes, exit
```

Because the operation does not echo the character on the screen, you have to request a screen display operation for that purpose.

INT 16H Function 11H: Determine Whether a Character Is Present

This operation is the same as function 01H, except that this one accepts the additional extended functions from the enhanced keyboard.

If an entered character is present in the keyboard buffer, the operation clears the zero flag and delivers the character to the AL and its scan code to the AH; the entered character remains in the buffer. If no character is present, the operation sets the zero flag and does not wait. Note that the operation provides a look-ahead feature, because the character remains in the keyboard buffer until function 10H reads it.

INT 16H Function 12H: Return the Current Keyboard Shift Status

This operation is similar to function 02H, which delivers to the AL the status of the keyboard shift from the BIOS data area at location 417H (40:17H). The operation also delivers the extended shift status to the AH, where a 1-bit means the following:

BIT	KEY	BIT	KEY
7	SysReq pressed	3	Right Alt pressed
6	Caps Lock pressed	2	Right Ctrl pressed
5	Num Lock pressed	1	Left Alt pressed
4	Scroll Lock pressed	0	Left Ctrl pressed

EXTENDED FUNCTION KEYS AND SCAN CODES

An extended function key such as <F1> or <Home> requests an action rather than delivers a character. There is nothing in the system design that compels these keys to perform a specific action: As the programmer, you determine, for example, that pressing <Home> is to set the cursor at the top left corner of the screen or that pressing <End> sets the cursor at the end of text on the screen. You could as easily program these keys to perform wholly unrelated operations.

Each key has a designated *scan code*, beginning with 01 for <Esc>. (See Appendix F for a complete list of these codes.) By means of the scan codes, a program may determine the source of any keystroke. For example, a program could issue INT 16H function 10H to request input of one character. The operation responds in one of two ways, depending on whether you press a character key or an extended function key. For a character, such as the letter A, the operation delivers these two items:

1. In the AH register, the scan code for the letter A, 1EH.
2. In the AL register, the ASCII character A (41H).

The keyboard contains two keys each for such characters as −, +, and *. Pressing the asterisk key, for example, sets the character code 2AH in the AL and one of two scan codes in the AH, depending on which key was pressed: 09H for the asterisk above the number 8, or 29H for the asterisk by the numeric keypad. The following example tests the scan code to determine which asterisk was pressed:

```
CMP  AL,2AH     ;Asterisk?
JNE  H30        ;  no, exit
CMP  AH,09H     ;Scan code on #8 key?
JE   H40        ;  yes, exit
```

If you press an extended function key, such as <Ins>, the operation delivers these two items:

1. In the AH register: The scan code for <Ins>, 52H.
2. In the AL register: Zero, or E0H for a new control key on the enhanced keyboard.

After an INT 16H operation (and some INT 21H operations), you can test the AL. If it contains 00H or E0H, the request is for an extended function; otherwise, the operation has delivered a character. The following example tests for an extended function key:

```
MOV  AH,10H     ;Request keyboard input
INT  16H        ;Call interrupt service
CMP  AL,00H     ;Extended function?
JE   K20        ;  yes, exit
CMP  AL,0E0H    ;Extended function?
JE   K20        ;  yes, exit
```

In the next example, if a user presses the <Home> key (scan code 47H), the cursor is set to row 0, column 0:

```
      MOV  AH,10H     ;Request keyboard input
      INT  16H        ;Call interrupt service
      CMP  AL,00H     ;Extended function?
      JE   K30        ; yes, bypass
      CMP  AL,0E0H    ;Extended function?
      JNE  K90        ;  no, exit
K30:  CMP  AH,47H     ;Scan code for <Home>?
      JNE  K90        ;  no, exit
      MOV  AH,02H     ;Request
      MOV  BH,00      ;  set cursor
      MOV  DX,00      ;  to 00:00
      INT  10H        ;Call interrupt service
```

Function keys <F1>–<F10> generate scan codes 3BH–44H, respectively, and <F11> and <F12> generate 85H and 86H. The following example tests for function key <F10>:

```
CMP  AH,44H     ;Function key <F10>?
JE   H50        ;  yes, exit
```

At H50, the program could perform any required action.

Keyboard Exercise

The following DEBUG exercise examines the effects of keying in various characters. Use the command A 100 to key in these instructions:

```
MOV  AH,10 (or 00 for an 83-key keyboard)
INT  16
JMP  100
```

Use the P (Proceed) command to execute the INT operation. Key in various normal characters with <Shift> and with <Ctrl>, and compare the results in the AH (scan code) and the AL (character) with the list in Appendix F.

PROGRAM: SELECTING FROM A MENU

The next program displays a menu with a drop shadow as explained in Chapter 10, and shown in Figure 11-1. The menu itself is defined in the data segment within a double-lined box. A user presses <UpArrow> or <DownArrow> and <Enter> to select an item from the menu.

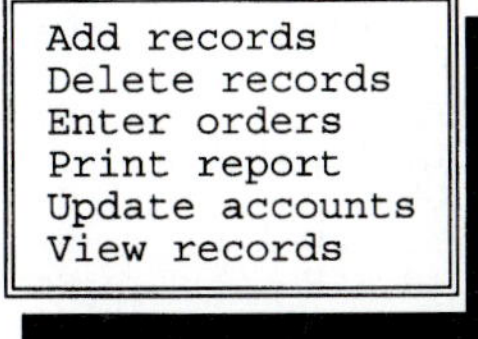

Figure 11-1 Menu with Drop Shadow

The program is listed in Figure 11-2. The procedures and what actions they perform are follows:

- A10MAIN calls Q10CLEAR to clear the screen, calls B10MENU to display the menu and to set the first item to reverse video, and calls C10INPT to accept keyboard input.
- B10MENU displays the full set of menu selections. It first uses INT 10H function 09H to display the shadow box: 8 rows of 19 shadow characters (0DBH). The procedure then displays the menu defined in the data segment as MENU on top of the shadow box but offset 1 row and column.
- C10INPT uses INT 16H for input: <DownArrow> to move down the menu, <UpArrow> to move up the menu, <Enter> to accept a menu item, and <Esc> to quit. All other keyboard entries are ignored. The routine wraps the cursor around, so that

```
TITLE     A11SELMU (EXE) Select item from menu
; ----------------------------------------------------
          .MODEL SMALL
          .STACK 64
; ----------------------------------------------------
          .DATA
TOPROW    EQU    00                    ;Top row of menu
BOTROW    EQU    07                    ;Bottom row of menu
LEFCOL    EQU    16                    ;Left column of menu
COL       DB     00                    ;Screen column
ROW       DB     00                    ;Screen row
COUNT     DB     ?                     ;Characters per line
ATTRIB    DB     ?                     ;Screen attribute
NINTEEN   DB     19                    ;Width of menu
MENU      DB     0C9H, 17 DUP(0CDH), 0BBH
          DB     0BAH, ' Add records      ', 0BAH
          DB     0BAH, ' Delete records   ', 0BAH
          DB     0BAH, ' Enter orders     ', 0BAH
          DB     0BAH, ' Print report     ', 0BAH
          DB     0BAH, ' Update accounts ', 0BAH
          DB     0BAH, ' View records     ', 0BAH
          DB     0C8H, 17 DUP(0CDH), 0BCH
PROMPT    DB     09, 'To select an item, use <Up/Down Arrow>'
          DB     ' and press <Enter>.'
          DB     13, 10, 09, 'Press <Esc> to exit.'
; ----------------------------------------------------
          .CODE
.386
A10MAIN   PROC   FAR
          MOV    AX,@data              ;Initialize segment
          MOV    DS,AX                 ;  registers
          MOV    ES,AX
          CALL   Q10CLEAR              ;Clear screen
          MOV    ROW,BOTROW+2          ;Set row
          MOV    COL,00                ;  and column
          CALL   Q20CURS               ;  for cursor
          MOV    AH,40H                ;Request display
          MOV    BX,01                 ;Handle for screen
          MOV    CX,81                 ;Number of characters
          LEA    DX,PROMPT             ;Address of prompt
          INT    21H                   ;Call interrupt service
A10LOOP:
          CALL   B10MENU               ;Display menu
          MOV    COL,LEFCOL+1
          CALL   Q20CURS               ;Set cursor
          MOV    ROW,TOPROW+1          ;Set row to top item
          MOV    ATTRIB,16H            ;Set reverse video
          CALL   D10DISP               ;Highlight current menu line
          CALL   C10INPUT              ;Provide for menu selection
          CMP    AL,0DH                ;Enter key pressed?
          JE     A10LOOP               ;  yes, continue
          MOV    AX,0600H              ;Esc pressed (indicates end)
          CALL   Q10CLEAR              ;Clear screen
          MOV    AX,4C00H              ;End of processing
          INT    21H
A10MAIN   ENDP
```

Figure 11-2a Selecting an Item from a Menu

```
;               Display full menu:
;               -----------------
B10MENU  PROC   NEAR
         MOV    ROW,TOPROW+1       ;Set top row of shadow
B20:
         MOV    COL,LEFCOL+1       ;Set left column of shadow
         CALL   Q20CURS            ;Set cursor next column
         MOV    AH,09H             ;Request display
         MOV    AL,0DBH            ;Shadow character
         MOV    BH,00              ;Page 0
         MOV    BL,60H             ;Black on brown
         MOV    CX,19              ;19 characters
         INT    10H
         INC    ROW                ;Next row
         CMP    ROW,BOTROW+2       ;All rows displayed?
         JNE    B20                ;No, repeat
         MOV    ROW,TOPROW         ;Set top row of menu
         LEA    SI,MENU            ;Address of menu
         MOV    ATTRIB,71H         ;Blue on white
B30:
         MOV    COL,LEFCOL         ;Set left column of menu
         MOV    COUNT,19           ;No. of cols to display
B40:
         CALL   Q20CURS            ;Set cursor next column
         MOV    AH,09H             ;Request display
         MOV    AL,[SI]            ;Get character from menu
         MOV    BH,00              ;Page 0
         MOV    BL,71H             ;Blue on white
         MOV    CX,01              ;One character
         INT    10H
         INC    COL                ;Set for next column,
         INC    SI                 ;  next character
         DEC    COUNT              ;Last character?
         JNZ    B40                ;No, repeat
         INC    ROW                ;Next row
         CMP    ROW,BOTROW+1       ;All rows displayed?
         JNE    B30                ;  No, repeat
         RET                       ;  Yes, return
B10MENU  ENDP
;                 Accept input for request:
;                 ------------------------
C10INPUT PROC   NEAR
         MOV    AH,10H             ;Request keyboard
         INT    16H                ;  input
         CMP    AH,50H             ;Down arrow?
         JE     C20
         CMP    AH,48H             ;Up arrow?
         JE     C30
         CMP    AL,0DH             ;Enter key?
         JE     C90
         CMP    AL,1BH             ;Escape key?
         JE     C90
         JMP    C10INPUT           ;None, retry
C20:     MOV    ATTRIB,71H         ;Blue on white
         CALL   D10DISP            ;Set old line to normal video
         INC    ROW                ;Increment for next row
         CMP    ROW,BOTROW-1       ;Past bottom row?
         JBE    C40                ;  no, ok
         MOV    ROW,TOPROW+1       ;  yes, reset
         JMP    C40
```

Figure 11-2b Selecting an Item from a Menu

```
C30:        MOV     ATTRIB,71H          ;Blue on white
            CALL    D10DISP             ;Set old line to normal video
            DEC     ROW
            CMP     ROW,TOPROW+1        ;Below top row?
            JAE     C40                 ;  no, ok
            MOV     ROW,BOTROW-1        ;  yes, reset
C40:        CALL    Q20CURS             ;Set cursor
            MOV     ATTRIB,17H          ;White on blue
            CALL    D10DISP             ;Set new line to reverse video
            JMP     C10INPUT
C90:        RET
C10INPUT    ENDP
;                   Set menu line to normal/highlight:
;                   ----------------------------------
D10DISP     PROC    NEAR
            MOVZX   AX,ROW              ;Row tells which line to set
            MUL     NINTEEN             ;Multiply by length of line
            LEA     SI,MENU+1           ;  for selected menu line
            ADD     SI,AX
            MOV     COUNT,17            ;Characters to display
D20:
            CALL    Q20CURS             ;Set cursor next column
            MOV     AH,09H              ;Request display
            MOV     AL,[SI]             ;Get character from menu
            MOV     BH,00               ;Page 0
            MOV     BL,ATTRIB           ;New attribute
            MOV     CX,01               ;One character
            INT     10H
            INC     COL                 ;Next column
            INC     SI                  ;Set for next character
            DEC     COUNT               ;Last character?
            JNZ     D20                 ;  no, repeat
            MOV     COL,LEFCOL+1        ;Reset column to left
            CALL    Q20CURS             ;Set cursor
            RET
D10DISP     ENDP
;                    Clear screen:
;                    ------------
Q10CLEAR    PROC    NEAR
            MOV     AX,0600H
            MOV     BH,61H              ;Blue on brown
            MOV     CX,0000             ;Full screen
            MOV     DX,184FH
            INT     10H                 ;Call BIOS
            RET
Q10CLEAR    ENDP

;                    Set cursor row:column:
;                    ---------------------
Q20CURS     PROC    NEAR
            MOV     AH,02H
            MOV     BH,00               ;Page 0
            MOV     DH,ROW              ;Row
            MOV     DL,COL              ;Column
            INT     10H
            RET
Q20CURS     ENDP
            END     A10MAIN
```

Figure 11-2c Selecting an Item from a Menu

trying to move the cursor above the first menu line sets it to the last line, and vice versa. The routine also calls D10DISP to reset the previous menu line to normal video and the new (selected) menu line to reverse video.

- D10DISP displays the currently selected line according to an attribute (normal or reverse video) that has been provided.
- Q10CLEAR clears the entire screen and sets it to blue foreground and brown background.

The program illustrates menu selection in a simple manner; a full program would execute a routine for each selected item. You'll get a better understanding of this program by typing it in as an .ASM file, assembling it, and testing it.

BIOS INT 09H AND THE KEYBOARD BUFFER

When you press a key, the keyboard's processor generates the key's scan code and requests INT 09H. This interrupt (at location 36 of the interrupt services table) points to an interrupt-handling routine in ROM BIOS. The routine issues a request for input from port 96 (60H): IN AL,60H. The BIOS routine reads the scan code and compares it with entries in a scan code table for the associated ASCII character (if any). The routine combines the scan code with its associated ASCII character and delivers the two bytes to the keyboard buffer. Figure 11-3 illustrates this procedure.

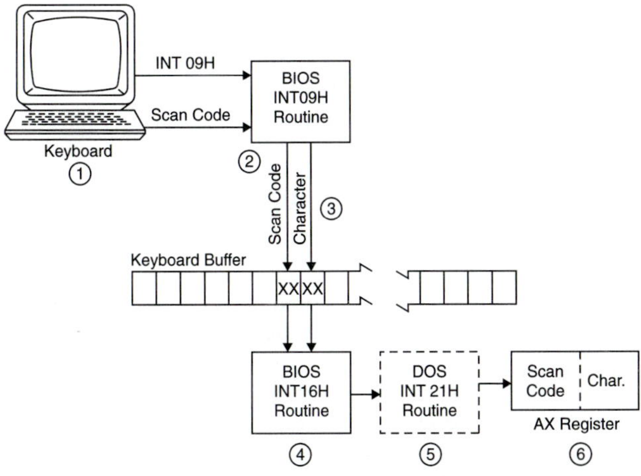
INT 09H
Scan Code
BIOS INT09H Routine
Keyboard
①
②
Scan Code
Character
③
Keyboard Buffer
XX XX
BIOS INT16H Routine
DOS INT 21H Routine
Scan Code
Char.
AX Register
④
⑤
⑥
① Keyboard generates INT 09H.
② INT 09H operation accepts scan code from keyboard and finds its associated character (if any).
③ INT 09H delivers character and scan code to the keyboard buffer.
④ & ⑤ Program requests INT 16H either directly or via INT 21H.
⑥ INT 16H accesses buffer and delivers character to AL and scan code to AH.

Figure 11-3 Keyboard Buffer

Note that INT 09H handles the keyboard status bytes at 40:17H, 40:18H and 40:96H for <Shift>, <Alt>, and <Ctrl>. Although pressing these keys generates INT 09H, the interrupt routine sets the appropriate bits in the status bytes, but doesn't deliver any characters to the keyboard buffer. Also, INT 09H ignores undefined keystroke combinations.

When you *press* a key, the keyboard processor automatically generates a scan code and issues INT 09H. When you *release* the key within one-half second, it generates a second scan code (the value of the first code plus 1000 0000B, which sets the leftmost bit) and issues another INT 09H. The second scan code tells the interrupt routine that you have released the key. If you hold the key for more than one-half second, the keyboard process becomes typematic; that is, it automatically repeats the key operation.

The keyboard buffer requires one address (the head of the buffer) to tell INT 16H from where to read the next character and another address (the tail of the buffer) to tell INT 09H where to store the next character. The two addresses are offsets within segment 40[0]H. The following describes the contents of the buffer:

ADDRESS	EXPLANATION
41AH	Address of the current head of the buffer, the next position for INT 16H to read a character.
41CH	Address of the current tail of the buffer, the next position for INT 09H to store an entered character.
41EH	Address of the beginning of the keyboard buffer itself. The buffer contains 16 words (32 bytes), although it can be longer, and holds keyboard characters and their associated scan codes as entered. Subsequently, INT 16H will read each character and its scan code and deliver them to the program. Two bytes are required for each character and scan code.

When you type a character, INT 09H advances the tail. When INT 16H reads a character, it advances the head. In this way, the process is circular, with the head continually chasing the tail.

When the buffer is *empty* (INT 16H has read all the stored characters), the head and tail are at the same address. In the following example, a user has keyed ahead the characters 'abc<Enter>'. INT 09H stores the characters as follows:

- 'a' in the buffer at 41EH and its scan code 1EH at 41FH;
- 'b' in the buffer at 420H and its scan code 30H at 421H;
- 'c' in the buffer at 422H and its scan code 2EH at 423H;
- the <Enter> at 424H and its scan code E0H at 425H.

At this point, INT 09H has advanced the tail to 426H:

```
 a   1EH   b   30H   c   2EH <Ent> E0H  . . .
 |    |    |    |    |    |    |    |    |
41E  41F  420  421  422  423  424  425  426
```

Once the program has issued INT 16H five times, it has read all the characters and advanced the tail to 426H; because the tail has the same address as the head, the buffer is now empty.

When the user keys in 15 characters, the buffer is *full,* and the tail is immediately behind the head. To see this, suppose the user now types ahead 'fghijklmnopqrs<Enter>'. INT 09H stores the characters beginning with the tail at 426H and circles around to store the '<Enter>' at 422H. The tail is now advanced to 424H, immediately before the head at 426H:

```
 r   s  <Ent> *   f   g   h   i   j   k   l   m   n   o   p   q
 |   |    |   |   |   |   |   |   |   |   |   |   |   |   |   |
41E 420  422 424 426 428 42A 42C 42E 430 432 434 436 438 43A 43C
```

At this point, INT 09H does not accept any more typed characters and, indeed, accepts only 15 at most, although the buffer holds 16. (Can you tell why? If INT 09H were to accept another character, it would advance the tail to the same address as the head, and INT 16H would incorrectly suppose that the buffer is empty.)

The Shift, Ctrl, and Alt Keys

INT 09H also handles the keyboard status byte at 40:17H in the BIOS data area, as well as at 40:18H and 40:96H for the enhanced keyboard. When you press <Shift>, <Ctrl>, or <Alt>, the BIOS routine sets the appropriate bit to 1, and when you release the key, it clears the bit to 0. Your program may test whether any of the control keys are pressed by means of INT 16H function 02H or by direct reference to the status byte.

The .COM program in Figure 11-4 illustrates the use of direct reference to the status byte at 40:17H. The program uses the SEGMENT AT feature to define the BIOS data area as, in effect, a dummy segment. KBSTATE identifies the location of the keyboard status byte at 40:17H. The code segment contains the following procedures:

- A10MAIN initializes the address of BIOSDATA in the ES (because the DS contains the segment address of the defined data), waits for the user to press a key and, if other than <Enter>, calls B10TEST. Pressing <Enter> tells the program to end.
- B10TEST transfers the keyboard status byte to the BL:
  ```
  MOV BL,ES:KBSTATE
  ```
  The ES: segment override operation tells the assembler to relate the offset address of KBSTATE with the segment address in the ES. If any of the <Shift>, <Ctrl>, or <Alt> keys were pressed, the procedure calls C10DISP. Note that just pressing a control key alone does not satisfy INT 16H; you have to press it in common with another key that causes a valid keyboard entry, such as <Shift>+<A>, <Ctrl>+<F1>, etc. (See Appendix F.) The keyboard status byte reflects the action of the control key.
- C10DISP displays the appropriate message for the pressed control key.

You could modify this program to test as well for the enhanced keyboard status bytes at 40:18H and 40:96H.

```
TITLE      A11KBSTA (COM) Testing Alt, Shift, & Ctrl
BIODATA    SEGMENT AT 40H              ;Locate BIOS data area
           ORG  17H                    ; and
KBSTATE    DB  ?                       ; status byte
BIODATA    ENDS

CODESG     SEGMENT PARA
           ASSUME  CS:CODESG,DS:BIODATA
           ORG  100H
BEGIN:     JMP  A10MAIN
ALTKEY     DB   'Alt key pressed', '$'
CTRLKEY    DB   'Ctrl key pressed', '$'
SHIFKEY    DB   'Shift key pressed', '$'

A10MAIN    PROC
           MOV  AX,BIODATA             ;Initialize seg. address
           MOV  ES,AX                  ; of BIODATA in ES
A30:
           MOV  AH,10H                 ;Request keyboard entry
           INT  16H
           CMP  AL,0DH                 ;User requests end?
           JE   A90                    ; yes, exit
           CALL B10TEST
           JMP  A30                    ;Repeat
A90:
           MOV  AX,4C00H               ;End processing
           INT  21H
A10MAIN    ENDP

B10TEST    PROC
           MOV  BL,ES:KBSTATE          ;Get keyboard status byte
           TEST BL,00000011B           ;Either Shift pressed?
           JZ   B20                    ; no, bypass
           LEA  DX,SHIFKEY
           CALL C10DISP
B20:
           TEST BL,00000100B           ;Ctrl key pressed?
           JZ   B30                    ; no, bypass
           LEA  DX,CTRLKEY
           CALL C10DISP
B30:
           TEST BL,00001000B           ;Alt key pressed?
           JZ   B90                    ; no, bypass
           LEA  DX,ALTKEY
           CALL C10DISP
B90:
           RET
B10TEST    ENDP

C10DISP    PROC
           MOV  AH,09H                 ;Request display
           INT  21H
           RET
C10DISP    ENDP
CODESG     ENDS
           END  BEGIN
```

Figure 11-4 Checking the Keyboard Status Byte

KEYING IN THE FULL ASCII CHARACTER SET

The entire ASCII set consists of 256 characters numbered 0 through 255 (FFH). Many of these are standard displayable characters, from ASCII 20H (space) through ASCII 7EH (the tilde character ~). Because of keyboard limitations, most of the 256 ASCII characters are not represented on it. You can, however, key in any of the ASCII codes 01 through 255 by holding down <Alt> and keying in the appropriate code as a decimal value on the numeric keypad. The system stores your entered value as two bytes in the keyboard buffer: The first is the generated ASCII character and the second is zero. For example, <Alt>+001 delivers 01H, and <Alt>+255 delivers FFH. You could use INT 16H with DEBUG's A command to examine the effect of entering various values:

```
100  MOV  AH,10
102  INT  16
104  JMP  100
```

See Appendix B for a complete table of ASCII values.

KEY POINTS

- The shift status bytes in the BIOS data area at 40:17H and 40:18H indicate the current status of such keys as <Ctrl>, <Alt>, <Shift>, <CapsLock>, <NumLock>, and <ScrollLock>.
- INT 21H keyboard operations provide a variety of services to echo or not echo characters on the screen, to recognize or ignore <Ctrl>+<Break>, and to accept scan codes.
- INT 16H provides the basic BIOS keyboard operations for accepting characters from the keyboard buffer. For a character key, the operation delivers the character to the AL and the key's scan code to the AH. For an extended function key, the operation delivers 00H or E0H to the AL and the key's scan code to the AH.
- The scan code is a unique number assigned to each key that enables the system to identify the source of a pressed key and enables a program to check for extended function keys such as <Home>, <PgUp>, and <Arrow>.
- BIOS data area at 40:1EH contains the keyboard buffer, which allows you to type ahead up to 15 characters before a program requests input.
- When you press a key, the keyboard's processor generates the key's scan code and requests INT 09H. When you release the key, it generates a second scan code (the first code plus 10000000B, which sets the leftmost bit) to tell INT 09H that the key is released.
- BIOS INT 09H retrieves a scan code from the keyboard. The operation uses the scan code to generate an associated ASCII character, which it delivers to the keyboard buffer area. BIOS may also set the status for <Ctrl>, <Alt>, or <Shift>.

QUESTIONS

11-1. (a) What is the location of the first byte of the keyboard shift status in the BIOS data area? (b) What do the contents 00000010 mean? (c) What do the contents 00001100 mean?

11-2. Describe the features of the following functions for INT 21H keyboard input: (a) 01H; (b) 07H; (c) 08H; (d) 0AH.

11-3. Explain the differences among INT 16H functions 00H, 10H, and 11H.

11-4. Provide the scan codes for the following keyboard functions: (a) Home; (b) PgDn; (c) DownArrow; (d) function key F8.

11-5. Use DEBUG to examine the effects of entered keystrokes. To request entry of assembly statements, type A 100 and key in the following instructions:

```
MOV AH,10 (or AH,00)
INT 16
JMP 100
```

Use U 100,104 to unassemble the program, and use the P command to get DEBUG to execute through the INT. Execution stops, waiting for your input. Press any key and examine the AH and AL registers. Continue typing a variety of keys. Press Q to quit DEBUG.

11-6. Code the instructions for INT 16H to accept a keystroke; if <PgUp>, set the cursor to column 0, row 0.

11-7. Revise Figure 11-2 to provide for the following features: (a) Revise the drop shadow from full shadow to three-quarter dots on (B2H). (b) After the initial clearing of the screen, display a prompt that asks users to press <F1> for a menu screen. (c) When <F1> is pressed, display the menu. (d) Allow users to select menu items also by pressing the first character (upper- or lowercase) of each item. (e) On request of an item, display a message for that particular selection, such as "Procedure to Delete Records." (f) Add a last line to the menu containing the item "Exit from program" that allows users to end processing. You'll also have to revise the procedure B10MENU to handle the display of another row.

11-8. Under what circumstances does an INT 09H occur?

11-9. Explain in simple terms how INT 09H handles <Alt> and <Ctrl> differently from the way it handles the standard keyboard keys.

11-10. (a) Where is the BIOS memory location of the keyboard buffer? (b) What is the buffer's size, in bytes? (c) How many keyboard characters can it contain?

11-11. Explain the effect of the following occurrences in the keyboard buffer: (a) The address of the head and tail are the same; (b) the address of the tail immediately follows the head.

11-12. Revise Figure 11-4 for the following requirements: (a) Test also for <CapsLock> and <NumLock>; (b) transfer the contents of the second byte of the keyboard shift status to the BH; (c) test also for <LeftAlt> and <LeftCtrl> pressed, and display an appropriate message.

PART D—DATA MANIPULATION

12 PROCESSING STRING DATA

Objective: To explain the special instructions used to process string data.

INTRODUCTION

Up to this chapter, the instructions presented have handled data defined as only one byte, word, or doubleword. It is often necessary, however, to move or compare data fields that exceed these lengths. For example, you may want to compare descriptions or names in order to sort them into ascending sequence. Items of this type are known as *string data* and may be in either character or numeric format. Assembly language provides these string instructions for processing string data internally:

MOVS	Moves one byte, word, or doubleword from one location in memory to another.
LODS	Loads from memory a byte into the AL, a word into the AX, or a doubleword into the EAX.
STOS	Stores the contents of the AL, AX, or EAX registers into memory.
CMPS	Compares byte, word, or doubleword memory locations.
SCAS	Compares the contents of the AL, AX, or EAX with the contents of a memory location.

Two other string operations, INS and OUTS, are covered in Chapter 21. An associated instruction, the REP prefix, causes a string instruction to perform repetitively so that it may process any number of bytes, words, or doublewords a specified number of times.

FEATURES OF STRING OPERATIONS

A string instruction can specify the repetitive processing of one byte, word, or doubleword (80386 and later) at a time. Thus you could select a byte operation for a string with an odd number of bytes and a word operation for a string with an even number of bytes. Each string instruction has a byte, word, and doubleword version and assumes use of the ES:DI or DS:SI pair of registers.

The string instructions expect that the DI and SI contain valid offset addresses that reference bytes in memory. The SI register is normally associated with the DS (data segment) register as DS:SI. The DI register is always associated with the ES (extra segment) register as ES:DI. For this reason, MOVS, STOS, CMPS, and SCAS require that an .EXE program initialize the ES register, usually, but not necessarily, with the same address as that in the DS register:

```
MOV  AX,@data     ;Get address of data segment,
MOV  DS,AX        ;  store it in DS
MOV  ES,AX        ;  and in ES
```

Figure 12-1 shows the registers associated with each string instruction.

There are basically two ways to code string instructions:

1. In Figure 12-1, the second column shows the basic format for each operation, which uses the implied operands listed in the third column (if you code an instruction as MOVS, you include the operands—for example, as MOVS BYTE1,BYTE2, where the definition of the operands indicates the length of the move). A later section, "Alternative Coding for String Instructions," describes this format in more detail.
2. The second way to code string instructions is the standard practice, as shown in the fourth, fifth, and sixth columns of Figure 12-1. You load the addresses of the operands in the DI and SI registers and code the instruction without operands, for example, as:

```
LEA    DI,BYTE2     ;Address of BYTE2
LEA    SI,BYTE1     ;Address of BYTE1
MOVSB               ;Move BYTE1 to BYTE2
```

REP: REPEAT STRING PREFIX

The REP prefix immediately before a string instruction, such as REP MOVSB, provides for repeated execution based on an initial count that you set in the CX register. REP executes the string instruction, decrements the CX, and repeats this operation until the count in the CX is zero. In this way, you can process strings of virtually any length.

Oper-ation	Basic Instruction	Implied Operands	Byte Operation	Word Operation	Doubleword Operation
Move	MOVS	ES:DI,DS:SI	MOVSB	MOVSW	MOVSD
Load	LODS	AX,DS:SI	LODSB	LODSW	LODSD
Store	STOS	ES:DI,AX	STOSB	STOSW	STOSD
Compare	CMPS	DS:SI,ES:DI	CMPSB	CMPSW	CMPSD
Scan	SCAS	ES:DI,AX	SCASB	SCASW	SCASD

Figure 12-1 Formats for the String Instructions

The direction flag (DF) determines the direction of a repeated operation:

- For processing from left to right (the normal practice), use CLD to clear the DF to zero.
- For processing from right to left, use STD to set the DF to 1.

In the following example, assume that the DS and ES are both initialized with the address of the data segment, as shown earlier. A REP MOVSB operation moves (or rather, copies) the 25 bytes of DATASTR1 to DATASTR2:

```
DATASTR1  DB    25 DUP('*')    ;Sending field
DATASTR2  DB    25 DUP(' ')    ;Receiving field
          ...
          CLD                  ;Clear direction flag
          MOV   CX,25          ;Initialize for 25 bytes
          LEA   DI,DATASTR2    ;Initialize receiving address
          LEA   SI,DATASTR1    ;Initialize sending address
          REP  MOVSB           ;Copy DATASTR1 to DATASTR2
```

During execution, CMPS and SCAS also set status flags, so that the operations can end immediately on finding a specified condition. The variations of REP for this purpose are the following:

- REP Repeat the operation until the CX is decremented to zero.
- REPE or REPZ Repeat the operation while the zero flag (ZF) indicates equal/zero. Stop when the ZF indicates not equal/zero or when the CX is decremented to zero.
- REPNE or REPNZ Repeat the operation while the ZF indicates not equal/zero. Stop when the ZF indicates equal or zero or when the CX is decremented to zero.

The use of word and doubleword operations can provide faster processing. We'll now examine each string operation in detail.

MOVS: MOVE STRING INSTRUCTION

MOVSB, MOVSW, and MOVSD combined with a REP prefix and a length in the CX can move any number of characters. Although you don't code the operands, the instruction looks like this:

[label:]	REP MOVSn	[ES:DI,DS:SI]

For the receiving string, the segment:offset registers are the ES:DI; for the sending string, the segment:offset registers are the DS:SI. As a result, at the start of an .EXE program, initialize the ES register along with the DS register, and prior to executing the MOVS, use LEA to initialize the DI and SI registers. Depending on the direction flag, MOVS increments or decrements the DI and SI registers by 1 for byte, 2 for word, and 4 for doubleword. The following example illustrates moving 10 words:

```
MOV   CX,10          ;Number of words
LEA   DI,STRING2     ;Address of STRING2
LEA   SI,STRING1     ;Address of STRING1
REP  MOVSW          ;Move 10 words
```

The instructions equivalent to the REP MOVSW operation are:

```
      JCXZ  J90       ;Bypass if CX initially zero
J30:  MOV  AX,[SI]    ;Get word from STRING1
      MOV  [DI],AX    ;Store word in STRING2
      ADD  DI,2       ;Increment for next word
      ADD  SI,2       ;
      LOOP J30        ;Decrement CX and repeat
J90:  ...
```

Earlier, Figure 6-2 illustrated moving a 9-byte field. The program could also have used MOVSB for this purpose. In Figure 12-2, the procedure B10MVSB uses MOVSB to move a 10-byte field, HEADG1, 1 byte at a time to HEADG2. The first instruction, CLD, clears the direction flag to zero so that the MOVSB processes data from left to right. The direction flag is normally zero at the start of execution, but CLD is coded here as a precaution.

The two LEA instructions load the SI and DI registers with the offset addresses of HEADG1 and HEADG2, respectively. Because the loader for a .COM program automatically initializes the DS and ES registers, the segment:offset addresses are correct for ES:DI and DS:SI. A MOV instruction initializes the CX with 10 (the length of HEADG1 and of HEADG2). The instruction REP MOVSB now performs the following:

- Moves the leftmost byte of HEADG1 (addressed by DS:SI) to the leftmost byte of HEADG2 (addressed by ES:DI);
- Increments the DI and SI by 1 for the next bytes to the right;
- Decrements the CX by 1;
- Repeats this operation, 10 loops in all, until the CX becomes zero.

Because the direction flag is zero and MOVSB increments DI and SI, each iteration processes 1 byte farther to the right, as HEADG1+1 to HEADG2+1, and so on. At the end of execution, the CX contains 00, the DI contains the address of HEADG2+10, and the SI contains the address of HEADG1+10—both 1 byte past the end of the name.

```
TITLE      A12MOVST (COM)  Use of MOVSn string operations
           .MODEL SMALL
           .CODE
           ORG    100H
BEGIN:     JMP    SHORT A10MAIN
; ---------------------------------------------------------------
HEADG1     DB     'Cybernauts'           ;Data items
HEADG2     DB     10 DUP(' ')
HEADG3     DB     10 DUP(' ')
; ---------------------------------------------------------------
A10MAIN    PROC   NEAR                   ;Main procedure
           CALL   B10MVSB                ;MVSB subroutine
           CALL   C10MVSW                ;MVSW subroutine
           MOV    AX,4C00H               ;End of processing
           INT    21H
A10MAIN    ENDP
;                 Use of MOVSB:
;                 ------------
B10MVSB    PROC   NEAR
           CLD                           ;Left to right
           MOV    CX,10                  ;Move 10 bytes,
           LEA    DI,HEADG2              ;  HEADG1 to HEADG2
           LEA    SI,HEADG1
           REP MOVSB
           RET
B10MVSB    ENDP
;                 Use of MOVSW:
;                 ------------
C10MVSW    PROC   NEAR
           CLD                           ;Left to right
           MOV    CX,05                  ;Move 5 words,
           LEA    DI,HEADG3              ;  HEADG2 to HEADG3
           LEA    SI,HEADG2
           REP MOVSW
           RET
C10MVSW    ENDP
           END    BEGIN
```

Figure 12-2 Using MOVS String Operations

If the direction flag is 1, MOVSB would decrement DI and SI, causing processing to occur from right to left. But in that case, to move the contents correctly, you would have to initialize the SI with HEADG1+9 and the DI with HEADG2+9.

The next procedure in Figure 12-2, C10MVSW, uses MOVSW to move five words from HEADG2 to HEADG3. At the end of execution, the CX contains 00, the DI contains the address of HEADG3+10, and the SI contains the address of HEADG2+10.

Because MOVSW increments the DI and SI registers by 2, the operation requires only 5 loops. For processing *right to left*, set the direction flag and initialize the SI with HEADG1+8 and the DI with HEADG2+8.

LODS: LOAD STRING INSTRUCTION

LODS simply loads the AL with a byte, the AX with a word, or the EAX with a doubleword from memory. The memory address is subject to the DS:SI registers, although you can override the SI. Depending on the direction flag, the operation also increments or decrements the SI by 1 for byte, 2 for word, and 4 for doubleword.

Because one LODS operation fills the register, there is no practical reason to use the REP prefix with it. For most purposes, a simple MOV instruction is adequate. But MOV generates 3 bytes of machine code, whereas LODS generates only 1, although it requires that you initialize the SI register. You could use LODS to step through a string 1 byte, word, or doubleword at a time, examining successively for a particular character.

The instructions equivalent to LODSB are

```
MOV  AL,[SI]      ;Transfer byte to AL
INC  SI           ;Increment SI for next byte (sets flags)
```

In Figure 12-3, the data area defines a 10-byte field named HEADG1 containing the value "Cybernauts" and another 10-byte field named HEADG2. The objective is to transfer the bytes from HEADG1 to HEADG2 in reverse sequence, so that HEADG2 contains "stuanrebyC." LODSB is used to access 1 byte at a time from HEADG1 into the AL, and the instruction MOV [DI],AL transfers the bytes to HEADG2, from right to left.

STOS: STORE STRING INSTRUCTION

STOS stores the contents of the AL, AX, or EAX register into a byte, word, or doubleword in memory. The memory address is always subject to the ES:DI registers. Depending on the direction flag, STOS also increments or decrements the DI register by 1 for byte, 2 for word, and 4 for doubleword.

```
TITLE     A12LODST (COM)  Use of LODSB string operation
          .MODEL  SMALL
          .CODE
          ORG     100H
BEGIN:    JMP     SHORT A10MAIN
; ---------------------------------------------------------------
HEADG1    DB      'Cybernauts'      ;Data items
HEADG2    DB      10 DUP(20H)
; ---------------------------------------------------------------
A10MAIN   PROC    NEAR              ;Main procedure
          CLD                       ;Left to right
          MOV     CX,10
          LEA     SI,HEADG1         ;Load address of HEADG1
          LEA     DI,HEADG2+9       ;Load address of HEADG2+9
A20:      LODSB                     ;Get character in AL,
          MOV     [DI],AL           ;  store in HEADG2,
          DEC     DI                ;  right to left
          LOOP    A20               ;Ten characters?
          MOV     AX,4C00H          ;  yes, exit
          INT     21H
A10MAIN   ENDP
          END     BEGIN
```

Figure 12-3 Using LODSB String Operation

A practical use of STOS with a REP prefix is to initialize a data area to any specified value, such as clearing a display area to blanks. You set the number of bytes, words, or doublewords in the CX. The instructions equivalent to REP STOSB are:

```
        JCXZ     P30          ;Jump if CX zero
P20:    MOV      [DI],AL      ;Store AL in memory
        INC/DEC  DI           ;Increment or decrement (sets flags)
        LOOP     P20          ;Decrement CX and repeat
P30:    ...                   ;Operation complete
```

The STOSW instruction in Figure 12-4 repeatedly stores a word containing 2020H (blanks) five times through HEADG1. The operation stores the AL in the first byte and the AH in the next byte (that is, reversed). At the end, all of HEADG1 is blank, the CX contains 00, and the DI contains the address of HEADG1+10.

```
TITLE     A12STOST (COM)  Use of STOSW string operation
          .MODEL SMALL
          .CODE
          ORG     100H
BEGIN:    JMP     SHORT A10MAIN
; ---------------------------------------------------------
HEADG1    DB      'Cybernauts'          ;Data item
; ---------------------------------------------------------
A10MAIN   PROC    NEAR                  ;Main procedure
          CLD                           ;Left to right
          MOV     AX,2020H              ;Move
          MOV     CX,05                 ;5 blank words
          LEA     DI,HEADG1             ;to HEADG1
          REP STOSW
          MOV     AX,4C00H              ;End of processing
          INT     21H
A10MAIN   ENDP
          END     BEGIN
```

Figure 12-4 Using STOSW String Operation

PROGRAM: USING LODS AND STOS TO TRANSFER DATA

The program in Figure 12-5 illustrates the use of both the LODS and STOS instructions. The example is similar to the program in Figure 10-4, which transfers characters and attributes directly to the video display area, except that Figure 12-5 contains these differences:

- For the video area, the program uses video page 2 rather than page 1.
- In B10PROC, it uses STOSW to store characters and associated attributes in the video area, instead of this instruction and its accompanying two DEC instructions that decrement the DI:
  `MOV WORD PTR [VIDAREA+DI],AX`
- It defines an item named PROMPT in the data segment, prompting the user to "Press any key . . . ", to be used at the end of processing.
- On completion of processing, the procedure C10PROMPT transfers the defined prompt to the video display area. To this end, it uses LODSB to access characters one

```
TITLE    A12DRVID (EXE)  Direct video display
         .MODEL SMALL
; ---------------------------------------------------------
VIDSEG   SEGMENT AT 0BA00H          ;Page 2 of video area
VIDAREA  DB  1000H DUP(?)
VIDSEG   ENDS
; ---------------------------------------------------------
         .DATA
PROMPT   DB      'Press any key...'
; ---------------------------------------------------------
         .STACK 64
; ---------------------------------------------------------
         .CODE
A10MAIN  PROC    FAR
         MOV     AX,@data           ;Addressability for
         MOV     DS,AX              ;  data segment
         MOV     AX,VIDSEG          ;  and for
         MOV     ES,AX              ;  video area
         ASSUME  ES:VIDSEG
         MOV     AH,0FH             ;Request get
         INT     10H                ;  and save
         PUSH    AX                 ;  current mode
         PUSH    BX                 ;  and page
         MOV     AH,00H             ;Request set
         MOV     AL,03              ;  mode 03, clear screen
         INT     10H
         MOV     AH,05H             ;Request set
         MOV     AL,02H             ;  page #02
         INT     10H
         CALL    B10PROC            ;Process display area
         CALL    C10PROMPT          ;Display user prompt
         CALL    D10INPT            ;Provide for input
         MOV     AH,05H             ;Restore
         POP     BX                 ;original
         MOV     AL,BH              ;page number
         INT     10H
         POP     AX                 ;Restore video
         MOV     AH,00H             ;mode (in AL)
         INT     10H
         MOV     AX,4C00H           ;End of processing
         INT     21H
A10MAIN  ENDP
;                Store character & attribute in video area:
;                ---------------------------------------
B10PROC  PROC    NEAR
         MOV     AL,41H             ;Character to display
         MOV     AH,01H             ;Attribute
         MOV     DI,660             ;Start of display area
B30:     MOV     CX,60              ;Characters per row
         REP STOSW                  ;Repeat 60 times
         INC     AH                 ;Next attribute
         INC     AL                 ;Next character
         ADD     DI,40              ;Indent for next row
         CMP     AL,51H             ;Last character to display?
         JNE     B30                ;  no, repeat
         RET                        ;  yes, return
B10PROC  ENDP
```

Figure 12-5 Using Direct Video Display

```
;                   Move prompt to video area:
;                   -------------------------
C10PROMPT PROC   NEAR
          MOV    AH,03H                 ;New attribute in AH
          MOV    CX,16                  ;Characters to display
          MOV    DI,3840                ;Location in display area
          LEA    SI,PROMPT              ;Address of prompt
C20:      LODSB                         ;Character into AL
          STOSW                         ;Store in display area
          LOOP   C20                    ;16 times
          RET                           ;Return
C10PROMPT ENDP
;                   Accept input:
;                   -------------
D10INPT   PROC   NEAR
          MOV    AH,10H                 ;Request keyboard
          INT    16H                    ;  input
          RET
D10INPT   ENDP
          END    A10MAIN
```

Figure 12-5 Using Direct Video Display

at a time from PROMPT into the AL and uses STOSW to transfer each character and its associated attribute from the AX into the video area.

CMPS: COMPARE STRING INSTRUCTION

CMPS compares the contents of one memory location (addressed by DS:SI) with that of another memory location (addressed by ES:DI). Depending on the direction flag, CMPS also increments or decrements the SI and DI registers, by 1 for byte, 2 for word, and 4 for doubleword. The operation sets the AF, CF, OF, PF, SF, and ZF flags. When combined with a REPnn prefix and a length in the CX, CMPS can successively compare strings of any length.

But note that CMPS provides an *alphanumeric* comparison, that is, a comparison according to ASCII values. The operation is not suited to algebraic comparisons, which consist of signed numeric values.

Consider the comparison of two strings containing "Jean" and "Joan." A comparison from left to right, one byte at a time, results in the following:

J : J   Equal
e : o   Unequal (e is low)
a : a   Equal
n : n   Equal

A comparison of the entire 4 bytes ends with a comparison of "n" with "n" (equal). Now since the two names are not identical, the operation should end as soon as it makes a comparison between two different characters. For this purpose, the REP variation, REPE (Repeat on Equal), repeats the operation as long as the comparison is between equal characters, or until the CX register equals zero. The coding for repeated 1-byte comparisons is REPE CMPSB.

Figure 12-6 consists of two examples that use CMPSB. The first example compares HEADG1 with HEADG2, which contain the same values. The CMPSB operation therefore continues for the entire 10 bytes. At the end of execution, the CX contains 00, the DI contains the address of HEADG2+10, the SI contains the address of HEADG1+10, the sign flag is positive, and the zero flag indicates equal or zero.

The second example compares HEADG2 with HEADG3, which contain different values. The CMPSB operation terminates after comparing the first byte and results in a high/unequal condition: The CX contains 09, the DI contains the address of HEADG3+1, the SI contains the address of HEADG2+1, the sign flag is positive, and the zero flag indicates unequal.

The first example results in equal or zero and (for illustrative reasons only) moves 01 to the BH register. The second example results in unequal and moves 02 to the BL register. If you use DEBUG to trace the instructions, you'll see 0102 in the BX at the end of execution.

Warning!: These examples use CMPSB to compare data one byte at a time. If you use CMPSW to compare data a word at a time, you have to initialize CX to 5. But that's not the problem. When comparing words, CMPSW reverses the bytes. For example, let's compare the names SAMUEL and ARNOLD. For the initial comparison of words, instead of comparing SA with AR, the operation compares AS with RA. So, instead of the name SAMUEL indicating a higher value, it incorrectly compares as lower. CMPSW works correctly only if the compared fields contain unsigned numeric data defined as DW, DD, or DQ (that is, with the data stored in reversed-byte sequence).

```
TITLE     A12CMPST (COM)  Use of CMPS string operations
          .MODEL SMALL
          .CODE
          ORG    100H
BEGIN:    JMP    SHORT A10MAIN
; ---------------------------------------------------------
HEADG1    DB     'Cybernauts'      ;Data items
HEADG2    DB     'Cybernauts'
HEADG3    DB     10 DUP(' ')
; ---------------------------------------------------------
A10MAIN   PROC   NEAR              ;Main procedure
          CLD                      ;Left to right
          MOV    CX,10             ;Initialize for 10 bytes
          LEA    DI,HEADG2
          LEA    SI,HEADG1
          REPE CMPSB               ;Compare HEADG1 : HEADG2
          JNE    A20               ;  not equal, bypass
          MOV    BH,01             ;  equal, set BH
A20:
          MOV    CX,10             ;Initialize for 10 bytes
          LEA    DI,HEADG3
          LEA    SI,HEADG2
          REPE CMPSB               ;Compare HEADG2 : HEADG3
          JE     A30               ;  equal, exit
          MOV    BL,02             ;  not equal, set BL
A30:
          MOV    AX,4C00H          ;End of processing
          INT    21H
A10MAIN   ENDP
          END    BEGIN
```

Figure 12-6 Using CMPS String Operations

SCAS: SCAN STRING INSTRUCTION

SCAS differs slightly from CMPS in that SCAS *scans* a string for a specified byte, word, or doubleword value. SCAS compares the contents of a memory location (addressed by ES:DI) with the contents of the AL, AX, or EAX. Depending on the direction flag, SCAS also increments or decrements the DI register by 1 for byte, 2 for word, and 4 for doubleword. At the end of execution, SCAS sets the AF, CF, OF, PF, SF, and ZF flags. When combined with a REPnn prefix and a length in the CX, SCAS can scan any string length.

SCAS would be particularly useful for a text-editing application in which the program has to scan for punctuation, such as periods, commas, and blanks.

The program in Figure 12-7 scans HEADG1 for the lowercase letter 'r'. Because the SCASB operation is to continue scanning while the comparison is not equal or until the CX is zero, the operation in this case is REPNE SCASB.

```
TITLE     A12SCAST (COM)  Use of SCASB string operation
          .MODEL SMALL
          .CODE
          ORG    100H
BEGIN:    JMP    SHORT A10MAIN
; -----------------------------------------------------
HEADG1    DB     'Cybernauts'            ;Data item
; -----------------------------------------------------
A10MAIN   PROC   NEAR                    ;Main procedure
          CLD                            ;Left to right
          MOV    AL,'r'
          MOV    CX,10                   ;Scan HEADG1
          LEA    DI,HEADG1               ;  for 'r'
          REPNE  SCASB
          JNE    A20                     ;If found,
          MOV    AL,03                   ;  store 03 in AL
A20:
          MOV    AH,4CH
          INT    21H                     ;End of processing
A10MAIN   ENDP
          END    BEGIN
```

Figure 12-7 Using SCASB String Operation

When scanning the string "Cybernauts" in HEADG1, SCASB finds a match on the fifth comparison. If you use DEBUG to trace the instructions, at the end of execution of the REP SCASB operation you will see that the zero flag shows zero, the CX is decremented to 05, and the DI is incremented by 05. (The DI is incremented 1 byte past the actual location of the 'r'.)

The program stores 03 in the AL register (for illustrative reasons) to indicate that the character was found.

SCASW scans for a word in memory that matches the word in the AX register. If you used LODSW or MOV to transfer a word into the AX register, the first byte would be in the AL and the second byte in the AH. Because SCASW compares the bytes in reversed sequence, the operation works correctly.

EXAMPLE: USING SCAN AND REPLACE

You may also want to replace a specific character with another character, for example, to clear editing characters such as paragraph and end-of-page symbols from a document. The following example scans TSTDATA for an asterisk (*) and replaces it with a blank. If SCASB locates an asterisk, it ends the operation. TSTDATA contains an asterisk at TSTDATA+5, where the blank is to be inserted, although SCASB will have incremented the DI register to TSTDATA+6. Decrementing the DI by 1 [DI-1] provides the correct address to insert the blank replacement character.

```
DATALEN   EQU 13                       ;Length of TSTDATA
TSTDATA   DB  'Extra*innings'
          ...
          CLD                          ;Set left to right
          MOV AL,'*'                   ;Search character
          MOV CX,DATALEN               ;Length of TSTDATA
          LEA DI,TSTDATA               ;Address of TSTDATA
          REPNE SCASB                  ;Scan TSTDATA
          JNE E20                      ;Character found?
          MOV BYTE PTR[DI-1],20H       ;Yes, replace with blank
E20:      ...
```

ALTERNATIVE CODING FOR STRING INSTRUCTIONS

As discussed earlier, if you code a string instruction explicitly with a B, W, or D suffix, such as MOVSB, MOVSW, or MOVSD, the assembler assumes the correct length and does not require operands. You can also use the basic instruction formats for the string operations. For an instruction such as MOVS, which has no suffix to indicate byte, word, or doubleword, the operands must indicate the length. For example, if CHAR1 and CHAR2 are defined as DB, the instruction

```
REP MOVS CHAR1,CHAR2
```

implies a repeated move of the byte beginning at CHAR2 to the byte beginning at CHAR1.

Another format allows you to refer to the segment registers explicitly and to use the PTR directive. If you load the DI and SI registers with the addresses of CHAR1 and CHAR2, you can code the MOVS instruction as

```
LEA  DI,CHAR2
LEA  SI,CHAR1
REP  MOVS ES:BYTE PTR[DI],DS:[SI]
```

Few programs are coded this way, and these formats are covered here just for the record.

DUPLICATING A PATTERN

The STOS instruction is useful for setting an area according to a specific byte, word, or doubleword value. However, for repeating a pattern that exceeds these lengths, you can use MOVS with a minor modification. Let's say that you want to set a display line to the following pattern:

```
|****||****||****||****||****|  . . .
```

Rather than define the entire pattern repetitively, you need only define the first six bytes immediately preceding the display line. Here are the instructions:

```
PATTERN  DB    '|****|'       ;Pattern to be duplicated
DISAREA  DB    42 DUP(?)      ;Display area
         ...
         CLD                  ;Left to right
         MOV   CX,21          ;21 words
         LEA   DI,DISAREA     ;Destination
         LEA   SI,PATTERN     ;Source
         REP   MOVSW          ;Move characters
```

On execution, MOVSW moves the first word of PATTERN (|*) to the first word of DISAREA and then moves the second (**) and third (*|) words:

```
|****||****|
↑     ↑
PATTERN  DISAREA
```

At this point, the DI contains the address of DISAREA+6, and the SI contains the address of PATTERN+6, which is also the same address as DISAREA. The operation now automatically duplicates the pattern by moving the first word of DISAREA to DISAREA+6, DISAREA+2 to DISAREA+8, DISAREA+4 to DISAREA+10, and so forth. Eventually the pattern is duplicated through to the end of DISAREA:

You can use this technique to duplicate a pattern any number of times. The pattern itself may be any length, but must immediately precede the destination field.

PROGRAM: RIGHT ADJUSTING A SCREEN DISPLAY

The program in Figure 12-8 illustrates most of the material described in this chapter. The procedures perform the following:

- A10MAIN Initializes the segment registers, calls B10INPT, C10SCAS, D10RGHT, and E10CLNM.

```
TITLE      A12RIGHT (EXE)  Right adjust displayed names
           .MODEL SMALL
           .STACK 64
           .DATA
NAMEPAR    LABEL  BYTE              ;Name parameter list
MAXNLEN    DB     31                ;Maximum length
ACTNLEN    DB     ?                 ;No. of chars entered
NAMEINP    DB     31 DUP(' ')       ;Name

PROMPT     DB     'Name?', '$'
NAMEDIS    DB     31 DUP(' '), 13, 10, '$'
ROW        DB     00
           .CODE
.386
A10MAIN    PROC   FAR               ;Main procedure
           MOV    AX,@data          ;Initialize
           MOV    DS,AX             ;  data segment
           MOV    ES,AX
           MOV    AX,0600H
           CALL   Q10SCR            ;Clear screen
           SUB    DX,DX             ;Set cursor 00,00
           CALL   Q20CURS
A20LOOP:
           CALL   B10INPT           ;Request input of name
           TEST   ACTNLEN,0FFH      ;No name? (indicates end)
           JZ     A90               ;  yes, exit
           CALL   C10SCAS           ;Scan for asterisk
           CMP    AL,'*'            ;Found?
           JE     A20LOOP           ;  yes, bypass
           CALL   D10RGHT           ;Right adjust name
           CALL   E10CLNM           ;Clear name
           JMP    A20LOOP
A90:       MOV    AX,4C00H          ;End of processing
           INT    21H
A10MAIN    ENDP
;                 Prompt for input:
;                 ----------------
B10INPT    PROC
           MOV    AH,09H
           LEA    DX,PROMPT         ;Display prompt
           INT    21H
           MOV    AH,0AH
           LEA    DX,NAMEPAR        ;Accept input
           INT    21H
           RET
B10INPT    ENDP
;                  Scan name for asterisk:
;                  ----------------------
C10SCAS    PROC
           CLD                      ;Left to right
           MOV    AL,'*'            ;Character for scan
           MOV    CX,30             ;Set 30-byte scan
           LEA    DI,NAMEINP
           REPNE SCASB              ;Asterisk found?
           JE     C20               ;  no,  exit
           MOV    AL,20H            ;  yes, clear * in AL
C20:       RET
C10SCAS    ENDP
```

Figure 12-8 Right Adjusting on the Screen

```
;               Right adjust and display name:
;               -----------------------------
D10RGHT  PROC
         STD                        ;Right to left
         MOVZX  CX,ACTNLEN          ;Length in CX for REP
         LEA    SI,NAMEINP          ;Calculate rightmost
         ADD    SI,CX               ;  position
         DEC    SI                  ;  of input name
         LEA    DI,NAMEDIS+30       ;Right pos'n of display name
         REP MOVSB                  ;Move string right to left
         MOV    DH,ROW
         MOV    DL,48
         CALL   Q20CURS             ;Set cursor
         MOV    AH,09H
         LEA    DX,NAMEDIS          ;Display name
         INT    21H

         CMP    ROW,20              ;Bottom of screen?
         JAE    D20                 ;  no,
         INC    ROW                 ;  increment row
         JMP    D90
D20:
         MOV    AX,0601H            ;  yes,
         CALL   Q10SCR              ;  scroll and
         MOV    DH,ROW              ;  set cursor
         MOV    DL,00
         CALL   Q20CURS
D90:     RET
D10RGHT  ENDP
;               Clear name:
;               ----------
E10CLNM  PROC
         CLD                        ;Left to right
         MOV    AX,2020H
         MOV    CX,15               ;Clear 15 words
         LEA    DI,NAMEDIS
         REP STOSW
         RET
E10CLNM  ENDP
;               Scroll screen:
;               -------------
Q10SCR   PROC                       ;AX set on entry
         MOV    BH,30               ;Color attribute
         MOV    CX,00
         MOV    DX,184FH
         INT    10H
         RET
Q10SCR   ENDP
;               Set cursor row/col:
;               ------------------
Q20CURS  PROC                       ;DX set on entry
         MOV    AH,02H
         SUB    BH,BH
         INT    10H
         RET
Q20CURS  ENDP
         END    A10MAIN
```

Figure 12-8 Right Adjusting on the Screen

- B10INPT Accepts a name up to 30 characters in length and displays it at the top of the screen.
- C10SCAS Uses SCASB to scan the name and bypasses any input containing an asterisk.
- D10RGHT Uses the length in ACTNLEN in the input parameter list to calculate the rightmost character of the name, and MOVSB right adjusts each entered name to the right of the screen, one under the other, as follows:

```
    Willie Mays
  Mickey Mantle
 Frank Robinson
```

- E10CLNM Uses STOSW to clear the keyboard input area.

KEY POINTS

- For the string instructions MOVS, STOS, CMPS, and SCAS, be sure that your .EXE programs initialize the ES register.
- For string instructions, use the suffixes B, W, or D for handling byte, word, or doubleword strings.
- Initialize the direction flag for the required direction of processing: Clear (CLD) for left to right or set (STD) for right to left.
- Doublecheck your initialization of the DI and SI registers. For example, MOVS implies operands DI,SI, whereas CMPS implies operands SI,DI.
- Initialize the CX register for REP to process the required number of bytes, words, or doublewords.
- For normal processing, use REP with MOVS and STOS, and use a conditional REP (REPE or REPNE) with CMPS and SCAS.
- CMPSW and SCASW reverse the bytes in words that are compared.
- To process right to left, addressing begins at the rightmost byte of the field. For example, if a field named COTITLE is 10 bytes long, then for processing bytes, the load address for LEA is COTITLE+9. For processing words, however, the address is COTITLE+8 because the string operation initially accesses COTITLE+8 and COTITLE+9.

QUESTIONS

12-1. The string operations assume that the operands relate to the ES:DI or DS:SI registers. Identify the registers for the following: (a) CMPS (operands 1 and 2); (b) MOVS (operands 1 and 2); (c) LODS (operand 1).

12-2. For string operations using REP, (a) how do you set the number of repetitions that are to occur? (b) How do you set processing right to left?

12-3. The chapter gives the instructions equivalent to (a) MOVSB, (b) LODSB, and (c) STOSB, each with a REP prefix. For each case, provide the equivalent code for processing words.

12-4. Revise the program in Figure 12-2. (a) Convert the program from .COM to .EXE format; (b) initialize the ES register; (c) change the MOVSB and MOVSW operations to move data from right to left. Use DEBUG to trace through the procedures, and note the contents of the data segment and registers.

12-5. For what conditions do each of the following instructions test? (a) REPE COMPSB; (b) REPNE SCASB.

12-6. Use the following data definitions and for parts (a)-(f) code the unrelated string operations:

```
DESCRIP DB  'Data Tech Advisors'
OUTAREA DB  18 DUP(' ')
```

(a) Move DESCRIP to OUTAREA, from left to right.

(b) Move DESCRIP to OUTAREA, from right to left.

(c) Load the fifth and sixth bytes of DESCRIP into the AX.

(d) Store the AX beginning at OUTAREA+10.

(e) Compare DESCRIP with OUTAREA (they will be unequal).

(f) Scan DESCRIP for the first blank character and, if found, move it to the BH.

12-7. Revise Figure 12-7 so that the operation scans HEADG1 for "na" as a pair of characters. A check of HEADG1 discloses that "na" does not appear as a word, as shown by the following: /Cy/be/rn/au/ts/. Two possible solutions are: (a) Use SCASW twice. The first SCASW begins at HEADG1 and the second SCASW begins at HEADG1+1; (b) or use SCASB and on finding an "n," compare the byte that follows it for an "a."

12-8. Define a 5-byte field containing the hex value C9CDCDCDBB. Use MOVSB to duplicate this field 20 times into a 100-byte area, and display the result.

13 ARITHMETIC I: PROCESSING BINARY DATA

Objective: To cover the requirements for addition, subtraction, multiplication, and division of binary data.

INTRODUCTION

This chapter covers addition, subtraction, multiplication, and division and the use of unsigned and signed numeric data. The chapter also provides many examples and warnings of various pitfalls for the unwary traveler in the realm of computer arithmetic. Chapter 14 covers special requirements involved with conversion between binary and ASCII data formats.

Although we are accustomed to performing arithmetic in decimal (base 10) format, a microcomputer performs its arithmetic only in binary (base 2). Further, the limitation of 16-bit registers on pre-80386 processors involves special treatment for large values.

Instructions described in this chapter are:

ADC	ADD with carry	IDIV	Divide signed
ADD	Add	IMUL	Multiply signed
CBW	Convert byte to word	MUL	Multiply unsigned
CDQ	Convert doubleword to quadword	NEG	Negate
CWD	Convert word to doubleword	SBB	Subtract with borrow
CWDE	Convert word to extended doubleword	SUB	Subtract
DIV	Divide unsigned		

PROCESSING UNSIGNED AND SIGNED DATA

Some numeric fields—for example, a customer number and the day of the month—are unsigned. Some signed numeric fields—for example, customer's balance owing and an algebraic number—may contain positive or negative values. Other signed numeric fields—for example, an employee rate of pay and the value of pi—are supposed to be always positive.

For unsigned data, where all bits are intended to be data bits, a 16-bit register can contain a maximum of 65,535. For signed data, where the leftmost bit is a sign bit, the register can contain a maximum of 32,767. But note that the ADD and SUB instructions do not distinguish between unsigned and signed data and, indeed, simply add and subtract bits.

The following example illustrates the addition of two binary numbers, with the values shown as both unsigned and signed. The top number contains a 1-bit to the left; for unsigned data, the bits represent 249, whereas for signed data, the bits represent −7. The addition does not set the overflow or carry flags:

BINARY	UNSIGNED DECIMAL	SIGNED DECIMAL	OF	CF
11111001	249	-7		
+00000010	+ 2	+2		
11111011	251	-5	0	0

In this example, the binary result of the addition is the same for both unsigned and signed data. However, the bits in the unsigned field represent decimal 251, whereas the bits in the signed field represent decimal −5. In effect, the contents of a field mean whatever you intend them to mean and you handle them accordingly.

Arithmetic Carry

An arithmetic operation transfers the resulting sign bit (0 or 1) to the carry flag. If the sign bit is a 1, then, in effect, the carry flag is set. Where a carry occurs on unsigned data, the result is invalid. The following example of addition causes a carry:

BINARY	UNSIGNED DECIMAL	SIGNED DECIMAL	OF	CF
11111100	252	-4		
+00000101	+ 5	+5		
(1)00000001	1	1	0	1
	(invalid)	(valid)		

The operation on the unsigned data is invalid because of the carry out of a data bit, whereas the operation on the signed data is valid.

Arithmetic Overflow

An arithmetic operation sets the overflow flag when a carry *into* the sign bit does not carry out, or a carry *out* occurs with no carry in. If an overflow occurs on signed data, the result is invalid (because of an overflow into the sign bit). The following example of addition causes an overflow:

```
              UNSIGNED     SIGNED
   BINARY     DECIMAL      DECIMAL   OF   CF
  01111001      121         +121
 +00001011     + 11         + 11
  10000100      132         -124      1    0
              (valid)     (invalid)
```

An add operation may set both the carry and the overflow flag. In the next example, the carry makes the operation on unsigned data invalid, and the overflow makes the operation on signed data invalid:

```
                 UNSIGNED     SIGNED
      BINARY     DECIMAL      DECIMAL   OF   CF
     11110110      246          -10
    +10001001     +137         -119
  (1)01111111      127         +127      1    1
                (invalid)    (invalid)
```

The upshot of all this is that you must have a good idea as to the magnitude of the numbers that your program will handle, and you define and process fields accordingly.

ADDITION AND SUBTRACTION

The ADD and SUB instructions perform simple addition and subtraction of binary data. The general formats for ADD and SUB are:

[label:]	ADD/SUB	register,register
[label:]	ADD/SUB	memory,register
[label:]	ADD/SUB	register,memory
[label:]	ADD/SUB	register,immediate
[label:]	ADD/SUB	memory,immediate

An ADD or SUB operation sets or clears the overflow and carry flags, as described in the previous section. As with other instructions, there are no direct memory-to-memory operations. The following example uses the AX register to add CURRAIN to RAINFALL:

```
CURRAIN    DW   123            ;Define CURRAIN
RAINFALL   DW   25             ;Define RAINFALL
           ...
           MOV  AX,CURRAIN     ;Move CURRAIN to AX
           ADD  AX,RAINFALL    ;Add RAINFALL to AX
           MOV  RAINFALL,AX    ;Move AX to RAINFALL
```

As described in Chapter 1, a negative binary number is represented in two's complement form by reversing the bits of the positive number and adding 1. Figure 13-1 provides

```
TITLE    A13ADD (COM)ADD and SUB operations
         .MODEL SMALL
         .CODE
         ORG    100H
BEGIN:   JMP    SHORT A10MAIN
; ----------------------------------------------------------
BYTE1    DB     64H                ;Data items
BYTE2    DB     40H
BYTE3    DB     16H
WORD1    DW     4000H
WORD2    DW     2000H
WORD3    DW     1000H
; ----------------------------------------------------------
A10MAIN  PROC   NEAR               ;Main procedure:
         CALL   B10ADD             ;Call ADD routine
         CALL   C10SUB             ;Call SUB routine
         MOV    AX,4C00H           ;End processing
         INT    21H
A10MAIN  ENDP

;               Examples of ADD bytes:
;               ---------------------
B10ADD   PROC
         MOV    AL,BYTE1
         MOV    BL,BYTE2
         ADD    AL,BL              ;Register-to-register
         ADD    AL,BYTE3           ;Memory-to-register
         ADD    BYTE1,BL           ;Register-to-memory
         ADD    BL,10H             ;Immediate-to-register
         ADD    BYTE1,25H          ;Immediate-to-memory
         RET
B10ADD   ENDP

;               Examples of SUB words:
;               ---------------------
C10SUB   PROC
         MOV    AX,WORD1
         MOV    BX,WORD2
         SUB    AX,BX              ;Register-from-register
         SUB    AX,WORD3           ;Memory-from-register
         SUB    WORD1,BX           ;Register-from-memory
         SUB    BX,1000H           ;Immediate-from-register
         SUB    WORD1,256H         ;Immediate-from-memory
         RET
C10SUB   ENDP
         END    BEGIN
```

Figure 13-1 Examples of ADD and SUB

examples of ADD and SUB for processing byte and word values. The procedure B10ADD uses ADD to process bytes and the procedure C10SUB uses SUB to process words.

Overflows

Be alert for overflows in arithmetic operations, especially for signed data. Because a byte provides for only a sign bit and 7 data bits (from −128 to +127), an arithmetic operation can easily exceed the capacity of a 1-byte register. And a sum in the AL register that exceeds its capacity may cause unexpected results. For example, if the AL contains 60H, then the instruction

```
ADD   AL,20H
```

generates a sum of 80H in the AL. Having added two positive values, we expect the sum to be positive, but the operation sets the overflow flag to overflow and the sign flag to negative. The reason? The value 80H, or binary 10000000, is a negative number; instead of +128, the sum is −128. The problem is that the AL register is too small for the sum, which should be in the full AX register, as shown in the next section.

EXTENDING VALUES IN A REGISTER

In the previous section, we saw how adding 20H to the value 60H in the AL caused an incorrect sum. A better solution would be for the AX to represent the full sum. The instruction for this purpose is CBW (Convert Byte to Word), which automatically propagates the sign bit of the AL (0 or 1) through the AH. Note that CBW is restricted to the use of the AX.

In the next example, CBW extends the sign (0) in the AL through the AH, which generates 0060H in the AX. The example then adds 20H to the AX (rather than to the AL) and generates the correct result in the AX: 0080H, or +128:

```
                                          AH  AL
...                                       xx  60H
CBW              ;Extend AL sign into AH  00  60
ADD   AX,20H     ;Add to AX               00  80
```

This example has the same numeric result as the one in the previous section, but the addition in the AX does not treat it as an overflow or as negative. Still, although a full word in the AX allows for a sign bit and 15 data bits, the AX is limited to values from −32,768 to +32,767.

Extending Words and Doublewords

The CWD (Convert Word to Doubleword) instruction is used to extend a 1-word signed value to a doubleword by duplicating the sign bit of the AX through the DX. Here is an example:

```
MOV   AX,WORD1     ;Move word to AX
CWD                ;Extend word to DX:AX
```

The CWDE (Convert Word to Extended Doubleword, for the 80386 and later) instruction is used to extend a 1-word signed value to a doubleword by duplicating the sign bit of the AX through the EAX. Here is an example:

```
MOV   AX,WORD1     ;Move word to AX
CWDE               ;Extend word to EAX
```

The CDQ (Convert Doubleword to Quadword, for the 80386 and later) instruction is used to extend a doubleword signed value to a quadword by duplicating the sign bit of the EAX through the EDX. Here is an example:

```
MOV   EAX,DBWORD   ;Move doubleword to EAX
CDQ                ;Extend doubleword to EAX:EDX
```

PERFORMING ARITHMETIC ON DOUBLEWORD VALUES

As we have seen, large numeric values may exceed the capacity of a word, in effect requiring multiword capacity. A major requirement in multiword arithmetic is reverse-byte and reverse-word sequence. Recall that the assembler automatically converts the contents of defined numeric words into reverse-byte sequence, so that, for example, a definition of 0134H becomes 3401H. The simplest way of defining a doubleword is as a DD. The following example adds and stores doublewords values:

```
DBWORD1  DD 0123BC62H        ;Define doublewords
DBWORD2  DD 0012553AH        ;
DBWORD3  DD 0                ;
         ...
         MOV EAX,DBWORD1     ;Add and
         ADD EAX,DBWORD2     ; store
         MOV DBWORD3,EAX     ; doublewords
```

The assembler automatically arranges the defined data in reverse-byte (and word) sequence. For some applications, however, the data may be defined as *word* values. For DBWORD1 defined in the previous example, you have to define the words as adjacent but in reverse order:

```
DW   0BC62H
DW   0123H
```

The assembler then converts these definitions into reverse-byte sequence as |62 BC|23 01|, suitable for doubleword arithmetic. Let's examine two ways to perform arithmetic on these values. The first is simple and specific, whereas the second is more sophisticated and general.

In Figure 13-2, the procedure B10DWD illustrates adding one pair of words (WORD1A and WORD1B) to a second pair (WORD2A and WORD2B) and storing the sum in a third pair (WORD3A and WORD3B). In effect, the operation is to add values, such as the following:

```
Initial value:    0123 BC62H
Add:              0012 553AH
                  ----------
Total:            0136 119CH
```

Because of the reverse-byte sequence in memory, the program defines the values with the words adjacent but reversed: BC62 0123 and 553A 0012, respectively. The assembler then stores these doubleword values in memory in proper reverse-byte sequence:

```
WORD1A and WORD1B:    62BC 2301
WORD2A and WORD2B:    3A55 1200
```

The procedure B10DWD first adds WORD2A to WORD1A in the AX (the low-order portions) and stores the sum in WORD3A. It next adds WORD2B to WORD1B (the high-order portions) in the AX, along with the carry from the previous addition. It then stores the sum in WORD3B. Let's examine the operations in detail. The first MOV and ADD operations reverse the bytes in the AX and add the leftmost words:

```
TITLE       A13DBADD (COM)  Adding doublewords
            .MODEL SMALL
            .CODE
            ORG     100H
BEGIN:      JMP     SHORT A10MAIN
; -----------------------------------------------------
WORD1A      DW      0BC62H              ;Data items
WORD1B      DW      0123H
WORD2A      DW      553AH
WORD2B      DW      0012H
WORD3A      DW      ?
WORD3B      DW      ?
; -----------------------------------------------------
A10MAIN     PROC    NEAR                ;Main procedure
            CALL    B10DWD              ;Call 1st ADD
            CALL    C10DWD              ;Call 2nd ADD
            MOV     AX,4C00H            ;End processing
            INT     21H
A10MAIN     ENDP
;                   Example of ADD doublewords:
;                   -------------------------
B10DWD      PROC
            MOV     AX,WORD1A           ;Add leftmost word
            ADD     AX,WORD2A
            MOV     WORD3A,AX
            MOV     AX,WORD1B           ;Add rightmost word
            ADC     AX,WORD2B           ;  with carry
            MOV     WORD3B,AX
            RET
B10DWD      ENDP
;                   Generalized add operation:
;                   ------------------------
C10DWD      PROC
            CLC                         ;Clear carry flag
            MOV     CX,02               ;Set loop count
            LEA     SI,WORD1A           ;Leftmost word
            LEA     DI,WORD2A           ;Leftmost word
            LEA     BX,WORD3A           ;Leftmost word of sum
C20:
            MOV     AX,[SI]             ;Move word to AX
            ADC     AX,[DI]             ;Add with carry to AX
            MOV     [BX],AX             ;Store word
            INC     SI                  ;Adjust addresses for
            INC     SI                  ;  next word to right
            INC     DI
            INC     DI
            INC     BX
            INC     BX
            LOOP    C20                 ;Repeat for next word
            RET
C10DWD      ENDP
            END     BEGIN
```

Figure 13-2 Adding Multiword Values

```
WORD1A:     BC62H
WORD2A:    +553AH
Total:  (1)119CH (9C11H is stored in WORD3A)
```

Because the sum of WORD1A plus WORD2A exceeds the capacity of the AX, a carry occurs, and the carry flag is set to 1. Next, the example adds the words at the right, but this time using ADC (Add with Carry) instead of ADD. ADC adds the two values and, because the carry flag is set, adds 1 to the sum:

```
WORD1B        0123H
WORD2B       +0012H
Plus carry   +    1H
             ------
Total         0136H (stored in WORD3B as 3601H)
```

By using DEBUG to trace the arithmetic, you can see the sum 0136H in the AX and the reversed values 9C11H in WORD3A and 3601H in WORD3B.

Also in Figure 13-2, the more sophisticated procedure C10DWD provides an approach to adding values of any length, although here it adds the same pairs of words as before, WORD1A:WORD1B and WORD2A:WORD2B. The procedure uses the SI, DI, and BX as base registers for the addresses of WORD1A, WORD2A, and WORD3A, respectively. It loops once through the instructions for each pair of words to be added—in this case, two times. The first loop adds the leftmost words, and the second loop adds the rightmost words. Because the second loop is to process the words to the right, the addresses in the SI, DI, and BX registers are incremented by 2. Two INC instructions perform this operation for each register. INC (rather than ADD) is used for a good reason: The instruction ADD reg,02 would clear the carry flag and would cause an incorrect answer, whereas INC does not affect the carry flag.

Because of the loop, there is only one add instruction, ADC. At the start, a CLC (Clear Carry) instruction ensures that the carry flag is initially clear. The results in WORD3A, WORD3B, and the AX are the same as the previous example.

To make this method work, be sure to (1) define the words adjacent to each other, (2) initialize the CX to the number of words to be added, and (3) process words from left to right.

For multiword subtraction, the instruction equivalent to ADC is SBB (Subtract with Borrow). Simply replace ADC with SBB in the procedure C10DWD.

Here are the general formats for ADC and SBB:

[label:]	ADC/SBB	register,register
[label:]	ADC/SBB	memory,register
[label:]	ADC/SBB	register,memory
[label:]	ADC/SBB	register,immediate
[label:]	ADC/SBB	memory,immediate

You could add quadwords using the technique covered earlier for adding multiwords; that is, define two pairs of adjacent doublewords and use the EAX register.

MULTIPLICATION

For multiplication, the MUL instruction handles unsigned data, and the IMUL (Integer Multiplication) instruction handles signed data. Both instructions affect the carry and overflow flags. As programmer, you have control over the format of the data you process, and you have the responsibility of selecting the appropriate multiply instruction. The general format for MUL and IMUL is

[label:]	MUL/IMUL	register/memory

The basic multiplication operations are byte times byte, word times word, and (80386 and later processors) doubleword times doubleword.

Byte Times Byte

For multiplying two 1-byte values, the multiplicand is in the AL register, and the multiplier is a byte in memory or another register. For the instruction MUL DL, the operation multiplies the contents of the AL by the contents of the DL. The generated product is in the AX register. The operation ignores and erases any data that may already be in the AH.

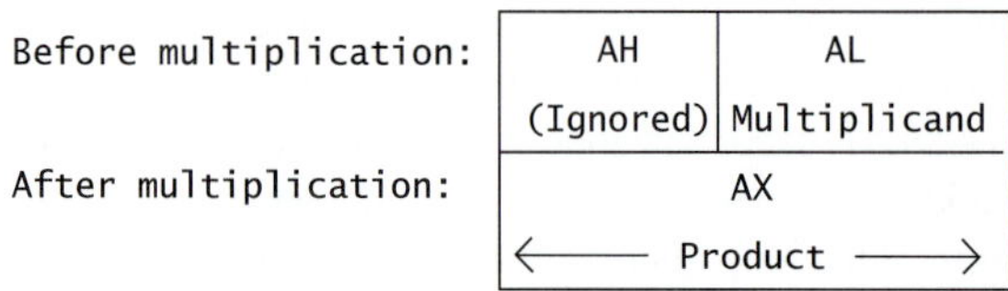

Word Times Word

For multiplying two 1-word values, the multiplicand is in the AX register and the multiplier is a word in memory or another register. For the instruction MUL DX, the operation multiplies the contents of the AX by the contents of the DX. The generated product is a doubleword that requires two registers: the high-order (leftmost) portion in the DX and the low-order (rightmost) portion in the AX. The operation ignores and erases any data that may already be in the DX.

	DX	AX
Before multiplication:	(Ignored)	Multiplicand
After multiplication:	High product	Low product

Doubleword Times Doubleword

For multiplying two doubleword values, the multiplicand is in the EAX register and the multiplier is a doubleword in memory or another register. The product is generated in the EDX:EAX pair. The operation ignores and erases any data already in the EDX.

	EDX	EAX
Before multiplication:	(Ignored)	Multiplicand
After multiplication:	High product	Low product

Field Sizes

The operand of MUL or IMUL references only the multiplier, which determines the field sizes. The instruction assumes that the multiplicand is in the AL, AX, or EAX, depending on the size of the multiplier. In the following examples, the multiplier is in a register:

INSTRUCTION	MULTIPLIER	MULTIPLICAND	PRODUCT
MUL CL	byte	AL	AX
MUL BX	word	AX	DX:AX
MUL EBX	doubleword	EAX	EDX:EAX

In the next examples, the multipliers are defined in memory:

```
BYTE1   DB  ?
WORD1   DW  ?
DWORD1  DD  ?
```

INSTRUCTION	MULTIPLIER	MULTIPLICAND	PRODUCT
MUL BYTE1	BYTE1	AL	AX
MUL WORD1	WORD1	AX	DX:AX
MUL DWORD1	DWORD1	EAX	EDX:EAX

Unsigned Multiplication: MUL

The purpose of the MUL instruction is to multiply unsigned data. In Figure 13-3, B10MUL gives three examples of the use of MUL: byte times byte, word times word, and word times byte. The first example multiplies 80H (128) by 40H (64). The product in the AX is 2000H (8,192). The second example generates 1000 0000H in the DX:AX registers.

The third example involves word times byte and requires extending BYTE1 to a word. Because the values are supposed to be unsigned, the example assumes that bits in the AH register are to be zero. (The problem with using CBW here is that the leftmost bit of the AL could be 1, and propagating 1-bits in the AH would result in a larger unsigned value.) The product in the DX:AX is 0040 0000H.

The fourth example uses the EAX for doubleword multiplication.

Signed Multiplication: IMUL

The purpose of the IMUL (Integer Multiplication) instruction is to multiply signed data. In Figure 13-3, C10IMUL gives the same three examples as B10MUL, but replacing MUL with IMUL.

The first example multiplies 80H (a negative number) by 40H (a positive number). The product in the AX register is E000H. Using the same data, MUL generates a product of 2000H, so you can see the difference between using MUL and using IMUL. MUL treats 80H as +128, whereas IMUL treats 80H as −128. The product of −128 times +64 is −8192H, which equals E000H. (Try converting E000H to bits, reverse the bits, add 1, and add up the bit values.)

```
TITLE     A13MULT (COM)  MUL and IMUL operations
          .MODEL SMALL
          .CODE
          ORG    100H
BEGIN:    JMP    SHORT A10MAIN
; -------------------------------------------------------------
BYTE1     DB     80H
BYTE2     DB     40H
WORD1     DW     8000H
WORD2     DW     2000H
DWORD1    DD     80000000
DWORD2    DD     20000000
; -------------------------------------------------------------
.386
A10MAIN   PROC   NEAR              ;Main procedure
          CALL   B10MUL            ;Call MUL  routine
          CALL   C10IMUL           ;Call IMUL routine
          MOV    AX,4C00H          ;End processing
          INT    21H
A10MAIN   ENDP
;                Examples of MUL:
;                ---------------
B10MUL    PROC
          MOV    AL,BYTE1          ;Byte x byte
          MUL    BYTE2             ;  product in AX

          MOV    AX,WORD1          ;Word x word
          MUL    WORD2             ;  product in DX:AX

          MOV    AL,BYTE1          ;Byte x word
          SUB    AH,AH             ;  extend multiplicand in AH
          MUL    WORD1             ;  product in DX:AX

          MOV    EAX,DWORD1        ;Doubleword x
          MUL    DWORD2            ;  doubleword
          RET
B10MUL    ENDP
;                Examples of IMUL:
;                ----------------
C10IMUL   PROC
          MOV    AL,BYTE1          ;Byte x byte
          IMUL   BYTE2             ;  product in AX

          MOV    AX,WORD1          ;Word x word
          IMUL   WORD2             ;  product in DX:AX

          MOV    AL,BYTE1          ;Byte x word
          CBW                      ;  extend multiplicand in AH
          IMUL   WORD1             ;  product in DX:AX

          MOV    EAX,DWORD1        ;Doubleword x
          IMUL   DWORD2            ;  doubleword
          RET
C10IMUL   ENDP
          END    BEGIN
```

Figure 13-3 Multiplying Unsigned and Signed Values

The second example multiplies 8000H (a negative value) by 2000H (a positive value). The product in the DX:AX is F000 0000H, which is the negative of the product that MUL generated.

The third example extends BYTE1 to a word in the AX. Because the values are supposed to be signed, the example uses CBW to extend the leftmost sign bit into the AH register: 80H in the AL becomes FF80H in the AX. Because the multiplier, WORD1, is also negative, the product should be positive. And indeed it is: 0040 0000H in the DX:AX—the same result as MUL, which multiplied two unsigned numbers.

The fourth example uses the EAX for doubleword multiplication.

In effect, if the multiplicand and multiplier have the same sign bit, MUL and IMUL generate the same product. But if the multiplicand and multiplier have different sign bits, MUL produces a positive product and IMUL produces a negative product. The upshot is that your program must know the format of the data and use the appropriate instructions.

You may find it worthwhile to use DEBUG to trace through these examples.

PERFORMING DOUBLEWORD MULTIPLICATION

Conventional multiplication involves multiplying byte by byte, word by word, or doubleword by doubleword. As we have already seen, the maximum signed value in a word is +32,767. Multiplying larger values on pre-80386 processors involves additional steps. The approach on these processors is to multiply each word separately and then add each product together. The following example multiplies a four-digit decimal number by a two-digit number:

```
  1,365
x    12
 ------
 16,380
```

What if you could multiply only two-digit numbers? Then you could multiply the 13 and the 65 by 12 separately, like this:

```
   13       65
x  12    x  12
  ---      ---
  156      780
```

Next, add the two products; but remember, since the 13 is in the hundreds position, its product is actually 15,600:

```
 15,600   (13 x 12 x 100)
+   780   (65 x 12)
 ------
 16,380
```

An assembly program can use this same technique, except that the data consists of words (4 digits) in hexadecimal format. Let's now examine the requirements for multiplying doubleword by word and doubleword by doubleword.

Doubleword by Word

In Figure 13-4, B10XMUL multiplies a doubleword by a word. The multiplicand, MULTCAN, consists of two words containing 3206H and 2521H, respectively. The reason for defining two DWs instead of a DD is to facilitate addressing for MOV instructions that

```
TITLE      A13DWMUL (COM)  Multiplication of doublewords
           .MODEL SMALL
           .CODE
           ORG     100H
BEGIN:     JMP     SHORT A10MAIN
; ------------------------------------------------------
MULTCAN    DW      2521H              ;Data items
           DW      3206H
MULTPLR    DW      0A26H
           DW      6400H
PRODUCT    DW      0
           DW      0
           DW      0
           DW      0
; ------------------------------------------------------
A10MAIN    PROC    NEAR               ;Main procedure
           CALL    B10XMUL            ;Call 1st multiply
           CALL    C10CLEAR           ;Clear product
           CALL    D10XMUL            ;Call 2nd multiply
           MOV     AX,4C00H           ;End processing
           INT     21H
A10MAIN    ENDP
;                  Doubleword x word:
;                  -----------------
B10XMUL    PROC
           MOV     AX,MULTCAN         ;Multiply left word
           MUL     MULTPLR+2          ;  of multiplicand
           MOV     PRODUCT,AX         ;Store product
           MOV     PRODUCT+2,DX

           MOV     AX,MULTCAN+2       ;Multiply right word
           MUL     MULTPLR+2          ;  of multiplicand
           ADD     PRODUCT+2,AX       ;Add to stored product
           ADC     PRODUCT+4,DX
           RET
B10XMUL    ENDP
;                  Clear product area:
;                  ------------------
C10CLEAR   PROC
           MOV     PRODUCT,0000       ;Clear words
           MOV     PRODUCT+2,0000     ;  left to right
           MOV     PRODUCT+4,0000
           MOV     PRODUCT+6,0000
           RET
C10CLEAR   ENDP
;                  Doubleword x doubleword:
;                  -----------------------
D10XMUL    PROC
           MOV     AX,MULTCAN         ;Multiplicand word 1
           MUL     MULTPLR            ;  x multiplier word 1
           MOV     PRODUCT+0,AX       ;Store product
           MOV     PRODUCT+2,DX

           MOV     AX,MULTCAN         ;Multiplicand word 1
           MUL     MULTPLR+2          ;  x multiplier word 2
           ADD     PRODUCT+2,AX       ;Add to stored product
           ADC     PRODUCT+4,DX
           ADC     PRODUCT+6,00       ;Add any carry
```

Figure 13-4a Multiplying Multiword Values

move words to the AX register. The values are defined in reverse-word sequence, and the assembler stores each word in reverse-byte sequence. Thus MULTCAN, which has a defined value of 32062521H, is stored as 21250632H.

```
            MOV     AX,MULTCAN+2        ;Multiplicand word 2
            MUL     MULTPLR             ;  x multiplier word 1
            ADD     PRODUCT+2,AX        ;Add to stored product
            ADC     PRODUCT+4,DX
            ADC     PRODUCT+6,00        ;Add any carry

            MOV     AX,MULTCAN+2        ;Multiplicand word 2
            MUL     MULTPLR+2           ;  x multiplier word 2
            ADD     PRODUCT+4,AX        ;Add to product
            ADC     PRODUCT+6,DX
            RET
D10XMUL     ENDP
            END     BEGIN
```

Figure 13-4b Multiplying Multiword Values

The multiplier, MULTPLR+2, contains 6400H. The field for the generated product, PRODUCT, provides for three words. The first MUL operation multiplies MULTPLR+2 and the left word of MULTCAN; the product is hex 0E80 E400H, stored in PRODUCT+2 and PRODUCT+4. The second MUL multiplies MULTPLR+2 and the right word of MULTCAN; the product is 138A 5800H. The routine then adds the two products, like this:

```
Product 1:   0000 0E80 E400
Product 2:  +138A 5800
Total:       138A 6680 E400
```

Because the first ADD may cause a carry, the second add is ADC (Add with Carry). Because numeric data is stored in reversed byte format, PRODUCT will actually contain 00E4 8066 8A13. The routine requires that the first word of PRODUCT initially contains zero.

Doubleword by Doubleword

Multiplying two doublewords on pre-80386 processors involves four multiplications:

MULTIPLICAND		MULTIPLIER
word 2	×	word 2
word 2	×	word 1
word 1	×	word 2
word 1	×	word 1

You add each product in the DX and AX to the appropriate word in the final product. In Figure 13-4, D10XMUL gives an example. MULTCAN contains 3206 2521H, MULTPLR contains 6400 0A26H, and PRODUCT provides for four words.

Although the logic is similar to multiplying doubleword by word, this problem requires an additional feature. Following the ADD/ADC pair is another ADC that adds 0 to PRODUCT. The first ADC itself could cause a carry, which subsequent instructions would clear. The second ADC, therefore, adds 0 if there is no carry and adds 1 if there is a carry. The final ADD/ADC pair does not require an additional ADC: Because PRODUCT is large enough for the final generated answer, there is no carry.

The final product is 138A 687C 8E5C CCE6, stored in PRODUCT with the bytes reversed. Try using DEBUG to trace through this example.

SPECIAL MULTIPLICATION INSTRUCTIONS

The 80286 and later processors have additional IMUL formats that provide for immediate operands and allow for generating products in registers other than the AX. You can use these instructions for either signed or unsigned multiplication, since the results are the same. The values must be all the same length: 16 or (for the 80386 and later) 32 bits.

16-Bit IMUL Operation

For the 16-bit IMUL, the first operand (a register) contains the multiplicand, and the second operand (an immediate value) is the multiplier. The product is generated in the first operand. A product that exceeds the register causes the carry and overflow flags to be set. The general format for this 16-bit IMUL operation is

[label:]	IMUL	register,immediate

32-Bit IMUL Operation

The 32-bit IMUL has three operands: The second operand (memory) contains the multiplicand, and the third operand (an immediate value) contains the multiplier. The product is generated in the first operand (a register). The general format for the 32-bit IMUL is

[label:]	IMUL	register,memory,immediate

16/32-Bit IMUL Operation

The 80386 and later processors provide yet another IMUL format for 16- or 32-bit operations. The first operand (a register) contains the multiplicand, and the second operand (register/memory) contains the multiplier. The product is generated in the first operand.

[label:]	IMUL	register,register/memory

Here are examples of these three IMUL instructions:

Size	Instruction	Multiplicand	Multiplier	Product
16-bit	IMUL DX,25	DX	25	DX
32-bit	IMUL ECX,MULTCAND,25	MULTCAND	25	ECX
16/32-bit	IMUL BX,CX	BX	CX	BX

MULTIPLICATION BY SHIFTING

For multiplying by a power of 2 (2, 4, 8, etc.), you may gain faster processing simply by shifting left the necessary number of bits. For the 8088/8086, a shift greater than 1 requires that you load the shift value in the CL register. In the following examples, the multiplicand is in the AX:

```
Multiply by 2 (shift left 1):    SHL AX,01
Multiply by 8 (shift left 3):    MOV CL,03    ;8088/8086
                                 SHL AX,CL    ;
Multiply by 8 (shift left 3):    SHL AX,03    ;80286 and later
```

The following routine for an 80286 or later processor could be useful for left shifting a doubleword product in the DX:AX registers. Although specific to a 4-bit shift, it could be adapted to other values:

```
SHL  DX,04    ;Shift DX to left 4 bits
MOV  BL,AH    ;Store AH in BL
SHL  AX,04    ;Shift AX to left 4 bits
SHR  BL,04    ;Shift BL to right 4 bits
OR   DL,BL    ;Insert 4 bits from BL in DL
```

Be especially careful not to shift off a significant digit.

DIVISION

For division, the DIV (Divide) instruction handles unsigned data and IDIV (Integer Divide) handles signed data. You are responsible for selecting the appropriate divide instruction. The general format for DIV/IDIV is

[label:]	DIV/IDIV	register/memory

The basic divide operations are byte into word, word into doubleword, and (80386 and later) doubleword into quadword.

Byte into Word

Here, the dividend is in the AX and the divisor is a byte in memory or another register. The operation stores the remainder in the AH and the quotient in the AL. Because a 1-byte quotient is very small—a maximum of +255 (FFH) if unsigned and +127 (7FH) if signed—this operation has limited use.

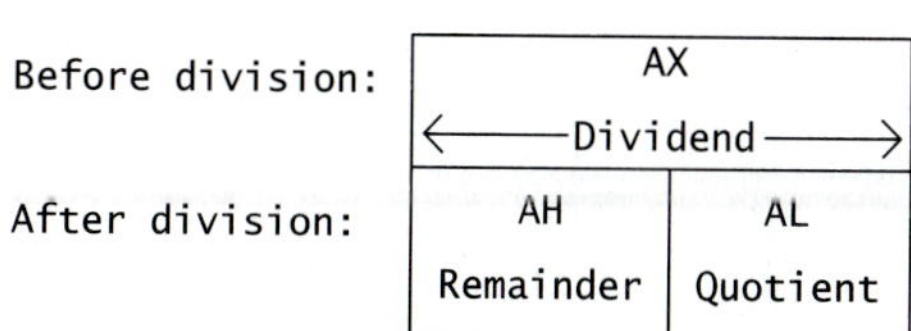

Word into Doubleword

For this operation, the dividend is in the DX:AX pair and the divisor is a word in memory or another register. The operation stores the remainder in the DX and the quotient in the AX. The 1Dword quotient allows a maximum of +32,767 (FFFFH) if unsigned and +16,383 (7FFFH) if signed.

	DX	AX
Before division:	High dividend	Low dividend
After division:	Remainder	Quotient

Doubleword into Quadword

For dividing a doubleword into a quadword, the dividend is in the EDX:EAX pair and the divisor is a doubleword in memory or another register. The operation stores the remainder in the EDX and the quotient in the EAX.

	EDX	EAX
Before division:	High dividend	Low dividend
After division:	Remainder	Quotient

Field Sizes

The operand of DIV/IDIV references the divisor, which determines the field sizes. In the following DIV examples, the divisors are in a register, which determines the type of operation:

OPERATION	DIVISOR	DIVIDEND	QUOTIENT	REMAINDER
DIV CL	byte	AX	AL	AH
DIV CX	word	DX:AX	AX	DX
DIV EBX	doubleword	EDX:EAX	EAX	EDX

In the following DIV examples, the divisors are defined in memory:

```
BYTE1   DB ?
WORD1   DW ?
DWORD1  DD ?
        ...            DIVISOR  DIVIDEND  QUOTIENT  REMAINDER
        DIV BYTE1      BYTE1    AX        AL        AH
        DIV WORD1      WORD1    DX:AX     AX        DX
        DIV DWORD1     DWORD1   EDX:EAX   EAX       EDX
```

Remainder. If you divide 13 by 3, the result is 4 1/3, where the quotient is 4 and the true remainder is 1. Note that a calculator (and a high-level programming language) would deliver a quotient of 4.333 . . . , which consists of an integer portion (4) and a fraction portion (.333). The values 1/3 and .333 are fractions, whereas the 1 is a remainder.

```
TITLE      A13DIV (COM)  DIV and IDIV operations
           .MODEL  SMALL
           .CODE
           ORG     100H
BEGIN:     JMP     SHORT A10MAIN
; -------------------------------------------------------------
BYTE1      DB      80H               ;Data items
BYTE3      DB      16H
WORD1      DW      2000H
WORD2      DW      0010H
WORD3      DW      1000H
; -------------------------------------------------------------
A10MAIN    PROC    NEAR              ;Main procedure
           CALL    B10DIV            ;Call DIV  routine
           CALL    C10IDIV           ;Call IDIV routine
           MOV     AX,4C00H          ;End processing
           INT     21H
A10MAIN    ENDP
;                  Examples of DIV:
;                  ---------------
B10DIV     PROC
           MOV     AX,WORD1          ;Word / byte
           DIV     BYTE1             ;  rmdr:quot in AH:AL
           MOV     AL,BYTE1          ;Byte / byte
           SUB     AH,AH             ;  extend dividend in AH
           DIV     BYTE3             ;  rmdr:quot in AH:AL

           MOV     DX,WORD2          ;Doubleword / word
           MOV     AX,WORD3          ;  dividend in DX:AX
           DIV     WORD1             ;  rmdr:quot in DX:AX
           MOV     AX,WORD1          ;Word / word
           SUB     DX,DX             ;  extend dividend in DX
           DIV     WORD3             ;  rmdr:quot in DX:AX
           RET
B10DIV     ENDP
;                  Examples of IDIV:
;                  ----------------
C10IDIV    PROC
           MOV     AX,WORD1          ;Word / byte
           IDIV    BYTE1             ;  rmdr:quot in AH:AL
           MOV     AL,BYTE1          ;Byte / byte
           CBW                       ;  extend dividend in AH
           IDIV    BYTE3             ;  rmdr:quot in AH:AL

           MOV     DX,WORD2          ;Doubleword / word
           MOV     AX,WORD3          ;  dividend in DX:AX
           IDIV    WORD1             ;  rmdr:quot in DX:AX
           MOV     AX,WORD1          ;Word / word
           CWD                       ;  extend dividend in DX
           IDIV    WORD3             ;  rmdr:quot in DX:AX
           RET
C10IDIV    ENDP
           END     BEGIN
```

Figure 13-5 Dividing Unsigned and Signed Values

Using DIV for Unsigned Division

The purpose of the DIV instruction is to divide unsigned data. In Figure 13-5, the procedure B10DIV gives four examples of DIV: byte into word, byte into byte, word into doubleword, and word into word. The first example divides 2000H (8092) by 80H (128). The remainder in the AH is 00H, and the quotient in the AL is 40H (64).

The second example requires extending BYTE1 to a word. Because the value is supposed to be unsigned, the example assumes that bits in the AH register are to be zero. The remainder in the AH is 12H, and the quotient in the AL is 05H.

In the third example, the remainder in the DX is 1000H, and the quotient in the AX is 0080H.

The fourth DIV requires extending WORD1 to a doubleword in the DX register. After the division, the remainder in the DX is 0000H and the quotient in the AX is 0002H.

Using IDIV for Signed Division

The purpose of the IDIV instruction is to divide signed data. In Figure 13-5, C10IDIV gives the same four examples as B10DIV, but replacing DIV with IDIV. The first example divides 2000H (positive) by 80H (negative). The remainder in the AH is 00H, and the quotient in the AL is C0H (−64). (Using the same data, DIV resulted in a quotient of +64.) The results, in hex, of the remaining three examples of IDIV are:

IDIV EXAMPLE	REMAINDER (DX)	QUOTIENT (AX)
2	EE (-18)	FB (-5)
3	1000 (4096)	0080 (128)
4	0000	0002

Only Example 4 produces the same answer as did DIV. In effect, if the dividend and divisor have the same sign bit, DIV and IDIV generate the same result. But if the dividend and divisor have different sign bits, DIV generates a positive quotient and IDIV generates a negative quotient.

You may find it worthwhile to use DEBUG to trace through these examples.

Overflows and Interrupts

DIV and IDIV operations assume that the quotient is significantly smaller than the original dividend. As a consequence, the operation can easily cause an overflow; when it does, an interrupt occurs, with unpredictable results. Dividing by zero always causes an interrupt. But dividing by 1 generates a quotient that is the same as the dividend and could also cause an interrupt.

Here's a useful rule: If the divisor is a byte, its contents must be greater than the left byte (AH) of the dividend; if the divisor is a word, its contents must be greater than the left word (DX) of the dividend; if the divisor is a doubleword, its contents must be greater than the left doubleword (EDX) of the dividend. The following illustration uses a divisor of 1, although other values could serve:

DIVIDE OPERATION	DIVIDEND	DIVISOR	QUOTIENT
Word by byte:	0123	01	(1)23
Doubleword by word:	0001 4026	0001	(1)4026

In both cases, the generated quotient exceeds its available space. You may be wise to include a test prior to a DIV or IDIV operation, as shown in the next two examples. In the first, DIVBYTE is a 1-byte divisor, and the dividend is already in the AX:

```
CMP   AH,DIVBYTE      ;Compare AH to divisor
JNB   F50             ;Bypass if not smaller
DIV   DIVBYTE         ;Divide word by byte
```

In the second example, DIVWORD is a 1-word divisor, and the dividend is in the DX:AX:

```
CMP   DX,DIVWORD      ;Compare DX to divisor
JNB   F70             ;Bypass if not smaller
DIV   DIVWORD         ;Divide doubleword by word
```

For IDIV, the logic should account for the fact that either dividend or divisor could be negative. Because the absolute value of the divisor must be the smaller of the two, you could use the NEG instruction to set a negative value temporarily to positive and restore the sign after the division.

Division by Subtraction

If a quotient is too large for the divisor, you could perform division by means of successive subtraction. That is, subtract the divisor from the dividend, increment a quotient value by 1, and continue subtracting until the dividend is less than the divisor. In the following example, the dividend is in the AX, the divisor is in the BX, and the quotient is developed in the CX:

```
        SUB CX,CX     ;Clear quotient
D20:    CMP AX,BX     ;If dividend < divisor,
        JB  D30       ; exit
        SUB AX,BX     ;Subtract divisor from dividend
        INC CX        ;Add 1 to quotient
        JMP D20       ;Repeat
D30:    ...           ;Quotient in CX, remainder in AX
```

At the end of the routine, the CX contains the quotient and the AX contains the remainder. The example is intentionally primitive to demonstrate the technique. If the quotient is in the DX:AX pair, include these two operations:

1. At D20, compare AX to BX only if DX is zero.
2. After the SUB instruction, insert SBB DX,00.

Note that a very large quotient and a small divisor may cause thousands of loops at a cost of processing time.

DIVISION BY SHIFTING

For division by a power of 2 (2, 4, 8, and so on), you may gain faster processing simply by shifting right the required number of bits. For the 8088/8086, a shift greater than 1 requires a shift value in the CL register. The following examples assume that the dividend is in the AX:

```
Divide by 2  (shift right 1):  SHR AX,01
Divide by 8  (shift right 3):  MOV CL,03     ;8088/8086
```

```
                                SHR AX,CL      ;
      Divide by 8  (shift right 3):  SHR CL,03      ;80286 and later
```

The following routine for an 80286 or later processor could be useful for right shifting a doubleword product in the DX:AX pair. Although specific to a 4-bit shift, it could be adapted to other values:

```
SHR   AX,04      ;Shift AX to right 4 bits
MOV   BL,DL      ;Store DL in BL
SHR   DX,04      ;Shift DX to right 4 bits
SHL   BL,04      ;Shift BL to left 4 bits
OR    DL,BL      ;Insert 4 bits from BL in DL
```

REVERSING THE SIGN

The NEG (negate) instruction reverses the sign of a binary value, from positive to negative and vice versa. In effect, NEG reverses the bits, just like NOT, and then adds 1 for proper two's complement notation. The general format for NEG is

[label:]	NEG	register/memory

Here are some unrelated examples:

```
NEG   CL          ;8 bits
NEG   BX          ;16 bits
NEG   EDX         ;32 bits
NEG   BINVAL      ;Byte or word in memory
```

Reversing the sign of a 32-bit (or larger) value involves more steps. Assume that the DX:AX pair contains a 32-bit binary number. NEG cannot act on the DX:AX pair concurrently, and using it on both registers would invalidly add 1 to both. Instead, use NOT to flip the bits, and use ADD and ADC to add the 1 for two's complement:

```
NOT   DX        ;Flip bits
NOT   AX        ;Flip bits
ADD   AX,1      ;Add 1 to AX
ADC   DX,0      ;Add carry to DX
```

One minor problem remains: It is all very well to perform arithmetic on binary data that the program itself defines or on data already in binary form on a disk file. However, data that enters a program from a keyboard is in ASCII format. Although ASCII data is suitable for displaying and printing, it requires special adjusting for arithmetic—a topic discussed in the next chapter.

THE NUMERIC DATA PROCESSOR

This section provides a general introduction to the numeric data processor; a full discussion is outside the scope of the book. The system board contains a socket for an Intel Numeric

Data Processor, known as a coprocessor. The 8087 coprocessor operates in conjunction with an 8088/86, the 80287 with an 80286, the 80387 with an 80386, and so forth.

The coprocessor has its own instruction set and floating-point hardware for performing such operations as exponentiation and logarithmic and trigonometric operations. The eight 80-bit floating-point registers can represent numeric values up to 10 to the 400th power. The coprocessor's mathematical processing is rated about 100 times faster than a regular processor.

The 8087 consists of eight 80-bit registers, R1-R8, in the following format:

S	exponent		significand	
79	78	64	63	0

Each register has an associated 2-bit tag that indicates its status:

00 Contains a valid number
01 Contains a zero value
10 Contains an invalid number
11 Is empty

The coprocessor recognizes seven types of numeric data:

1. *Word integer:* 16 bits of binary data.

S	number	
15	14	0

2. *Short integer:* 32 bits of binary data.

S	number	
31	30	0

3. *Long integer:* 64 bits of binary data.

S	number	
63	62	0

4. *Short real:* 32 bits of floating-point data.

S	exponent		significand	
31	30	23	22	0

5. *Long real:* 64 bits of floating-point data.

S	exponent		significand	
63	62	52	51	0

6. *Temporary real:* 80 bits of floating-point data.

S	exponent		significand	
79	78	64	63	0

7. *Packed decimal:* 18 significant decimal digits.

S	zeros		significand	
79	78	72	71	0

Types 1, 2, and 3 are common binary two's-complement formats. Types 4, 5, and 6 represent floating-point numbers. Type 7 contains 18 4Dbit decimal digits. You can load any of these formats from memory into a coprocessor register and can store the register contents into memory. However, for its calculations, the coprocessor converts all formats in its registers into temporary real. Data is stored in memory in reverse-byte sequence.

The processor requests a specific operation and delivers numeric data to the coprocessor, which performs the operation and returns the result. For assembling, use the appropriate .80x86 directive.

The INT 11H instruction can help determine the presence of a coprocessor. The operation delivers the equipment status to the AX, where bit 1 on means that a coprocessor is present.

KEY POINTS

- The maximum signed values for 1-byte accumulators are +127 and −128.
- For multiword addition, use ADC to account for any carry from a previous ADD. If the operation is performed in a loop, use CLC to initialize the carry flag to zero.
- Use MUL for unsigned data and IMUL for signed data.
- With MUL, if a multiplier is defined as a byte, the multiplicand is AL; if the multiplier is a word, the multiplicand is AX; if the multiplier is a doubleword, the multiplicand is EAX.
- Shift left (SHL or SAL) for multiplying by powers of 2.
- Use DIV for unsigned data and IDIV for signed data.
- For division, be especially careful of overflows. The divisor must be greater than the contents of the AH if the divisor is a byte, DX if the divisor is a word, or EDX if the divisor is a doubleword.

- With DIV, if a divisor is defined as a byte, the dividend is AX; if the divisor is a word, the dividend is DX:AX; if the divisor is a doubleword, the dividend is EDX:EAX.
- Shift right for dividing by powers of 2—SHR for unsigned fields and SAR for signed fields.

QUESTIONS

13-1. For both unsigned and signed data, (a) what are the maximum values in a byte and (b) what is the maximum value in a word?

13-2. Distinguish between a carry and an overflow as a result of an arithmetic operation.

13-3. For the following binary additions, show the sums as binary numbers and as unsigned and signed decimal numbers, plus show the settings of the overflow and carry flags:

```
(a) 00110011  (b) 01110110  (c) 11010110
   +00011000     +00011001     +01011001
```

13-4. Revise Figure 13-2 so that the routine adds three pairs of words instead of two. Define the additional words as WORD3A and WORD3B and change the old WORD3A and WORD3B to WORD4A and WORD4B.

For Questions 5-8, refer to the following data, with words properly defined in reverse sequence:

```
VALUE1  DW  0153H
        DW  1624H
VALUE2  DW  0328H
        DW  3C44H
RESULT  DW  0
        DW  0
        DW  0
```

13-5. Code the instructions to add the following: (a) the word VALUE1 to the word VALUE2; (b) the doubleword beginning at VALUE1 to the doubleword at VALUE2.

13-6. Explain the effect of the following related instructions:

```
STC
MOV  DX,VALUE1
ADC  DX,VALUE2
```

13-7. Code the instructions to multiply (MUL) the following: (a) the word VALUE1 by the word VALUE2; (b) the doubleword beginning at VALUE1 by the word VALUE2. Store the product in RESULT.

13-8. Code the instructions to divide (DIV) the following: (a) the word VALUE1 by 36; (b) the doubleword beginning at VALUE1 by the word VALUE2.

13-9. What divisors other than zero cause overflow errors?

13-10. Refer to the section "Multiplication by Shifting," which illustrates shifting left 4 bits. Revise the example for a left shift of 2 bits.

14 ARITHMETIC II: PROCESSING ASCII AND BCD DATA

Objective: To examine ASCII and BCD data formats, to perform arithmetic in these formats, and to cover conversions between these formats and binary.

INTRODUCTION

The natural data format for arithmetic on a computer is binary. As seen in Chapter 13, binary format causes no major problems, as long as the program itself defines the data. However, much of the numeric data that a program must process is in a form other than binary. For example, numeric data enters a program from a keyboard as ASCII characters, in base-10 format. Similarly, the display of numeric values on a screen is in ASCII format.

A related numeric format, *binary-coded decimal (BCD),* has occasional uses and appears as unpacked and as packed. The PC provides a number of instructions that facilitate simple arithmetic and conversion between formats. This chapter also covers techniques for converting ASCII data into binary format to perform arithmetic, as well as techniques for converting the binary results back into ASCII format for viewing. The program at the end of the chapter combines much of the material covered in Chapters 1 through 13.

If you have programmed in a high-level language such as C, you are used to the compiler accounting for the radix (decimal or binary) point. However, the computer does not recognize a radix point in an arithmetic field, so that you as an assembly language programmer have to account for its position.

Instructions introduced in this chapter are:

AAA	ASCII Adjust After Addition
AAS	ASCII Adjust After Subtraction
AAM	ASCII Adjust After Multiplication
AAD	ASCII Adjust for Division
DAA	Decimal Adjustment After Addition
DAS	Decimal Adjustment After Subtraction

DATA IN DECIMAL FORMAT

To this point, we have handled numeric values in binary and ASCII formats. The PC system also supports binary-coded decimal (BCD) format, which allows for some limited arithmetic operations. Two uses for BCD format are:

1. BCD permits proper rounding of numbers with no loss of precision, a feature that is particularly useful for handling dollars and cents. (Rounding of binary numbers that represent dollars and cents may cause a loss of precision.)
2. BCD is often a simpler format for performing arithmetic on small values entered from a keyboard or for output on the screen or printer.

A BCD digit consists of four bits that represent the decimal digits 0 through 9:

Binary	BCD digit	Binary	BCD digit
0000	0	0101	5
0001	1	0110	6
0010	2	0111	7
0011	3	1000	8
0100	4	1001	9

You can store BCD digits as unpacked or as packed:

1. *Unpacked BCD* contains a single BCD digit in the lower (rightmost) four bits of each byte, with zeros in the upper four bits. Note that although ASCII format is also in a sense "unpacked," it isn't called that.
2. *Packed BCD* contains two BCD digits, one in the upper four bits and one in the lower four bits. This format is commonly used for arithmetic using the numeric coprocessor, defined by the DT directive as 10 bytes.

Let's examine the representation of the decimal number 1,527 in the three decimal formats:

Format	Contents	Length
ASCII	31 35 32 37	Four bytes
Unpacked BCD	01 05 02 07	Four bytes
Packed BCD	15 27	Two bytes

The processor performs arithmetic on ASCII and BCD values one digit at a time. You have to use special instructions for converting between the two formats.

PROCESSING ASCII DATA

Because data that you enter from a keyboard is in ASCII format, the representation in memory of an entered decimal value such as 1234 is 31323334H. But performing arithmetic on the ASCII value involves the AAA and AAS instructions:

[label:]	AAA	;ASCII Adjust After Addition
[label:]	AAS	;ASCII Adjust After Subtraction

These instructions are coded without operands and automatically adjust an ASCII value in the AX register. The adjustment occurs because an ASCII value represents an unpacked base-10 number, whereas the processor performs base-2 arithmetic.

Adding ASCII Numbers

Consider the effect of adding the ASCII numbers 8 (38H) and 4 (34H):

```
       38H
      +34H
Total  6CH
```

The sum 6CH is neither a correct ASCII nor a correct binary value. However, ignore the leftmost 6, and add 6 to the rightmost hex C: Hex C plus 6 = hex 12, the correct answer in terms of decimal numbers. Why add 6? Because that's the difference between hexadecimal (16) and decimal (10). Although a little oversimplified, it does indicate the way in which AAA performs its adjustment.

The AAA operation checks the rightmost hex digit (4 bits) of the AL register. If the digit is between A and F or the auxiliary carry flag (AF) is 1, the operation adds 6 to the AL register, adds 1 to the AH register, and sets the carry (CF) and auxiliary carry flags to 1. In all cases, AAA clears the leftmost hex digit of the AL to zero.

As an example, assume that the AX contains 0038H and the BX contains 0034H. The 38 in the AL and the 34 in the BL represent two ASCII bytes that are to be added. The sum of the 8 and the 4 should be 12. Addition and adjustment are as follows:

```
ADD  AL,BL     ;Add 34H to 38H, equals 006CH
AAA            ;Adjust for ASCII Add, equals 0102H
```

Because after the ADD the rightmost hex digit of the AL is C, AAA adds 6 to the AL, adds 1 to the AH, sets the CF and AF flags, and clears to zero the leftmost hex digit of the AL. The result in the AX is now 0102H.

To restore the ASCII representation, simply insert 3s in the leftmost hex digits of the AH and AL to get 3132H, or decimal 12:

```
OR  AX,3030H    ;Result is now 3132H
```

In the next example, the AF flag affects the result. This time, the ADD operation adds 39H to 39H in the AL, giving 72H and setting the AF (because of the carry from bit 3 to bit 4). Although the value in the rightmost four bits is only 2, because the AF is set, AAA adds 6 to the AL, adds 1 to the AH, and clears the leftmost hex digit of the AL. The result in the AX is now corrected as 0108 (or 18).

All that is very well for adding 1-byte ASCII numbers. Adding multibyte ASCII numbers, however, requires a loop that processes from right to left (low order to high order) and accounts for carries. The example in Figure 14-1 adds two 3-byte ASCII numbers, ASCVAL1 and ASCVAL2, and produces a 4-byte sum, ASCTOT. Note the following points:

- A CLC instruction at the start of B10ADD zeros the CF flag.
- Following B20, ADC is used for addition because an ADD may cause a carry that should be added to the next (left) byte.
- A MOVZX instruction clears the AH on each loop because each AAA may add 1 to the AH. ADC, however, accounts for any carry. Note that the use of XOR or SUB to clear the AH would change the CF flag.
- When looping is complete, the procedure moves the AH (containing either a final 00 or 01) to the leftmost byte of ASCTOT.
- At the end, ASCTOT contains 01020702H. To insert ASCII 3 in each byte, the program calls C10CONV, which loops through ASCTOT in memory and ORs each byte with 30H. The result is 31323732H, or decimal 1272, which the program displays before ending.

The routine did not use OR after AAA to insert leftmost 3s, because OR sets the carry flag and changes the effect for the ADC instructions. A solution that saves the flag settings is to push (PUSHF) the flags register, execute the OR, and then pop (POPF) the flags to restore them:

```
ADC     AL,[DI]     ;Add with carry
AAA                 ;Adjust for ASCII
PUSHF               ;Save flags
OR      AL,30H      ;Insert ASCII 3
POPF                ;Restore flags
MOV    [BX],AL      ;Store sum
```

Subtracting ASCII Numbers

The AAS instruction works like AAA. AAS checks the rightmost hex digit (4 bits) of the AL. If the digit is between A and F or the auxiliary carry is 1, the operation subtracts 6 from the AL, subtracts 1 from the AH, and sets the auxiliary (AF) and carry (CF) flags. In all cases, AAS clears the leftmost hex digit of the AL to zero.

The next two examples assume that ASCVAL1 contains 39H and ASCVAL2 contains 35H. The first example subtracts ASCVAL2 (35H) from ASCVAL1 (39H). AAS does not need to make an adjustment, because the rightmost hex digit is less than hex A:

```
TITLE      A14ASCAD (COM)  Adding ASCII numbers
           .MODEL SMALL
           .CODE
.386
           ORG     100H
BEGIN:     JMP     SHORT A10MAIN
; ----------------------------------------------------------
ASCVAL1    DB      '548'             ;ASCII items
ASCVAL2    DB      '724'
ASCTOT     DB      '0000', '$'
; ----------------------------------------------------------
A10MAIN    PROC    NEAR
           CALL    B10ADD
           CALL    C10CONV
           MOV     AH,09H            ;Request display
           LEA     DX,ASCTOT         ;  total
           INT     21H
           MOV     AX,4C00H          ;End processing
           INT     21H
A10MAIN    ENDP
;                  Add ASCII values:
;                  ----------------
B10ADD     PROC    NEAR
           CLC                       ;Clear carry flag
           LEA     SI,ASCVAL1+2      ;Initialize ASCII numbers
           LEA     DI,ASCVAL2+2
           LEA     BX,ASCTOT+3
           MOV     CX,03             ;Initialize 3 loops
B20:
           MOVZX   AX,[SI]           ;Load ASCII byte in AX
           ADC     AL,[DI]           ;Add (with carry)
           AAA                       ;Adjust for ASCII
           MOV     [BX],AL           ;Store sum
           DEC     SI
           DEC     DI
           DEC     BX
           LOOP    B20               ;Loop 3 times
           MOV     [BX],AH           ;At end, store carry
           RET
B10ADD     ENDP
;                  Convert binary to ASCII:
;                  -----------------------
C10CONV    PROC    NEAR
           LEA     BX,ASCTOT+3       ;Convert ASCTOT
           MOV     CX,04             ;  to ASCII
C20:
           OR      BYTE PTR[BX],30H
           DEC     BX
           LOOP    C20               ;Loop 4 times
           RET
C10CONV    ENDP
           END     BEGIN
```

Figure 14-1 Adding ASCII Numbers

```
                        AX     AF  CF
MOV   AL,ASCVAL1      ;0039
SUB   AL,ASCVAL2      ;0004    0   0
AAS                   ;0004    0   0
OR    AL,30H          ;0034
```

The second example subtracts ASCVAL1 (39H) from ASCVAL2 (35H). Because the rightmost digit of the result is hex C, AAS subtracts 6 from the AL, subtracts 1 from the AH, and sets the AF and CF flags:

```
                          AX    AF  CF
MOV    AL,ASCVAL2      ;0035
SUB    AL,ASCVAL1      ;00FC    1   1
AAS                    ;FF06    1   1
```

The answer, which should be −4, is FF06H, its ten's complement, which has little value.

PROCESSING UNPACKED BCD DATA

Multiplication and division of ASCII numbers require that you first convert the numbers into unpacked BCD format. You can use the AAM and AAD instructions to perform arithmetic directly on unpacked BCD numbers:

[label:]	AAM	;ASCII Adjust After Multiplication
[label:]	AAD	;ASCII Adjust Before Division

Multiplying ASCII Numbers

The AAM instruction corrects the result of multiplying ASCII data in the AX register. However, you must first clear the 3 in the leftmost hex digit of each byte, thus converting the value to unpacked BCD. For example, the ASCII number 31323334 becomes 01020304 as unpacked BCD. Also, because the adjustment is only one byte at a time, you can multiply only 1-byte fields and have to perform the operation repetitively in a loop. Use only the MUL (unsigned multiplication), not the IMUL, operation.

AAM divides the AL by 10 (0AH) and stores the quotient in the AH and the remainder in the AL. For example, suppose that the AL contains 35H and the CL contains 39H. The following code multiplies the contents of the AL by the CL and converts the result to ASCII format:

```
INSTRUCTION               COMMENT                  AX    CL
AND   CL,0FH   ;Convert CL to 09                  0035  09
AND   AL,0FH   ;Convert AL to 05                  0005  09
MUL   CL       ;Multiply AL by CL                 002D  09
AAM            ;Convert AX to unpacked BCD        0405
OR    AX,3030H ;Convert AX to ASCII               3435
```

The MUL operation generates 45 (002DH) in the AX. AAM divides this value by 10, generating a quotient of 04 in the AH and a remainder of 05 in the AL. The OR instruction then converts the unpacked BCD value to ASCII format.

Figure 14-2 depicts multiplying a 4-byte ASCII multiplicand by a 1-byte ASCII multiplier. Because AAM can accommodate only 1-byte operations, the procedure B10MULT steps through the multiplicand one byte at a time, from right to left. At the end, the unpacked BCD product is 0108090105, which a loop in C10CONV converts to true ASCII format as 3138393135, or decimal 18,915. The program displays the product before it ends processing.

If the multiplier is greater than one byte, you have to provide yet another loop that steps through the multiplier. In that case, it may be simpler to convert the ASCII data to binary format, as covered in a later section.

```
TITLE      A14ASCMU (COM)  Multiplying ASCII numbers
           .MODEL SMALL
           .CODE
           ORG    100H
BEGIN:     JMP    A10MAIN
;-------------------------------------------------
MULTCAN    DB     '3783'            ;ASCII items
MULTPLR    DB     '5'
ASCPROD    DB     5 DUP(0), '$'
;-------------------------------------------------
A10MAIN    PROC   NEAR
           CALL   B10MULT
           CALL   C10CONV
           MOV    AH,09H            ;Request display
           LEA    DX,ASCPROD
           INT    21H
           MOV    AX,4C00H          ;End processing
           INT    21H
A10MAIN    ENDP
;                 Multiply ASCII numbers:
;                 ----------------------
B10MULT    PROC   NEAR
           MOV    CX,04             ;Initialize 4 loops
           LEA    SI,MULTCAN+3
           LEA    DI,ASCPROD+4
           AND    MULTPLR,0FH       ;Clear ASCII 3
B20:
           MOV    AL,[SI]           ;Load ASCII character
           AND    AL,0FH            ;Clear ASCII 3
           MUL    MULTPLR           ;Multiply
           AAM                      ;Adjust for ASCII
           ADD    AL,[DI]           ;Add to
           AAA                      ;  stored
           MOV    [DI],AL           ;  product
           DEC    DI
           MOV    [DI],AH           ;Store product carry
           DEC    SI
           LOOP   B20               ;Loop 4 times
           RET
B10MULT    ENDP
;                 Convert product to ASCII:
;                 ------------------------
C10CONV    PROC   NEAR
           LEA    BX,ASCPROD+4      ;Right to left,
           MOV    CX,05             ;  5 bytes
C20:
           OR     BYTE PTR[BX],30H
           DEC    BX
           LOOP   C20               ;Loop 4 times
           RET
C10CONV    ENDP
           END    BEGIN
```

Figure 14-2 Multiplying ASCII Numbers

Dividing ASCII Numbers

The AAD instruction provides a correction of an ASCII dividend prior to dividing. Just as with AAM, you first clear the leftmost 3s from the ASCII bytes to create unpacked BCD format. AAD allows for a 2-byte dividend in the AX. The divisor can be only a single byte containing 01 to 09.

Assume that the AX contains the ASCII value 28 (3238H) and the CL contains the divisor, ASCII 7 (37H). The following instructions perform the adjustment and division:

```
INSTRUCTION        COMMENT                    AX    CL
AND  CL,0FH        ;Convert to unpacked BCD   3238  07
AND  AX,0F0FH      ;Convert to unpacked BCD   0208
AAD                ;Convert to binary         001C
DIV  CL            ;Divide by 7               0004
```

AAD multiplies the AH by 10 (0AH), adds the product 20 (14H) to the AL, and clears the AH. The result, 001CH, is the hex representation of decimal 28.

Figure 14-3 allows for dividing a 1-byte divisor into a 4-byte dividend. The procedure B10DIV steps through the dividend from left to right. LODSB gets a byte from DIVDND into the AL (via the SI), and STOSB stores bytes from the AL into QUOTNT (via the DI). The remainder stays in the AH register so that AAD can adjust it in the AL. At the end, the quotient, in unpacked BCD format, is 00090204, and the remainder in the AH is 02. The procedure C10CONV converts the quotient to ASCII format as 30393234 (from left to right this time). The program displays the ASCII quotient, 0924, before ending.

If the divisor is greater than one byte, you have to provide yet another loop to step through the divisor. Better yet, see the later section "Conversion of ASCII to Binary Format."

PROCESSING PACKED BCD DATA

In the preceding example of ASCII division, the quotient was 00090204. If you compress this value, keeping only the right digit of each byte, the result is 0924, now in packed BCD format. You can also perform addition and subtraction on packed BCD data. For this purpose, there are two adjustment instructions, DAA and DAS:

[label:]	DAA	;Decimal Adjustment After Addition
[label:]	DAS	;Decimal Adjustment After Subtraction

DAA corrects the result of adding two packed BCD values in the AL, and DAS corrects the result of subtracting them. Once again, you have to process the BCD fields one byte (two digits) at a time.

The BCD sum in the AL consists of two 4-bit digits. If the value of the rightmost digit exceeds 9 or the AF flag is set, DAA adds 6 to the AL and sets the AF. If the value in the AL now exceeds 99H or the CF is set, DAA adds 60H to the AL and sets the CF. Otherwise, it clears the AF and CF. The following example should clarify this procedure.

Consider adding the BCD values 057836 and 069427. With the CF flag cleared to 0, start the addition with the rightmost pair of digits.

```
TITLE       A14ASCDV (COM)  Dividing ASCII numbers
            .MODEL SMALL
            .CODE
            ORG     100H
BEGIN:      JMP     SHORT A10MAIN
;---------------------------------------------------------------
DIVDND      DB      '3698'              ;ASCII items
DIVSOR      DB      '4'
ASCQUOT     DB      4 DUP(0), '$'
;---------------------------------------------------------------
A10MAIN     PROC    NEAR
            CALL    B10DIV
            CALL    C10CONV
            MOV     AH,09H              ;Display
            LEA     DX,ASCQUOT          ;  quotient
            INT     21H
            MOV     AX,4C00H            ;End processing
            INT     21H
A10MAIN     ENDP
;                   Divide ASCII numbers:
;                   --------------------
B10DIV      PROC    NEAR
            MOV     CX,04               ;Initialize 4 loops
            SUB     AH,AH               ;Clear left byte of dividend
            AND     DIVSOR,0FH          ;Clear divisor of ASCII 3
            LEA     SI,DIVDND
            LEA     DI,ASCQUOT
B20:
            LODSB                       ;Load ASCII byte
            AND     AL,0FH              ;Clear ASCII 3
            AAD                         ;Adjust for divide
            DIV     DIVSOR              ;Divide
            STOSB                       ;Store quotient
            LOOP    B20                 ;Four times?
            RET                         ;  yes, exit
B10DIV      ENDP
;                   Convert product to ASCII:
;                   ------------------------
C10CONV     PROC    NEAR
            LEA     BX,ASCQUOT          ;Leftmost byte,
            MOV     CX,04               ;  4 bytes
C20:
            OR      BYTE PTR[BX],30H  ;Clear ASCII 3
            INC     BX                  ;Next byte
            LOOP    C20                 ;Loop 4 times
            RET                         ;Exit
C10CONV     ENDP
            END     BEGIN
```

Figure 14-3 Dividing ASCII Numbers

	BCD	HEX	BINARY	STORED BCD
First ADC, clears CF	36	36	0011 0110	
	27	27	0010 0111	
	63	5D	0101 1101	
DAA adds 06H, sets AF			0000 0110	
			0110 0011	63
Second ADC, sets CF	78	78	0111 1000	
	94	94	1001 0100	
	(1)72	(1)0C	(1)0000 1100	
DAA adds 06H, sets AF			0000 0110	

```
                                                 0001 0010
DAA adds 60H (because                            0110 0000
  CF set), sets CF                               0111 0010      72
Third ADC, adds 1          05          05        0000 0101
 (because CF set),         06          06        0000 0110
 clears CF                  1           1        0000 0001
                           12          0C        0000 1100
DAA adds 06H, sets AF                            0000 0110
                                                 0001 0010      12
```

The BCD sum is now correctly stored as 127263.

The program in Figure 14-4 illustrates the foregoing example of BCD addition. The procedure B10CONV converts the ASCII values ASCVAL1 and ASCVAL2 to the packed BCD values BCDVAL1 and BCDVAL2, respectively. Processing, which is from right to left, could just as easily be from left to right. Also, processing words is easier than processing bytes because you need two ASCII bytes to generate one packed BCD byte. However, the use of words does require an even number of bytes in the ASCII field.

The procedure C10ADD performs a loop three times to add the packed BCD numbers to BCDSUM. The final total is 00127263H, which you can confirm with DEBUG—use D DS:114.

CONVERTING ASCII DATA TO BINARY FORMAT

Performing arithmetic in ASCII or BCD format is suitable only for short fields. For most arithmetic purposes, it is more practical to convert such numbers into binary format. In fact, it is easier to convert from ASCII directly to binary than to convert from ASCII to BCD to binary.

Conversion from ASCII to binary is based on the fact that an ASCII number is in base 10 and the computer performs arithmetic in base 2. Here is the procedure:

1. Start with the rightmost byte of the ASCII field and process from right to left.
2. Strip the 3 from the left hex digit of each ASCII byte, thereby forming a packed BCD number.
3. Multiply the first BCD digit by 1, the second by 10 (0AH), the third by 100 (64H), and so forth, and sum the products.

The following example converts ASCII number 1234 to binary:

```
        Decimal                  Hexadecimal
     Step       Product        Step      Product
4 × 1 =            4       4 ×  01H =       4H
3 × 10 =          30       3 ×  0AH =      1EH
2 × 100 =        200       2 ×  64H =      C8H
1 × 1000 =      1000       1 × 3E8H =     3E8H
Total:          1234         04D2H
```

```
TITLE    A14BCDAD (COM)  Convert ASCII to BCD and add
         .MODEL SMALL
         .CODE
.386
         ORG     100H
BEGIN:   JMP     SHORT A10MAIN
;--------------------------------------------------
ASCVAL1  DB      '057836'          ;ASCII data items
ASCVAL2  DB      '069427'
BCDVAL1  DB      '000'             ;BCD data items
BCDVAL2  DB      '000'
BCDSUM   DB      4 DUP(0)
;--------------------------------------------------
A10MAIN  PROC    NEAR
         LEA     SI,ASCVAL1+4      ;Initialize for ASCVAL1
         LEA     DI,BCDVAL1+2
         CALL    B10CONV           ;Call convert routine
         LEA     SI,ASCVAL2+4      ;Initialize for ASCVAL2
         LEA     DI,BCDVAL2+2
         CALL    B10CONV           ;Call convert routine
         CALL    C10ADD            ;Call add routine
         MOV     AX,4C00H          ;End processing
         INT     21H
A10MAIN  ENDP
;                Convert ASCII to BCD:
;                --------------------
B10CONV  PROC
         MOV     CX,03             ;No. of words to convert
B20:     MOV     AX,[SI]           ;Get ASCII pair
         XCHG    AH,AL
         SHL     AL,04             ;Shift off
         SHL     AX,04             ;  ASCII 3s
         MOV     [DI],AH           ;Store BCD digits
         SUB     SI,02
         DEC     DI
         LOOP    B20               ;Three times?
         RET                       ;  yes, return
B10CONV  ENDP
;                Add BCD numbers:
;                ---------------
C10ADD   PROC
         XOR     AH,AH             ;Clear AH
         LEA     SI,BCDVAL1+2      ;Initialize
         LEA     DI,BCDVAL2+2      ;  BCD
         LEA     BX,BCDSUM+3       ;  addresses
         MOV     CX,03             ;3-byte fields
         CLC
C20:
         MOV     AL,[SI]           ;Get BCDVAL1 (or LODSB)
         ADC     AL,[DI]           ;Add BCDVAL2
         DAA                       ;Decimal adjust
         MOV     [BX],AL           ;Store in BCDSUM
         DEC     SI
         DEC     DI
         DEC     BX
         LOOP    C20               ;Loop 3 times
         RET
C10ADD   ENDP
         END     BEGIN
```

Figure 14-4 Converting and Adding BCD Numbers

Try checking that the sum 04D2H really equals decimal 1234. In Figure 14-5, the procedure B10CONV converts ASCII number 1234 to its binary equivalent. An LEA instruction

```
TITLE      A14ASCBI (COM)  Convert ASCII to binary format
           .MODEL SMALL
           .CODE
           ORG    100H
BEGIN:     JMP    SHORT A10MAIN
; ----------------------------------------------------------
ASCVAL     DB     '1234'             ;Data items
BINVAL     DW     0
ASCLEN     DW     4
MULFACT    DW     1
; ----------------------------------------------------------
A10MAIN    PROC   NEAR               ;Main procedure
           CALL   B10CONV
           MOV    AX,4C00H
           INT    21H                ;End processing
A10MAIN    ENDP

B10CONV    PROC   NEAR
           MOV    BX,10              ;Mult factor
           MOV    CX,04              ;Count for loop
           LEA    SI,ASCVAL+3        ;Address of ASCVAL
B20:
           MOV    AL,[SI]            ;Select ASCII character
           AND    AX,000FH           ;Remove 3-zone
           MUL    MULFACT            ;Multiply by 10 factor
           ADD    BINVAL,AX          ;Add to binary
           MOV    AX,MULFACT         ;Calculate next
           MUL    BX                 ;  10 factor
           MOV    MULFACT,AX
           DEC    SI                 ;Last ASCII character?
           LOOP   B20                ;  no, continue
           RET                       ;  yes, return
B10CONV    ENDP
           END    BEGIN
```

Figure 14-5 Converting ASCII Numbers to Binary Format

initializes the address of the rightmost byte of the ASCII field, ASCVAL+3, in the SI register. The instruction at B20 that moves the ASCII byte to the AL is

```
MOV AL,[SI]
```

The operation uses the address of ASCVAL+3 to copy the rightmost byte of ASCVAL into the AL. Each iteration of the loop decrements the SI by 1 and references the next byte to the left. The loop repeats for each of the four bytes of ASCVAL. Also, each iteration multiplies MULFACT by 10 (0AH), giving multipliers of 1, 10 (0AH), 100 (64H), and so forth. At the end, BINVAL contains the correct binary value, D204H, in reverse-byte sequence, which you can confirm with DEBUG.

The routine is coded for clarity; for faster processing, the multiplier could be stored in the DI register.

CONVERTING BINARY DATA TO ASCII FORMAT

To print or display the result of binary arithmetic, you have to convert it into ASCII format. The operation involves reversing the previous step: Instead of multiplying, continue dividing the binary number by 10 (0AH) until the quotient is less than 10. Each remainder, which can be only 0 through 9, successively generates the ASCII number. As an example, let's convert 4D2H back into decimal format:

Divide by 10	Quotient	Remainder
A ⟌ 4D2	7B	4
A ⟌ 7B	C	3
A ⟌ C	1	2

Because the quotient (1) is now less than the divisor (0AH), the operation is complete. The remainders from right to left, along with the last quotient, form the BCD result: 1234. All that remains is to store these digits in memory with ASCII 3s, as 31323334.

The program in Figure 14-6 converts binary number 04D2H to ASCII format. The procedure B10CONV divides the binary number successively by 10, until the remaining quotient is less than 10 (0AH), and stores the generated hex digits in ASCII format as 31323334, which the program displays before ending. You may find it useful, if not downright entertaining, to reproduce this program and trace its execution step by step.

```
TITLE     A14BINAS (COM)  Convert binary data to ASCII
          .MODEL SMALL
          .CODE
          ORG     100H
BEGIN:    JMP     SHORT A10MAIN
; ----------------------------------------------------------
ASCVAL    DB      4 DUP(' '), '$' ;Data items
BINVAL    DW      04D2H
; ----------------------------------------------------------
A10MAIN   PROC    NEAR                ;Main procedure
          CALL    B10CONV
          MOV     AH,09H              ;Display
          LEA     DX,ASCVAL           ;  ASCII value
          INT     21H
          MOV     AX,4C00H            ;End processing
          INT     21H
A10MAIN   ENDP

B10CONV   PROC    NEAR
          MOV     CX,0010             ;Division factor
          LEA     SI,ASCVAL+3         ;Address of ASCVAL
          MOV     AX,BINVAL           ;Get binary amount
B20:
          CMP     AX,CX               ;Value < 10?
          JB      B30                 ;  yes, exit
          XOR     DX,DX               ;Clear upper quotient
          DIV     CX                  ;Divide by 10
          OR      DL,30H
          MOV     [SI],DL             ;Store ASCII character
          DEC     SI
          JMP     B20
B30:
          OR      AL,30H              ;Store last quotient
          MOV     [SI],AL             ;  as ASCII character
          RET
B10CONV   ENDP
          END     BEGIN
```

Figure 14-6 Converting Binary Numbers to ASCII Format

SHIFTING AND ROUNDING A PRODUCT

Suppose your product contains three decimal places and you have to round it and reduce it to two decimal places. As an example, if the product is 17.385, add 5 to the rightmost (unwanted) decimal position, and shift right one digit:

```
Product:           17.385
Add 5:            + 0.005
Rounded product:  17.390 = 17.39
```

If (a) the product is 17.3855, add 50 and shift two digits, and if (b) the product is 17.38555, add 500 and shift three digits:

```
(a) 17.3855              (b) 17.38555
  + 0.0050                 + 0.00500
    17.3905 = 17.39          17.39055 = 17.39
```

Further, a number with six decimal places requires adding 5,000 and shifting four digits, and so forth. Now, because a computer normally processes binary data, 17.385 appears as 43E9H. Adding 5 to 43E9H gives 43EEH, or 17390 in decimal format. So far, so good. But shifting one binary digit results in 21F7H, or 8695—indeed, the shift simply halves the value. You require a shift that is equivalent to shifting *right* one decimal digit. You can accomplish this shift by dividing the rounded binary value by 10, or hex A: Hex 43EE divided by hex A = 6CBH. Conversion of 6CBH to a decimal number gives 1739. Now just insert a decimal point in the correct position, and you can display the rounded, shifted value as 17.39.

By this method, you can round and shift any binary number. For three decimal places, add 5 and divide by 10; for four decimal places, add 50 and divide by 100. Perhaps you have noticed a pattern: The rounding factor (5, 50, 500, etc.) is always one-half of the value of the shift factor (10, 100, 1,000, etc.).

Of course, the radix point in a binary number is implied and is not actually present.

PROGRAM: CONVERTING ASCII DATA

The program in Figure 14-7 allows users to enter the number of hours worked and the rate of pay for employees and displays the calculated wage. For brevity, the program omits some error checking that would otherwise be included. The procedures are as follows:

A10MAIN	Handles initialization and invokes the procedures for entering data and calculating wage.
B10INPT	Accepts hours and rate of pay in ASCII format from the keyboard. These values may contain a decimal point.
C10HOUR	Initializes conversion of ASCII hours to binary.
D10RATE	Initializes conversion of ASCII rate to binary.
E10MULT	Performs the multiplication, rounding, and shifting. A wage with zero, one, or two decimal places does not require rounding or shifting.

```
TITLE       A14SCREMP (EXE) Enter hours and rate, display wage
            .MODEL SMALL
            .STACK 64
            .DATA
LEFCOL      EQU     28                  ;Equates for screen
RITCOL      EQU     52                  ;  locations
TOPROW      EQU     10
BOTROW      EQU     14

HRSPAR      LABEL   BYTE                ;Hours parameter list:
MAXHLEN     DB      6                   ;
ACTHLEN     DB      ?                   ;
HRSFLD      DB      6 DUP(?)            ;

RATEPAR     LABEL   BYTE                ;Rate parameter list:
MAXRLEN     DB      6                   ;
ACTRLEN     DB      ?                   ;
RATEFLD     DB      6 DUP(?)            ;

MESSG1      DB      'Hours worked? '
MESSG2      DB      'Rate of pay?  '
MESSG3      DB      'Wage =  '
ASCWAGE     DB      10 DUP(30H), 13, 10
MESSG4      DB      'Press any key to continue or Esc to quit'

ADJUST      DW      ?                   ;Data items
BINVAL      DW      00
BINHRS      DW      00
BINRATE     DW      00
COL         DB      00
DECIND      DB      00
MULT10      DW      01
NODEC       DW      00
ROW         DB      00
SHIFT       DW      ?
TENWD       DW      10
; -----------------------------------------------------------
.386
            .CODE
A10MAIN     PROC    FAR
            MOV     AX,@data            ;Initialize DS
            MOV     DS,AX               ;  and ES registers
            MOV     ES,AX
            CALL    Q10SCR              ;Clear screen
A20LOOP:
            CALL    Q30WIN              ;Clear window
            CALL    Q20CURS             ;Set cursor
            CALL    B10INPT             ;Accept hours & rate
            CALL    C10HOUR             ;Convert hours to binary
            CALL    D10RATE             ;Convert rate to binary
            CALL    E10MULT             ;Calculate wage, round
            CALL    F10WAGE             ;Convert wage to ASCII
            CALL    G10DISP             ;Display wage
            CALL    H10PAUS             ;Pause for user
            CMP     AL,1BH              ;Esc pressed?
            JNE     A20LOOP             ;  no, continue
            CALL    Q10SCR              ;  yes, clear screen
            MOV     AX,4C00H            ;End processing
            INT     21H
A10MAIN     ENDP
```

Figure 14-7a Displaying Employee Wages

```
;               Input hours & rate:
;               -------------------
B10INPT  PROC   NEAR
         MOV    ROW,TOPROW+1        ;Set cursor
         MOV    COL,LEFCOL+3
         CALL   Q20CURS
         INC    ROW
         MOV    AH,40H              ;Request display
         MOV    BX,01               ;File handle
         MOV    CX,14               ;No. of characters
         LEA    DX,MESSG1           ;Prompt for hours
         INT    21H
         MOV    AH,0AH
         LEA    DX,HRSPAR           ;Accept hours
         INT    21H
         MOV    COL,LEFCOL+3        ;Set column
         CALL   Q20CURS
         INC    ROW
         MOV    AH,40H              ;Request display
         MOV    BX,01               ;File handle
         MOV    CX,14               ;No. of characters
         LEA    DX,MESSG2           ;Prompt for rate
         INT    21H
         MOV    AH,0AH
         LEA    DX,RATEPAR          ;Accept rate
         INT    21H
         RET
B10INPT  ENDP
;               Process hours:
;               --------------
C10HOUR  PROC   NEAR
         MOV    NODEC,00
         MOVZX  CX,ACTHLEN
         LEA    SI,HRSFLD-1         ;Set right position
         ADD    SI,CX               ;  of hours
         CALL   J10ASBI             ;Convert to binary
         MOV    AX,BINVAL
         MOV    BINHRS,AX
         RET
C10HOUR  ENDP
;               Process rate:
;               -------------
D10RATE  PROC   NEAR
         MOVZX  CX,ACTRLEN
         LEA    SI,RATEFLD-1        ;Set right position
         ADD    SI,CX               ;  of rate
         CALL   J10ASBI             ;Convert to binary
         MOV    AX,BINVAL
         MOV    BINRATE,AX
         RET
D10RATE  ENDP
;               Multiply, round, and shift:
;               ---------------------------
E10MULT  PROC   NEAR
         MOV    CX,05
         LEA    DI,ASCWAGE          ;Set ASCII wage
         MOV    AX,3030H            ;  to 30s
         CLD
         REP STOSW
```

Figure 14-7b Displaying Employee Wages

```
          MOV    SHIFT,10
          MOV    ADJUST,00
          MOV    CX,NODEC
          CMP    CL,06             ;If more than 6
          JA     E40               ;  decimals, error
          DEC    CX
          DEC    CX
          JLE    E30               ;Bypass if 0, 1, 2 decs
          MOV    NODEC,02
          MOV    AX,01
E20:
          MUL    TENWD             ;Calculate shift factor
          LOOP   E20
          MOV    SHIFT,AX
          SHR    AX,1              ;Calculate round value
          MOV    ADJUST,AX
E30:
          MOV    AX,BINHRS
          MUL    BINRATE           ;Calculate wage
          ADD    AX,ADJUST         ;Round wage
          ADC    DX,00
          CMP    DX,SHIFT          ;Product too large
          JB     E50               ;  for DIV?
E40:
          XOR    AX,AX             ;Clear AX
          JMP    E70
E50:
          CMP    ADJUST,00         ;Shift required?
          JZ     E80               ;  no, bypass
          DIV    SHIFT             ;Shift wage
E70:      XOR    DX,DX             ;Clear remainder
E80:      RET
E10MULT   ENDP
;                Convert wage to ASCII:
;                ---------------------
F10WAGE   PROC   NEAR
          LEA    SI,ASCWAGE+7      ;Set decimal point
          MOV    BYTE PTR[SI],'.'
          ADD    SI,NODEC          ;Set right start pos'n
F30:
          CMP    BYTE PTR[SI],'.'
          JNE    F40               ;Bypass if at dec pos'n
          DEC    SI
F40:
          CMP    DX,00             ;If DX:AX < 10,
          JNZ    F50
          CMP    AX,0010           ;  operation finished
          JB     F60
F50:
          DIV    TENWD             ;Remainder is ASCII digit
          OR     DL,30H
          MOV    [SI],DL           ;Store ASCII character
          DEC    SI
          SUB    DX,DX             ;Clear remainder
          JMP    F30
F60:
          OR     AL,30H            ;Store last ASCII
          MOV    [SI],AL           ;  character
          RET
F10WAGE   ENDP
```

Figure 14-7c Displaying Employee Wages

```
;                   Display wage:
;                   ------------
G10DISP   PROC      NEAR
          MOV       COL,LEFCOL+3        ;Set column
          CALL      Q20CURS
          MOV       CX,09
          LEA       SI,ASCWAGE
G20:                                    ;Clear leading zeros
          CMP       BYTE PTR[SI],30H
          JNE       G30                 ;  to blanks
          MOV       BYTE PTR[SI],20H
          INC       SI
          LOOP      G20
G30:
          MOV       AH,40H              ;Request display
          MOV       BX,01               ;File handle
          MOV       CX,19               ;No. of characters
          LEA       DX,MESSG3           ;Wage
          INT       21H
          RET
G10DISP   ENDP
;                   Pause for user:
;                   --------------
H10PAUS   PROC      NEAR
          MOV       COL,20              ;Set cursor
          MOV       ROW,22
          CALL      Q20CURS
          MOV       AH,40H              ;Request display
          MOV       BX,01               ;File handle
          MOV       CX,40               ;No. of characters
          LEA       DX,MESSG4           ;Display pause
          INT       21H
          MOV       AH,10H              ;Request reply
          INT       16H
          RET
H10PAUS   ENDP
;                   Convert ASCII to binary:
;                   -----------------------
J10ASBI   PROC      NEAR
          MOV       MULT10,0001
          MOV       BINVAL,00
          MOV       DECIND,00
          XOR       BX,BX               ;Clear BX
J20:
          MOV       AL,[SI]             ;Get ASCII character
          CMP       AL,'.'              ;Bypass if dec point
          JNE       J40
          MOV       DECIND,01
          JMP       J50
J40:
          AND       AX,000FH
          MUL       MULT10              ;Multiply by factor
          ADD       BINVAL,AX           ;Add to binary
          MOV       AX,MULT10           ;Calculate next
          MUL       TENWD               ;  factor x 10
          MOV       MULT10,AX
          CMP       DECIND,00           ;Reached decimal point?
          JNZ       J50
          INC       BX                  ;  yes, add to count
```

Figure 14-7d Displaying Employee Wages

```
J50:
          DEC     SI
          LOOP    J20
          CMP     DECIND,00          ;End of loop
          JZ      J90                ;Any decimal point?
          ADD     NODEC,BX           ;  yes, add to total
J90:      RET
J10ASBI   ENDP
;                 Scroll whole screen:
;                 -------------------
Q10SCR    PROC    NEAR
          MOV     AX,0600H
          MOV     BH,30H             ;Attribute
          MOV     CX,00
          MOV     DX,184FH
          INT     10H
          RET
Q10SCR    ENDP
;                 Set cursor row:column:
;                 ---------------------
Q20CURS   PROC    NEAR
          MOV     AH,02H
          MOV     BH,00              ;Page 0
          MOV     DH,ROW             ;Set row,
          MOV     DL,COL             ;  column
          INT     10H
          RET
Q20CURS   ENDP
;                 Scroll display window:
;                 ---------------------
Q30WIN    PROC    NEAR
          MOV     AX,0605H           ;Five rows
          MOV     BH,16H             ;Attribute
          MOV     CH,TOPROW
          MOV     CL,LEFCOL
          MOV     DH,BOTROW
          MOV     DL,RITCOL
          INT     10H
          RET
Q30WIN    ENDP
          END     A10MAIN
```

Figure 14-7e Displaying Employee Wages

F10WAGE	Inserts the decimal point, determines the rightmost position to begin storing ASCII characters, and converts the binary wage to ASCII.
G10DISP	Clears leading zeros of wage to blanks and displays the wage.
H10PAUS	Displays the calculated wage until the user presses a key. Pressing <Esc> tells the program to discontinue processing.
J10ASBI	Converts ASCII to binary (a common routine for hours and for rate) and determines the number of decimal places in the entered value.
Q10SCR	Scrolls the whole screen and sets it to black on cyan.
Q30WIN	Scrolls a window in the middle of the screen where hours, rate, and wage are displayed as brown on blue.

Limitations. A limitation of this program is that the total number of decimal places in hours and in rate of pay must be 6 or less. Another limitation is the magnitude of the wage itself. If hours and rate contain a total that exceeds six decimal places, or if the wage exceeds about 6,553.50, the program clears the wage to zero. In practice, a program would print a warning message or would contain procedures to overcome these limitations.

Error checking. A program designed for users other than the programmer not only should produce warning messages, but also should validate hours and rate of pay. The only valid characters are the numbers 0 through 9 and one decimal point. For any other character, the program should display a message and redisplay the input prompt. A useful instruction for validating is XLAT, which Chapter 15 covers.

In practice, test your program thoroughly for all possible conditions, such as zero values, extremely high and low values, and negative values.

Negative values. Some applications involve negative amounts, especially for reversing and correcting entries. You could allow a minus sign following a value, such as 12.34−, or preceding the value, as −12.34. The program could then check for a minus sign during conversion to binary. On the other hand, you may want to leave the binary number positive and simply set an indicator to record the fact that the amount is negative. When the arithmetic is complete, the program, if required, can insert a minus sign to the left or right of the ASCII field.

If you want the binary number to be negative, convert the ASCII input to binary as usual. (See the section "Reversing the Sign" in Chapter 13 for changing the sign of a binary field.) And watch out for using IMUL and IDIV to handle signed data. For rounding a negative amount, subtract 5 instead of adding 5.

KEY POINTS

- An ASCII field requires one byte for each character. For a numeric field, the rightmost half-byte contains the digit, and the leftmost half-byte contains 3.
- Clearing the leftmost 3s of an ASCII number to 0s converts it to unpacked binary-coded decimal (BCD) format.
- Compressing ASCII characters to two digits per byte converts the field to packed binary-coded decimal (BCD) data.
- After an ASCII add, use AAA to adjust the answer; after an ASCII subtract, use AAS to adjust the answer.
- Before an ASCII multiplication, convert the multiplicand and multiplier to unpacked BCD by clearing the leftmost hex 3s to 0s. After the multiplication, use AAM to adjust the product.
- Before an ASCII division, convert the dividend and divisor to unpacked BCD by clearing the leftmost hex 3s, and use AAD to adjust the dividend.
- For most arithmetic purposes, convert ASCII numbers to binary. When converting from ASCII to binary format, check that the ASCII characters are valid: 30 though 39, a decimal point, and possibly a minus sign.

QUESTIONS

14-1. Assume that the AX contains ASCII 8 (0038H) and the DX contains ASCII 6 (0036H). Explain the results of each of the following unrelated operations:

```
(a) ADD AX,35H   (b)  ADD AX,DX
    AAA               AAA
(c) SUB AX,DX    (d)  SUB AX,0BH
    AAS               AAS
```

14-2. Use hex notation to show the decimal value 3796 in the following formats: (a) ASCII; (b) unpacked BCD; (c) packed BCD.

14-3. An unpacked BCD field named BCDAMT contains 02050904H. Code a loop that causes its contents to be proper ASCII 32353934H.

14-4. A field named ASCAMT1 contains the ASCII decimal value 215, and another field named ASCAMT2 contains ASCII 4. Code the instructions to multiply the ASCII numbers and to store the product in ASCPROD.

14-5. Use the same fields as in Question 14-4 to divide ASCAMT1 by ASCAMT2 and store the quotient in ASCQUOT.

14-6. Provide the manual calculations for the following: (a) Convert ASCII decimal value 39846 to binary, and show the result in hex format; (b) convert the hex value back to ASCII.

14-7. Code and run a program that determines a computer's memory size (see INT 12H in Chapter 3), converts the size to ASCII format, and displays it on the screen as follows:

```
Memory size is nnn bytes
```

15 DEFINING AND PROCESSING TABLES

Objective: To cover the requirements for defining tables, performing searches of tables, and sorting table entries.

INTRODUCTION

Many program applications require *tables* or *arrays* containing such data as names, descriptions, quantities, and rates. This chapter begins by defining some conventional tables and then covers methods for searching through them. Techniques for searching tables are subject to the way in which the tables are defined, and many methods of defining and searching other than those given here are possible. The definition and use of tables largely involves applying what you have already learned. Other commonly used features are the use of sorting, which rearranges the sequence of data in a table, and the use of linked lists, which use pointers to locate items in a table.

The only instruction introduced in this chapter is XLAT (Translate).

DEFINING TABLES

To facilitate searching through them, most tables are arranged in a consistent manner, with each entry defined with the same format (character or numeric), with the same length, and in either ascending or descending order.

A table that you have been using throughout this book is the definition of the stack, which in the following is a table of 64 uninitialized words, where the name STACK refers to the first word of the table:

```
STACK DW  64 DUP(?)
```

The following two tables, MONTABL and CUSTABL, initialize character and numeric values, respectively. MONTABL defines alphabetic abbreviations of the months, whereas CUSTABL defines a table of customer numbers:

```
MONTABL  DB 'Jan', 'Feb',  'Mar', ..., 'Dec'
CUSTABL  DB  205, 208, 209, 212, 215, 224,  . . .
```

All entries in MONTABL are three characters, and all entries in CUSTABL are three digits. But note that the assembler converts the decimal numbers to binary format and, provided that they don't exceed the value 255, stores them each in one byte.

A table may also contain a mixture of numeric and character values, provided that their definitions are consistent. In the following table of stock items, each numeric entry (stock number) is 2 digits (1 byte), and each character entry (stock description) is 9 bytes:

```
STOKTBL DB 12, 'Computers', 14, 'Paper....', 17, 'Diskettes', ...
```

The four dots following the description "Paper" are to show that spaces should be present; that is, spaces, not dots, are to be keyed in the description. For added clarity, you may code each table entry on a separate line:

```
STOKTBL DB 12, 'Computers'
        DB 14, 'Paper....'
        DB 17, 'Diskettes'
        ...
```

The next example defines a table with 100 entries, each initialized to 15 blanks (1500 bytes):

```
STORETBL DB 100 DUP(15 DUP(' '))
```

A program could use this table to store up to 100 values that it has generated internally, or it could use the table to store the contents of up to 100 entries that it accepts from a keyboard or reads from a disk file.

Tables on Disk

In real-world situations, many programs are table driven. Tables are stored as disk files, which any number of programs may require for processing. To this end, a program can read a table file from disk into an "empty" table defined for that purpose. The reason for this practice is because the contents of tables change over time. If each program defines its own tables, any changes require that all programs redefine the tables and be reassembled. With table files on disk, a change to a table simply involves changing the contents of the file. Chapter 17 gives an example of a table file.

Now let's examine different ways to use tables in programs.

DIRECT ADDRESSING OF TABLE ENTRIES

Suppose that a user enters a numeric month such as 03 and that a program is to convert it to alphabetic format—in this case, March. The routine to perform this conversion involves defining a table of alphabetic months, all of equal length. The length of each entry should be that of the longest name, September, in this format:

```
MONTBL DB 'January..'
       DB 'February.'
       DB 'March....'
       ...
       DB 'December.'
```

The entry 'January' is at MONTBL+00, 'February' is at MONTBL+09, 'March' is at MONTBL+18, and so forth. To locate month 03, the program has to perform the following steps:

1. Convert the entered month from ASCII 33 to binary 3.
2. Deduct 1 from this number: $3 - 1 = 2$ (because month 01 is at MONTBL+00)
3. Multiply the new number by 9 (the length of each entry): $2 \times 9 = 18$.
4. Add this product (18) to the address of MONTBL; the result is the address of the required description: MONTBL+18, where the entry "March" begins.

This technique is known as *direct table addressing.* Because the algorithm calculates the required table address directly, the program does not have to search successively through each entry in the table.

Direct Addressing, Example 1: Table of Months

The program in Figure 15-1 provides an example of a direct access of a table with the names of the months. The procedure B10CONV assumes 11 (November) as input and converts the month from ASCII to binary format like this:

```
Load ASCII month in AX =               3131H
Use 3030 for XOR (unpacked month) =    0101H
If leftmost byte nonzero, clear =      0001H
    and add 0AH (decimal 10) =         000BH   (decimal 11)
```

The procedure C10LOC determines the actual location of entries in the table:

```
Deduct 1 from month in the AX =        000AH   (decimal 10)
Multiply by 9 (length of entries) =    005AH   (decimal 90)
Add address of table (MONTBL) =        MONTBL+5AH
```

The procedure transfers the description ("November") from the table to ALFMON, where D10DISP displays it. One way to improve this program is to accept numeric months from the keyboard and to verify that the values are between 01 and 12, inclusive.

```
TITLE      A15DIREC (COM)  Direct table addressing
           .MODEL SMALL
           .CODE
           ORG     100H
BEGIN:     JMP     SHORT A10MAIN
; -------------------------------------------------------
NINE       DB      9
MONIN      DB      '11'
ALFMON     DB      9 DUP (20H)
MONTBL     DB      'January  ', 'February ', 'March    '
           DB      'April    ', 'May      ', 'June     '
           DB      'July     ', 'August   ', 'September'
           DB      'October  ', 'November ', 'December '
; -------------------------------------------------------
.386
A10MAIN    PROC    NEAR              ;Main procedure
           CALL    B10CONV           ;Convert to binary
           CALL    C10LOC            ;Locate month
           CALL    D10DISP           ;Display alpha month
           MOV     AX,4C00H          ;End processing
           INT     21H
A10MAIN    ENDP
;                  Convert ASCII to binary:
B10CONV    PROC
           MOV     AH,MONIN          ;Set up month
           MOV     AL,MONIN+1
           XOR     AX,3030H          ;Clear ASCII 3s
           CMP     AH,00             ;Month 01-09?
           JZ      B20               ;  yes, bypass
           XOR     AH,AH             ;  no,  clear AH,
           ADD     AL,10             ;  correct for binary
B20:       RET
B10CONV    ENDP
;                  Locate month in table:
C10LOC     PROC
           LEA     SI,MONTBL
           DEC     AL                ;Correct for table
           MUL     NINE              ;Multiply AL by 9
           ADD     SI,AX
           MOVZX   CX,NINE           ;Initialize 9-char move
           CLD
           LEA     DI,ALFMON
           REP MOVSB                 ;Move 9 characters
           RET
C10LOC     ENDP
;                  Display alpha month:
D10DISP    PROC
           MOV     AH,40H            ;Request display
           MOV     BX,01             ;File handle
           MOV     CX,09             ;9 characters
           LEA     DX,ALFMON
           INT     21H
           RET
D10DISP    ENDP
           END     BEGIN
```

Figure 15-1 Direct Table Addressing: Example 1

Direct Addressing, Example 2: Tables of Months and Days

The program in Figure 15-2 retrieves today's date from the system and displays it. INT 21H function 2AH delivers the following binary values:

```
TITLE     A15DISDA (EXE) Display day of week and month
          .MODEL  SMALL
          .STACK  64
          .DATA
SAVEDAY   DB      ?
SAVEMON   DB      ?
TEN       DB      10
ELEVEN    DB      11
TWELVE    DB      12
DAYSTBL   DB      'Sunday, $   ', 'Monday, $   '
          DB      'Tuesday, $  ', 'Wednesday, $'
          DB      'Thursday, $ ', 'Friday, $   '
          DB      'Saturday, $ '
MONTBL    DB      'January $  ', 'February $ ', 'March $    '
          DB      'April $    ', 'May $      ', 'June $     '
          DB      'July $     ', 'August $   ', 'September $'
          DB      'October $  ', 'November $ ', 'December $ '
; -----------------------------------------------------------
          .CODE
A10MAIN   PROC    FAR
          MOV     AX,@data        ;Initialize
          MOV     DS,AX           ;  segment registers
          MOV     ES,AX
          MOV     AX,0600H
          CALL    Q10SCR          ;Clear screen
          CALL    Q20CURS         ;Set cursor
          MOV     AH,2AH          ;Get today's date
          INT     21H
          MOV     SAVEMON,DH      ;Save month
          MOV     SAVEDAY,DL      ;Save day of month
          CALL    B10DAYWK        ;Display day of week
          CALL    C10MONTH        ;Display month
          CALL    D10DAYMO        ;Display day
          CALL    E10INPT         ;Wait for input
          CALL    Q10SCR          ;Clear screen
          MOV     AX,4C00H        ;End processing
          INT     21H
A10MAIN   ENDP
;                 Display day of week:
;                 -------------------
B10DAYWK  PROC    NEAR
          MUL     TWELVE          ;Day (in AL) x 12
          LEA     DX,DAYSTBL      ;Address of table
          ADD     DX,AX           ;  plus offset
          MOV     AH,09H          ;Request display
          INT     21H
          RET
B10DAYWK  ENDP
;                 Display month:
;                 -------------
C10MONTH  PROC    NEAR
          MOV     AL,SAVEMON      ;Get month
          DEC     AL              ;Decrement by 1
          MUL     ELEVEN          ;Multiply by entry length
          LEA     DX,MONTBL       ;Address of table
          ADD     DX,AX           ;  plus offset
          MOV     AH,09H          ;Request display
          INT     21H
          RET
C10MONTH  ENDP
```

Figure 15-2a Direct Table Addressing: Example 2

```
.386
;               Display day of month:
;               ---------------------
D10DAYMO  PROC   NEAR
          MOVZX  AX,SAVEDAY      ;Get day
          DIV    TEN             ;Convert from binary
          OR     AX,3030H        ;  to ASCII
          MOV    BX,AX           ;Save ASCII day
          MOV    AH,02H          ;Request display
          MOV    DL,BL           ;  first digit
          INT    21H
          MOV    AH,02H          ;Request display
          MOV    DL,BH           ;Second digit
          INT    21H
          RET
D10DAYMO  ENDP
;               Wait for keyboard input:
;               ------------------------
E10INPT   PROC   NEAR
          MOV    AH,10H          ;Request input
          INT    16H             ;Call BIOS
          RET
E10INPT   ENDP
;               Scroll screen:
;               --------------
Q10SCR    PROC   NEAR
          MOV    AX,0600H        ;Request scroll
          MOV    BH,17H          ;White on blue
          MOV    CX,0000
          MOV    DX,184FH
          INT    10H             ;Call BIOS
          RET
Q10SCR    ENDP
;               Set cursor:
;               -----------
Q20CURS   PROC   NEAR
          MOV    AH,02H          ;Request set cursor
          MOV    BH,00           ;Page
          MOV    DH,10           ;Row
          MOV    DL,24           ;Column
          INT    10H             ;Call BIOS
          RET
Q20CURS   ENDP
          END    A10MAIN
```

Figure 15-2b Direct Table Addressing: Example 2

AL = Day of week (where Sunday = 0) DH = Month (01–12)

CX = Year (not used by this program) DL = Day of month (01–31)

The program uses these values to display the alphabetic day of the week and the month in the form "Wednesday, September 12." To this end, the program defines a table of days of the week named DAYSTBL, beginning with Sunday, and a table of months named MONTBL, beginning with January.

Entries in DAYSTBL are 12 bytes long, with each description followed by a comma, blank, $ sign, and padded with blanks to the right. INT 21H function 09H displays all characters up to the $ sign; the comma and blank are followed on the screen by the month. The procedure B10DAYWK multiplies the day of the week by 12 (the length of each entry in DAYSTBL). The product is an offset into the table, where, for example, Sunday is at

DAYSTBL+0, Monday is at DAYSTBL+12, and so forth. The day is displayed directly from the table.

Entries in MONTBL are 11 bytes long, with each description followed by a blank, and $ sign, and padded with blanks to the right. The procedure C10MONTH first decrements the month by 1 so that, for example, month 01 becomes entry zero in MONTBL. It then multiplies the month by 11 (the length of each entry in MONTBL). The product is an offset into the table, where, for example, January is at MONTBL+0, February at MONTBL+11, and so forth. The procedure displays the month directly from the table.

The procedure D10DAYMO divides the day of the month by 10 to convert it from binary to ASCII format. Because the maximum value for day is 31, the quotient and the remainder can each be only one digit. (For example, 31 divided by 10 gives a quotient of 3 and a remainder of 1.) INT 21H function 02H displays each of the two characters, including the leading zero for days less than 10; suppressing the leading zero involves some minor program changes.

At the end, the program waits for the user to press a key before it ends processing.

Although direct table addressing is very efficient, it works best when entries are in sequence and in a predictable order. Thus it would work well for entries that are in the order 01, 02, 03, . . . , or 106, 107, 108, . . . , or even 05, 10, 15,. . . . However, few applications provide such a neat arrangement of table values. The next section examines tables with values that are sequential, but not in a predictable order.

SEARCHING A TABLE

Some tables consist of unique numbers with no apparent pattern. A typical example is a table of stock items with nonconsecutive numbers such as 034, 038, 041, 139, and 145. Another type of table—such as an income tax table—contains ranges of values. The following sections examine both of these types of tables and the requirements for searching them.

Tables with Unique Entries

The stock item numbers for most businesses are usually not in consecutive order. Rather, they tend to be grouped by category, perhaps with a leading number to indicate furniture or appliance or to indicate that it is located in a certain department. Also, over time, some items are deleted from stock and other items are added. As an example, let's define a table with stock numbers and their related descriptions. These could be defined in separate tables, such as

```
STOKNOS   DB '05','10','12', ...
STOKDESC  DB 'Excavators', 'Lifters...', 'Presses...' , ...
```

Each step in a search could increment the address of the first table by 2 (the length of each entry in STOKNOS) and the address of the second table by 10 (the length of each entry in STOKDESC). Or, a procedure could keep a count of the number of loops executed and, on finding a match with a certain key stock number, multiply the count by 10 and use this product as an offset to the address of STOKDESC.

On the other hand, it may be clearer to define stock numbers and descriptions in the same table, with one line for each pair of items:

```
STOKTBL  DB '05','Excavators'
         DB '10','Lifters...'
         DB '12','Presses...'
         ...
```

The program in Figure 15-3 defines this table with six pairs of stock numbers and descriptions. The search routine at the start of B10TABLE begins comparing the first byte of the input stock number, STOKNIN, with the first byte of stock number in the table. The results of the comparison can be low, high, or equal.

1. *Low.* If the comparison of the first or second bytes is low, the program determines that the stock number is not in the table and at B40 could display an error message (not coded). For example, the program compares input stock item 01 with table item 05; the first byte is equal, but because the second byte is low, the program determines that the item is not in the table.
2. *High.* If the comparison of the first or second bytes is high, the program has to continue the search; to compare the input stock item with the next stock item in the table, it increments the SI, which contains the table address. For example, the program compares input stock item 06 with table item 05. The first byte is equal, but the second byte is high, so it compares the input with the next item in the table: stock item 06 with table item 10. The first byte is low, so the program determines that the item is not in the table.
3. *Equal.* If both the first and second bytes are equal, the stock number is found. For example, the program compares input stock item 10 with table item 05. The first byte is high, so it compares the input with the next item in the table: Stock item 10 with table item 10. Because the first byte is equal and the second is equal, the program has found the item; at B50 it calls C10DISP, which copies the description from the table into DESCRN, where it is displayed.

The search loop performs a maximum of six comparisons. If the number of loops exceeds six, the stock number is known to be not in the table.

The table could also define unit prices. The user keys in stock number and quantity sold. The program could locate the stock item in the table, calculate amount of sale (quantity sold times unit price), and display description and amount of sale.

In Figure 15-3, the item number is 2 characters and the description is 10. Programming details would vary for different numbers of entries and different lengths of entries. For example, to compare 3-byte fields, you could use REPE CMPSB, although REPE involves the CX register, which LOOP already uses.

Tables with Ranges

Income tax provides a typical example of a table with ranges of values. Consider the following hypothetical table of taxable income, tax rates, and adjustment factors:

```
TITLE     A15TABSR (COM)  Table search Using CMP
          .MODEL  SMALL
          .CODE
          ORG     100H
BEGIN:    JMP     SHORT A10MAIN
; -----------------------------------------------------
STOKNIN   DB      '12'                   ;Input stock no.
STOKTBL   DB      '05','Excavators'      ;Start of table
          DB      '10','Lifters   '      ;
          DB      '12','Presses   '      ;
          DB      '15','Valves    '      ;
          DB      '23','Processors'      ;
          DB      '27','Pumps     '      ;End of table
DESCRIP   DB      10 DUP(?)              ;Save area
; -----------------------------------------------------
A10MAIN   PROC    NEAR
          CALL    B10TABLE
          MOV     AX,4C00H          ;End processing
          INT     21H
A10MAIN   ENDP

B10TABLE  PROC    NEAR
          MOV     CX,06             ;Initialize compares
          LEA     SI,STOKTBL
B20:
          MOV     AL,STOKNIN
          CMP     AL,[SI]           ;Stock#(1) : table
          JNE     B30               ;Not equal, exit
          MOV     AL,STOKNIN+1      ;Equal:
          CMP     AL,[SI+1]         ;  stock#(2) : table
          JE      B50               ;  equal, found
B30:      JB      B40               ;Low, not in table
          ADD     SI,12             ;High, get next entry
          LOOP    B20
B40:                                ;Not in table
;         ...                       ;Display error message
          JMP     B90
B50:
          CALL    C10DISP
B90:      RET
B10TABLE  ENDP

C10DISP   PROC    NEAR              ;Display description
          MOV     CX,05             ;Length of description
          LEA     DI,DESCRIP        ;Address of description
          INC     SI
          INC     SI                ;Extract description
          REP MOVSW                 ;  from table
          MOV     AH,40H            ;Request display
          MOV     BX,01             ;File handle
          MOV     CX,10             ;10 characters
          LEA     DX,DESCRIP        ;Stock description
          INT     21H
          RET
C10DISP   ENDP
          END     BEGIN
```

Figure 15-3 Searching a Table Using CMP

TAXABLE INCOME($)	RATE	ADJUSTMENT FACTOR
0-1,000.00	.10	0.00
1,000.01-2,500.00	.15	050.00
2,501.01-4,250.00	.18	125.00
4,250.01-6,000.00	.20	260.00
6,000.01 and over	.23	390.00

In the tax table, rates increase as taxable income increases. The adjustment factor compensates for our calculating tax at the high rate, whereas lower rates apply to lower levels of income. Entries for taxable income contain the maximum income for each step:

```
TAXTBL  DD 100000, 10, 00000
        DD 250000, 15, 05000
        DD 425000, 18, 12500
        DD 600000, 20, 26000
        DD 999999, 23, 39000
```

To perform a search of the table, the program compares the taxpayer's actual taxable income starting with the first entry in the table and does the following, according to the results of the comparison:

- High: Not yet found; increment for the next entry in the table.
- Low or equal: Found; use the associated rate and adjustment factor. Calculate the tax deduction as (taxable income × table rate) − adjustment factor. Note that the last entry in the table contains the maximum value (999999), which always correctly forces an end to the search.

Searching a Table Using String Comparisons

REPE CMPS is useful for comparing item numbers that are two or more bytes long. The program in Figure 15-4 defines STOKTBL, but this time revised as a 3-byte stock number. Because STOKNIN is the first field in the data area and STOKTBL is next, they appear in the data segment as follows:

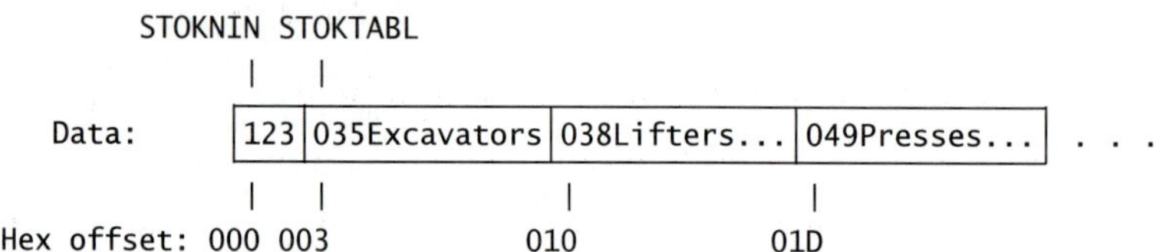

The last entry in the table contains stock item '999' (the highest possible stock number) to force the search to end. The program could have used LOOP to force an end of search, but REPE makes the CX unavailable for LOOP. The search routine compares STOKNIN (arbitrarily defined to contain 123) with each table entry, as follows:

STOKNIN	TABLE ENTRY	RESULT OF COMPARISON
123	035	High, check next entry
123	038	High, check next entry

```
                             TITLE  A15STRSR (EXE)  Table search using CMPSB
                                    .MODEL  SMALL
                                    .STACK  64
                             ; ---------------------------------------------
                                    .DATA
0000  31 32 33               STOKNIN  DB     '123'
0003 30 33 35 45 78 63       STOKTBL  DB     '035','Excavators' ;Define table
     61 76 61 74 6F 72
     73
0010 30 33 38 4C 69 66                DB     '038','Lifters   '
     74 65 72 73 20 20
     20
001D 30 34 39 50 72 65                DB     '049','Presses   '
     73 73 65 73 20 20
     20
002A 31 30 32 56 61 6C                DB     '102','Valves    '
     76 65 73 20 20 20
     20
0037 31 32 33 50 72 6F                DB     '123','Processors'
     63 65 73 73 6F 72
     73
0044 31 32 37 50 75 6D                DB     '127','Pumps     '
     70 73 20 20 20 20
     20
0051 39 39 39                         DB     '999', 10 DUP(' ')    ;End table
     000A[ 20 ]
005E 000A[ ?? ]              DESCRN   DB     10 DUP(?)             ;Save area
                             ; ---------------------------------------------
                                      .CODE
0000                         A10MAIN  PROC   FAR
0000  B8 ---- R                       MOV    AX,@data       ;Initialize
0003  8E D8                           MOV    DS,AX          ;  segment
0005  8E C0                           MOV    ES,AX          ;  registers
0007  E8 000F R                       CALL   B10TABLE
000A  B8 4C00                         MOV    AX,4C00H       ;End processing
000D  CD 21                           INT    21H
000F                         A10MAIN  ENDP

000F                         B10TABLE PROC   NEAR
000F  FC                              CLD
0010  8D 3E 0003 R                    LEA    DI,STOKTBL     ;Initialize table
0014                         B20:                           ;  address
0014  B9 0003                         MOV    CX,03          ;Compare 3 bytes
0017  8D 36 0000 R                    LEA    SI,STOKNIN     ;Init stock# addr
001B  F3/ A6                          REPE CMPSB            ;Stock# : table
001D  74 09                           JE     B30            ;  equal, exit
001F  72 0D                           JB     B40            ;  low, not entry
0021  03 F9                           ADD    DI,CX          ;Add CX to offset
0023  83 C7 0A                        ADD    DI,10          ;Next table item
0026  EB EC                           JMP    B20
0028                         B30:
0028  E8 002F R                       CALL   C10DISPL       ;Display descr'n
002B  EB 01 90                        JMP    B90
002E                         B40:
                             ;        <Display error message>
002E                         B90:
002E  C3                              RET
002F                         B10TABLE ENDP
```

Figure 15-4a Searching a Table Using CMPSB

```
123        049        High, check next entry
123        102        High, check next entry
123        123        Equal, entry found
```

```
002F                     C10DISPL PROC  NEAR
002F  B9 0005                     MOV   CX,05          ;Set to move 5 words
0032  8B F7                       MOV   SI,DI
0034  8D 3E 005E R                LEA   DI,DESCRN      ;Addr of descr'n
0038  F3/ A5                      REP MOVSW            ;Get descr'n
003A  B4 40                       MOV   AH,40H         ;Request display
003C  BB 0001                     MOV   BX,01          ;File handle
003F  B9 000A                     MOV   CX,10          ;10 characters
0042  8D 16 005E R                LEA   DX,DESCRN      ;Stock description
0046  CD 21                       INT   21H
0048  C3                          RET
0049                     C10DISPL ENDP
                                  END   A10MAIN
```

Figure 15-4b Searching a Table Using CMPSB

The procedure B10TABLE initializes the DI to the offset address of STOKTBL (003), the CX to the length (03) of each stock item, and the SI to the offset of STOKNIN (000). As long as the bytes contain equal values, the CMPSB operation compares byte for byte, and automatically increments the DI and SI registers for the next bytes. A comparison with the first table entry (123:035) ends with a high comparison after the first byte; the DI contains 004, the SI contains 001, and the CX contains 02.

For the second comparison, the DI should contain 010 and the SI should contain 000. Correcting the SI simply involves reloading the address of STOKNIN. To correct the address of the table entry that should be in the DI, however, the increment depends on whether the comparison ended after one, two, or three bytes. The CX contains the number of the remaining uncompared bytes, in this case, 02. Adding the CX value plus the length of the stock description (that of the previously compared stock item) gives the offset of the next table item, as follows:

```
Address in DI after CMPSB:           004H
Add remaining length in CX:        + 02H
Add length of stock description:   + 0AH
Next offset address in table:        010H
```

Because the CX contains the number of the remaining uncompared bytes (if any), the arithmetic works for all cases and ends after one, two, or three comparisons. On an equal comparison, the CX contains 00, and the DI is already incremented to the address of the required description. The procedure calls C10DISPL, where a REP MOVSW operation copies the description into DESCRN in order to display it.

Tables with Variable-Length Entries

It is possible to define a table with variable-length entries. A special delimiter character such as 00H could follow each entry, and FFH could distinguish the end of the table. The SCAS instruction is suitable for scanning for the delimiters. However, you must be sure that no byte within an entry contains the bit configuration of a delimiter; for example, an arithmetic binary amount may contain any possible bit configuration.

THE XLAT (TRANSLATE) INSTRUCTION

The XLAT instruction translates the contents of a byte into another predefined value. You could use XLAT, for example, to validate the contents of data items or, if you transfer data between a PC and an IBM mainframe computer, to translate data between ASCII and EBCDIC formats. The general format for XLAT is

[label:]	XLAT	;No operand

XLAT expects that the address of the table is in the BX register and the byte to be translated is in the AL. The following example converts ASCII numbers 0–9 into EBCDIC format. Because the representation of 0–9 in ASCII is 30–39 and in EBCDIC is F0–F9, you could use an OR operation to make the change. However, let's also convert all other characters to a blank, which is 40H in EBCDIC. To use XLAT, you define a translation table that accounts for all 256 possible characters, with EBCDIC codes inserted in the ASCII positions; that is, the EBCDIC characters in the ASCII locations and EBCDIC blanks in all other locations. Because the number 0 is ASCII 30H, the EBCDIC numbers begin in the table at location 30H, or decimal 48:

```
XLTABLE  DB  48 DUP(40H)                          ;EBCDIC blanks
         DB  0F0H,0F1H,0F2H,0F3H, ...,0F9H        ;EBCDIC 0-9
         DB  198 DUP(40H)                         ;EBCDIC blanks
```

The following example performs the initialization and translation of an ASCII item named ASCNO into EBCDIC format:

```
LEA   BX,XLTABLE     ;Address of table in BX
MOV   AL,ASCNO       ;Character to translate in AL
XLAT                 ;Translate to EBCDIC
```

XLAT uses the AL value as an offset address; in effect, the BX contains the starting address of the table, and the AL contains an offset value within the table. If the AL value is 00, for example, the table address would be XLTABLE+0 (the first byte of XLTABLE containing 40H). XLAT would replace the 00 in the AL with 40H from the table.

Note that the first DB in XLTABLE defines 48 bytes, addressed as XLTABLE+00 through XLTABLE+47. The second DB in XLTABLE defines data beginning at XLTABLE+48. If the AL value is 32H (decimal 50), the table address is XLTABLE+50; this location contains F2 (EBCDIC 2), which XLAT would insert in the AL register.

The program in Figure 15-5 modifies XLTABLE so that it converts ASCII minus sign (2D) and decimal point (2E) to EBCDIC (60 and 4B, respectively) and now loops through a 6-byte ASCII field. Initially, ASCNO contains −31.5 followed by a blank, or hex 2D33312E3520. At the end of the loop, EBCNO should contain hex 60F3F14BF540, which you can verify by means of DEBUG.

```
            page    60,132
TITLE       A15XLATE (COM)   Translate ASCII to EBCDIC
            .MODEL SMALL
            .CODE
            ORG     100H
BEGIN:      JMP     A10MAIN
; -------------------------------------------------------
ASCNO       DB      '-31.5 '           ;ASCII item to convert
EBCNO       DB      6 DUP(' ')         ;Converted EBCDIC item
XLTABLE     DB      45 DUP(40H)        ;Translate table
            DB      60H, 4BH
            DB      40H
            DB      0F0H,0F1H,0F2H,0F3H,0F4H
            DB      0F5H,0F6H,0F7H,0F8H,0F9H
            DB      198 DUP(40H)
; -------------------------------------------------------
A10MAIN     PROC    NEAR
            LEA     SI,ASCNO           ;Address of ASCNO
            LEA     DI,EBCNO           ;Address of EBCNO
            MOV     CX,06              ;Length of items
            LEA     BX,XLTABLE         ;Address of table
A20:
            LODSB                      ;Get ASCII char in AL
            XLAT                       ;Translate character
            STOSB                      ;Store AL in EBCNO
            LOOP    A20                ;Repeat 6 times
;           ...
            MOV     AX,4C00H           ;End processing
            INT     21H
A10MAIN     ENDP
            END     BEGIN
```

Figure 15-5 Converting ASCII Numbers to EBCDIC

PROGRAM: DISPLAYING HEX AND ASCII CHARACTERS

The program in Figure 15-6 displays all 256 hex values (00–FF), including most of their related ASCII symbols, for example, both the ASCII symbol S and its hex representation, 53. The full display appears on the screen as a 16-by-16 matrix:

```
00 01 02 03 04 05 06 07 08 09 0A 0B 0C 0D 0E 0F
 .  .  .  .  .  .  .  .  .  .  .  .  .  .  .  .
 .  .  .  .  .  .  .  .  .  .  .  .  .  .  .  .
 .  .  .  .  .  .  .  .  .  .  .  .  .  .  .  .
F0 F1 F2 F3 F4 F5 F6 F7 F8 F9 FA FB FC FD FE FF
```

As shown in Figure 8-1, displaying ASCII symbols causes no serious problem. However, displaying the hex representation of an ASCII value is more involved. For example, you have to convert 00H to 3030H, 01H to 3031H, and so forth.

The program defines HEXCTR initially with 00 and subsequently increments it by 1 for each of the 256 ASCII characters. The procedure B10HEX splits HEXCTR into its two hex digits. For example, if HEXCTR contains 4FH, the routine would extract the hex 4, which XLAT uses for the translation. The value returned to the AL is 34H. The routine then extracts the F and translates it to 46H. The result, 3446H, is displayed on the screen as 4F.

```
TITLE     A15ASCHX (COM)  Display ASCII and hex characters
          .MODEL SMALL
          .CODE
.386
          ORG     100H
BEGIN:    JMP     SHORT A10MAIN
; -----------------------------------------------------------
DISPROW   DB      16 DUP(5 DUP(' ')), 13
HEXCTR    DB      00
XLATAB    DB      30H,31H,32H,33H,34H,35H,36H,37H,38H,39H
          DB      41H,42H,43H,44H,45H,46H
; -----------------------------------------------------------
A10MAIN   PROC    NEAR                 ;Main procedure
          CALL    Q10CLR               ;Clear screen
          LEA     SI,DISPROW
A20LOOP:
          CALL    B10HEX               ;Translate
          CALL    C10DISPL             ;  and display
          CMP     HEXCTR,0FFH          ;Last hex value (FF)?
          JE      A50                  ;  yes, terminate
          INC     HEXCTR               ;  no,  incr next hex
          JMP     A20LOOP
A50:      MOV     AX,4C00H             ;End processing
          INT     21H
A10MAIN   ENDP
;                 Convert ASCII to hex:
;                 --------------------
B10HEX    PROC    NEAR
          MOVZX   AX,HEXCTR            ;Get hex pair in AX
          SHR     AX,04                ;Shift off right hex digit
          LEA     BX,XLATAB            ;Set table address
          XLAT                         ;Translate hex
          MOV     [SI],AL              ;Store left character

          MOV     AL,HEXCTR
          AND     AL,0FH               ;Clear left hex digit
          XLAT                         ;Translate hex
          MOV     [SI]+1,AL            ;Store right character
          RET
B10HEX    ENDP
;                 Display as hex characters:
;                 -------------------------
C10DISPL  PROC    NEAR                 ;
          MOV     AL,HEXCTR            ;Get hex character
          MOV     [SI]+3,AL
          CMP     AL,1AH               ;EOF character?
          JE      C20                  ;  yes, bypass
          CMP     AL,07H               ;Lower than 7?
          JB      C30                  ;  yes, ok
          CMP     AL,10H               ;Higher/equal 16?
          JAE     C30                  ;  yes, ok
C20:                                   ;Else force blank
          MOV     BYTE PTR [SI]+3,20H
C30:
          ADD     SI,05                ;Next location in row
          LEA     DI,DISPROW+80
          CMP     DI,SI                ;Filled up row?
          JNE     C40                  ;  no, bypass
```

Figure 15-6a Displaying ASCII and Hex Values

```
                MOV     AH,40H              ;Yes, request display
                MOV     BX,01               ;  file handle
                MOV     CX,81               ;  entire row
                LEA     DX,DISPROW
                INT     21H
                LEA     SI,DISPROW          ;Reset display row
C40:            RET
C10DISPL        ENDP

;                       Clear screen:
Q10CLR          PROC    NEAR
                MOV     AX,0600H            ;Request scroll
                MOV     BH,61H              ;Attribute
                MOV     CX,0000
                MOV     DX,184FH
                INT     10H
                RET
Q10CLR          ENDP
                END     BEGIN
```

Figure 15-6b Displaying ASCII and Hex Values

The procedure C10DISPL converts non-ASCII characters to blanks. Because INT 21H function 40H treats 1AH as an end-of-file character, the program also changes it to blank. The procedure displays a full row of 16 characters and ends after displaying the 16th row.

There are many other ways of converting hex digits to ASCII characters; for example, you could experiment with shifting and comparing.

SORTING TABLE ENTRIES

Often, an application requires *sorting* data in a table into ascending or descending sequence. For example, a user may want a list of stock descriptions in ascending sequence, or a list of sales agents' total sales in descending sequence. There are a number of table sort routines, varying from relatively slow processing but clear, to fast processing but obscure. The routine presented in this section is fairly efficient and could serve for most table sorting.

A general approach to sorting a table is to compare a table entry with the entry immediately following it. If the comparison is high, exchange the entries. Continue in this fashion, comparing entry 1 with entry 2, entry 2 with entry 3, and so on to the end of the table, exchanging where necessary. If you made any exchanges, repeat the entire process from the start of the table, comparing entry 1 with entry 2 again, and so forth. At any point, if you proceed through the entire table without making an exchange, you know that the table is sorted into sequence.

In the following pseudocode, SWAP is an item that indicates whether an exchange was made (YES) or not made (NO).

```
T10:    Initialize address of last entry in the table
T20:    Set SWAP to NO
        Initialize address of start of the table
T30:    Table entry > next entry?
```

```
        Yes: Exchange entries
             Set SWAP to YES
    Increment for next entry in the table
    At end of the table?
        No:  Jump to T30
        Yes: Does SWAP = YES?
             Yes:  Jump to T20 (repeat sort)
             No:   End of sort
```

The program in Figure 15-7 allows a user to key in up to 30 names from the keyboard, which the program stores in a table named NAMETAB. It contains the following procedures:

- A10MAIN calls B10ENTER to accept a name from the keyboard, calls C10STOR to store the name in a table and, when all the names are keyed in, calls D10SORT and F10DISP.
- B10ENTER prompts the user to key in a name, accepts it, and fills it to the right with blanks. When all the names are keyed in, the user just presses <Enter>, with no name.
- C10STOR stores each name successively in the table.
- D10SORT and E10XCHG sort the table of names into ascending sequence.
- F10DISP displays the sorted table.

Note that the table entries are all fixed-length 20 bytes; a routine for sorting variable-length data would be more complicated.

LINKED LISTS

A *linked list* contains data in what are called cells, like entries in a table, but in no specified sequence. To facilitate forward searches, each cell contains a *pointer* that indicates the location of the next entry in the list. (A cell may also contain a pointer to the preceding entry so that searching may proceed in either direction.) The method facilitates additions and deletions to a list without the need for expanding and contracting it.

Consider a linked list that contains cells with part number (4-byte ASCII value), unit price (binary word), and a pointer (binary word) to the next part number in the sequence. Thus each entry is 8 bytes in length. The pointer is an offset from the start of the list. The linked list begins at offset 0000, the second item in the series is at 0024, the third is at 0032, and so forth:

OFFSET	PART NO.	PRICE	LOCATION OF NEXT PART NO.
0000	0103	12.50	0024
0008	1720	08.95	0016
0016	1827	03.75	0000
0024	0120	13.80	0032
0032	0205	25.00	0008

```
            page 60,132
TITLE       A15NMSRT (EXE)  Sort names entered from terminal
            .MODEL SMALL
            .STACK 64
; -------------------------------------------------------
            .DATA
NAMEPAR     LABEL   BYTE                 ;Name parameter list:
MAXNLEN     DB      21                   ;  maximum length
NAMELEN     DB      ?                    ;  no. of chars entered
NAMEFLD     DB      21 DUP(' ')          ;  name

CRLF        DB      13, 10
ENDADDR     DW      ?
MESSG1      DB      'Name? '
NAMECTR     DB      00
NAMETAB     DB      30 DUP(20 DUP(' ')) ;Name table
NAMESAV     DB      20 DUP(?), 13, 10
SWAPPED     DB      00
; -------------------------------------------------------
            .CODE
A10MAIN     PROC    FAR
            MOV     AX,@data             ;Initialize DS and
            MOV     DS,AX                ;  ES registers
            MOV     ES,AX
            CLD
            CALL    Q10CLR               ;Clear screen
            CALL    Q20CURS              ;Set cursor
            LEA     DI,NAMETAB
A20LOOP:
            CALL    B10ENTER             ;Accept name from KB
            CMP     NAMELEN,00           ;Any more names?
            JZ      A30                  ;  no,  go to sort
            CMP     NAMECTR,30           ;30 names entered?
            JE      A30                  ;  yes, go to sort
            CALL    C10STOR              ;Store entered name in table
            JMP     A20LOOP
A30:                                     ;End of input
            CALL    Q10CLR               ;Clear screen
            CALL    Q20CURS              ;  and set cursor
            CMP     NAMECTR,01           ;One or no name entered?
            JBE     A40                  ;  yes, exit
            CALL    D10SORT              ;Sort stored names
            CALL    F10DISP              ;Display sorted names
A40:        MOV     AX,4C00H             ;End processing
            INT     21H
A10MAIN     ENDP
;                   Accept name as input:
;                   --------------------
B10ENTER    PROC
            MOV     AH,40H               ;Request display
            MOV     BX,01                ;File handle
            MOV     CX,06                ;6 characters
            LEA     DX,MESSG1            ;Prompt
            INT     21H
            MOV     AH,0AH
            LEA     DX,NAMEPAR           ;Accept name
            INT     21H
```

Figure 15-7a Sorting a Table of Names

```
                MOV     AH,40H              ;Request display
                MOV     BX,01               ;File handle
                MOV     CX,02               ;2 characters
                LEA     DX,CRLF             ;Return/line feed
                INT     21H

                MOV     BH,00               ;Clear characters after name
                MOV     BL,NAMELEN          ;Get count of chars
                MOV     CX,21
                SUB     CX,BX               ;Calc remaining length
B20:
                MOV     NAMEFLD[BX],20H     ;Set name to blank
                INC     BX
                LOOP    B20
                RET
B10ENTER        ENDP
;                       Store name in table:
;                       --------------------
C10STOR         PROC
                INC     NAMECTR             ;Add to number of names
                CLD
                LEA     SI,NAMEFLD
                MOV     CX,10               ;Ten words
                REP MOVSW                   ;Name (SI) to table (DI)
                RET
C10STOR         ENDP
;                       Sort names in table:
;                       --------------------
D10SORT         PROC
                SUB     DI,40               ;Set up stop address
                MOV     ENDADDR,DI
D20:
                MOV     SWAPPED,00          ;Set up start
                LEA     SI,NAMETAB          ; of table
D30:
                MOV     CX,20               ;Length of compare
                MOV     DI,SI
                ADD     DI,20               ;Next name for compare
                MOV     AX,DI
                MOV     BX,SI
                REPE CMPSB                  ;Compare name to next
                JBE     D40                 ;  no exchange
                CALL    E10XCHG             ;  exchange
D40:
                MOV     SI,AX
                CMP     SI,ENDADDR          ;End of table?
                JBE     D30                 ;  no, continue
                CMP     SWAPPED,00          ;Any swaps?
                JNZ     D20                 ;  yes, continue
                RET                         ;  no, end of sort
D10SORT         ENDP
;                       Exchange table entries:
;                       -----------------------
E10XCHG         PROC
                MOV     CX,10               ;Number of characters
                LEA     DI,NAMESAV
                MOV     SI,BX
                REP MOVSW                   ;Move lower item to save
```

Figure 15-7b Sorting a Table of Names

```
                MOV     CX,10               ;Number of characters
                MOV     DI,BX
                REP MOVSW                   ;Move higher item to lower

                MOV     CX,10
                LEA     SI,NAMESAV
                REP MOVSW                   ;Move save to higher item
                MOV     SWAPPED,01          ;Signal exchange made
                RET
E10XCHG         ENDP
;                       Display sorted names:
;                       --------------------
F10DISP         PROC
                LEA     SI,NAMETAB
K20:
                LEA     DI,NAMESAV          ;Init'ze start of table
                MOV     CX,10               ;Count for loop
                REP MOVSW
                MOV     AH,40H              ;Request display
                MOV     BX,01               ;File handle
                MOV     CX,22               ;20 characters + CR/LF
                LEA     DX,NAMESAV
                INT     21H
                DEC     NAMECTR             ;Is this last one?
                JNZ     K20                 ;  no, loop
                RET                         ;  yes, exit
F10DISP         ENDP
;                       Clear screen:
;                       ------------
Q10CLR          PROC
                MOV     AX,0600H
                MOV     BH,61H              ;Attribute
                MOV     CX,00               ;Full screen
                MOV     DX,184FH
                INT     10H
                RET
Q10CLR          ENDP
;                       Set cursor:
;                       ----------
Q20CURS         PROC
                MOV     AH,02H              ;Request set cursor
                MOV     BH,00               ;Page 0
                MOV     DX,00               ;Location 00:00
                INT     10H
                RET
Q20CURS         ENDP
                END     A10MAIN
```

Figure 15-7c Sorting a Table of Names

The item at offset 0016 contains 0000 as the next address, either to indicate the end of the list or to make the list circular.

The program in Figure 15-8 uses the contents of the defined linked list, LINKLST, to locate a specified part number, in this case, 1720. The search begins with the first item in the table. The logic for using CMPSB is similar to that in Figure 15-4. The procedure B10LINK compares the part number (1720) with each item in the table, according to the results of the comparison:

- *Low:* The item is not in the table.

```
TITLE      A15LNKLS (EXE)  Use of a Linked List
           .MODEL SMALL
           .STACK 64               ;Define stack
           .DATA
PARTNO     DB     '1720'           ;Part number
LINKLST    DB     '0103'           ;Linked list table
           DW     1250, 24
           DB     '1720'
           DW     0895, 16
           DB     '1827'
           DW     0375, 00
           DB     '0120'
           DW     1380, 32
           DB     '0205'
           DW     2500, 08
; ---------------------------------------------------------
                  .CODE            ;Define code segment
A10MAIN    PROC   FAR
           MOV    AX,@data         ;Set address of data
           MOV    DS,AX            ;   segment in DS
           MOV    ES,AX            ;   and ES register
           CALL   B10LINK
           MOV    AX,4C00H         ;End processing
           INT    21H
A10MAIN    ENDP

B10LINK    PROC   NEAR
           CLD
           LEA    DI,LINKLST       ;Initialize table address
B20:
           MOV    CX,04            ;Set to compare 4 bytes
           LEA    SI,PARTNO        ;Init'ze part# address
           REPE   CMPSB            ;Part# : table
           JE     B30              ;  equal, exit
           JB     B40              ;  low, not in table
           ADD    DI,CX            ;Add CX value to offset
           ADD    DI,02            ;Get offset of next item
           MOV    DX,[DI]
           LEA    DI,LINKLST
           ADD    DI,DX
           CMP    DX,00            ;Last table entry?
           JNE    B20
           JMP    B40
B30:
;                 <Item Found>
           JMP    B90
B40:
;                 <Display error message>

B90:       RET
B10LINK    ENDP
           END    A10MAIN
```

Figure 15-8 Using a Linked List

- *High:* The procedure gets the offset from the table for the next item to be compared. If the offset is not zero, the comparison is repeated for the next item; if the offset is zero, the search ends without finding a match.
- *Equal:* The item is found.

A more complete program could allow a user at a keyboard to enter any part number and could display the price as an ASCII value.

THE TYPE, LENGTH, AND SIZE OPERATORS

The assembler supplies a number of special operators that you may find useful. For example, the length of a table may change from time to time and you may have to modify a program to account for the new definition and add routines that check for the end of the table. The use of the TYPE, LENGTH, and SIZE operators can help reduce the number of instructions that have to be changed.

Consider this definition of a table with 12 words:

```
RAINTBL  DW   12 DUP(?)    ;Table with 12 words
```

The program can use the TYPE operator to determine the definition (DW in this case), the LENGTH operator to determine the DUP factor (12), and the SIZE operator to determine the number of bytes ($12 \times 2 = 24$). The following examples illustrate the three operators:

```
MOV  AX,TYPE RAINTBL      ;AX = 0002H (2 bytes)
MOV  BX,LENGTH RAINTBL    ;BX = 000CH (12 bytes)
MOV  CX,SIZE RAINTBL      ;CX = 0018H (24 bytes)
```

You may use the values that LENGTH and SIZE return to end a search or a sort of a table. For example, if the SI register contains the incremented offset address of a search, you may test this offset using

```
CMP  SI,SIZE RAINTBL
```

Chapter 26 describes the TYPE, LENGTH, and SIZE operators in detail.

KEY POINTS

- For most purposes, a table contains related entries with the same length and data format.
- A table is based on its data format; for example, entries may be character or numeric and typically each the same length.
- The maximum numeric value for a DB is 256 and that numeric DW and DD reverse the bytes. Also, CMP and CMPSW assume that words contain bytes in reverse sequence.
- If a table is subject to frequent changes, or if several programs reference the table, store it on disk. An updating program can handle changes to the table. Any program can then load the table from disk, and the programs need not be changed.
- Under direct table addressing, the program calculates the address of a table entry and accesses that entry directly.

- When searching a table, a program successively compares a data item against each entry in the table until it finds a match.
- The XLAT instruction facilitates translating data from one format to another.

QUESTIONS

15-1. Distinguish between processing a table by direct addressing and by searching.

15-2. Define a table named TEMPTBL with 365 words, initialized to (a) zeros for binary data; (b) blanks for character data.

15-3. Define three separate related tables that contain the following data: (a) ASCII item numbers 05, 09, 12, 19, and 23; (b) item descriptions of videotape, receivers, modems, keyboards, and diskettes; (c) item prices 12.50, 93.75, 87.45, 79.35, and 15.95.

15-4. Revise Question 15-3 so that all the data is in the same table. For the first item, define its number and description on the first line and its price on the second line; for the second item, define them on lines three and four, and so forth.

15-5. Revise Figure 15-1 so that it accepts the month from the keyboard in numeric (ASCII) format. If the entry is valid (01–12), locate and display the alphabetic month; otherwise, display an error message. Allow for any number of keyboard entries; end processing when the user replies to the prompt with only <Enter>. Also, revise the table so that a '$' sign follows each entry. Instead of transferring the description to ALFMON, the program should display it directly from the table.

15-6. Code a program that allows a user to enter item numbers (ITEMIN) and quantities (QTYIN) from the keyboard. Use the table defined in Question 15-4, and include a search routine that uses ITEMIN to locate an item number in the table. Extract the description and price from the table. Calculate the value (quantity × price) of each sale, and display description and value on the screen.

15-7. Using the description table defined in Question 15-3, write a program that (a) moves the contents of the table to another (empty) table; (b) sorts the contents of this new table into ascending sequence; (c) displays each description on one row of the screen. Provide for scrolling the screen.

15-8. Revise Figure 15-5 to reverse the process—that is, translate EBCDIC data to ASCII format. The EBCDIC characters to translate are minus sign (60H), decimal point (4BH), and numbers 0–9 (F0H–F9H). All other characters are to be translated to ASCII blank. For data, use a string of EBCDIC hex characters containing F0F0F1F24BF5F060 (defined as 0F0H, 0F1H, etc.), which are to be translated to ASCII format and displayed. The hex result should be 303031322E35302D.

15-9. Write a program to provide simple encryption of data. Define an 80-byte data area named CRYPDATA containing any ASCII data. Arrange a translation table to convert the data somewhat randomly, for example, A to M, B to R, C to X, and so forth. Provide for all 256 possible byte values. Arrange a second translation table that reverses (decrypts) the data. The program should perform the following actions: (a) Display the original contents of CRYPDATA on a line; (b) encrypt CRYPDATA and display the encrypted data on a second line, (c) decrypt CRYPDATA and display the decrypted data on a third line (which should be identical to the first line).

PART E—ADVANCED INPUT/OUTPUT

16 DISK STORAGE I: ORGANIZATION

Objective: To examine the basic formats for hard disk and diskette storage, the boot record, directory, and file allocation table.

INTRODUCTION

A serious programmer has to be familiar with the technical details of disk organization, particularly for developing utility programs that examine the contents of diskettes and hard disks.

This chapter explains the concepts of tracks, sectors, and cylinders and gives the capacities of some commonly used devices. Also covered is the organization of important data recorded at the beginning of a disk, including the boot record (which helps the system load the operating system from disk into memory), the directory (which contains the name, location, and status of each file on the disk), and the file allocation table (or FAT, which allocates disk space for files).

Where a reference to a disk or diskette is required, this text uses the general term *disk.*

DISK CHARACTERISTICS

For processing records on disks, you need some familiarity with the terms and characteristics of disk organization. A diskette has two sides (or surfaces), whereas a hard disk contains a number of two-sided disks on a spindle.

Tracks and Sectors

Each side of a diskette or hard disk contains a number of concentric *tracks,* numbered beginning with 00, the outermost track. Each track is formatted into *sectors* of 512 bytes, where the data is stored.

Both diskettes and hard disk devices are run by a *controller* that handles the placement of the read-write heads on the disk surface and the transfer of data between disk and memory. There is a read-write head for each disk surface. For both diskette and hard disk, a request for a read or a write causes the disk drive controller to move the read-write heads (if necessary) to the required track. The controller then waits for the required sector on the spinning surface to reach the head, at which point the read or write operation takes place. For a read operation, for example, the controller reads each bit from the sector as it passes the read/write head. Figure 16-1 illustrates these features.

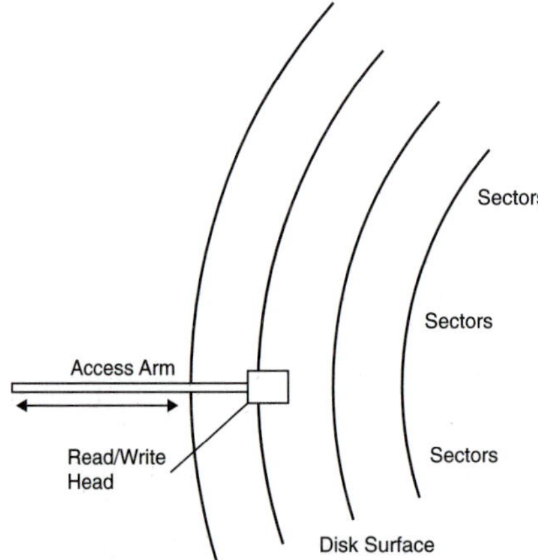

Figure 16-1 Disk Surface and Read/Write Head

There are two main differences between a hard disk and a diskette drive. For hard disk, the read-write head rides just above the disk surface without ever touching it, whereas for diskette, the read-write head actually touches the surface. Also, a hard disk device rotates constantly, whereas a diskette device starts and stops for each read/write operation.

Cylinders

A *cylinder* is a vertical set of all of the tracks with the same number on each surface of a diskette or hard disk. Thus cylinder 0 is the set of all tracks numbered 0 on every side, cylinder 1 is the set of all tracks numbered 1, and so forth. For a diskette, then, cylinder 0 consists of track 0 on side 1 and track 0 on side 2; cylinder 1 consists of track 1 on side 1 and track 1 on side 2; and so forth. Side number and head are the same; for example, disk head 1 accesses the data on side 1.

When writing a file, the controller fills all the tracks on a cylinder and then advances the read-write heads to the next cylinder. For example, the system fills all of diskette cylinder 0 (all the sectors on track 0, sides 1 and 2), and then advances to cylinder 1, side 1.

As seen, a reference to disk sides (heads), tracks, and sectors is by number. Side and track numbers begin with 0, but sectors may be numbered in one of two ways:

1. *Physical sector:* Sector numbers on each track begin with 1, so that the first sector on the disk is addressed as cylinder 0, head/side 0, sector 1, the next as cylinder 0, head/side 0, sector 2, and so forth.
2. *Relative sector:* Sectors may be numbered relative to the start of the disk, so that the first sector on the disk, on cylinder 0, track 0, is addressed as relative sector 0, the next one as relative sector 1, up to the last sector on the disk.

Different disk operations may use one or the other method, depending on how accessing is to be performed.

Disk Controller

The disk controller, which is located between the processor and the disk drive, handles all communication between them. The controller accepts data from the processor and converts the data into a form that is usable by the device. For example, the processor may send a request for data from a specific cylinder-head-sector. The role of the controller is to provide the appropriate commands to move the access arm to the required cylinder, select the read/write head, and accept the data from the sector when the data reaches the read-write head.

While the controller is performing its work, the processor is freed for other tasks. Under this approach, the controller handles only one bit at a time. However, the controller can also perform faster I/O by bypassing the processor entirely and transferring data directly to and from memory. The method of transferring a large block of data in this manner is known as *direct memory access (DMA).* To this end, the processor provides the controller with the read or write command, the address of the I/O buffer in memory, the number of sectors to transfer, and the numbers of the cylinder, head, and starting sector. With this method, the processor has to wait until the DMA is complete, because only one component at a time can use the memory path.

Clusters

A *cluster* is a group of sectors that the system treats as a unit of storage space. A cluster size is always a power of 2, such as 1, 2, 4, or 8 sectors. On a disk device that supports one sector per cluster, sector and cluster are the same. A disk with two sectors per cluster would look like this:

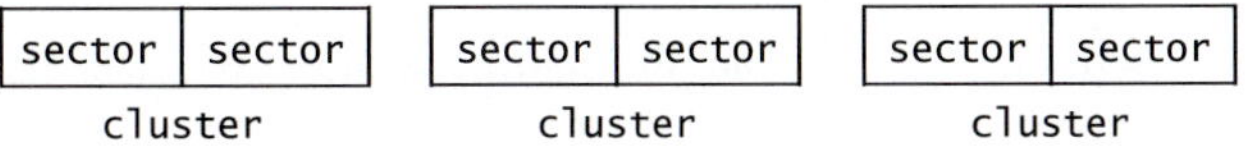

And a disk with four sectors per cluster would look like this:

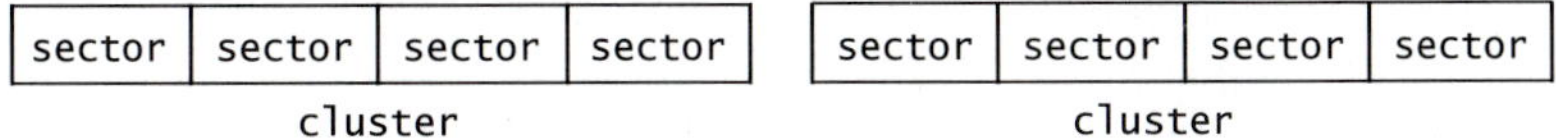

A hard disk typically has four sectors per cluster. A file begins on a cluster boundary and requires a minimum of one cluster, even if the file occupies only one of the four sectors. A cluster may also overlap from one track to another.

A 100-byte file (small enough to fit on one sector) stored on disk with four sectors per cluster uses $4 \times 512 = 2{,}048$ bytes of storage, although only one sector would contain data. For each file, the system stores its clusters in ascending sequence, although a file may be fragmented so that it resides, for example, in clusters 8, 9, 10, 14, 17, and 18.

Disk Capacity

Here are common diskette storage capacities:

Capacity	Tracks per Side (Cylinders)	Sectors per Track	Bytes per Sector	Total, Two Sides	Sectors per Cluster
5.25" 360KB	40	9	512	368,640	2
5.25" 1.2MB	80	15	512	1,228,800	1
3.5" 720KB	80	9	512	737,280	2
3.5" 1.44MB	80	18	512	1,474,560	1
3.5" 2.88MB	80	36	512	2,949,120	–

For hard disks, capacities vary considerably by device and by partition. Useful operations for determining the number of cylinders, sectors per track, or read-write heads include INT 21H functions 1FH and 440DH with minor code 60H, both covered in Chapter 18.

THE DISK SYSTEM AREA AND DATA AREA

Certain sectors are reserved for the purpose of supplying information about the files on the disk. The organization of diskettes and hard disks varies according to their capacity. A hard disk and some diskettes are formatted as self-booting—that is, they enable processing to start when the power is turned on or when a user presses the Ctrl + Alt + Del keys. The general organization of a disk consists of a system area, followed by a data area that comprises the rest of the disk.

System Area

The *system area* is the first area of a disk, on the outermost track(s) beginning with side 0, track 0, sector 1. The information that the system stores and maintains in its system area is used to determine, for example, the starting location of each file stored on the disk. The three components of the system area are:

1. Boot record
2. File allocation table (FAT)
3. Directory

The system area and the data area are organized like this:

Boot record	FAT	Directory	System files	User files

←System area→ |←Data area→

The following list gives the organization of various diskette devices, showing the starting and ending sector numbers for the boot record, FAT, and directory. Sectors are identified by relative sector number, where relative sector 0 is cylinder 0, track 0, sector 1, the first sector on the device (explained earlier in the section "Cylinders"):

Device	Boot	FAT	Directory	Sectors/Cluster
5.25" 360KB	0	1-4	5-11	2
5.25" 1.2MB	0	1-14	15-28	1
3.5" 720KB	0	1-6	7-13	2
3.5" 1.44MB	0	1-18	19-32	1

For hard disk, the locations of the boot record and the FAT are usually the same as for diskette, whereas the size of the FAT and the location of the directory vary by device.

A formatted diskette contains the following information in terms of beginning physical and relative sectors:

	720K (9 sectors/track)				1.44MB (18 sectors/track)			
File	Cyl.	Side	Sector	Relative Sector	Cyl.	Side	Sector	Relative Sector
Boot record	0	0	1	0	0	0	1	0
FAT1	0	0	2	1	0	0	2	1
FAT2	0	0	4	4	0	0	11	10
Directory	0	0	8	7	0	1	2	19
Data area	0	1	6	1	0	1	16	33

Data files on 720K diskettes begin on cylinder 0, side 1, sectors 6 through 9. The system stores records next on cylinder 1, side 0, then cylinder 1, side 1, then cylinder 2, side 0, and so forth. This feature of filling data on opposite sides (in the same cylinder) before proceeding to the next cylinder reduces the motion of the disk head and is the method used on both diskettes and hard disks.

Data Area

The *data area* for a bootable disk or diskette begins with two system files named IO.SYS and MSDOS.SYS (for MS-DOS) or IBMBIO.COM and IBMDOS.COM (for IBM PC-DOS). When you use FORMAT /S to format a disk, DOS copies its system files onto the first sectors of the data area. User files either immediately follow the system files or, if there are no system files, begin at the start of the data area.

The next sections explain the boot record, directory, and FAT.

THE BOOT RECORD

The boot record contains the instructions that load (or "boot") the system files IO.SYS, MS-DOS.SYS, and COMMAND.COM (if present) from disk into memory. All formatted disks contain a boot record even if the system files are not stored on it. The boot record contains the following information, in order of offset address:

00H	Short or far jump to the bootstrap routine at offset 1EH or 3EH in the boot record
03H	Manufacturer's name and DOS version number when boot was created
0BH	Bytes per sector, usually 200H (512)
0DH	Sectors per cluster (1, 2, 4, or 8)
0EH	Reserved sectors
10H	Number of copies of the FAT (1 or 2)
11H	Number of root directory entries
13H	Total number of sectors if volume is less than 32 MB
15H	Media descriptor byte (same as first byte of the FAT, described later)
16H	Number of sectors for the FAT
18H	Number of sectors per track
1AH	Number of read-write heads (sides or surfaces)
1CH	Number of hidden sectors
1EH	Bootstrap loader routine for DOS versions through 3.3
20H	Total number of sectors if volume is greater than 32 MB
24H	Physical drive number (for diskette, A = 0; for hard disk, 80H = drive C, etc.)
25H	Reserved by the system
26H	Extended boot sector signature (contains 29H)
27H	Volume ID
2BH	Volume label
36H	Reserved by the system
3EH–1FFH	As of DOS 4.0, the bootstrap loader begins here

DOS 4.0 extended the boot record with additional fields from 20H through 1FFH. The original boot record is 20H (32) bytes, whereas the extended version is 200H (512) bytes.

THE DIRECTORY

All files on a disk begin on a cluster boundary, which is the first sector of the cluster. For each file, DOS creates a 32-byte (20H) directory entry that describes the name of the file, the date it was created, its size, and the location of its starting cluster. Directory entries have the following format:

BYTE	PURPOSE
00H-07H	*Filename,* as defined in the program that created the file. The first byte can also indicate the file status: • 00H File has never been used • 05H First character of filename is actually E5H • 2EH Entry is for a subdirectory • E5H File has been deleted
08H-0AH	*Filename extension,* such as EXE or ASM
0BH	*File attribute,* defining the type of file (note that a file may have more than one attribute): • 00H Normal file • 01H File that can only be read (read-only) • 02H Hidden file, not displayed by a directory search • 04H System file, not displayed by a directory search • 08H Volume label (if this is a volume label record, the label itself is in the filename and extension fields) • 10H Subdirectory • 20H Archive file, which indicates whether the file was rewritten since the last update. (As an example, code 07H would mean a system file (04H) that is read only (01H) and hidden (02H).)
0CH-15H	Reserved by the system.
16H-17H	*Time of day* when the file was created or last updated; stored as 16 bits in binary format as |hhhhhmmmmmmsssss|.
18H-19H	*Date* when the file was created or last updated, stored as 16 bits in binary format as |yyyyyyym|mmmddddd|. The year can be 000–119 (with 1980 as the starting point), the month can be 01–12, and the day can be 01–31.
1AH-1BH	*Starting cluster* of the file. The number is relative to the last two sectors of the directory. Where there are no system files, the first data file begins at relative cluster 002. The actual side, track, and cluster depend on disk capacity. A zero entry means that the file has no space allocated to it.
1CH-1FH	*Size of the file* in bytes. When you create a file, the system calculates and stores its size in this field.

For numeric fields that exceed one byte in the directory, data is stored with the bytes in reverse sequence.

THE FILE ALLOCATION TABLE

The purpose of the FAT is to allocate disk space for files. The FAT contains an entry for each cluster on the disk. When you create a new file or revise an existing file, the system revises the associated FAT entries according to the location of the file on disk. The FAT begins at sector 2, immediately following the boot record. On a disk where a cluster consists of four sectors, the same number of FAT entries can reference four times as much data as disks where a cluster consists of one sector. Consequently, the use of clusters with multiple sectors reduces the number of entries in the FAT and enables the system to address a larger disk storage space.

The original designers provided for two copies of the FAT (FAT1 and FAT2), presumably because FAT2 could be used if FAT1 became corrupted. However, although FAT2 is still maintained, its use has never been implemented. The earlier section "Disk System Area and Data Area" includes both FAT1 and FAT2 in the FAT storage requirements. All other discussions in this book concern FAT1.

First Entry in the FAT

The first byte of the FAT, the media descriptor, indicates the type of device (see also byte 15H in the boot record), including the following:

F0H	3.5", two-sided, 18 sectors/track (1.44MB) and 3.5", two-sided, 36 sectors/track (2.88MB)
F8H	Hard disk (including RAM disk)
F9H	3.5", two-sided, 9 sectors/track (720KB) and 5.25", two-sided, 15 sectors/track (1.2MB)
FCH	5.25", one-sided, 9 sectors/track (180KB)
FDH	5.25", two-sided, 9 sectors/track (360KB)
FFH	5.25", two-sided, 8 sectors/track (320KB)

Note that F0H and F9H each identify two different disk formats.

Second Entry in the FAT

The second FAT entry contains FFFFH for diskette FATs that support 12-bit FAT entries and FFFFFFH for hard disks that support 16-bit FAT entries. The first two FAT entries look like this:

1.44MB diskette	F0	FF	FF	. .	. .	. .	. .	. .	. . .	. .
Hard disk	F8	FF	FF	FF	. .	. .	. .	. .	. . .	. .

As already described, the first field on a disk is the boot record, followed by the FAT and then the directory. The data area is next. The entire picture is as follows:

```
| cluster 0 | cluster 1 | cluster 2 | cluster 3 |  . . .  | cluster n |
|<-directory area->|<------------- data area --------------------->|
```

You would expect that the data area would be the starting point for clusters; however, the first two cluster numbers (0 and 1) point to the directory, so that the data area for stored data files begins with cluster number 2. The reason for this odd state of affairs will soon be made clear.

Pointer Entries in the FAT

Following the first two FAT entries are *pointer entries* that relate to every cluster in the data area. The directory (at 1AH–1BH) contains the location of the first cluster for a file, and the FAT contains a chain of pointer entries for each succeeding cluster.

The entry length for diskettes is 3 hex digits (1 1/2 bytes, or 12 bits), but for hard disk it is 4 hex digits (2 bytes, or 16 bits). Each FAT pointer entry indicates the use of a particular cluster according to the following format:

12 BITS	16 BITS	EXPLANATION
000	0000	Referenced cluster is currently unused
nnn	nnnn	Relative number of next cluster for a file
FF0–FF6	FFF0–FFF6	Reserved cluster
FF7	FFF7	Unusable (bad track)
FFF	FFFF	Last cluster of a file

The first two entries for a 1.44MB diskette (a 12-bit FAT) look like this:

```
FAT entry:          | F0F | FF. |. . .|. . .| . . . |. . .| . . . | . . . |. . .|
Relative cluster:      0     1     2     3     4      5      6      . . .   end
```

The term "relative cluster" means the cluster to which the FAT entry points. In a sense, the first two FAT entries (0 and 1) point to the last two clusters in the directory, which have been assigned as the start of clusters; the directory indicates the size and starting cluster for files.

The directory contains the starting cluster number for each file and a chain of FAT pointer entries that indicate the location of the next cluster, if any, at which the file continues. A pointer entry containing (F)FFFH indicates the last cluster for the file.

Sample FAT Entries

The following examples should help clarify the FAT structure. Suppose a diskette contains only one file, named CUSTOMER.FIL, that is fully stored on clusters 2, 3, and 4. The directory entry for this file contains the filename CUSTOMER, the extension FIL, 00H to indicate a normal file, the creation date, 0002H for the location of the first relative cluster of the file, and an entry for the size of the file in bytes. The 12-bit FAT entry would appear as follows, except that pairs of bytes would be reversed:

FAT entry:	F0F	FFF	003	004	FFF	...	...	. . .	...
Relative cluster:	0	1	2	3	4	5	6	. . .	end

For the first two FAT entries, F0 indicates a two-sided nine-sectored (1.44MB) diskette, followed by FFFFH. For a program to read CUSTOMER.FIL sequentially from disk into memory, the system takes the following steps:

- For the first cluster, searches the disk directory for the filename CUSTOMER and extension FIL, extracts from the directory the location of the first relative cluster (2) of the file, and delivers its contents (data from the sectors) to the program in main memory.
- For the next cluster, accesses the FAT pointer entry that represents relative cluster 2. From the diagram, this entry contains 003, meaning that the file continues on relative cluster 3. The system delivers the contents of this cluster to the program.
- For the last cluster, accesses the FAT pointer entry that represents relative cluster 3. This entry contains 004, meaning that the file continues on relative cluster 4. The system delivers the contents of this cluster to the program.

The FAT entry for relative cluster 4 contains FFFH to indicate that no more clusters are allocated for the file. The system has now delivered all the file's data, from clusters 2, 3, and 4.

We've just seen how FAT entries work in principle; now let's see how they work in terms of reversed-byte sequence, where a little more ingenuity is required.

Handling 12-Bit FAT Entries in Reversed-Byte Sequence

Following is the same example of FAT entries for CUSTOMER.FIL just covered, but now with pointer entries in reversed-byte sequence. The 12-bit FAT for this file looks like this:

FAT entry:	F0F	FFF	034	000	FF0	Fxx	. . .
Relative cluster:	0	1	2	3	4	5	

But what's needed now to decipher the entries is to represent them according to *relative byte* rather than cluster:

FAT entry:	F0	FF	FF	03	40	00	FF	0F	. . .
Relative byte:	0	1	2	3	4	5	6	7	

Here are the steps used to access the clusters:

- To process the first FAT entry, multiply 2 (the file's first cluster as recorded in the directory) by 1.5 (the length of FAT entries) to get 3. (For programming, multiply by 3 and shift right one bit.) Access the word at bytes 3 and 4 in the FAT. These bytes contain 03 40, which, when reversed, are 4003. Because cluster 2 was an even number, use the last three digits, so that 003 is the second cluster for the file.

- For the third cluster, multiply cluster number 3 by 1.5 to get 4. Access FAT bytes 4 and 5. These contain 40 00, which, when reversed, are 0040. Because cluster 3 was an odd number, use the first three digits, so that 004 is the third cluster for the file.
- For the fourth cluster, multiply cluster 4 by 1.5 to get 6. Access FAT bytes 6 and 7. These contain FF 0F, which, when reversed, are 0FFF. Because cluster 4 was an even number, use the last three digits, FFF, which mean that this is the last entry. (Whew!)

Handling 16-Bit FAT Entries

As mentioned earlier, following the media descriptor for hard disk is FFFFFFH. FAT pointer entries are 16 bits long and begin with bytes 3 and 4, which represent cluster 2. The directory entry provides the starting clusters for files, and pointer entry FFFFH indicates end-of-file. Determining the cluster number from each FAT entry is simple, although the bytes in each entry are in reverse sequence.

As an example of 16-bit FAT entries, suppose the only file on a particular hard disk occupies four clusters (at 4 sectors per cluster, or 16 sectors in all). According to the directory, the file starts at cluster 2. Each FAT pointer entry is a full word, so that reversing the bytes involves only the one entry. Here is the FAT, with pointer entries in reversed-byte sequence:

FAT entry:	F8FF	FFFF	0300	0400	0500	FFFF	. . .
Relative cluster:	0	1	2	3	4	5	

The FAT entry for relative cluster 2, 0300, reverses as 0003 for the next cluster. The FAT entry for relative cluster 3, 0400, reverses as 0004 for the next cluster. Continue with the chain of remaining entries in this fashion through to the entry for cluster number 5.

If your program has to determine the type of disk that is installed, it can check the media descriptor in the boot sector directly or, preferably, could use INT 21H function 1BH or 1CH.

EXERCISE: EXAMINING THE FAT

Let's use DEBUG to examine the FAT for a disk. For this exercise, you'll need two formatted blank 3.5" diskettes with 720K and 1.44MB capacities, without the system files copied on them. Copy two files onto each disk. The first file should be larger than 512 bytes and smaller than 1,024 bytes, to fit onto two sectors; A04ASM1.ASM is suggested. The second file should be larger than 1,536 bytes and smaller than 2,048 bytes to fit onto four sectors; A10DRVID.ASM is suggested. You'll see that the FATs for the two diskettes are similar, but not identical.

Procedure for the 720K Disk

First insert the 720K diskette in drive A (or B if necessary). Load DEBUG and key in the L (load) command (more fully explained in Appendix E):

```
L 100 0 0 20 (for drive B, use L 100 1 0 20)
```

The L command entries are:

- 100H is the starting offset in DEBUG's segment where the data is to be read in.
- The first 0 means use drive A (or 1 for drive B).
- The second 0 means read data beginning with relative sector 0.
- 20 means read 20H (32) sectors.

You can now examine the boot record, directory, and FAT for this diskette. To start the display, key in the command D 100. Because the file is stored beginning at offset 100H, you can locate the records this way:

1. The boot record is at the start, at 100H.
2. The FAT follows the boot sector: 100H + 200H (1 sector, 200H or 512 bytes) = 300H.
3. The directory follows the FAT: 300H + [6 sectors × 200H] = F00H.

The boot record. Some of the fields on the boot record are:

- Segment offset 103H shows the manufacturer's name and DOS version when the FAT was created.
- Offset 10BH shows the number of bytes per sector (where 0002H reverses as 0200H, or 512 bytes).
- Offset 115H is the media descriptor, F9H for this diskette.

Check out the other fields.

The Directory. For the directory, key in the command D F00, where:

- Offset F00H contains the filename for the first file, A04ASM1.ASM.
- Offset F1AH gives the starting cluster number (0200, or 0002) for this file.
- Offset F1CH-F1FH gives the size of the file in bytes.
- Offset F20H begins the entry for the second file, A10DRVID.ASM. Note that F3AH shows its starting cluster as 0300, or 0003.

The FAT. For the FAT, key in the command D 300, which should display:

FAT entry:	F9	FF	FF	FF	4F	00	FF	0F	...
Relative byte:	0	1	2	3	4	5	6	7	

- F9 is the media descriptor.
- FF FF at bytes 1 and 2 is the content of the second field.

The pointer entries beginning at byte 3 can be calculated like this:

- For the first file, multiply 2 (its first cluster according to the directory) by 1.5 to get 3. Access offset bytes 3 and 4 in the FAT, which contain FF 4F, and reverse the bytes to get 4FFF. Because cluster 2 was an even number, use the last three digits, FFF, which tell you that there are no more clusters for this file.
- For the second file, multiply 3 (its first cluster according to the directory) by 1.5 to get 4. Access offset bytes 4 and 5 in the FAT, which contain 4F 00, and reverse the bytes to get 004F. Because cluster 3 was an odd number, use the first three digits, 004, which identify the next cluster in the series. Multiply cluster 4 by 1.5 to get 6. Access offset bytes 6 and 7 in the FAT, which contain FF 0F, and reverse the bytes to get 0FFF. Because cluster 4 was an even number, use the first three digits, FFF, which indicate the end of the data.

Procedure for the 1.44MB Disk

Now insert the 1.44MB diskette in drive A, and enter the DEBUG command L 100 0 0 30. (Load 30H sectors because there's more FAT on 1.44MB diskettes.) The boot record begins at 100H and the FAT follows at 100H + 200H = 300H. Because the FAT for a 1.44MB diskette is 18 sectors long, the directory is at 300H + (12H × 200H) = 2700H.

The boot record. Use D 100 to display the boot record. Note that the media descriptor byte at 115H is F0 and the number of sectors per cluster (at 10DH) is 1.

The directory. For the directory, key in the command D 2700. The first file name is at 2700H and its starting cluster (2) is at 271A. The second file name is at 2720H and its starting cluster (4) is at 273A. (The starting cluster for the second file on the 720K diskette was 3 because that format has two sectors per cluster, whereas a 1.44MB diskette has one sector per cluster.)

The FAT. For the FAT, enter the command D 300, which should display:

FAT entry:	F0	FF	FF	03	F0	FF	05	60	00	07	F0	FF
Relative byte:	0	1	2	3	4	5	6	7	8	9	10	11

According to the directory, the first file starts at cluster 2, so multiply 2 by 1.5 to get relative byte 3. Bytes 3 and 4 contain 03 F0, which reverse as F003. Because cluster 2 was an even number, use the last three digits, 003. Cluster 3 × 1.5 is 4; relative bytes 4 and 5 contain F0 FF, which reverse as FFF0. Because cluster 3 was an odd number, use the first three digits, FFF, which indicate the end of the file. We now know that the file resides on clusters 2 and 3.

Use the same technique to trace through the chain for the second file, which begins with cluster 4, or relative byte 6.

INT 21H provides some supporting services for programs to access information about the directory and the FAT, including functions 47H (Get Current Directory) and 1BH and 1CH (Get FAT Information), described in Chapter 18.

PROCESSING FILES ON DISK

Data on disk is stored in the form of a *file,* just as you have stored your programs. Although there is no restriction on the kind of data that you may keep in a file, a typical user file would consist of *records* for customers, inventory supplies, or name-and-address lists. Each record contains information about a particular customer or inventory item. Within a file, all records are usually (but not necessarily) the same length and format. A record contains one or more fields that provide information about the record. Records for a customer file, for example, could contain such fields as customer number, customer name, and amount owing. The records could be in ascending sequence by customer number, as follows:

#1	name	amt		#2	name	amt		#3	name	amt	. . .	#n	name	amt

Processing for files on hard disk is similar to that for diskette; for both, you have to supply a path name to access files in subdirectories.

Interrupt Services for Disk Input/Output

A number of special interrupt services support disk input/output. A program that writes (or *creates*) a file first causes the system to generate an entry for it in the directory. When all the file's records have been written, the program *closes* the file so that the system can complete the directory entry for the size of the file.

A program that is to read a file first *opens* the file to ensure that it exists. Once the program has read all the records, it should close the file, making it available to other programs. Because of the directory's design, you may process records in a disk file either sequentially (one record after another, successively) or randomly (records retrieved as requested, throughout the file).

The *highest level* of disk processing is via INT 21H, which supports disk accessing by means of a directory and "blocking" and "unblocking" of records. This method performs some preliminary processing before linking to BIOS. Chapter 17 covers the use of DOS operations to write and read disk files, and Chapter 18 discusses various operations that support directories and disk files.

The *lowest level* of disk processing is via BIOS interrupt 13H, which involves direct addressing of track and sector numbers, and is covered in Chapter 19.

KEY POINTS

- Each side of a diskette or hard disk contains a number of concentric tracks, starting with track number 00. Each track is formatted into sectors of 512 bytes, starting with sector number 1.
- A cylinder is the set of all tracks with the same number on each side.

- A sector may be referenced by cylinder-head or by relative sector number.
- A cluster is a group of sectors that the system treats as a unit of storage space. A cluster size is always a power of 2, such as 1, 2, 4, or 8 sectors. A file begins on a cluster boundary and requires a minimum of one cluster.
- Regardless of size, all files begin on a cluster boundary.
- The boot record contains the instructions that load (or "boot") the system files IOSYS.SYS, MSDOS.COM, and COMMAND.COM from disk into memory.
- The directory contains an entry for each file on a disk and indicates the filename, extension, file attribute, time, date, starting sector, and file size.
- The purpose of the file allocation table (FAT) is to allocate disk space for files. The FAT begins at sector 2 immediately following the boot record and contains one entry for each cluster for each file in the directory.

QUESTIONS

16-1. What is the length in bytes of a standard sector?

16-2. What is a cylinder?

16-3. What is the purpose of a disk controller?

16-4. (a) What is a cluster? (b) What is its purpose? (c) What is the disk space (in terms of bytes) used for each of cluster sizes 1, 2, 4, and 8?

16-5. Show how to calculate the capacity of a diskette, based on the number of cylinders, sectors per track, and bytes per sector, for (a) a 3.5", 1.44MB diskette and (b) a 5.25", 360KB diskette.

16-6. What are the three parts of the disk system area?

16-7. (a) What is the purpose of the boot record? (b) Where is it located? (c) How can you use it to determine the number of sectors per track?

16-8. How does the directory indicate a deleted file?

16-9. What is the indication in the directory for (a) a normal file; (b) a read-only file; (c) a system file?

16-10. What is the additional effect on a diskette or hard disk when you use FORMAT /S to format?

16-11. Consider a file with a size of 3,165 (decimal) bytes. (a) Where does the system store the size? (b) What is the size in hexadecimal format? Show the value as the system stores it.

16-12. Where and how does the FAT indicate that the device on which it resides is on (a) a hard disk; (b) a 3.5", 1.44MB diskette; (c) a 5.25", 360KB diskette?

16-13. How does the FAT indicate 12-bit entries and 16-bit entries?

17 DISK STORAGE II: WRITING AND READING FILES

Objective: To cover the use of file handles and the operations for writing and reading disk files sequentially and randomly.

INTRODUCTION

The original services for processing disk files used a method called file control blocks (FCBs). This method, although still supported by DOS, can address drives and filenames, but not subdirectories. Succeeding DOS versions introduced a number of extended services that are simpler and more capable than their original counterparts. Some of these operations involve the use of an ASCIIZ string to initially identify a drive, path, and filename; a file handle for subsequent accessing of the file; and special return codes to identify errors.

Although no new assembly language instructions are required, this chapter introduces a number of INT 21H services for processing disk files. Here they are, arranged by category:

OPERATIONS USING FILE HANDLES	OPERATIONS USING FCBS
3CH Create file	0FH Open file
3DH Open file	10H Close file
3EH Close file	14H Read record
3FH Read record	15H Write record
40H Write record	16H Create file
42H Move file pointer	21H Read record randomly
OTHER SERVICES	22H Write record randomly
INT 25H Absolute read	27H Read block randomly
INT 26H Absolute write	28H Write block randomly

The chapter covers the services for writing and reading disk files, and Chapter 18 covers the various support services required for handling disk drives, directories, and files. As a reminder, the term cluster denotes a group of one or more sectors of data, depending on the device.

ASCIIZ STRINGS

When using many of the extended services for disk processing, you first provide the system with the address of an *ASCIIZ string* containing the filespec: the location of the disk drive, directory path, and filename (all optional and within apostrophes), followed by a byte of hex zeros; thus the name ASCIIZ string. The maximum length of the string is 128 bytes.

The following example defines a drive and filename:

```
PATHNAM1 DB 'E:\A17RANRD.ASM',00H
```

This example defines a drive, subdirectory, and filename:

```
PATHNAM2 DB 'F:\UTILITY\A17RANRD.EXE',00H
```

The backslash, which may also be a forward slash, acts as a path separator. A byte of zeros terminates the string. For interrupts that require an ASCIIZ string, load its offset address in the DX register, for example, as LEA DX,PATHNAM1.

FILE HANDLES

As discussed in Chapter 9, you may use file handles directly for certain standard devices: 00 = input, 01 = output, 02 = error output, 03 = auxiliary device, and 04 = printer. Other I/O services involve the use of a file handle for operations that access files; for these, you have to request the file handle number from the system. A disk file must first be opened; unlike transferring data from the keyboard or to the screen, the system has to address disk files through its directory and FAT entries and must update these entries. During program execution, each file referenced must be assigned its own unique file handle.

The system delivers a file handle when you open a file for input or create a file for output. The operations involve the use of an ASCIIZ string and INT 21H function 3CH or 3DH. The file handle is a unique 1-word number returned in the AX that you save in a word data item and use for all subsequent requests to access the file. Typically, the first file handle returned is 05, the second is 06, and so forth.

The PSP contains a default file handle table that provides for 20 handles (thus the nominal limit for opened files), but you can use INT 21H function 67H to increase the limit, as explained in Chapter 24.

ERROR RETURN CODES

The file handle operations for disk deliver a *completion status* via the carry flag and the AX register. A successful operation clears the carry flag to zero and performs other appropriate functions. An unsuccessful operation sets the carry flag to 1 and returns an error code in the AX, depending on the operation. Figure 17-1 lists error codes 01–36; other codes are concerned with networking.

01	Invalid function number	20	Unknown unit
02	File not found	21	Drive not ready
03	Path not found	22	Unknown command
04	Too many files open	23	CRC data error
05	Access denied	24	Bad request structure length
06	Invalid handle	25	Seek error
07	Memory control block destroyed	26	Unknown media type
08	Insufficient memory	27	Sector not found
09	Invalid memory block address	28	Printer out of paper
10	Invalid environment	29	Write fault
11	Invalid format	30	Read fault
12	Invalid access code	31	General failure
13	Invalid data	32	Sharing violation
15	Invalid drive specified	33	Lock violation
16	Attempt to remove directory	34	Invalid disk change
17	Not same device	35	FCB unavailable
18	No more files	36	Sharing buffer overflow
19	Write-protected disk		

Figure 17-1 Major Disk Error Return Codes

If these errors aren't enough, you can also use INT 59H for additional information about errors. (See Chapter 18.)

The following sections cover the requirements for creating, writing, and closing disk files.

FILE POINTERS

The system maintains a separate *file pointer* for each file that a program is processing. The create and open operations initialize the value of the file pointer to zero, the file's starting location. The file pointer subsequently accounts for the current offset location within the file.

Each read/write operation causes the system to increment the file pointer by the number of bytes transferred. The file pointer then points to the location of the next record to be accessed. File pointers facilitate both sequential and random processing. For random accessing of a record, you can use INT 21H function 42H (covered in a later section) to set the file pointer to any location in the file.

USING FILE HANDLES TO CREATE DISK FILES

The procedure for writing a disk file is the following:

1. Use an ASCIIZ string to get a file handle from the system;
2. Use INT 21H function 3CH to create the file;
3. Use INT 21H function 40H to write records in the file;
4. At the end, use INT 21H function 3EH to close the file.

INT 21H Function 3CH: Create File

For *creating* a new file or overwriting an old file with the same name, first use INT 21H function 3CH. Load the CX with the required file attribute (covered in Chapter 16) and the DX with the address of the ASCIIZ string (the location on disk of the new file). Here's an example that creates a normal file on drive E with attribute 0:

```
PATHNAM1  DB   'E:\ACCOUNTS.FIL',00H
FILHAND1  DW   ?                ;File handle
          ...
          MOV AH,3CH            ;Request create file
          MOV CX,00             ;Normal attribute
          LEA DX,PATHNAM1       ;ASCIIZ string
          INT 21H               ;Call interrupt service
          JC  error             ;Special action if error
          MOV FILHAND1,AX       ;Save handle in word
```

For a valid operation, the system creates a directory entry with the given attribute, clears the carry flag, and sets the handle for the file in the AX. Use this file handle for all subsequent accesses of the file. The named file is opened with its file pointer set to zero and is now available for writing. If a file with the given name already exists in the path, the operation sets up a zero length for overwriting the new file on the old one.

For error conditions, the operation sets the carry flag and returns a code in the AX: 03, 04, or 05 (see Figure 17-1). Code 05 means that either the directory is full or the referenced filename has the read-only attribute. Be sure to check the carry flag first. For example, creating a file probably delivers handle 05 to the AX, which could easily be confused with error code 05, access denied. Related services for creating a file are INT 21H functions 5AH and 5BH, covered in Chapter 18.

INT 21H Function 40H: Write Record

For *writing* records on disk, use INT 21H function 40H. Load the BX with the stored file handle, the CX with the number of bytes to write, and the DX with the address of the output area. The following example uses the file handle from the preceding create operation to write a 256-byte record from OUTAREA:

```
FILHAND1  DW   ?                ;File handle
OUTAREA   DB   256 DUP(' ')     ;Output area
          ...
          MOV AH,40H            ;Request write record
          MOV BX,FILHAND1       ;File handle
          MOV CX,256            ;Record length
          LEA DX,OUTAREA        ;Address of output area
          INT 21H               ;Call interrupt service
          JC  error2            ;Special action if error
          CMP AX,256            ;All bytes written?
          JNE error3            ;If not, error
```

A valid operation writes the record onto disk, increments the file pointer, clears the carry flag, and sets the AX to the number of bytes actually written. A full disk may cause the number written to differ from the number requested but, because the system does not report this condition as an error, you have to test the value returned in the AX. An invalid operation sets the carry flag and returns to the AX error code 05 (access denied) or 06 (invalid handle).

INT 21H Function 3EH: Close File

When you have finished writing a file, you have to *close* it. Load the file handle in the BX, and use INT 21H function 3EH:

```
MOV  AH,3EH          ;Request close file
MOV  BX,FILHAND1     ;File handle
INT  21H             ;Call interrupt service
```

A successful close operation writes any remaining records still in the memory buffer and updates the FAT and the directory with the date and file size. An unsuccessful operation sets the carry flag and returns in the AX the only possible error code, 06 (invalid handle).

Program: Creating a Disk File

The program in Figure 17-2 creates a file from names that a user keys in. Its major procedures are the following:

- A10MAIN Calls B10CREAT, C10PROC and, if at the end of input, calls F10CLSE.
- B10CREAT Uses INT 21H function 3CH to create the file and saves the handle in a data item named HANDLE.
- C10PROC Accepts input from the keyboard and clears positions from the end of the name to the end of the input area.
- D10SCRL Scrolls the screen when near the bottom row.
- E10WRIT Uses INT 21H function 40H to write records.
- F10CLSE At the end of processing, uses INT 21H function 3EH to close the file in order to create a proper directory entry.

The input area is 30 bytes, followed by 2 bytes for the Enter (0DH) and Line Feed (0AH) characters, for 32 bytes in all. The program writes the 32 bytes as a fixed-length record. You could omit the Enter/Line Feed characters, but you should include them if you want to sort the records in the file, because the DOS SORT program requires these characters to indicate the end of records. For this example, the command to sort the records from NAMEFILE.DAT into ascending sequence in NAMEFILE.SRT could be

```
SORT F:<NAMEFILE.DAT >NAMEFILE.SRT
```

(SORT processes from NAMEFILE.DAT to NAMEFILE.SRT.)

```
            page 60,132
TITLE       A17CRFIL (EXE)  Create disk file of names
            .MODEL  SMALL
            .STACK  64
; ----------------------------------------------------
            .DATA
NAMEPAR     LABEL   BYTE              ;Parameter list:
MAXLEN      DB      30                ;Maximum length
NAMELEN     DB      ?                 ;Actual length
NAMEREC     DB      30 DUP(' '), 0DH, 0AH ;Entered name,
                                      ;  CR/LF for writing
ERRCDE      DB      00                ;Error indicator
HANDLE      DW      ?                 ;File handle
PATHNAM     DB      'F:\NAMEFILE.DAT', 0
PROMPT      DB      'Name? '
ROW         DB      01
OPNMSG      DB      '*** Open error  ***', 0DH, 0AH
WRTMSG      DB      '*** Write error ***', 0DH, 0AH
; ----------------------------------------------------
            .CODE
A10MAIN     PROC   FAR
            MOV     AX,@data          ;Initialize data
            MOV     DS,AX             ;  segment
            MOV     ES,AX
            MOV     AX,0600H
            CALL    Q10SCR            ;Clear screen
            CALL    Q20CURS           ;Set cursor
            CALL    B10CREAT          ;Create file
            CMP     ERRCDE,00         ;Create error?
            JZ      A20LOOP           ;  yes, continue
            JMP     A90               ;  no,  exit
A20LOOP:
            CALL    C10PROC
            CMP     NAMELEN,00        ;End of input?
            JNE     A20LOOP           ;  no,  continue
            CALL    F10CLSE           ;  yes, close,
A90:        MOV     AX,4C00H          ;End processing
            INT     21H
A10MAIN     ENDP

;                   Create disk file:
;                   ----------------
B10CREAT    PROC    NEAR
            MOV     AH,3CH            ;Request create
            MOV     CX,00             ;Normal
            LEA     DX,PATHNAM
            INT     21H
            JC      B20               ;Error?
            MOV     HANDLE,AX         ;  no, save handle
            RET
B20:                                  ;  yes,
            LEA     DX,OPNMSG         ;  error message
            CALL    X10ERR
            RET
B10CREAT    ENDP
```

Figure 17-2a Using a Handle to Create a File

Note two points. (1) The Enter/Line Feed characters are included after each record only to facilitate the sort and could otherwise be omitted. (2) Each record could be in variable-length format, only up to the end of the name; this would involve some extra programming, as you'll see later.

```
;                   Accept input:
;                   ------------
C10PROC     PROC    NEAR
            MOV     AH,40H              ;Request display
            MOV     BX,01               ;Handle
            MOV     CX,06               ;Length of prompt
            LEA     DX,PROMPT           ;Display prompt
            INT     21H

            MOV     AH,0AH              ;Request input
            LEA     DX,NAMEPAR          ;Accept name
            INT     21H
            CMP     NAMELEN,00          ;Is there a name?
            JZ      C90                 ;  no, exit
            MOV     AL,20H              ;Blank for storing
            SUB     CH,CH
            MOV     CL,NAMELEN          ;Length
            LEA     DI,NAMEREC
            ADD     DI,CX               ;Address + length
            NEG     CX                  ;Calculate remaining
            ADD     CX,30               ;  length
            REP STOSB                   ;Set to blank
            CALL    E10WRIT             ;Write disk record
            CALL    D10SCRL             ;Check for scroll
C90:
            RET
C10PROC     ENDP
;                   Check for scroll:
;                   ----------------
D10SCRL     PROC    NEAR
            CMP     ROW,18              ;Bottom of screen?
            JAE     D20                 ;  yes, bypass
            INC     ROW                 ;  no,  add to row
            JMP     D90
D20:
            MOV     AX,0601H            ;Scroll one row
            CALL    Q10SCR
D90:        CALL    Q20CURS             ;Reset cursor
            RET
D10SCRL     ENDP
;                   Write disk record:
;                   -----------------
E10WRIT     PROC    NEAR
            MOV     AH,40H              ;Request write
            MOV     BX,HANDLE
            MOV     CX,32               ;30 for name, 2 for CR/LF
            LEA     DX,NAMEREC
            INT     21H
            JNC     E20                 ;Valid write?
            LEA     DX,WRTMSG           ;  no,
            CALL    X10ERR              ;  call error routine
            MOV     NAMELEN,00
E20:
            RET
E10WRIT     ENDP
```

Figure 17-2b Using a Handle to Create a File

```
;                   Close disk file:
;                   ----------------
F10CLSE   PROC      NEAR
          MOV       NAMEREC,1AH        ;Set EOF mark
          CALL      E10WRIT
          MOV       AH,3EH             ;Request close
          MOV       BX,HANDLE
          INT       21H
          RET
F10CLSE ENDP
;                   Scroll screen:
;                   --------------
Q10SCR    PROC      NEAR               ;AX set on entry
          MOV       BH,1EH             ;Set yellow on blue
          MOV       CX,0000
          MOV       DX,184FH
          INT       10H                ;Scroll
          RET
Q10SCR    ENDP
;                   Set cursor:
;                   -----------
Q20CURS   PROC      NEAR
          MOV       AH,02H             ;Request
          MOV       BH,00              ;  set cursor
          MOV       DH,ROW             ;Row
          MOV       DL,00              ;Column
          INT       10H
          RET
Q20CURS   ENDP
;                   Display disk error message:
;                   ---------------------------
X10ERR    PROC      NEAR               ;DX contains
          MOV       AH,40H             ;  address of message
          MOV       BX,01              ;Handle for screen
          MOV       CX,21              ;Length
          INT       21H
          MOV       ERRCDE,01          ;Set error code
          RET
X10ERR    ENDP
          END       A10MAIN
```

Figure 17-2b Using a Handle to Create a File

USING FILE HANDLES TO READ DISK FILES

This section covers the requirements for opening and reading disk files using file handles. The procedure for reading a disk file is the following:

1. Use an ASCIIZ string to get a file handle from the system.
2. Use INT 21H function 3DH to open the file.
3. Use INT 21H function 3FH to read records from the file.
4. At the end, use INT 21H function 3EH to close the file.

INT 21H Function 3DH: Open File

If your program is to read a file, first use INT 21H function 3DH to open it. This operation checks that a file by the given name actually exists. Load the DX with the address of the required ASCIIZ string, and set the AL with an access code:

BITS	REQUEST	BITS	REQUEST
0–2	000 = read only 001 = write only 010 = read/write	3 4–6 7	1 = Reserved Sharing mode Inheritance flag

Before reading a file, be sure to use function 3DH to open the file, not function 3CH to create it. The following example opens a file for reading:

```
FILHAND2 DW  ?      ;File handle
         ...
         MOV  AH,3DH          ;Request open file
         MOV  AL,00           ;Read only
         LEA  DX,PATHNM1      ;ASCIIZ string
         INT  21H             ;Call interrupt service
         JC   error4          ;Special action if error
         MOV  FILHAND2,AX     ;Save handle in word
```

If a file with the given name exists, the operation sets the record length to 1 (which you can override), assumes the file's current attribute, sets the file pointer to 0 (the start of the file), clears the carry flag, and returns a handle for the file in the AX. Use this file handle for all subsequent accesses of the file.

If the file does not exist, the operation sets the carry flag and returns an error code in the AX: 02, 03, 04, 05, or 12 (see Figure 17-1). Be sure to check the carry flag first. For example, creating a file probably delivers handle 05 to the AX, which could easily be confused with error code 05, access denied.

INT 21H Function 3FH: Read Record

To read records, use INT 21H function 3FH. Load the file handle in the BX, the number of bytes to read in the CX, and the address of the input area in the DX. The following example uses the file handle from the preceding example to read a 512-byte record:

```
FILHAND2  DW   ?
INAREA    DB   512 DUP(' ')
          ...
          MOV  AH,3FH          ;Request read record
          MOV  BX,FILHAND2     ;File handle
          MOV  CX,512          ;Record length
          LEA  DX,INAREA       ;Address of input area
          INT  21H             ;Call interrupt service
          JC   error5          ;Special action if error
          CMP  AX,00           ;Zero bytes read?
          JE   endfile         ; yes, end of file
```

A valid operation delivers the record to the program, clears the carry flag, and sets the AX to the number of bytes actually read. Zero in the AX means an attempt to read from the end of the file; this is a warning, not an error. An invalid read sets the carry flag and returns to the AX error code 05 (access denied) or 06 (invalid handle).

Because the system limits the number of files open at one time, a program that successively reads a number of files should close them as soon as it is through with them.

Program: Reading a Disk File Sequentially

The program in Figure 17-3 reads the file created by the program in Figure 17-2 and sorted by the DOS SORT command. Here are the main procedures:

- A10MAIN Calls B10OPEN, C10READ, D10DISP and, if at the end, closes the file and ends processing.
- B10OPEN Uses INT 21H function 3DH to open the file and saves the handle in a data item named HANDLE,
- C10READ Issues INT 21H function 3FH, which uses the handle to read the records.
- D10DISP Displays the records and scrolls the screen. Because Enter and Line Feed characters already follow each record, the program does not have to advance the cursor when displaying records.

USING FILE HANDLES FOR RANDOM PROCESSING

The preceding discussion on processing disk files sequentially is adequate for creating a file, for printing its contents, and for making changes to small files. Some applications, however, involve accessing a particular record on a file, such as information from a few employees or inventory parts.

To update a file with new data, a program that is restricted to sequential processing may have to read every record in the file up to the one that is required. For example, to access the 300th record in a file, sequential processing could involve reading through the preceding 299 records before delivering the 300th (although the system could begin at a specific record number).

The general solution is to use *random processing,* in which a program can directly access any given record in a file. Although you create a file sequentially, you may access the records sequentially or randomly.

When a program first requests a record randomly, the read operation uses the directory to locate the sector in which the record resides, reads the entire sector from disk into a buffer, and delivers the required record to the program.

In the next example, records are 128 bytes long and four to a sector. A request for random record number 21 causes the following four records to be read from the sector into the buffer:

record #20	record #21	record #22	record #23

When the program requests the next record randomly, such as number 23, the operation first checks the buffer. Because the record is already there, it is transferred directly to the

```
TITLE      A17RDFIL (EXE)  Read disk records sequentially
           .MODEL  SMALL
           .STACK  64
           .DATA
ENDCDE     DB      00                ;End process indicator
HANDLE     DW      ?
IOAREA     DB      32 DUP(' ')
OPENMSG    DB      '*** Open error ***', 0DH, 0AH
PATHNAM    DB      'F:\NAMEFILE.SRT',0
READMSG    DB      '*** Read error ***', 0DH, 0AH
ROW        DB      00
;--------------------------------------------------------
           .CODE
A10MAIN    PROC    FAR
           MOV     AX,@data          ;Initialize
           MOV     DS,AX             ;  segment
           MOV     ES,AX             ;  registers
           MOV     AX,0600H
           CALL    Q10SCR            ;Clear screen
           CALL    Q20CURS           ;Set cursor
           CALL    B10OPEN           ;Open file
           CMP     ENDCDE,00         ;Valid open?
           JNZ     A90               ;  no, exit
A20LOOP:
           CALL    C10READ           ;Read disk record
           CMP     ENDCDE,00         ;Normal read?
           JNZ     A80               ;  no,  exit
           CALL    D10DISP           ;  yes, display name,
           JMP     A20LOOP           ;  continue
A80:       MOV     AH,3EH            ;Request close file
           MOV     BX,HANDLE         ;
           INT     21H
A90:       MOV     AX,4C00H          ;End processing
           INT     21H
A10MAIN    ENDP
;                  Open file:
;                  ---------
B10OPEN    PROC    NEAR
           MOV     AH,3DH            ;Request open
           MOV     AL,00             ;Normal file
           LEA     DX,PATHNAM
           INT     21H
           JC      B20               ;Error?
           MOV     HANDLE,AX         ;  no, save handle,
           JMP     B90               ;  return
B20:
           MOV     ENDCDE,01         ;  yes,
           LEA     DX,OPENMSG        ;  display
           CALL    X10ERR            ;  error message
B90:       RET
B10OPEN    ENDP
;                  Read disk record:
;                  ----------------
C10READ    PROC   NEAR
           MOV     AH,3FH            ;Request read
           MOV     BX,HANDLE
           MOV     CX,32             ;30 for name, 2 for CR/LF
           LEA     DX,IOAREA
           INT     21H
           JC      C20               ;Error on read?
```

Figure 17-3a Reading Records Sequentially

```
         CMP     AX,00            ;End of file?
         JE      C30
         CMP     IOAREA,1AH       ;EOF marker?
         JE      C30              ;  yes, exit
         JMP     C90
C20:                              ;  no,
         LEA     DX,READMSG       ;  invalid read
         CALL    X10ERR
C30:     MOV     ENDCDE,01        ;Force end
C90:     RET
C10READ  ENDP
;                Display name:
;                -------------
D10DISP  PROC    NEAR
         MOV     AH,40H           ;Request display
         MOV     BX,01            ;Set handle
         MOV     CX,32            ;  and length
         LEA     DX,IOAREA
         INT     21H
         CMP     ROW,20           ;Bottom of screen?
         JAE     D80              ;  yes, bypass
         INC     ROW              ;  no, increment row
         JMP     D90
D80:
         MOV     AX,0601H
         CALL    Q10SCR           ;Scroll
         CALL    Q20CURS          ;Set cursor
D90:     RET
D10DISP  ENDP
;                Scroll screen:
;                --------------
Q10SCR   PROC    NEAR             ;AX set on entry
         MOV     BH,1EH           ;Set color
         MOV     CX,0000
         MOV     DX,184FH         ;Request scroll
         INT     10H
         RET
Q10SCR   ENDP
;                Set cursor:
;                -----------
Q20CURS  PROC    NEAR
         MOV     AH,02H           ;Request set
         MOV     BH,00            ;  cursor
         MOV     DH,ROW           ;  row
         MOV     DL,00            ;  column
         INT     10H
         RET
Q20CURS  ENDP
;                Display disk error message:
;                ---------------------------
X10ERR   PROC    NEAR
         MOV     AH,40H           ;DX contains address
         MOV     BX,01            ;Handle for screen
         MOV     CX,20            ;Length
         INT     21H              ;  of message
         RET
X10ERR   ENDP
         END     A10MAIN
```

Figure 17-3b Reading Records Sequentially

program. If the program requests a record number that is not in the buffer, the operation uses the directory to locate the sector containing the record, reads the entire sector into the buffer, and delivers the record to the program. In this case, requesting random record numbers that are close together in the file results in fewer disk accesses.

INT 21H Function 42H: Move File Pointer

The open operation initializes the file pointer to zero, and subsequent sequential reads and writes increment it for each record processed. You can use function 42H (Move File Pointer) to set the file pointer anywhere within a file and then use other services for random retrieval or updating of records.

To request function 42H, set the file handle in the BX and the required offset as bytes in the CX:DX. For an offset up to 65,535 bytes, set zero in the CX and the offset value in the DX. Also, set a *method code* in the AL that tells the operation the point from which to take the offset:

00 Take the offset from the start of the file.

01 Take the offset from the current location of the file pointer, which could be anywhere within the file, including at the start.

02 Take the offset from the end-of-file. You can use this method code for adding records to the end-of-file. Or you can determine the file size by clearing the CX:DX to zero and using method code 02.

The following example moves the pointer 1,024 bytes from the start of a file:

```
MOV  AH,42H        ;Request move pointer
MOV  AL,00         ;  to start of file
MOV  BX,HANDLE1    ;Set file handle
MOV  CX,00         ;Upper portion of offset
MOV  DX,1024       ;Lower portion of offset
INT  21H           ;Call interrupt service
JC   error         ;Special action if error
```

A valid operation clears the carry flag and delivers the new pointer location in the DX:AX. You may then perform a read or write operation for random processing. An invalid operation sets the carry flag and returns in the AX code 01 (invalid method code) or 06 (invalid handle).

Program: Reading a Disk File Randomly

The program in Figure 17-4 reads the file created in Figure 17-2. By keying in a relative record number that is within the bounds of the file, a user can request any record in the file to be displayed on the screen. If the file contains 24 records, then valid record numbers are 01 through 24. A number entered from the keyboard is in ASCII format and in this case should be only one or two digits.

```
TITLE      A17RDRAN (EXE)  Read disk records randomly
           .MODEL  SMALL
           .STACK  64
           .DATA
HANDLE     DW      ?                     ;File handle
RECINDX    DW      ?                     ;Record index
ERRCDE     DB      00                    ;Read error indicator
PROMPT     DB      'Record number? '
IOAREA     DB      32 DUP(' ')           ;Disk record area
PATHNAM    DB      'F:\NAMEFILE.SRT',0
OPENMSG    DB      '*** Open error ***', 0DH, 0AH
READMSG    DB      '*** Read error ***', 0DH, 0AH
ROW        DB      00
COL        DB      00

RECDPAR    LABEL   BYTE                  ;Input parameter list:
MAXLEN     DB      3                     ;  maximum length
ACTLEN     DB      ?                     ;  actual length
RECDNO     DB      3 DUP(' ')            ;  record number

;--------------------------------------------------------
           .CODE
.386
A10MAIN    PROC    FAR
           MOV     AX,@data              ;Initialize
           MOV     DS,AX                 ;  segment
           MOV     ES,AX                 ;  registers
           MOV     AX,0600H
           CALL    Q10SCRN               ;Clear screen
           CALL    Q20CURS               ;Set cursor
           CALL    B10OPEN               ;Open file
           CMP     ERRCDE,00             ;Valid open?
           JNZ     A90                   ;  no, exit
A20LOOP:
           CALL    C10RECN               ;Request record #
           CMP     ACTLEN,00             ;Any more requests?
           JE      A90                   ;  no, exit
           CALL    D10READ               ;Read disk record
           CMP     ERRCDE,00             ;Normal read?
           JNZ     A30                   ;  no,  bypass
           CALL    E10DISP               ;  yes, display name,
A30:
           JMP     A20LOOP               ;  continue
A90:       MOV     AX,4C00H              ;End processing
           INT     21H
A10MAIN    ENDP
;                  Open file:
;                  ---------
B10OPEN    PROC    NEAR
           MOV     AH,3DH                ;Request open
           MOV     AL,00                 ;Normal file
           LEA     DX,PATHNAM
           INT     21H
           JC      B20                   ;Error?
           MOV     HANDLE,AX             ;  no, save handle
           RET
```

Figure 17-4a Reading a Disk File Randomly

```
B20:      MOV     ERRCDE,01          ;  yes,
          LEA     DX,OPENMSG         ;  display
          CALL    X10ERR             ;  error message
          RET
B10OPEN   ENDP
;                 Get record number:
;                 -----------------
C10RECN   PROC    NEAR
          MOV     AH,40H             ;Request display promp
          MOV     BX,01              ;File handle
          MOV     CX,15              ;15 characters
          LEA     DX,PROMPT
          INT     21H
          MOV     AH,0AH             ;Request input
          LEA     DX,RECDPAR         ;  of record number
          INT     21H
          CMP     ACTLEN,01          ;Check length 0, 1, 2
          JB      C40                ;Length 0, terminate
          JA      C20
          XOR     AH,AH              ;Length 1
          MOV     AL,RECDNO
          JMP     C30
C20:
          MOV     AH,RECDNO          ;Length 2
          MOV     AL,RECDNO+1
C30:
          AND     AX,0F0FH           ;Clear ASCII 3s
          AAD                        ;Convert to binary
          DEC     AX                 ;Adjust (1st record is
          SHL     AX,05              ;Multiply by 16
          MOV     RECINDX,AX         ;Save index
C40:
          MOV     COL,20
          CALL    Q20CURS
          RET
C10RECN   ENDP
;                 Read disk record randomly:
;                 -------------------------
D10READ   PROC    NEAR
          MOV     AH,42H             ;Request set file poi
          MOV     AL,00              ;  to start of file
          MOV     BX,HANDLE          ;File handle
          MOV     CX,00              ;Upper portion of offs
          MOV     DX,RECINDX         ;Lower portion of offs
          INT     21H
          JC      D20                ;Error condition?
                                     ;  yes, bypass
          MOV     AH,3FH             ;Request read
          MOV     BX,HANDLE
          MOV     CX,32              ;30 for name, 2 for CI
          LEA     DX,IOAREA
          INT     21H
          JC      D20                ;Error on read?
          CMP     IOAREA,1AH         ;EOF marker?
          JE      D30                ;  yes, exit
          JMP     D90
D20:      LEA     DX,READMSG         ;Invalid read
          CALL    X10ERR             ;Display message
```

Figure 17-4b Reading a Disk File Randomly

The program is organized as follows:

- A10MAIN Calls B10OPEN, C10RECN, D10READ, and E10DISP; ends when the user has no more requests.

```
D30:        MOV     ERRCDE,01           ;Force end
D90:        RET
D10READ     ENDP
;                   Display name:
;                   ------------
E10DISP     PROC    NEAR
            MOV     AH,40H              ;Request display
            MOV     BX,01               ;Set handle
            MOV     CX,32               ;  and length
            LEA     DX,IOAREA
            INT     21H
            MOV     COL,00              ;Clear column
            CMP     ROW,20              ;Bottom of screen?
            JAE     E20                 ;  yes, bypass
            INC     ROW                 ;  no, increment row
            JMP     E90
E20:
            MOV     AX,0601H
            CALL    Q10SCRN             ;Scroll
            CALL    Q20CURS             ;Set cursor
E90:        RET
E10DISP     ENDP
;                   Scroll screen:
;                   -------------
Q10SCRN     PROC    NEAR                ;AX set on entry
            MOV     BH,1EH              ;Set color
            MOV     CX,0000
            MOV     DX,184FH            ;Request scroll
            INT     10H
            RET
Q10SCRN     ENDP
;                   Set cursor:
;                   ----------
Q20CURS     PROC    NEAR
            MOV     AH,02               ;Request set
            MOV     BH,00               ;  cursor
            MOV     DH,ROW              ;  row
            MOV     DL,COL              ;  column
            INT     10H
            RET
Q20CURS     ENDP
;                   Display disk error message:
;                   --------------------------
X10ERR      PROC    NEAR
            MOV     AH,40H              ;DX contains address
            MOV     BX,01               ;Handle
            MOV     CX,20               ;Length
            INT     21H                 ;  of message
            INC     ROW
            RET
X10ERR      ENDP
            END     A10MAIN
```

Figure 17-4c Reading a Disk File Randomly

- B10OPEN Opens the file and gets the file handle.
- C10RECN Accepts a record number from the keyboard and checks its length in the parameter list. There are three possible lengths:

  00 End of processing requested

  01 One-digit request, stored in the AL

  02 Two-digit request, stored in the AX

  The procedure has to convert the ASCII number to binary. Because the number is in the AX, the AAD instruction works well for this purpose. The system recognizes location

0 as the beginning of a file. The program deducts 1 from the actual number (so that a user request, for example, for record 1 becomes record 0), multiplies the value by 16 (the length of records in the file), and stores the result in a field called RECINDX.

For example, if the entered number is ASCII 12, the AX would contain 3132. An AND instruction converts this value to 0102, AAD further converts it to 000C (12), and SHL effectively multiplies the number by 16 to get C0 (192). An improvement would be for the procedure to validate the input number (01–24).

- D10READ Uses function 42H and the relative record location from RECINDX to set the file pointer and issues function 3FH to deliver the required record to the program in IOAREA.
- E10DISP Displays the retrieved record.

PROGRAM: PROCESSING AN ASCII FILE

The preceding examples created files and read them, but you may also want to process ASCII files created by an editor or word processing program. You need to know the organization of the directory and FAT and the way in which the system stores data in a sector. The data in an .ASM file, for example, is stored exactly the way you key it in, including the characters for Tab (09H), Enter (0DH), and Line Feed (0AH). To conserve disk space, the spaces that appear on the screen immediately preceding a Tab character or spaces on a line to the right of an Enter character are not stored. The following illustrates an instruction as entered from a keyboard:

```
<Tab>MOV<Tab>AH,09<Enter>
```

The hex representation for this ASCII data would be

```
094D4F560941482C30390D0A
```

where 09H is Tab, 0DH is Enter, and 0AH is Line Feed. When an editor or word processing program reads the file, the Tab, Enter, and Line Feed characters automatically adjust the cursor on the screen.

Let's now examine the program in Figure 17-5, which reads and displays the file A17RDFIL.ASM (from Figure 17-3), one sector at a time. The program performs much the same functions as DOS TYPE, where each line displays everything up to the Enter/Line Feed characters.

- A10MAIN Calls B10OPEN, C10READ to read the first sector, and D10XFER, and closes the file at the end.
- B10OPEN Opens the file, saves the file handle, and determines the size of the file (based on the low-order portion of the file size in the AX).
- C10READ Reads a full sector of data into SECTOR.
- D10XFER Transfers data from the sector to a display line, calls E10DISP to display it, calls C10READ for the next sector, and continues processing until reaching the end of the file.

```
TITLE      A17RDASC (EXE)   Read/display an ASCII file
           .MODEL SMALL
           .STACK 64
           .DATA
DISAREA    DB      120 DUP(' ')        ;Display area
ENDCDE     DW      00                  ;End process indicator
FILESIZE   DW      0                   ;File size (low-order)
HANDLE     DW      0                   ;File handle
OPENMSG    DB      '*** Open error ***'
PATHNAM    DB      'F:\A20PRTAS.ASM', 0
ROW        DB      00
SECTOR     DB      512 DUP(' ')        ;Input area
; ---------------------------------------------------------------
           .CODE
A10MAIN    PROC    FAR                 ;Main procedure
           MOV     AX,@data            ;Initialize
           MOV     DS,AX               ;  segment
           MOV     ES,AX               ;  registers
           MOV     AX,0600H
           CALL    Q10SCR              ;Clear screen
           CALL    Q20CURS             ;Set cursor
           CALL    B10OPEN             ;Open file
           CMP     ENDCDE,00           ;Valid open?
           JNE     A90                 ;  no,  exit
           CALL    C10READ             ;Yes, read 1st disk sector
           CMP     ENDCDE,00           ;End-file, no data?
           JE      A90                 ;  yes, exit
           CALL    D10XFER             ;Display/read
A90:
           MOV     AH,3EH              ;Request close file
           MOV     BX,HANDLE
           INT     21H
           MOV     AX,4C00H            ;End processing
           INT     21H
A10MAIN    ENDP
;                  Open disk file:
;                  --------------
B10OPEN    PROC    NEAR
           MOV     AH,3DH              ;Request open
           MOV     AL,00               ;Read only
           LEA     DX,PATHNAM
           INT     21H
           JNC     B20                 ;Test carry flag,
           CALL    X10ERR              ;  error if set
           RET
B20:       MOV     HANDLE,AX           ;Save handle
           MOV     AH,42H              ;Request set pointer
           MOV     AL,02               ;  to end of file
           MOV     BX,HANDLE           ;  to determine
           MOV     CX,0                ;  file size
           MOV     DX,CX               ;
           INT     21H
           MOV     FILESIZE,AX         ;Save size (low-order)
           MOV     AH,42H              ;Reset file pointer
           MOV     AL,00               ;  to start of file
           MOV     DX,CX               ;
           INT     21H
           RET
B10OPEN    ENDP
```

Figure 17-5a Reading an ASCII File

```
;               Read disk sector:
;               ----------------
C10READ  PROC   NEAR
         MOV    AH,3FH             ;Request read
         MOV    BX,HANDLE          ;Device
         MOV    CX,512             ;Length
         LEA    DX,SECTOR          ;Buffer
         INT    21H
         MOV    ENDCDE,AX          ;Save status
         RET
C10READ  ENDP
;               Transfer data to display line:
;               -----------------------------
D10XFER  PROC   NEAR
         CLD                       ;Set left-to-right
         LEA    SI,SECTOR
D20:     LEA    DI,DISAREA
D30:
         LEA    DX,SECTOR+512
         CMP    SI,DX              ;End of sector?
         JNE    D40                ; no,  bypass
         CALL   C10READ            ; yes, read next
         CMP    ENDCDE,00          ;End of file?
         JE     D80                ; yes, exit
         LEA    SI,SECTOR
D40:
         LEA    DX,DISAREA+80
         CMP    DI,DX              ;End of DISAREA?
         JB     D50                ; no,  bypass
         MOV    [DI],0D0AH         ; yes, set CR/LF,
         CALL   E10DISP            ; and display
         LEA    DI,DISAREA
D50:
         LODSB                     ;[SI] to AL, INC SI
         STOSB                     ;AL to [DI], INC DI
         DEC    FILESIZE           ;All chars processed?
         JZ     D80                ; yes, exit
         CMP    AL,0AH             ;Line feed?
         JNE    D30                ; no,  loop
         CALL   E10DISP            ; yes, display
         JMP    D20
D80:     CALL   E10DISP            ;Display last line
D90:     RET
D10XFER  ENDP
;               Display line:
;               ------------
E10DISP  PROC   NEAR
         MOV    AH,40H             ;Request display
         MOV    BX,01              ;Handle
         LEA    CX,DISAREA         ;Calculate
         NEG    CX                 ; length of
         ADD    CX,DI              ; line
         LEA    DX,DISAREA
         INT    21H
         CMP    ROW,22             ;Bottom of screen?
         JAE    E20                ; no, exit
         INC    ROW
         JMP    E90
```

Figure 17-5b Reading an ASCII File

```
E20:        MOV     AX,0601H            ;Scroll
            CALL    Q10SCR
            CALL    Q20CURS
E90:        RET
E10DISP     ENDP
;                   Scroll screen:
;                   -------------
Q10SCR      PROC    NEAR                ;AX set on entry
            MOV     BH,1EH              ;Set color attribute
            MOV     CX,0000             ;Scroll
            MOV     DX,184FH
            INT     10H
            RET
Q10SCR      ENDP
;                   Set cursor:
;                   ----------
Q20CURS     PROC    NEAR
            MOV     AH,02H              ;Request set
            MOV     BH,00               ;  cursor
            MOV     DH,ROW
            MOV     DL,00
            INT     10H
            RET
Q20CURS     ENDP
;                   Display disk error message:
;                   --------------------------
X10ERR      PROC    NEAR
            MOV     AH,40H              ;Request display
            MOV     BX,01               ;Handle
            MOV     CX,18               ;Length
            LEA     DX,OPENMSG
            INT     21H
            MOV     ENDCDE,01           ;Error indicator
            RET
X10ERR      ENDP
            END     A10MAIN
```

Figure 17-5c Reading an ASCII File

The procedure transfers one byte at a time from SECTOR to DISAREA, where the characters are to be displayed. It has to check for the end of a sector (to read another sector) and the end of the display area. For conventional ASCII files, such as .ASM files, each line is relatively short and is sure to end with Enter/Line Feed. NonDASCII files, such as .EXE and .OBJ files, do not have lines, so the program has to check for the end of DISAREA to avoid moving data into the area that follows. The program is intended to display only ASCII files, but the test for the end of DISAREA is insurance against unexpected file types.

These are the steps:

1. Initialize the address of SECTOR and the address of DISAREA.
2. If at the end of SECTOR, read the next sector. If at the end-of-file, exit; otherwise initialize the address of SECTOR.
3. If at the end of DISAREA, force an Enter/Line Feed, display the line, and initialize DISAREA.
4. Get a character from SECTOR and store it in DISAREA.
5. If all the characters have been processed, exit.
6. If the character is Line Feed (0AH), display the line and go to step 2; otherwise go to step 3.

- E10DISP Displays the data in the display line up to and including the Line Feed. Because lines in an ASCII file are in variable-length format, you have to scan for the end of each line before displaying it. (The monitor accepts Tab characters (09H) and automatically sets the cursor on the next location evenly divisible by eight.)

  Scrolling can be a problem. If you perform no special tests to determine whether you have reached the bottom of screen, the operation automatically displays new lines over old and, if the old line is longer, old characters still appear to the right. For proper scrolling, you have to count rows and test whether you are at the bottom of the screen.
- X10ERR Displays a message for a disk error.

Try running this program under DEBUG with an appropriate drive number and ASCII file. After each disk input, display the contents of the input area and see how your records are formatted. Enhancements to this program would be to prompt a user to key in the filename and extension and to use the full DX:AX for the file size.

ABSOLUTE DISK I/O

The purpose of the DOS INT 25H and 26H instructions is to enable *absolute* reads and writes to process a disk directly, for example, in recovering a damaged file. In this case, you do not define file handles or FCBs, and you lose the convenience of directory handling and blocking or deblocking of records that INT 21H provides. Note that INT 21H function 44H (covered in Chapter 18) provides a similar service and has superseded INT 25H and 26H.

Because these operations treat all records as if they were the size of a sector, they directly access a whole sector or block of sectors. Disk addressing is in terms of relative record number (relative sector). To determine a relative record number on two-sided diskettes with 9 sectors per track, count each sector from track 0, sector 1, as follows:

TRACK	SECTOR	RELATIVE RECORD NUMBER
0	1	0 (the first sector on the disk)
0	2	1
1	1	9
1	9	17
2	9	26

A formula for determining the relative record number on diskettes with 9 sectors is

```
Relative record number = (track x 9) + (sector - 1)
```

Thus the relative record number for track 2, sector 9, is

```
(2 x 9) + (9 - 1) = 18 + 8 = 26
```

Here is the required coding for disk partitions that are less than 32 MBs:

```
MOV   AL,drive#      ;0 for A, 1 for B, etc.
MOV   BX,addr        ;Address of parameter block
MOV   CX,sectors     ;Number of sectors to read/write
MOV   DX,sector#     ;Beginning relative sector number
INT   25H or 26H     ;Absolute read or write
```

```
JC    [error]        ;CF is set on an error
POPF                 ;Pop flags
```

INT 25H and 26H destroy all registers except the segment registers and use the carry flag to indicate a successful (0) or unsuccessful (1) operation. An unsuccessful operation returns one of the following nonzero codes to the AL:

```
10000000  Attachment failed to respond
01000000  Seek operation failed
00001000  Bad CRC read on diskette
00000100  Requested sector not found
00000011  Attempt to write on write-protected diskette
00000010  Other error
```

The INT operation pushes the flags onto the stack. Because the original flags are still on the stack upon returning from the operation, pop them after checking the carry flag.

Since DOS 4.0, you can use INT 25H and 26H to access disk partitions that exceed 32 megabytes. The DX is not used, and the BX points to a 10-byte parameter block in the following format:

```
00H-03H  32-bit sector number
04H-05H  Number of sectors to read/write
06H-07H  Offset address of buffer
08H-09H  Segment address of buffer
```

DISK SERVICES USING FILE CONTROL BLOCKS

This section briefly covers the FCB services for creating disk files and processing them sequentially and randomly. These services were introduced by the first version of DOS and are still available under all versions.

Disk processing for the FCB services involves defining a file control block (FCB) that defines the file and a disk transfer area (DTA) that defines records. You provide the system with the DTA address for all disk I/O operations. Because the FCB method does not support file handles or path names, its use is restricted to processing files in the current directory. Also, FCB operations do not use the error codes listed in Figure 17-1 and they do not clear or set the carry flag to indicate success or failure. (A variation of FCBs exist in the program segment prefix (PSP)).

File Control Block

The FCB, which you define in the data area, contains the following information about the file and its records (you initialize bytes 00–15 and 32–36, whereas the system sets bytes 17–31):

0   *Disk drive.* For most FCB operations, 00 is the default drive, 01 is drive A, 02 is drive B, and so forth.

1–8   *Filename.* The name of the file, left adjusted, with trailing blanks, if any.

9–11	*Filename extension.* Left adjusted if fewer than three characters.
12–13	*Current block number.* A block consists of 128 records. Read/write operations use the current block number and current record number (byte 32) to locate a particular record. The number is relative to the beginning of the file, where the first block is 0, the second is 1, and so forth.
14–15	*Logical record size.* An open operation initializes the record size to 128 (80H), although you may change it to your own required record size.
16–19	*File size.* The file size from the directory, which your program may read, but should not change.
20–21	*Date.* The date from the directory, when the file was created or last updated.
22–31	*Reserved,* not available to the program.
32	*Current record number.* The current record number (0–127) within the current block (see bytes 12–13). The system uses the current block and record to locate records in the file.
33–36	*Relative record number.* For random read/write, this entry must contain a relative record number. Because of the limit on the maximum file size (1,073,741,824 bytes), a file with a short record size can contain more records and may have a higher maximum relative record number than a file with a longer record size. If the record size is greater than 64, byte 36 contains 00H.

Preceding the FCB is an optional 7-byte extension, which you may use for processing files with special attributes. To use the extension, code the first byte with FFH, the second byte with the file attribute, and the remaining 5 bytes with hex zeros.

Using FCBs To Create Disk Files

A program using these disk services defines an FCB for each file referenced. Disk operations require the address of the FCB in the DX register and use this address to access fields within the FCB. Operations include create file, set disk transfer area (DTA), write record, and close file.

INT 21H function 16H: create file. On initialization, a program uses INT 21H function 16H to create a new FCB file:

```
MOV  AH,16H        ;Request create
LEA  DX,FCBname    ;  FCB disk file
INT  21H           ;Call interrupt service
```

The operation searches the directory for a filename that matches the entry in the FCB. If one is found, it reuses the space in the directory and, if none is found, it searches for a vacant entry. The operation then initializes the file size to zero and opens the file. The open step checks for available disk space and sets one of the following return codes in the AL: 00H = space is available; FFH = no space is available. Open also initializes the FCB current block number to zero and sets a default value in the FCB record size of 128 (80H) bytes. Before writing a record, you may override these defaults with your own values.

The disk transfer area. The disk transfer area (DTA) identifies the location where you store records for writing on disk. Because the FCB contains the record size, the DTA does not require a delimiter to indicate the end of the record. Only one DTA may be active at any time. Use function 1AH to supply the system with the address of the DTA:

```
MOV   AH,1AH          ;Request set address
LEA   DX,DTAname      ;  of DTA
INT   21H             ;Call interrupt service
```

If a program processes only one disk file, it needs to initialize the DTA only once for its entire execution. For processing more than one file, it must initialize the appropriate DTA immediately before each read/write.

INT 21H function 15H: write record. To write a disk record sequentially under the FCB method, use function 15H:

```
MOV   AH,15H          ;Request write FCB record
LEA   DX,FCBname      ;  sequentially
INT   21H             ;Call interrupt service
```

The write operation uses the information in the FCB and the address of the current DTA. If the record is the size of a sector, the operation writes it. Otherwise, the operation fills records into a buffer area that is the length of a sector and writes the buffer when it is full. For example, if each record is 128 bytes long, the operation fills the buffer with 4 records ($4 \times 128 = 512$) and then writes the buffer into an entire disk sector.

A successful write operation adds the record size to the file size field and increments the current record number by 1. When the current record number exceeds 127, the operation clears it to 0 and increments the current block number. The operation returns a code in the AL: 00H = write was successful; 01H = disk is full; 02H = DTA is too small for the record.

INT 21H function 10H: close file. When finished writing records, you may write an end-of-file marker (1AH in the first byte of a special last record), and then use function 10H to close the file:

```
MOV   AH,10H          ;Request close the
LEA   DX,FCBname      ;  FCB file
INT   21H             ;Call interrupt service
```

The close operation writes on disk any partial data still in the disk buffer, updates the directory with the date and file size, and returns a code to the AL: 00H = close was successful; FFH = file was not in the correct location in the directory, perhaps caused by a user changing a diskette.

Using FCBs For Sequential Reading of Disk Files

A program that reads a disk file defines the FCB exactly like the one used to create the file. Sequential read operations include open file, set DTA, read record, and close file.

INT 21H function 0FH: Open file. Function 0FH opens a file for input:

```
MOV  AH,0FH          ;Request open
LEA  DX,FCBname      ;  the FCB file
INT  21H             ;Call interrupt service
```

The open operation checks that the directory contains an entry with the filename and extension defined in the FCB. If the entry is not in the directory, the operation returns FFH in the AL. If the entry is present, the operation returns 00H in the AL and sets the actual file size, date, current block number (0), and record size (80H) in the FCB. You may subsequently override this record size.

The disk transfer area. The DTA defines an area for receiving input records, in the same format used to create the file. Use function 1AH to set the address of the DTA, as you do for creating the file.

INT 21H function 14H: read record. Use function 14H to read an FCB disk record sequentially:

```
MOV  AH,14H          ;Request read FCB record
LEA  DX,FCBname      ;  sequentially
INT  21H             ;Call interrupt service
```

The operation returns a code in the AL: 00 = successful read; 01 = end of file, no data was read; 02 = DTA is too small; 03 = end of file, record was read partially and filled out with zeros. A successful read operation uses the information in the FCB to deliver the disk record, beginning at the address of the DTA. An attempt to read past the last record of the file causes the operation to signal an end-of-file condition that sets the AL to 01H, for which you should test.

Using FCBs for Random Processing

The requirements for random processing involve inserting the required record number in the relative record field (bytes 33–36) and issuing a random read/write command. To locate a record randomly, the system converts the relative record number to the current block (bytes 12–13) and current record (byte 32).

INT 21H function 21H: read record randomly. The open operation and setting of the DTA are the same for both random and sequential processing. For example, for a program that is to read relative record number 05 randomly, insert 05000000H in the relative record number and request function 21H:

```
MOV AH,21H          ;Request FCB
LEA DX,FCBname      ;  random read
INT 21H             ;Call interrupt service
```

The operation returns a code in the AL: 00 = successful read; 01 = end of file, no more data available; 02 = DTA too small; 03 = record has been partially read and filled out with zeros. A successful operation converts relative record number to current block and record, uses this value to locate the required disk record, and delivers it to the DTA. A faulty response can be caused by an invalid relative record number or an incorrect address in the DTA or FCB.

INT 21H function 22H: write record randomly. The create operation and setting of the DTA are the same for both random and sequential processing. With relative record number initialized in the FCB, use function 22H to write a record randomly:

```
MOV  AH,22H        ;Request FCB random
LEA  DX,FCBname    ;  write
INT  21H           ;Call interrupt service
```

The operation returns a code in the AL: 00 = successful write; 01 = disk full; 02 = DTA too small.

Random Block Processing

If a program has sufficient space, one random block operation can write an entire file from the DTA onto disk or can read the entire file from disk into the DTA. You first open the file and initialize the DTA. You may then begin processing with any valid relative record number and any number of records, although the block must be within the file's range of records.

INT 21H function 28H: write block randomly. Use function 28H for a random block write of an FCB file:

```
MOV  AH,28H        ;Request FCB random block write
MOV  CX,records    ;Set number of records
LEA  DX,FCBname    ;Address of FCB
INT  21H           ;Call interrupt service
```

The operation converts the relative record number to the current block and record, which it uses to determine the starting disk location and returns a code in the AL: 00 = successful write of all records; 01 = no records written because of insufficient disk space; 02 = DTA too small. A valid operation sets the relative record, current block, and current record for the next record number.

INT 21H Function 27H: read block randomly. Use function 27H for a random block read of an FCB file:

```
MOV  AH,27H        ;Request FCB random block read
MOV  CX,records    ;Initialize number of records
LEA  DX,FCBname    ;Address of FCB
INT  21H           ;Call interrupt service
```

The operation returns a code in the AL: 00 = successful read of all records; 01 = has read to end of file, last record is complete; 02 = DTA too small, read not completed; 03 = end of file, has read a partial record. The operation stores in the CX the actual number of records read and sets the relative record, current block, and current record for the next record.

KEY POINTS

- Many of the disk services reference an ASCIIZ string that consists of a directory path followed by a byte of hex zeros.
- On errors, many of the disk functions set the carry flag and return an error code in the AX.
- The system maintains a file pointer for each file that a program is processing. The create and open operations set the value of the file pointer to zero, the file's starting location.
- The create function 3CH is used prior to writing a file, and open function 3DH prior to reading a file.
- The create and open functions return a file handle that you use for subsequent file accessing.
- A program that has completed writing a file should close it so that the system may update the directory.
- A program using original INT 21H functions for disk I/O defines a file control block (FCB) for each file that it accesses.
- An FCB block consists of 128 records. The current block number, combined with the current record number, indicates the disk record to be processed.
- For an FCB, the disk transfer area (DTA) is the location of the record that is to be written or read. Initialize each DTA prior to execution of a read/write operation.

QUESTIONS

Of the following questions, the first 10 concern disk operations involving file handles, and the remainder involve FCB disk operations.

17-1. What are the error return codes for (a) invalid handle; (b) path not found; (c) write-protected disk?

17-2. Define an ASCIIZ string named ASCPATH for a file named PATIENT.LST on drive D.

17-3. For the file in Question 17-2, each record contains patient number (5 characters), name (20), street address (20), city (20), date of birth (mmddyy), M/F code, room number (2), and bed number (2). Provide the instructions to (a) define an item named FHANDLE for the file handle; (b) define the fields for the patient record; (c) create the file; (d) write a record from PATNTOUT; and (e) close the file. Include tests for errors.

17-4. For the file in Question 17-3, code the instructions to (a) open the file and (b) read each record into PATNTIN and display it. Complete the program and provide data to test it.

17-5. Revise the program in Figure 17-5 so that a user at a keyboard can key in a filename, which the program uses to locate the file and to display its contents. Provide for any number of requests and for pressing only <Enter> to cause processing to end.

17-6. Under what circumstances should you close a file that is used only for input?

17-7. Write a program that allows a user to key in part numbers (3 characters), part descriptions (12 characters), and unit prices (xxx.xx) on a terminal. The program is to use file handles to create a disk file containing this information. Remember to convert the price from ASCII to binary. Following is sample input data:

```
Part Description  Price    Part Description Price
|023|Assemblers  |00315|  |122|Lifters     |10520|
|024|Linkages    |00430|  |124|Processors  |21335|
|027|Compilers   |00525|  |127|Labelers    |00960|
|049|Compressors |00920|  |232|Bailers     |05635|
|114|Extractors  |11250|  |237|Grinders    |08250|
|117|Haulers     |00630|  |999|            |00000|
```

17-8. Write a program that displays the contents of the file created in Question 17-7. It will have to convert the binary value for the price to ASCII format.

17-9. Using the file created in Question 17-7, write a program for the following requirements: (a) Read all the records into a table in memory; (b) request a user to key in part number and quantity; (c) search the table for part number; (d) if the part number is found, use the table price to calculate the value of the part (quantity × price); (e) display description and calculated value. Allow any number of keyboard requests.

17-10. Revise the program in Question 17-8 so that it does random disk processing. Define a table of the valid part numbers. Request a user to key in a part number, which the program locates in the table. Use the offset in the table to calculate the offset in the file, and use INT 21H function 42H to move the file pointer. Display description and price. Request the user to enter quantity sold; then calculate and display amount of sale (quantity × price).

17-11. Provide the full set of instructions (MOV through INT 21H) for the following FCB operations: (a) create; (b) set DTA; (c) sequential write; (d) open; (e) sequential read.

17-12. A program uses the record size to which the FCB open operation defaults. (a) How long is this record size? (b) How many records would a sector contain? (c) How many records would a diskette contain, assuming it is stored on four tracks with 9 sectors per track? (d) If the file in part (c) is being read sequentially, how many physical disk accesses will occur?

18 DISK STORAGE III: INT 21H FUNCTIONS FOR SUPPORTING DISKS AND FILES

Objective: To examine the various INT 21H operations involved in supporting the use of disk drives and files.

INTRODUCTION

This chapter introduces a number of useful operations involved with the handling of disk drives, the directory, the FAT, and disk files.

OPERATIONS HANDLING DISK DRIVES

0DH: Reset disk drive

0EH: Select default drive

19H: Get default drive

1BH, 1CH: Get drive information

1FH: Get default drive parameter block (DPB)

2EH: Set/reset disk verify

32H: Get drive parameter block (DPB)

36H: Get free disk space

4400H: Get device information

4401H: Set device information

4404H: Read control data from drive

4405H: Write control data to drive

4406H: Check input status

4407H: Check output status
4408H: Determine if removable media for device
440DH minor code 41H: Write disk sector
440DH minor code 61H: Read disk sector
440DH minor code 42H: Format track
440DH minor code 46H: Set media ID
440DH minor code 60H: Get device parameters
440DH minor code 66H: Get media ID
440DH minor code 68H: Sense media type
54H: Get verify state
59H: Get extended error

OPERATIONS HANDLING DISK FILES

29H: Parse filename
41H: Delete file
43H: Get/set file attribute
45H, 46H: Duplicate file handle
4EH, 4FH: Find matching file
56H: Rename file
57H: Get/set file date/time
5AH, 5BH: Create temporary/new file

OPERATIONS HANDLING THE DIRECTORY AND FAT

39H: Create subdirectory
3AH: Remove subdirectory
3BH: Change current directory
47H: Get current directory

Error codes cited in this chapter refer to the list in Figure 17-1.

OPERATIONS HANDLING DISK DRIVES

INT 21H Function 0DH: Reset Disk Drive

Normally, closing a file causes the operation to write all remaining records and update the directory. Under special circumstances, such as between program steps or on an error condition, a program may use function 0DH to reset a disk drive:

```
MOV  AH,0DH    ;Request reset disk
INT  21H       ;Call interrupt service
```

The operation flushes all file buffers and resets the read/write heads to cylinder 0; it does not automatically close the files and returns no values.

INT 21H Function 0EH: Select Default Disk Drive

The main purpose of function 0EH is to select a drive as the current default. To use it, set the drive number in the DL, where 0 = drive A, 1 = B, and so forth:

```
MOV  AH,0EH     ;Request set default
MOV  DL,03      ;  drive D
INT  21H        ;Call interrupt service
```

The operation delivers the number of drives (all types, including RAM disks) to the AL. Because the system requires at least two logical drives A and B, it returns the value 02 for a 1-drive system. (Use INT 11H for determining the actual number of drives.)

INT 21H Function 19H: Get Default Disk Drive

This function determines the default disk drive:

```
MOV  AH,19H     ;Request default drive
INT  21H        ;Call interrupt service
```

The operation returns a drive number in the AL, where 0 = A, 1 = B, and so forth. You could move this number directly into your program for accessing a file from the default drive, although some disk operations assume that 1 = drive A and 2 = drive B.

INT 21H Function 1BH: Get Information for Default Drive

This operation, now superseded by function 36H, returns information about the default drive:

```
MOV  AH,1BH     ;Request information re drive
INT  21H        ;Call interrupt service
```

Because the operation changes the DS, you should PUSH it before the interrupt and POP it after. A successful operation returns the following information:

AL	Number of sectors per cluster
BX	Pointer (DS:BX) to the first byte (media descriptor) in the FAT
CX	Size of the physical sector, usually 512
DX	Number of clusters on the disk

The product of the AL, CX, and DX gives the capacity of the disk. An unsuccessful operation returns FFH in the AL.

INT 21H Function 1CH: Get Information for Specific Drive

This operation, now superseded by function 36H, returns information about a specific drive. To use it, insert the required drive number in the DL, where 0 = default, 1 = A, and so forth:

```
MOV  AH,1CH     ;Request disk information
MOV  DL,drive   ;Device number
INT  21H        ;Call interrupt service
```

The operation is otherwise identical to function 1BH.

INT 21H Function 1FH: Get Default Drive Parameter Block (DPB)

The drive parameter block (DPB) is a data area containing the following low-level information about the data structure of the drive:

OFFSET	SIZE	CONTENTS
00H	Byte	Drive number (0 = A, etc.)
01H	Byte	Logical unit for driver
02H	Word	Sector size in bytes
04H	Byte	Sectors per cluster minus 1
05H	Byte	Sectors per cluster (power of 2)
06H	Word	First relative sector of the FAT
08H	Byte	Number of copies of the FAT
09H	Word	Number of root directory entries
0BH	Word	First relative sector of first cluster
0DH	Word	Highest cluster number plus 1
0FH	Word	Sectors occupied by each FAT
11H	Word	First relative sector of the directory
13H	Dword	Address of device driver
17H	Byte	Media descriptor
18H	Byte	Access flag (0 if disk was accessed)
19H	Dword	Pointer to next parameter block
1DH	Word	Last allocated cluster
1FH	Word	Number of free clusters

PUSH the DS before issuing this function, and POP it after returning:

```
PUSH  DS
MOV   AH,1FH     ;Request address of DPB
INT   21H        ;Call interrupt service
...   (access the DPB)
POP   DS
```

A valid operation clears the AL and returns an address in the DS:BX that points to the DPB for the default drive. For an error, the AL is set to FFH. See also function 32H.

INT 21H Function 2EH: Set/Reset Disk Write Verification

This function allows you to verify disk write operations, that is, whether the data was properly written. The operation sets a switch that tells the system to verify the disk controller's cyclical redundancy check (CRC), a sophisticated form of parity checking. Loading 00 in the AL sets verify off and 01 sets verify on. The switch stays set until another operation changes it. Here is an example:

```
MOV  AH,2EH      ;Request verify (or MOV AX,2E01H)
MOV  AL,01       ;Set verify on
INT  21H         ;Call interrupt service
```

The operation does not return any value; it simply sets a switch. The system subsequently responds to invalid write operations. Because a disk drive rarely records data incorrectly and the verification causes some delay, the operation is most useful where recorded data is especially critical. A related function, 54H, returns the current setting of the verify switch.

INT 21H Function 32H: Get Drive Parameter Block (DPB)

To get the DPB, load the drive number in the DX (where 0 = default, 1 = A, etc.). (See function 1FH; other than requesting a specific drive, this function is identical.)

INT 21H Function 36H: Get Free Disk Space

This function delivers information about the space on a disk device. To use it, load the drive number (0 = default, 1 = A, 2 = B, etc.) in the DL:

```
MOV  AH,36H      ;Request free disk space
MOV  DL,0        ;  for default drive
INT  21H         ;Call interrupt service
```

A successful operation returns the following: AX = number of sectors per cluster; BX = number of available clusters; CX = number of bytes per sector; DX = total number of clusters on device. The product of AX, CX, and DX gives the capacity of the disk. For an invalid device number, the operation returns FFFFH in the AX. The operation does not set or clear the carry flag.

INT 21H Function 44H: I/O Control for Devices

This elaborate service, IOCTL, communicates information between a program and an open device. To use it, load a subfunction value in the AL to request one of a number of actions. A valid operation clears the carry flag. An error, such as invalid file handle, sets the carry flag and returns a standard error code to the AX. The major IOCTL subfunctions follow.

INT 21H Function 4400H: Get Device Information

This operation returns information about a file or device:

```
MOV  AX,4400H     ;Request device information
MOV  BX,handle    ;Handle of file or device
INT  21H          ;Call interrupt service
```

A valid operation clears the carry flag and returns a value in the DX, where bit 7 = 0 means that the handle indicates a file, and bit 7 = 1 means a device. The other bits have this meaning for file or device:

FILE (Bit 7 = 0):

0–5 Drive number (0 = A, 1 = B, etc.)

6 1 = file not written to

DEVICE (Bit 7 = 1):

0 Standard console input

1 Standard console output

2 Null device

3 Clock device

4 Special device

5 0 = ASCII mode, 1 = binary mode

6 For input, 0 = end of file returned

An error sets the carry flag and returns code 01, 05, or 06 in the AX.

INT 21H Function 4401H: Set Device Information

This operation sets device information, as shown for function 4400H. To use it, load the file handle in the BX and the bit setup in the DL for bits 0–7. An error sets the carry flag and returns code 01, 05, 06, or 0DH in the AX.

INT 21H Function 4404H: Read Control Data from Drive

This operation reads control data from a block-device driver (disk drive). To use it, load the drive (0 = default, 1 = A, etc.) in the BL, the number of bytes to read in the CX, and the address of the data area in the DX. A successful operation returns to the AX the number of bytes transferred. An error sets the carry flag and returns code 01, 05, or 0DH in the AX.

INT 21H Function 4405H: Write Control Data to Drive

This operation writes control data to a block-device driver. The setup is otherwise the same as for function 4404H.

INT 21H Function 4406H: Check Input Status

This service checks whether a file or device is ready for input. To use it, load the handle in the BX. A valid operation returns one of the following codes in the AL:

- Device: 00H = not ready or FFH = ready
- File: 00H = EOF reached or FFH = EOF not reached

An error sets the carry flag and returns code 01, 05, or 06 in the AX.

INT 21H Function 4407H: Check Output Status

This service determines whether a file or device is ready for output. A valid operation returns one of the following codes in the AL:

- Device: 00H = not ready or FFH = ready
- File: 00H = ready or FFH = ready

An error sets the carry flag and returns code 01, 05, or 06 in the AX.

INT 21H Function 4408H: Determine If Removable Media for Device

This service determines whether the device contains removable media, such as diskette. To use it, load the BL with the drive number (0 = default, 1 = A, etc.). A valid operation clears the carry flag and returns one of the following codes in the AX: 00H = removable device or 01H = fixed device. An error sets the carry flag and returns code 01 or 0FH (invalid drive number) in the AX.

INT 21H Function 440DH, Minor Code 41H: Write Disk Sector

This operation writes data from a buffer to one or more sectors on disk. To use it, load these registers:

```
MOV  AX,440DH         ;Request write disk sector
MOV  BX,drive         ;Drive (0 = default, 1 = A, etc.)
MOV  CH,08H           ;Device category = 08H
MOV  CL,41H           ;Minor code = write track
LEA  DX,devblock      ;Address of device block
INT  21H              ;Call interrupt service
```

The address returned in the DX points to a device block with the following format:

```
devblock  LABEL BYTE         ;Device block:
specfunc  DB  0              ;  Special functions (zero)
rwhead    DW  head           ;  Read/write head
rwcyl     DW  cylinder       ;  Cylinder
rwsect1   DW  sector         ;  Starting sector
rwsects   DW  number         ;  Number of sectors
rwbuffr   DW  buffer         ;  Offset address of buffer
          DW  SEG _DATA      ;  Address of data segment
```

The entry named rwbuffr provides the address of the buffer in segment:offset (DS:DX) format, stored in reverse-word sequence. The SEG operator indicates the definition of a segment, in this case the data segment, _DATA. The buffer identifies the data area to be written and should be the length of the number of sectors × 512, such as

```
WRBUFFER  DB  1024 DUP (?)    ;Output buffer
```

A successful operation clears the carry flag and writes the data. Otherwise, the operation sets the carry flag and returns error code 01, 02, or 05 in the AX.

INT 21H Function 440DH, Minor Code 42H: Format Track

To use this function to format tracks, set these registers:

```
MOV  AX,440DH      ;Request format track
MOV  BX,drive      ;Drive (0 = default, 1 = A, etc.)
MOV  CH,08         ;Device category (08)
MOV  CL,42H        ;Minor code = format track
LEA  DX,block      ;Address of block (DS:DX)
INT  21H           ;Call interrupt service
```

The address returned in the DX points to a block with the following format:

```
blkname  LABEL BYTE    ;Disk information block:
specfun  DB    0       ;  Special function, code 0
diskhd   DW    ?       ;  Disk head
cylindr  DW    ?       ;  Cylinder
tracks   DW    ?       ;  Number of tracks
```

A successful operation clears the carry flag and formats the tracks. Otherwise, the operation sets the carry flag and returns error code 01, 02, or 05 in the AX.

INT 21H Function 440DH, Minor Code 46H: Set Media ID

For using this function to set the media ID, set these registers:

```
MOV  AX,440DH      ;Request set media ID
MOV  BX,drive      ;Drive (0 = default, 1 = A, etc.)
MOV  CH,08         ;Device category (08)
MOV  CL,46H        ;Minor code = set media ID
LEA  DX,block      ;Address of block (DS:DX)
INT  21H           ;Call interrupt service
```

The address returned in the DX points to a media block with the following format:

```
blkname  LABEL BYTE          ;Media block:
infolev  DW    0             ;  Information level = 0
serialn  DD    ??            ;  Serial number
volabel  DB    11 DUP (?)    ;  Volume label
filetyp  DB    8 DUP (?)     ;  Type of FAT
```

The field named filetyp contains the ASCII value FAT12 or FAT16, with trailing blanks. A successful operation clears the carry flag and sets the ID. Otherwise, the operation sets the carry flag and returns error code 01, 02, or 05 in the AX. (See also function 440DH, minor code 66H.)

INT 21H Function 440DH, Minor Code 60H: Get Device Parameters

For using this function to get device parameters, set these registers:

```
MOV  AX,440DH      ;Request get device parameters
MOV  BX,drive      ;Drive (0 = default, 1 = A, etc.)
```

```
MOV  CH,08          ;Device category (08)
MOV  CL,60H         ;Minor code = get parameters
LEA  DX,block       ;Address of block (DS:DX)
INT  21H            ;Call interrupt service
```

The address returned in the DX points to a device parameter block (DPB) with the following format:

```
specfun  DB  ?    ;Special functions (0 or 1)
devtype  DB  ?    ;Device type
devattr  DW  ?    ;Device attribute
cylindr  DW  ?    ;Number of cylinders
medityp  DB  ?    ;Media type
bytesec  DW  ?    ;Bytes per sector
secclus  DB  ?    ;Sectors per cluster
ressect  DW  ?    ;Number of reserved sectors
fats     DB  ?    ;Number of FATs
rootent  DW  ?    ;Number of root directory entries
sectors  DW  ?    ;Total number of sectors
mediads  DB  ?    ;Media descriptor
fatsecs  DW  ?    ;Number of sectors per FAT
sectrak  DW  ?    ;Sectors per track
heads    DW  ?    ;Number of heads
hidsect  DD  ?    ;Number of hidden sectors
exsects  DD  ?    ;Number of sectors if sectors field = 0
```

If the field named specfun is 0, the information is about the default medium in the drive; if 1, the information is about the current medium. A successful operation clears the carry flag and delivers the data. Otherwise, the operation sets the carry flag and returns error code 01, 02, or 05 in the AX.

INT 21H Function 440DH, Minor Code 61H: Read Disk Sector

This operation reads data from one or more sectors on disk to a buffer. To use it, set the CL with minor code 61H; otherwise, technical details for the operation are identical to those for minor code 41H, which writes sectors. Figure 18-1, covered later, illustrates the function.

INT 21H Function 440DH, Minor Code 66H: Get Media ID

For using this function to get the media ID, set these registers:

```
MOV  AX,440DH       ;Request media ID
MOV  BX,drive       ;Drive (0 = default, 1 = A, etc.)
MOV  CH,08          ;Device category (08)
MOV  CL,66H         ;Minor code = get media ID
LEA  DX,block       ;Address of block (DS:DX)
INT  21H            ;Call interrupt service
```

The address returned in the DX points to a media block:

```
blkname  LABEL  BYTE          ;Media block:
infolev  DW     0             ; Information level = 0
serialn  DD     ?             ; Serial number
volabel  DB     11 DUP (?)    ; Volume label
filetyp  DB     8 DUP (?)     ; Type of FAT
```

A successful operation clears the carry flag and sets the ID. The field named filetyp contains the ASCII value FAT12 or FAT16, with trailing blanks. Otherwise, the operation sets the carry flag and returns error code 01, 02, or 05 in the AX. (See also function 440DH, minor code 46H.)

INT 21H Function 440DH, Minor Code 68H: Sense Media Type

To use this function to request the media type, set these registers:

```
MOV  AX,440DH    ;Request media type
MOV  BX,drive    ;Drive (0 = default, 1 = A, etc.)
MOV  CH,08       ;Device category (08)
MOV  CL,68H      ;Minor code = get media type
LEA  DX,block    ;Address of block (DS:DX)
INT  21H         ;Call interrupt service
```

The address returned in the DX points to a 2-byte media block to receive data:

```
default  DB  ?    ;01 for default value, 02 for other
medatyp  DB  ?    ;02 = 720K, 07 = 1.44MB, 09 = 2.88MB
```

A successful operation clears the carry flag and sets the type. Otherwise, the operation sets the carry flag and returns error code 01 or 05 in the AX.

Other IOCTL operations for function 44H, not covered here, are concerned with file sharing.

INT 21H Function 54H: Get Verify State

This service can determine the status of the disk write-verify flag. (See function 2EH for setting the switch.) The operation returns 00H to the AL for verify off or 01H for verify on. There is no error condition.

INT 21H Function 59H: Get Extended Error

This operation provides additional information about errors after execution of INT 21H services that set the carry flag, FCB services that return FFH, and INT 24H error handlers. The operation returns the following:

```
AX = Extended error code    BL = Suggested action
BH = Error class            CH = Location
```

Also, the operation clears the carry flag and—watch for this—destroys the contents of the CL, DI, DS, DX, ES, and SI registers. PUSH all required registers prior to this interrupt, and POP them afterward. The following sections explain the errors:

Extended error code (AX). Returns some 90 or more error codes; code 00 means that the previous INT 21H operation resulted in no error.

Error class (BH). Provides the following information:

01H	Out of resource, such as storage channel
02H	Temporary situation (not an error), such as a locked file condition that should go away
03H	Lack of proper authorization
04H	System software error, not this program
05H	Hardware failure
06H	Serious system error, not this program
07H	Error in this program, such as inconsistent request
08H	Requested item not found
09H	Improper file or disk format
0AH	File or item is locked
0BH	Disk error, such as CRC error or wrong disk
0CH	File or item already exists
0DH	Unknown error class

Action (BL). Provides information on the action to take:

01	Retry a few times; may have to ask user to terminate.
02	Pause first and retry a few times.
03	Ask user to reenter proper request.
04	Close files and terminate the program.
05	Terminate the program immediately; do not close files.
06	Ignore the error.
07	Request user to perform an action (such as change diskette) and retry the operation.

Location (CH). Provides additional information on locating an error:

01	Unknown situation, can't help	04	Serial device problem
02	Disk storage problem	05	Memory problem
03	Network problem		

PROGRAM: READING DATA FROM SECTORS

The program in Figure 18-1 illustrates the use of IOCTL function 44H subfunction 0DH minor code 61H. The program reads data from a sector into a buffer in memory and dis-

```
TITLE     A18RDSCT (EXE)  Read disk sector
          .MODEL  SMALL
          .STACK  64
          .DATA
ROW       DB      00
COL       DB      00
XLATAB    DB      30H,31H,32H,33H,34H,35H,36H,37H,38H,39H
          DB      41H,42H,43H,44H,45H,46H
READMSG   DB      '*** Read error ***', 0DH, 0AH

RDBLOCK   DB      0                  ;Block
RDHEAD    DW      0                  ;  structure
RDCYLR    DW      0                  ;
RDSECT    DW      8                  ;
RDNOSEC   DW      1                  ;
RDBUFFR   DW      IOBUFFR            ;
          DW      SEG _DATA          ;
IOBUFFR   DB      512 DUP(' ') ;Disk sector area
;----------------------------------------------------------
.386
          .CODE
A10MAIN   PROC    FAR
          MOV     AX,@data           ;Initialize
          MOV     DS,AX              ;  segment
          MOV     ES,AX              ;  registers
          CALL    Q10SCR             ;Clear screen
          CALL    Q20CURS            ;Set cursor
          CALL    B10READ            ;Get sector data
          JNC     A80                ;If valid read, bypass
          LEA     DX,READMSG         ;If invalid, display
          CALL    X10ERR             ;  error message
          JMP     A90
A80:
          CALL    C10DISP            ;Convert and display
A90:      MOV     AX,4C00H           ;End processing
          INT     21H
A10MAIN   ENDP
;                 Read sector data:
;                 -----------------
B10READ   PROC    NEAR
          MOV     AX,440DH      ;IOCTL for block device
          MOV     BX,01         ;Drive A
          MOV     CH,08         ;Device category
          MOV     CL,61H        ;Read sector
          LEA     DX,RDBLOCK    ;Address of block structure
          INT     21H
          RET
B10READ   ENDP
;                 Display sector data:
;                 -------------------
C10DISP   PROC    NEAR
          LEA     SI,IOBUFFR
C20:
          MOV     AL,[SI]
          SHR     AL,04              ;Shift off right hex digit
          LEA     BX,XLATAB          ;Set table address
          XLAT                       ;Translate hex
          CALL    Q30DISPL
```

Figure 18-1a Reading Disk Sectors

```
          INC    COL
          MOV    AL,[SI]
          AND    AL,0FH              ;Clear left hex digit
          XLAT                       ;Translate hex
          CALL   Q30DISPL
          INC    SI
          INC    COL
          CMP    COL,64              ;Rightmost screen loc
          JBE    C20                 ;No, repeat
          INC    ROW                 ;Yes, increment row
          MOV    COL,00
          CALL   Q20CURS
          CMP    ROW,15              ;At last row?
          JBE    C20                 ;No, repeat
          RET
C10DISP   ENDP
;                Scroll screen:
;                -------------
Q10SCR    PROC   NEAR
          MOV    AX,0600H            ;Request scroll
          MOV    BH,1EH              ;Set attribute
          MOV    CX,0000
          MOV    DX,184FH
          INT    10H
          RET
Q10SCR    ENDP
;                Set cursor:
;                ----------
Q20CURS   PROC   NEAR
          MOV    AH,02H              ;Request set
          MOV    BH,00               ;  cursor
          MOV    DH,ROW              ;  row
          MOV    DL,COL              ;  column
          INT    10H
          RET
Q20CURS   ENDP
;                Display character:
;                -----------------
Q30DISPL  PROC   NEAR
          MOV    AH,02H              ;Request display
          MOV    DL,AL               ;  character
          INT    21H
          RET
Q30DISPL  ENDP
;                Display disk error message:
;                --------------------------
X10ERR    PROC   NEAR
          MOV    AH,40H              ;DX contains address
          MOV    BX,01               ;Handle
          MOV    CX,20               ;Length
          INT    21H                 ;  of message
          INC    ROW
          RET
X10ERR    ENDP
          END    A10MAIN
```

Figure 18-1b Reading Disk Sectors

plays each input byte as a pair of hex characters, as was done in Figure 15-6. The block structure in the data segment, RDBLOCK, arbitrarily specifies a head, cylinder, and starting sector, which you can change for your own purposes. RDBUFFR defines two addresses:

1. IOBUFFR is the offset address of the input buffer, which provides for one sector (512 bytes) of data.

2. SEG _DATA uses the SEG operator to identify the address of the data segment for the IOCTL operation.

   Major procedures in the code segment are:

- A10MAIN Calls B10READ and, if a valid operation, calls C10DISP.
- B10READ Uses the IOCTL operation to read the data from the sector into IOBUFFR. (The test for a valid read is made on returning from the procedure.)
- C10DISP Converts each byte in IOBUFFR into two hex characters for displaying. Two XLAT instructions handle the conversion for each half-byte. The routine displays 16 rows of 32 pairs of characters in columns 0–63 and rows 0–15.

You could enhance this program by allowing a user at the keyboard to request any sector.

OPERATIONS HANDLING THE DIRECTORY AND THE FAT

INT 21H Function 39H: Create Subdirectory

This service creates a subdirectory, just like the DOS command MKDIR. To use it, load the DX with the address of an ASCIIZ string containing the drive and directory pathname—it's that simple:

```
ASCstrg DB  'd:\pathname',00H      ;ASCIIZ string
        ...
        MOV  AH,39H                ;Request create subdirectory
        LEA  DX,ASCstrg            ;Address of ASCIIZ string (DS:DX)
        INT  21H                   ;Call interrupt service
```

A valid operation clears the carry flag; an error sets the carry flag and returns code 03 or 05 in the AX.

INT 21H Function 3AH: Remove Subdirectory

This service deletes a subdirectory, just like the DOS command RMDIR. Note that you cannot delete the current (active) directory or a subdirectory containing files. Load the DX with the address of an ASCIIZ string containing the drive and directory pathname:

```
ASCstrg  DB  'd:\pathname',00H ;ASCIIZ string
         ...
         MOV AH,3AH       ;Request delete subdirectory
         LEA DX,ASCstrg   ;Address of ASCIIZ string (DS:DX)
         INT 21H          ;Call interrupt service
```

A valid operation clears the carry flag; an error sets the carry flag and returns code 03, 05, or 10H in the AX.

INT 21H Function 3BH: Change Current Directory

This service changes the current directory to one that you specify, just as the DOS command CHDIR does. To use it, load the DX with the address of an ASCIIZ string containing the new drive and directory pathname:

```
ASCstrg  DB    'd:\pathname',00H ;ASCIIZ string
         ...
         MOV   AH,3BH            ;Request change directory
         LEA   DX,ASCstrg        ;Address of ASCIIZ string (DS:DX)
         INT   21H               ;Call interrupt service
```

A valid operation clears the carry flag; an error sets the carry flag and returns code 03 in the AX.

INT 21H Function 47H: Get Current Directory

This function determines the current directory for any drive. To use it, define a buffer space large enough to contain the longest possible pathname (64 bytes), and load its address in the SI. Identify the drive in the DL by 0 = default, 1 = A, 2 = B, and so forth:

```
buffer  DB   64 DUP(20H)     ;64-byte buffer space
        ...
        MOV  AH,47H          ;Request get directory
        MOV  DL,drive        ;Drive
        LEA  SI,buffer       ;Address of buffer (DS:DI)
        INT  21H             ;Call interrupt service
```

A valid operation clears the carry flag and delivers the name of the current directory (but not the drive) to the buffer as an ASCIIZ string, such as PCPROGS\TESTDATA0. A byte containing 00H identifies the end of the pathname. If the requested directory is the root, the value returned is only a byte of 00H. In this way, you can get the current pathname for using to access any file in a subdirectory. An invalid drive number sets the carry flag and returns error code 0FH in the AX.

INT 21H Function 56H: Rename File or Directory

See the next section for this function.

PROGRAM: DISPLAYING THE DIRECTORY

The program in Figure 18-2 illustrates the use of two of the functions described in the preceding section. The procedures perform the following:

- A10MAIN Calls B10DRIV and C10PATH, and waits for a keyboard entry before ending.
- B10DRIV Uses function 19H to get the default drive in the AL register. The drive is returned as 0 (for A), 1 (for B), and so forth. To adjust the number to its alphabetic equiv-

```
TITLE      A18GETDR (COM)  Get current directory
           .MODEL SMALL
           .CODE
           ORG    100H
BEGIN:     JMP    SHORT A10MAIN
; ----------------------------------------------------
PATHNAM    DB     64 DUP(' ')      ;Current pathname
; ----------------------------------------------------
A10MAIN    PROC   NEAR
           CALL   B10DRIV          ;Get/display drive
           CALL   C10PATH          ;Get/display path
           MOV    AH,10H           ;Pause until user
           INT    16H              ;  presses a key
           MOV    AX,4C00H         ;End processing
           INT    21H
A10MAIN    ENDP
;                 Get default drive:
;                 -----------------
B10DRIV    PROC   NEAR;
           MOV    AH,19H           ;Request default drive
           INT    21H
           ADD    AL,41H           ;Change hex no. to letter
           MOV    DL,AL            ;  0=A, 1=B, etc.
           CALL   D10DISP          ;Display drive number,
           MOV    DL,':'
           CALL   D10DISP          ;  colon,
           MOV    DL,'\'
           CALL   D10DISP          ;  backslash
           RET
B10DRIV    ENDP
;                 Get pathname for current directory:
;                 ----------------------------------
C10PATH    PROC   NEAR;
           MOV    AH,47H           ;Request pathname
           MOV    DL,00
           LEA    SI,PATHNAM
           INT    21H
C20:
           CMP    BYTE PTR [SI],00H ;End of pathname?
           JE     C90              ;  yes, exit
           MOV    AL,[SI]          ;Display pathname
           MOV    DL,AL            ;  one byte at
           CALL   D10DISP          ;  a time
           INC    SI
           JMP    C20              ;Repeat
C90:       RET
C10PATH    ENDP
;                 Display single character:
;                 ------------------------
D10DISP    PROC   NEAR             ;DL set on entry
           MOV    AH,02H           ;Request display
           INT    21H
           RET
D10DISP    ENDP
           END     BEGIN
```

Figure 18-2 Getting the Current Directory

alent, the procedure simply adds 41H, so that 00 becomes 41H (A), 01 becomes 42H (B), and so forth. It then displays the drive letter followed by a colon and backslash (n:\).

- C10PATH Uses function 47H to get the pathname for the current directory. The procedure tests immediately for the 00H ASCIIZ delimiter, because a default to the root directory would deliver only that character. Otherwise, the routine displays each character up to the delimiter.

- D10DISP Displays a single character.

The program intentionally contains only features necessary to get it to work; a full program would include, for example, clearing the screen and setting colors.

OPERATIONS HANDLING DISK FILES

This section describes the operations that process disk files.

INT 21H Function 29H: Parse Filename

This service converts a command line containing a file specification (filespec) of the form d:filename.ext into FCB format. The function can accept a filespec from a user, for example, for copying and deleting files. To use it, load the SI register (used as DS:SI) with the address of the filespec to be parsed, the DI (used as ES:DI) with the address of an area where the operation is to generate the FCB format, and the AL with a bit value that controls the parsing method:

```
MOV  AH,29H         ;Request parse filename
MOV  AL,code        ;Parsing method
LEA  DI,FCBname     ;Address of FCB (ES:DI)
LEA  SI,filespec    ;Address of filespec (DS:SI)
INT  21H            ;Call interrupt service
```

The codes for the parsing method are:

BIT	VALUE	ACTION
0	0	Means that filespec begins in the first byte.
0	1	Scan past separators (such as blanks) to find the filespec.
1	0	Set drive ID byte in the generated FCB: missing drive = 00, A = 01, B = 02, and so forth.
1	1	Change drive ID byte in the generated FCB only if the parsed filespec specifies a drive. In this way, an FCB can have its own default drive.
2	0	Change filename in the FCB as required.
2	1	Change filename in the FCB only if the filespec contains a valid filename.
3	0	Change filename extension as required.
3	1	Change extension only if filespec contains a valid extension.
4–7	0	Must be zero.

For valid data, function 29H creates a standard FCB format for the filename and extension, with an 8-character filename filled out with blanks if necessary, a 3-character extension filled out with blanks if necessary, and no period between them.

The operation recognizes standard punctuation and converts the wild cards * and ? into a string of one or more characters. For example, PROG12.* becomes PROG12bb??? (2 blanks to fill out filename and ??? for the extension). The AL returns one of the following codes: 00H = no wild cards encountered; 01H = wild cards converted; or FFH = invalid drive specified.

After the operation, the DS:SI contains the address of the first byte after the parsed filespec, and the ES:DI contains the address of the first byte of the FCB. For a failed operation, the byte at DI+1 is blank, although the operation attempts to convert almost anything you throw at it.

To make this operation work with file handles, further editing includes deleting blanks and inserting a period between filename and extension.

INT 21H Function 41H: Delete File

This function deletes a file (but not read-only) from within a program. Load the address in the DX of an ASCIIZ string containing the device path and filename, with no wild-card references:

```
ASCstrng  DB   'd:\pathname',00H ;ASCIIZ string
          ...
          MOV  AH,41H            ;Request delete file
          LEA  DX,ASCstrng       ;Address of ASCIIZ string (DS:DX)
          INT  21H               ;Call interrupt service
```

A valid operation clears the carry flag, marks the filename in the directory as deleted, and releases the file's allocated disk space in the FAT. An error sets the carry flag and returns code 02, 03, or 05 in the AX.

INT 21H Function 43H: Get or Set File Attribute

You can use this operation either to get or set a file attribute in the directory. The operation requires the address of an ASCIIZ string containing the drive, path, and filename for the requested file. (Or use the default directory if no path is given.)

Get file attribute. To *get* the file attribute, load the AL with code 00, as shown by the following example:

```
ASCstrng  DB   'd:\pathname',00H ;ASCIIZ string
          ...
          MOV  AH,43H            ;Request
          MOV  AL,00             ; get attribute
          LEA  DX,ASCstrng       ;ASCIIZ string (DS:DX)
          INT  21H               ;Call interrupt service
```

A valid operation clears the carry flag, clears the CH, and returns the current attribute to the CL:

BIT	ATTRIBUTE	BIT	ATTRIBUTE
0	Read-only file	3	Volume label
1	Hidden file	4	Subdirectory
2	System file	5	Archive file

An error sets the carry flag and returns code 02 or 03 to the AX.

Set file attribute. To *set* the file attribute, load the AL with code 01 and attribute bit(s) in the CX. You may change read-only, hidden, system, and archive files, but not the volume label or subdirectory. The following example sets hidden and archive attributes for a file:

```
MOV  AH,43H         ;Request
MOV  AL,01          ;  set attributes,
MOV  CX,22H         ;  hidden and archive
LEA  DX,ASCstrng    ;ASCIIZ string (DS:DX)
INT  21H            ;Call interrupt service
```

A valid operation clears the carry flag and sets the directory entry to the attribute in the CX. An invalid operation sets the carry flag and returns code 02, 03, or 05 to the AX.

INT 21H Function 45H: Duplicate a File Handle

The purpose of this service is to give a file more than one handle. The uses of old versus new handles are identical—the handles reference the same file, file pointer, and buffer area. One use is to request a file handle and use that handle to close the file. This action causes the system to flush the buffer and update the directory. You can then use the original file handle to continue processing the file. Here is an example of function 45H:

```
MOV  AH,45H       ;Request duplicate handle
MOV  BX,handle    ;Current handle to be duplicated
INT  21H          ;Call interrupt service
```

A successful operation clears the carry flag and returns the next available file handle in the AX. An error sets the carry flag and returns error code 04 or 06 to the AX. (See also function 46H.)

INT 21H Function 46H: Force Duplicate of a File Handle

This service is similar to function 45H, except that this one can assign a specific file handle. You could use the service to redirect output, for example, to another path. To use it, load the BX with the original handle and the CX with the second handle. A successful operation clears the carry flag. An error sets the carry flag and returns error code 04 or 06 to the AX. Some combinations may not work; for example, handle 00 is always keyboard input, 04 is printer output, and 03 (auxiliary) cannot be redirected. (See also function 45H.)

INT 21H Function 4EH: Find First Matching File

You can use function 4EH to begin a search in a directory for the first of (probably) related files and use function 4FH to continue searching for succeeding files of the group. You have to define a 43-byte buffer for the operation to return the located directory entry and issue function 1AH (set DTA) before using this service. For beginning the search, set the CX with the file attribute of the filename(s) to be returned—any combination of read only (bit 0), hidden (bit 1), system (bit 2), volume label (bit 3), directory (bit 4), or archive (bit 5). Load the DX with the address of an ASCIIZ string containing the filespec; the string may (and probably would) contain the wild-card characters ? and *. For example, a request for filespec E:\ASMPROGS\A12*.ASM causes the operation to begin with the first file that matches the string. Here's an example:

```
DTAname   DB   43 DUP(?)
ASCstrng  DB   'ASCIIZ string',00H
          ...
          MOV  AH,1AH        ;Request set DTA
          LEA  DX,DTAname    ;Area for DTA (DS:DX)
          INT  21H           ;Call interrupt service
          MOV  AH,4EH        ;Request first match
          MOV  CX,00H        ;Normal attribute
          LEA  DX,ASCstrng   ;ASCIIZ string (DS:DX)
          INT  21H           ;Call interrupt service
```

An operation that locates a match clears the carry flag and fills the 43-byte (2BH) DTA with the following:

```
FILEDTA    LABEL   BYTE           ;File DTA:
           DB      21 DUP(20H)    ; Reserved for subsequent search
FILATTR    DB      0              ; File attribute
FILTIME    DW      0              ; File time
FILDATE    DW      0              ; File date
LOSIZE     DW      0              ; File size: low word
HISIZE     DW      0              ; File size: high word
FILNAME    DB      13 DUP(20H)    ; Name and extension as an ASCIIZ
                                    string, followed by hex 00
```

An error sets the carry flag and returns code 02, 03, or 12H. If you plan to use function 4FH subsequently, do not change the contents of the DTA.

A unique use for function 4EH is to determine whether a reference is to a filename or to a subdirectory. For example, if the returned attribute is 10H, the reference is to a subdirectory. The operation also returns the size of the file, which is illustrated in Figure 20-2. You may use function 4EH to determine the size of a file and function 36H to check the space available for writing it. This operation supersedes the obsolete function 11H.

INT 21H Function 4FH: Find Next Matching File

Before using this service, issue function 4EH to begin the search in a directory and then function 4FH to continue searching:

```
MOV  AH,4FH     ;Request next match
INT  21H        ;Call interrupt service
```

A successful operation clears the carry flag and returns to the AX codes 00 (filename found) or 18 (no more files). An error sets the carry flag and returns code 02, 03, or 12H to the AX.

This operation supersedes the now-obsolete function 12H. Figure 18-3 later illustrates functions 4EH and 4FH.

INT 21H Function 56H: Rename File or Directory

This service can rename a file or directory from within a program. To use it, load the DX with the address of an ASCIIZ string containing the old drive, path, and name of the file or directory to be renamed. Load the DI (combined as ES:DI) with the address of an ASCIIZ string containing the new drive, path, and name, with no wild cards. Drive numbers, if used, must be the same in both strings. Because the paths need not be the same, the operation can both rename a file and move it to another directory on the same drive:

```
oldstrng  DB   'd:\oldpath\oldname', 00H
newstrng  DB   'd:\newpath\newname', 00H
          ...
          MOV  AH,56H             ;Request rename file/directory
          LEA  DX,oldstrng        ;DS:DX
          LEA  DI,newstrng        ;ES:DI
          INT  21H                ;Call interrupt service
```

A successful operation clears the carry flag; an error sets the carry flag and returns in the AX code 02, 03, 05, or 11H.

INT 21H Function 57H: Get/Set a File's Date and Time

This service enables a program to get or set the date and time for an open file. The formats for time and date are the same as those in the directory:

BITS FOR TIME	BITS FOR DATE
0BH-0FH Hours	09H-0FH Year (relative to 1980)
05H-0AH Minutes	05H-08H Month
00H-04H Seconds	00H-04H Day of month

Seconds are in the form of the number of 2-second increments, 0–29. Load the request (0 = get or 1 = set) in the AL and the file handle in the BX. For requesting set, load the time in the CX and the date in the DX. Following is an example:

```
MOV  AH,57H        ;Request set
MOV  AL,01         ;  file's date and time
MOV  BX,handle     ;File handle
MOV  CX,time       ;New time
MOV  DX,date       ;New date
INT  21H           ;Call interrupt service
```

A valid operation clears the carry flag; a get operation returns the time in the CX and date in the DX, whereas a set operation changes the date and time entries for the file. An invalid operation sets the carry flag and returns in the AX error code 01 or 06.

INT 21H Function 5AH: Create a Temporary File

This service would be useful for a program that creates temporary files, especially in networks, where the names of other files may be unknown and the program is to avoid accidentally overwriting them. The operation creates a file with a unique name within the path.

To use this service, load the CX with the required file attribute—any combination of read only (bit 0), hidden (bit 1), system (bit 2), volume label (bit 3), directory (bit 4), and archive (bit 5). Load the DX with the address of an ASCIIZ path—drive (if necessary), the subdirectory (if any), a backslash, and 00H, followed by 13 blank bytes for the new filename:

```
ASCpath  DB   'd:\pathname\', 00H, 13 DUP(20H)
         ...
         MOV  AH,5AH              ;Request create file
         MOV  CX,attribute        ;File attribute
         LEA  DX,ASCpath          ;ASCIIZ path
         INT  21H                 ;Call interrupt service
```

A successful operation clears the carry flag, delivers the file handle to the AX, and appends the new filename to the ASCIIZ string beginning at the 00H byte. An invalid operation sets the carry flag and returns code 03, 04, or 05 in the AX.

INT 21H Function 5BH: Create a New File

This service creates a file only if the named file does not already exist; otherwise it is identical to function 3CH (Create File). You could use function 5BH whenever you don't want to overwrite an existing file. A valid operation clears the carry flag and returns the file handle in the AX. An invalid operation (including finding an identical filename) sets the carry flag and returns code 03, 04, 05, or 50H in the AX.

PROGRAM: SELECTIVELY DELETING FILES

The program in Figure 18-3 illustrates the use of functions 4EH and 4FH to find all filenames in the directory and function 41H to delete selected files. The program assumes drive F:, which you may change, and consists of the following procedures:

- A10MAIN Calls procedures B10FIRST, C10NEXT, D10DISPL, and E10DELET.
- B10FIRST Sets the DTA for function 4EH and finds the first matched entry in the directory.
- C10NEXT Finds succeeding matched entries in the directory.
- D10DISPL Displays the names of the files and asks whether they are to be deleted.
- E10DELET Accepts a reply Y (yes) to delete the file, N (no) to keep it, or <Enter> to end processing, and deletes the files requested.

As a precaution during testing, use temporary copied files.

```
TITLE     A18SELDL (COM)  Select and delete files
CODESG    SEGMENT PARA 'Code'
          .MODEL SMALL
          .CODE
          ORG    100H
BEGIN:    JMP    A10MAIN
; ---------------------------------------------------------------
TAB       EQU    09
LF        EQU    10
CR        EQU    13
CRLF      DB     CR, LF
PATHNAM   DB     'F:\*.*', 00H
DELMSG    DB     TAB, 'Delete '
ENDMSG    DB     CR, LF, 'No more directory entries', CR, LF
ERRMSG1   DB     'Invalid path/file'
ERRMSG2   DB     'Write-protected disk'
PROMPT    DB     'Y = Delete, N = Keep, Ent = Exit', CR, LF
DISKAREA  DB     43 DUP(20H)
; ---------------------------------------------------------------
A10MAIN   PROC   NEAR                 ;Main procedure
          CALL   Q10SCRN              ;Clear screen
          CALL   Q20CURS              ;Set cursor
          CALL   B10FIRST             ;  directory entry
          CMP    AX,00H               ;If no entries,
          JNE    A90                  ;  exit
          MOV    CX,34                ;Length of prompt
          LEA    DX,PROMPT            ;Display initial prompt
          CALL   Q30LINE
A20:
          CALL   D10DISPL             ;Display filename
          CALL   E10DELET             ;Delete if requested
          CMP    AL,0FFH              ;Request for finish?
          JE     A90                  ;  yes, exit
          MOV    CX,02                ;Length of data
          LEA    DX,CRLF              ;Set cursor on
          CALL   Q30LINE              ;  next line
          CALL   C10NEXT              ;Get next directory entry
          CMP    AX,00H               ;Any more entries?
          JE     A20                  ;  yes, loop
A90:      MOV    AX,4C00H             ;End processing
          INT    21H
A10MAIN   ENDP
;                Find first entry in directory:
;                ----------------------------
B10FIRST  PROC   NEAR
          MOV    AH,1AH               ;Get DTA for function
          LEA    DX,DISKAREA          ;  calls
          INT    21H
          MOV    AH,4EH               ;Locate first directory
          MOV    CX,00                ;  entry
          LEA    DX,PATHNAM           ;Address of ASCIIZ string
          INT    21H
          JNC    B90                  ;Valid operation?
          PUSH   AX                   ;  no,
          MOV    CX,17                ;  display ending
          LEA    DX,ERRMSG1           ;  message
          CALL   Q30LINE              ;
          POP    AX
B90:      RET
B10FIRST  ENDP
```

Figure 18-3a Selectively Deleting Files

```
;                Find succeeding entries in directory:
;                -------------------------------------
C10NEXT   PROC   NEAR                  ;Read directory entry
          MOV    AH,4FH                ;Get next
          INT    21H
          CMP    AX,00H                ;More entries?
          JE     C90                   ;  yes, bypass
          PUSH   AX                    ;  no,
          MOV    CX,29                 ;  display ending
          LEA    DX,ENDMSG             ;  message
          CALL   Q30LINE               ;
          POP    AX
C90:      RET
C10NEXT   ENDP
;                Display message and filename:
;                -----------------------------
D10DISPL  PROC   NEAR
          MOV    CX,08                 ;Length of message
          LEA    DX,DELMSG             ;Display delete message
          CALL   Q30LINE
          LEA    SI,DISKAREA+1EH       ;Start of filename
D30:      MOV    DL,[SI]               ;Get char for display
          CALL   Q40CHAR
          INC    SI                    ;Next character
          CMP    BYTE PTR [SI],00H ;Hex zero stopper?
          JNE    D30                   ;  no, get next char
          MOV    DL,'?'                ;  yes, exit
          CALL   Q40CHAR
          RET
D10DISPL  ENDP
;                Delete record if requested:
;                ---------------------------
E10DELET  PROC   NEAR
          MOV    AH,10H                ;Accept 1-character
          INT    16H                   ;  reply (y/n)
          CMP    AL,0DH                ;Enter character?
          JE     E50                   ;  yes, exit
          OR     AL,00100000B          ;Force lowercase
          CMP    AL,'y'                ;Delete requested?
          JNE    E90                   ;  no, bypass
          MOV    AH,41H                ;  yes,
          LEA    DX,DISKAREA+1EH       ;  address of filename
          INT    21H                   ;  delete entry
          JNC    E90                   ;Valid delete?
          MOV    CX,20                 ;  no, display
          LEA    DX,ERRMSG2            ;  warning message
          CALL   Q30LINE               ;
E50:      MOV    AL,0FFH               ;End-of-process indicator
E90:      RET
E10DELET  ENDP
;                Screen functions:
;                ----------------
Q10SCRN   PROC   NEAR
          MOV    AX,0600H              ;Request clear screen
          MOV    BH,1EH                ;Set attribute
          MOV    CX,00
          MOV    DX,184FH
          INT    10H
          RET
Q10SCRN   ENDP
```

Figure 18-3b Selectively Deleting Files

```
Q20CURS   PROC   NEAR
          MOV    AH,02H          ;Request
          MOV    BH,00           ;   set cursor
          MOV    DH,00           ;Row 0
          MOV    DL,10           ;Column 10
          INT    10H
          ---
```

Figure 18-3c Selectively Deleting Files

KEY POINTS

- Operations involved with handling disk drives include reset, select default, get drive information, get free disk space, and the extensive operation I/O control for devices.
- Operations involved with handling the directory and FAT include create subdirectory, remove subdirectory, change current directory, and get current directory.
- Operations involved with handling disk files (other than create, open, read, and write) include rename file, get/set attribute, find matching file, and get/set date/time.

QUESTIONS

Use DEBUG for these questions. Key in the A 100 command and the required assembler instructions. Examine any values returned in the registers.

18-1. The following questions involve disk drives:

(a) Function 19H to determine the current default disk drive.
(b) Function 1BH for information about the current default disk drive.
(c) Function 1FH for information about the default DPB.
(d) Function 36H to determine the amount of free disk space.
(e) Function 4400H to get information on the device in use.
(f) Function 4408H to determine whether any media in use are removable.
(g) Function 440DH minor code 60H to get the device parameters.
(h) Function 440DH minor code 66H to get the media ID.

18-2. The following questions involve directories:

(a) Function 39H to create a subdirectory. For safety, you could create it on a RAM disk or diskette. Use any name.
(b) Function 56H to rename the subdirectory.
(c) Function 3AH to remove the subdirectory.

18-3. The following questions involve disk files (use a copied file for this exercise):

(a) Function 43H to get the attribute from a file on a diskette.
(b) Function 56H to rename the file.
(c) Function 43H to set the attribute to hidden.
(d) Function 57H to get the file's date and time.
(e) Function 41H to delete the file.

18-4. Write a small program from within DEBUG that simply executes INT 21H function 29H (Parse Filename). Provide for the filespec at 81H and the FCB at 5CH; both are in the PSP immediately before the program. Enter various filespecs, such as D:PROG1.DOC, PROG2, PROG3.*, and C:*.ASM. Check the results at offset 5CH after each execution of the parse.

19 DISK STORAGE IV: INT 13H DISK FUNCTIONS

Objective: To examine the basic programming requirements for using the BIOS INT 13H functions to format, verify, read from, and write to disks.

INTRODUCTION

In Chapters 17 and 18, we examined the use of the INT 21H services for disk processing. You can also process directly at the BIOS level, although BIOS supplies no automatic use of the directory or blocking and deblocking of records. BIOS disk operation INT 13H treats data as the size of a sector and handles disk addressing in terms of actual track and sector numbers. INT 13H disk operations involve resetting reading, writing, verifying, and formatting the drive.

Most of the INT 13H operations are for experienced software developers who are aware of the potential danger in their misuse. Also, BIOS versions may vary according to the processor used and even by computer model.

This chapter introduces the following INT 13H functions:

00H	Reset disk/diskette system	0CH	Seek cylinder
01H	Read disk/diskette status	0DH	Alternate disk reset
02H	Read sectors	0EH	Read sector buffer
03H	Write sectors	0FH	Write sector buffer
04H	Verify sectors	15H	Get disk/diskette type
05H	Format tracks	16H	Change of diskette status
08H	Get drive parameters	17H	Set diskette type

09H	Initialize drive	18H	Set media type for format
0AH	Read extended sector buffer	19H	Park disk heads
0BH	Write extended sector buffer		

BIOS STATUS BYTE

Most of the INT 13H functions clear or set the carry flag on success or failure and return a status code to the AH register. BIOS maintains information in its data area about each device and its status. The *status byte* shown in Figure 19-1 reflects the indicator bits to be found in the BIOS data area at 40:41H for the Diskette Drive Data Area and at 40:74H for the Hard Disk Data Area. (See Chapter 25 for details.)

Code	Status
00H	No error
01H	Bad command, not recognized by the controller
02H	Address mark on disk not found
03H	Writing on protected disk attempted
04H	Invalid track/sector
05H	Reset operation failed
06H	Diskette removed since last access
07H	Drive parameters wrong
08H	Direct memory access (DMA) overrun (data accessed too fast to enter)
09H	DMA across a 64K boundary attempted on read/write
10H	Bad CRC on a read encountered (error check indicated corrupted data)
20H	Controller failed (hardware failure)
40H	Seek operation failed (hardware failure)
80H	Device failed to respond (diskette: drive door open or no diskette; hard disk: time out)
AAH	Drive not ready
BBH	Undefined error
CCH	Write fault

Figure 19-1 INT 13H Status Codes

If a disk operation returns an error, a program's usual action is to reset the disk (function 00H) and to retry the operation three times. If there is still an error, the program could display a message and give the user a chance to change the diskette, if that's the solution to the problem.

BASIC INT 13H DISK OPERATIONS

This section covers the basic INT 13H disk operations, each requiring a function code in the AH register.

INT 13H Function 00H: Reset Disk System

Use this operation after a preceding disk operation has reported a serious error. The operation performs a hard reset on the diskette or hard drive controller; that is, the next time the drive is accessed, it first resets to cylinder 0. For a diskette, set the DL to the drive number (0 = drive A, etc.), and for hard disk set the DL to a value of 80H or higher (80H = the first drive, 81H = the second, etc.). An example of the use of function 00H is as follows:

```
MOV  AH,00H     ;Request reset disk
MOV  DL,80H     ;Hard disk
INT  13H        ;Call interrupt service
```

A valid operation clears the carry flag; an error sets the carry flag and returns a status code in the AH. Function 0DH is a related operation.

INT 13H Function 01H: Read Disk Status

This operation gives you another chance to examine the status of the most recent disk operation. (See status byte in Figure 19-1.) Set the DL to the usual code (0 = drive A, etc.) for diskette and a value of 80H or more (80H = the first drive, etc.) for hard disk. This operation returns to the AL the status code that the last disk operation would have returned to the AH. The operation, which should always be valid, clears the carry flag and returns its own status code, 00H, in the AH.

INT 13H Function 02H: Read Disk Sectors

This operation reads a specified number of sectors on the same track directly into memory. To use it, initialize the following registers:

AL	Number of sectors, up to the maximum for a track
CH	Cylinder/track number (numbers begin with 0)
CL	Bits 7–6 Cylinder/track number (high-order two bits) Bits 5–0 Starting sector number (numbers begin with 1)
DH	Head/side number (0 or 1 for diskette)
DL	Drive number for diskette (0 = A) or hard drive (80H or higher)
ES:BX	Address of an I/O buffer in the data area, which should be large enough for all the sectors to be read. (BX in this case is subject to the ES.)

The following example reads one sector into an area named INSECT:

```
INSECT  DB   512 DUP(?)     ;Area for input
        ...
        MOV  AH,02H         ;Request read sector
        MOV  AL,01          ;One sector
        LEA  BX,INSECT      ;Input buffer (ES:BX)
        MOV  CH,05          ;Track 05
        MOV  CL,03          ;Sector 03
        MOV  DH,00          ;Head 00
        MOV  DL,03          ;Drive 03 (D)
        INT  13H            ;Call interrupt service
```

A valid operation clears the carry flag and returns to the AL the number of sectors that the operation has actually read. The contents of the DS, BX, CX, and DX registers are preserved. An error sets the carry flag and returns the status code in the AH; reset the drive (function 00H) and retry the operation.

For most situations, you specify only one sector or all sectors for a track. Initialize the CH and CL, and increment them to read the sectors sequentially. Once the sector number exceeds the maximum for a track, you have to reset it to 01 and either increment the track number on the same side of the disk or increment the head number for the next side.

Testing Whether a Diskette Is Ready

A program may issue a request for accessing a diskette that has not yet been inserted. A standard practice is to attempt the operation three times before displaying a message to the user. The example that follows uses INT 13H function 02H in an attempt to read a sector of data. Try using DEBUG to enter the instructions (but not the comments) and test the code with and without a diskette present in drive A. For an installed diskette, the operation should read the contents of the disk's boot record, 512 (200H) bytes, beginning at location DS:200H. The code is:

```
0100   MOV CX,03       ;Count for loop
0103   PUSH CX         ;Save count
0104   MOV AX,0201     ;Request read one sector
0107   MOV BX,0200     ;Input address
010A   MOV CX,0001     ;Track and sector numbers
010D   MOV DX,0000     ;Head and drive numbers
0110   INT 13          ;Call interrupt service
0112   POP CX          ;Restore count
0113   JNC 118         ;If no error, exit
0115   CLC             ;If error,
0116   LOOP 103        ;  try 3 times
0118   NOP             ;That's it
```

INT 13H Function 03H: Write Sectors

This operation, the opposite of function 02H, writes a specified area from memory (512 bytes or a multiple of 512) onto designated formatted sectors. To use it, load the registers and handle processing just as for function 02H. A valid operation clears the carry flag and delivers to the AL the number of sectors that were written; the contents of the DS, BX, CX, and DX registers are preserved. An error sets the carry flag and returns a status code in the AH; reset the drive and retry the operation.

PROGRAM: USING INT 13H TO READ SECTORS

The program in Figure 19-2 uses INT 13H to read sectors from disk into memory. Note that there is no open operation or file handle. The major data areas are:

```
TITLE     A19BIORD (EXE)  Read disk sectors via BIOS
          .MODEL  SMALL
          .STACK  64
; -------------------------------------------------------
          .DATA
CURADR    DW      0301H            ;Beginning track-sector
ENDADR    DW      0401H            ;Ending track-sector
ENDCDE    DB      00               ;End process indicator
READMSG   DB      '*** Read error ***'
SECTIN    DB      512 DUP(' ')     ;Input area for sector
SIDE      DB      00
; -------------------------------------------------------
          .CODE
A10MAIN   PROC    FAR
          MOV     AX,@data         ;Initialize
          MOV     DS,AX            ;  segment
          MOV     ES,AX            ;  registers
          MOV     AX,0600H         ;Request scroll
A20LOOP:
          CALL    Q10SCRN          ;Clear screen
          CALL    Q20CURS          ;Set cursor
          CALL    B10ADDR          ;Calculate disk address
          MOV     CX,CURADR
          MOV     DX,ENDADR
          CMP     CX,DX            ;At ending sector?
          JE      A90              ;  yes, exit
          CALL    C10READ          ;Read disk record
          CMP     ENDCDE,00        ;Normal read?
          JNZ     A90              ;  no,  exit
          CALL    D10DISP          ;Display sector
          JMP     A20LOOP          ;Repeat
A90:      MOV     AX,4C00H
          INT     21H              ;End processing
A10MAIN   ENDP
;                 Calculate next disk address:
;                 ----------------------------
B10ADDR   PROC    NEAR
          MOV     CX,CURADR        ;Get track/sector
          CMP     CL,10            ;Past last sector?
          JNE     B90              ;  no, exit
          MOV     CL,01            ;Set sector to 1
          CMP     SIDE,00          ;Bypass if side 0
          JE      B20
          INC     CH               ;Increment track
B20:
          XOR     SIDE,01          ;Change side
          MOV     CURADR,CX
B90:      RET
B10ADDR   ENDP
;                 Read disk sector:
;                 ----------------
C10READ   PROC    NEAR
          MOV     AH,02H           ;Request read
          MOV     AL,01            ;Number of sectors
          LEA     BX,SECTIN        ;Address of buffer
          MOV     CX,CURADR        ;Track/sector
          MOV     DH,SIDE          ;Side
          MOV     DL,00            ;Drive A
          INT     13H
```

Figure 19-2a Using INT 13H to Read Disk Sectors

```
          CMP     AH,00           ;Normal read?
          JZ      C90             ;Yes, exit
          MOV     ENDCDE,01       ;No,
          CALL    X10ERR          ;  invalid read
C90:
          INC     CURADR          ;Increment sector
          RET
C10READ ENDP
;                 Display sector:
;                 --------------
D10DISP   PROC    NEAR
          MOV     AH,40H          ;Request display
          MOV     BX,01           ;Handle
          MOV     CX,512          ;Length
          LEA     DX,SECTIN       ;Address of input
          INT     21H
          MOV     AH,10H          ;Wait for keyboard
          INT     16H             ;  entry
          RET
D10DISP   ENDP
;                 Clear screen:
;                 ------------
Q10SCRN   PROC    NEAR
          MOV     AX,0600H        ;Request scroll
          MOV     BH,1EH          ;Set attribute
          MOV     CX,0000         ;Full screen
          MOV     DX,184FH
          INT     10H
          RET
Q10SCRN   ENDP
;                 Set cursor:
;                 ----------
Q20CURS   PROC    NEAR
          MOV     AH,02H          ;Request set
          MOV     BH,00           ;  cursor
          MOV     DX,0000
          INT     10H
          RET
Q20CURS   ENDP
;                 Display disk error message:
;                 --------------------------
X10ERR    PROC    NEAR
          MOV     AH,40H          ;Request display
          MOV     BX,01           ;Handle
          MOV     CX,18           ;Length of message
          LEA     DX,READMSG
          INT     21H
          RET
X10ERR    ENDP
          END     A10MAIN
```

Figure 19-2b Using INT 13H to Read Disk Sectors

CURADR Contains the beginning track (03) and sector (01), which the program increments.

ENDADR contains the ending track (04) and sector (01). The total number of sectors is 9 (for track 3) $\times$ 2 (for two sides) $=$ 18. One way to enhance the program would be to prompt the user for the starting and ending track and sector.

SECTIN Defines 512 bytes as an area for reading in a sector.

The main procedures are:

A10MAIN	Calls B10ADDR, C10READ, and D10DISP, and ends after reading the last requested sector.
B10ADDR	Calculates each disk address in terms of side, track, and sector. When the sector number reaches 10, the routine resets the sector to 01. If the side is 1, the program increments the track number; the side number is then changed, from 0 to 1 or ; from 1 to 0. This process works only for diskettes (because they are two-sided) that contain 9 sectors per track.
C10READ	Reads a disk sector from drive A: (which you may change) into SECTIN and increments the sector number for a valid read operation.
D10DISP	Displays the contents of the currently read sector. The display acts on CR, Tab, etc, and the procedure waits for the user to press a key before continuing.

Try running this program under DEBUG. Trace through the instructions that initialize the segment registers. For the input operation, adjust the starting and ending sectors to the location of the disk's FAT. (See Chapter 16.) Use G (Go) to execute the program, and examine the FAT and directory entries in the SECTIN.

As an alternative to DEBUG, your program could convert the ASCII characters in the input area to their hex equivalents and display the hex values just as DEBUG does. (See also the program in Figure 15-6.) In this way, you could examine the contents of any sector—even hidden ones—and could allow a user to enter changes and write the changed sector back onto disk.

Note that when INT 21H creates a file, it inserts records in available clusters, which may not be contiguous on disk. For that reason, you can't expect INT 13H to read the file sequentially, although you could access the FAT entries for the location of the next cluster.

OTHER INT 13H DISK OPERATIONS

The following describes additional INT 13H disk services.

INT 13H Function 04H: Verify Sectors

This operation simply checks that the specified sectors can be read and performs a cyclical redundancy check (CRC). When an operation writes to a sector, the disk controller calculates and writes a CRC checksum immediately following the sector, based on the bits that are set. You can use function 04H to read the sector, recalculate the checksum, and compare it with the stored value. Note that the verification consists of recalculating the checksum rather than checking that the byte values in the sector agree with the output data in memory. You could use this function after a write (function 03H) to ensure more reliable output, although at a cost of more processing time.

Load the registers just as for function 02H, but since the operation does not perform true verification of the written data, there is no need to set an address in the ES:BX. A successful operation clears the carry flag and returns to the AL the number of sectors actually verified; the contents of the DS, BX, CX, and DX are preserved. An error sets the carry flag and returns a status code in the AH; reset the drive and retry the operation.

INT 13H Function 05H: Format Tracks

Read/write operations require information on formatting to locate and process a requested sector. This operation formats tracks according to one of four different sizes. Prior to execution of the operation, use function 17H to set the diskette type and function 18H to set the media type. For formatting diskettes, initialize these registers:

AL	Number of sectors to format
CH	Cylinder/track number (numbers begin with 0)
DH	Head/side number (0 or 1 for diskette)
DL	Drive number for diskette (0 = A) or hard drive (80H or higher)
ES:BX	Segment:offset address that points to a group of address fields for a track. For each diskette sector on a track, there must be one 4-byte entry of the form T/H/S/B, where Byte 0 T = Cylinder/track number 1 H = Head/side number 2 S = Sector number 3 B = Bytes per sector (00H = 128, 01H = 256, 02H = 512, 03H= 1024)

For example, if you format track 03, head 00, and 512 bytes per sector, the first entry for the track is hex 03000102, followed by one entry for each remaining sector.

The operation clears (if valid) or sets (if invalid) the carry flag and returns the status code in the AH.

INT 13H Function 08H: Get Disk Drive Parameters

This useful function returns information about a disk drive. To use it, load the drive number in the DL (0 = A, 1 = B for diskette and 80H or higher for hard disk). A successful operation returns the following:

BL	Diskette type (01H = 360K, 02H = 1.2M, 03H = 720K, 04H = 1.44M)
CH	High cylinder/track number
CL	Bits 0–5 = high sector number Bits 6–7 = high-order 2 bits of cylinder number
DH	High head number
DL	Number of drives attached to the controller
ES:DI	For diskettes, the segment:offset address of an 11-byte

diskette drive parameter table. Two relevant fields are:
Offset 3 gives bytes per sector (00H = 128, 01H = 256, 02H = 512, 03H = 1024)
Offset 4 gives sectors per track

You can use the DEBUG command D ES:offset (the offset returned in the DI) to display the values. The operation clears (if valid) or sets (if invalid) the carry flag and returns the status code in the AH.

INT 13H Function 09H: Initialize Drive

BIOS performs this function when you boot up your computer, according to its own hard disk table. The DL contains the drive number (80H or higher). The operation clears (if valid) or sets (if invalid) the carry flag and returns the status in the AH. BIOS INT 41H and INT 46H are related operations.

INT 13H Function 0AH: Read Extended Sector Buffer

The sector buffer on hard disks includes the 512 bytes of data plus 4 bytes for an error correction code (ECC), used for error checking and correcting the data. This function can read the whole sector buffer rather than just the data portion. To read an extended buffer, load these registers:

AL	Number of sectors (up to the maximum for the drive)
ES:BX	Segment:offset address of the input buffer
CH	Cylinder/track number
CL	Bits 0–5 = high sector number Bits 6–7 = high-order 2 bits of cylinder number
DH	Head/side number
DL	Drive number (80H or higher)

A successful operation returns to the AL the number of sectors transferred. The operation clears (if valid) or sets (if invalid) the carry flag and returns a status code in the AH.

INT 13H Function 0BH: Write Extended Sector Buffer

This function is similar to function 0AH, except that, rather than read the sector buffer, it writes it (including the ECC code) onto disk.

INT 13H Function 0CH: Seek Disk Cylinder

This function positions the read/write head on a hard disk at a specified cylinder (track), but does not transfer any data. To seek a cylinder, load these registers:

CH	Cylinder/track number
CL	Bits 0–5 = sector number Bits 6–7 = high-order 2 bits of cylinder/track number

DH Head/side number

DL Drive (80H or higher)

The operation clears (if valid) or sets (if invalid) the carry flag and returns a status code in the AH.

INT 13H Function 0DH: Alternate Disk Reset

This operation is similar to function 00H, except that this one is restricted to hard disks. Load the drive (80H or higher) in the DL. The operation resets the read/write access arm to cylinder 0. It clears (if valid) or sets (if invalid) the carry flag and returns a status code in the AH.

INT 13H Function 0EH: Read Sector Buffer

This operation is similar to function 0AH, except that this one reads the 512-byte data portion of the sector and not the ECC bytes.

INT 13H Function 0FH: Write Sector Buffer

This operation is similar to function 0BH, except that this one writes only the 512-byte data portion of the sector, not the ECC bytes.

INT 13H Functions 10H: Test for Drive Ready; 11H: Recalibrate Hard Drive; 12H: ROM Diagnostics; 13H: Drive Diagnostics; and 14H: Controller Diagnostics

These functions perform internal diagnostics and report specified information for BIOS and for advanced utility programs. The operations clear (if valid) or set (if invalid) the carry flag and return a status code in the AH.

INT 13H Function 15H: Get Disk Type

This function returns information about a disk drive. To use it, load the DL with the drive (0 = A, etc. for diskette or 80H or higher for hard disk). A valid operation returns one of the following codes in the AH:

00H No drive/disk present

01H Diskette drive that does not sense a change of diskette

02H Diskette drive that senses a change of diskette

03H Hard disk drive

For return code 03 in the AH, the CX:DX pair contains the total number of disk sectors on the drive. The operation clears or sets the carry flag, and returns error codes in the AH.

INT 13H Function 16H: Change of Diskette Status

This function checks for a change of diskette for systems that can sense a change (see also function 15H). To use this service, load the DL with the drive number (0 = A, etc.). The operation returns one of the following codes in the AH:

00H	No change of diskette (carry flag = 0)
01H	Invalid diskette parameter (carry flag = 1)
06H	Diskette changed (carry flag = 1)
80H	Diskette drive not ready (carry flag = 1)

Status codes 01H and 80H are errors that set the carry flag, whereas 06H is a valid status that also sets the carry flag—a potential source of confusion.

INT 13H Function 17H: Set Diskette Type

This operation sets up the combination of drive and diskette. Use function 17H along with function 05H for disk formatting. To use this service, load the drive number (0 = A, etc.) in the DL and the diskette type in the AL. Diskette types include:

01H	360K diskette in 360K drive
02H	360K diskette in 1.2M drive
03H	1.2M diskette in 1.2M drive
04H	720K diskette in 720K drive
05H	1.44M diskette in 1.44M drive

The operation clears (if valid) or sets (if invalid) the carry flag and returns the status in the AH.

INT 13H Function 18H: Set Media Type for Format

Use this operation immediately before executing function 05H. To set the media type, load these registers:

CH	Number of tracks (low-order 8 bits)
CL	Number of tracks (high 2 bits in bits 7–6), sectors per track (bits 5–0)
DL	Drive (0 = A, etc.)

A valid operation returns in the ES:DI a pointer to an 11-byte diskette parameter table. (See function 08H.) The operation clears (if valid) or sets (if invalid) the carry flag and returns the status in the AH.

INT 13H Function 19H: Park Disk Heads

This operation requires the drive number in the DL (80H and higher for hard disk). The operation clears (if valid) or sets (if invalid) the carry flag and returns the status in the AH.

KEY POINTS

- BIOS INT 13H provides direct access to tracks and sectors.
- INT 13H does not supply automatic directory handling, end-of-file operations, or blocking and deblocking of records.
- The verify sector operation performs an elementary check of data written at some cost of processing time.
- A program should check for the status byte after each INT 13H disk operation.

QUESTIONS

19-1. What are the two major disadvantages of using BIOS INT 13H? That is, why is the use of INT 21H usually preferred?

19-2. Under what circumstances would a programmer use INT 13H?

19-3. Most INT 13H operations return a status code. (a) Where is the code returned? (b) What does code 00H mean? (c) What does code 04H mean?

19-4. What is the standard procedure for an error returned by INT 13H? That is, how do you check for an error and what action do you take?

19-5. Code the instructions to reset the diskette controller.

19-6. Code the instructions to read the diskette status.

19-7. Using memory address DISKIN, drive B, head 0, track 5, and sector 4, code the instructions for INT 13H to read three sectors.

19-8. Using memory address DATAOUT, drive A, head 0, track 7, and sector 3, code the instructions for INT 13H to write one sector. Be sure to use a spare diskette for this exercise.

19-9. After the write operation in Question 19-8, how would you check for an attempt to write on a protected disk?

19-10. Based on Question 19-8, code the instructions to verify the write operation.

20 FACILITIES FOR PRINTING

Objective: To describe the requirements for printing using the various interrupt operations.

INTRODUCTION

Compared to screen and disk handling, printing appears to be a relatively simple process. There are only a few operations involved, all done either through DOS INT 21H or BIOS INT 17H. Special commands to the printer include Form Feed, Line Feed, Tab, and Carriage Return.

A printer must understand a signal from the processor, for example, to eject to a new page, to feed one line down a page, or to tab across a page. The processor also must understand a signal from a printer indicating that it is busy or out of paper. Unfortunately, many types of printers respond differently to signals from a processor, and one of the more difficult tasks for software specialists is to interface their programs to such printers.

This chapter introduces the following interrupt operations for handling the printer:

INT 21H FUNCTIONS	INT 17H FUNCTIONS
40H Print characters	00H Print character
05H Print character	01H Initialize port
	02H Get printer port status

COMMON PRINTER CONTROL CHARACTERS

Standard characters that control printing on all common printers for the PC include the following:

DECIMAL	HEX	FUNCTION
09	09H	Horizontal Tab
10	0AH	Line Feed (advance one line)
12	0CH	Form Feed (advance to next page)
13	0DH	Carriage Return (return to left margin)

Horizontal tab. The Horizontal Tab (09H) control character causes the printer to advance the current print position to the next tab stop (usually, if set, every 8 positions). The command works only on printers that have the feature and when the printer tabs are set up. You can issue a string of blank characters to get around a printer's inability to tab.

Line feed. The Line Feed (0AH) control character advances the printer by a single line and two successive line feeds cause a double space.

Form feed. Initializing the paper when you power up a printer determines the starting position for the top of a page. The default length for a page is 11 inches, which provides 66 lines at 6 lines per inch. Neither the processor nor the printer automatically checks for the bottom of a page. Whether you use cut sheets on a laser printer or continuous forms, as programmer you are responsible for directing the printer to begin printing on the next page. To control paging, count the lines as they print, and on reaching the maximum for the page (such as 60 lines), issue a Form Feed (0CH) command, and then reset the program's line count to 0 or 1.

At the end of printing, deliver a Line Feed or Form Feed command to force the printer to print the last line still in its buffer. Issuing a form feed at the end of printing ensures that the last sheet feeds out of the printer.

Carriage return. The Carriage Return (0DH) control character, normally accompanied with a Line Feed, resets the printer to its leftmost margin. This character is known as <Enter> or <Return> on the keyboard and as CR on the screen.

INT 21H FUNCTION 40H: PRINT CHARACTERS

We have already used file handles in the chapters on screen handling and disk processing. For printing with INT 21H function 40H, load these registers:

AH	Function 40H	CX	Number of characters to print
BX	File handle 04	DX	Address of the data to be printed

The following example prints 27 characters from a data item named HEADING beginning at the leftmost margin. The Carriage Return (0DH) and Line Feed (0AH) characters immediately following the text in HEADING cause the printer to reset to column 0 and advance 1 line:

```
HEADING  DB   'Mountain Outfitting Corp.', 0DH, 0AH
         ...
         MOV  AH,40H          ;Request printing
         MOV  BX,04           ;Handle 04 for printer
         MOV  CX,27           ;Send 27 characters
         LEA  DX,HEADING      ;Address of print area
         INT  21H             ;Call interrupt service
```

A successful operation prints the text, clears the carry flag, and returns in the AX the number of characters printed. An unsuccessful operation sets the carry flag and returns in the AX error code 05 (access denied) or 06 (invalid handle). An end-of-file marker (Ctrl-Z or 0AH) in the transmitted data also causes the operation to end.

Two conditions that intercept an attempt to print are:

1. The printer power is not turned on. The system displays
   "Write Fault Error Writing Device PRN"
   "Abort Retry Ignore Fail"
2. Out of paper or a paper jam. The system displays
   "Printer out of paper error writing device PRN"

PROGRAM: PRINTING WITH PAGE OVERFLOW AND HEADINGS

The program in Figure 9-2 accepts names from a user at the keyboard and displays them down the screen. The program in Figure 20-1 is similar to that one but instead directs the names to the printer. Each printed page contains a heading followed by a double space and the entered names in the following format:

```
List of Employee Names    Page 01
Annie Hall
Fanny Hill
Danny Rose
...
```

The program counts each line printed and, on nearing the bottom of a page, ejects the form to the top of the next page. The major procedures are the following:

- A10MAIN Calls B10INPT and C10PRINT and ends processing when the user presses only <Enter>.
- B10INPT Prompts for and accepts a name from the keyboard.
- C10PRINT If at the end of a page (60 lines), calls M10PAGE; prints the name (its length is based on the actual length in the keyboard input parameter list).
- D10PAGE Advances to a new page; prints the heading; resets line count and adds to page count.
- P10OUT Common routine that handles requests to print.

```
TITLE     A20PRTNM (EXE)  Accept entered names and print
          .MODEL  SMALL
          .STACK  64
          .DATA
NAMEPAR   LABEL   BYTE              ;Keyboard parameter list:
MAXNLEN   DB      20                ;  maximum length of name
NAMELEN   DB      ?                 ;  actual length entered
NAMEFLD   DB      20 DUP(' ')       ;  name entered
                                    ;Heading line:
HEADG     DB      'List of Employee Names    Page  '
PAGECTR   DB      '01', 0DH, 0AH, 0AH

FFEED     DB      0CH               ;Form feed
LFEED     DB      0DH, 0AH          ;CR, line feed
LINECTR   DB      01
PROMPT    DB      'Name? '
; -----------------------------------------------------------
          .CODE
A10MAIN   PROC    FAR
          MOV     AX,@data          ;Initialize
          MOV     DS,AX             ;  segment
          MOV     ES,AX             ;  registers
          CALL    Q10CLR            ;Clear screen
          CALL    D10PAGE           ;Page heading
A20LOOP:
          MOV     DX,0000           ;Set cursor to 00,00
          CALL    Q20CURS
          CALL    B10INPT           ;Accept input of name
          CALL    Q10CLR
          CMP     NAMELEN,00        ;Name entered?
          JE      A30               ;  no, exit
          CALL    C10PRINT          ;  yes, prepare printing
          JMP     A20LOOP
A30:      MOV     CX,01             ;End of processing:
          LEA     DX,FFEED          ;  one character
          CALL    P10OUT            ;  for form feed,
          MOV     AX,4C00H          ;  exit
          INT     21H
A10MAIN   ENDP
;                 Accept input of name:
;                 --------------------
B10INPT   PROC    NEAR
          MOV     AH,40H            ;Request display
          MOV     BX,01             ;
          MOV     CX,05             ;  5 characters,
          LEA     DX,PROMPT         ;  prompt message
          INT     21H
          MOV     AH,0AH            ;Request keyboard
          LEA     DX,NAMEPAR        ;  input
          INT     21H
          RET
B10INPT   ENDP
;                 Prepare for printing:
;                 --------------------
C10PRINT  PROC    NEAR
          CMP     LINECTR,60        ;End of page?
          JB      C20               ;  no,  bypass
          CALL    D10PAGE           ;  yes, print heading
```

Figure 20-1a Printing with Page Overflow and Headings

```
C20:        MOV    CH,00
            MOV    CL,NAMELEN           ;Set no. of characters
            LEA    DX,NAMEFLD           ;Set address of name
            CALL   P10OUT               ;Print name
            MOV    CX,02                ;Request CR,
            LEA    DX,LFEED             ;  line feed
            CALL   P10OUT
            INC    LINECTR              ;Add to line count
            RET
C10PRINT    ENDP
;                  Page heading routine:
;                  --------------------
D10PAGE     PROC   NEAR
            CMP    WORD PTR PAGECTR,3130H  ;First page?
            JE     D30                  ;  yes, bypass
            MOV    CX,01                ;
            LEA    DX,FFEED             ;  no,
            CALL   P10OUT               ;  form feed,
            MOV    LINECTR,03           ;  reset line count
D30:
            MOV    CX,37                ;Length heading, page
            LEA    DX,HEADG             ;Address of heading
            CALL   P10OUT
            INC    PAGECTR+1            ;Add to page count
            CMP    PAGECTR+1,3AH        ;Page no. = hex 3A?
            JNE    D90                  ;  no,  bypass
            MOV    PAGECTR+1,30H        ;  yes, set to ASCII
            INC    PAGECTR              ;
D90:        RET
D10PAGE     ENDP
;                  Print routine:
;                  -------------
P10OUT      PROC   NEAR                 ;CX and DX set on entry
            MOV    AH,40H               ;Request print
            MOV    BX,04                ;Handle
            INT    21H
            RET
P10OUT      ENDP
;                  Clear screen:
;                  ------------
Q10CLR      PROC   NEAR
            MOV    AX,0600H             ;Request scroll
            MOV    BH,60H               ;Attribute
            MOV    CX,0000              ;From 00,00
            MOV    DX,184FH             ;  to 24,79
            INT    10H
            RET
Q10CLR      ENDP
;                  Set cursor row/col:
;                  ------------------
Q20CURS     PROC   NEAR                 ;DX set on entry
            MOV    AH,02H               ;Request set cursor
            MOV    BH,00                ;Page number 0
            INT    10H
            RET
Q20CURS     ENDP
            END    A10MAIN
```

Figure 20-1b Printing with Page Overflow and Headings

At the beginning of execution, it is necessary to print a heading, but not to eject to a new page. To this end, D10PAGE bypasses the form feed if PAGECTR contains 01, its initial value. PAGECTR is defined as DB '01', which generates an ASCII number, 3031H. The procedure increments PAGECTR by 1 so that it becomes, progressively, 3032, 3033, and so forth. The value is valid up to 3039 and then becomes 303A, which would print as a zero and a colon. At this point, the routine resets the 3AH to 30H and adds 1 to the leftmost byte, so that 303AH becomes 3130H, or decimal value 10.

Placing a test for the end of the page *before* (rather than after) printing a name ensures that the last page has at least one name under the title.

PROGRAM: PRINTING ASCII FILES AND HANDLING TABS

A common procedure, performed, for example, by the video adapter, is to replace a Tab character (09H) with blanks through to the next location evenly divisible by 8. Thus tab stops could be at locations 8, 16, 24, and so forth, so that all locations between 0 and 7 tab to 8, those between 8 and 15 tab to 16, and so forth. Some printers, however, ignore Tab characters. DOS PRINT, for example, which prints ASCII files (such as assembly source programs), has to check each character that it sends to the printer. If the character is a Tab, the program inserts blanks up to the next tab position.

The program in Figure 20-2 requests a user to key in the name of a file and prints the contents of the file. The program is similar to the one in Figure 17-3 that displays records, but goes a step further in replacing tab stops for the printer with blanks. Following are three examples of tab stops, for print positions 1, 9, and 21, and the logic for setting the next tab position:

```
Present print location:        1          9          21
Binary value:              00000001   00001001   00010101
Clear rightmost 3 bits:    00000000   00001000   00010000
Add 8:                     00001000   00010000   00011000
New tab location:              8         16          24
```

The program is organized as follows:

- A10MAIN Calls B10PROMP, C10OPEN, D10READ, and E10XFER.
- B10PROMP Requests the user to key in a filename. Pressing only <Enter> indicates that the user is finished.
- C10OPEN Opens the requested disk file for input. If the operation is valid, the procedure uses INT 21H function 42H to determine the file size (uses only the low-order portion, with a maximum of 65,535 bytes).
- D10READ Reads a sector from the file.
- E10XFER Checks the input data for end of sector, end of file, end of display area, Line Feed, and Tab. Basically, the procedure sends regular characters to the print area and handles the logic for handling tab stops. The procedure also determines the end of file by decrementing the stored file size by 1 for each character processed.
- P10PRINT Prints the output line and clears it to blanks.

You could modify the program to count the lines printed and force a form feed when near the bottom of a page, at line 60 or so. You could also use an editor program to embed Form Feed characters directly in your ASCII files, at the exact location where you want a

```
          page 60,132
TITLE     A20PRTAS (EXE)  Read and print disk records
          .MODEL SMALL
          .STACK 64
; -----------------------------------------------------
          .DATA
PATHPAR   LABEL  BYTE               ;Parameter list for
MAXLEN    DB     32                 ;  input of
NAMELEN   DB     ?                  ;  filename
FILENAME  DB     32 DUP(' ')

FILEDTA   LABEL  BYTE               ;File DTA
          DB     26 DUP(20H)        ;Reserved
FILESIZE  DW     0                  ;File size (low-order)
          DW     0                  ;File size (high-order
          DB     13 DUP(20H)        ;Rest of file DTA

COUNT     DW     00
ENDCDE    DW     00                 ;End process indicator
FFEED     DB     0CH
HANDLE    DW     0
OPENMSG   DB     '*** Open error ***', 0DH, 0FH
PRTAREA   DB     120 DUP(' ')       ;Print area
PROMPT    DB     'Name of file? '
ROW       DB     0                  ;Screen row
SECTOR    DB     512 DUP(' ')       ;Input area for file
; -----------------------------------------------------
          .CODE
.386
A10MAIN   PROC   FAR                ;Main procedure
          MOV    AX,@data           ;Initialize
          MOV    DS,AX              ;  segment
          MOV    ES,AX              ;  registers
          CALL   Q10SCR             ;Clear screen
A20LOOP:
          MOV    ENDCDE,00          ;Initialize
          CALL   B10PROMP           ;Request filename
          CMP    NAMELEN,00         ;Any request?
          JE     A90                ;  no, exit
          CALL   C10OPEN            ;Open file, get handle
          CMP    ENDCDE,00          ;Valid open?
          JNE    A20LOOP            ;  no, request again
          CALL   D10READ            ;Read 1st disk sector
          CMP    ENDCDE,00          ;End-of-file, no data?
          JE     A80                ;  yes, request next
          CALL   E10XFER            ;Print/read
A80:
          MOV    AH,3EH             ;Close file
          MOV    BX,HANDLE
          INT    21H
          JMP    A20LOOP            ;Repeat processing
A90:
          MOV    AX,4C00H           ;End processing
          INT    21H
A10MAIN   ENDP
```

Figure 20-2a Printing an ASCII File

page break, such as at the end of a procedure; the usual method is to hold down the Alt key and press numbers on the numeric keypad, such as 012 for Form Feed.

You could revise the program for INT 21H function 05H to send each character directly to the printer, thereby eliminating the definition and use of the print area.

```
;               Request file name:
;               -----------------
B10PROMP  PROC   NEAR
          CALL   Q20CURS            ;Set cursor
          MOV    AH,40H             ;Prompt for filename
          MOV    BX,01              ;Handle for screen
          MOV    CX,13              ;No. of characters
          LEA    DX,PROMPT
          INT    21H
          MOV    AH,0AH             ;Accept filename
          LEA    DX,PATHPAR
          INT    21H
          MOVZX  BX,NAMELEN         ;Insert zero at end
          MOV    FILENAME[BX],0     ; of filespec
          RET
B10PROMP  ENDP
;               Open disk file:
;               --------------
C10OPEN   PROC   NEAR
          MOV    AH,3DH             ;Request open
          MOV    AL,00              ;Read only
          LEA    DX,FILENAME
          INT    21H
          JNC    C20                ;Test carry flag,
          CALL   X10ERR             ; error if set
          JMP    C90
C20:
          MOV    HANDLE,AX          ;Save handle
          MOV    AH,1AH             ;Set DTA
          LEA    DX,FILEDTA         ;
          INT    21H                ;
          MOV    AH,4EH             ;Find file
          MOV    CX,0               ; and get
          LEA    DX,FILENAME        ; file size
          INT    21H
C90:      RET
C10OPEN   ENDP
;               Read disk sector:
;               ----------------
D10READ   PROC   NEAR
          MOV    AH,3FH             ;Request read
          MOV    BX,HANDLE          ;Device
          MOV    CX,512             ;Length
          LEA    DX,SECTOR          ;Buffer
          INT    21H
          MOV    ENDCDE,AX
          RET
D10READ   ENDP
;               Transfer data to print line:
;               ---------------------------
E10XFER   PROC   NEAR
          CLD                       ;Set left-to-right
          LEA    SI,SECTOR          ;Initialize
E20:
          LEA    DI,PRTAREA
          MOV    COUNT,00
```

Figure 20-2b Printing an ASCII File

```
E30:        LEA     DX,SECTOR+512
            CMP     SI,DX              ;End of sector?
            JNE     E40                ;  no,  bypass
            CALL    D10READ            ;  yes, read next
            CMP     ENDCDE,00          ;End of file?
            JE      E90                ;  yes, exit
            LEA     SI,SECTOR
E40:
            MOV     BX,COUNT
            CMP     BX,120             ;At end of print area?
            JB      E50                ;  no,  bypass
            MOV     [DI+BX],0D0AH      ;  yes, set CR/LF
            CALL    P10PRNT
            LEA     DI,PRTAREA         ;Reinitialize
            MOV     COUNT,00
E50:
            LODSB                      ;[SI] to AL, INC SI
            MOV     BX,COUNT
            MOV     [DI+BX],AL         ;Character to print line
            INC     BX
            DEC     FILESIZE           ;All chars processed?
            JZ      E90                ;  yes, exit
            CMP     AL,0AH             ;Line feed?
            JNE     E60                ;  no,  bypass
            CALL    P10PRNT            ;  yes, call print
            JMP     E20
E60:
            CMP     AL,09H             ;Tab character?
            JNE     E70                ;  no, bypass
            DEC     BX                 ;  yes, reset BX
            MOV     BYTE PTR [DI+BX],20H ;Clear tab to blank
            AND     BX,0FFF8H          ;Clear rightmost 3 bits,
            ADD     BX,08              ;  add 8 for tab stop
E70:
            MOV     COUNT,BX
            JMP     E30
E90:
            MOV     BX,COUNT           ;End of file
            MOV     BYTE PTR [DI+BX],0CH   ;Form feed
            CALL    P10PRNT            ;Print last line
            RET
E10XFER     ENDP
;                   Print line:
;                   ----------
P10PRNT     PROC    NEAR
            MOV     AH,40H             ;Request print
            MOV     BX,04
            MOV     CX,COUNT           ;Length
            INC     CX
            LEA     DX,PRTAREA
            INT     21H
            MOV     AX,2020H           ;Clear print line
            MOV     CX,60
            LEA     DI,PRTAREA
            REP STOSW
            RET
P10PRNT     ENDP
```

Figure 20-2c Printing an ASCII File

```
;               Scroll screen:
;               ------------
Q10SCR    PROC  NEAR
          MOV   AX,0600H            ;Request scroll
          MOV   BH,1EH              ;Set attribute
          MOV   CX,0000
          MOV   DX,184FH
          INT   10H
          RET
Q10SCR    ENDP
;               Set cursor:
;               ----------
Q20CURS   PROC  NEAR
          MOV   AH,02H              ;Request set
          MOV   BH,00               ;  cursor
          MOV   DH,ROW              ;Row
          MOV   DL,10               ;Column 10
          INT   10H
          INC   ROW                 ;Next screen row
          RET
Q20CURS   ENDP
;               Display disk error message:
;               --------------------------
X10ERR    PROC  NEAR
          CALL  Q20CURS             ;Set cursor
          MOV   AH,40H              ;Request display
          MOV   BX,01               ;Handle
          MOV   CX,20               ;Length
          LEA   DX,OPENMSG          ;Error message
          INT   21H
          MOV   ENDCDE,01           ;Error indicator
          RET
X10ERR    ENDP
          END   A10MAIN
```

Figure 20-2d Printing an ASCII File

INT 21H FUNCTION 05H: PRINT CHARACTER

The original INT 21H function 05H also provides print facilities. To use it, load function 05H in the AH register and the character that you want to print in the DL, as follows:

```
MOV  AH,05H      ;Request print character
MOV  DL,char     ;Character to print
INT  21H         ;Call interrupt service
```

These instructions are adequate for sending a single character to the printer. However, printing typically involves a full or partial line of text and requires the program to step through a line formatted in the data area.

The following example illustrates printing a full line. It first initializes the address of HEADING in the SI register and sets the CX to the length of HEADING. The loop at P20 then extracts each character successively from HEADING and sends it to the printer. Because the first character in HEADING is a Form Feed and the last two characters are Line Feeds, the heading prints at the top of a new page and is followed by a double space. The code is as follows:

```
HEADING  DB    0CH,'Mountain Outfitting Corp.',0DH,0AH,0AH
         ...
```

```
            MOV   CX,29          ;Initialize length and
            LEA   SI,HEADING     ; address of heading
P20:
            MOV   AH,05H         ;Request print
            MOV   DL,[SI]        ;  character from heading
            INT   21H            ;Call interrupt service
            INC   SI             ;Next character in heading
            LOOP  P20            ;Loop 29 times
```

If the printer is not turned on, the system displays a message, "Out of paper". If you turn on the power, the program begins printing correctly. You can also press Ctrl+Break to cancel execution of the print operation.

SPECIAL PRINTER CONTROL CHARACTERS

We have already examined the use of the basic printer control characters, Tab, Line Feed, Form Feed, and Carriage Return. Other commands suitable for most printers are the following:

DECIMAL	HEX	ACTION
08	08	Backspace
11	0B	Vertical Tab
14	0E	Turn on expanded mode
15	0F	Turn on condensed mode
18	12	Turn off condensed mode
20	14	Turn off expanded mode

Some print commands require a preceding Esc (escape) character (1BH):

1B	30	Set line spacing to 8 lines per inch
1B	32	Set line spacing to 6 lines per inch
1B	45	Set on emphasized printing mode
1B	46	Set off emphasized printing mode

You can send control characters to the printer in two ways:

1. Define control characters in the data area. The following sets condensed mode, sets 8 lines per inch, prints a title, and causes a carriage return and line feed:
```
HEADING  DB  0FH, 1BH, 30H, 'Mountain Outfitting Corp.', 0DH, 0AH
```
2. Use function 05H to send the characters to the printer:
```
MOV  AH,05H    ;Request print
MOV  DL,0FH    ;Request condensed mode
INT  21H       ;Call interrupt service
```

All subsequent characters print in condensed mode until the program sends another command that resets the mode.

The foregoing commands do not necessarily work for all printer models. Check your manual for the printer's specific commands.

INT 17H FUNCTIONS FOR PRINTING

INT 17H provides facilities for printing at the BIOS level. Valid printer ports for LPT1, LPT2, and LPT3 are 0 (the default), 1, and 2, respectively. INT 17H provides three functions, as specified in the AH register:

1. Issue function 02H first to determine the printer's status, via a selected port number. Include this status test before every attempt to print. If the printer is available, then
2. Issue function 01H to initialize the printer port, and
3. Issue function 00H operations to send characters to the printer.

The operations return the printer status to the AH, with one or more bits set to 1:

BIT	CAUSE	BIT	CAUSE
0	Time out	5	Out of paper
3	Input/output error	6	Acknowledged from printer
4	Selected	7	Not busy

If the printer is already switched on and ready, the operation returns 90H (binary 10010000): The printer is not busy, but is selected, a valid condition. Printer errors are bit 5 (out of paper) and bit 3 (output error). If the printer is not switched on, the operation returns B0H, or binary 10110000, indicating "Out of paper".

INT 17H Function 00H: Print a Character

This operation causes printing of one character and allows for printer ports 0, 1, or 2. To use it, load the character in the AL and the printer port number in the DX:

```
MOV  AH,00H     ;Request print
MOV  AL,char    ;Character to be printed
MOV  DX,00      ;Select printer port 0
INT  17H        ;Call interrupt service
```

The operation returns the status to the AH register. The recommended practice is to use function 02H first to check the printer status.

INT 17H Function 01H: Initialize the Printer Port

This operation selects a port, resets the printer, and initializes it for data. The following example selects port 0:

```
MOV  AH,01H     ;Request initialize port
MOV  DX,00      ;Select printer port 0
INT  17H        ;Call interrupt service
```

Because the operation sends a Form Feed character to the printer, you can use it to set the forms to the top-of-page position, although most printers do this automatically when turned on. The operation returns a status code in the AH.

INT 17H Function 02H: Get Printer Port Status

The purpose of this operation is to determine the status of the printer. The following example selects port 0:

```
MOV   AH,02H          ;Request read port
MOV   DX,00           ;Select printer port 0
INT   17H             ;Call interrupt service
TEST  AH,00101001B    ;Ready?
JNZ   errormsg        ;  no, display message
```

The operation returns the same printer port status as function 01H. When the program runs, if the printer is not initially turned on, BIOS is unable to return a message automatically—your program is supposed to test and act upon the printer status. If your program does not check the status, your only indication is the cursor blinking. If you turn on the printer at this point, some of the output data is lost. Consequently, before executing any BIOS print operations, check the port status; if there is an error, display a message. (INT 21H performs this checking automatically, although its message, "Out of paper," applies to various conditions.) When the printer is switched on, the message no longer appears and printing begins normally with no loss of data.

At any time, a printer may run out of forms or may be inadvertently switched off. If you are writing a program for others to use, include a status test (function 02H) before every attempt to print.

KEY POINTS

- After printing is completed, use a Line Feed or Form Feed command to clear the printer buffer.
- INT 21H function 40H prints strings of characters, whereas INT 21H function 05H and BIOS INT 17H print a single character at a time.
- The system displays a message if there is a printer error, although BIOS returns only a status code. When using BIOS INT 17H, use function 02H to check the printer status before printing.

QUESTIONS

20-1. Provide the printer control characters for (a) Carriage Return; (b) Line Feed; (c) Form Feed; (d) Horizontal Tab.

20-2. Code a program using INT 21H function 40H for the following requirements: (a) Eject the forms to the next page; (b) print your name; (c) perform a carriage return and a line feed, and print your street address; (d) perform a carriage return and line feed, and print your city and state; (e) eject the forms.

20-3. Revise Question 20-2 to use INT 21H function 05H.

20-4. Define a heading line that provides for a carriage return and form feed operation, sets condensed mode, defines a title (any name), and turns off condensed mode.

20-5. Revise Question 20-3 so that the name is printed in expanded mode, street and address in condensed mode, and city-state in normal size but emphasized mode.

20-6. INT 17H for printing returns an error code in the AH. What do the following codes mean? (a) 08H; (b) 10H; (c) 90H.

20-7. Revise Question 20-2 to use INT 17H. Include a test for the printer status.

20-8. Revise Question 20-2 so that the program performs parts (b), (c), and (d) five times.

20-9. Revise Figure 20-1 to run under INT 21H function 05H.

20-10. Revise Figure 20-2 so that it also displays the printed lines.

21 OTHER INPUT/OUTPUT FACILITIES

Objective: To describe the programming requirements for the mouse and the use of ports.

INTRODUCTION

This chapter describes the use of the mouse, accessing the PC's ports, the IN and OUT instructions, and generating sound through the PC's speaker. The instructions that are introduced are:

- INT 33H for mouse handling
- IN/INS and OUT/OUTS for accessing ports

MOUSE FEATURES

The mouse is a commonly used pointing device controlled by a software interface known as a driver that is normally installed by an entry in the CONFIG.SYS or AUTOEXEC.BAT file. The driver must be installed so that a program can recognize and respond to the mouse's actions.

Some basic mouse definitions follow:

- *Pixel:* The smallest addressable element on a screen. For text mode 03, for example, there are 8 pixels per byte.

- *Mouse pointer:* In text mode, the pointer is a flashing block, in reverse video; in graphics mode, the pointer is an arrowhead.
- *Mickey:* A unit of measure for movement of the mouse, approximately 1/200 of an inch.
- *Mickey count:* The number of mickeys the mouse ball rolls horizontally or vertically. The mouse driver uses the mickey count to move the pointer on the screen a certain number of pixels.
- *Threshold speed:* The speed in mickeys per second that the mouse must move to double the speed of the pointer on the screen. The default is 64 mickeys per second.

All mouse operations within a program are performed by standard INT 33H functions of the form

```
MOV  AX,function     ;Request mouse function
...                  ;Parameters (if any)
INT  33H             ;Call mouse driver
```

Note that unlike other INT operations that use the AH register, INT 33H functions are loaded in the *full AX register.*

The first mouse instruction that a program issues should be function 00H, which simply initializes the interface between the mouse driver and the program. Typically, you need issue this command just once, at the start of the program. Following function 00H, the program should execute function 01H, which causes the mouse pointer to appear on the screen. After that, you have a choice of a wide range of mouse operations.

MOUSE FUNCTIONS

The following are the mouse functions available for INT 33H, of which relatively few are commonly used:

00H	Initialize the mouse
01H	Display the mouse pointer
02H	Conceal the mouse pointer
03H	Get button status and pointer location
04H	Set pointer location
05H	Get button-press information
06H	Get button-release information
07H	Set horizontal limits for pointer
08H	Set vertical limits for pointer
09H	Set graphics pointer type
0AH	Set text pointer type
0BH	Read mouse-motion counters
0CH	Install interrupt handler for mouse events

0DH	Turn on light pen emulation
0EH	Turn off light pen emulation
0FH	Set mickey-to-pixel ratio
10H	Set pointer exclusion area
13H	Set double-speed threshold
14H	Swap mouse-event interrupt
15H	Get buffer size for mouse driver state
16H	Save mouse driver state
17H	Restore mouse driver state
18H	Install alternative handler for mouse events
19H	Get address of alternative handler
1AH	Set mouse sensitivity
1BH	Get mouse sensitivity
1CH	Set mouse interrupt rate
1DH	Select display page for pointer
1EH	Get display page for pointer
1FH	Disable mouse driver
20H	Enable mouse driver
21H	Reset mouse driver
22H	Set language for mouse driver messages
23H	Get language number
24H	Get mouse information

COMMON INT 33H OPERATIONS

In this section, we examine the more common INT 33H operations required for most programs that use a mouse.

Function 00H: Initialize the Mouse

This is the first command that a program issues for handling a mouse, and needs to be executed only once. Simply load the AX with function 00H, and issue INT 33H. The operation requires no input parameters, but returns these values:

- AX = 0000H if no mouse support is available or FFFFH if support is available
- BX = the number of mouse buttons (if support is available)

If mouse support is available, the operation *initializes the mouse driver* as follows:

- Sets the mouse pointer to the center of the screen
- Conceals the mouse pointer if it is visible

- Sets the mouse pointer display page to zero
- Sets the mouse pointer according to the screen mode: rectangle and inverse color for text or arrow shape for graphics
- Sets the mickey-to-pixel ratio, where horizontal ratio = 8 to 8 and vertical ratio = 16 to 8
- Sets the horizontal and vertical limits for the pointer to their minimum and maximum values
- Enables light pen emulation mode
- Sets the double-speed threshold to 64 mickeys per second, which you can change.

Function 01H: Display the Mouse Pointer

After issuing function 00H, use this operation to cause the mouse pointer to be displayed on the screen. The operation requires no input parameters and returns no values.

The mouse driver maintains a pointer flag that determines whether or not to display the pointer. It displays the pointer if the flag is zero and conceals it for any other value. Initially, the value is −1; function 01H increments the flag, thus causing the pointer to be displayed. (See also function 02H.)

Function 02H: Conceal the Mouse Pointer

The standard practice is to issue this function at the end of a program's execution, to cause the pointer to be concealed. The operation requires no input parameters and returns no values.

The pointer flag is displayed when it contains a zero value and is concealed for any other value. This function decrements the flag to force it to be concealed.

Function 03H: Get Button Status and Pointer Location

This function returns useful information about the mouse. It requires no input parameters, but returns these values:

- BX = Status of buttons, according to bit location, as follows:
  Bit 0 Left button (0 = up, 1 = pressed down)
  Bit 1 Right button (0 = up, 1 = pressed down)
  Bit 2 Center button (0 = up, 1 = pressed down)
  Bits 3–15 Reserved for internal use
- CX = Horizontal (x) coordinate
- DX = Vertical (y) coordinate

The horizontal and vertical coordinates are expressed in terms of *pixels,* even in text mode (8 per byte for video mode 03). The values are always within the minimum and maximum limits for the pointer.

Function 04H: Set Pointer Location

Use this operation to set the horizontal and vertical coordinates for the mouse pointer on the screen (the values for the location are in terms of pixels—8 per byte for video mode 03):

```
MOV  AX,04H           ;Request set mouse pointer
MOV  CX,horiz-locn    ;Horizontal location
MOV  DX,vertl-locn    ;Vertical location
INT  33H              ;Call mouse driver
```

The operation sets the pointer at the new location, adjusted as necessary if outside the minimum and maximum limits.

Example: Basic Mouse Operations

The following example illustrates the use of the mouse instructions covered to this point:

```
MOV   AX,00H    ;Request initialize mouse
INT   33H       ;Call mouse driver
CMP   AX,00H    ;Mouse available?
JE   exit       ;  no, exit
MOV   AX,01H    ;Request show mouse pointer
INT   33H       ;Call mouse driver
MOV   AX,04H    ;Request set mouse pointer
MOV   CX,24     ;Horizontal location
MOV   DX,16     ;Vertical location
INT   33H       ;Call mouse driver
...
MOV   AX,02H    ;Request hide mouse pointer
INT   33H       ;Call mouse driver
```

Function 05H: Get Button-Press Information

To use this function to return information about button presses, set the BX with the button number, where 0 = left, 1 = right, and 2 = center:

```
MOV  AX,05H          ;Request press information
MOV  BX,button-no    ;Button number
INT  33H             ;Call mouse driver
```

The operation returns the up/down status of all buttons and the press count and location of the requested button:

- AX = Status of buttons, according to bit location, as follows:
  Bit 0 Left button (0 = up, 1 = pressed down)
  Bit 1 Right button (0 = up, 1 = pressed down)
  Bit 2 Center button (0 = up, 1 = pressed down)

Bits 3–15 Reserved for internal use

- BX = Button-press counter
- CX = Horizontal (x) coordinate of last button press
- DX = Vertical (y) coordinate of last button press

The operation resets the button-press counter to zero.

Function 06H: Get Button-Release Information

To use this function to return information about button releases, set the BX with the button number (0 = left, 1 = right, and 2 = center):

```
MOV  AX,06H           ;Request release information
MOV  BX,button-no     ;Button number
INT  33H              ;Call mouse driver
```

The operation returns the up/down status of all buttons and the release count and location of the requested button, as follows:

- AX = Status of buttons, according to bit location, as follows:
  Bit 0 Left button (0 = up, 1 = pressed down)
  Bit 1 Right button (0 = up, 1 = pressed down)
  Bit 2 Center button (0 = up, 1 = pressed down)
  Bits 3–15 Reserved for internal use
- BX = Button release counter
- CX = Horizontal (x) coordinate of last button release
- DX = Vertical (y) coordinate of last button release

The operation resets the button release counter to zero.

Function 07H: Set Horizontal Limits for Pointer

You can use this operation to set the minimum and maximum horizontal limits for the pointer:

```
MOV  AX,07H          ;Request set horizontal limit
MOV  CX,min-locn     ;Minimum limit
MOV  DX,max-locn     ;Maximum limit
INT  33H             ;Call mouse driver
```

If the minimum value is greater than the maximum, the operation arbitrarily exchanges the values. If necessary, the operation also moves the pointer to within the new area. See also functions 08H and 10H.

Function 08H: Set Vertical Limits for Pointer

You can use this operation to set the minimum and maximum vertical limits for the pointer.

```
MOV  AX,08H          ;Request set vertical limit
MOV  CX,min-locn     ;Minimum limit
MOV  DX,max-locn     ;Maximum limit
INT  33H             ;Call mouse driver
```

If the minimum value is greater than the maximum, the operation arbitrarily exchanges the values. If necessary, the operation also moves the pointer inside the new area. See also functions 07H and 10H.

Function 0BH: Read Mouse-Motion Counters

This operation returns the horizontal and vertical mickey count since the last call to the function (within the range −32,768 to +32,767). Returned values are:

- CX = Horizontal count (a positive value means travel to the right, negative means to the left)
- DX = Vertical count (a positive value means travel downwards, negative means upwards)

Function 0CH: Install Interrupt Handler for Mouse Events

Your program may need to determine automatically when a mouse-related activity (or event) has occurred. The purpose of function 0CH is to provide an *event handler* whereby the mouse software interrupts your program and calls the event handler, which performs its required function and returns to your program's point of execution on completion of the task.

Load the CX with an event mask to indicate the actions for which the handler is to respond and the ES:DX with the segment:offset address of the interrupt handler routine:

```
MOV  AX,0CH          ;Request interrupt handler
LEA  CX,mask         ;Address of event mask
LEA  DX,handler      ;Address of handler (ES:DX)
INT  33H             ;Call mouse driver
```

Define the event mask with bits set as required:

0 = mouse pointer moved	4 = right button released
1 = left button pressed	5 = center button pressed
2 = left button released	6 = center button released
3 = right button pressed	7–15 = reserved, define as 0

Define the interrupt handler as a FAR procedure. The mouse driver uses a far call to enter the interrupt handler with these registers set:

- AX = The event mask as defined, except that bits are set only if the condition occurred
- BX = Button state (if set, bit 0 means left button down, bit 1 means right button down, and bit 2 means center button down)

- CX = Horizontal (x) coordinate
- DX = Vertical (y) coordinate
- SI = Last vertical mickey count
- DI = Last horizontal mickey count
- DS = Data segment for the mouse driver

On the program's entry into the interrupt handler, push all registers and initialize the DS register to the address of your data segment. Within the handler, use only *BIOS,* not DOS, interrupts. On exit, pop all registers.

Function 10H: Set Pointer Exclusion Area

This operation defines a screen area in which the pointer is not displayed:

```
MOV  AX,10H         ;Request set exclusion area
MOV  CX,upleft-x    ;Upper left x coordinate
MOV  DX,upleft-y    ;Upper left y coordinate
MOV  SI,lowrgt-x    ;Lower right x coordinate
MOV  DI,lowrgt-y    ;Lower right y coordinate
INT  33H            ;Call mouse driver
```

To replace the exclusion area, call the function again with different parameters, or reissue function 00H or 01H.

Function 13H: Set Double-Speed Threshold

This operation sets the threshold speed at which the pointer motion on the screen is doubled. Load the DX with the new value (the default is 64 mickeys per second). (See also function 1AH.)

Function 1AH: Set Mouse Sensitivity

Sensitivity concerns the number of mickeys that the mouse needs to move before the pointer is moved. Function 1AH sets the horizontal and vertical mouse motion in terms of the number of mickeys per 8 pixels, as well as the threshold speed at which the pointer motion on the screen is doubled (see also functions 0FH, 13H, and 1BH):

```
MOV  AX,1AH          ;Request set mouse sensitivity
MOV  BX,horzon       ;Horizontal mickeys (default = 8)
MOV  CX,vertic       ;Vertical mickeys (default = 16)
MOV  DX,threshold    ;Threshold speed (default = 64)
INT  33H             ;Call mouse driver
```

Function 1BH: Get Mouse Sensitivity

This operation returns the horizontal and vertical mouse motion in terms of number of mickeys per 8 pixels as well as the threshold speed at which the pointer motion on the screen is doubled. (See function 1AH for the registers and values that are returned.)

Function 1DH: Select Display Page for Pointer

The page for video display is set with INT 10H function 05H. For mouse operations, set the page number in the BX and issue INT 33H function 1DH.

Function 1EH: Get Display Page for Pointer

This operation returns the current video display page in the BX.

Function 24H: Get Mouse Information

This operation returns information about the version and type of mouse that is installed:

- BH = Major version number
- BL = Minor version number
- CH = Mouse type (1 = bus mouse, 2 = serial mouse, 3 = InPort mouse, 4 = PS/2 mouse, and 5 = HP mouse)

PROGRAM: USING THE MOUSE

The program in Figure 21-1 displays the horizontal and vertical positions of the pointer as a user moves the mouse. The main procedures are:

- A10MAIN Initializes the program, calls B10INIT, C10PTR, D10CONV, and Q30DISP, and ends processing when the user presses the left button.
- B10INIT Issues INT 33H function 00H to initialize the mouse (or to indicate that no mouse driver is present) and issues function 01H to cause the mouse pointer to display.
- C10PTR Issues function 03H to check and exit if the user has pressed the left button. If not pressed, the program converts the horizontal and vertical positions from pixel values to binary numbers (by shifting the values 3 bits to the right, effectively dividing by 8). If the location is the same as when it was previously checked, the routine repeats issuing function 03H; if the location has changed, control returns to the calling procedure.
- D10CONV Converts the binary values for horizontal and vertical screen locations to displayable ASCII characters. Note that with 8 pixels per byte, the horizontal value returned at screen column 79 (the rightmost location) is 79 × 8 = 632. The procedure divides this value by 8 to get, in this case, 79, the maximum case. Consequently, the conversion can correctly assume that values returned are within 0 through 79.
- E10HIDE Hides the pointer immediately before the program ends processing.
- Q30DISP Displays the horizontal and vertical values at the center of the screen as X = col and Y = row.

One way to improve this program would be to issue function 0CH to set an interrupt handler. In this way, the required instructions are automatically invoked whenever the mouse is active.

```
          page 60,132
TITLE     A21MOUSE (EXE)  Handling the mouse
          .MODEL SMALL
          .STACK 64
          .DATA
XBINARY   DW     0                 ;Binary X coordinate
YBINARY   DW     0                 ;Binary Y coordinate
ASCVAL    DW     ?                 ;ASCII field

;         Screen display fields:
DISPDATA  LABEL  BYTE
XMSG      DB     'X = '            ;X message
XASCII    DW     ?                 ;X ASCII value
          DB     '  '              ;
YMSG      DB     'Y = '            ;Y message
YASCII    DW     ?                 ;Y ASCII value
.286
          .CODE
A10MAIN   PROC   FAR
          MOV    AX,@data          ;Initialize
          MOV    DS,AX             ;  DS register
          CALL   Q10CLEAR          ;Clear screen
          CALL   B10INIT           ;Initialize mouse
          CMP    AX,00             ;Mouse installed?
          JE     A90               ;  no, exit
A20:
          CALL   C10PTR            ;Get mouse pointer
          CMP    BX,01             ;Button pressed?
          JE     A80               ;  yes, exit
          CALL   Q20CURS           ;Set cursor
          MOV    AX,XBINARY        ;
          CALL   D10CONV           ;X to ASCII
          MOV    AX,ASCVAL         ;
          MOV    XASCII,AX         ;
          MOV    AX,YBINARY        ;
          CALL   D10CONV           ;Y to  ASCII
          MOV    AX,ASCVAL         ;
          MOV    YASCII,AX         ;
          CALL   Q30DISP           ;Display X and Y values
          JMP    A20               ;Repeat
A80:
          CALL   E10HIDE           ;Hide mouse pointer
A90:
          CALL   Q10CLEAR          ;Clear screen
          MOV    AX,4C00H          ;End processing
          INT    21H
A10MAIN   ENDP
;                Initialize mouse pointer:
;                ------------------------
B10INIT   PROC   NEAR
          MOV    AX,00H            ;Request initialize
          INT    33H               ;  mouse
          CMP    AX,00             ;Mouse installed?
          JE     B90               ;  no, exit
          MOV    AX,01H            ;Show pointer
          INT    33H
B90:
          RET                      ;Return to caller
B10INIT   ENDP
```

Figure 21-1a Printing with Page Overflow and Headings

```
;                       Get mouse pointer location:
;                       --------------------------
C10PTR      PROC        NEAR
C20:        MOV         AX,03H              ;Get pointer location
            INT         33H
            CMP         BX,01               ;Right button pressed?
            JE          C90                 ;  yes, means exit
            SHR         CX,03               ;Divide pixel value
            SHR         DX,03               ;  by 8
            CMP         CX,XBINARY          ;Has pointer location
            JNE         C30                 ;  changed?
            CMP         DX,YBINARY          ;
            JE          C20                 ;  no, repeat operation
C30:        MOV         XBINARY,CX          ;  yes, save new locatior
            MOV         YBINARY,DX          ;
C90:        RET                             ;Return to caller
C10PTR      ENDP
;                       Convert binary to ASCII:
;                       -----------------------
D10CONV     PROC        NEAR                ;AX = binary X or Y
            MOV         ASCVAL,2020H        ;Clear ASCII field
            MOV         CX,10               ;Set divide factor
            LEA         SI,ASCVAL+1         ;Load ASCVAL address
            CMP         AX,CX               ;Compare location to 10
            JB          D20                 ;  lower, bypass
            DIV         CL                  ;  higher, divide by 10
            OR          AH,30H              ;Insert ASCII 3s
            MOV         [SI],AH             ;Store in rightmost byte
            DEC         SI                  ;Decr address of ASCVAL
D20:        OR          AL,30H              ;Insert ASCII 3s
            MOV         [SI],AL             ;Store in leftmost byte
            RET                             ;Return to caller
D10CONV     ENDP
;                       Hide mouse pointer before ending:
;                       --------------------------------
E10HIDE     PROC        NEAR
            MOV         AX,02H              ;Request hide pointer
            INT         33H
            RET                             ;Return to caller
E10HIDE     ENDP
;                       Screen operations:
;                       -----------------
Q10CLEAR    PROC        NEAR
            MOV         AX,0600H            ;Request clear screen
            MOV         BH,30H              ;Colors
            MOV         CX,00               ;Full
            MOV         DX,184FH            ;  screen
            INT         10H
            RET                             ;Return to caller
Q10CLEAR    ENDP

Q20CURS     PROC        NEAR
            MOV         AH,02H              ;Set cursor
            MOV         BH,0                ;Page 0
            MOV         DH,0                ;Row
            MOV         DL,25               ;Column
            INT         10H
            RET                             ;Return to caller
Q20CURS     ENDP
```

Figure 21-1b Using the Mouse

```
Q30DISP  PROC  NEAR
         MOV   AH,40H            ;Request display
         MOV   BX,01             ;Screen handle
         MOV   CX,14             ;Number of characters
         LEA   DX,DISPDATA       ;Display area
         INT   21H
         RET                     ;Return to caller
Q30DISP  ENDP
         END   A10MAIN
```

Figure 21-1c Using the Mouse

PORTS

A *port* is a device that connects a processor to the external world. Through a port, a processor receives a signal from an input device and sends a signal to an output device. Ports are identified by their addresses, in the range of 0H–3FFH, or 1,024 ports in all. Note that these addresses are not conventional memory addresses. You can use the IN and OUT instructions to handle I/O directly at the port level.

IN transfers data from an input port to the AL if a byte and to the AX if a word, whereas OUT transfers data to an output port from the AL if a byte and from the AX if a word. The general formats are

[label:]	IN	accum-reg,port
[label:]	OUT	port,accum-reg

You can specify a port address either *statically* or *dynamically*:

Statically. Use an operand from 0 through 255 directly as

```
Input   IN  AL,port#    ;Input one byte from port
Output  OUT port#,AX    ;Output one word to port
```

Dynamically. Use the contents of the DX register, 0 through 65,535, indirectly. You can use this method to process consecutive port addresses by incrementing the DX. The following example uses port 60H:

```
MOV DX,60H    ;Port 60H (keyboard)
IN  AL,DX     ;Get byte from port
```

Some of the major port addresses are:

020H–023H	Interrupt mask registers
040H–043H	Timer/counter
060H	Input from the keyboard
061H	Speaker (bits 0 and 1)
200H--20FH	Game controller
278H–27FH	Parallel port adapter LPT3
2F8H–2FFH	Serial port COM2

378H–37FH	Parallel port adapter LPT2
3B0H–3BBH	Monochrome display adapter
3BCH–3BFH	Parallel port adapter LPT1
3C0H–3CFH	VGA/EGA
3D0H–3DFH	Color graphics adapter (CGA)
3F0H–3F7H	Disk controller
3F8H–3FFH	Serial port COM1

Although the standard practice is to use DOS and BIOS interrupts, you may safely bypass BIOS when you access ports 21H, 40–42H, 60H, 61H, and 201H. For example, on bootup, a ROM BIOS routine scans the system for the addresses of the serial and parallel port adapters. If the serial port addresses are found, BIOS places them in its data area, beginning at memory location 40:00H; if the parallel port addresses are found, BIOS places them in its data area, beginning at location 40:08H. Each location has space for four 1-word entries. The BIOS table for a system with two serial ports and two parallel ports could look like this:

```
40:00 F803 COM1        40:08 7803 LPT1
40:02 F802 COM2        40:0A 7802 LPT2
40:04 0000 unused      40:0C 0000 unused
40:06 0000 unused      40:0E 0000 unused
```

For example, to use BIOS INT 17H to print a character, insert the printer port number in the DX register:

```
MOV  AH,00H      ;Request print
MOV  AL,char     ;Character to print
MOV  DX,0        ;Printer port 0 = LPT1
INT  17H         ;Call interrupt service
```

Some programs allow for printing only via LPT1. If you have two printer ports installed as LPT1 and LPT2, you could use the program in Figure 21-2 to reverse (toggle) their addresses in the BIOS table. In the program, BIOSDAT defines the BIOS data area, and PARLPRT defines the first of the four word-size port addresses.

STRING INPUT/OUTPUT

You can also transfer data (on the 80286 and later) by means of the INSn and OUTSn string instructions. These work much like the string instructions covered in Chapter 12.

The INSn Instruction

The instructions for the INSn operation are:

```
INSTRUCTION        EXAMPLE
INS                INS ES:destination,DX
INSB               REP INSB
```

```
          page 60,132
TITLE     A21PORT (COM)  Switch printer ports LPT1 & 2
BIOSDAT   SEGMENT AT 40H            ;BIOS data area
          ORG    8H                 ;Printer port addresses
PARLPRT   DW     4 DUP(?)           ;4 words
BIOSDAT   ENDS

CODESG    SEGMENT PARA 'code'
          ASSUME DS:BIOSDAT,CS:CODESG
          ORG    100H
BEGIN:
          MOV    AX,BIOSDAT         ;Init address of BIOS
          MOV    DS,AX              ;  data area in DS

          MOV    AX,PARLPRT(0)      ;LPT1 address to AX
          MOV    BX,PARLPRT(2)      ;LPT2 address to BX
          MOV    PARLPRT(0),BX      ;Exchange
          MOV    PARLPRT(2),AX      ;  addresses
          MOV    AX,4C00H           ;End processing
          INT    21H
CODESG    ENDS
          END    BEGIN
```

Figure 21-2 Switching Printer Ports

```
INSW            REP INSW
INSD (80386+)   REP INSD
```

The receiving data (or destination) is a "string" addressed by ES:DI, and the DX contains the address of the input port. The normal practice is to use INSn with the REP prefix and the CX containing the number of items (bytes, words, or doublewords) to be received. If the direction flag (DF) is clear, the DI is incremented by the size of each item received; if the DF is set, the DI is decremented.

The following example illustrates the INSn operation:

```
MOV  CX,no-bytes        ;Number of bytes
LEA  DI,destination     ;String destination (ES:DI)
MOV  DX,port-no         ;Port number
REP INSB                ;Receive bytes
```

The OUTSn Instruction

The instructions for the OUTSn operation are:

INSTRUCTION	EXAMPLE
OUTS	OUTS DX,DS:source
OUTSB	REP OUTSB
OUTSW	REP OUTSW
OUTSD (80386+)	REP OUTSD

The sending data (or source) is a string addressed by DS:SI, and the DX contains the address of the output port. The normal practice is to use OUTSn with the REP prefix and the CX containing the number of items (bytes, words, or doublewords) to be sent. If the direction flag (DF) is clear, the SI is incremented by the size of each item received; if the DF is set, the SI is decremented.

The following example illustrates the OUTSn operation:

```
MOV   CX,no-bytes     ;Number of bytes
LEA   SI,source       ;String destination (DS:SI)
MOV   DX,port-no      ;Port number
REP   OUTSB           ;Send bytes
```

GENERATING SOUND

The PC generates sound by means of a built-in permanent magnet speaker. You can select one of two ways to drive the speaker or combine both ways: (1) Use bit 1 of port 61H to activate the Intel 8255A-5 Programmable Peripheral Interface (PPI) chip, or (2) use the gating of the Intel 8353-5 Programmable Interval Timer (PIT). The clock generates a 1.19318-Mhz signal. The PPI controls gate 2 at bit 0 of port 61H.

The program in Figure 21-3 generates a series of notes in ascending frequency. DURTION provides the length of each note, and TONE determines the frequency. The program initially accesses port 61H and saves the value that the operation delivers. A CLI instruction clears the interrupt flag to enable a constant tone. The interval timer generates a clock tick of 18.2 ticks per second that (unless you code CLI) interrupts execution of your program and causes the tone to wobble.

The contents of TONE determine its frequency; high values cause low frequencies and low values cause high frequencies. After the routine B10SPKR plays each note, it increases the frequency of TONE by means of a right shift of 1 bit (effectively halving its value). Because decreasing TONE in this example reduces how long it plays, the routine also increases DURTION by means of a left shift of 1 bit (effectively doubling its value).

The program ends when TONE is reduced to 0. The initial values in DURTION and TONE have no technical significance. You can experiment with other values and try executing the program without the CLI instruction.

You could use any variation of the logic to play a sequence of notes, in order, for example, to draw a user's attention. You could also revise the program as per Question 21-7.

KEY POINTS

- In text mode, the mouse pointer is a flashing block, in reverse video; in graphics mode, the pointer is an arrowhead.
- Mouse operations use INT 33H, with a function code loaded in the AX.
- The first mouse operation to execute should be function 00H, which initializes the mouse driver.
- Function 01H is required to display the mouse pointer, 03H to get the button status, and 04H to get the pointer location.
- Through a port, a processor receives a signal from an input device and sends a signal to an output device. Ports are identified by their addresses, in the range 0H–3FFH, or 1,024 in all.

```
            page 60,132
TITLE       A21SOUND (COM)  Produce sound from speaker
SOUNSG      SEGMENT PARA 'Code'
            ASSUME CS:SOUNSG,DS:SOUNSG,SS:SOUNSG
            ORG     100H
BEGIN:      JMP     SHORT A10MAIN
; -----------------------------------------------------
DURTION     DW      10000            ;Length of tone
TONE        DW      512H             ;Frequency
; -----------------------------------------------------
A10MAIN     PROC    NEAR
            IN      AL,61H           ;Get port data
            PUSH    AX               ;  and save
            CLI                      ;Clear interrupts
            CALL    B10SPKR          ;Produce sound
            POP     AX               ;Reset
            OUT     61H,AL           ;  port value
            STI                      ;Reset interrupts
            MOV     AX,4C00H         ;End
            INT     21H              ;  processing
A10MAIN     ENDP

B10SPKR     PROC    NEAR
B20:        MOV     DX,DURTION       ;Set duration of sound
B30:
            AND     AL,11111100B     ;Clear bits 0 & 1
            OUT     61H,AL           ;Transmit to speaker
            MOV     CX,TONE          ;Set length
B40:
            LOOP    B40              ;Time delay
            OR      AL,00000010B     ;Set bit 1 on
            OUT     61H,AL           ;Transmit to speaker
            MOV     CX,TONE          ;Set length
B50:
            LOOP    B50              ;Time delay
            DEC     DX               ;Reduce duration
            JNZ     B30              ;Continue?
            SHL     DURTION,1        ;  no, increase length
            SHR     TONE,1           ;Reduce frequency
            JNZ     B20              ;Now zero?
            RET                      ;  yes, return
B10SPKR     ENDP

SOUNSG      ENDS
            END     BEGIN
```

Figure 21-3 Generating Sound

- The PC generates sound by means of a built-in permanent magnet speaker. You can select one of two ways to drive the speaker or combine both ways.

QUESTIONS

21-1. Explain these terms: (a) mickey; (b) mickey count; (c) mouse pointer.

21-2. Provide the INT 33H function for each of the following mouse operations:
   (a) Conceal the mouse pointer
   (b) Get button-release information
   (c) Set pointer location

(d) Install interrupt handler for mouse events
(e) Get button-press information
(f) Read mouse-motion counters

21-3. Explain the purpose of the mouse pointer flag.

21-4. Code the instructions for the following requirements:
(a) Initialize the mouse
(b) Display the mouse pointer
(c) Get mouse information
(d) Set the mouse pointer on row 16, to the center column
(e) Get mouse sensitivity
(f) Get button status and pointer location
(g) Conceal the mouse pointer.

21-5. Combine the requirements in Question 21-4 into a full program. You can run the program under DEBUG, although at times DEBUG may scroll the pointer off the screen.

21-6. Refer to Figure 21-2 and revise the instructions so that the program reverses the addresses for COM1 and COM2.

21-7. Revise the program in Figure 21-3 for the following requirements: Generate notes that decrease in frequency; initialize TONE to 01 and DURTION to a high value. On each loop, increase the value in TONE, decrease the value in DURTION, and end the program when DURTION equals 0.

PART F—ADVANCED PROGRAMMING

22 DEFINING AND USING MACROS

Objective: To explain the definition and use of macro instructions.

INTRODUCTION

For each symbolic instruction that you code, the assembler generates one machine-language instruction. On the other hand, for each coded statement in a high-level language such as C or BASIC, the compiler may generate many machine-language instructions. In this regard, you can think of a high-level language as consisting of a set of *macro* statements.

The assembler has facilities that you can use to define macros. You define a unique name for the macro, along with the set of assembly language instructions that the macro is to generate. Then, wherever you need to code the set of instructions, simply code the name of the macro, and the assembler automatically generates your defined instructions.

Macros are useful for the following purposes:

- To simplify and reduce the amount of repetitive coding.
- To reduce errors caused by repetitive coding.
- To make an assembly program more readable.

Examples of functions that may be implemented by macros are input/output operations that load registers and perform interrupts, conversions of ASCII and binary data, multiword arithmetic operations, and string-handling routines.

Here is the basic format of a *macro definition:*

macroname	MACRO [parameter list] [instructions] ENDM	;Define macro ;Body of macro ;End of macro

The MACRO directive on the first line tells the assembler that the instructions that follow, up to ENDM, are to be part of a macro definition. The ENDM ("end macro") directive ends the macro definition. The instructions between MACRO and ENDM comprise the body of the macro definition.

To include a macro within your program, you first define it or copy it from a macro library. The macro definition appears before the coding of any segment.

TWO SIMPLE MACRO DEFINITIONS

Let's first examine a simple macro definition that initializes the segment registers for an .EXE program:

```
INITZ  MACRO              ;Define macro
       MOV   AX,@data     ; } Body of
       MOV   DS,AX        ; } macro
       MOV   ES,AX        ; } definition
       ENDM               ;End of macro
```

The name of this macro is INITZ, although any other unique valid name is acceptable. The names referenced in the macro definition—@data, AX, DS, and ES—must be defined elsewhere in the program or must otherwise be known to the assembler.

You may subsequently use the macro instruction INITZ in the code segment where you want to initialize the registers. When the assembler encounters the macro instruction INITZ, it scans a table of symbolic instructions and, failing to find an entry, checks for macro instructions. Because the program contains a definition of the macro INITZ, the assembler substitutes the body of the definition, generating the instructions—the *macro expansion.* A program would use the macro instruction INITZ only once, although other macros are designed to be used any number of times, and each time the assembler generates the macro expansion.

Let's also define a second macro named FINISH that handles normal exiting from a program:

```
FINISH  MACRO             ;Define macro
        MOV   AX,4C00H    ;  Request
        INT   21H         ;  end of processing
        ENDM              ;End of macro
```

Figure 22-1 provides a listing of the assembled program that defines and uses both INITZ and FINISH. This particular assembler version lists the macro expansion with the number 1 to the left of each instruction to indicate that a macro instruction generated it.

```
                                        page 60,132
                                 TITLE  A22MACR1 (EXE)  Simple macros
                                 ; ------------------------------------
                                 INITZ  MACRO               ;Define macro
                                        MOV   AX,@data      ;Initialize segment
                                        MOV   DS,AX         ;  registers
                                        MOV   ES,AX
                                        ENDM                ;End macro

                                 FINISH MACRO               ;Define macro
                                        MOV   AX,4C00H      ;End processing
                                        INT   21H
                                        ENDM                ;End macro
                                 ; -----------------------------------------------
                                        .MODEL SMALL
                                        .STACK 64
                                        .DATA
0000 54 65 73 74 20 6D           MESSGE DB    'Test macro instruction',13,10,'$'
     61 63 72 6F 20 69
     6E 73 74 72 75 63
     74 69 6F 6E 0D 0A
     24
                                 ; -----------------------------------------------
                                        .CODE
0000                             BEGIN  PROC   FAR
                                        INITZ               ;Macro instruction
0000 B8 ---- R     1                    MOV   AX,@data      ;Initialize segment
0003 8E D8         1                    MOV   DS,AX         ;  registers
0005 8E C0         1                    MOV   ES,AX
0007 B4 09                              MOV   AH,09H        ;Request display
0009 8D 16 0000 R                       LEA   DX,MESSGE     ;Message
000D CD 21                              INT   21H
                                        FINISH
000F B8 4C00       1                    MOV   AX,4C00H      ;End processing
0012 CD 21         1                    INT   21H
0014                             BEGIN  ENDP
                                        END   BEGIN
```

Figure 22-1 Simple Assembled Macro Instructions

(TASM shows the '1' at the far left of the listing.) A macro expansion indicates only instructions for which object code is generated, so that directives like ASSUME or PAGE coded in the macro definition would not appear.

It's hardly worth bothering to define a macro that is to be used only once, but you could catalog the macro in a library for use with all programs. A later section explains how to catalog macros in a library and how to include them automatically in a program.

USING PARAMETERS IN MACROS

To make a macro more flexible, you can define parameters in the operand as *dummy arguments.* The following macro definition named PROMPT provides for the use of INT 21H function 09H to display messages:

```
PROMPT  MACRO MESSGE        ;Dummy argument
        MOV   AH,09H
        LEA   DX,MESSGE
        INT   21H
        ENDM                ;End of macro
```

When using this macro instruction, you have to supply the name of the message, which references a data area terminated by a dollar sign.

A dummy argument in a macro definition tells the assembler to match its name with any occurrence of the same name in the macro body. For example, the dummy argument MESSGE also occurs in the LEA instruction. Let's say that the program defines a prompt named MESSAGE2 as

```
MESSAGE2 DB  'Enter the date as mm/dd/yy'
```

You now want to use the macro instruction PROMPT to display MESSAGE2. To this end, you supply the name MESSAGE2 as a parameter:

```
PROMPT  MESSAGE2
```

The parameter (MESSAGE2) in the macro instruction matches the dummy argument (MESSGE) in the original macro definition:

```
Macro definition:  PROMPT MACRO MESSGE  (argument)
                                   |
Macro instruction:    PROMPT  MESSAGE2  (parameter)
```

The assembler has already matched the argument in the original macro definition with operand in the LEA statement. It now substitutes the parameter(s) of the macro instruction MESSAGE2 with the dummy argument, MESSGE, in the macro definition. The assembler substitutes MESSAGE2 for the occurrence of MESSGE in the LEA instruction and would substitute it for any other occurrence of MESSGE.

The macro definition and macro expansion are shown in full in Figure 22-2. The program also defines the macros INITZ and FINISH at the start and uses them in the code segment.

A dummy argument may contain any valid name, including a register name such as CX. You may define a macro with any number of dummy arguments, separated by commas, up to column 120 of a line (depending on the assembler version). The assembler substitutes parameters of the macro instruction for dummy arguments in the macro definition, entry for entry, from left to right.

MACRO COMMENTS

You may code comments in a macro definition to clarify its purpose. A semicolon or a COMMENT directive indicates a comment line. The following example of a comment uses semicolons:

```
PROMPT  MACRO  MESSGE
;       This macro permits a display of messages
        MOV   AH,09H       ;Request display
        LEA   DX,MESSGE    ;  prompt
        INT   21H
        ENDM
```

```
                                      page   60,132
                               TITLE  A22MACR2 (EXE)  Use of parameters
                               ; ------------------------------------------
                               INITZ  MACRO            ;Define macro
                                      MOV   AX,@data   ;Initialize segment
                                      MOV   DS,AX      ;  registers
                                      MOV   ES,AX
                                      ENDM             ;End macro

                               PROMPT MACRO MESSGE     ;Define macro
                                      MOV   AH,09H     ;Request display
                                      LEA   DX,MESSGE  ;  prompt
                                      INT   21H
                                      ENDM             ;End macro

                               FINISH MACRO            ;Define macro
                                      MOV   AX,4C00H   ;End processing
                                      INT   21H
                                      ENDM             ;End macro
                               ; ------------------------------------------
                                      .MODEL SMALL
                                      .STACK 64
                                      .DATA
0000 43 75 73 74 6F 6D         MESSG1 DB    'Customer name?', '$'
     65 72 20 6E 61 6D
     65 3F 24
000F 43 75 73 74 6F 6D         MESSG2 DB    'Customer address?', '$'
     65 72 20 61 64 64
     72 65 73 73 3F 24
                               ; ------------------------------------------
                                      .CODE
0000                           BEGIN  PROC  FAR
                                      INITZ
0000 B8 ---- R     1                  MOV   AX,@data   ;Initialize segment
0003 8E D8         1                  MOV   DS,AX      ;  registers
0005 8E C0         1                  MOV   ES,AX
                                      PROMPT MESSG2
0007 B4 09         1                  MOV   AH,09H     ;Request display
0009 8D 16 000F R  1                  LEA   DX,MESSG2  ;  prompt
000D CD 21         1                  INT   21H
                                      FINISH
000F B8 4C00       1                  MOV   AX,4C00H   ;End processing
0012 CD 21         1                  INT   21H
0014                           BEGIN  ENDP
                                      END   BEGIN
```

Figure 22-2 Using Macro Parameters

Because the default is to list only instructions that generate object code, the assembler does not automatically display a comment when it expands a macro definition. If you want a comment to appear within an expansion, use the listing directive .LALL ("list all," including the leading period) prior to requesting the macro instruction:

```
.LALL
PROMPT MESSAGE1
```

A macro definition could contain a number of comments, but you may want to list some and suppress others. Still use .LALL to list them, but code double semicolons (;;) before comments that are always to be suppressed. (The assembler's default is .XALL, which causes a listing only of instructions that generate object code.)

On the other hand, you may not want to list any of the source code of a macro expansion, especially if the macro instruction is used several times in a program. In that case, code the listing directive .SALL ("suppress all"), which reduces the size of the printed program, although it has no effect on the size of the generated object program.

A listing directive holds effect throughout a program until another listing directive is encountered. You can place them in a program to cause some macros to list only the generated object code (.XALL), some to list both object code and comments (.LALL), and some to suppress listing both object code and comments (.SALL). For .LALL and .SALL, TASM Ideal mode uses the terms %MACS and %NOMACS. MASM 6.0 introduced the terms .LISTMACROALL, LISTMACRO, and .NOLISTMACRO for .LALL, .XALL, and .SALL, respectively.

The program in Figure 22-3 illustrates the preceding features. It contains the macros INITZ, FINISH, and PROMPT, described earlier. The code segment contains the listing directive .SALL to suppress listing the expansion of INITZ and FINISH and the first expansion of PROMPT. For the second use of PROMPT, the listing directive .LALL causes the assembler to list the comment and the expansion of the macro. But note that in the macro definition for PROMPT, the comment in the macro expansion containing a double semicolon (;;) is not listed.

USING A MACRO WITHIN A MACRO DEFINITION

A macro definition may contain a reference to another defined macro. Consider a simple macro named INT21 that loads a function in the AH register and issues INT 21H:

```
INT21  MACRO FUNCTN
       MOV   AH,FUNCTN
       INT   21H
       ENDM
```

To use this INT21 macro to accept input from the keyboard, code

```
LEA   DX,NAMEPAR
INT21 0AH
```

The generated code for INT21 would load function 0AH into the AH and issue INT 21H for keyboard input. Now suppose you have another macro, named DISP, that loads INT 21H function 02H in the AH register to display a character:

```
DISP  MACRO CHAR
      MOV   AH,02H
      MOV   DL,CHAR
      INT   21H
      ENDM
```

To display a question mark, for example, code the macro as DISP '?'. But you could change DISP to take advantage of the INT21 macro by referring to INT21 within DISP's macro definition:

```
                              page   60,132
                        TITLE   A22MACR3 (EXE)  Use of .LALL & .SALL
                        ; -----------------------------------------
                        INITZ  MACRO                ;Define macro
                               MOV   AX,@data       ;Initialize segment
                               MOV   DS,AX          ;  registers
                               MOV   ES,AX
                               ENDM  ;End macro

                        PROMPT MACRO  MESSGE
                        ;This macro displays any message
                        ;;Generates code that requests display
                               MOV   AH,09H         ;Request display
                               LEA   DX,MESSGE      ;  prompt
                               INT   21H
                               ENDM

                        FINISH MACRO                ;Define macro
                               MOV   AX,4C00H       ;End processing
                               INT   21H
                               ENDM  ;End macro
                        ; -----------------------------------------
                               .MODEL  SMALL
                               .STACK  64
                               .DATA
0000 43 75 73 74 6F 6D  MESSG1 DB    'Customer name?', 13, 10, '$'
     65 72 20 6E 61 6D
     65 3F 0D 0A 24
0011 43 75 73 74 6F 6D  MESSG2 DB    'Customer address?', 13, 10, '$'
     65 72 20 61 64 64
     72 65 73 73 3F 0D
     0A 24
                        ; -----------------------------------------
                               .CODE
0000                    BEGIN  PROC  FAR
                               .SALL
                               INITZ
                        PROMPT MESSG1
                               .LALL
                        PROMPT MESSG2
  1                     ;This macro displays any message
000F B4 09          1          MOV   AH,09H         ;Request display
0011 8D 16 0011 R   1          LEA   DX,MESSG2      ;  prompt
0015 CD 21          1          INT   21H
                               .SALL
                               FINISH
001C                    BEGIN  ENDP
                               END   BEGIN
```

Figure 22-3 Listing and Suppression of Macro Expansion

```
DISP   MACRO CHAR
       MOV   DL,CHAR
       INT21 02H
       ENDM
```

Now if you code the DISP macro as DISP '?', the assembler generates

```
MOV  DL,'?'
MOV  AH,02H
INT  21H
```

THE LOCAL DIRECTIVE

Some macros require the definition of data items and instruction labels within the macro definition itself. However, if you use the macro more than once in the same program, and the assembler defines the data item or label for each occurrence, the duplicate names would cause the assembler to generate an error message. To ensure that each generated name is unique, code the LOCAL directive immediately after the MACRO statement, even before comments. Its general format is

```
LOCAL dummy-1, dummy-2, ...     ;One or more dummy arguments
```

Figure 22-4 illustrates the use of LOCAL. The purpose of the program is to perform division by successive subtraction. The routine subtracts the divisor from the dividend and adds 1 to the quotient until the dividend is less than the divisor. The procedure requires two labels: COMP for the loop address and OUT for exiting the procedure on completion. Both COMP and OUT are defined as LOCAL and may have any valid names.

In the macro expansion, the generated symbolic label for COMP is ??0000 and for OUT is ??0001. If you use the DIVIDE macro instruction again in the same program, the symbolic labels for the next macro expansion would become ??0002 and ??0003, respectively. In this way, the feature ensures that each label generated within a program is unique.

INCLUDING MACROS FROM A LIBRARY

Defining macros such as INITZ, FINISH, and PROMPT and using them just once in a program is not very productive. The standard approach is to catalog your macros in a disk library under a descriptive name, such as MACRO.LBY. You simply have to gather all your macro definitions into one or more files that you store on disk:

```
INITZ   MACRO
        ...
        ENDM
        ...
PROMPT  MACRO  MESSGE
        ...
        ENDM
```

You can use an editor or word processor to write the file, but be sure it is an unformatted ASCII file. The following examples assume that the file is stored on drive F: under the name MACRO.LBY. Your programs can now use any of the cataloged macros, but instead of coding MACRO definitions at the start of the program, use an INCLUDE directive like this:

```
INCLUDE F:\MACRO.LBY
```

The assembler accesses the file named MACRO.LBY on drive F: and includes *all* the cataloged macro definitions into the program, although your program may need only some of them. The assembled listing will contain a copy of the macro definitions, indicated by the letter C in column 30 of the .LST file for some assembler versions.

```
                                     page  60,132
                              TITLE  A22MACR4 (EXE)  Use of LOCAL
                              ; -----------------------------------------------
                              INITZ  MACRO               ;Define macro
                                     MOV   AX,@data      ;Initialize segment
                                     MOV   DS,AX         ;  registers
                                     MOV   ES,AX
                                     ENDM                ;End macro
                              DIVIDE MACRO  DIVIDEND,DIVISOR,QUOTIENT
                                     LOCAL COMP
                                     LOCAL OUT
                              ;      AX = div'd, BX = divisor, CX = quotient
                                     MOV   AX,DIVIDEND ;Set dividend
                                     MOV   BX,DIVISOR  ;Set divisor
                                     SUB   CX,CX       ;Clear quotient
                              COMP:
                                     CMP   AX,BX         ;Dividend < divisor?
                                     JB    OUT           ;  yes, exit
                                     SUB   AX,BX         ;Dividend - divisor
                                     INC   CX            ;Add to quotient
                                     JMP   COMP
                              OUT:
                                     MOV   QUOTIENT,CX ;Store quotient
                                     ENDM                ;End macro
                              FINISH MACRO               ;Define macro
                                     MOV   AX,4C00H      ;End processing
                                     INT   21H
                                     ENDM                ;End macro
                              ; -----------------------------------------------
                                     .MODEL SMALL
                                     .STACK 64
                                     .DATA
0000 0096                     DIVDND DW     150          ;Dividend
0002 001B                     DIVSOR DW    27            ;Divisor
0004 0000                     QUOTNT DW    ?             ;Quotient
                              ; -----------------------------------------------
                                     .CODE
0000                          BEGIN  PROC  FAR
                                     .SALL
                                     INITZ
                                     .LALL
                              DIVIDE DIVDND,DIVSOR,QUOTNT
                       1      ;      AX = div'd, BX = divisor, CX = quotient
0007 A1 0000 R         1             MOV   AX,DIVDND     ;Set dividend
000A  8B 1E 0002 R     1             MOV   BX,DIVSOR     ;Set divisor
000E  2B C9            1             SUB   CX,CX         ;Clear quotient
0010                   1      ??0000:
0010  3B C3            1             CMP   AX,BX         ;Dividend < divisor?
0012  72 05            1             JB    ??0001        ;  yes, exit
0014  2B C3            1             SUB   AX,BX         ;Dividend - divisor
0016  41               1             INC   CX            ;Add to quotient
0017  EB F7            1             JMP   ??0000
0019                   1      ??0001:
0019  89 0E 0004 R     1             MOV   QUOTNT,CX     ;Store quotient
                                     .SALL
                                     FINISH
0022                          BEGIN  ENDP
                                     END   BEGIN
```

Figure 22-4 Using the LOCAL Directive

Because some assemblers involve a two-pass operation, you can use the following statements to cause INCLUDE to occur only during pass 1 (instead of both passes):

```
IF1
        INCLUDE F:\MACRO.LBY
ENDIF
```

IF1 and ENDIF are conditional directives. IF1 tells the assembler to access the named library only on pass 1 of the assembly. ENDIF terminates the IF logic. A copy of the macro definition no longer appears on the listing—a saving of both time and space. (MASM versions 6.0 and on do not need directives that refer to two passes, whereas TASM will take more than one pass if you use /m in the command line at assembly time.)

The program in Figure 22-5 contains the previously described IF1, INCLUDE, and ENDIF statements, although the assembler lists only the ENDIF in the LST file. The macro instructions used in the code segment, INITZ, FINISH, and PROMPT, are cataloged in MACRO.LBY as a disk file by means of an editor program.

```
          page 60,132
TITLE     A22MACR5 (EXE)   Test of INCLUDE
     IF1
          INCLUDE F:A22MACRO.LBY
     ENDIF
; ----------------------------------------
          .MODEL SMALL
          .STACK 64
          .DATA
MESSGE    DB      'Test of macro','$'
; ----------------------------------------
          .CODE
BEGIN     PROC    FAR
          INITZ
          PROMPT MESSGE
          FINISH
BEGIN     ENDP
          END     BEGIN
```

Figure 22-5 Using Library INCLUDE

The placement of INCLUDE is not critical, but it must appear before any macro instruction that references an entry in the library.

The PURGE Directive

Execution of an INCLUDE statement causes the assembler to include all the macro definitions that are in the specified library. Suppose, however, that a library contains the macros INITZ, FINISH, PROMPT, and DIVIDE, but a program requires only INITZ and FINISH. The PURGE directive enables you to "delete" the unwanted macros PROMPT and DIVIDE from the current assembly:

```
IF1
       INCLUDE D:\MACRO.LBY     ;Include full library
ENDIF
PURGE   PROMPT,DIVIDE           ;Delete unneeded macros
...
INITZ   ...                     ;Use remaining macros
```

The PURGE operation facilitates only the assembly of a program and has no effect on the macros stored in the library.

CONCATENATION

The ampersand (&) character tells the assembler to join (concatenate) text or symbols. In the following macro, an ampersand facilitates generating a MOVSB, MOVSW, or MOVSD instruction:

```
STRMOVE  MACRO   TAG
         REP MOVS&TAG
         ENDM
```

A user could code this macro instruction as STRMOVE B, STRMOVE W, or STRMOVE D. The assembler then concatenates the parameter B, W, or D with the MOVS instruction, to produce REP MOVSB, REP MOVSW, or REP MOVSD, respectively. (This somewhat trivial example is offered for illustrative purposes.)

REPETITION DIRECTIVES

The repetition directives REPT, IRP, and IRPC cause the assembler to repeat a block of statements up to the directive's terminating ENDM statement. (MASM 6.0 introduced the terms REPEAT, FOR, and FORC for REPT, IRP, and IRPC, respectively.) These directives do not have to be contained in a MACRO definition, but if they are, you code an ENDM to end each repetition directive and another ENDM to end the MACRO definition.

REPT: Repeat Directive

The REPT (or REPEAT) directive causes the assembler to repeat a block of statements up to ENDM according to the number of times in the expression entry:

```
REPT expression
```

The first example generates the DEC instruction four times:

```
REPT  4
      DEC SI
ENDM
```

The second example initializes the value N to 0 and then repeats the generation of DB N five times:

```
N =    0
REPT   5
   N =    N + 1
   DB     N
ENDM
```

The operation generates five DB statements, DB 1 through DB 5. A use for REPT could be to define a table or part of a table. The next example defines a macro that uses REPT for beeping the speaker five times:

```
BEEPSPKR  MACRO
          MOV   AH,02H    ;Request output
          MOV   DL,07     ;Beep character
          REPT 5          ;Repeat five times
            INT 21H       ;Call interrupt service
          ENDM            ;End of REPT
          ENDM            ;End of MACRO
```

IRP: Indefinite Repeat Directive

The IRP directive causes the assembler to repeat a block of instructions up to ENDM. Its general format is

```
IRP  dummy,<arguments>
```

The arguments, contained in angle brackets, consist of any number of valid symbols, including string, numeric, or arithmetic constants. The assembler generates a block of code for each argument. For the first example, the assembler generates DB 3, DB 9, DB 17, DB 25, and DB 28:

```
IRP  N,<3,9,17,25,28>
  DB   N
ENDM
```

For the second example, the assembler generates a PUSH statement for each of the specified registers:

```
IRP  REG <AX, BX, CX, DX>
  PUSH  REG
ENDM
```

IRPC: Indefinite Repeat Character Directive

The IRPC (or FORC) directive causes the assembler to repeat a block of statements up to ENDM. Its general format is

```
IRPC  dummy,string
```

The assembler generates a block of code for each character in the string. In the following example, the assembler generates DW 3 through DW 8:

```
IRPC  N,345678
  DW    N
ENDM
```

CONDITIONAL DIRECTIVES

Assembly language supports a number of conditional directives. An earlier example used IF1 to include a library entry only during pass 1 of an assembly. Conditional directives are most useful within a macro definition, but are not limited to that purpose. Every IFnn directive must have a matching ENDIF to terminate a tested condition. One optional ELSE may provide an alternative action. Here is the general format for the IF family of conditional directives:

```
IFxx      (condition)
...                        }    conditional
ELSE      (optional)       }
...                        }      block
ENDIF     (end of IF)
```

Omission of ENDIF causes the error message "Undeterminated conditional." If the assembler finds that a condition is found true, it executes the conditional block up to the ELSE or, if no ELSE is present, up to the ENDIF. If the condition is found false, the assembler executes the conditional block following the ELSE; if no ELSE is present, it does not generate any of the conditional block.

The following explains how the assembler handles the conditional directives:

- IF expression If the expression evaluates to a nonzero value, assemble the statements within the conditional block.
- IFE expression If the expression evaluates to a zero, assemble the statements within the conditional block.
- IF1 (no expression) If processing pass 1, act on the statements in the conditional block.
- IF2 (no expression) If processing pass 2, act on the statements in the conditional block.
- IFDEF symbol If the symbol is defined in the program or is declared as EXTRN, process the statements in the conditional block.
- IFNDEF symbol If the symbol is not defined or is not declared as EXTRN, process the statements in the conditional block.
- IFB <argument> If the argument is blank, process the statements in the conditional block. The argument requires angle brackets.
- IFNB <argument> If the argument is not blank, process the statements in the conditional block. The argument requires angle brackets.
- IFIDN <arg-1>,<arg-2> If the argument-1 string is identical to the argument-2 string, process the statements in the conditional block. The arguments require angle brackets.
- IFDIF <arg-1>,<arg-2> If the argument-1 string is different from the argument-2 string, process the statements in the conditional block. The arguments require angle brackets.

IF and IFE can use the relational operators EQ (equal), NE (not equal), LT (less than), LE (less than or equal), GT (greater than), and GE (greater than or equal) as, for example, in the statement

```
IF expression1  EQ expression2
```

Here's a simple example of the use of IFNB (if not blank). INT 21H function 3CH enables a program to end processing and to deliver a return code in the AL. The following example revises the FINISH macro used earlier to provide for a return code:

```
FINISH  MACRO   RETCODE
        MOV     AH,3CH        ;Request end processing
          IFNB    <RETCODE>
            MOV     AL,RETCODE
          ENDIF
        INT     21H           ;Call interrupt service
        ENDM
```

Here's another example of the use of IFNB. All INT 21H requests require a function in the AH register, and some requests also require a value in the DX. The macro INT21 defined earlier uses IFNB to test for a nonblank argument for the DX; if the result is true (the argument is nonblank), the assembler generates the MOV instruction that loads the DX:

```
INT21  MACRO  FUNCTN,DXADDRES
       MOV    AH,FUNCTN
       IFNB   <DXADDRES>
       MOV    DX,OFFSET DXADDRES
ENDIF
INT       21H
ENDM
```

Using INT21 for simple keyboard input of one character requires only loading the AH with a value, in this case, function 01H:

```
INT21  01
```

The assembler generates MOV AH,01 and INT 21H. Keyboard input of a character string requires function 0AH in the AH and the input address in the DX. You could code the INT21 macro as

```
INT21  0AH,IPFIELD
```

The assembler then generates both the MOV AH,0AH, the MOV DX,OFFSET address, and the INT 21H instructions.

The EXITM Directive

A macro definition may contain a conditional directive that tests for a serious condition. If the condition is true, the assembler is to exit from any further expansion of the macro. The EXITM directive serves this purpose:

```
IFxx   [condition]
...   (invalid condition)
EXITM
...
ENDIF
```

If the assembler encounters EXITM in an expansion of a macro instruction, it discontinues the macro expansion and resumes processing after ENDM. You can also use EXITM to end REPT, IRP, and IRPC directives, even if they are contained within a macro definition.

Macro Using IF and IFNDEF Conditions

The skeleton program in Figure 22-6 contains a macro definition named DIVIDE that generates a routine to perform division by successive subtraction. A user has to code the DIVIDE macro instruction with parameters for the dividend, divisor, and quotient, in that order. The macro uses IFNDEF to check whether these data items are actually defined in the program. For any item not defined, the macro increments a field arbitrarily named CNTR. (CNTR could have any valid name and is for temporary use in the macro definition.) After checking the three parameters, the macro checks CNTR for nonzero:

```
      IF    CNTR
;       Macro expansion terminated
      EXITM
      ENDIF
```

If CNTR has been set to a nonzero value, the assembler generates the comment and exits (EXITM) from any further expansion of the macro. Note that an initial instruction clears CNTR to 0 and also that the IFNDEF blocks need only to set CNTR to 1 rather than increment it.

If the conditions pass all the tests safely, the assembler generates the macro expansion. In the code segment, the second DIVIDE macro instruction contains an invalid dividend and quotient and generates only comments. A way to improve the macro would be to test whether the divisor is nonzero and whether the dividend and divisor have the same sign. For these purposes, use assembly instructions rather than conditional directives because the conditions occur when the program is executed, not when it is assembled.

Macro Using IFIDN Condition

The skeleton program in Figure 22-7 contains a macro definition named MOVIF that generates MOVSB or MOVSW, depending on the parameter supplied. A user has to code the macro instruction with the parameter B (byte) or W (word) to indicate whether MOVS is to become MOVSB or MOVSW. The two occurrences of IFIDN in the macro definition are

```
IFIDN  <&TAG>,<B>      IFIDN  <&TAG>,<W>
REP  MOVSB             REP MOVSW
...                    ...
```

The first IFIDN generates REP MOVSB if you code MOVIFB as a macro instruction, and the second IFIDN generates REP MOVSW if you code MOVIFW. If a user does not supply B or W, the assembler generates a comment and default to MOVSB. (The normal use of the ampersand (&) operator is for concatenation.)

The three examples of MOVIF in the code segment test for B, for W, and for an invalid condition. Don't attempt to execute the program as it stands, because the DI and SI

```
                                 page   60,132
                         TITLE   A22MACR6 (EXE)  Test of IF and IFNDEF
                         ; -------------------------------------------
                         INITZ   MACRO                ;Define macro
                                 MOV    AX,@data      ;Initialize segment
                                 MOV    DS,AX         ;  registers
                                 MOV    ES,AX
                                 ENDM                 ;End macro
                         FINISH  MACRO                ;Define macro
                                 MOV    AX,4C00H      ;End processing
                                 INT    21H
                                 ENDM                 ;End macro
                         DIVIDE  MACRO  DIVIDEND,DIVISOR,QUOTIENT
                                 LOCAL  COMP
                                 LOCAL  OUT
                                 CNTR    = 0
                         ;       AX = div'nd, BX = div'r, CX = quot't
                                 IFNDEF DIVIDEND
                         ;              Dividend not defined
                                 CNTR    = CNTR +1
                                 ENDIF
                                 IFNDEF DIVISOR
                         ;              Divisor not defined
                                 CNTR    = CNTR +1
                                 ENDIF
                                 IFNDEF QUOTIENT
                         ;              Quotient not defined
                                 CNTR    = CNTR + 1
                                 ENDIF
                                 IF     CNTR
                         ;              Macro expansion terminated
                                 EXITM
                                 ENDIF
                                 MOV    AX,DIVIDEND ;Set dividend
                                 MOV    BX,DIVISOR  ;Set divisor
                                 SUB    CX,CX       ;Clear quotient
                         COMP:
                                 CMP    AX,BX       ;Dividend < divisor?
                                 JB     OUT         ;  yes, exit
                                 SUB    AX,BX       ;Dividend - divisor
                                 INC    CX          ;Add to quotient
                                 JMP    COMP
                         OUT:
                                 MOV    QUOTIENT,CX ;Store quotient
                                 ENDM
                         ; -------------------------------------------
                                 .MODEL SMALL
                                 .STACK 64
                                 .DATA
0000  0096               DIVDND  DW     150         ;Dividend
0002  001B               DIVSOR  DW     27          ;Divisor
0004  0000               QUOTNT  DW     ?           ;Quotient
                         ; -------------------------------------------
                                 .CODE
0000                     BEGIN   PROC   FAR
                                 .SALL
                                 INITZ
                                 .LALL
```

Figure 22-6a Using the IF and IFNDEF Directives

```
                                    DIVIDE DIVDND,DIVSOR,QUOTNT
= 0000                      1       CNTR   = 0
                            1  ;    AX = div'nd, BX = div'r, CX = quot't
0007  A1 0000 R             1       MOV    AX,DIVDND    ;Set dividend
000A  8B 1E 0002 R          1       MOV    BX,DIVSOR    ;Set divisor
000E  2B C9                 1       SUB    CX,CX        ;Clear quotient
0010                        1  ??0000:
0010  3B C3                 1       CMP    AX,BX        ;Dividend < divisor?
0012  72 05                 1       JB     ??0001       ;  yes, exit
0014  2B C3                 1       SUB    AX,BX        ;Dividend - divisor
0016  41                    1       INC    CX           ;Add to quotient
0017  EB F7                 1       JMP    ??0000
0019                        1  ??0001:
0019  89 0E 0004 R          1       MOV    QUOTNT,CX    ;Store quotient
                                    DIVIDE DIDND,DIVSOR,QUOT
= 0000                      1       CNTR   = 0
                            1  ;    AX = div'nd, BX = div'r, CX = quot't
                            1       IFNDEF DIDND
                            1  ;           Dividend not defined
= 0001                      1       CNTR   = CNTR +1
                            1       ENDIF
                            1       IFNDEF QUOT
                            1  ;           Quotient not defined
= 0002                      1       CNTR   = CNTR + 1
                            1       ENDIF
                            1       IF     CNTR
                            1  ;           Macro expansion terminated
                            1       EXITM
                                    .SALL
                                    FINISH
0022                           BEGIN ENDP
                                    END    BEGIN
```

Figure 22-6b Using the IF and IFNDEF Directives

registers have to contain proper values for the MOVS instructions. Admittedly, this macro is not very useful, since its purpose is to illustrate the use of conditional directives in a simple manner. By now, however, you should be able to develop some meaningful macros.

KEY POINTS

- A macro definition requires a MACRO directive, a block of one or more statements known as the body that the macro definition is to generate, and an ENDM directive to end the definition.
- A macro instruction is the use of the macro in a program. The code that a macro instruction generates is the macro expansion.
- The .SALL, .LALL, and .XALL directives control the listing of comments and the object code generated in a macro expansion.
- The LOCAL directive facilitates using names within a macro definition and must appear immediately after the macro statement.
- The use of dummy arguments in a macro definition allows a user to code parameters for more flexibility.
- A macro library makes cataloged macros available to other programs.
- Conditional directives enable you to validate macro parameters.

```
                                   page  60,132
                           TITLE   A22MACR7 (EXE)  Tests of IFIDN
                           ; -------------------------------------------
                           INITZ   MACRO              ;Define macro
                                   MOV   AX,@data     ;Initialize segment
                                   MOV   DS,AX        ;  registers
                                   MOV   ES,AX
                                   ENDM               ;End macro

                           MOVIF   MACRO TAG          ;Define macro
                                   IFIDN <&TAG>,<B>
                                   REP MOVSB          ;Move bytes
                                   EXITM
                                   ENDIF
                                   IFIDN <&TAG>,<W>
                                   REP MOVSW          ;Move words
                                   ELSE
                           ;       No B or W tag, default to B
                                   REP MOVSB          ;Move bytes
                                   ENDIF
                                   ENDM               ;End of macro

                           FINISH MACRO               ;Define macro
                                   MOV   AX,4C00H     ;End processing
                                   INT   21H
                                   ENDM               ;End macro
                           ; -------------------------------------------
                                   .MODEL SMALL
                                   .STACK 64
                                   .CODE
0000                       BEGIN   PROC  FAR
                                   .LALL
                                   INITZ
0000  B8 ---- R   1                MOV   AX,@data     ;Initialize segment
0003  8E D8       1                MOV   DS,AX        ;  registers
0005  8E C0       1                MOV   ES,AX
                                   MOVIF B
                  1                IFIDN  <B>,<B>
0007  F3/ A4      1                REP MOVSB          ;Move bytes
                  1                EXITM
                                   MOVIF W
                  1                IFIDN  <W>,<W>
0009  F3/ A5      1                REP MOVSW          ;Move words
                  1                ENDIF
                                   MOVIF
                  1                ELSE
                  1        ;       No B or W tag, default to B
000B  F3/ A4      1                REP MOVSB          ;Move bytes
   1                               ENDIF
                                   .LALL
                                   FINISH
0012                       BEGIN   ENDP
                                   END   BEGIN
```

Figure 22-7 Using the IFIDN Directive

QUESTIONS

22-1. Under what circumstances would the use of macros be recommended?

22-2. Code the first and last lines for a simple macro named BIGMACRO.

22-3. Distinguish between the body of a macro definition and the macro expansion.

22-4. What is a dummy argument?

22-5. Code the directives for the following statements: (a) List only instructions that generate object code; (b) suppress all instructions that a macro generates.

22-6. Code two macro definitions that perform multiplication: (a) MULTBYTE is to generate code that multiplies a byte by a byte; (b) MULTWORD is to generate code that multiplies a word by a word. Include the multiplicands and multipliers as dummy arguments in the macro definition. Test the execution of the macros with a small program that also defines the required data fields.

22-7. Store the macros defined in Question 22-6 in a macro library. Revise the program to INCLUDE the library entries during pass 1 of the assembly.

22-8. Write a macro named PRINT17 that uses INT 17H to print. The macro should include a test for the status of the printer and should provide for any defined print line with any length.

22-9. Revise the macro in Figure 22-6 so that it generates code to bypass the division if the divisor is zero when the program executes.

22-10. Write, assemble, and test a program that uses the macros named MULTBYTE, MULTWORD, and PRINT17. (a) Define two 1-byte fields named BYTE1 and BYTE2 and two 1-word fields named WORD1 and WORD2, all containing numeric data. (b) Use MULTBYTE to multiply the 1-byte fields and use MULTWORD to multiply the 1-word fields. (c) Convert the products into ASCII format and use PRINT17 to print them.

23 LINKING TO SUBPROGRAMS

Objective: To cover the programming techniques involved in linking and executing separately assembled programs.

INTRODUCTION

Up to this chapter, all of our programs have consisted of one stand-alone assembled module. It is possible, however, to develop a program that consists of a main program linked with one or more separately assembled subprograms. The following are reasons for organizing a program into subprograms:

- To link between languages—for example, to combine the ease of coding in a high-level language with the processing efficiency of assembly language.
- To facilitate the development of large projects, in which different teams produce their modules separately.
- To overlay parts of a program during execution because of the program's large size.

Each program is assembled separately and generates its own unique object (.OBJ) module. The linker then links the object modules into one combined executable (.EXE) module. Typically, the main program is the one that begins execution, and it calls one or more subprograms. Subprograms in turn may call other subprograms.

Figure 23-1 shows two examples of a hierarchy of a main program and three subprograms. In part (a), the main program calls subprograms 1, 2, and 3. In part (b), the main program calls subprograms 1 and 2, and only subprogram 1 calls subprogram 3.

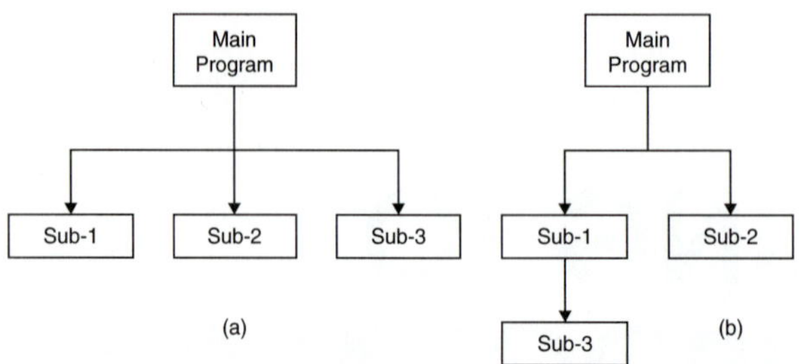

Figure 23-1 Program Hierarchy

There are numerous ways to organize subprograms, but the organization has to make sense to the assembler and linker. You also have to watch out for situations in which, for example, subprogram 1 calls subprogram 2, which calls subprogram 3, which in turn calls subprogram 1. This process, known as recursion, can be made to work but, if not handled carefully, can cause interesting execution bugs.

THE SEGMENT DIRECTIVE

This section covers a number of options used for coding the SEGMENT directive. The general format for the full SEGMENT directive is

seg-name	SEGMENT	[align] [combine] ['class']

The align, combine, and class types are described next.

Align Type

The align operator (if coded) tells the assembler to align the named segment beginning on a particular storage boundary:

- BYTE Byte boundary, for a segment of a subprogram that is to be combined with that of another program. Byte alignment is generally suitable for programs run on an 8088 processor.
- WORD Word boundary, for a segment of a subprogram that is to be combined with that of another program. Word alignment is generally suitable for programs run on 8086/80286 processors.
- DWORD Doubleword boundary, normally for the 80386 and later processors.
- PARA Paragraph boundary (divisible by 16, or 10H), the default and the most commonly used alignment for both main programs and subprograms.
- PAGE Page boundary (divisible by 256, or 100H).

Omitting the align operator from the first segment causes a default to PARA. Omitting it from succeeding segments also causes a default to PARA if the name is unique; if it is not unique, the default is the alignment type of the previously defined segment of the same name.

Combine Type

The combine operator (if coded) tells the assembler and linker whether to combine segments or to keep them separate. (You have already used the STACK combine type for .EXE programs.) Other combine types relevant to this chapter are NONE, PUBLIC, and COMMON:

- NONE The segment is to be logically separate from other segments, although they may all end up as physically adjacent. This type is the default for full segment directives.
- PUBLIC The linker is to combine the segment with all other segments that are defined as PUBLIC and have the same segment name and class. The assembler calculates offsets from the beginning of the first segment. In effect, the combined segment contains a number of sections, each beginning with a SEGMENT directive and ending with ENDS. This type is the default for simplified segment directives.
- COMMON If COMMON segments have the same name and class, the linker gives them the same base address. During execution, the second segment overlays the first one. The largest segment determines the length of the common area.

Class Type

You have already used the class names 'Stack,' 'Data,' and 'Code.' You can assign the same class name to related segments so that the assembler and linker group them together. That is, they are to appear as segments one after the other, but are not combined into one segment unless the PUBLIC combine option is also coded. The class entry may contain any valid name, contained in single quotes, although the name 'Code' is recommended for the code segment.

The following two unrelated SEGMENT statements generate identical results, namely, an independent code segment aligned on a paragraph boundary:

```
CODESG1  SEGMENT  PARA NONE 'Code'
CODESG2  SEGMENT  'Code' (defaults to PARA and NONE)
```

We explained fully defined segment directives in Chapter 4, but have used the simplified segment directives in subsequent chapters. Because full segment directives can provide tighter control when assembling and linking subprograms, most examples in this chapter use them.

Program examples in this and later chapters illustrate many of the Align, Combine, and Class options.

INTRASEGMENT CALLS

CALL instructions used to this point have been *intrasegment* calls; that is, the called procedure is in the same code segment as that of the calling procedure. An intrasegment CALL is *near* if the called procedure is defined as or defaults to NEAR (that is, within ± 32K).

The near CALL pushes the IP register onto the stack and replaces the IP with the offset of the destination address. Thus a near CALL references a (near) procedure within the same segment.

```
            CALL   nearproc     ;Near call: push IP,
            ...                 ;  link to nearproc
nearproc    PROC   NEAR
            ...
            RET/RETN            ;Near return: pop IP,
nearproc    ENDP                ;  return to caller
```

Now consider a near intrasegment CALL statement that consists of object code E8 2000, where E8 is the operation code for CALL and 2000 (0020) is the offset of a called procedure. The operation pushes the IP onto the stack and stores the 2000 as 0020 in the IP. The processor then combines the current segment address in the CS with the offset in the IP (CS:IP) for the next instruction to execute. On exit from the called procedure, a (near) RET pops the stored IP off the stack and into the IP so that the combined segment:offset address causes a return to the instruction following the CALL.

An intrasegment call may be near, as described, or far if the call is to a procedure defined as far within the same segment. RET is near if it appears in a NEAR procedure and far if it appears in a FAR procedure. You can code these instructions as RETN or RETF, respectively.

INTERSEGMENT CALLS

A CALL is classed as *far* if the called procedure is defined as FAR or as EXTRN, often but not necessarily in another segment. The far CALL first pushes the contents of the CS register onto the stack and inserts the new segment address in the CS. It then pushes the IP onto the stack and inserts a new offset address in the IP. (The pushed CS:IP values provide the address of the instruction immediately following the CALL.) In this way, both addresses of the code segment and the offset are saved for the return from the called procedure. A call to another segment is always an *intersegment* far call.

```
         CALL   farproc     ;Far call: push CS and IP,
         ...                ;  link to farproc
farproc  PROC   FAR
         ...
         RET/RETF           ;Far return: pop IP and CS,
farproc  ENDP               ;  return to caller
```

Consider an intersegment CALL statement that consists of object code 9A 0002 AF04. Hex 9A is the operation code for a far CALL, 0002 (or 0200) is the offset, and AF04 (or 04AF) is the new segment address. The operation pushes the current IP onto the stack and stores the new offset 0002 as 0200 in the IP. It next pushes the current CS onto the stack and stores the new segment address AF04 as 04AF in the CS. The processor then combines the current segment address in the CS with the offset in the IP (CS:IP) for the effective address of the first instruction to execute in the called subprogram:

```
Address in code segment:  04AF0H
Offset in IP:            + 0200H
Effective address:        04CF0H
```

On exit from the called procedure, an intersegment (far) RET reverses the CALL operation, popping both the original IP and CS addresses back into their respective registers. The CS:IP pair now points to the address of the instruction following the original CALL, where execution resumes.

The basic difference then between a near and a far CALL is that a near CALL replaces only the IP offset, whereas a far CALL replaces both the CS segment address and the IP offset. A near RET/RETN is associated with a near CALL and a far RET/RETF with a far CALL.

THE EXTRN AND PUBLIC ATTRIBUTES

In Figure 23-2, the main program (MAINPROG) calls a subprogram (SUBPROG). The requirement here is for an intersegment CALL.

```
          EXTRN   SUBPROG:FAR
MAINPROG  PROC    FAR
          ...
          CALL    SUBPROG
          ...
MAINPROG  ENDP
--------------------------------
          PUBLIC  SUBPROG
SUBPROG   PROC    FAR
          ...
          ...
          RETF
SUBPROG   ENDP
```

Figure 23-2 Intersegment Call

The CALL in MAINPROG has to know that SUBPROG exists outside MAINPROG (or else the assembler generates an error message that SUBPROG is an undefined symbol). The directive EXTRN SUBPROG:FAR notifies the assembler that any reference to SUBPROG is to a FAR label that in this case is defined externally, in another assembly. Because the assembler has no way of knowing what the address will be at execution time, it generates "empty" object code operands in the far CALL (the listing shows zeros for the offset and hyphens for the segment), which the linker subsequently is to fill:

```
MASM:  9A 0000 ---- E    ;E = external
TASM:  9A 00000000se     ;se = external segment
```

SUBPROG in its turn contains a PUBLIC directive that tells the assembler and linker that another module has to know the address of SUBPROG. In a later step, when both MAINPROG and SUBPROG are successfully assembled into separate object modules, they may be linked as follows:

```
LINK/TLINK D:MAINPROG+D:SUBPROG,D:,CON
```

The linker matches EXTRNs in one object module with PUBLICs in the other and inserts any required offset addresses. It then combines the two object modules into one executable module. If unable to match references, the linker supplies error messages, which you should watch for before attempting to execute the module.

The EXTRN/EXTERN Directive

The EXTRN directive tells the assembler that the named item—a data item, procedure, or label—is defined in another assembly. (MASM 6.0 introduced the term EXTERN.) It has the following format:

```
EXTRN/EXTERN name:type [, ... ]
```

You can define more than one name up to the end of the line or code additional EXTRN statements. The other assembly module in its turn must define the name and identify it as PUBLIC. The type entry must be valid in terms of the actual definition of a name:

- ABS identifies a constant value.
- BYTE, WORD, and DWORD identify data items that one module references but another module defines.
- NEAR and FAR identify a procedure or instruction label that one module references but another module defines.
- A name defined by an EQU.

The PUBLIC Directive

The PUBLIC directive tells the assembler and linker that the address of a specified symbol defined in the current assembly is to be available to other modules. The general format for PUBLIC is

```
PUBLIC symbol [, ... ]
```

You can define more than one symbol up to the end of the line or code additional PUBLIC statements. The symbol entry can be a label (including PROC labels), a variable, or a number. Invalid entries include register names and EQU symbols that define values greater than 2 bytes.

The calling of far procedures and the use of EXTRN and PUBLIC should offer little difficulty, although some care is required for making data defined in one module known in other modules.

Let's now examine three different ways of making data known between programs: using EXTRN and PUBLIC, defining common data in subprograms, and passing parameters.

USING EXTRN AND PUBLIC FOR AN ENTRY POINT

The program in Figure 23-3 consists of a main program, A23MAIN1, and a subprogram, A23SUB1, both using full segment directives. The main program defines segments for the stack, data, and code. The data segment defines QTY and PRICE. The code segment

```
                        TITLE    A23MAIN1 (EXE)  Call subprogram
                                 EXTRN  A23SUB1:FAR
                        ; ------------------------------------------
0000                    STACKSG  SEGMENT PARA STACK 'Stack'
0000 0040[????]                  DW     64 DUP(?)
0080                    STACKSG  ENDS
                        ; ------------------------------------------
0000                    DATASG   SEGMENT PARA 'Data'
0000 0140               QTY      DW     0140H
0002 2500               PRICE    DW     2500H
0004                    DATASG   ENDS
                        ; ------------------------------------------
0000                    CODESG   SEGMENT PARA 'Code'
0000                    BEGIN    PROC   FAR
                                 ASSUME CS:CODESG,DS:DATASG,SS:STACKSG
0000 B8 ---- R                   MOV    AX,DATASG
0003 8E D8                       MOV    DS,AX
0005 A1 0002 R                   MOV    AX,PRICE        ;Set up price
0008 8B 1E 0000 R                MOV    BX,QTY          ;  and quantity
000C 9A 0000 ---- E              CALL   A23SUB1         ;Call subprogram
0011 B8 4C00                     MOV    AX,4C00H        ;End processing
0014 CD 21                       INT    21H
0016                    BEGIN    ENDP
0016                    CODESG   ENDS
                                 END    BEGIN

Segments and Groups:
        N a m e         Length   Align     Combine   Class
CODESG . . . . . . . .  0016     PARA      NONE      'CODE'
DATASG . . . . . . . .  0004     PARA      NONE      'DATA'
STACKSG  . . . . . . .  0080     PARA      STACK     'STACK'
Symbols:
        N a m e         Type     Value     Attr
A23SUB1  . . . . .      L FAR    0000      External
BEGIN  . . . . . .      F PROC   0000      CODESG    Length = 0016
PRICE  . . . . . .      L WORD   0002      DATASG
QTY  . . . . . . .      L WORD   0000      DATASG
---------------------------------------------------------------------
                        TITLE    A23SUB1 Called subprogram
0000                    CODESG   SEGMENT PARA 'Code'
0000                    A23SUB1  PROC   FAR
                                 ASSUME CS:CODESG
                                 PUBLIC A23SUB1
0000 F7 E3                       MUL    BX        ;AX = price, BX = qty
0002 CB                          RETF             ;DX:AX = product
0003                    A23SUB1  ENDP
0003                    CODESG   ENDS
                                 END    A23SUB1

Segments and Groups:
        N a m e         Length   Align     Combine   Class
CODESG . . . . . . . .  0003     PARA      NONE      'CODE'
Symbols:
        N a m e         Type     Value     Attr
A23SUB1  . . . . . . .  F PROC   0000      CODESG  Global Length = 0003
---------------------------------------------------------------------
```

Figure 23-3a Using EXTRN and PUBLIC

```
Link Map
Object Modules: A23MAIN1+A23SUB1

 Start  Stop   Length Name           Class
00000H 0007FH 00080H STACKSG         STACK
00080H 00083H 00004H DATASG          DATA
00090H 000A5H 00016H CODESG          CODE <-- Note 2 code
000B0H 000B2H 00003H CODESG          CODE <--   segments

Program entry point at 0009:0000
```

Figure 23-3b Using EXTRN and PUBLIC

loads the AX with PRICE and the BX with QTY and then calls the subprogram. An EXTRN in the main program identifies the entry point to the subprogram as A23SUB1:FAR.

The subprogram contains a PUBLIC statement (after the ASSUME) that makes A23SUB1 known to the linker as the entry point for execution. This subprogram simply multiplies the contents of the AX (price) by the BX (quantity) and develops the product in the DX:AX pair as 002E 4000H.

Because the subprogram does not define any data, it does not need a data segment; it could, but only the subprogram itself would recognize the data.

The SS and SP registers in the subprogram contain the same addresses as those in the main program. As a result, the subprogram references the stack defined in the main program, and so does not define a stack. Because the linker requires the definition of at least one stack for an .EXE program, the stack in the main program serves this purpose.

Now let's examine the symbol tables following each assembly. Note that the symbol table for the main program shows A23SUB1 as Far and External. The symbol table for the subprogram shows A23SUB1 as F (for Far) and Global. The term *global* implies that the name is known to other subprograms outside A23SUB1.

The link map at the end of the listing shows the organization of the program in memory. Note that there is 1 stack and 1 data segment, but 2 code segments (one for each assembly) at different starting addresses, because their combine types are NONE. These segments appear in the sequence that you enter in the LINK command. In this example, the code segment for the main program (normally first) starts at offset 00090H and the code segment for the subprogram at 000B0H.

A trace of program execution disclosed that the CS register for A23MAIN1 contained 0F20[0] and the instruction CALL A23SUB1 generated

```
9A 0000 220F (expect your segment value to differ)
```

The machine code for an intersegment CALL is 9AH. The operation pushes the IP register onto the stack and loads 0000 (the first operand of the CALL) in the IP. It then pushes the CS containing 0F20[0] onto the stack and loads 0F22[0] (the second operand) in the CS. (We are showing the register contents in normal, not reversed, byte order.)

The CS:IP pair direct the next instruction to execute at 0F22[0] plus 0000. What is at 0F220? It's the entry point to A23SUB1 at its first executable instruction, which you can calculate. The main program began with the CS register containing 0F20[0].

According to the map, the main code segment offset begins at offset 00090H and the subprogram offset begins at offset 000B0H, 20H bytes apart. Adding the main program's CS value plus 20H supplies the effective address of the subprogram's code segment:

```
CS address for A23MAIN1:    0F200H
Size of A23MAIN1:          +00020H
CS address for A23SUB1:     0F220H
```

The program loader determines this address just as we have and substitutes it in the CALL operand. A23SUB1 multiplies the two values in the AX and BX, with the product in the DX:AX, and makes a far return (RETF) to A23MAIN1 (because the return is to a FAR procedure).

DEFINING THE CODE SEGMENT AS PUBLIC

Figure 23-4 provides a variation of Figure 23-3. There is one change in the main program, A23MAIN2, and one change in the subprogram, A23SUB2, both involving the use of PUBLIC in the SEGMENT directive for both code segments:

```
CODESG SEGMENT PARA PUBLIC 'Code'
```

Interesting results appear in the link map and the CALL object code. In the symbol table following each assembly, the combine type for CODESG is PUBLIC, whereas in Figure 23-3 it was NONE. Also, the link map at the end now shows only one code segment. The fact that both segments have the same name (CODESG), class ('Code'), and PUBLIC attribute caused the linker to combine the two logical code segments into one physical code segment. Further, a trace of machine execution showed that the CALL is far; that is, even though the call is within the same segment, it is to a FAR procedure, as defined:

```
9A 2000 200F (expect your segment address to differ)
```

This far CALL stores 2000H in the IP as 0020H and 200FH in the CS register as 0F20[0]. Because the subprogram shares a common code segment with the main program, the CS register is set to the same starting address, 0F20H. But the CS:IP for A23SUB2 now provides the following effective address:

```
CS address for A23MAIN2 and A23SUB2:  0F200H
IP offset for A23SUB2:               + 0020H
Effective address of A23SUB2:          0F220H
```

The code segment of the subprogram therefore presumably begins at 0F220H. Is this correct? The link map doesn't make the point clear, but you can infer the address from the listing of the main program, which ends at offset 0015H. (The map shows 16H, which is the next available location.) Because the code segment for the subprogram is defined as PARA, it begins on a paragraph boundary (evenly divisible by 10H, so that the rightmost digit is 0):

```
                    TITLE     A23MAIN2 (EXE)  Call subprogram
                              EXTRN  A23SUB2:FAR
                    ; -------------------------------------------
0000                STACKSG   SEGMENT PARA STACK 'Stack'
0000 0040[????]               DW     64 DUP(?)
0080                STACKSG   ENDS
                    ; -------------------------------------------
0000                DATASG    SEGMENT PARA 'Data'
0000 0140           QTY       DW     0140H
0002 2500           PRICE     DW     2500H
0004                DATASG    ENDS
                    ; -------------------------------------------
0000                CODESG    SEGMENT PARA PUBLIC 'Code'
0000                BEGIN     PROC   FAR
                              ASSUME CS:CODESG,DS:DATASG,SS:STACKSG
0000 B8 ---- R                MOV    AX,DATASG
0003 8E D8                    MOV    DS,AX
0005 A1 0002 R                MOV    AX,PRICE       ;Set up price
0008 8B 1E 0000 R             MOV    BX,QTY         ; and quantity
000C 9A 0000 ---- E           CALL   A23SUB2        ;Call subprogram
0011 B8 4C00                  MOV    AX,4C00H       ;End processing
0014 CD 21                    INT    21H
0016                BEGIN     ENDP
0016                CODESG    ENDS
                              END    BEGIN

Segments and Groups:
    N a m e         Length    Align     Combine   Class
CODESG . . . . . . . 0016     PARA      PUBLIC    'CODE'
DATASG . . . . . . . 0004     PARA      NONE      'DATA'
STACKSG  . . . . . . 0080     PARA      STACK     'STACK'
Symbols:
    N a m e           Type    Value      Attr
A23SUB2  . . . . . . L FAR    0000      External
BEGIN  . . . . . . . F PROC   0000      CODESG  Length = 0016
PRICE  . . . . . . . L WORD   0002      DATASG
QTY  . . . . . . . . L WORD   0000      DATASG
---------------------------------------------------------------------

                    TITLE     A23SUB2 Called subprogram
                    ; --------------------------------
0000                CODESG    SEGMENT PARA PUBLIC 'Code'
0000                A23SUB2   PROC   FAR
                              ASSUME CS:CODESG
                              PUBLIC A23SUB2
0000 F7 E3                    MUL    BX        ;AX = price, BX = qty
0002 CB                       RETF             ;DX:AX = product
0003                A23SUB2   ENDP
0003                CODESG    ENDS
                              END    A23SUB2

Segments and Groups:
    N a m e         Length    Align  Combine  Class
CODESG . . . . . . . 0003     PARA   PUBLIC   'CODE'
Symbols:
    N a m e           Type    Value   Attr
A23SUB2  . . . . . . F PROC   0000   CODESG  Global  Length = 0003
```

Figure 23-4a Code Segment Defined as PUBLIC

```
Link Map
Object Modules: A23MAIN2+A23SUB2

 Start   Stop    Length Name       Class
 00000H 0007FH 00080H STACKSG    STACK
 00080H 00083H 00004H DATASG     DATA
 00090H 000B2H 00023H CODESG     CODE <-- 1 code
                                          segment
 Program entry point at 0009:0000
```

Figure 23-4b Code Segment Defined as PUBLIC

```
| main program ....(unused) | subprogram |
|             |             |
0F200        141F0        0F220
```

The linker sets the subprogram at the first paragraph boundary immediately following the main program, at offset 00020H. Therefore, just as was calculated, the code segment of the subprogram begins at 0F200H plus 0020H, or 0F220H.

Now let's examine this same program defined with simplified segment directives.

USING SIMPLIFIED SEGMENT DIRECTIVES

Figure 23-5 shows the previous program now defined with simplified segment directives. Figure 23-4 defines the code segments as PUBLIC, whereas Figure 23-5 defaults to PUBLIC, so that both examples generate one code segment. However, the use of simplified segment directives causes some significant differences. First, the linker has rearranged the segments (as shown in the map) in sequence of code, data, and stack, although this has no effect on program execution. Second, the subprogram's code segment (_TEXT) aligns on a word (rather than paragraph) boundary. A trace of machine execution showed the following object code for the CALL:

```
9A 1600 170F (expect your segment address to differ)
```

This time, the new offset value is 16H, and the segment address is 0F17H. Because the subprogram shares a common code segment with the main program, the CS register is set to the same starting address, 0F17(0), for both. You may calculate the effective address of A23SUB3 as follows:

```
CS address for A23MAIN3 and A23SUB3:    F170H
IP offset for A23SUB3:                 + 016H
Effective address of A23SUB3:           F186H
```

You can infer the address from the listing of the main program, which ends at offset 0015H. (The map shows 16H, which is the next available location.) Because the map shows the main code segment beginning at 00000H, the next word boundary following 0015H is at 00016H, where A23SUB3 begins.

```
                          TITLE     A23MAIN3 (EXE)  Call subprogram
                                    .MODEL   SMALL
                                    .STACK   64
                                    EXTRN    A23SUB3:FAR
                          ; ------------------------------------------
                                    .DATA
0000 0140                 QTY       DW       0140H
0002 2500                 PRICE     DW       2500H
                          ; ------------------------------------------
                                    .CODE
0000                      BEGIN     PROC     FAR
0000 B8 ---- R                      MOV      AX,@data
0003 8E D8                          MOV      DS,AX
0005 A1 0002 R                      MOV      AX,PRICE       ;Set up price
0008 8B 1E 0000 R                   MOV      BX,QTY         ;  and quantity
000C 9A 0000 ---- E                 CALL     A23SUB3        ;Call subprogram
0011 B8 4C00                        MOV      AX,4C00H       ;End processing
0014 CD 21                          INT      21H
0016                      BEGIN     ENDP
                                    END      BEGIN

Segments and Groups:
     N a m e              Length    Align       Combine    Class
DGROUP . . . . . . . .    GROUP
 _DATA . . . . . . . .    0004      WORD        PUBLIC     'DATA'
 STACK . . . . . . . .    0040      PARA        STACK      'STACK'
 _TEXT  . . . . . . . .   0016      WORD        PUBLIC     'CODE'
Symbols:
     N a m e              Type      Value       Attr
A23SUB3  . . . . . . .    L FAR     0000        External
BEGIN  . . . . . . . .    F PROC    0000        _TEXT  Length = 0016
PRICE  . . . . . . . .    L WORD    0002        _DATA
QTY  . . . . . . . . .    L WORD    0000        _DATA
------------------------------------------------------------------------

                          TITLE     A23SUB3 Called subprogram
                                    .MODEL SMALL
                                    .CODE
0000                      A23SUB3   PROC    FAR
                                    PUBLIC A23SUB3
0000 F7 E3                          MUL     BX         ;AX = price, BX = qty
0002 CB                             RETF               ;DX:AX = product
0003                      A23SUB3   ENDP
                                    END     A23SUB3

Segments and Groups:
     N a m e              Length    Align       Combine    Class
DGROUP . . . . . . . .    GROUP
 _DATA . . . . . . . .    0000      WORD        PUBLIC     'DATA'
 _TEXT  . . . . . . . .   0003      WORD        PUBLIC     'CODE'

Symbols:
     N a m e              Type      Value       Attr
A23SUB3  . . . . . . .    F PROC    0000        _TEXT  Global  Length=0003

------------------------------------------------------------------------
```

Figure 23-5a Using Simplified Segment Directives

DEFINING COMMON DATA AS PUBLIC

A common programming requirement is to process data in one module that is defined in another module. Let's modify the preceding examples so that, although the main program still defines QTY and PRICE, the subprogram (rather than the main program)

```
Link Map
Object Modules: A23MAIN3+A23SUB3

Start  Stop   Length Name       Class
00000H 00018H 00019H _TEXT      CODE <-- code segment
0001AH 0001DH 00004H _DATA      DATA          first
00020H 0005FH 00040H STACK      STACK

Program entry point at 0000:0000
```

Figure 23-5b Using Simplified Segment Directives

loads their values into the BX and AX. Figure 23-6 gives the revised coding, with the following changes:

- The main program, A23MAIN4, defines QTY and PRICE as PUBLIC. The data segment is also defined with the PUBLIC attribute. Note in the symbol table the global attribute for QTY and PRICE.
- The subprogram, A23SUB4, defines both QTY and PRICE as EXTRN and as WORD. This definition informs the assembler of the length of the two fields. The assembler can generate the correct operation code for the MOV instructions, but the linker will have to complete the operands. (In the subprogram's symbol table, PRICE and QTY are now classed as external.)

The assembler lists the MOV instructions in the subprogram as

```
A1 0000 E        MOV AX,PRICE
8B 1E 0000 E     MOV BX,QTY
```

Object code A1 means move a word from memory to the AX, whereas 8B means move a word from memory to the BX. (AX operations often require fewer bytes.) For A23SUB4, the assembler has no way of knowing the locations of QTY and PRICE, so it has stored zeros in the operands for both MOVs. Tracing through program execution reveals that the linker has completed the object code operands as follows:

```
A1 0200
8B 1E 0000
```

The object code is now identical to that generated for the three preceding programs, where the MOV instructions are in the calling program. This is a logical result because the operands in all three programs reference the same data segment address in the DS register and the same offset values.

The main program and the subprogram may define other data items, but only those defined as PUBLIC and EXTRN would be known in common to them.

DEFINING DATA IN BOTH PROGRAMS

In the preceding example, A23MAIN4 defined QTY and PRICE, whereas A23SUB4 did not define any data. The reason A23SUB4 can reference A23MAIN4's data is because it has preserved the address of the data segment in the DS register, which still points to

```
                        TITLE     A23MAIN4 (EXE)  Call subprogram
                                  EXTRN  A23SUB4:FAR
                                  PUBLIC QTY,PRICE
                        ; -------------------------------------------
0000                    STACKSG   SEGMENT PARA STACK 'Stack'
0000 0040[????]                   DW      64 DUP(?)
0080                    STACKSG   ENDS
                        ; -------------------------------------------
0000                    DATASG    SEGMENT PARA PUBLIC 'Data'
0000 0140               QTY       DW      0140H
0002 2500               PRICE     DW      2500H
0004                    DATASG    ENDS
                        ; -------------------------------------------
0000                    CODESG    SEGMENT PARA PUBLIC 'Code'
0000                    BEGIN     PROC    FAR
                                  ASSUME CS:CODESG,DS:DATASG,SS:STACKSG
0000 B8 ---- R                    MOV     AX,DATASG
0003 8E D8                        MOV     DS,AX
0005 9A 0000 ---- E               CALL    A23SUB4        ;Call subprogram
000A B8 4C00                      MOV     AX,4C00H       ;End processing
000D CD 21                        INT     21H
000F                    BEGIN     ENDP
000F                    CODESG    ENDS
                                  END     BEGIN

Segments and Groups:
    N a m e             Length    Align    Combine    Class
CODESG . . . . . .       000F     PARA     PUBLIC     'CODE'
DATASG . . . . . .       0004     PARA     PUBLIC     'DATA'
STACKSG  . . . . .       0080     PARA     STACK      'STACK'
Symbols:
    N a m e              Type     Value     Attr
A23SUB4  . . . . .      L FAR     0000     External
BEGIN  . . . . . .      F PROC    0000     CODESG     Length = 000F
PRICE  . . . . . .      L WORD    0002     DATASG     Global
QTY  . . . . . . .      L WORD    0000     DATASG     Global
-------------------------------------------------------------------------

                        TITLE     A23SUB4 Called subprogram
                                  EXTRN  QTY:WORD, PRICE:WORD
                        ; -----------------------------------
0000                    CODESG    SEGMENT PARA PUBLIC 'CODE'
0000                    A23SUB4   PROC    FAR
                                  ASSUME CS:CODESG
                                  PUBLIC A23SUB4
0000 A1 0000 E                    MOV     AX,PRICE
0003 8B 1E 0000 E                 MOV     BX,QTY
0007 F7 E3                        MUL     BX            ;DX:AX = product
0009 CB                           RETF                  ;Return to caller
000A                    A23SUB4   ENDP
000A                    CODESG    ENDS
                                  END     A23SUB4
```

Figure 23-6a Common Data in Subprograms

A23MAIN4's data segment. (The only segment address changed was that of the code segment.) But programs are not always so simple, and subprograms often not only have to define their own data, but also have to reference data in the calling program, as the next example shows.

In a variation on the preceding program, Figure 23-7 defines QTY in A23MAIN5, but defines PRICE in A23SUB5. From inside A23MAIN5, PRICE does not exist, although A23SUB5 has to know the location of both items. A23SUB5's code segment has to retrieve

```
Segments and Groups:
    N a m e          Length   Align  Combine    Class
CODESG . . . . . .    000A    PARA    PUBLIC    'CODE'
Symbols:
    N a m e           Type    Value    Attr
A23SUB4  . . . . .  F PROC    0000     CODESG  Global  Length = 000A
PRICE  . . . . . .  V WORD    0000     External
QTY  . . . . . . .  V WORD    0000     External
--------------------------------------------------------------------
```

```
Link Map
Object Modules: A23MAIN4+A23SUB4

Start  Stop   Length Name           Class
00000H 0007FH 00080H STACKSG        STACK
00080H 00083H 00004H DATASG         DATA
00090H 000A9H 0001AH CODESG         CODE

Program entry point at 0009:0000
```

Figure 23-6b Common Data in Subprograms

QTY right away, while the DS register still contains the address of A23MAIN5's data segment. A23SUB5 then pushes the DS onto the stack and loads the DS with the address of its own data segment. A23SUB5 can now get PRICE and perform the multiplication of QTY and PRICE.

Before returning to A23MAIN5, A23SUB5 has to pop the DS off the stack so that A23MAIN5 can access its own data segment. (Technically, this is not really necessary in the current example, because A23MAIN5 happens to end processing immediately, but we'll do it as a standard practice.)

As a final note, you could make both data segments PUBLIC, with the same name and class. In that case, the linker would combine them, and A23SUB5 wouldn't have to push and pop the DS, because the programs would use the same data segment and DS address. We'll leave this variation as an exercise for you to revise and trace under DEBUG. A23SUB5's code segment could look like this:

```
EXTRN   QTY:WORD
ASSUME  CS:CODESG,DS:DATASG
PUBLIC  A23SUB5
MOV     AX,PRICE        ;PRICE in own data segment
MOV     BX,QTY          ;QTY in A23MAIN5
MUL     BX              ;Product in DX:AX
RETF                    ;Far return
```

PASSING PARAMETERS TO A SUBPROGRAM

Another way of making data known to a called subprogram is by *passing parameters,* in which a program passes data physically via the stack. In this case, ensure that each PUSH references a word (or doubleword on advanced systems), in either memory or a register.

The *stack frame* is the portion of the stack that the calling program uses to pass parameters and that the called subprogram uses for accessing the parameters. The called

```
                        TITLE    A23MAIN5 (EXE)  Call subprogram
                                 EXTRN  A23SUB5:FAR
                                 PUBLIC QTY
                        ; ----------------------------------------------
0000                    STACKSG  SEGMENT PARA STACK 'Stack'
0000 0040[????]                  DW      64 DUP(?)
0080                    STACKSG  ENDS
                        ; ----------------------------------------------
0000                    DATASG   SEGMENT PARA 'Data'
0000 0140               QTY      DW      0140H
0002                    DATASG   ENDS
                        ; ----------------------------------------------
0000                    CODESG   SEGMENT PARA 'Code'
0000                    BEGIN    PROC   FAR
                                 ASSUME CS:CODESG,DS:DATASG,SS:STACKSG
0000 B8 ---- R                   MOV    AX,DATASG
0003 8E D8                       MOV    DS,AX
0005 9A 0000 ---- E              CALL   A23SUB5       ;Call subprogram
000A B8 4C00                     MOV    AX,4C00H      ;End processing
000D CD 21                       INT    21H
000F                    BEGIN    ENDP
000F                    CODESG   ENDS
                                 END    BEGIN

Segments and Groups:
    N a m e           Length     Align  Combine  Class
CODESG . . . . . .     000F      PARA    NONE    'CODE'
DATASG . . . . . .     0002      PARA    NONE    'DATA'
STACKSG  . . . . .     0080      PARA    STACK   'STACK'
Symbols:
    N a m e            Type      Value   Attr
A23SUB5  . . . . .     L FAR     0000    External
BEGIN  . . . . . .     F PROC    0000    CODESG  Length = 000F
QTY  . . . . . . .     L WORD    0000    DATASG  Global
--------------------------------------------------------------------

                        TITLE    A23SUB5 Called subprogram
                                 EXTRN   QTY:WORD
                        ; ----------------------------------------------
0000                    DATASG   SEGMENT PARA 'Data'
0000 2500               PRICE    DW      2500H
0002                    DATASG   ENDS
                        ; ----------------------------------------------
0000                    CODESG   SEGMENT PARA 'CODE'
0000                    A23SUB5  PROC   FAR
                                 ASSUME CS:CODESG
                                 PUBLIC A23SUB5
0000 8B 1E 0000 E                MOV    BX,QTY        ;Get QTY from CALLMUL
0004 1E                          PUSH   DS            ;Save CALLMUL's DS
                                 ASSUME DS:DATASG
0005 B8 ---- R                   MOV    AX,DATASG     ;Set up own DS
0008 8E D8                       MOV    DS,AX         ;Price from own
000A A1 0000 R                   MOV    AX,PRICE      ;  data segment
000D F7 E3                       MUL    BX            ;DX:AX = product
000F 1F                          POP    DS            ;Restore CALLMUL's DS
0010 CB                          RETF                 ;Return to caller
0011                    A23SUB5  ENDP
0011                    CODESG   ENDS
                                 END     A23SUB5
```

Figure 23-7a Defining Data in Both Programs

```
Segments and Groups:
    N a m e          Length  Align    Combine  Class
CODESG . . . . . . . 0011     PARA    NONE     'CODE'
DATASG . . . . . . . 0002     PARA    NONE     'DATA'
Symbols:
    N a m e          Type    Value    Attr
A23SUB5  . . . . . . F PROC   0000    CODESG  Global  Length = 0011
PRICE  . . . . . . . L WORD   0000    DATASG
QTY  . . . . . . . . V WORD   0000    External
```

```
Link Map
Object Modules: A23MAIN5+A23SUB5

Start  Stop   Length Name                Class
00000H 0007FH 00080H STACKSG             STACK
00080H 00081H 00002H DATASG              DATA
00090H 00091H 00002H DATASG              DATA
000A0H 000AEH 0000FH CODESG              CODE
000B0H 000C0H 00011H CODESG              CODE

Program entry point at 000A:0000
```

Figure 23-7b Defining Data in Both Programs

subprogram may also use the stack frame for temporary storage of local data. The BP register acts as a frame pointer. For passing parameters, we'll make use of both the BP and SP registers.

In Figure 23-8, the calling program A23MAIN6 pushes both PRICE and QTY prior to calling the subprogram A23SUB6. Initially, the SP contained the size of the stack, 80H. Each word pushed onto the stack decrements the SP by 2. After the CALL, the stack frame appears as follows:

. . .	1200	200F	4001	0025
	78	7A	7C	7E

1. A PUSH loaded PRICE (2500H) onto the stack frame at offset 7EH.
2. A PUSH loaded QTY (0140H) onto the stack frame at offset 7CH.
3. CALL pushed the contents of the CS (0F20H for this execution) onto the stack frame at 7AH. Because the subprogram is PUBLIC, the linker combines the two code segments, and the CS address is the same for both.
4. CALL also pushed the contents of the IP register, 0012H, onto the stack frame at 78H.

The called program requires the use of the BP to access the parameters in the stack frame. Its first action is to save the contents of the BP for the calling program, so it pushes the BP onto the stack. In this example, the BP happens to contain zero, which PUSH stores in the stack at offset 76H:

0000	1200	200F	4001	0025
76	78	7A	7C	7E

```
                          TITLE     A23MAIN6 (EXE)  Passing parameters
                                    EXTRN  A23SUB6:FAR
                          ; ---------------------------------------------
0000                      STACKSG   SEGMENT PARA STACK 'Stack'
0000 0040[????]                     DW      64 DUP(?)
0080                      STACKSG   ENDS
                          ; ---------------------------------------------
0000                      DATASG    SEGMENT PARA 'Data'
0000 0140                 QTY       DW      0140H
0002 2500                 PRICE     DW      2500H
0004                      DATASG    ENDS
                          ; ---------------------------------------------
0000                      CODESG    SEGMENT PARA PUBLIC 'Code'
0000                      BEGIN     PROC    FAR
                                    ASSUME  CS:CODESG,DS:DATASG,SS:STACKSG
0000 B8 ---- R                      MOV     AX,DATASG
0003 8E D8                          MOV     DS,AX
0005 FF 36 0002 R                   PUSH    PRICE         ;Save price
0009 FF 36 0000 R                   PUSH    QTY           ;  and quantity
000D 9A 0000 ---- E                 CALL    A23SUB6       ;Call subprogram
0012 B8 4C00                        MOV     AX,4C00H      ;End processing
0015 CD 21                          INT     21H
0017                      BEGIN     ENDP
0017                      CODESG    ENDS
                                    END     BEGIN

Segments and Groups:
    N a m e               Length   Align   Combine   Class
CODESG . . . . . . . . .  0017     PARA    PUBLIC    'CODE'
DATASG . . . . . . . . .  0004     PARA    NONE      'DATA'
STACKSG  . . . . . . . .  0080     PARA    STACK     'STACK'
Symbols:
    N a m e               Type     Value    Attr
A23SUB6  . . . . . . . .  L FAR    0000     External
BEGIN  . . . . . . . . .  F PROC   0000     CODESG   Length = 0017
PRICE  . . . . . . . . .  L WORD   0002     DATASG
QTY  . . . . . . . . . .  L WORD   0000     DATASG
-----------------------------------------------------------------------

                          TITLE     A23SUB6 Called subprogram
0000                      CODESG    SEGMENT PARA PUBLIC 'Code'
0000                      A23SUB6   PROC    FAR
                                    ASSUME  CS:CODESG
                                    PUBLIC  A23SUB6
0000 55                             PUSH    BP
0001 8B EC                          MOV     BP,SP
0003 8B 46 08                       MOV     AX,[BP+8]      ;Get price
0006 8B 5E 06                       MOV     BX,[BP+6]      ;Get quantity
0009 F7 E3                          MUL     BX             ;DX:AX = product
000B 5D                             POP     BP
000C CA 0004                        RETF    4              ;Return to caller
000F                      A23SUB6   ENDP
000F                      CODESG    ENDS
                                    END
```

Figure 23-8a Passing Parameters

The program then inserts the contents of the SP (0076H) into the BP because the BP (but not the SP) is usable as an index register. Because the BP now also contains 0076H, PRICE is in the stack at BP + 8 (offset 7EH), and QTY is at BP + 6 (offset 7CH). We know these relative locations because we pushed 3 words (6 bytes) onto the stack after QTY was pushed. The routine transfers PRICE and QTY from the stack to the AX and BX, respectively, and performs the multiplication.

```
Segments and Groups:
    N a m e          Length    Align     Combine Class
CODESG . . . . . . . 000F      PARA      PUBLIC    'CODE'
Symbols:
    N a m e          Type      Value      Attr
A23SUB6  . . . . . . F PROC    0000      CODESG  Global  Length=000F
--------------------------------------------------------------------
```

```
          Link Map
          Object Modules: A23MAIN6+A23SUB6

          Start   Stop    Length Name                Class
          00000H 0007FH 00080H STACKSG              STACK
          00080H 00083H 00004H DATASG               DATA
          00090H 000BEH 0002FH CODESG               CODE

          Program entry point at 0009:0000
```

Figure 23-8b Passing Parameters

Before returning to the calling program, the subprogram pops the BP (returning the zero address to the BP), which increments the SP by 2, from 76H to 78H.

The last instruction, RETF, is a far return to the calling program, which performs the following:

- Pops the word now at the top of the stack frame (1200H) to the IP and increments the SP by 2, from 78H to 7AH.
- Pops the word now at the top (0F20) onto the CS and increments the SP by 2, from 7AH to 7CH.

Because of the two passed parameters at offsets 7CH and 7EH, the return instruction is coded as RETF 4. The 4, known as a *pop-value,* contains the number of bytes in the passed parameters (two 1-word parameters in this case). RETF adds the pop-value to the SP, correcting it to 80H. In effect, because the parameters in the stack are no longer required, the operation "discards" them and returns correctly to the calling program. Note that although the POP and RET operations increment the SP, they don't actually erase the contents of the stack.

If you follow the general rules discussed in this chapter, you should be able to link a program consisting of more than two assembly modules and to make data known in all the modules. But watch out for the size of the stack: For large programs with many PUSH and CALL operations, defining 64 words could be a wise precaution.

Chapter 24 covers some important concepts on memory management and executing overlay programs. Chapter 26 provides additional features of segments, including defining more than one code or data segment in the same assembly module and the use of GROUP to combine these into a common segment.

LINKING PASCAL WITH AN ASSEMBLY LANGUAGE PROGRAM

This section explains how to link a Pascal program to an assembly subprogram. The simple Pascal program in Figure 23-9 links to an assembly subprogram whose sole purpose is to set the cursor. The Pascal program is compiled to produce an .OBJ module, and the

```
program p23pascl ( input, output );

  procedure set_curs( const row: integer;
                      const col: integer ); extern;
  var
       temp_row:      integer;
       temp_col:      integer;

  begin
       write( 'Enter cursor row: ' );
       readln( temp_row );

       write( 'Enter cursor column: ' );
       readln( temp_col );

       set_curs( temp_row, temp_col );
       write( 'New cursor location' );
  end.

----------------------------------------------------------

TITLE     A23SETCR  Assembler subprogram called by Pascal
          PUBLIC SET_CURS
;
;    SET_CURS: Set cursor on screen at passed location
;    Passed:   const row        Row and column where
;              const col        cursor is to be set
;    Returned: Nothing
;
CODESEG   SEGMENT PARA PUBLIC 'CODE'
SET_CURS  PROC    FAR
          ASSUME  CS:CODESEG
          PUSH    BP            ;Caller's BP register
          MOV     BP,SP         ;Point to parameters passed

          MOV     SI,[BP+8]     ;SI points to row
          MOV     DH,[SI]       ;Move row to DH

          MOV     SI,[BP+6]     ;SI points to column
          MOV     DL,[SI]       ;Move column to DL

          MOV     AH,02H        ;Request set cursor
          MOV     BH,0          ;Video page
          INT     10H

          POP     BP            ;Return to caller
          RETF    4
SET_CURS  ENDP
CODESEG   ENDS
          END
```

Figure 23-9 Linking Pascal to Assembler

assembly program is assembled to produce an .OBJ module. The linker then combines these two .OBJ modules into one .EXE executable module.

The Pascal program defines two items named temp_row and temp_col and accepts entries for row and column from the keyboard into these variables. The program defines the name of the assembly subprogram as set_curs and defines the two parameters as extern. It sends the addresses of temp_row and temp_col as parameters to the subprogram to set the cursor to that location. The Pascal statement that "calls" the name of the subprogram and passes the parameters is

```
set_curs( temp_row, temp_col );
```

Values pushed onto the stack are the calling program's stack pointer, the return segment pointer, the return offset, and the addresses of the two passed parameters. The following shows the offsets for each entry in the stack:

00 Caller's stack pointer
02 Caller's return segment pointer
04 Caller's return offset
06 Address of second parameter
08 Address of first parameter

Because the assembly subprogram has to use the BP register, you have to push the BP onto the stack to save its address for the return to the Pascal calling program. Note that the steps in the called subprogram are similar to those in the program in Figure 23-7.

The SP register normally addresses entries in the stack. But since you cannot use the SP to act as an index register, the step after pushing the BP is to move the address in the SP to the BP. This step enables you to use the BP as an index register to access entries in the stack frame.

The next step is to access the addresses of the two parameters in the stack frame. The first passed parameter, the row, is at offset 08H in the stack frame and can be accessed by BP + 08H. The second passed parameter, the column, is at offset 06H and can be accessed by BP + 06H.

Each of the two addresses in the stack frame has to be transferred to one of the available index registers: BX, DI, or SI. This example uses [BP + 08] to move the address of the row to the SI and then uses [SI] to move the contents of the passed parameter to the DH register.

The column is transferred to the DL register in a similar way. Then the subprogram uses the row and column in the DX register for INT 10H to set the cursor. On exit, the subprogram pops the BP. The RET instruction requires an operand value that is two times the number of parameters—in this case, 2 × 2, or 4. Values are automatically popped off the stack and control transfers back to the calling program.

If you change a segment register, be sure to PUSH it on entry into and POP it on exit from the subprogram. The recommended practice for a Pascal call is to preserve the DI, SI, BP, DS, and SS registers. You can also use the stack to pass values from a subprogram to a calling program. Although the subprogram in Figure 23-9 doesn't return values, Pascal would expect a subprogram to return them as a single word in the AX or as a pair of words in the DX:AX.

This trivial program produces a module larger than 20K bytes. A compiler language typically generates considerable overhead regardless of the size of the source program.

Other Pascal versions do not necessarily follow the conventions used here. The appropriate standard is that described in the compiler manual, usually in a section whose title begins with "Interfacing . . . " or "Mixed Languages . . . ".

LINKING C WITH AN ASSEMBLY LANGUAGE PROGRAM

The problem with describing the linkage of C to an assembly program is that versions of C have different conventions. (For precise requirements, refer to your C manual.) Some points of interest are the following:

- For versions of C that are sensitive to uppercase and lowercase, the name of the assembly module should be in the same case as the C program's reference.
- Most versions of C pass parameters onto the stack in a sequence that is the *reverse* of that of other languages. Consider, for example, the C statement

  ```
  Adds (m, n);
  ```

  The statement pushes n and then m onto the stack in that order and calls Adds. On return from the called module, the C module (not the assembly module) adds 4 to the SP to discard the passed parameters. The typical procedure in the called assembly module for accessing the two passed parameters is as follows:

  ```
  PUSH  BP
  MOV   BP,SP
  MOV   DH,[BP+4]
  MOV   DL,[BP+6]
  ...
  POP   BP
  RET
  ```

- Some versions of C require that an assembly module that changes the DI and SI registers should push them on entry into and pop them on exit from the assembler subprogram.
- The assembly module should return values, if required, as one word in the AX or two words in the DX:AX pair.
- For some versions of C, an assembly program that sets the DF flag should clear it (CLD) before returning.

Linking Microsoft C with Microsoft Assembler

Naming conventions. In Microsoft C and assembler, the assembly modules must use a naming convention for segments and variables that is compatible with that in C. All assembler references to functions and variables in the C module must begin with an underscore (_). Further, because C is *case sensitive,* the assembly module should use the same case (upper or lower) for any variable names in common with the C module.

Registers. The assembly module must preserve the original values in the BP, SP, CS, DS, SS, DI, and SI registers.

Passing parameters. There are two methods of passing parameters:

1. By *reference,* either as near (an offset in the default segment) or as far (an offset in another segment). The called assembly module can directly alter the value defined in the C module.

2. By *value,* in which the C caller passes a copy of the variable on the stack. The called assembly module can alter the passed value, but has no access to the original C value. If there is more than one parameter, C pushes them onto the stack starting with the rightmost parameter.

Compatibility of data types. The following list shows the types of C variables and their equivalent assembler types:

C DATA TYPE	MASM 5.X TYPE	MASM 6.X TYPE
char	DB	BYTE
unsigned short/int	DW	WORD
int, short	DW	SWORD
unsigned long	DD	DWORD
long	DD	SDWORD

Returned values. The called assembly module uses the following registers for any returned values:

C DATA TYPE	REGISTER
char	AL
short, near, int (16 bit)	AX
short, near, int (32 bit)	EAX
long, far (16 bit)	DX:AX
long, far (32 bit)	EDX:EAX

On return from the called module, issue RET with no pop value.

Compiling and assembling. Use the same memory model for both languages. The assembly .MODEL statement indicates the C convention, such as .MODEL SMALL,C. Also, use the appropriate assembly switch to preserve the case of (nonlocal) names.

Linking Turbo C with Turbo Assembler

Language interfaces. Turbo C provides two ways of interfacing with Turbo Assembler—by separate modules and by inline code:

1. *Separate modules.* For this conventional method, you code the C and assembly programs separately. Use TCC to compile the C module, TASM to assemble the assembly module, and TLINK to link them.
2. *Inline assembly code.* To compile the C module, you request TCC.EXE (the command version of Turbo C). Simply insert assembly statements, preceded by the keyword asm, in the source code, as, for example,

```
asm INC WORD PTR FLDX
```

Segments. The code segment must be named _TEXT. The data segments (two if required) are named _DATA for data that is to be initialized on entry to a block and _BSS for uninitialized data.

Naming conventions. The Turbo Assembler modules must use a naming convention for segments and variables that is compatible with that of Turbo C. All assembler references to functions and variables in the C module must begin with an underscore (_). Further, since C is case sensitive, the assembly module should use the same case (upper or lower) for any variable names in common with the C module.

Registers. The assembly module may freely use the AX, BX, CX, DX, ES, and flags registers. It may also use the BP, SP, CS, DS, SS, DI, and SI registers provided that it saves (pushes) and restores (pops) them.

Passing parameters. Turbo C passes parameters by value. If there is more than one parameter, Turbo C pushes them onto the stack from right to left.

Return. The assembly program simply uses RET (with no pop-value) to return to the C module. The C module pops the stack on reentry to it.

Example of a C Program

The program in Figure 23-10 illustrates linking a Turbo C program with an assembly module. The program performs the same actions as the Pascal program in the previous section: The C program accepts values from the keyboard for row and column and passes them to the assembler subprogram. The assembler subprogram in its turn sets the cursor and returns to the C module.

KEY POINTS

- The align operator tells the assembler to align the named segment beginning on a particular storage boundary.
- The combine operator tells the assembler and linker whether to combine segments or to keep them separate.
- You can assign the same class name to related segments so that the assembler and linker group them together.
- An intrasegment CALL is near if the called procedure is defined as or defaults to NEAR (within 32K). An intrasegment call may be far if the call is to a far procedure within the same segment.
- An intersegment CALL calls a procedure in another segment and is defined as FAR or as EXTRN.
- In a main program that calls a subprogram, define the entry point as EXTRN; in the subprogram, define the entry point as PUBLIC.

```
#include <stdio.h>

int main (void)
{
   int temp_row, temp_col;

   printf ("Enter cursor row: ");
   scanf ("%d", &temp_row);

   printf ("Enter cursor column: ");
   scanf ("%d", &temp_col);

   set_curs (temp_row, temp_col);
   printf ("New cursor location\n");
}
--------------------------------------------------------
;
; Use small memory model for C: near code, near data
; Use 'standard' segment names, and group directive

_DATA      segment word 'DATA'
row        equ     [bp+4]          ;Parameters
col        equ     [bp+6]          ;  (arguments)
_DATA      ends


_TEXT      SEGMENT BYTE PUBLIC 'CODE'
DGROUP     GROUP   _DATA
           ASSUME  CS:_TEXT, DS:DGROUP, SS:DGROUP

           PUBLIC  _set_curs
_set_curs  PROC    NEAR
           PUSH    BP              ;Caller's BP register
           MOV     BP,SP           ;Point to parameters

           MOV     AH,02H          ;Request set cursor
           MOV     BX,0            ;Video page 0
           MOV     DH,ROW          ;Row from BP+4
           MOV     DL,COL          ;Column from BP+6
           INT     10H             ;Call interrupt

           POP     BP              ;Restore BP
           RETF                    ;Return to caller
_set_curs  ENDP
_TEXT      ENDS
           END
```

Figure 23-10 Linking C to Assembler

- To link two code segments into one segment, define them with the same name, the same class, and the PUBLIC combine type.
- It is generally easier (but not necessary) to define common data in the main program. The main program defines the common data as PUBLIC, and the subprogram (or subprograms) defines the common data as EXTRN.

QUESTIONS

23-1. Give four reasons for organizing a program into subprograms.

The next three questions refer to the general format for the SEGMENT directive:

```
seg-name SEGMENT [align] [combine] ['class']
```

23-2. (a) What is the default for the SEGMENT directive's align option? (b) What is the effect of the BYTE option? (That is, what action does the assembler take?)

23-3. (a) What is the default for the SEGMENT directive's combine option? (b) Why would you use its PUBLIC option? (c) Why would you use its COMMON option?

23-4. (a) What is normally the code segment's class option for the SEGMENT directive? (b) If two segments have the same class but not the PUBLIC combine option, what is the effect? (c) If two segments have the same class and both have the PUBLIC combine option, what is the effect?

23-5. Explain the difference between an intrasegment call and an intersegment call.

23-6. A program named MPROG23 is to call a subprogram named SCALC23. (a) What statement in MPROG23 informs the assembler that the name SCALC23 is defined outside its own assembly? (b) What statement in SCALC23 is required to make its name known to MPROG23?

23-7. Assume that MPROG23 in Question 23-6 has defined three data items as DWs: QUANTITY (stock quantity on hand), UNITCOST (unit cost), and STVALUE (stock value). SCALC23 is to divide STVALUE by QUANTITY and is to store the quotient in UNITCOST. (a) How does MPROG23 inform the assembler that the three data items are to be known outside this assembly? (b) How does SCALC23 inform the assembler that the three data items are defined in another module?

23-8. Combine Questions 23-6 and 23-7 into a working program and test it.

23-9. Revise Question 23-8 so that MPROG23 passes all three data items as parameters. Note, however, that SCALC23 is to return the calculated price intact in its parameter.

23-10. Expand Question 23-9 so that MPROG23 accepts stock quantity and value from the keyboard, subprogram SBINRY23 converts the ASCII amounts to binary, subprogram SCALC23 calculates the price, and subprogram SASCII23 converts the binary price to ASCII and displays the result.

24 MEMORY MANAGEMENT

Objective: To explain how the system manages memory and loads programs for execution.

INTRODUCTION

This chapter describes the boot procedure, system initialization, program segment prefix, environment, memory control, program loader, and resident programs. The operations introduced are INT 2FH function 4A01H Multiplex Interrupt and these INT 21H functions:

25H Set interrupt vector	49H Free allocated memory
31H Keep program	4AH Modify allocated memory block
3306H Get DOS version	4BH Load or execute a program
34H Get address of DOS busy flag	51H Get address of current PSP
35H Get interrupt vector	52H Get address of internal DOS list
48H Allocate memory	58H Get/set memory allocation strategy

THE MAIN DOS PROGRAMS

The four major DOS programs are the boot record, IO.SYS, MSDOS.SYS, and COMMAND.COM:

1. The *boot record* is on track 0, sector 1, of any disk that you format with FORMAT /S. When you start up the computer, the system automatically executes the boot record, which, in turn, loads IO.SYS from disk into memory.

2. *IO.SYS* is a low-level interface to the BIOS routines in ROM. On startup, it determines the status of the computer's devices and equipment, sets addresses in the interrupt vector table for interrupts up to 20H, and handles input/output between memory and external devices. It also loads MSDOS.SYS.
3. *MSDOS.SYS* is a high-level interface to programs that sets addresses in the interrupt vector table for interrupts 20H through 3FH. Its services include managing the directory and files on disk, blocking/deblocking disk records, and INT 21H functions. It also loads COMMAND.COM.
4. *COMMAND.COM* consists of three portions that are loaded into memory either permanently or temporarily during a session:
   a. The functions of the *resident portion* include handling the following interrupts: INT 22H (Terminate Address); INT 23H (Ctrl+Break Handler); INT 24H (Error detection on Disk Read/Write); and INT 27H (Terminate but Stay Resident (TSR)).
   b. When the system starts up, *the initialization portion* processes the AUTOEXEC file and determines the segment address where programs are to be loaded for execution. Because none of the initialization routines is required again during a session, the first program loaded from disk overlays this portion.
   c. The *transient portion* is loaded into a high area of memory, which may be overlaid with other requested programs. This portion displays the familiar screen prompt and accepts and executes such requests as DIR and COPY. It also contains the loader facility that loads .COM and .EXE programs from disk into memory for execution.

   Normal program termination causes a return to the resident portion of COMMAND.COM. If the executed program overlaid the transient portion, the resident portion reloads it into memory.

Figure 24-1 shows a map of memory after the system programs have been loaded. Details vary by system.

THE HIGH-MEMORY AREA

The processor uses a number of address lines to access memory. For the 80286 and later, line number A20 can address a 64K space known as the *high-memory area (HMA),* from FFFF:10H through FFFF:FFFFH, just above the 1-megabyte address.

When the processor runs in real (8086) mode, it normally disables the A20 line so that addresses that exceed this limit wrap around to the beginning of memory. Enabling the A20 line permits addressing locations in the HMA. As of DOS 5.0, you can ask CONFIG.SYS to relocate system files from low memory to the HMA, thereby freeing space for user programs. You can use INT 21H function 3306H (Get DOS Version), to determine the presence of system files in the HMA:

```
MOV  AX,3306H     ;Request DOS version
INT  21H          ;Call interrupt service
```

Beginning Address	Contents
F0000H	System ROM area
E0000H	ROM BIOS
D0000H	ROM BIOS
C0000H	ROM BIOS
B0000H	Video buffers
A0000H	Video buffers
xxxx0H	Transient portion of COMMAND.COM, at top of RAM
	. . .
	User programs
	Resident programs (if any)
xxxx0H	Resident portion of COMMAND.COM
xxxx0H	MSDOS.SYS and IO.SYS
00500H	DOS communication area
00400H	BIOS data area
00000H	Interrupt vector table

Note: Conventional memory is from 00000H to A0000H (640K).
Upper memory area is from A0000H up to FFFF0H (one meg).
High memory area (HMA) is 64K from FFFF0H through FFFFFH.
Extended memory is above HMA.

Figure 24-1 Map of Base Memory

The operation returns the following values in registers:

- BL = Major version number (as n in version n.2)
- BH = Minor version number (as 2 in version n.2)
- DL = Revision number in the three low bits (2-0)
- DH = DOS version flags, where bit 4 set to 1 means in HMA

INT 2FH (Multiplex Interrupt), among its many services, provides a check (via function 4A01H) for available space in the HMA:

```
MOV AX,4A01H     ;Request space in HMA
INT 2FH          ;Call multiplex interrupt
```

The operation returns the following values in registers:

- BX = Number of free bytes available in the HMA (zero if COMMAND.COM is not loaded high)
- ES:DI = Address of the first free byte in the HMA (FFFF:FFFF if DOS is not loaded high)

THE PROGRAM SEGMENT PREFIX

The program loader loads .COM and .EXE programs for execution into a program segment and creates a PSP at offset 00H and the program itself at offset 100H of the segment. The PSP contains the following fields, according to relative position:

00–01H	An INT 20H instruction (CD20H) to facilitate the return to the system
02–03H	The segment address of the last paragraph of memory allocated to the program, as xxxx0. For example, 640K is indicated as 00A0H, meaning A0000[0].
04–09H	Reserved by the system
0A–0DH	Terminate address (segment address for INT 22H)
0E–11H	Ctrl+Break exit address (segment address for INT 23H)
12–15H	Critical error exit address (segment address for INT 24H)
16–17H	Reserved by the system
18–2BH	Default file handle table
2C–2DH	Segment address of program's environment
2E–31H	Reserved by the system
32–33H	Length of the file handle table
34–37H	Far pointer to the handle table
38–4FH	Reserved by the system
50–51H	Call to INT 21H function (INT 21H and RETF)
52–5BH	Reserved by the system
5C–6BH	Parameter area 1, formatted as a standard unopened FCB (#1)
6C–7FH	Parameter area 2, formatted as standard unopened FCB (#2); overlaid if the FCB at 5CH is opened
80–FFH	Buffer for a default DTA

PSP 18-2BH: Default File Handle Table

Each byte in the 20-byte default file handle table refers to an entry in a system table that defines the related device or driver. Initially, the table contains 0101010002FF . . . FF, where the first 01 refers to the keyboard, the second 01 to the screen, and so forth:

TABLE	DEVICE	HANDLE	DEVICE
01	Console	0	Keyboard (standard input)
01	Console	1	Screen (standard output)
01	Console	2	Screen (standard error)
00	COM1 (serial port)	3	Auxiliary
02	Printer	4	Standard printer
FF	Unassigned	5	Unassigned

The table of 20 handles explains why the system allows a maximum of 20 files open at one time. Normally, the word at PSP offset 32H contains the length of the table (14H, or 20), and 34H contains its segment address in the form IP:CS, where the IP is 18H (the offset in the PSP) and the CS is the segment address of the PSP.

Programs that need more than 20 open files have to release memory (INT 21H function 4AH) and use function 67H (set maximum handle count):

```
MOV  AH,67H       ;Request more handles
MOV  BX,count     ;New number (20 to 65,535)
INT  21H          ;Call interrupt service
```

The amount of memory required is 1 byte per handle, rounded up to the next byte paragraph plus 16 bytes. The operation creates the new handle table outside the PSP and updates PSP locations 32H and 34H. An invalid operation sets the carry flag and sets an error code in the AX.

PSP 2C-2DH: Segment Address of Environment

Every program loaded for execution has a related *environment* that the system stores in memory, beginning on a paragraph boundary before the program segment. The default size is 160 bytes, with a maximum of 32K. The environment contains such system commands as COMSPEC, PATH, PROMPT, and SET that are applicable to the program.

PSP 5C-6BH: Standard Unopened FCB #1

You may make a request for program execution including a file name, such as MASM E:PROG1.ASM. The program loader *formats* this area as FCB #1, with 05H (for drive E) followed by the file name (8 characters) and extension (3 characters). Omission of a drive and file name causes the loader to set the first byte to 00H (the default) and the rest of the FCB to blanks (20H).

PSP 6C-7FH: Standard Unopened FCB #2

You may also request program execution including two file names, such as COPY C:FILEA.DOC,D:FILEB.DOC. The program loader formats this area as FCB #2 for the *second* filename entered, with 04H (for drive D) followed by the file name (8 characters) and extension (3 characters).

PSP 80-FFH: Default DTA Buffer

The program loader initializes the *default buffer* for the DTA with the full text (if any) that you key in after the requested program name, such as MASM or COPY. The first byte contains the number of keys (if any) pressed immediately *after* the program name that is keyed in. Following the number are the characters (if any) keyed in, and then any "garbage" left in memory from a previous program.

The following four examples should clarify the contents and purpose of FCB #1, FCB #2, and the DTA.

Example 1: Command with No Operand

Suppose that you request a program named CALCIT.EXE to execute by keying in CALCIT <Enter>. When the program loader constructs the PSP, it sets up FCB #1, FCB #2, and the default DTA as:

```
5CH FCB #1: 00 20 20 20 20 20 20 20 20 20 20 20 ...
6CH FCB #2: 00 20 20 20 20 20 20 20 20 20 20 20 ...
80H DTA:    00 0D ...
```

FCB #1 and FCB #2: These are both dummy FCBs. Their first byte, 00H, refers to the default drive number. The subsequent bytes for filename and extension are blank, because there is no typed text following the program name.

DTA: The first byte contains the number of bytes keyed in after the name CALCIT, not including the <Enter>. Because no keys other than <Enter> were pressed, the number is zero. The second byte contains 0DH, for <Enter>.

Example 2: Command with Text Operand

Suppose that you want to execute a program named COLOR and pass a parameter "BY" that tells the program to set the color to blue (B) on a yellow (Y) background. You type the program name followed by the parameter: COLOR BY. The program loader then formats the PSP as follows:

```
5CH FCB #1: 00 42 59 20 20 20 20 20 20 20 20 20 ...
6CH FCB #2: 00 20 20 20 20 20 20 20 20 20 20 20 ...
80H DTA:    03 20 42 59 0D ...
```

FCB #1: This field contains 00H as the default drive and 4259H (BY) as the (presumed) filename. Note that the program loader doesn't know whether the filename is valid.

DTA: The bytes mean a length of 3, followed by a space, "BY," and 0DH for <Enter>. Other than the length, this field contains exactly what was typed after the program name COLOR.

Example 3: Command with a Filename Operand

Many programs allow you to type a filename after the program name. If you key in, for example, DEL D:CALCIT.OBJ <Enter>, the PSP contains the following:

```
5CH FCB #1: 04 43 41 4C 43 49 54 20 20 4F 42 4A ...
                C  A  L  C  I  T        O  B  J
6CH FCB #2: 00 20 20 20 20 20 20 20 20 20 20 20 ...
80H DTA:    0D 20 44 3A 43 41 4C 43 49 54 2E 4F 42 4A 0D ...
                   D  :  C  A  L  C  I  T  .  O  B  J
```

FCB #1: The first byte indicates the drive number (04 = D), followed by the name of the file, CALCIT, that the program is to reference. Next are two blanks that complete the 8-character filename and, finally, the extension, OBJ, without the leading dot.

DTA: The length of 13 (0DH) is followed by exactly what was typed, including 0DH for <Enter>.

Example 4: Command with Two Filename Operands

Consider entering a command followed by two operands, such as

```
COPY A:FILEA.ASM D:FILEB.ASM
```

The program loader sets the FCBs and DTA with the following:

```
5CH FCB #1: 01 46 49 4C 45 41 20 20 20 41 53 4D ...
                F  I  L  E  A           A  S  M
6CH FCB #2: 04 46 49 4C 45 42 20 20 20 41 53 4D ...
                F  I  L  E  B           A  S  M
80H DTA:    10 20 41 3A 46 49 4C 45 41 2E 41 53 4D 20 etc...
                   A  :  F  I  L  E  A  .  A  S  M    etc...
```

FCB #1. The first byte, 01, refers to drive A, followed by the first filename.

FCB #2. The first byte, 04, refers to drive D, followed by the second filename.

DTA. The DTA contains the number of characters keyed in (10H), a space (20H), A:FILEA.ASM D:FILEB.ASM, and 0DH for <Enter>.

Accessing the PSP

By determining the address of the PSP, you can access it in order to process specified files or to take special action. Because an .EXE program can't always assume that its code segment immediately follows the PSP, you can request INT 21H function 51H to deliver to the BX register the segment address of the current PSP. The following statements get the address of the PSP and save it in the ES register:

```
MOV AH,51H      ;Request address of PSP
INT 21H         ;Call interrupt service
MOV ES,BX       ;Save PSP address in ES
```

You may now use the ES to access data in the PSP:

```
CMP ES:BYTE PTR[80H],0     ;Check PSP buffer
JE  EXIT                   ;  zero, no data
```

To locate the DTA for a .COM program, simply set 80H in the BX, DI, or SI register and access the contents:

```
MOV   SI,80H            ;Address of DTA
CMP   BYTE PTR[SI],0    ;Check buffer (DS:SI)
JE    EXIT              ;  zero, no data
```

Program Example: Accessing the PSP

The partial .COM program in Figure 24-2 sets the attribute of a requested file to normal (00H). A user would key in the program name followed by the name of the file, such as A24ATTRB d:filename.ext. The program scans the DTA for the <Enter> character and replaces it with a byte of hex zeros, creating an ASCIIZ string. A user could also type in the directory path.

```
TITLE  A24ATTRB (.COM)  Set file attribute to normal
       .MODEL SMALL
       .CODE
       ORG    100H
BEGIN  PROC   NEAR
       MOV    AL,0DH                ;Search character <Enter>
       MOV    CX,21                 ;Number of bytes
       MOV    DI,82H                ;Start address in PSP
       REPNZ SCASB                  ;Scan for <Enter>
       JNZ    A90                   ;Not found, error
       DEC    DI                    ;Found:
       MOV    BYTE PTR [DI],0 ;Replace with 00H
       MOV    AH,43H                ;Request
       MOV    AL,01                 ;  set attribute
       MOV    CX,00                 ;  to normal
       MOV    DX,82H                ;ASCIIZ string in PSP
       INT    21H                   ;Call interrupt service
       JC     A90                   ;Write error?...
;      ...
A90:          ...                   ;Error processing
BEGIN  ENDP
       END    BEGIN
```

Figure 24-2 Setting the File Attribute

MEMORY BLOCKS

The system allows any number of programs such as RAMDISK and MOUSE to be loaded and to stay resident while other programs are executing. The system sets up one or two *memory blocks* for each loaded program. Immediately preceding each memory block is an *arena header* (or *memory control record*) beginning on a paragraph boundary and containing the following fields:

00–00H	Code, where 4DH ('M') means more blocks to follow and 5AH ('Z') means zero blocks to follow (the last block). (This is a useful interpretation, but not necessarily the original intention.)
01–02H	Segment address of the owner's PSP. 0800H means that the segment belongs to MSDOS.SYS, and 0000H means that it is released and available.
03–04H	Length of the memory block, in paragraphs.
05–07H	Reserved.
08–0FH	Filename of owner, in ASCIIZ format since DOS 4.0.

A forward linked list connects memory blocks. The *first* memory block, set up and owned by MSDOS.SYS, contains DOS file buffers, FCBs used by file handle functions, and device drivers loaded by DEVICE commands in CONFIG.SYS.

The *second* memory block is the resident portion of COMMAND.COM with its own PSP. A few special programs such as FASTOPEN and SHARE may be loaded before COMMAND.COM.

The *third* memory block is the master environment containing the COMSPEC command, PROMPT commands, PATH commands, and any strings set by SET.

Succeeding blocks include any resident (TSR) programs and the currently executing program. Each of these programs has two blocks; the first is a copy of the environment, and the second is a program segment with the PSP and the executable module.

INT 21H Function 52H: Get Address of Internal DOS List

The arena header for the first memory block, which belongs to MSDOS.SYS, can be located by means of an undocumented feature: INT 21H function 52H. The system table of addresses begins with these entries, each in doubleword (DD) format:

00H	DD	Address of first drive parameter block
04D	DD	Address of list of system file tables
08H	DD	Address of CLOCK$ device driver
0CH	DD	Address of CON device driver
. . .		

Function 52H returns the segment address of the list of file tables (the second entry) in the ES and an offset in the BX. ES:[BX-4] therefore points to the preceding entry, a doubleword in IP:CS format that contains the address of the first arena header.

To find subsequent memory blocks in the chain:

1. Use the address of the arena header for the memory block.
2. Add 1 to the segment address of the arena header to get the start of its memory block. (The arena header is 10H bytes long.)
3. Add the length of the memory block from offsets 03–04H of the arena header. You now have the segment address of the next arena header.

To determine the paragraphs of memory available to the system for the last program, find the arena header containing "Z" in byte 0, and perform the preceding calculations. The last block has available to it all remaining higher memory.

Example: Tracing Memory Blocks

If you use DEBUG to trace through memory blocks on your own system, you can use DEBUG's H (Hex) command for hexadecimal arithmetic. Use it like this: H hex-value1,hex-value2. The H command returns the sum and the difference of the two values.

For the following example, DEBUG displayed the required memory contents. (Watch out for reversed-byte sequence.) The trace proceeded as follows:

1. Function 52H returned 02CC[0] in the ES and 0026H in the BX. Because you want the four bytes to the left at 0022H, use D 02CC:22 to display the address of the arena header for the first memory block in IP:CS format. This turns out to be 00 00 56 0B, and the address is therefore 0B56[0].
2. Use D B56:0 to display the first arena header:
   ```
   4D 08 00 AE 05 ...
   ```
   The 4D ("M") means more memory blocks follow, 0800 (0008H) tells us that the memory block belongs to MSDOS.SYS, and AE05 (05AEH) is the length of the memory block.
3. Locate the second arena header (COMMAND.COM):
   ```
   Location of first arena header:    B56[0]
   Add 1 paragraph:                  + 1[0]
   Add length of its memory block:  + 5AE[0]
   Location of next arena header:    1105[0]
   ```
   Use D 1105:0 to display the second arena header:
   ```
   4D 06 11 64 01 ...
   ```
   You could also examine the contents of COMMAND.COM at this point.
4. Locate the third arena header, the master environment:
   ```
   Location of previous arena header:    1105[0]
   Add 1 paragraph:                        + 1[0]
   Add length of its memory block:       +164[0]
   Location of next arena header:        126A[0]
   ```
   Use D 126A:0 to display the third arena header: 4D . . . .

You could follow the same procedure to examine the contents of the master environment and locate any remaining memory blocks. Note that succeeding programs have two memory blocks each: one for their environment and one for their program segment. The last arena header has 5AH ("Z") in its first byte. If you display from within DEBUG, this is its own memory block, because DEBUG would be the last program loaded in memory.

Handling Upper Memory Blocks

Since DOS 5.0, CONFIG.SYS may contain a DOS=UMB (upper memory block) statement for allocating memory to programs above conventional memory, between the 640K and the 1-megabyte boundaries. The statement causes the system to establish a dummy arena header 16 bytes before the 640K boundary and marked as owned. Its size field contains a value large enough to bypass any video buffers and ROM routines.

In this way, you can step up from the last arena header in conventional memory to locate memory blocks in upper memory. Within upper memory, other arena headers marked as owned are also used to bypass any areas already used by ROM or video.

MEMORY ALLOCATION STRATEGY

INT 21H function 58H provides a number of strategies to determine where in memory to load a program.

Function 5800H: Get Memory Allocation Strategy

This operation allows queries to the memory allocation strategy:

```
MOV  AX,5800H      ;Request get strategy
INT  21H           ;Call interrupt service
```

The operation clears the carry flag and returns the strategy in the AX:

- 00H = First fit (the default): Search from the lowest address in conventional memory for the first available block that is large enough to load the program.
- 01H = Best fit: Search for the smallest available block in conventional memory that is large enough to load the program.
- 02H = Last fit: Search from the highest address in conventional memory for the first available block.
- 40H = First fit, high only: Search from the lowest address in upper memory for the first available block.
- 41H = Best fit, high only: Search for the smallest available block in upper memory.
- 42H = Last fit, high only: Search from the highest address in upper memory for the first available block.
- 80H = First fit, high: Search from the lowest address in upper memory for the first available block. If none is found, search conventional memory.
- 81H = Best fit high: Search for the smallest available block in upper memory. If none is found, search conventional memory.
- 82H = Last fit, high: Search from the highest address in upper memory for the first available block. If none is found, search conventional memory.

Best fit and last fit strategies are appropriate to multitasking systems, which could have fragmented memory because of programs running concurrently. When a program finishes processing, its memory is released to the system.

Function 5801H: Set Memory Allocation Strategy

This operation allows changes to the memory allocation strategy. To set a strategy, set the AL with code 01 and the BX with the strategy code. An error sets the carry flag and returns 01 (invalid function) in the AX.

Function 5802H: Get Upper Memory Link

This operation indicates whether a program can allocate memory from the upper memory area (above 640K). The operation clears the carry flag and returns one of the following codes to the AL: 00H means the area is not linked and you cannot allocate, and 01H means the area is linked, you can allocate.

Function 5803H: Set Upper Memory Link

This operation can link or unlink the upper memory area and, if the area is linked, can allocate memory from it:

```
MOV  AX,5803H        ;Request
MOV  BX,linkflag     ;  link/unlink
INT  21H             ;  upper memory area
```

The link flag parameter has the following meaning: 00H = unlink the area and 01H = link the area. A successful operation clears the carry flag and allows a program to allocate memory from it. An error sets the carry flag and returns to the AX code 01 (CONFIG.SYS did not contain DOS=UMB) or 07 (memory links damaged).

THE PROGRAM LOADER

On loading .COM and .EXE programs, the program loader performs the following steps:

1. Sets up memory blocks for the program's environment and for the program segment
2. Creates a program segment prefix at location 00H of the program segment and loads the program at 100H.

Other than these steps, the load and execute steps differ for .COM and .EXE programs. A major difference is that the linker inserts a special header record in an .EXE file when storing it on disk, and the program loader uses this record for loading.

Loading and Executing a .COM Program

Because the organization of a .COM file is relatively simple, the program loader needs to know only that the file extension is .COM. As described earlier, a program segment prefix precedes .COM and .EXE programs loaded in memory. The first two bytes of the PSP contain the INT 20H instruction (return to DOS). On loading a .COM program, the program loader

- Sets the four segment registers with the address of the first byte of the PSP.
- Sets the stack pointer (SP) to the end of the 64K segment, offset FFFEH (or to the end of memory if the segment is not large enough), and pushes a zero word on the stack.
- Sets the instruction pointer to 100H (the size of the PSP) and allows control to proceed to the address generated by CS:IP, the first location immediately following the PSP. This is the first byte of your program, and it should contain an executable instruction. Figure 24-3 illustrates this initialization.

Loading and Executing an .EXE Program

As stored on disk by the linker, an .EXE module consists of two parts: a *header record* containing control and relocation information; and the actual *load module*.

The header is a minimum of 512 bytes and may be longer if there are many relocatable items. The header contains information about the size of the executable module, where it is to be loaded in memory, the address of the stack, and relocation offsets to be inserted

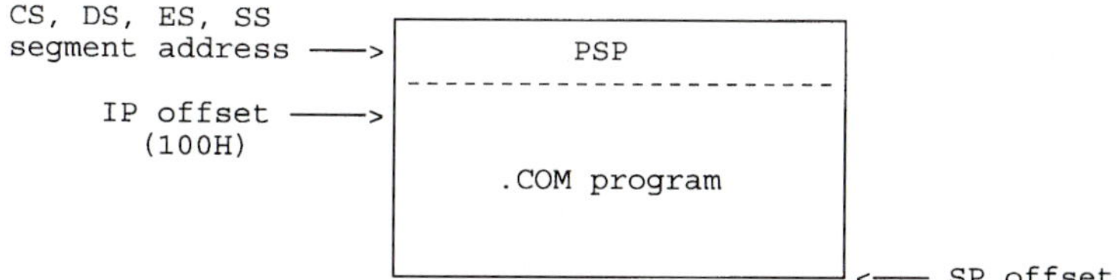

Figure 24-3 Initialization of a .COM program

into incomplete machine addresses. In the following list, the term *block* refers to a 512-byte area in memory:

00–01H	Hex 4D5A ('MZ') identifies an .EXE file.
02–03H	Number of bytes in the last block of the .EXE file.
04–05H	Size of the file including the header, in 512-byte block increments. For example, if the size is 1,025, this field contains 2 and 02–03H contains 1.
06–07H	Number of relocation table items (see 1CH).
08–09H	Size of the header, in 16-byte (paragraph) increments, to help the program loader locate the start of the executable module following the header. The minimum number is 20H (32) (32 × 16 = 512 bytes).
0A–0BH	Minimum count of paragraphs that must reside above the end of the program when it is loaded.
0C–0DH	High/low loader switch. When linking, you decide whether the program is to load for execution at a low (the usual) or a high memory address. The value 0000H indicates high. Otherwise, this location contains the maximum count of paragraphs that must reside above the end of the loaded program.
0E–0F	Offset location in the executable module of the stack segment.
10–11H	The defined size of the stack as an offset that the loader is to insert in the SP register when transferring control to the executable module.
12–13H	Checksum value—the sum of all the words in the file (ignoring overflows), used as a validation check for possible lost data.
14–15H	Offset (usually, but not necessarily, 00H) that the loader is to insert in the IP register when transferring control to the executable module.
16–17H	Offset of the code segment within the executable module that the loader inserts in the CS register. The offset is relative to the other segments, so that if the code segment is first, the offset would be zero.

18–19H	Offset of the relocation table (see the item at 1CH).
1A–1BH	Overlay number, where zero (the usual) means that the .EXE file contains the main program.
1CH–end	Relocation table containing a variable number of relocation items, as identified at offset 06–07H. Positions 06–07H of the header indicate the number of items in the executable module that are to be relocated. Each relocation item, beginning at header 1CH, consists of a 2-byte offset value and a 2-byte segment value.

The system constructs memory blocks for the environment and the program segment. Following are the steps that the program loader performs when loading and initializing an .EXE program:

- Reads the formatted part of the header into memory.
- Calculates the size of the executable module (total file size in position 04H minus header size at position 08H) and reads the module into memory at the start segment.
- Reads the relocation table items into a work area and adds the value of each item to the start segment value.
- Sets the DS and ES registers to the segment address of the PSP.
- Sets the SS register to the address of the PSP, plus 100H (the size of the PSP), plus the SS offset value (at 0EH). Also, sets the SP register to the value at 10H, the size of the stack.
- Sets the CS to the address of the PSP plus 100H (the size of the PSP), plus the CS offset value in the header (at 16H) to the CS. Also, sets the IP with the offset at 14H. The CS:IP pair provides the starting address of the code segment and, in effect, program execution. Figure 24-4 illustrates this initialization.

After the preceding steps, the loader is finished with the .EXE header and discards it. The CS and SS registers are set correctly, but your program has to set the DS and ES for its own data segment:

```
MOV  AX,datasegname     ;Set DS and ES registers
MOV  DS,AX              ;  to address
MOV  ES,AX              ;  of data segment
```

Example: Loading an .EXE Program

Consider the following Link Map that the linker generated for an .EXE program:

```
Start    Stop   Length  Name        Class

00000H  0003AH  003BH  CSEG         Code
00040H  0005AH  001BH  DSEG         Data
00060H  0007FH  0020H  STACK        Stack

Program entry point at 0000:0000
```

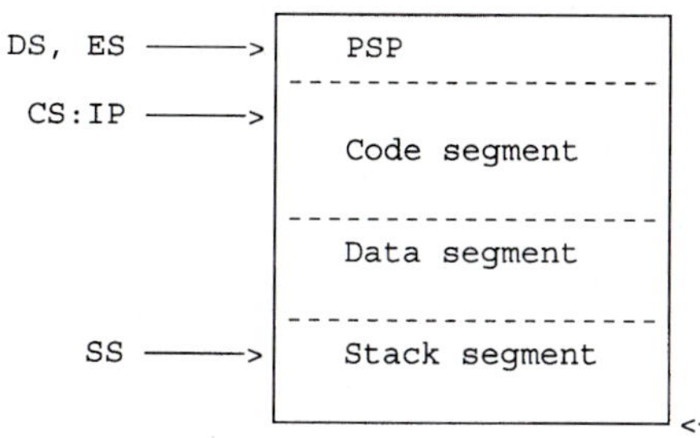

Figure 24-4 Initialization of an .EXE program

The map provides the *relative* (not actual) location of each of the three segments. Note that some systems arrange these segments in alphabetic sequence by name. According to the map, the code segment (CSEG) is to start at 00000H—its relative location is the beginning of the executable module, and its length is 003BH bytes. The data segment, DSEG, begins at 00040H and has a length of 001BH. The 00040H is the first address following CSEG that aligns on a paragraph boundary (a boundary evenly divisible by 10H). The stack segment, STACK, begins at 00060H, the first address following DSEG that aligns on a paragraph boundary.

DEBUG can't display a header record after a program is loaded for execution, because the loader replaces the header record with the PSP. However, you can use DEBUG's L command to load a sector from disk and the D command to display it. For example, load beginning at CS:100 from drive A: (0), relative sector 3, and one sector (512 bytes): L 100 0 3 1. The header for the program we are examining contains the following relevant information, according to hex location (numeric data is in reverse-byte sequence):

00H	Hex 4D5A ("MZ")
02H	Number of bytes in last block: 5B00H (or 005BH)
04H	Size of file, including header, in 512-byte blocks: 0200H (0002 × 512 = 1,024 bytes)
06H	Number of relocation table items following formatted portion of header: 0100H (that is, 0001)
08H	Size of header, in 16-byte increments: 2000H (0020H = 32, and 32 × 16 = 512 bytes)
0CH	Load in low memory: FFFFH
0EH	Offset location of stack segment: 6000H, or 0060H
10H	Offset to insert in SP: 2000H, or 0020H
14H	Offset for IP: 0000H
16H	Offset for CS: 0000H
18H	Offset for the relocation table: 1E00H, or 001EH

When DEBUG loaded this program, the registers contained the following values:

```
SP = 0020  DS = 138F  ES = 138F
SS = 13A5  CS = 139F  IP = 0000
```

For .EXE modules, the loader sets the DS and ES to the address of the PSP and sets the CS, IP, SS, and SP to values from the header record. Let's see how the loader initializes these registers.

CS:IP Registers

According to the DS register, when the program loaded, the address of the PSP was 138F[0]H. Because the PSP is 100H bytes long and the code segment is first (at offset 0), the code segment follows the PSP immediately at 139F[0]H. You can see the offset at location 16H in the header. The loader uses these values to initialize the CS register:

```
Start address of PSP (see DS):     138F0H
Length of PSP:                     + 100H
Offset of code segment                 0H
                                   ______
Address of code segment            139F0H
```

The CS now provides the starting address of the code portion (CSEG) of the program. You can use the DEBUG display command D CS:0000 to view the machine code of a program in memory. The code is identical to the hex portion of the assembler's .LST printout, other than operands that .LST tags as R. Also, the loader sets the IP with 0000H, the offset from 14H in the header.

SS:SP Registers

The loader used the value 60H in the header (at 0EH) for setting the address of the stack in the SS register:

```
Start address of PSP (see DS):                  138F0H
Length of PSP:                                  + 100H
Offset of stack (see location 0EH in header):   +  60H
                                                ______
Address of stack:                               13A50H
```

The loader used 20H from the header (at 10H) to initialize the stack pointer to the length of the stack. In this example, the stack was defined as DW 16 DUP(?), that is, sixteen 2-byte fields = 32, or 20H. The SP points to the current top of the stack.

DS Register

The loader uses the DS register to establish the starting point for the PSP at 138F[0]. Because the header does not contain a starting address for the DS, your program has to initialize it:

```
0004 B8 ---- R     MOV AX,DSEG
0007 8E D8         MOV DS,AX
```

The assembler left unfilled the machine address of DSEG, which has become an entry in the header's relocation table (which begins at 1EH). The loader calculates the DS address as follows:

```
CS address:                 139F0H
Plus offset for the DS:        40H
DS address:                 13A30H
```

DEBUG shows the completed instruction as B8 A313. The loader stores A313 in the DS as 13A3. We now have these values at the start of execution:

REGISTER	ADDRESS	MAP OFFSET
CS	139F[0]H	00H
DS	13A3[0]H	40H
SS	13A5[0]H	60H

As an exercise, trace any of your linked .EXE programs with DEBUG and note the changed values in the registers:

INSTRUCTION	REGISTERS CHANGED
MOV AX,DSEG	IP and AX
MOV DS,AX	IP and DS
MOV ES,AX	IP and ES

The DS now contains the correct address of the data segment. You can use D DS:00 to view the contents of the data segment and use D SS:00 to view the contents of the stack.

ALLOCATING AND FREEING MEMORY

INT 21H services allow you to *allocate, release,* and *modify* the size of an area of memory. You most likely would use these services for resident programs and programs that load other programs for execution. Because DOS was designed as a single-user environment, a program that needs to load another program for execution has to release some of its memory space.

INT 21H Function 48H: Allocate Memory

To allocate memory for a program, request function 48H, and set the BX with the number of required paragraphs:

```
MOV  AH,48H            ;Request allocate memory
MOV  BX,paragraphs     ;Number of paragraphs
INT  21H               ;Call interrupt service
```

The operation begins at the first memory block and steps through each block until it locates a space large enough for the request, usually at the high end of memory.

A successful operation clears the carry flag and returns in the AX the segment address of the allocated memory block. An unsuccessful operation sets the carry flag and returns in the AX an error code (07 = memory block destroyed or 08 = insufficient memory) and in the BX the size, in paragraphs, of the largest block available. A memory block destroyed means that the operation found a block in which the first byte was not 'M' or 'Z'.

INT 21H Function 49H: Free Allocated Memory

Function 49H frees allocated memory; it is commonly used to release a resident program. Load in the ES the segment address of the block to be returned:

```
MOV  AH,49H             ;Request free allocated memory
LEA  ES,seg-address     ;Address of block for paragraphs
INT  21H                ;Call interrupt service
```

A successful operation clears the carry flag and stores 00H in the second and third bytes of the memory block, meaning that it is no longer in use. An unsuccessful operation sets the carry flag and returns in the AX an error code (07 = memory block destroyed and 09 = invalid memory block address).

INT 21H Function 4AH: Modify Allocated Memory Block

Function 4AH can increase or decrease the size of a memory block. Initialize the BX with the number of paragraphs to retain for the program and the ES with the address of the PSP:

```
MOV  AH,4AH             ;Request modify allocated memory
MOV  BX,paragraphs      ;Number of paragraphs
LEA  ES,PSP-address     ;Address of PSP
INT  21H                ;Call interrupt service
```

A program can calculate its own size by subtracting the end of the last segment from the address of the PSP. You'll have to ensure that you use the last segment if your linker rearranges segments in alphabetic sequence.

A successful operation clears the carry flag. An unsuccessful operation sets the carry flag and returns in the AX an error code (07 = memory block destroyed, 08 = insufficient memory, and 09 = invalid memory block address) and returns in the BX the maximum possible size (if an attempt to increase the size was made). A wrong address in the ES can cause error 07.

LOADING OR EXECUTING A PROGRAM FUNCTION

Let's now examine how to get an executing program to load and, in turn, to execute a subprogram. Function 4BH enables a program to load a subprogram into memory for execution. Load these registers:

- AL = Function code for one of the following: 00H = load and execute, 01H = load program, 03H = load overlay, 05H = set execution state (not covered in this text)
- ES:BX = Address of a parameter block
- DS:DX = Address of the path name for the called subprogram, an ASCIIZ string in uppercase letters.

Here are the instructions to load the subprogram:

```
MOV  AH,4BH             ;Request load subprogram
MOV  AL,code            ;Function code (load only)
```

```
LEA  BX,para-block      ;Address of parameter block
LEA  DX,path            ;Address of path name
INT  21H                ;Call interrupt service
```

An invalid operation sets the carry flag and returns an error code in the AX.

AL = 00H: Load and Execute

This operation loads an .EXE or .COM program into memory, establishes a program segment prefix for it, and transfers control to it for execution. Because all registers, including the SS, are changed, the operation is not for novices. The parameter block addressed by the ES:BX has the following format:

OFFSET	PURPOSE
00H	Address of environment-block segment to be passed at PSP+2CH. A zero address means that the loaded program is to inherit the environment of its parent.
02H	Doubleword pointer to command line for placing at PSP+80H.
06H	Doubleword pointer to default FCB #1 for passing at PSP+5CH.
0AH	Doubleword pointer to default FCB #2 for passing at PSP+6CH.

The doubleword pointers have the form offset:segment address.

AL = 01H: Load Program

The operation loads an .EXE or .COM program into memory and establishes a program segment prefix for it, but does not transfer control to it for execution. The parameter block addressed by the ES:BX has the following format:

OFFSET	PURPOSE
00H:	Address of environment-block segment to be passed at PSP+2CH. If the address is zero, the loaded program is to inherit the environment of its parent.
02H	Doubleword pointer to command line for placing at PSP+80H.
06H	Doubleword pointer to default FCB #1 for passing at PSP+5CH.
0AH	Doubleword pointer to default FCB #2 for passing at PSP+6CH.
0EH	Starting stack address
12H	Starting code segment address

The doubleword pointers are addressed in the form offset:segment.

AL = 03H: Load Overlay

This operation loads a program or block of code, but does not establish a PSP or begin execution of the program or block. Thus the requested program could be an overlay. The parameter block addressed by the ES:BX has the following format:

Offset 00H Word segment address where file is to be loaded

Offset 02H Word relocation factor to apply to the image

An error sets the carry flag and returns an error code in the AX, described in Figure 18-1.

Program: Load and Execute

The program in Figure 24-5 requests the system to perform the DIR command for drive D. The program first uses function 4AH to reduce its memory requirements to its actual size—the difference between its last (dummy) segment ZNDSEG and the start of its PSP. Note that at this point, the ES still contains the address of the PSP, as loaded on entry. (The ASSUME statements preceding and following MOV BX,SEG ZNDSEG appear to be required for MASM 5.1, but not for some other assemblers.) The module is 80 bytes in size, so that the PSP (10H paragraphs) and the program (8 paragraphs) total 18H paragraphs.

Function 4BH with code 00 in the AL handles the loading and execution of COMMAND.COM. The program displays the directory entries for drive D.

INT 21H Function 4DH: Get Subprogram Return Value

This operation retrieves the return value that the last subprogram delivered when it terminated by function 4CH or 31H. The returned values are:

- AH contains the subprogram's termination method, where 00H = normal termination, 01H = terminated by Ctrl+C, 02H = critical device error, and 03H = terminated by function 31H (keep program).
- AL contains the return value from the subprogram.

PROGRAM OVERLAYS

The program in Figure 24-6 uses the same service (4BH) as that in Figure 24-5, but this time just to load a program into memory without executing it. The process consists of a main program, A24CALLV, and two subprograms, A24SUB1 and A24SUB2. A24CALLV contains these segments:

```
STACKSG   SEGMENT   PARA   STACK   'Stack1'
DATASG    SEGMENT   PARA   'Data1'
CODESG    SEGMENT   PARA   'Code1'
ZENDSG    SEGMENT                          ;Dummy (empty) segment
```

A24SUB1 is linked with and called by A24CALLV. Its segments are:

```
DATASG    SEGMENT   PARA   'Data2'
CODESG    SEGMENT   PARA   'Code2'
```

```
TITLE     A24EXDIR (EXE) INT 21H function 4BH to execute DIR
; -------------------------------------------------------------------
SSEG      SEGMENT PARA STACK 'Stack'
          DW      32(?)
SSEG      ENDS
; -------------------------------------------------------------------
DSEG      SEGMENT PARA 'Data'
PARAREA   LABEL   BYTE                ;Parameter block for load/exe
          DW      0                   ;  address of envir. string
          DW      OFFSET DIRCOM       ;  pointer to command line
          DW      DSEG
          DW      OFFSET FCB1         ;  pointer to default FCB1
          DW      DSEG
          DW      OFFSET FCB2         ;  pointer to default FCB2
          DW      DSEG
DIRCOM    DB      17,'/C DIR D:',13,0   ;Command line
FCB1      DB      16 DUP(0)
FCB2      DB      16 DUP(0)
PROGNAM   DB      'C:\COMMAND.COM',0    ;Location of COMMAND.COM
DSEG      ENDS
; -------------------------------------------------------------------
CSEG      SEGMENT PARA 'Code'
          ASSUME  CS:CSEG,DS:DSEG,SS:SSEG,ES:DSEG
A10MAIN   PROC    FAR
          MOV     AH,4AH              ;Reduce allocated memory spac
          ASSUME  CS:ZNDSEG
          MOV     BX,SEG ZNDSEG       ;Ending segment
          ASSUME  CS:CSEG
          MOV     CX,ES               ;  minus start of
          SUB     BX,CX               ;  program segment
          INT     21H
          JC      A20ERR              ;Not enough space?
          MOV     AX,DSEG             ;Yes,
          MOV     DS,AX               ;  set DS and ES
          MOV     ES,AX
          MOV     AH,4BH              ;Request load
          MOV     AL,00               ;  and execute
          LEA     BX,PARAREA          ;  COMMAND.COM
          LEA     DX,PROGNAM
          INT     21H
          JC      A30ERR              ;Execute error?
          MOV     AL,00               ;OK, no error code
          JMP     A90XIT
A20ERR:
          MOV     AL,01               ;Error code 1
          JMP     A90XIT
A30ERR:
          MOV     AL,02               ;Error code 2
          JMP     A90XIT
A90XIT:
          MOV     AH,4CH              ;Request
          INT     21H                 ;  end processing
A10MAIN   ENDP
CSEG      ENDS

ZNDSEG    SEGMENT                     ;Dummy segment
ZNDSEG    ENDS
          END     A10MAIN
```

Figure 24-5 Executing DIR from Within a Program

```
TITLE      A24CALLV (EXE)  Call subprogram and overlay
           EXTRN   A24SUB1:FAR
; ---------------------------------------------------
STACKSG    SEGMENT PARA STACK 'Stack1'
           DW      64 DUP(?)
STACKSG    ENDS
; ---------------------------------------------------
DATASG     SEGMENT PARA 'Data1'
PARABLK    LABEL   WORD                 ;Parameter block
           DW      0                    ;
           DW      0                    ;
FILENAM    DB      'F:\A24SUB2.EXE',0
ERRMSG1    DB      'Modify mem error'
ERRMSG2    DB      'Allocate error  '
ERRMSG3    DB      'Seg call error  '
DATASG     ENDS
; ---------------------------------------------------
CODESG     SEGMENT PARA 'Code1'
A10MAIN    PROC    FAR
           ASSUME  CS:CODESG,DS:DATASG,SS:STACKSG
           MOV     AX,DATASG
           MOV     DS,AX
           CALL    Q10SCR               ;Scroll screen
           CALL    A24SUB1              ;Call subprogram 1

           MOV     AH,4AH               ;Shrink memory
           ASSUME  CS:ZENDSG
           MOV     BX,SEG ZENDSG        ;Address of end program
           ASSUME  CS:CODESG
           MOV     CX,ES                ;Address of PSP
           SUB     BX,CX                ;Size of this program
           INT     21H
           JC      A20ERR               ;If error, exit

           MOV     AX,DS                ;Initialize ES for
           MOV     ES,AX                ;  this service
           MOV     AH,48H               ;Allocate memory for overlay
           MOV     BX,40                ;40 paragraphs
           INT     21H
           JC      A30ERR               ;If error, exit
           MOV     PARABLK,AX           ;Save segment address

           MOV     AH,4BH               ;Load subprogram 2
           MOV     AL,03                ;  with no execute
           LEA     BX,PARABLK
           LEA     DX,FILENAM
           INT     21H
           JC      A50ERR               ;If error, exit
           MOV     AX,PARABLK           ;Exchange two words
           MOV     PARABLK+2,AX         ;  of PARABLK
           MOV     PARABLK,20H          ;Set CS offset to 20H
           LEA     BX,PARABLK
           CALL    DWORD PTR [BX]       ;Call subprogram 2
           JMP     A90
A20ERR:
           CALL    Q20SET               ;Set cursor
           LEA     DX,ERRMSG1
           CALL    Q30DISP              ;Display message
           JMP     A90
```

Figure 24-6a Calling a Subprogram and Overlay

```
A30ERR:
        CALL    Q20SET          ;Set cursor
        LEA     DX,ERRMSG2
        CALL    Q30DISP         ;Display message
        JMP     A90
A50ERR:
        CALL    Q20SET          ;Set cursor
        LEA     DX,ERRMSG3
        CALL    Q30DISP         ;Display message
        JMP     A90
A90:
        MOV     AX,4C00H        ;End processing
        INT     21H
A10MAIN ENDP
;               Video screen services:
;               ---------------------
Q10SCR  PROC    NEAR
        MOV     AX,0600H        ;Request scroll
        MOV     BH,1EH          ;Set attribute
        MOV     CX,0000
        MOV     DX,184FH
        INT     10H
        RET
Q10SCR  ENDP

Q20SET  PROC    NEAR
        MOV     AH,02H          ;Request set
        MOV     BH,00           ;  cursor
        MOV     DH,12
        MOV     DL,00
        INT     10H
        RET
Q20SET  ENDP

Q30DISP PROC    NEAR            ;DX set on entry
        MOV     AH,40H          ;Request display
        MOV     BX,01           ;Handle
        MOV     CX,16           ;Length
        INT     21H
        RET
Q30DISP ENDP
CODESG  ENDS

ZENDSG  SEGMENT                 ;Dummy (empty) segment
ZENDSG  ENDS
        END     A10MAIN
----------------------------------------------------------

TITLE   A24SUB1  Called subprogram
DATASG  SEGMENT PARA 'Data2'
SUBMSG  DB      'Subprogram 1 reporting'
DATASG  ENDS

CODESG  SEGMENT PARA 'Code2'
A24SUB1 PROC    FAR
        ASSUME  CS:CODESG,DS:DATASG
        PUBLIC  A24SUB1
        PUSH    DS              ;Save caller's DS
```

Figure 24-6b Calling a Subprogram and Overlay

```
         MOV      AX,DATASG          ;Initialize DS
         MOV      DS,AX
         MOV      AH,02H             ;Request set
         MOV      BH,00              ;  cursor
         MOV      DH,05
         MOV      DL,00
         INT      10H
         MOV      AH,40H             ;Request display
         MOV      BX,01              ;Handle
         MOV      CX,22              ;Length
         LEA      DX,SUBMSG          ;Message
         INT      21H
         POP      DS                 ;Restore DS for caller
         RET
A24SUB1  ENDP
CODESG   ENDS
         END
-----------------------------------------------------------

TITLE    A24SUB2 Called overlay subprogram
DATASG   SEGMENT PARA 'Data'
SUBMSG   DB       'Subprogram 2 reporting'
DATASG   ENDS

CODESG   SEGMENT PARA 'Code'
A24SUB2  PROC     FAR
         ASSUME   CS:CODESG,DS:DATASG
         PUSH     DS                 ;Save caller's DS
         MOV      AX,CS              ;Set address of first
         MOV      DS,AX              ;  segment in DS
         MOV      AH,02H             ;Request set
         MOV      BH,00              ;  cursor
         MOV      DH,10
         MOV      DL,00
         INT      10H
         MOV      AH,40H             ;Request display
         MOV      BX,01              ;Handle
         MOV      CX,22              ;Length
         LEA      DX,SUBMSG          ;Message
         INT      21H
         POP      DS                 ;Restore caller's DS
         RET
A24SUB2  ENDP
CODESG   ENDS
         END
```

Figure 24-6c Calling a Subprogram and Overlay

A24CALLV's segments are linked first—that's why their class names differ: 'Data1', 'Data2', 'Code1', 'Code2', and so forth. Here's the link map for A24CALLV+A24SUB1:

Start	Stop	Length	Name	Class
00000H	0007FH	00080H	STACKSG	Stack1
00080H	000C2H	00043H	DATASG	Data1
000D0H	0016DH	0009FH	CODESG	Code1
00170H	00170H	00000H	ZENDSG	
00170H	00185H	00016H	DATASG	Data2
00190H	001AFH	00020H	CODESG	Code2

A24SUB2 is also called by A24CALLV, but is linked separately. Its segments are:

```
DATASG   SEGMENT   PARA   'Data'
CODESG   SEGMENT   PARA   'Code'
```

A24SUB2's link map looks like this (along with a warning about no stack segment):

```
Start  Stop   Length Name      Class
00000H 00015H 00016H DATASG    Data
00020H 0003EH 0001FH CODESG    Code
```

When the program loader transfers A24CALLV+A24SUB1 into memory for execution, A24CALLV calls and executes A24SUB1 in normal fashion. The near CALL initializes the IP correctly, but because A24SUB1 has its own data segment, it has to push A24CALLV's DS and establish its own DS address. A24SUB1 sets the cursor, displays a message, pops the DS, and returns to A24CALLV.

To overlay A24SUB2 on A24SUB1, A24CALLV has to *shrink* its own memory space, because the system has given it all available memory. A24CALLV's highest segment is ZENDSG, which is empty. A24CALLV subtracts the address of its PSP (still in the ES) from the address of ZENDSG. The difference is 270H (27H paragraphs), calculated as the size of the PSP (100H) plus the offset of ZENDSG (170H), which is delivered to the system by function 4AH.

INT 21H function 48H then allocates memory to allow space for A24SUB2 to be loaded (overlaid) on top of A24SUB1, arbitrarily set to 40H paragraphs. The operation returns the loading address in the AX register, which A24CALLV stores in PARABLK. This is the first word of a parameter block to be used by function 4BH.

Function 4BH with code 03 in the AL loads A24SUB2 into memory. Note the definition in the data segment: F:\A24SUB2.EXE,0. Function 4BH references CS and PARABLK—the first word contains the segment address where the overlay is to be loaded and the second word is an offset, in this case, zero. A diagram may help make these steps clearer:

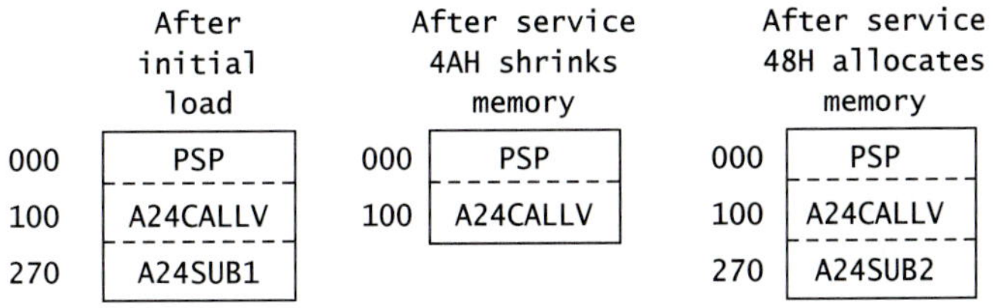

```
         After              After service         After service
        initial             4AH shrinks           48H allocates
         load                 memory                memory
000  |    PSP     |    000 |    PSP     |    000 |    PSP     |
     |- - - - - - |        |- - - - - - |        |- - - - - - |
100  | A24CALLV   |    100 | A24CALLV   |    100 | A24CALLV   |
     |- - - - - - |                              |- - - - - - |
270  | A24SUB1    |                         270  | A24SUB2    |
```

The far CALL to A24SUB2 requires a reference defined as IP:CS, but PARABLK is in the form CS:IP. The CS value is therefore moved to the second word, and 20H is stored in the first word for the IP, because the link map shows that value as the offset of A24SUB2's code segment. The next instructions load the address of PARABLK in the BX and call A24SUB2:

```
LEA  BX,PARABLK          ;Address of PARABLK
CALL DWORD PTR [BX]      ;Call A24SUB2
```

Note that A24CALLV doesn't reference A24SUB2 by name in its code segment and so doesn't require an EXTRN statement specifying A24SUB2. Because A24SUB2 has its own data segment, it first pushes the DS onto the stack and initializes its own address. But A24SUB2 wasn't linked with A24CALLV. As a result, the instruction MOV AX,DATASG would set the AX only with the offset address of DATASG, 0[0]H, and not its segment address. We do know that CALL set the CS with the address of the first segment, which (according to the Link Map) happens to be the address of the data segment. Copying the CS to the DS gives the correct address in the DS. Note that if A24SUB2's code and data segments are arranged in a different sequence, the coding has to be revised accordingly.

A24SUB2 sets the cursor, displays a message, pops the DS, and returns to A24CALLV.

RESIDENT PROGRAMS

A number of programs are designed to reside in memory while other programs run, and you can activate their services through special keystrokes. You load resident programs before activating other normal processing programs. They are almost always .COM programs and are also known as "terminate but stay resident" (TSR) programs.

The easy part of writing a resident program is getting it to reside. Instead of normal termination, you cause it to exit by means of INT 21H function 31H (Keep Program). The operation requires the size of the program in the DX register:

```
MOV  AH,31H          ;Request TSR
MOV  DX,prog-size    ;Size of program
INT  21H             ;Call interrupt service
```

When you execute the initialization routine, the system reserves the memory block where the program resides and loads subsequent programs higher in memory.

The not-so-easy part of writing a resident program involves activating it after it is resident, because it is not a program internal to the system, as are CLS, COPY, and DIR. A common approach is to modify the interrupt vector table so that the resident program interrupts all keystrokes, acts on a special keystroke or combination, and passes on all other keystrokes. The effect is that a resident program typically, but not necessarily, consists of the following parts:

1. A section that redefines locations in the interrupt vector table.
2. An initialization procedure that executes only the first time the program runs and that performs the following:
   - Replaces the address in the interrupt vector table with its own address;
   - Establishes the size of the portion of the program that is to remain resident; and

   - Uses an interrupt that tells the system to end executing the current program and to attach the specified portion of the program in memory.
3. A procedure that remains resident and that is activated, for example, by such actions as special keyboard input or the timer clock.

In effect, the initialization procedure sets up all the conditions to make the resident program work and then allows itself to be erased. The organization of memory now appears as follows:

- Rest of available memory
- Initialization portion of program (overlaid by next program)
- Resident portion of program (stays in memory)
- COMMAND.COM
- IO.SYS and MSDOS.SYS
- Interrupt vector table

A resident program may use two INT 21H functions for accessing the interrupt vector table, because there is no assurance that more advanced computers will have the interrupt table located beginning at location 0000H.

INT 21H Function 35H: Get Interrupt Vector

To retrieve the address in the interrupt vector table of a particular interrupt, load the AL with the required interrupt number:

```
MOV  AH,35H      ;Request get interrupt vector
MOV  AL,int#     ;Interrupt number
INT  21H         ;Call interrupt service
```

The operation returns the address of the interrupt in the ES:BX as segment:offset. For conventional memory, a request for the address of INT 09H, for example, returns 00H in the ES and 24H (36) in the BX.

INT 21H Function 25H: Set Interrupt Vector

To set a new interrupt, load the required interrupt number in the AL and the new address in the DX:

```
MOV  AH,25H        ;Request set interrupt vector
MOV  AL,int#       ;Interrupt number
LEA  DX,newaddr    ;New address for interrupt
INT  21H           ;Call interrupt service
```

The operation replaces the present address of the interrupt with the new address. In effect, then, when the specified interrupt occurs, processing links to your (resident) program, rather than to the normal interrupt address.

```
TITLE    A24TSTNM (COM)  Resident program
BIODATA  SEGMENT AT 40H          ;BIOS data area
         ORG    17H
KBSTAT   DB     ?                ;Keyboard status byte
BIODATA  ENDS
;        ------------------------------------------------------
CODESG   SEGMENT PARA
         ASSUME  CS:CODESG,DS:BIODATA
         ORG    100H
BEGIN:
         JMP    B10INIT          ;Jump to initialization
SAVINT9  DD     ?                ;INT 09H address
A10TEST:
         PUSH   AX               ;Save registers
         PUSH   CX
         PUSH   DS

         MOV    AX,BIODATA       ;Segment address of
         MOV    DS,AX            ;  BIOS data area
         MOV    AL,KBSTAT        ;Get keyboard flag
         TEST   AL,00100000B     ;NumLock state?
         JZ     A30EXIT          ;No, exit

         IN     AL,60H           ;Get keystroke from port
         CMP    AL,71            ;Scan code < 71?
         JL     A30EXIT          ;  yes, exit
         CMP    AL,83            ;Scan code > 83?
         JG     A30EXIT          ;  yes, exit
                                 ;Must be from numeric keypad
         MOV    AL,10110110B     ;Set frequency
         OUT    43H,AL
         MOV    AX,1000
         OUT    42H,AL
         MOV    AL,AH
         OUT    42H,AL
         IN     AL,61H           ;Turn on speaker
         MOV    AH,AL
         OR     AL,03
         OUT    61H,AL
         MOV    CX,9000          ;Set duration
A20PAUSE:
         LOOP   A20PAUSE
         MOV    AL,AH            ;Turn off speaker
         OUT    61H,AL
A30EXIT:
         POP    DS               ;Restore registers
         POP    CX
         POP    AX
         JMP    CS:SAVINT9       ;Resume INT 09H

;               Initialization routine:
B10INIT:        ;--------------------
         CLI                     ;Prevent further interrupts
         MOV    AH,35H           ;Get address of INT 09H
         MOV    AL,09H           ;  in ES:BX
         INT    21H
         MOV    WORD PTR SAVINT9,BX ;  and save it
         MOV    WORD PTR SAVINT9+2,ES
```

Figure 24-7a Resident Program

```
        MOV     AH,25H
        MOV     AL,09H          ;Set new address for INT 09H
        MOV     DX,OFFSET A10TEST ;  in A10TEST
        INT     21H

        MOV     AH,31H          ;Request stay resident
        MOV     DX,OFFSET B10INIT ;Set size of resident portion
        STI                     ;Restore interrupts
        INT     21H
CODESG  ENDS
        END     BEGIN
```

Figure 24-7b Resident Program

Example of a Resident Program

The resident program in Figure 24-7 named A24TSTNM beeps if you use the numeric keypad when NumLock is on. Its purpose is to warn you that you are typing a number rather than, say, pressing an arrow key to move the cursor. This program has to intercept INT 09H (Keyboard Input) to check for the key pressed.

The following points about the resident program are of interest:

BIODATA defines the BIOS data segment beginning at 40[0]—in particular, the keyboard flags byte, called here KBSTAT, which reflects the status of the keyboard. Bit 5 on (1) means that NumLock is on.

CODESG begins the code segment of A24TSTNM. The first executable instruction, JMP B10INIT, transfers execution past the resident portion to the B10INIT procedure near the end. This routine first uses CLI to prevent any further interrupts that may happen to occur at this time. It then uses INT 21H function 35H to locate the address of INT 09H in the interrupt vector table. The operation returns the address in the ES:BX, which the B10INIT routine stores in INT9SAV. Next, function 25H sets the program's own address for INT 09H in the interrupt table, A10TEST, the entry point to the resident program. In effect, the program saves INT 09H's address and replaces it with its own address. The last step establishes the size of the resident portion (all the code up to B10INIT) in the DX and uses INT 21H function 31H (Terminate but Stay Resident) to exit. The code from B10INIT to the end gets overlaid by the next program that is loaded for execution.

A10TEST is the name of the resident procedure that is activated when a user presses a key. The system transfers execution to the address of INT 09H in the interrupt vector table, which has been changed to the address of A10TEST. Because the interrupt may happen, for example, while the user is in DOS or an editor or word processing program, A24TSTNM has to save the registers that it uses. The program accesses the keyboard flag to determine whether NumLock is on and whether the numeric keypad was pressed (a keyboard scan code between 71 and 83 inclusive). If so, the program beeps the speaker. (The use of the speaker is explained in Chapter 21, under the section "Generating Sound.") Final instructions involve restoring the pushed registers—in reverse sequence—and jumping to INT9SAV, which contains the original INT 09H address. Control is now released back to the interrupt.

The next example should help make the procedure clear. First, here's an explanation of a conventional operation without a TSR intercepting the interrupt:

1. A user presses a key, and the keyboard sends INT 09H to BIOS.
2. BIOS uses the address of INT 09H in the interrupt vector table to locate its BIOS routine.
3. Control then transfers to the BIOS routine.
4. The routine gets the character and, if a standard character, delivers it to the keyboard buffer.

Next is the procedure for the resident program:

1. A user presses a key, and the keyboard sends INT 09H to BIOS.
2. BIOS uses the address of INT 09H in the interrupt vector table to locate its BIOS routine.
3. But the table now contains the address of A10TEST in the resident program, to which control transfers.
4. If NumLock is on and the character is a numeric keypad number, A10TEST beeps the speaker.
5. A10TEST exits by jumping to the original saved INT 09H address, which transfers control to the BIOS routine.
6. The BIOS routine gets the character and, if a standard character, delivers it to the keyboard buffer.

Try using DEBUG to examine the results of executing this program. Use D 0:20 to display the contents of the interrupt table at 20H (36), where the interrupt address for INT 09H is stored. The first word is the offset and the second word is the segment address, both in reverse-byte sequence. For example, if the stored address is 0701 EF05, then use D 107:05EF to view the contents of the stored address. The display should begin with 50511EB8, which is the start of the machine code for A10TEST in the resident program.

You can modify or expand this program for your own purposes. A few programs that also replace the table address of INT 09H do not allow concurrent use of a resident program such as this one.

INT 21H Function 34H: Get Address of DOS Busy Flag

Although this interrupt is used internally by DOS, some TSRs use it when requesting a DOS interrupt to check whether another interrupt is currently active. Because DOS is not reentrant (that is, you cannot enter DOS while it is active), the TSR has to wait until DOS is no longer busy, as indicated by the busy flag, inDOS.

```
MOV  AH,34H              ;Request busy
INT  21H                 ;Call interrupt service
```

```
CMP   ES:BYTE PTR[BX],0    ;Test if flag is zero
JE    ...
```

The service returns the address of inDOS in the ES:BX. The flag contains the number of DOS functions currently active, where 0 means none. You may enter DOS only if inDOS is 0.

KEY POINTS

- The boot record is on track 0, sector 1, of any disk that you use FORMAT /S to format. When you initiate the system, it automatically loads the boot record from disk into memory. The boot record then loads IO.SYS from disk into memory.
- IO.SYS is a low-level interface to the BIOS routines in ROM. On initiation, IO.SYS determines the status of all devices and equipment associated with the computer and sets interrupt vector table addresses for interrupts up to 20H. IO.SYS also handles I/O between memory and external devices.
- MSDOS.SYS is a high-level interface to programs that is loaded into memory after IO.SYS. Its operations include setting interrupt vector table addresses for interrupts 20H through 3FH, managing the directory and files on disk, handling blocking and deblocking of disk records, and handling INT 21H functions.
- COMMAND.COM handles the various system commands and runs requested .COM, .EXE, and .BAT files. It consists of a small resident portion, an initialization portion, and a transient portion. COMMAND.COM is responsible for loading executable programs from disk into memory.
- The .EXE module that the linker creates consists of a header record containing control and relocation information and the actual load module.
- On loading either a .COM or an .EXE program, the system sets up memory blocks for the program's environment and for the program segment. Preceding each memory block is a 16-byte arena header beginning on a paragraph boundary. The program loader also creates a PSP at location 00H of the program segment and loads the program at 100H.
- On loading a .COM program, the loader sets the segment registers with the address of the PSP, sets the stack pointer to the end of the segment, pushes a zero word onto the stack, and sets the instruction pointer to 100H (the size of the PSP). Control then proceeds to the address generated by CS:IP, the first location immediately following the PSP.
- On loading an .EXE program, the loader reads the header record into memory, calculates the size of the executable module, and reads the module into memory at the start segment. It adds the value of each relocation table item to the start segment value. It sets the DS and ES to the segment address of the PSP; sets the SS to the address of the PSP plus 100H plus the SS offset value; sets the SP to the size of the stack, and sets the CS to the address of the PSP, plus 100H, plus the CS offset value

in the header. The loader also sets the IP with the offset at 14H. The CS:IP pair provide the starting address of the code segment for program execution.

- Useful fields within the PSP include parameter area 1 at 5CH, parameter area 2 at 6CH, and default disk transfer area at 80H.
- Load a resident program before activating other normal processing programs. Exit by means of INT 21H function 31H, which requires the size of the program in the DX.

QUESTIONS

24-1. (a) What is the location of the boot record? (b) What is its purpose?

24-2. Explain the purpose of IO.SYS.

24-3. Explain the purpose of MSDOS.SYS.

24-4. Where, generally, are the following portions of COMMAND.COM located in memory and what is their purpose? (a) Resident; (b) transient.

24-5. (a) Where does the system store the program segment prefix? (b) What is its size?

24-6. A user types in the instruction FORGE E:SLIM.ASM to request execution of the FORGE program. Show the hex contents in the program's PSP at (a) 5CH, parameter area 1 (FCB #1), and (b) 80H, the default DTA.

24-7. Your program has to determine what PATH commands are set for its environment. Explain where the program may find its own environment. (The request is for the program's environment, not the DOS master environment.)

24-8. A .COM program is loaded for execution with its PSP beginning at location 2CD4[0]H. What address does the program loader store in each of the following registers (ignore reverse-byte notation): (a) CS; (b) DS; (c) ES; (d) SS.

24-9. A link map for an .EXE program shows the following:

```
Start  Stop   Length Name   Class
00000H 0003FH 00040H STACK  STACK
00040H 0006BH 0002CH CODESG CODE
00070H 0009CH 0002DH DATASG DATA
```

The loader loads the program with the PSP beginning at location 1B38[0]H. Showing calculations where appropriate, determine the contents of each of the registers at the time of loading (ignore reverse-byte notation): (a) SS; (b) SP; (c) CS; (d) DS; (e) ES.

24-10. An arena header begins at location 10A4[0] and contains the following: 4D C00E 0A00. . . . (a) What does the 4D (M) mean to the system? (b) How would the contents differ if this were the last memory block? (c) What is the memory location of the next arena header? Show your calculations.

24-11. Resident programs commonly intercept keyboard input. Where and what exactly is this intercepted address?

24-12. In what two significant ways does the coding for terminating a resident program differ from terminating a normal program?

PART G—REFERENCE CHAPTERS

25 BIOS DATA AREAS AND PROGRAM INTERRUPTS

Objective: To describe the BIOS data areas and interrupt services for BIOS and DOS.

INTRODUCTION

BIOS contains an extensive set of input/output routines and tables that indicate the status of the system's devices. Both DOS and user programs can request BIOS routines for communication with devices attached to the system. The method of interfacing with BIOS is by means of software interrupts. This chapter examines the data areas (or tables) that BIOS supports, the interrupt procedure, and BIOS interrupts 00H through 1BH and DOS interrupts 20H through 33H.

THE BOOT PROCESS

On the PC, ROM resides beginning at location FFFF0H. Turning on the power causes a "cold boot." The processor enters a reset state, sets all memory locations to zero, performs a parity check of memory, and sets the CS register to FFFF[0]H and the IP register to zero. The first instruction to execute is therefore at FFFF:0, the entry point to BIOS. BIOS also stores the value 1234H at 40[0]:72H to signal a subsequent Ctrl+Alt+Del ("warm reboot") not to perform the preceding power-on self-test.

BIOS checks the various ports to identify and initialize devices that are attached, including INT 11H (equipment determination) and INT 12H (memory size determination).

Then, beginning at location 0 of conventional memory, BIOS establishes the interrupt vector table that contains addresses of interrupt routines.

Next, BIOS determines whether a disk containing the system files is present and, if so, it executes INT 19H to access the first disk sector containing the bootstrap loader. This program is a temporary operating system to which the BIOS routine transfers control after loading it into memory. The bootstrap has only one task: to load the first part of the real operating system into memory. The system files IO.SYS, MSDOS.SYS, and COMMAND.COM are then loaded from disk into memory.

THE BIOS DATA AREA

BIOS maintains its own 256-byte (100H) data area in lower memory beginning at segment address 40[0]H, with fields containing data in reverse-byte sequence. A worthwhile exercise is to use DEBUG to examine these fields, which are listed next by offset.

Serial Port Data Area

- 00H–07H Four words, addresses of up to four serial ports, COM1-COM4.

Parallel Port Data Area

- 08H–0FH Four words, addresses of up to four parallel ports, LPT1–LPT4.

System Equipment Data Area

- 10H–11H Equipment status, a primitive indication of the status of installed devices. You can issue INT 11H, which returns the following in the AX:

BIT	DEVICE
15,14	Number of parallel ports attached
11–9	Number of RS232 serial adapters
7,6	Number of diskette devices, where bit 00 = 1, 01 = 2, 10 = 3, and 11 = 4
5,4	Initial video mode. Bit values are 00 = unused, 01 = 40 × 25 color, 10 = 80 × 25 color, 11 = 80 × 25 monochrome
2	Pointing device (mouse), where 1 = installed
1	1 = math coprocessor is present
0	1 = diskette drive is present

Miscellaneous Data Area

- 12H Manufacturer's test flags

Memory Size Data Area

- 13H–14H Amount of memory on system board, in kilobytes
- 15H–16H Amount of expansion memory, in kilobytes

Keyboard Data Area 1

- 17H First byte of the current shift status:

BIT	ACTION	BIT	ACTION
7	Insert active	3	Alt pressed
6	CapsLock active	2	Ctrl pressed
5	NumLock active	1	Left shift pressed
4	Scroll Lock active	0	Right shift pressed

"Active" means that the key was already pressed and set on. "Pressed" means that the key was being held down when BIOS stored the status.

- 18H Second byte of the current shift status:

BIT	ACTION	BIT	ACTION
7	Insert pressed	3	Ctrl/NumLock pressed
6	CapsLock pressed	2	SysReq pressed
5	NumLock pressed	1	Left Alt pressed
4	Scroll Lock pressed	0	Left Ctrl pressed

- 19H Alternate keyboard entry for ASCII characters.
- 1AH–1BH Pointer to keyboard buffer head
- 1CH–1DH Pointer to keyboard buffer tail
- 1EH–3DH Keyboard buffer (32 bytes)

Diskette Drive Data Area

- 3EH Disk seek status. Bit number 0 refers to drive A, 1 to B, 2 to C, and 3 to D. A bit value of 0 means that the next seek is to reposition to cylinder 0 to recalibrate the drive.
- 3FH Disk motor status. If bit 7 = 1, a write operation is in progress. Bit number 0 refers to drive A, 1 to B, 2 to C, and 3 to D; a bit value of 0 means that the motor is on.
- 40H Motor count for time-out until motor is turned off
- 41H Disk status, indicating an error on the last diskette drive operation:

00H No error
01H Invalid drive parameter
02H Address mark not found
03H Write-protect error
04H Sector not found
09H Attempt to make DMA across 64K boundary
0CH Media type not found
10H CRC error on read
20H Controller error

06H Diskette change line active	40H Seek failed
08H DMA overrun	80H Drive not ready

- 42H-48H Diskette drive controller status

Video Data Area 1

- 49H Current video mode, indicated by a 1-bit:

BIT	MODE	BIT	MODE
7	Monochrome	3	80 × 25 color
6	640 × 200 monochrome	2	80 × 25 monochrome
5	320 × 200 monochrome	1	40 × 25 color
4	320 × 200 color	0	40 × 25 monochrome

- 4AH–4BH Number of columns on the screen
- 4CH–4DH Size of the video page buffer
- 4EH–4FH Starting offset of the video buffer
- 50H–5FH Eight words for the current starting location for each of 8 pages, numbered 0–7
- 60H–61H Starting and ending line of the cursor
- 62H Currently active display page
- 63H–64H Port address of the active display, where monochrome is 03B4H and color is 03D4H
- 65H Current setting of the video mode register
- 66H Current color palette

System Data Area

- 67H–68H Data-edge time count
- 69H–6AH Cyclical redundancy check (CRC) register
- 6BH Last input value
- 6CH–6DH Lower half of timer
- 6EH–6FH Higher half of timer
- 70H Timer overflow (1 if timer has passed midnight)
- 71H Ctrl+Break keys set bit 7 to 1
- 72H–73H Memory reset flag. If the contents are 1234H, Ctrl+Alt+Del keys cause a "warm" reboot

Hard Disk Data Area

- 74H Status of last hard disk operation (details in Chapter 19)
- 75H Number of hard disks attached

Time-Out Data Area

- 78H–7BH Time-out for parallel ports (LPT1–LPT4)
- 7CH–7FH Time-out for serial ports (COM1–COM4)

Keyboard Data Area 2

- 80H–81H Offset address for start of keyboard buffer
- 82H–83H Offset address for end of keyboard buffer

Video Data Area 2

- 84H Number of rows on the screen (minus 1)
- 85H Character height, in scan lines
- 86H–8AH Miscellaneous video information

Diskette/Hard Disk Data Area

- 8BH–95H Controller and error status

Keyboard Data Area 3

- 96H Keyboard mode state and type flags

BIT	ACTION	BIT	ACTION
7	Read ID in progress	3	Right Alt pressed
6	Last code was ACK	2	Right Ctrl pressed
5	Force NumLock if read ID and KBX	1	Last scan code was E0
4	Extended keyboard installed	0	Last scan code was E1

- 97H Keyboard LED Flags (bit 0 = ScrollLock, 1 = NumLock, and 2 = CapsLock)

Real-Time Clock Data Area

- 98H–A7H Status of wait flags

Save Pointer Data Area

- A8H–ABH Pointers to various BIOS tables

Miscellaneous Data Area 2

- ACH–FFH Reserved by the system for internal use

INTERRUPT SERVICES

An interrupt operation suspends execution of a program so that the system can take special action. You have already used a number of interrupts for video display, disk I/O, printing, and resident programs. The interrupt routine executes and normally returns control to the interrupted procedure, which then resumes execution. BIOS handles INT 00H–1FH, whereas DOS handles INT 20H–3FH.

Interrupt Vector Table

When the computer powers up, BIOS and DOS establish an interrupt vector table in locations 000H–3FFH of conventional memory. The table provides for 256 (100H) interrupts, each with a related 4-byte offset:segment address in the form IP:CS. The operand of an interrupt instruction such as INT 05H identifies the type of request. Since there are 256 entries, each 4 bytes long, the table occupies the first 1,024 bytes of memory, from 00H through 3FFH. Each address in the table relates to a BIOS or DOS routine for a specific interrupt type. Thus bytes 0–3 contain the address for interrupt 0, bytes 4–7 for interrupt 1, and so forth:

INT 00H	INT 01H	INT 02H	INT 03H	INT 04H	INT 05H	INT 06H	...
IP:CS	IP:CS	IP:CS	IP:CS	IP:CS	IP:CS	IP:CS	...
00H	04H	08H	0CH	10H	14H	18H	...

Executing an Interrupt

An interrupt pushes onto the stack the contents of the flags register, the CS, and the IP. For example, the table address of INT 05H (which prints the video display area when a user presses Ctrl+PrtSc) is 0014H (05H $\times$ 4 = 14H). The operation extracts the 4-byte address from location 0014H and stores 2 bytes in the IP and 2 bytes in the CS. The address in the CS:IP then points to the start of a routine in the BIOS area, which now executes. The interrupt returns via an IRET (Interrupt Return) instruction, which pops the IP, CS, and flags from the stack and returns control to the instruction following the INT.

External and Internal Interrupts

An *external interrupt* is caused by a device that is external to the processor. The two lines that can signal external interrupts are the nonmaskable interrupt (NMI) line and the interrupt request (INTR) line. The NMI line reports memory and I/O parity errors. The processor always acts on this interrupt, even if you issue CLI to clear the interrupt flag in an attempt to disable external interrupts. The INTR line reports requests from external devices, namely interrupts 05H through 0FH, for the timer, keyboard, serial ports, fixed disk, diskette drives, and parallel ports.

An *internal interrupt* occurs as a result of the execution of an INT instruction or a divide operation that causes an overflow, execution in single-step mode, or a request for an external interrupt, such as disk I/O. Programs commonly use internal interrupts, which are nonmaskable, to access BIOS and DOS procedures.

BIOS INTERRUPTS

This section covers BIOS interrupts 00H through 1BH. Other operations not covered can be executed only by BIOS.

INT 00H. Divide by Zero. Invoked by an attempt to divide by zero; displays a message and usually hangs the system. Program developers are familiar with this error because erasing a segment register may accidentally cause it.

INT 01H. Single Step. Used by DEBUG and other debuggers to enable single-stepping through program execution.

INT 02H. Nonmaskable Interrupt. Used for serious hardware conditions, such as parity errors, that are always enabled. Thus a program issuing a CLI (Clear Interrupt) instruction does not affect these conditions.

INT 03H. Break Point. Used by debugging programs to stop execution. DEBUG's Go and Proceed commands set this interrupt at the appropriate stopping point in the program; DEBUG undoes single-step mode and allows the program to execute normally up to INT 03H, whereupon DEBUG resets single-step mode.

INT 04H. Overflow. May be caused by an arithmetic operation, although usually no action takes place.

INT 05H. Print Screen. Causes the contents of the video display area to print. Issuing INT 05H activates the interrupt internally, and pressing <Ctrl>+<PrtSc> activates it externally. The operation enables interrupts and saves the cursor position. No registers are affected. Address 50:00 in the BIOS data area contains the status of the operation.

INT 08H. System Timer. A hardware interrupt that updates the system time and (if necessary) date. A programmable timer chip generates an interrupt every 54.9254 milliseconds, about 18.2 times a second.

INT 09H. Keyboard Interrupt. Caused by pressing or releasing a key on the keyboard; described in detail in Chapter 11.

INT 0BH, INT 0CH. Serial Device Control. Control the COM1 and COM2 ports, respectively.

INT 0DH, INT 0FH. Parallel Device Control. Control the LPT2 and LPT1 ports, respectively.

INT 0EH. Diskette Control. Signals diskette activity, such as completion of an I/O operation.

INT 10H. Video Display. Accepts a number of functions in the AH for screen mode, setting the cursor, scrolling, and displaying; described in detail in Chapter 10.

INT 11H. Equipment Determination. Determines the optional devices on the system and returns the value at BIOS location 40:10H to the AX. (At power-up time, the system executes this operation and stores the AX in location 40:10H; see the earlier section "BIOS Data Area" for details.)

INT 12H. Memory Size Determination. Returns in the AX the size of base memory, in terms of contiguous kilobytes; for example, 640K memory is 0280H, as determined during power-on.

INT 13H. Disk Input/Output. Accepts a number of functions in the AH for disk status, read sectors, write sectors, verify, format, and get diagnostics; covered in Chapter 19.

INT 14H. Communications Input/Output. Provides byte stream I/O (that is, one bit at a time) to the RS232 communication port. The DX should contain the number of the RS232 adapter (0–3 for COM1, 2, 3, and 4, respectively). A number of functions are established through the AH register:

Function 00H. Initialize Communications Port. Set the following parameters in the AL, according to bit number:

BAUD RATE	PARITY	STOP BIT	WORD LENGTH
7 − 5	4 − 3	2	1 − 0
000 = 110	00 = none	0 = 1	10 = 7 bits
001 = 150	01 = odd	1 = 2	11 = 8 bits
010 = 300	10 = none		
011 = 600	11 = even		
100 = 1,200			
101 = 2,400			
110 = 4,800			
111 = 9,600			

The operation returns the status of the communications port in the AX. (See function 03H for details.) Here's an example that sets COM1 to 1,200 baud, no parity, 1 stop bit, and 8-bit data length:

```
MOV  AH,00H          ;Request initialize port
MOV  AL,10000011B    ;Parameters
MOV  DX,00           ;COM1 serial port
INT  14H             ;Call interrupt service
```

Function 01H. Transmit Character. Load the AL with the character that the routine is to transmit and the DX with the port number. On return, the operation sets the port status in the AH. (See function 03H.) If the operation is unable to transmit the byte, it also sets bit 7 of the AH, although the normal purpose of this bit is to report a time-out error. Be sure to execute function 00H before using this service.

Function 02H. Receive Character. Load the port number in the DX. The operation accepts a character from the communications line into the AL. It also sets the AH with the port status (see function 03) for error bits 7, 4, 3, 2, and 1. Thus a nonzero value in the AX indicates an input error. Be sure to execute function 00H before using this service.

Function 03H. Return Status of Communications Port. Load the port number in the DX. The operation returns the line status in the AH and modem status in the AL:

AH (LINE STATUS)	**AL (MODEM STATUS)**
7 Time out	7 Received line signal detect
6 Trans shift register empty	6 Ring indicator
5 Trans hold register empty	5 Data set ready
4 Break detect	4 Clear to send
3 Framing error	3 Delta receive line signal detect
2 Parity error	2 Trailing edge ring detector
1 Overrun error	1 Delta data set ready
0 Data ready	0 Delta clear to send

Other INT 14H functions are 04H (extended initialize) and 05H (extended communications port control).

INT 15H. System Services. This rather elaborate operation provides for a large number of functions in the AH, including the following:

21H	Power-on self-testing	88H	Determine extended memory size
43H	Read system status	89H	Switch processor to protected mode
84H	Joystick support	C2H	Mouse interface

For example, with function code 88H in the AH, INT 15H returns in the AX the number of kilobytes of extended memory. (For example, 0580H means 1408K bytes.) Because the operation exits without resetting interrupts, use it like this:

```
MOV  AH,88H     ;Request extended memory
INT  15H        ;  from BIOS
STI             ;Restore interrupts
```

INT 16H. Keyboard Input. Accepts a number of functions in the AH for basic keyboard input; covered in Chapter 10.

INT 17H. Printer Output. Provides a number of functions for printing via BIOS; discussed in Chapter 20.

INT 18H. ROM BASIC Entry. Called by BIOS if the system starts up with no disk containing the DOS system programs.

INT 19H. Bootstrap Loader. If a disk(ette) device is available with the DOS system programs, reads track 0, sector 1, into the boot location in memory at 7C00H and transfers control to this location. If there is no disk drive, transfers to the ROM BASIC entry point via INT 18H. It is possible to use this operation as a software interrupt; it does not clear the screen or initialize data in ROM BIOS.

INT 1AH. Read and Set Time. Reads or sets the time of day according to a function code in the AH:

- 00H = Read system timer clock. Returns the high portion of the count in the CX and the low portion in the DX. If the time has passed 24 hours since the last read, the operation sets the AL to a nonzero value.
- 01H = Set system timer clock. Load the high portion of the count in the CX and the low portion in the DX.
- 02H–07H. These functions handle the time and date for real-time clock services.

To determine how long a routine executes, you could set the clock to zero and then read it at the end of processing.

INT 1BH. Get Control on Keyboard Break. When Ctrl+Break keys are pressed, causes ROM BIOS to transfer control to its interrupt address, where a flag is set.

BIOS:DOS INTERFACE

The two system modules, IO.SYS and MSDOS.SYS, facilitate using BIOS. Because these modules provide much of the additional required processing, the DOS operations are generally easier to use than their BIOS counterparts and are generally more machine independent.

IO.SYS is a low-level interface to BIOS that facilitates reading data from external devices into memory and writing data from memory onto external devices.

MSDOS.SYS contains a file manager and provides a number of services. For example, when a user program requests INT 21H, the operation delivers information to MSDOS.SYS via the contents of registers. To complete the request, MSDOS.SYS may translate the information into one or more calls to IO.SYS, which in turn calls BIOS. The following shows the relationships:

```
    User            High level      Low level     ROM       External
  ---------
 | Program |
 | request | <---> |MSDOS.SYS| <---> |IO.SYS| <---> |BIOS| <---> |Device|
 | for I/O |
  ---------
```

DOS INTERRUPTS

Interrupts 20H through 3FH are reserved for DOS operations, as described in the following sections.

INT 20H. Terminate Program. An obsolete operation that ends execution of a .COM program, restores addresses for Ctrl+Break and critical errors, flushes register buffers, and returns control to DOS. On exit from this function, the CS should contain the address of the PSP. INT 21H function 4CH supersedes INT 20H.

INT 21H. DOS Function Request. Requires a function code in the AH and is described in detail in the next section.

INT 22H. Terminate Address. Copies the address of this interrupt into the program's PSP (at offset 0AH) when the program loader loads a program for execution. On program termination, the operation transfers control to the address of the interrupt. Your programs should not issue this interrupt.

INT 23H. Ctrl+Break Address. Designed to transfer control to a DOS routine (via PSP offset 0EH) when you press <Ctrl>+<Break> or <Ctrl>+<C>. The routine ends execution of a program or a batch file. A program could also change this address to that of its own routine to perform special action without ending the program. Your programs should not issue this interrupt.

INT 24H. Critical-error Handler. Used by the system to transfer control (via PSP offset 12H) when it recognizes a critical error (often in a disk or printer operation). Your programs should not issue this interrupt.

INT 25H. Absolute Disk Read. Reads the contents of one or more disk sectors; covered in Chapter 17, but superseded by INT 21H function 440DH, minor code 61H.

INT 26H. Absolute Disk Write. Writes data from memory to one or more disk sectors; covered in Chapter 17, but superseded by INT 21H function 440DH, minor code 41H.

INT 27H. Terminate but Stay Resident. Causes a .COM program on exit to remain in memory; superseded by INT 21H function 31H.

INT 2FH. Multiplex Interrupt. Involves communication between programs, such as communicating the status of a print spooler, the presence of a device driver, or system commands such as ASSIGN or APPEND. Chapter 24 describes function 4A01H, which checks the high-memory area for available space.

INT 33H. Mouse Handler. Provides services for handling a mouse. (See Chapter 21.)

INT 21H SERVICES

Following are the INT 21H services, which require a function code in the AH register:

00H. Terminate program. Basically the same as INT 20H and also superseded by INT 21H function 4CH.

01H. Keyboard input with echo. (See Chapter 11.)

02H. Display character. (See Chapter 9.)

03H. Communications input. Reads a character from the serial port into the AL; a primitive service, and BIOS INT 14H is preferred.

04H. Communications output. The DL contains the character to transmit; BIOS INT 14H is preferred.

05H. Printer output. (See Chapter 20.)

06H. Direct keyboard and display. (See Chapter 11.)

07H. Direct keyboard input without echo. (See Chapter 11.)

08H. Keyboard input without echo. (See Chapter 11.)

09H. Display string. (See Chapter 9.)

0AH. Buffered keyboard input. (See Chapter 11.)

0BH. Check keyboard status. (See Chapter 11.)

0CH. Clear keyboard buffer and invoke input. (See Chapter 11.)

0DH. Reset disk drive. (See Chapter 18.)

0EH. Select default disk drive. (See Chapter 18.)

0FH. Open FCB file. (See Chapter 17.)

10H. Close FCB file. (See Chapter 17.)

11H. Search for first matching disk entry. Obsolete and superseded by function 4EH.

12H. Search for next matching disk entry. Obsolete and superseded by function 4FH.

13H. Delete FCB file. Obsolete and superseded by function 41H.

14H. Read FCB sequential record. (See Chapter 17.)

15H. Write FCB sequential record. (See Chapter 17.)

16H. Create FCB file. (See Chapter 17.)

17H. Rename FCB file. Obsolete and superseded by function 56H.

19H. Determine default disk drive. (See Chapter 18.)

1AH. Set disk transfer area. (See Chapter 17.)

1BH. Get information for default drive. (See Chapter 18.)

1CH. Get information for specific drive. (See Chapter 18.)

1FH. Get default drive parameter block. (See Chapter 18.)

21H. Read FCB record randomly. (See Chapter 17.)

22H. Write FCB record randomly. (See Chapter 17.)

23H. Get FCB file size. Obsolete and superseded by function 42H.

24H. Set random FCB record field. (See Chapter 17.)

25H. Set interrupt vector. (See Chapter 24.) When a user presses <Ctrl>+<Break> or <Ctrl>+<C>, the normal procedure is for the program to terminate and return to the operating system. You may want your program to provide its own routine to handle this situation. The following example uses INT 21H function 25H to set the address for <Ctrl>+<Break> in the interrupt vector table (INT 23H) for its own routine, C10BRK. The routine could take any necessary action.

```
            MOV  AH,25H       ;Request set table address
            MOV  AL,23H       ;  for INT 23H
            LEA  DX,C10BRK    ;New address
            INT  21H          ;Call interrupt service
            ...
C10BRK:                       ;Ctrl+Break routine
            ...
            IRET              ;Interrupt return
```

26H. Create new program segment prefix. Superseded by function 4B00H.

27H. Read disk block randomly. (See Chapter 17.)

28H. Write disk block randomly. (See Chapter 17.)

29H. Parse filename. (See Chapter 18.)

2AH. Get system date. Returns these binary values: AL = day of week (Sunday = 0); CX = year (1980–2099); DH = month (01–12); DL = day (01–31).

2BH. Set system date. Load these binary values: CX = year (1980–2099); DH = month (01–12); DL = day (01–31). On return, the AL indicates a valid (00H) or invalid (FFH) operation.

2CH. Get system time. Returns these binary values: CH = hours, in 24-hour format (00–23, where midnight is 00); CL = minutes (00–59); DH = seconds (00–59); DL = hundredths of a second (00–99).

2DH. Set system time. Load these binary values: CH = hours, in 24-hour format (00–23, where midnight is 00); CL = minutes (00–59); DH = seconds (00–59); DL = hundredths of a second (00–99). On return, the AL indicates a valid (00H) or invalid (FFH) operation.

2EH. Set/reset disk verification. (See Chapter 18.)

2FH. Get address of current disk transfer area (DTA). (See Chapter 17 and see function 1AH for setting the address.)

30H. Get version number of DOS. (See also function 3306H.) Returns these values:

- AL = major number, such as n for version n.11.
- AH = minor number, such as hex B (11) for version n.11.
- BH = manufacturer number or version flag. If version flag is 08H, DOS runs in ROM.
- BL:CX = zero or 24-bit user serial number (manufacturer dependent).

31H. Terminate but stay resident. (See Chapter 24.)

32H. Get drive parameter block (DPB). (See Chapter 18.)

3300H. Get Ctrl+C state. If the Ctrl+C flag is off (0), causes the system to check for Ctrl+C only while handling character I/O functions 01H–0CH. If the flag is on (1), the system checks while handling other functions as well. To get the state, set subfunction 00H in the AL. The value returned in the DL is 00H = checking disabled or 01H = checking enabled.

3300H. Check Ctrl+C state. If the Ctrl+C flag is off (0), causes the system to check for Ctrl+C only while handling character I/O functions 01H–0CH. If the flag is on (1), the system checks while handling other functions as well. To set the state, set subfunction 01H in the AL, and set the state in the DL as 00H = set checking off or 01H = set checking on.

3305H. Get startup drive. Returns in the DL the drive (1 = A, etc.) used to load the system files.

3306H. Get DOS version (see also function 30H). Returns these values:

- BL = major version number, such as n for version n.11
- BH = minor version number, such as hex B (11) for version n.11
- DL = revision number in bits 2–0
- DH = DOS version flag (indicates whether the system is running in conventional memory, high-memory area, or ROM)

Although the SETVER command can fake the version number, function 3306H delivers the true version.

34H. Get DOS busy flag (inDOS) address. (See Chapter 24.)

35H. Get interrupt vector. (See Chapter 24.)

36H. Get free disk space. (See Chapter 18.)

38H. Get/set country-dependent information. Supports a number of functions concerning information specific to various countries, such as the symbol and format for the country's currency, separators for thousands and decimal places, and separators for the date and time. Load the DX for the operation: FFFFH to set the country code that the system is to use until further notice, or any other value to get the country code currently in use.

39H. Create subdirectory (MKDIR). (See Chapter 18.)

3AH. Remove subdirectory (RMDIR). (See Chapter 18.)

3BH. Change current directory (CHDIR). (See Chapter 18.)

3CH. Create file with handle. (See Chapter 17.)

3DH. Open file with handle. (See Chapter 17.)

3EH. Close file with handle. (See Chapter 17.)

3FH. Read file/device. (See Chapters 9 and 17.)

40H. Write file/device with handle. (See Chapters 9, 17, and 20.)

41H. Delete file from directory. (See Chapter 18.)

42H. Move file pointer. (See Chapter 17.)

43H. Check/change file attribute. (See Chapter 18.)

44H. I/O control for devices. Supports an extensive set of subfunctions for checking devices and reading and writing data, listed in the following functions:

4400H. Get device information. (See Chapter 18.)

4401H. Set device information. (See Chapter 18.)

4404H. Read control data from drive. (See Chapter 18.)

4405H. Write control data to drive. (See Chapter 18.)

4406H. Check input status. (See Chapter 18.)

4407H. Check output status. (See Chapter 18.)

4408H. Determine if removable media for device. (See Chapter 18.)

440DH. Minor Code 41H: Write disk sector. (See Chapter 18.)

440DH. Minor Code 61H: Read disk sector. (See Chapter 18.)

440DH. Minor Code 42H: Format track. (See Chapter 18.)

440DH. Minor Code 46H: Set media ID. (See Chapter 18.)

440DH. Minor Code 60H: Get device parameters. (See Chapter 18.)

440DH. Minor Code 66H: Get media ID. (See Chapter 18.)

440DH. Minor Code 68H: Sense media type. (See Chapter 18.)

45H. Duplicate a file handle. (See Chapter 18.)

46H. Force duplicate of handle. (See Chapter 18.)

47H. Get current directory. (See Chapter 18.)

48H. Allocate memory block. (See Chapter 24.)

49H. Free allocated memory block. (See Chapter 24.)

4AH. Set allocated memory block size. (See Chapter 24.)

4BH. Load/execute a program. (See Chapter 24.)

4CH. Terminate program. (See Chapter 4.) The standard operation for ending program execution.

4DH. Retrieve return code of a subprocess. (See Chapter 24.)

4EH. Find first matching directory entry. (See Chapter 18.)

4FH. Find next matching directory entry. (See Chapter 18.)

50H. Set address of program segment prefix (PSP). Load the BX with the offset address of the PSP for the current program. No values are returned.

51H. Get address of program segment prefix (PSP). Returns the offset address of the PSP for the current program. (See Chapter 24.)

52H. Get address of internal DOS list (undocumented, see Chapter 24).

54H. Get verify state. (See Chapter 18.)

56H. Rename a file. (See Chapter 18.)

57H. Get/set file date and time. (See Chapter 18.)

5800H. Get memory allocation strategy. (See Chapter 24.)

5801H. Set memory allocation strategy. (See Chapter 24.)

5802H. Get upper memory link. (See Chapter 24.)

5803H. Set upper memory link. (See Chapter 24.)

59H. Get extended error code. (See Chapter 18.)

5AH. Create a temporary file. (See Chapter 18.)

5BH. Create a new file. (See Chapter 18.)

5CH. Lock/unlock file access. Used for networking and multitasking environments.

5DH. Set extended error. Load the DX with the offset address of a table of information on errors. The next execution of function 59H (Get Extended Error Code) is to retrieve the table. (See function 59H in Chapter 18 for details.)

5EH. Local area network services. A subfunction in the AL specifies the service: 00H = Get machine name; 02H = Set printer setup; 03H: Get printer setup.

5FH. Local area network services. A subfunction in the AL specifies the service: 02H = Get assign-list entry; 03H = Make network connection; 04H = Cancel network connection.

62H. Get address of PSP. (Function 51H is an identical operation.)

65H. Get extended country information. Supports a number of subfunctions concerning information specific to various countries.

66H. Get/set global code page.

67H. Set maximum handle count. (See Chapter 24.)

68H. Commit file. (See Chapter 18.)

6CH. Extended open file. Combines functions 3CH (create file), 3DH (open file), and 5BH (create unique file). (See Chapter 18.)

KEY POINTS

- ROM resides beginning at location FFFF0H. Turning on the power causes a "cold boot." The processor enters a reset state, sets all memory locations to zero, performs a parity check of memory, and sets the CS register to FFFF[0]H and the IP register to zero. The first instruction to execute is therefore at FFFF:0, or FFFF0, the entry point to BIOS.
- On bootup, BIOS checks the various ports to identify and initialize devices that are attached. BIOS then establishes an interrupt vector table, beginning at location 0 of memory, that contains addresses for interrupts that occur. Two operations that BIOS

performs are equipment and memory size determination. If a disk containing the DOS system files is present, BIOS accesses the first disk sector containing the bootstrap loader. This program loads system files IO.SYS, MSDOS.SYS, and COMMAND.COM from disk into memory.

- BIOS maintains its own data area in lower memory beginning at segment address 40[0]H. Relevant data areas include those for serial port, parallel port, system equipment, keyboard, diskette drive, video control, hard disk, and real-time clock.
- The operand of an interrupt instruction such as INT 12H identifies the type of request. For each of the 256 possible types, the system maintains a 4-byte address in the interrupt services table at locations 0000H through 3FFH.
- BIOS interrupts range from 00H through 1FH and include print screen, timer, video control, diskette control, video display, equipment and memory size determination, disk I/O, keyboard input, communications, printer output, and bootstrap loader.
- INT 20H through 3FH are reserved for DOS operations.
- INT 21H handles such operations as keyboard input, display output, printer output, reset disk, open/close file, delete file, read/write record, terminate but stay resident, create subdirectory, and terminate program.

QUESTIONS

25-1. Distinguish between an external and an internal interrupt.

25-2. Distinguish between an NMI line and an INTR line.

25-3. (a) What is the memory location of the entry point to BIOS? (b) On power-up, how does the system direct itself to this address?

25-4. On bootup, BIOS performs INT 11H, 12H, and 19H. Explain the purpose of each interrupt.

25-5. Where is the beginning location of the BIOS data area?

25-6. The following binary values were noted in the BIOS data area. For each item, identify the field and explain the significance of the 1-bits.
(a) 10-11H: 01000100 01100111 (b) 17H: 01101010
(c) 18H: 00010010 (d) 96H: 00001010

25-7. The following hex values were noted in the BIOS data area. For each item, identify the field and explain the significance of the value.
(a) 00-03H: F8 03 F8 02 (b) 08-0BH: 78 03 00 00
(c) 13-14H: 80 02 (d) 15-16H: 00 10
(e) 4A-4BH: 50 00 (f) 60-61H: 0E 0D
(g) 84H: 18

25-8. Identify the following BIOS interrupts: (a) Memory size determination; (b) communications I/O; (c) get equipment status; (d) printer output; (e) keyboard input;

(f) disk I/O; (g) video display; (h) keyboard interrupt; (i) print screen; (j) divide by zero.

25-9. What INT operations are reserved for DOS?

25-10. Identify the functions for the following INT 21H services: (a) terminate but stay resident; (b) get address of interrupt table; (c) create subdirectory; (d) get free disk space; (e) get address of PSP; (f) communications input; (g) get system time; (h) rename a file.

25-11. Identify the following INT 21H functions: (a) 03H; (b) 09H; (c) 0DH; (d) 19H; (e) 2AH; (f) 31H; (g) 35H; (h) 39H; (i) 41H.

26 OPERATORS AND DIRECTIVES

Objective: To provide a detailed explanation of the assembly language operators and directives.

INTRODUCTION

The various assembly language features at first tend to be somewhat overwhelming. But once you have become familiar with the simpler and more common features described in earlier chapters, you should find the descriptions of the various type specifiers, operators, and directives in this chapter more easily understood and a handy reference. The assembly language manual contains a few other marginally useful features.

Note re Turbo Assembler: TASM can run either in MASM mode, which accepts the standard MASM specifications, or in Ideal mode, which in many cases uses somewhat different terms and rules and may not recognize the MASM specifications. This chapter identifies many of these exceptions.

TYPE SPECIFIERS

Type specifiers can provide the size of a data variable or the relative distance of an instruction label. Type specifiers that give the size of a data variable are BYTE, WORD, DWORD, FWORD, QWORD, and TBYTE. Those that give the distance of an instruction label are NEAR, FAR, and PROC. A near address, which is simply an offset, is assumed to be in the current segment; a far address, which consists of a segment:offset address, can be used to access data in another segment.

The PTR and THIS operators, as well as the COM, EXTRN, LABEL, and PROC directives, use type specifiers.

OPERATORS

An operator provides a facility for changing or analyzing operands during an assembly. Operators are divided into various categories:

- *Calculation operators:* Arithmetic, index, logical, shift, and structure field name.
- *Macro operators:* Various types, covered in Chapter 22.
- *Record operators:* MASK and WIDTH, covered later in this chapter under the RECORD directive.
- *Relational operators:* EQ, GE, GT, LE, LT, and NE.
- *Segment operators:* OFFSET, SEG, and segment override.
- *Type (or Attribute) operators:* HIGH, HIGHWORD, LENGTH, LOW, LOWWORD, PTR, SHORT, SIZE, THIS, and TYPE.

Because a knowledge of these categories is not necessary, we'll simply cover the operators in alphabetic sequence.

Arithmetic Operators

These operators include the familiar arithmetic signs and perform arithmetic during an assembly. In most cases, you could perform the calculation yourself, although the advantage of using these operators is that every time you change the program and reassemble it, the assembler automatically recalculates the values of the arithmetic operators. Following is a list of the operators, together with an example of their use and the effect obtained:

SIGN	TYPE	EXAMPLE	EFFECT
+	Addition	FLDA+25	Adds 25 to address of FLDA
+	Positive	+FLDA	Treats FLDA as positive
−	Subtraction	FLDB-FLDA	Calculates difference between two offset addresses
−	Negation	−FLDA	Reverses sign of FLDA
*	Multiplication	value*3	Multiplies value by 3
/	Division	value/3	Divides value by 3
MOD	Remainder	value1 MOD value2	Delivers remainder for value1/value2

Except for addition (+) and subtraction (−), all operators must be integer constants. The following related examples illustrate integer expressions:

```
value1 = 12 * 4          ;48
value1 = value1 / 6      ;48 / 6 = 8
value1 = -value1 - 3     ;(-8) - (3) = -11
```

HIGH and HIGHWORD Operators

The HIGH operator returns the high (leftmost) byte of an expression, and HIGHWORD (since MASM 6.0) returns the high word of an expression. (See also the LOW operator.) Here is an example:

```
EQUVAL  EQU  1234H
        . . .
        MOV  CL,HIGH EQUVAL    ;Load 12H in CL
```

Index Operators

For a direct memory reference, one operand of an instruction specifies the name of a defined data item, as shown by COUNTER in the instruction ADD CX,COUNTER. During execution, the processor locates the specified data item in memory by combining the data segment address in the DS with the offset value of the data item.

For indirect addressing of memory, an operand references a base or index register, constants, offset variables, and variables. The index operator, which uses square brackets, acts like a plus (+) sign. A typical use of indexing is to reference data items in tables. You can use the following operations to reference indexed memory:

- [Constant], i.e., an immediate number or name in square brackets. For example, load the fifth entry of PARTTBL into the CL (note that PARTTBL[0] is the first entry):

```
PARTTBL  DB   25 DUP(?)         ;Defined table
         . . .
         MOV  CL,PARTTBL[4]     ;Get fifth entry from PARTTBL
```

- Base register BX as [BX] in association with the DS segment register, and base register BP as [BP] in association with the SS segment register. For example, use the offset address in the BX (as DS:BX), and move the referenced item to the DX:

```
MOV  DX,[BX]     ;Base register DS:BX
```

- Index register DI as [DI] and index register SI as [SI], both in association with the DS segment register. For example, use the offset address in the SI (as DS:SI), and move the referenced item to the AX:

```
MOV  AX,[SI]     ;Index register DS:SI
```

- Combined index registers. For example, move the contents of the AX to the address determined by adding the DS address, the BX offset, the SI offset, and the constant 4:

```
MOV  [BX+SI+4],AX    ;Base + index + constant
```

The first operand in the preceding example could also be coded as [BX+SI]+4. You may combine these operands in any sequence, but don't combine two base registers [BX+BP] or two index registers [DI+SI]. Only the index registers must be in square brackets so that the assembler knows to treat it as an index entry.

LENGTH Operator

The LENGTH operator returns the number of entries defined by a DUP operator, as shown by the following MOV instruction:

```
PARTTBL  DW    10 DUP(?)
         ...
         MOV   DX,LENGTH PARTTBL     ;Return length 10 to DX
```

If the referenced operand does not contain a DUP entry, the operator returns the value 01 (a limit to its usefulness). (See also the SIZE and TYPE operators.)

Logical Operators

The logical operators perform logical operations on the bits in an expression:

OPERATOR	USED AS	EFFECT
AND	expression1 AND expression2	ANDs the bits
OR	expression1 OR expression2	ORs the bits
XOR	expression1 XOR expression2	Exclusive ORs the bits
NOT	NOT expression1	Reverses the bits

Here are two examples:

```
MOV  CL,00111100B AND 01010101B     ;CL = 00010100B
MOV  DL,NOT 01010101B               ;DL = 10101010B
```

LOW and LOWWORD Operators

The LOW operator returns the low (rightmost) byte of an expression, and LOWWORD (since MASM 6.0) returns the low word of an expression. (See also the HIGH operator.) Here is an example:

```
EQUVAL  EQU 1234H
        ...
        MOV CL,LOW EQUVAL    ;Load 34H in CL
```

OFFSET Operator

The OFFSET operator returns the offset address (that is, the relative address within the data segment or code segment) of a variable or label. The general format is

```
OFFSET variable or label
```

The following MOV returns the offset address of PARTTBL:

```
MOV DX,OFFSET PARTTBL
```

Note that LEA doesn't require OFFSET to return the same value:

```
LEA DX,PARTTBL
```

MASK Operator

See "RECORD Directive" in the later section "Directives."

PTR Operator

The PTR operator can be used on data variables and instruction labels. It uses the type specifiers BYTE, WORD, FWORD, DWORD, QWORD, and TBYTE to specify a size in an ambiguous operand or to override the defined type (DB, DW, DF, DD, DF, or DT) for variables. It also uses the type specifiers NEAR, FAR, and PROC to override the implied distance of labels. The general format for PTR is

```
type PTR expression
```

The type is the new attribute, such as BYTE. The expression is a variable or constant. Following are unrelated examples of the PTR operator (watch out for WORDA, where the assembler stores the bytes in reverse sequence):

```
BYTEA  DB   22H
       DB   35H
WORDA  DW   2672H                  ;Data stored as 7226
       ...
       MOV  AH,BYTE PTR WORDA       ;Move first byte (72)
       ADD  BL,BYTE PTR WORDA+1     ;Add second byte (26)
       MOV  BYTE PTR WORDA,05       ;Move 05 to first byte
       MOV  AX,WORD PTR BYTEA       ;Move two bytes (2235) to AX
       CALL FAR PTR[BX]             ;Call far procedure
```

A feature that performs a similar function to PTR is the LABEL directive, described later.

SEG Operator

The SEG operator returns the address of the segment in which a specified variable or label is placed. Programs that combine separately assembled segments would most likely use this operator. The general format is

```
SEG variable or label
```

The following MOV instructions return the address of the segment in which the referenced names are defined:

```
MOV  DX,SEG WORDA       ;Address of data segment
MOV  DX,SEG A10BEGIN    ;Address of code segment
```

Segment Override Operator

This operator, coded as a colon (:), calculates the address of a label or variable relative to a particular segment. Its general format is

```
segment:expression
```

The named segment can be any of the segment registers or a segment or group name. The expression can be a constant, an expression, or a SEG expression. These next examples override the default DS segment register:

```
MOV  BH,ES:10H      ;Access from ES + 10H
MOV  CX,SS:[BX]     ;Access from SS + offset in BX
```

An instruction may have a segment override operator apply to only one operand.

SHL and SHR Operators

The operators SHL and SHR shift an expression during an assembly. The general formats are

```
expression SHL/SHR count
```

In the following example, the SHR operator shifts the bit constant 3 bits to the right:

```
MOV  BL,01011101B SHR 3    ;Load 00001011B
```

Most likely, the expression would reference a symbolic name rather than a constant value.

SHORT Operator

The purpose of the SHORT operator is to modify the NEAR attribute of a JMP destination that is within +127 and −128 bytes. The format is

```
JMP SHORT label
```

The assembler reduces the machine code operand from two bytes to one. This feature is useful for near jumps that branch forward, since otherwise the assembler initially doesn't know the distance of the jump address and may assume two bytes for a near jump.

SIZE Operator

The SIZE operator returns the product of LENGTH times TYPE and is useful only if the referenced variable contains the DUP entry. Under TASM Ideal mode, the operation returns the actual number of bytes. The general format is

```
SIZE variable
```

See "TYPE Operator" for an example.

THIS Operator

The THIS operator creates an operand with segment and offset values that are equal to those of the current location counter. Its general format is

```
THIS type
```

The type specifier can be BYTE, WORD, DWORD, FWORD, QWORD, or TBYTE for variables and NEAR, FAR, or PROC for labels. THIS would typically be used with the EQU or equals sign (=) directives. The following example defines PARTREC:

```
PARTREC EQU  THIS BYTE
```

The effect is the same as if you used the LABEL directive as

```
PARTREC LABEL BYTE
```

TYPE Operator

The TYPE operator returns the number of bytes, according to the definition of the referenced variable. However, the operation always returns 1 for a string variable and 0 for a constant.

DEFINITION	NUMBER OF BYTES FOR NUMERIC VARIABLE
DB/BYTE	1
DW/WORD	2
DD/DWORD	4
DF/FWORD	6
DQ/QWORD	8
DT/TWORD	10
STRUC/STRUCT	Number of bytes defined by the structure
NEAR label	FFFFH
FAR label	FFFEH

The general format of TYPE is

```
TYPE variable or label
```

The following examples illustrate the TYPE, LENGTH, and SIZE operators:

```
BYTEA    DB   ?                   ;Define one byte
PARTTBL  DW   10 DUP(?)           ;Define 10 words
         ...
         MOV  AX,TYPE BYTEA       ;AX = 0001H
         MOV  AX,TYPE PARTTBL     ;AX = 0002H
         MOV  CX,LENGTH PARTTBL   ;CX = 000AH (10)
         MOV  DX,SIZE PARTTBL     ;DX = 0014H (20)
```

Because PARTTBL is defined as DW, TYPE returns 0002H, LENGTH returns 000AH (10) based on the DUP entry, and SIZE returns type times length, or 14H (20).

WIDTH Operator

See "RECORD Directive" in the following section.

DIRECTIVES

This section describes most of the assembler directives. Chapter 4 covered in detail the directives for defining data (DB, DW, etc.), and Chapter 22 covered the directives for macro instructions, so they aren't repeated here. Directives are divided into various categories:

- Code labels: ALIGN, EVEN, LABEL, and PROC.
- Conditional assembly: IF, ELSE, and others, covered in Chapter 21.
- Conditional errors: .ERR, .ERR1, and others.
- Data allocation: ALIGN, EQU, EVEN, LABEL, and ORG. DB, DW, DD, DF, DQ, and DT, covered in Chapter 4.
- Listing control: .CREF, .LIST, PAGE, SUBTTL (SUBTITLE), TITLE, .XCREF, and .XLIST, covered in this chapter. .LALL, .LFCOND, .SALL, .SFCOND, .TFCOND, and .XALL, covered in Chapter 22.
- Macros: ENDM, EXITM, LOCAL, MACRO, and PURGE, covered in Chapter 21.
- Miscellaneous: COMMENT, INCLUDE, INCLUDELIB, NAME, &OUT, and .RADIX.
- Processor: .8086, .286, .286P, .386, .386P, .8087, .287, .387, etc.
- Repeat blocks: IRP, IRPC, and REPT, covered in Chapter 22.
- Scope: COMM, EXTRN, and PUBLIC.
- Segment: .ALPHA, ASSUME, .DOSSEG, END, ENDS, GROUP, SEGMENT, and .SEQ.
- Simplified segment: .CODE, .CONST, .DATA, .DATA?, DOSSEG, .EXIT, .FARDATA, .FARDATA?, .MODEL, and .STACK.
- Structure/Record: ENDS, RECORD, STRUCT, TYPEDEF, UNION.

Because a knowledge of these categories is not necessary, we'll cover the directives (other than macro-related ones) in alphabetic sequence.

ALIGN Directive

The ALIGN directive causes the assembler to align the next data item or instruction on an address according to a given value. Alignment can facilitate the processor in accessing words and doublewords. The general format is

```
ALIGN number
```

The number must be a power of 2, such as 2, 4, 8, or 16. In the following example, the location counter is at 0005 when the ALIGN 4 statement causes the assembler to advance its location counter to the next address evenly divisible by 4:

```
0005  ALIGN  4
0008  DBWORD DD 0     ;Align on doubleword boundary
```

If the location counter is already at the required address, it is not advanced. The assembler fills unused bytes with zeros for data and NOPs for instructions. Note that ALIGN 2 has the same effect as EVEN.

.ALPHA Directive

The .ALPHA directive, placed at or near the start of a program, tells the assembler to arrange segments in alphabetic sequence, for compatibility with early assembler versions. You can also use the /A option on the assembler command line. (See also the DOSSEG and .SEQ directives.)

ASSUME Directive

ASSUME tells the assembler to associate segment names with the CS, DS, ES, and SS segment registers. Its general format is

```
ASSUME seg-reg:seg-name [, ...]
```

Valid segment register entries are CS, DS, ES, and SS, plus FS and GS on the 80386 and later processors. Valid segment names are those of segment registers, NOTHING, GROUP, and a SEG expression. One ASSUME statement may assign up to four segment registers, in any sequence. The simplified segment directives automatically generate an ASSUME.

In the following ASSUME statement, CODESG, DATASG, and STACK are the names the program has used to define the segments:

```
ASSUME  CS:CODESG,DS:DATASG,SS:STACK,ES:DATASG
```

Omission of a segment reference is the same as coding NOTHING. Use of the keyword NOTHING also cancels any previous ASSUME for a specified segment register:

```
ASSUME ES:NOTHING
```

Suppose that you neither assign the ES register nor use NOTHING to cancel it. Then, to reference an item in the data segment, an instruction operand may use the segment override operator (:) to reference the ES register, which must contain a valid segment address:

```
MOV  AX,ES:[BX]     ;Use indexed address
MOV  AX,ES:WORDA    ;Move contents of WORDA
```

.CODE Directive

This simplified segment directive defines the code segment. Its general format is

```
.CODE [name]
```

All executable code must be placed in this segment. For TINY, SMALL, and COMPACT models, the default segment name is _TEXT. The MEDIUM and LARGE memory models permit multiple code segments, which you distinguish by means of the name operand. (See also the .MODEL directive.)

COMM Directive

Defining a variable as COMM gives it both the PUBLIC and EXTRN attributes. In this way, you do not have to define the variable as PUBLIC in one module and EXTRN in another. The general format is

```
COMM [NEAR/FAR] label:size[:count]
```

- COMM is coded within a data segment.
- The NEAR or FAR attributes may be coded or allowed to default to one or the other, depending on the memory model.
- The label is the name of the variable. Note that the variable cannot have an initial value.
- The size can be any of the type specifiers BYTE, WORD, DWORD, QWORD, and TBYTE, or an integer specifying the number of bytes.
- The count indicates the number of elements for the variable. The default is 1.

The following examples define items with the COMM attribute:

```
COMM  NEAR  COMFLD1:WORD       ;Word size with COMM attribute
COMM  FAR   COMFLD2:BYTE:25    ;25 bytes with COMM attribute
```

COMMENT Directive

This directive is useful for multiple lines of comments. Its general format is

```
COMMENT delimiter [comments]
    [comments]
delimiter [comments]
```

The delimiter is the first nonblank character, such as % or +, following COMMENT. The comments terminate on the line on which the second delimiter appears. This example uses "+" as a delimiter:

```
COMMENT + This routine scans
          the keyboard input
          for invalid
        + characters.
```

TASM Ideal mode does recognize the COMMENT directive.

.CONST Directive

This simplified segment directive defines a data (or constant-data) segment with the 'const' class. (See also the .MODEL directive.)

.CREF Directive

This directive (the default) tells the assembler to generate a cross-reference table. It would be used following an .XCREF directive that caused suppression of the table.

.DATA and .DATA? Directives

These simplified segment directives define data segments. .DATA defines a segment for initialized near data; .DATA? defines a segment for uninitialized near data, usually used when linking to a high-level language. For a stand-alone assembly program, you may also define uninitialized near data in a .DATA segment. (See, in addition, the .FARDATA and .MODEL directives.)

DOSSEG/.DOSSEG Directive

There are a number of ways to control the sequence in which the assembler arranges segments. (Some early versions arrange them alphabetically.) You may code the .SEQ or .ALPHA directives at the start of a program, or you may enter the /S or /A options on the assembler command line. The DOSSEG (.DOSSEG since MASM 6.0) directive tells the assembler to ignore all other requests and to adopt the DOS segment sequence—basically, code, data, and stack. Code this directive at or near the start of the program, primarily to facilitate the use of the CODEVIEW debugger for stand-alone programs.

END Directive

The END directive is placed at the end of a source program. The general format is

```
END [start-address]
```

The optional start-address indicates the location in the code segment (usually the first instruction) where execution is to begin. The system loader uses this address to initialize the CS register. If your program consists of only one module, define a start-address. If it consists of a number of modules, only one (usually the first) has a start-address.

ENDP Directive

This directive indicates the end of a procedure, defined by PROC. Its general format is

```
MASM:                 proc-name  ENDP
TASM Ideal mode:  ENDP [proc-name]
```

The procedure name is the same as the one that defines the procedure.

ENDS Directive

This directive indicates the end of a segment (defined by SEGMENT) or a structure (defined by STRUC or STRUCT). Its general format is

```
MASM:                 seg-name  ENDS
TASM Ideal mode:  ENDS [seg-name]
```

The segment name is the same as the one that defines the segment or structure.

EQU Directive

The EQU directive is used to redefine a data name or variable with another data name, variable, or immediate value. The directive should be defined in a program before it is referenced. The formats for numeric and string a data differ:

```
Numeric equate: name EQU expression
String equate:  name EQU <string>
```

The assembler replaces each occurrence of the name with the operand. Because EQU is used for simple replacement, it takes no additional storage in the generated object program.

Examples of the use of EQU with numeric data are:

```
COUNTER  DW   0
SUM      EQU  COUNTER      ;Another name for COUNTER
TEN      EQU  10           ;Numeric value
         ...
         INC  SUM          ;Increment COUNTER
         ADD  SUM,TEN      ;Add 10 to COUNTER
```

Examples of the use of EQU with string data are:

```
PRODMSG  EQU  <'Enter product number:'>
BYPTR    EQU  <BYTE PTR>
         ...
MESSGE1  DB   PRODMSG           ;Replace with string
         ...
         MOV  SAVE,BYPTR [BX] ;Replace with string
```

The angle brackets make it easier to indicate a string operand.

.ERR Directives

These conditional error directives can be used to help test for errors during an assembly:

DIRECTIVE	ERROR FORCED
.ERR	When encountered
.ERR1	During pass 1 of an assembly
.ERR2	During pass 2 of an assembly
.ERRE	By true (0) expression
.ERRNZ	By false (not 0) expression
.ERRDEF	By defined symbol
.ERRNDEF	By not defined symbol
.ERRB	By blank string
.ERRNB	By not blank string
.ERRIDN[I]	By identical strings
.ERRDIF[I]	By different strings

You could use the preceding directives in macros and in conditional assembly statements. In the following conditional assembly statements, the assembler displays a message if the condition is not true:

```
IF      condition
        ...
ELSE    .ERR
        %OUT [message]
ENDIF
```

Since MASM 6.0, it is no longer necessary to refer to pass 1 (.ERR1) or pass 2 (.ERR2) of an assembly.

EVEN Directive

EVEN tells the assembler to advance its location counter if necessary so that the next defined data item or instruction is aligned on an even storage boundary. This feature facilitates processors that can access 16 or 32 bits at a time. (See also the ALIGN directive.)

In the following example, BYTELOCN is a 1-byte field on an even boundary, 0016. The location counter is now at 0017. EVEN causes the assembler to advance the location counter one byte to 0018, where the next data item, WORDLOCN, is defined:

```
0016  BYTELOCN  DB  ?
0017            EVEN  (Advance location counter)
0018  WORDLOCN  DW  ?
```

.EXIT Directive

You can use this directive in the code segment to generate program termination code. Its general format is

```
MASM:               .EXIT [return-value]
TASM Ideal mode: EXITCODE [return-value]
```

where a return-value of 0 means no problem and 1 means an error terminated processing. The generated code is

```
MOV  AH,4CH
MOV  AL,return-value    ;Generated if return-value coded
INT  21H
```

EXTRN/EXTERN Directive

The EXTRN (or EXTERN since MASM 6.0) directive informs the assembler and linker about data variables and labels that the current assembly references, but that another module (linked to the current one) defines. The general format is

```
EXTRN/EXTERN name:type [, ...]
```

The name is an item defined in another assembly and declared in it as PUBLIC. The type specifier can refer to either of the following:

- Data items: ABS (a constant), BYTE, WORD, DWORD, FWORD, QWORD, TBYTE. Code the EXTRN in the segment in which the item occurs.
- Distance: NEAR or FAR. Code NEAR in the segment in which the item occurs, and code FAR anywhere.

In the next example, the calling program defines CONVAL as PUBLIC and as a DW. The called subprogram identifies CONVAL (in another segment) as EXTRN and FAR.

Calling program:

```
DSEG1   SEGMENT
        PUBLIC CONVAL
        ...
CONVAL  DW ?
        ...
DSEG1   ENDS
```

Called subprogram:

```
        EXTRN CONVAL:FAR
DSEG2   SEGMENT
        ...
        MOV  AX,CONVAL
```

```
        ...
DSEG2   ENDS
```

See Chapter 23 for examples of EXTRN.

.FARDATA and .FARDATA? Directives

These simplified segment directives define data segments. .FARDATA defines a segment for initialized far data, and .FARDATA? defines a segment for uninitialized far data. For a stand-alone assembly program, you may also define uninitialized far data in a .FARDATA segment. (See also the .DATA and .MODEL directives.)

GROUP Directive

A program may contain several segments of the same type (code, data, or stack). The purpose of the GROUP directive is to collect segments of the same type under one name, so that they reside within one segment, usually a data segment. The general format is

```
name  GROUP  seg-name  [, seg-name], ...
```

The following GROUP combines DSEG1 and DSEG2 in the same assembly module:

```
GROUPX  GROUP     DSEG1, DSEG2
DSEG1   DSEGMENT  PARA 'Data'
        ASSUME    DS:GROUPX
        ...
DSEG1   ENDS
;
DSEG2   DSEGMENT  PARA 'Data'
        ASSUME    DS:GROUPX
        ...
DSEG2   ENDS
```

The effect of using GROUP is similar to giving the segments the same name and the PUBLIC attribute.

INCLUDE Directive

If you have sections of assembly code or macro instructions that various programs use, you may store them in separate disk files, available for use by any program. Consider a routine that converts ASCII code to binary is stored on drive E: in a file named CONVERT.LIB. To access the file, insert an INCLUDE statement such as

```
INCLUDE E:CONVERT.LIB
```

at the location in the source program where you would normally code the ASCII conversion routine. The assembler locates the file on disk and includes the statements in your program. (If the assembler cannot find the file, it issues an error message and ignores the INCLUDE.)

For each included line, the assembler prints a C (depending on version) in column 30 of the .LST file and begins the source code in column 33.

Chapter 22 gives a practical example of INCLUDE and explains how to use the directive only for pass 1 of an assembly.

LABEL Directive

The LABEL directive enables you to redefine the attribute of a data variable or instruction label. Its general format is

```
name  LABEL  type-specifier
```

For labels, you may use LABEL to redefine executable code as NEAR, FAR, or PROC, such as for a secondary entry point into a procedure. For variables, you can use the type specifiers BYTE, WORD, DWORD, FWORD, QWORD, or TBYTE, or a structure name, to redefine data items and the names of structures, respectively. For example, LABEL enables you to define a field as both DB and DW.

The following example illustrates the BYTE and WORD types:

```
BYTE1   LABEL  BYTE        ;Define first byte as BYTE1
WORD1   DW     2532H       ;Define first two bytes as WORD1
WORD2   LABEL  WORD        ;Define third and fourth bytes as WORD2
BYTE2   DB     25H         ;Define third byte as BYTE2
        DB     32H         ;Define fourth byte
        ...
        MOV    AL,BYTE1    ;Move 1st byte
        MOV    BX,WORD2    ;Move third and fourth bytes
```

The first MOV instruction moves only the first byte of WORD1. The second MOV moves the two bytes beginning at BYTE2. The PTR operator performs a similar function.

The next example uses LABEL with the NEAR operator. Although the normal way to code a near label is with a semicolon suffix, as A20CALC:, you can also code the label as A20CALC LABEL NEAR.

.LIST Directive

The .LIST directive (the default, and known as %LIST in TASM Ideal mode) causes the assembler to list the source program. You may have a block of code that you don't need listed because it is common to other programs. In this case, you may use the .XLIST (or .NOLIST) directive to discontinue the listing and then use .LIST to resume the listing. Use these directives with no operand.

.MODEL Directive

This simplified segment directive creates default segments and the required ASSUME and GROUP statements. Its general format is

```
.MODEL memory-model
```

The memory models are

TINY	Since MASM 6.0 and TASM 4.0, used for .COM programs.
SMALL	All data in one segment and all code in one segment.
MEDIUM	All data in one segment, but code in more than one segment.
COMPACT	Data in more than one segment, but code in one segment.
LARGE	Both data and code in more than one segment, but no array may exceed 64K.
HUGE	Both data and code in more than one segment, and arrays may exceed 64K.

The .STACK directive defines the stack, .CODE defines the code segment, and any or all of .DATA, .DATA?, .FARDATA, and .FARDATA? may define data segments. Here is an example:

```
.MODEL  SMALL
.STACK  120
.DATA
        [data items]
.CODE
        [instructions]
END
```

In TASM Ideal mode, the directive is MODEL (with no leading dot) and the segments are CODESEG, DATASEG, UDATASEG, FARDATA, and UFARDATA, respectively.

.NOLIST Directive (see .XLIST Directive)

ORG Directive

Consider a data segment with the following definitions:

OFFSET	NAME	OPERATION	OPERAND	LOCATION COUNTER
00	WORD1	DW	2542H	02
02	BYTE1	DB	36H	03
03	WORD2	DW	212EH	05
05	BYTE2	DD	00000705H	09

Initially, the assembler's location counter is set to 00. Because WORD1 is 2 bytes, the location counter is incremented to 02 for the location of the next item. Because BYTE1 is 1 byte, the location counter is incremented to 03, and so forth. You may use the ORG directive to change the contents of the location counter and, accordingly, the location of the next defined item. Its general format is

```
ORG expression
```

The expression must form a 2-byte absolute number and must not be a symbolic name. Suppose the following data items are defined immediately after BYTE2 in the previous definition:

OFFSET	NAME	OPERATION	OPERAND	LOCATION COUNTER
		ORG	0	00
00	BYTE3	DB	?	01
01	WORD3	DW	?	02
03	BYTE4	DB	?	04
		ORG	$+5	09

The first ORG resets the location counter to 00. The variables that follow—BYTE3, WORD3, and BYTE4—redefine the memory locations originally defined as WORD1, BYTE1, and WORD2, respectively:

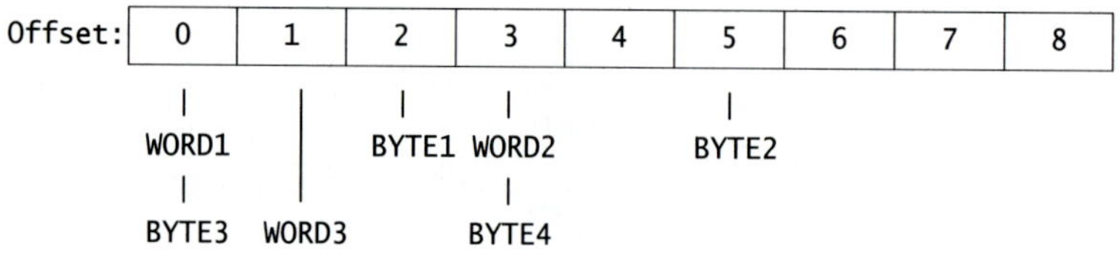

```
Offset: | 0 | 1 | 2 | 3 | 4 | 5 | 6 | 7 | 8 |
          |   |   |   |       |
        WORD1     BYTE1 WORD2 BYTE2
          |   |       |
        BYTE3 WORD3   BYTE4
```

An operand containing a dollar symbol ($), as in the last ORG, refers to the current value in the location counter. The operand $+5 therefore sets the location counter to 04 + 5, or 09, which is the same setting as after the definition of BYTE2.

A reference to WORD2 is to a 1-word field at offset 03, and a reference to BYTE4 is to a 1-byte field also at offset 03:

```
MOV  AX,WORD2    ;One word
MOV  AL,BYTE4    ;One byte
```

When you use ORG to redefine memory locations, be sure to reset the location counter to the correct value and that you account for all redefined memory locations. Also, the redefined variables should not contain defined constants—these would overlay constants on top of the original ones. ORG cannot appear within a STRUC definition.

%OUT/ECHO Directive

This directive tells the assembler to direct a message to the standard output device (usually the screen). (Since MASM 6.0, the name is ECHO.) The general format is

```
%OUT/ECHO message
```

The ".ERR Directives" section gives an example.

PAGE Directive

The PAGE directive at the start of a source program specifies the maximum number of lines to list on a page and the maximum number of characters on a line. Its general format is

```
PAGE  [[length],width]
```

The following example sets 60 lines per page and 132 characters per line:

```
PAGE 60,132
```

The number of lines per page may range from 10 to 255, and the number of characters per line may range from 60 to 132. Omission of a PAGE statement causes the assembler to assume PAGE 50,80. To force a page to eject at a specific line, such as at the end of a segment, code PAGE with no operand.

In TASM Ideal mode, PAGE with an operand is %PAGESIZE and PAGE with no operand is %NEWPAGE.

PROC Directive

A procedure is a block of code that begins with the PROC directive and terminates with ENDP. Although technically you may enter a procedure inline or by a JMP instruction, the normal practice is to use CALL to enter and RETN or RETF to exit. The CALL operand may be a NEAR or FAR type specifier.

A procedure that is in the same segment as the calling procedure is a NEAR procedure and is accessed by an offset:

```
proc-name  PROC  [NEAR]
```

An omitted operand defaults to NEAR. If a called procedure is external to the calling segment, it must be declared as PUBLIC, and you should use CALL to enter it.

For an .EXE program, the main PROC that is the entry point for execution must be FAR. Also, a called procedure under a different ASSUME CS value must have the FAR attribute:

```
           PUBLIC  proc-name
proc-name  PROC    FAR
```

A far label may be in another segment, which CALL accesses by a segment address and offset.

TASM Ideal mode defines PROC and ENDP like this:

```
PROC  proc-name [NEAR/FAR]
...
ENDP  [proc-name]
```

Processor Directives

These directives define the processors that the assembler is to recognize. The normal placement of processor directives is at the start of a source program, although you could code them inside a program at a point where you want a processor's features enabled or disabled.

- .8086 enables the 8086/8088 and 8087 coprocessor (the default mode).
- .186, .286, .386, .486, and .586 enable all the instruction sets up to and including the named processor and its associated coprocessor. That is, the directive permits instructions of earlier processors. (For example, .386 enables .387, .286, .186, and .8086.)
- .186P, .286P, .386P, .486P and .586P enable all the instruction sets just cited, plus the processor's privileged instructions. TASM Ideal mode uses the terms P8086 through P586 and P8087 through P587.

PUBLIC Directive

The purpose of the PUBLIC directive is to inform the assembler and linker that the identified symbols in an assembly are to be referenced by other modules linked with the current one. Its general format is

```
PUBLIC  symbol [, ... ]
```

The symbol can be a label, a number (up to two bytes), or a variable. See the "EXTRN Directive" section and Chapter 23 for examples.

RECORD Directive

The RECORD directive enables you to define patterns of bits, such as color patterns and switch indicators as one bit or as multibit. Its general format is

```
MASM:record-name RECORD field-name:width[=exp] [, ... ]
TASM Ideal mode: RECORD record name... .
```

The record name and field names may be any unique valid identifiers. Following each field name is a colon (:) and a width that specifies the number of bits. The range of the width entry is 1 to 32 bits. Lengths up to 8 become 8 bits, 9 to 16 become 16 bits, and 17 to 32 become 32 bits, with the contents right adjusted if necessary. The following example uses the RECORD directive to define BITREC:

```
BITREC RECORD BIT1:3,BIT2:7,BIT3:6
```

BIT1 defines the first 3 bits of BITREC, BIT2 defines the next 7, and BIT3 defines the last 6. The total is 16 bits, or 1 word. You may initialize values in a record as follows:

```
BITREC2 RECORD BIT1:3=101B,BIT2:7=0110110B,BIT3:6=011010B
```

Note that a RECORD definition does not actually generate any storage. Therefore, following a definition of RECORD in the data segment, you have to code another statement that allocates storage for the record. Define a unique valid name, the record name, and an operand consisting of angle brackets (the less-than and greater-than symbols):

```
DEFBITS BITREC <>
```

The allocation for DEFBITS generates object code AD9AH (stored as 9AAD) in the data segment. The angle brackets may also contain entries that redefine BITREC.

The program in Figure 26-1 defines BITREC as RECORD, but without initial values in the record fields. In this case, an allocation statement in the data segment as shown within angle brackets initializes each field.

Record-specific operators are WIDTH, shift count, and MASK. The use of these operators permits you to change a RECORD definition without having to change the instructions that reference it.

WIDTH operator. The WIDTH operator returns a width as the number of bits in a RECORD or in a RECORD field. For example, in Figure 26-1, following A20 are two examples of WIDTH. The first MOV returns the width of the entire RECORD BITREC (16 bits); the second MOV returns the width of the record field BIT2 (7 bits). In both cases, the assembler has generated an immediate operand for width.

Shift count. A direct reference to a RECORD field such as MOV CL,BIT2 does not refer to the contents of BIT2. (Indeed, that would be rather difficult.) Instead, the assembler generates an immediate operand that contains a shift count to help you isolate the field. The immediate value represents the number of bits that you would have to shift BIT2 to right adjust it. In Figure 26-1, the three examples following A30 return the shift count for BIT1, BIT2, and BIT3.

MASK operator. The MASK operator returns a mask of 1-bits representing the specified field and, in effect, defines the bit positions that the field occupies. For example, the MASK for each of the fields defined in BITREC is

FIELD	BINARY	HEX
BIT1	1110000000000000	E000
BIT2	0001111111000000	1FC0
BIT3	0000000000111111	003F

In Figure 26-1, the three instructions following A40 return the MASK values for BIT1, BIT2, and BIT3. The instructions following A50 and A60 isolate BIT2 and BIT1, respectively, from BITREC. A50 gets the record into the AX register and uses a MASK of BIT2 to AND it:

```
Record:         101 0110110 011010
AND MASK BIT2:  000 1111111 000000
Result:         000 0110110 000000
```

```
                 TITLE   A26RECOR (COM) Test of RECORD Directive
0000             CODESG  SEGMENT PARA 'Code'
                         ASSUME CS: CODESG,DS:CODESG,SS:CODESG
0100                     ORG    100H
0100 EB 02       BEGIN:  JMP     SHORT A10MAIN
                 ;------------------------------------------------------
                 BITREC RECORD BIT1:3,BIT2:7,BIT3:6          ;Define record
0102 AD9A        DEFBITS BITREC <101B,0110110B,011010B>      ;Init. record
                 ;------------------------------------------------------
0104             A10MAIN PROC NEAR
0104             A20:                                  ;Width:
0104 B7 10               MOV  BH,WIDTH BITREC          ;  of record (16)
0106 B0 07               MOV  AL,WIDTH BIT2            ;  of field (07)
0108             A30:                                  ;Shift count:
0108 B1 0D               MOV  CL,BIT1                  ;  hex 0D
010A B1 06               MOV  CL,BIT2                  ;      06
010C B1 00               MOV  CL,BIT3                  ;      00
010E             A40:                                  ;Mask:
010E B8 E000             MOV  AX,MASK BIT1             ;  hex E000
0111 BB 1FC0             MOV  BX,MASK BIT2             ;      1FC0
0114 B9 003F             MOV  CX,MASK BIT3             ;      003F
0117             A50:                                  ;Isolate BIT2:
0117 A1 0102 R           MOV  AX,DEFBITS               ;  get record
011A 25 1FC0             AND  AX,MASK BIT2             ;  clear BIT1 & 3
011D B1 06               MOV  CL,BIT2                  ;  get shift 06
011F D3 E8               SHR  AX,CL                    ;  shift right
0121             A60:                                     ;Isolate BIT1:
0121 A1 0102 R           MOV  AX,DEFBITS               ;  get record
0124 B1 0D               MOV  CL,BIT1                  ;  get shift 13
0126 D3 E8               SHR  AX,CL                    ;  shift right
0128 B8 4C00             MOV  AX,4C00H                 ;End processing
012B CD 21               INT  21H
012D             A10MAIN ENDP
012D             CODESG  ENDS
                         END BEGIN
---------------------------------------------------------------------------
Structures and Records:
 N a m e                 Width    # fields
                         Shift    Width   Mask    Initial
BITREC . . . . . . . . . 0010     0003
 BIT1  . . . . . . . . . 000D     0003    E000     0000
 BIT2  . . . . . . . . . 0006     0007    IFC0     0000
 BIT3  . . . . . . . . . 0000     0006    003F     0000
Segments and Groups:
 N a m e                 Length   Align   Combine  Class
CODESG . . . . . . . . .  012D    PARA      NONE   'CODE'
Symbols:
 N a m e                  Type    Value    Attr
A10MAIN . . . . . . . . . N PROC  0114    CODESG  Length = 0029
A20 . . . . . . . . . . . L NEAR  0104    CODESG
A30 . . . . . . . . . . . L NEAR  0108    CODESG
A40 . . . . . . . . . . . L NEAR  010E    CODESG
A50 . . . . . . . . . . . L NEAR  0117    CODESG
A60 . . . . . . . . . . . L NEAR  0121    CODESG
BEGIN . . . . . . . . . . L NEAR  0100    CODESG
BIT1 . . . . . . . . . . . 000D
BIT2 . . . . . . . . . . . 0006
BIT3 . . . . . . . . . . . 0000
DEFBITS  . . . . . . .  L WORD  0102    CODESG
```

Figure 26-1 Using the RECORD Directive

The effect is to clear all bits except those of BIT2. The next two instructions cause the AX to shift 6 bits so that BIT2 is right-adjusted:

```
0000000000110110 (0036H)
```

The example following A60 gets the record into the AX, and because BIT1 is the leftmost field, the routine simply uses its shift factor to shift right 13 bits:

```
0000000000000101 (0005H)
```

SEGMENT Directive

An assembly module consists of one or more segments, part of a segment, or even parts of several segments. The general format for a segment is

```
seg-name  SEGMENT [align] [combine] ['class']
          ...
seg-name  ENDS
```

TASM Ideal mode uses the format SEGMENT seg-name . . . .

All operands are optional. The following subsections describe the entries for align, combine, and class.

Align. The align operand indicates the starting boundary for a segment:

BYTE	Next address
WORD	Next even address (divisible by 2)
DWORD	Next doubleword address (divisible by 4)
PARA	Next paragraph (divisible by 16, or 10H)
PAGE	Next page address (divisible by 256, or 100H)

PARA is commonly used for all types of segments. BYTE and WORD can be used for segments that are to be combined within another segment, usually a data segment. DWORD is normally used for programs to be run on 80386 and later processors.

Combine. The combine operands NONE, PUBLIC, STACK, and COMMON indicate the way the linker is to handle a segment:

- NONE (default): The segment is to be logically separate from other segments, although it may end up physically adjacent to them. The segment is presumed to have its own base address.
- PUBLIC: LINK loads PUBLIC segments of the same name and class adjacent to one another. One base address is presumed for all such PUBLIC segments.
- STACK: LINK treats STACK the same as PUBLIC. There must be at least one STACK defined in a linked .EXE program. If there is more than one stack, the SP is set to the start of the first stack.

- COMMON: If COMMON segments have the same name and class, the linker gives them the same base address. During execution, the second segment overlays the first one. The largest segment, even if overlaid, determines the length of the common area.
- AT paragraph-address: The paragraph must be defined previously. The entry facilitates defining labels and variables at fixed offsets within fixed areas of memory, such as the interrupt table in low memory or the BIOS data area at 40[0]H. For example, the code in ROM defines the location of the video display area as

```
VIDEO_RAM SEGMENT AT 0B800H
```

The assembler creates a dummy segment that provides, in effect, an image of the memory locations.

'class'. The class entry can help the linker associate segments with different names, identify segments, and control their order. Class may contain any valid name, contained in single quotes. The linker uses the name to relate segments that have the same name and class. Typical examples are 'Data' and 'Code'. If you define a class as 'Code', the linker expects that segment to contain instruction code. Also, the CODEVIEW debugger expects the class 'Code' for the code segment.

The linker combines the following two segments with the same name (CSEG) and class ('Code') into one physical segment under the same segment register:

```
------------------------------------------
 Assembly  CSEG  SEGMENT PARA PUBLIC 'Code'
 module 1        ASSUME  CS:CSEG
                 ...
           CSEG  ENDS
------------------------------------------
 Assembly  CSEG  SEGMENT PARA PUBLIC 'Code'
 module 2        ASSUME  CS:CSEG
                 ...
           CSEG  ENDS
------------------------------------------
```

Because you may want to control the ordering of segments within a program, it is useful to understand how the linker handles the process. The original order of the segment names provides the basic sequence, which you may override by means of the PUBLIC attribute and class names. The following example shows two object modules (both modules contain a segment named DSEG1 with the PUBLIC attribute and identical class names) before linking:

```
module 1  SSEG   SEGMENT  PARA STACK
module 1  DSEG1  SEGMENT  PARA PUBLIC 'Data'
module 1  DSEG2  SEGMENT  PARA
module 1  CSEG   SEGMENT  PARA 'Code'
module 2  DSEG1  SEGMENT  PARA PUBLIC 'Data'
module 2  DSEG2  SEGMENT  PARA
module 2  CSEG   SEGMENT  PARA 'Code'
```

After the .OBJ modules are linked, the .EXE module looks like this:

```
module 1       CSEG   SEGMENT PARA 'Code'
module 2       CSEG   SEGMENT PARA 'Code'
modules 1 + 2  DSEG1  SEGMENT PARA PUBLIC 'Data'
module 1       DSEG2  SEGMENT PARA
module 2       DSEG2  SEGMENT PARA
module 1       SSEG   SEGMENT PARA STACK
```

You may nest segments, provided that one nested segment is completely contained within the other. In the following example, DSEG2 is completely contained within DSEG1:

```
DSEG1  SEGMENT
       ...      DSEG1 begins
DSEG2  SEGMENT
       ...      DSEG2 area
DSEG2  ENDS
       ...      DSEG1 resumes
DSEG1  ENDS
```

The .ALPHA, .SEQ, and DOSSEG directives and the assembler options /A and /S can also control the order of segments. (To combine segments into groups, see the GROUP directive.)

.SEQ Directive

This directive (the default), placed at or near the start of a program, tells the assembler to leave segments in their original sequence. (Some early assemblers rearranged segments in alphabetic sequence.) You may also use the assembler command line option /A. (See also the .ALPHA and DOSSEG directives.)

.STACK Directive

This simplified segment directive defines the stack. Its general format is

```
.STACK [size]
```

The default stack size is 1,024 bytes, which you may override. (See also the .MODEL directive.)

.STARTUP Directive

You can use this directive at the start of the code segment to initialize the DS, SS, and SP registers. TASM Ideal mode uses the term STARTUPCODE. See also the .EXIT directive.

STRUC/STRUCT Directive

The STRUC directive (STRUCT since MASM 6.0) facilitates defining related fields within a structure. Its general format is

```
struc-name  STRUC/STRUCT
                ...
      [ defined fields ]
                ...
struc-name  ENDS
```

A structure begins with its name and the directive STRUC and ends with the name and the directive ENDS. The assembler identifies the defined fields one after the other from the start of the structure. Valid entries are DB, DW, DD, DQ, and DT definitions with optional field names.

TASM Ideal mode uses the format STRUC struc-name.

In Figure 26-2, STRUC defines a parameter list named PARLIST for use with INT 21H function 0AH to input a name via the keyboard. Note that (like the RECORD directive) STRUC does not actually generate any storage. Therefore, an allocation statement is needed to allocate storage for the structure, making it addressable within the program:

```
PARAMS PARLIST  <>
```

The angle brackets (less-than and greater-than symbols) in the operand are empty in this example, but you may use them to redefine (or override) data within a structure.

Instructions may reference a structure directly by its name. To reference fields within a structure, instructions must qualify them by using the allocate name of the structure (PARAMS in the example), followed by a period that connects it with the field name, as, for example, MOV AL,PARAMS.ACTLEN.

You may also use the allocate statement (PARAMS in Figure 26-2) to redefine the contents of fields within a structure.

SUBTTL/SUBTITLE Directive

The SUBTTL directive (SUBTITLE since MASM 6.0 and %SUBTTL in TASM Ideal mode) causes a subtitle of up to 60 characters to print on line 3 of each page of an assembly source listing. You may code this directive any number of times. The general format is

```
SUBTTL/SUBTITLE  text
```

TEXTEQU Directive

The general format for this directive (introduced by MASM 6.0) is

```
TEXTEQU  [text-item]
```

The operand text-item can be a literal string, a constant preceded by %, or a string that a macro function has returned.

```
                        page 60,132
                    TITLE   A26STRUC (COM) Defining a structure
0000                CODESG SEGMENT PARA 'Code'
                        ASSUME  CS:CODESG,DS:CODESG,SS:CODESG
0100                    ORG   100H
0100 EB 30          BEGIN: JMP   SHORT MAIN
                    ;-----------------------------------------------
                    PARLIST STRUCT             ;Parameter list
0000 19             MAXLEN  DB     25          ;
0001 00             ACTLEN  DB     ?           ;
0002 0019 [20]      NAMEIN  DB     25 DUP(' ') ;
001B                PARLIST ENDS

0102 19             PARAMS  PARLIST <>         ;Allocate storage
0103 00
0104 0019 [20]
011D 57 68 61 74 20 69 PROMPT  DB     'What is the part no.?'
73 20 74 68 65 20
70 61 72 74 20 6E
6F 2E 3F
                    ;-----------------------------------------------
0132                MAIN    PROC   NEAR
0132 B4 40                  MOV    AH,40H      ;Request display
0134 BB 0001                MOV    BX,01
0137 B9 0015                MOV    CX,21       ;Length of prompt
013A 8D 16 011D R           LEA    DX,PROMPT   ;Address of prompt
013E CD 21                  INT    21H
0140 B4 0A                  MOV    AH,0AH      ;Accept keyboard
0142 8D 16 0102 R           LEA    DX,PARAMS   ; input
0146 CD 21                  INT    21H
0148 A0 0103 R              MOV    AL, PARAMS.ACTLEN
                    ;       ...                ;Length of input
014B B8 4C00                MOV    AX,4C00H    ;End processing
014E CD 21                  INT    21H
0150                MAIN    ENDP
0150                CODESG  ENDS
                            END    BEGIN

Structures and Records:
N a m e                 Width   # fields
                        Shift   Width    Mask      Initial
PARLIST . . . . . . . .001B    0003
 MAXLEN . . . . . . . .0000
 ACTLEN . . . . . . . .0001
 NAMEIN . . . . . . . .0002
Segments and Groups:
 N a m e                Length  Align    Combine   Class
CODESG . . . . . . . . 0150    PARA     NONE      'CODE'
Symbols:
 N a m e                Type    Value    Attr
BEGIN . . . . . . . . .L NEAR  0100     CODESG
MAIN . . . . . . . . . N PROC  0132     CODESG    Length = 001E
PARAMS . . . . . . . . L       0102     CODESG
PROMPT . . . . . . . . L BYTE  011D     CODESG
```

Figure 26-2 Using a Structure

TITLE Directive

The TITLE directive (%TITLE in TASM Ideal mode) causes a title of up to 60 characters to print on line 2 of each page of a source listing. You may code TITLE once, at the start according to the format TITLE text.

.XCREF/.NOCREF Directive

The .XCREF directive (.NOCREF since MASM 6.0) tells the assembler to suppress the cross-reference table. Its general format is

```
.XCREF/.NOCREF  [name [,name] ...]
```

Omitting the operand causes suppression of all entries in the table. You may also suppress the cross-reference of particular items. Here are examples of .XCREF and .CREF:

```
.XCREF              ;Suppress cross-reference
...
.CREF               ;Restore cross-reference
...
.XREF FLDA,FLDB     ;Suppress cross-reference of FLDA and FLDB.
```

.XLIST/.NOLIST Directive

You may use the .XLIST directive (named .NOLIST since MASM 6.0 and %NOLIST in TASM Ideal mode) anywhere in a source program to discontinue listing an assembled program. A typical situation would be where the statements are common to other programs and you don't need another listing. The .LIST directive (the default) resumes the listing. Use these directives with no operands.

27 THE PC INSTRUCTION SET

Objective: To explain machine code and to provide a description of the PC instruction set.

INTRODUCTION

This chapter explains machine code and provides a list of symbolic instructions with an explanation of their purpose.

Many instructions have a specific purpose, so that a 1-byte machine language instruction code is adequate. The following are examples:

```
MACHINE   SYMBOLIC
 CODE     INSTRUCTION          COMMENT
  40      INC AX          ;Increment AX
  50      PUSH AX         ;Push AX
  C3      RET (short)     ;Short return from procedure
  CB      RET (far)       ;Far return from procedure
  FD      STD             ;Set direction flag
```

None of these instructions makes a direct reference to memory. Instructions that specify an immediate operand, two registers, or a reference to memory are more complex and require two or more bytes of machine code.

Machine code has a special provision for indicating a particular register and another provision for referencing memory by means of an addressing mode byte.

REGISTER NOTATION

Instructions that reference a register may contain three bits that indicate the particular register and a *w-bit* that indicates whether the width is a byte (0) or a word (1). Also, only certain instructions may access the segment registers. Figure 27-1 shows the complete register notations. For example, bit value 000 means AH if the w bit is 0 and AX if it is 1.

General, Base, and Index Registers			Bits for Segment Registers	
Bits	w = 0	w = 1	000	ES
000	AL	AX/EAX	001	CS
001	CL	CX/ECX	010	SS
010	DL	DX/EDX	011	DS
011	BL	BX/EBX	100	FS
100	AH	SP	101	GS
101	CH	BP		
110	DH	SI		
111	BH	DI		

Figure 27-1

Here's the symbolic and machine code for a MOV instruction with a 1-byte immediate operand:

```
MOV  AH,00      10110 100 00000000
                    | |||
                    w reg = AH
```

In this case, the first byte of machine code indicates a width of 1 byte (w = 0) and refers to the AH register (100). Here's a MOV instruction that contains a 1-word immediate operand, along with its generated machine code:

```
MOV  AX,00      10111 000 00000000 00000000
                    | |||
                    w reg = AX
```

The first byte of machine code indicates a width of 1 word (w = 1) and refers to the AX register (000). For other instructions, w and reg may occupy different positions.

THE ADDRESSING MODE BYTE

The *mode* byte, when present, occupies the second byte of machine code and consists of the following three elements:

- mod A 2-bit mode, where the values 00, 01, and 10 refer to memory locations and 11 refers to a register
- reg A 3-bit reference to a register
- r/m A 3-bit reference to a register or memory, where r specifies which register and m indicates a memory address

Also, the first byte of machine code may contain a *d-bit* that indicates the direction (left/right) of flow. In the following example of adding the AX to the BX

```
ADD  BX,AX      00000011  11 011 000
                      ||  || ||| |||
                      dw mod reg r/m
```

d = 1 means that mod (11) and reg (011) describe the first operand and r/m (000) describes the second operand. Since w = 1, the width is a word. Therefore, the instruction is to add the AX (000) to the BX (011).

The second byte of the object code indicates most modes of addressing memory. You can use DEBUG to check the example this way: Key in the machine code as E 100 03 D8 and unassemble it with U 100,101.

Mod bits. The *two mod* bits distinguish between addressing of registers and memory. The following explains their purpose:

00 r/m bits give the exact addressing option; no offset byte.

01 r/m bits give the exact addressing option; one offset byte.

10 r/m bits give the exact addressing option; two offset bytes.

11 r/m specifies a register. The w-bit (in the operation code byte) determines whether a reference is to an 8-, 16-, or 32-bit register.

Reg bits. The three *reg bits,* in association with the w-bit, determine the actual width.

R/M bits. The three *r/m (register/memory) bits,* in association with the mod bits, determine the addressing mode, as shown in Figure 27-2.

r/m	mod=00	mod=01 or 10	mod=11 w=0	mod=11 w=1
000	BX+SI	DS:[BX+SI+disp]	AL	AX
001	BX+DI	DS:[BX+DI+disp]	CL	CX
010	BP+SI	SS:[BP+SI+disp]	DL	DX
011	BP+DI	SS:[BP+DI+disp]	BL	BX
100	SI	DS:[SI+disp]	AH	SP
101	DI	DS:[DI+disp]	CH	BP
110	Direct	SS:[BP+disp]	DH	SI
111	BX	DS:[BX+disp]	BH	DI

Figure 27-2

TWO-BYTE INSTRUCTIONS

The following 2-byte instruction adds the BX to the AX:

```
ADD  AX,BX      0000 0011  11 000 011
                       ||  || ||| |||
                       dw mod reg r/m
```

d = 1 — reg plus w describe the first operand (AX), and mod plus r/m plus w describe the second operand (BX).

w = 1 — The width is a word.

mod = 11 — The second operand is a register.

reg = 000 — The first operand is the AX register.

r/m = 011 — The second operand is the BX register.

The next example multiplies the AL by the BL:

```
MUL BL      11110110  11 100 011
                   |  || ||| |||
                   w mod reg r/m
```

The processor assumes that the multiplicand is in the AL if the multiplier is a byte, the AX if a word, and the EAX if a doubleword. The width (w = 0) is a byte, mod (11) references a register, and the register (r/m = 011) is the BL (011). Reg = 100 is not meaningful here.

THREE-BYTE INSTRUCTIONS

The following MOV generates three bytes of machine code:

```
MOV  mem-word,AX     10100011 mmmmmmmm mmmmmmmm
                           ||
                           dw
```

A move from the accumulator (AX or AL) needs to know only whether the operation is byte or word. In this example, w = 1 means a word, and the 16-bit AX is understood. (AL coded in the second operand would cause the w bit to be zero.) Bytes 2 and 3 contain the offset to the memory location. Using the accumulator register often generates a shorter instruction length and faster execution than the use of other registers.

FOUR-BYTE INSTRUCTIONS

The following 4-byte instruction multiplies the AL by a memory location:

```
MUL  mem-byte     11110110  00 100 110 mmmmmmmm mmmmmmmm
                         |  || ||| |||
                         w mod reg r/m
```

For this instruction, although reg is 100, the multiplicand is assumed to be in the AL. Mod = 00 indicates a memory reference, and r/m = 110 means a direct reference to memory; the two subsequent bytes provide the offset to the memory location.

The next example illustrates the LEA instruction, which specifies a word address:

```
LEA  DX,mem      10001101 00 010 110 mmmmmmmm mmmmmmmm
                          || ||| |||
                      LEA mod reg r/m
```

Reg = 010 designates the DX register; mod = 00 and r/m = 110 indicate a direct reference to a memory address; and the two subsequent bytes provide the offset to this location.

THE INSTRUCTION SET

This section covers the instruction set in alphabetic sequence, although closely related instructions are grouped together for convenience. In addition to the preceding discussion of mode byte and width bit, the following abbreviations are relevant:

addr	Address of a memory location
addr-high	Rightmost byte of an address
addr-low	Leftmost byte of an address
data	Immediate operand (8-bit if w = 0, 16-bit if w = 1)
data-high	Rightmost byte of an immediate operand
data-low	Leftmost byte of an immediate operand
disp	Displacement (offset value)
reg	Reference to a register

The 80286 and later processors support a number of specialized instructions not covered here: ARPL, BOUND, CLTS, ENTER, LAR, LEAVE, LGDT, LIDT, LLDT, LMSW, LSL, LTR, SGDT, SIDT, SLDT, SMSW, STR, VERR, and VERW. Instructions unique to the 80486 and later are BSWAP, INVD, WBINVD, and INVLPG, also not covered.

Abbreviations for flags are the following: AF = Auxiliary, CF = Carry, DF = Direction, IF = Interrupt, OF = Overflow, PF = Parity, SF = Sign, TF = Trap, and ZF = Zero.

AAA: ASCII Adjust After Addition

Operation. Corrects the sum (after an ADD) in the AL of two ASCII bytes. If the value of the rightmost four bits of the AL is greater than 9, or if the AF is set to 1, AAA adds 1 to the AH, adds 6 to the AL, and sets the AF and CF. Otherwise, the AF and CF are cleared. AAA always clears the leftmost four bits of the AL.

Flags. Affects AF and CF. (OF, PF, SF, and ZF are undefined.)

Source code. AAA (no operand)

Object code. `00110111`

AAD: ASCII Adjust Before Division

Operation. Adjusts an unpacked BCD value (dividend) in the AX prior to division. AAD multiplies the AH by 10, adds the product to the AL, and clears the AH. The resulting binary value in the AX is now equivalent to the original unpacked BCD value and is ready for a binary divide operation.

Flags. Affects PF, SF, and ZF. (AF, CF, and OF are undefined.)

Source code. AAD (no operand)

Object code. `|11010101|00001010|`

AAM: ASCII Adjust After Multiplication

Operation. Adjusts the product in the AL generated by using MUL to multiply two unpacked BCD digits. AAM divides the AL by 10 and stores the quotient in the AH and the remainder in the AL.

Flags. Affects PF, SF, and ZF. (AF, CF, and OF are undefined.)

Source code. AAM (no operand)

Object code. `|11010100|00001010|`

AAS: ASCII Adjust After Subtraction

Operation. Adjusts the difference in the AL (after a SUB) of two ASCII bytes. If the value of the rightmost four bits is greater than 9, or if the CF is 1, AAS subtracts 6 from the AL, subtracts 1 from the AH, and sets the AF and CF. Otherwise, the AF and CF are cleared. AAS always clears the leftmost four bits of the AL.

Flags. Affects AF and CF. (OF, PF, SF, and ZF are undefined.)

Source code. AAS (no operand)

Object code. `00111111`

ADC: Add with Carry

Operation. Typically used in multiword binary addition to carry an overflowed 1-bit into the next stage of arithmetic. ADC adds the contents of the CF (0/1) to the first operand, and then adds the second operand to the first, just like ADD. (See also SBB.)

Flags. Affects AF, CF, OF, PF, SF, and ZF.

Source code. ADC register/memory,register/memory/immediate

Object code. Three formats:

Reg/mem with register: `|000100dw|modregr/m|`
Immed to accumulator: `|0001010w|---data--|data if w=1|`
Immed to reg/mem: `|100000sw|mod010r/m|---data---|data if sw=01|`

ADD: Add Binary Numbers

Operation. Adds binary values from memory, register, or immediate to a register, or adds values in a register or immediate to memory. Values may be byte, word, or doubleword (80386 and later).

Flags. Affects AF, CF, OF, PF, SF, and ZF.

Source code. ADD register/memory,register/memory/immediate

Object code. Three formats:
Reg/mem with register: `|000000dw|modregr/m|`
Immed to accumulator: `|0000010w|--data--|data if w=1|`
Immed to reg/mem: `|100000sw|mod000r/m|---data---|data if sw=01|`

AND: Logical AND

Operation. Performs a logical AND operation on bits of two operands. Both operands are bytes, words, or doublewords (80386 and later), which AND matches bit for bit. For each pair of matched bits that are 1, the 1-bit in the first operand is set to 1; otherwise, the bit is cleared. (See also OR, XOR, and TEST.)

Flags. Affects CF (0), OF (0), PF, SF, and ZF. (AF is undefined.)

Source code. AND register/memory,register/memory/immediate

Object code. Three formats:
Reg/mem with register: `|001000dw|modregr/m|`
Immed to accumulator: `|0010010w|---data--|data if w=1|`
Immed to reg/mem: `|100000sw|mod 100 r/m|---data--|data if w=1`

BSF/BSR: Bit Scan Forward/Bit Scan Reverse (80386 and Later)

Operation. Scans a bit string for the first 1-bit. BSF scans from right to left, and BSR scans from left to right. The second operand (16 or 32 bits) contains the string to be scanned. If a 1-bit is found, the operation returns its position in the first operand's register and sets the ZF; otherwise it clears the ZF.

Flags. Affects ZF.

Source code. BSF/BSR register,register/memory

Object code. BSF: `|00001111|10111100|modregr/m|`
BSR: `|00001111|10111101|modregr/m|`

BT/BTC/BTR/BTS: Bit Test (80386 and Later)

Operation. Copies a specified bit into the CF. The first operand contains the bit string being tested and the second contains a value that indicates its position. BT simply copies the bit to the CF. The other instructions also copy the bit but act on the bit this way: BTC complements the bit by reversing its value in the first operand; BTR resets the bit by clearing it to zero; BTS sets the bit to 1. References are to 16- and 32-bit values.

Flags. Affects CF.

Source code. BT/BTC/BTR/BTS register/memory,register/immediate

Object code. Two formats:

Immed to reg: `|00001111|10111010|mod***r/m|`

Reg/mem to reg: `|00001111|10***010|modregr/m|`

`(*** means 100 = BT, 111 = BTC, 110 = BTR, 101 = BTS)`

CALL: Call a Procedure

Operation. Calls a near or far procedure. The assembler generates a near CALL if the called procedure is NEAR and a far CALL if the called procedure is FAR. A near CALL pushes the IP (the address of the next instruction) onto the stack; it then loads the IP with the destination offset address. A far CALL pushes the CS onto the stack and loads an intersegment pointer onto the stack; it then pushes the IP onto the stack and loads the IP with the destination offset address. On return, a subsequent RETN or RETF reverses these steps.

Flags. Affects none.

Source code. CALL register/memory

Object code. Four formats:

Direct within segment: `|11101000|disp-low |disp-high|`

Indirect within segment: `|11111111|mod010r/m|`

Indirect intersegment: `|11111111|mod011r/m|`

Direct intersegment: `|10011010|offset-low|offset-high|seg-low|seg-high|`

CBW: Convert Byte to Word

Operation. Extends a 1-byte signed value to a signed word by duplicating the sign (bit 7) of the AL through the bits in the AH. (See also CWD, CWDE, and CDQ.)

Flags. Affects none.

Source code. CBW (no operand)

Object code. `10011000`

CDQ: Convert Doubleword to Quadword (80386 and later)

Operation. Extends a 32-bit signed value to a 64-bit signed value by duplicating the sign (bit 31) of the EAX through the EDX. (See also CBW, CWD, and CWDE.)

Flags. Affects none.

Source code. CDQ (no operand)

Object code. `10011001`

CLC: Clear Carry Flag

Operation. Clears the CF so that, for example, ADC does not add a 1-bit. (See also STC.)

Flags. CF (becomes 0).

Source code. CLC (no operand)

Object code. `11111000`

CLD: Clear Direction Flag

Operation. Clears the DF, to cause string operations such as MOVS to process from left to right. (See also STD.)

Flags. DF (becomes 0).

Source code. CLD (no operand)

Object code. `11111100`

CLI: Clear Interrupt Flag

Operation. Clears the IF, to disable maskable external interrupts. (See also STI.)

Flags. IF (becomes 0).

Source code. CLI (no operand)

Object code. `11111010`

CMC: Complement Carry Flag

Operation. Complements the CF: reverses the CF bit value so that 0 becomes 1 and 1 becomes 0.

Flags. CF (reversed).

Source code. CMC (no operand)

Object code. `11110101`

CMP: Compare

Operation. Compares the binary contents of two data fields. CMP internally subtracts the second operand from the first and sets/clears flags, but does not store the result. Both operands are byte, word, or doubleword (80386 and later). CMP may compare register, memory, or immediate to a register or may compare register or immediate to memory. (CMP makes a numeric comparison; see CMPS for string comparisons.)

Flags. Affects AF, CF, OF, PF, SF, and ZF.

Source code. CMP register/memory,register/memory/immediate

Object code. Three formats:

Reg/mem with register: `|001110dw|modregr/m|`
Immed to accumulator: `|0011110w|---data--|data if w=1|`
Immed to reg/mem: `|100000sw|mod111r/m|---data----|data if sw=0|`

CMPS/CMPSB/CMPSW/CMPSD: Compare String

Operation. Compares strings of any length in memory. A REPn prefix normally precedes these instructions, along with a maximum value in the CX. CMPSB compares bytes, CMPSW compares words, and CMPSD (80386 and later) compares doublewords. The DS:SI address the first operand and the ES:DI address the second. If the DF is 0, the operation compares from left to right and increments the SI and DI by 1 for byte, 2 for word, and 4 for doubleword; if the DF is 1, it compares from right to left and decrements the SI and DI. REPn decrements the CX by 1 for each repetition. REPNE ends when the first match is found, REPE ends when the first nonmatch is found, or both end when the CX is decremented to 0; the DI and SI are advanced past the byte that caused termination. The last compare sets/clears the flags.

Flags. Affects AF, CF, OF, PF, SF, and ZF.

Source code. [REPnn] CMPSB/CMPSW/CMPSD (no operand)

Object code. `1010011w`

CMPXCHG: Compare and Exchange (80486 and Later)

Operation. Compares the second operand (AL, AX, or EAX) with the first operand (register/memory). If they are equal, CMPXCHG loads the second operand into the first operand and sets the ZF; if unequal, CMPXCHG loads the first operand into the second operand and clears the ZF.

Flags. Affects AF, CF, OF, PF, SF, and ZF.

Source code. CMPXCHG register/memory,AL/AX/EAX

Object code. `0F B0/r or 0F B1/r (hex)`

CMPXCHG8B: Compare and Exchange (Pentium and Later)

Operation. Compares the 64-byte EDX:EAX with the first operand (register/memory). If they are equal, CMPXCHG8B loads the EDX:EAX into the first operand and sets the ZF; if unequal, CMPXCHG8B loads the first operand into the EDX:EAX and clears the ZF.

Flags. Affects ZF.

Source code. CMPXCHG8B register/memory (one operand, 64 bytes)

Object code. `0F C7 (hex)`

CWD: Convert Word to Doubleword

Operation. Extends a 1-word signed value to a signed doubleword in the DX:AX by duplicating the sign (bit 15) of the AX through the DX, typically to generate a 32-bit dividend. (See also CBW, CWDE, and CDQ.)

Flags. Affects none.

Source code. CWD (no operand)

Object code. `10011001`

CWDE: Convert Word to Extended Doubleword (80386 and Later)

Operation. Extends a 1-word signed value to a doubleword in the EAX by duplicating the sign (bit 15) of the AX, typically to generate a 32-bit dividend. (See also CBW, CWD, and CDQ.)

Flags. Affects none.

Source code. CWDE (no operand)

Object code. `10011000`

DAA: Decimal Adjust After Addition

Operation. Corrects the result in the AL after an ADD or ADC adds two packed BCD items. If the value of the rightmost four bits is greater than 9, or if the AF is 1, DAA adds 6 to the AL and sets the AF. Next, if the value in the AL is greater than 99H, or if the CF is 1, DAA adds 60H to the AL and sets the CF. Otherwise, the AF and CF are cleared. The AL now contains a correct 2-digit packed decimal result. (See also DAS.)

Flags. Affects AF, CF, PF, SF, and ZF. (OF is undefined.)

Source code. DAA (no operand)

Object code. `00100111`

DAS: Decimal Adjust After Subtraction

Operation. Corrects the result in the AL after a SUB or SBB subtracts two packed BCD items. If the value of the rightmost four bits is greater than 9, DAS subtracts 60H from the AL and sets the CF. Otherwise, the AF and CF are cleared. The AL now contains a correct 2-digit packed decimal result. (See also DAA.)

Flags. Affects AF, CF, PF, SF, and ZF. (OF is undefined.)

Source code. DAS (no operand)

Object code. `00101111` (no operand)

DEC: Decrement by 1

Operation. Decrements 1 from a byte, word, or doubleword (80386 and later) in a register or memory and treats the value as an unsigned integer. (See also INC.)

Flags. Affects AF, OF, PF, SF, and ZF.

Source code. DEC register/memory

Object code. Two formats:
Register: `|01001reg|`
Reg/memory: `|1111111w|mod001r/m|`

DIV: Unsigned Divide

Operation. Divides an unsigned dividend by an unsigned divisor. DIV treats a leftmost 1-bit as a data bit, not a minus sign. Division by zero causes a zero-divide interrupt. (See also IDIV.) Here are the divide operations according to the size of the dividend:

Size	Dividend (Operand 1)	Divisor (Operand 2)	Quotient	Remainder	Example
16-bit	AX	8-bit reg/memory	AL	AH	DIV BH
32-bit	DX:AX	16-bit reg/memory	AX	DX	DIV CX
64-bit	EDX:EAX	32-bit reg/memory	EAX	EDX	DIV ECX

Flags. Affects AF, CF, OF, PF, SF, and ZF. (All undefined.)

Source code. DIV register/memory

Object code. `|1111011w|mod110r/m|`

ESC: Escape

Operation. Facilitates the use of coprocessors such as the 80x87 to perform special operations. ESC provides the coprocessor with an instruction and operand for execution. Note that as of version 6.1, MASM no longer supports ESC; instead, it generates the full required object code for coprocessor instructions.

Flags. Affects none.

Source code. ESC immediate,register/memory

Object code. `|11011xxx|modxxxr/m|`(x-bits refer to the coprocessor op code)

HLT: Enter Halt State

Operation. Causes the processor to enter a halt state while waiting for an interrupt; the CS and IP registers now point to the address of the instruction immediately following. When an interrupt occurs, the processor pushes the CS and IP onto the stack and executes the interrupt routine. On return, an IRET instruction pops the stack, and processing resumes following the original HLT.

Flags. Affects none.

Source code. HLT (no operand)

Object code. `11110100`

IDIV: Signed (Integer) Divide

Operation. Divides a signed dividend by a signed divisor. IDIV treats a leftmost bit as a sign (0 = positive, 1 = negative). Division by zero causes a zero-divide interrupt. (See CBW and CWD to extend the length of a signed dividend, and see also DIV.) Here are the divide operations according to the size of the dividend:

Size	Dividend (Operand 1)	Divisor (Operand 2)	Quotient	Remainder	Example
16-bit	AX	8-bit reg/memory	AL	AH	IDIV BH
32-bit	DX:AX	16-bit reg/memory	AX	DX	IDIV CX
64-bit	EDX:EAX	32-bit reg/memory	EAX	EDX	IDIV ECX

Flags. Affects AF, CF, OF, PF, SF, and ZF.

Source code. IDIV register/memory

Object code. `|1111011w|mod111r/m|`

IMUL: Signed (Integer) Multiply

Operation. Multiplies a signed multiplicand by a signed multiplier. IMUL treats a leftmost bit as the sign (0 = positive, 1 = negative). The operation assumes the multiplicand is in the AL, AX, or EAX, and takes its size from that of the multiplier. (See also MUL.) Here are the multiply operations according to the size of the multiplier:

Size	Multiplicand (Operand 1)	Multiplier (Operand 2)	Product	Example
8-bit	AL	8-bit register/memory	AX	IMUL BL
16-bit	AX	16-bit register/memory	DX:AX	IMUL BX
32-bit	EAX	32-bit register/memory	EDX:EAX	IMUL ECX

Flags. Affects CF and OF. (AF, PF, SF, and ZF are undefined.)

Source code. IMUL register/memory (all processors)

Object code. `|1111011w|mod101r/m|` (first format)
Three other IMUL formats are also available:

- IMUL register,immediate (80286 and later)
- IMUL register,register,immediate (80286 and later)
- IMUL register,register/memory (80386 and later)

IN: Input Byte or Word

Operation. Transfers from an input port a byte to the AL or a word to the AX. Code the port as a fixed numeric operand (as IN AX,port#) or as a variable in the DX (as IN AX,DX). Use the DX if the port number is greater than 256. (See also INS and OUT.)

Source code. IN AL/AX,portno/DX

Flags. Affects none.

Object code. Two formats:
Variable port: `|1110110w|`
Fixed port: `|1110010w|--port--|`

INC: Increment by 1

Operation. Increments by 1 a byte, word, or doubleword (80386 and later) in a register or memory and treats the value as an unsigned integer, coded, for example, as INC CX. (See also DEC.)

Flags. Affects AF, OF, PF, SF, and ZF.

Source code. INC register/memory

Object code. Two formats:
Register: `|01000reg|`
Reg/memory: `|1111111w|mod000r/m|`

INS/INSB/INSW/INSD: Input String (80286 and Later)

Operation. Receives a string (the destination) from a port. The destination is addressed by the ES:DI, and the DX contains the port number. The standard practice is to use INSn with the REP prefix, with the CX containing the number of items (as byte, word, or doubleword) to be received. Depending on the DF (0/1), the operation increments/decrements the DI according to the item size. (See also IN and OUTS).

Flags. Affects none.

Source code. [REP] INSB/INSW/INSD (no operand)

Object code. `|0110110w|`

INT: Interrupt

Operation. Interrupts processing and transfers control to one of the 256 interrupt (vector) addresses beginning at segment 0, offset 0. INT performs the following: (1) pushes the flags onto the stack and resets the IF and TF flags; (2) pushes the CS onto the stack and places the high-order word of the interrupt address in the CS; and (3) pushes the IP onto the stack and fills the IP with the low-order word of the interrupt address. For the 80386 and later, INT pushes a 16-bit IP for 16-bit segments and a 32-bit IP for 32-bit segments. IRET returns from the interrupt routine.

Flags. Clears IF and TF.

Source code. INT number

Object code. `|1100110v|--type--|`(if v = 0, type is 3)

INTO: Interrupt on Overflow

Operation. Causes an interrupt (usually harmless) if an overflow has occurred (the OF is set to 1) and performs an INT 04H. The interrupt address is at location 10H of the interrupt service table. (See also INT.)

Flags. Affects IF and TF.

Source code. INTO (no operand)

Object code. `11001110`

IRET/IRETD: Interrupt Return

Operation. Provides a far return from an interrupt routine. IRET performs the following procedure: (1) pops the word at the top of the stack into the IP, increments the SP by 2, and pops the top of the stack into the CS; (2) increments the SP by 2 and pops the top of the stack into the flags register. This procedure undoes the steps that the interrupt originally took and performs a return. For the 80386 and later, use IRETD (doubleword) to pop a 32-bit IP. (See also RET.)

Flags. Affects all.

Source code. IRET

Object code. 11001111 (no operand)

Jcondition: Jump on Condition

This section summarizes the conditional jump instructions that transfer to a stated operand if the tested flag condition is true. If true, the operation adds the operand offset to the IP and performs the jump; if not true, processing continues with the next instruction in sequence. For the 8086–80286, the jump must be short (−128 to 127 bytes); for the 80386 and later, the assembler assumes a near jump (−32,768 to 32,767 bytes), but you may use the SHORT operator to force a short jump. The operations test the flags but do not change them. The source code is *Jcondition label.* All object codes are of the form |distnnnn|--disp--|, where *disp* bits are 0111 for short jumps and 1000 for near jumps.

In the first list, the instructions are typically used after a compare operation, which compares the first operand to the second.

SOURCE CODE	OBJECT CODE	FLAGS CHECKED	USED AFTER COMPARISON
JA	|dist0111|	CF = 0, ZF = 0	Unsigned data, above (higher)
JAE	|dist0011|	CF = 0	Unsigned data, above/equal
JB	|dist0010|	CF = 1	Unsigned data, below (lower)
JBE	|dist0110|	CF = 1 or AF = 1	Unsigned data, below/equal
JE	|dist0100|	ZF = 1	Signed/unsigned data, equal
JG	|dist1111|	ZF = 0, SF = OF	Signed data, greater
JGE	|dist1101|	SF = OF	Signed data, greater/equal
JL	|dist1100|	SF not= OF	Signed data, lower
JLE	|dist1110|	ZF = 1 or SF not= OF	Signed data, lower/equal
JNA	|dist0110|	CF = 1 or AF = 1	Unsigned data, not above
JNAE	|dist0010|	CF = 1	Unsigned data, not above/equal
JNB	|dist0011|	CF = 0	Unsigned data, not below
JNBE	|dist0111|	CF = 0, ZF = 0	Unsigned data, not below/equal
JNE	|dist0101|	ZF = 0	Signed/unsigned, not equal
JNG	|dist1110|	ZF = 1 or SF not= OF	Signed data, not greater
JNGE	|dist1100|	SF not= OF	Signed data, not greater/equal
JNL	|dist1101|	SF = OF	Signed data, not lower
JNLE	|dist1111|	ZF = 0, SF = OF	Signed data, not lower/equal

In the second list, the instructions are typically used after a an arithmetic or other operation, which clears or sets bits according to the result.

SOURCE CODE	OBJECT CODE	FLAGS CHECKED	USED TO TEST
JC	|dist0010|	CF = 1	If CF set (same as JB/JNAE)
JNC	|dist0011|	CF = 0	If CF off (same as JAE/JNB)
JNO	|dist0001|	OF = 0	If OF off
JNP	|dist1011|	PF = 0	If no (odd) parity: odd number of bits set in low-order 8 bits
JNS	|dist1001|	SF = 0	If sign is positive
JNZ	|dist0101|	ZF = 0	If signed/unsigned data not zero
JO	|dist0000|	OF = 1	If OF set
JP	|dist1010|	PF = 1	If even parity: even number of bits set in low order 8 bits
JPE	|dist1010|	PF = 1	Same as JP
JPO	|dist1011|	PF = 0	Same as JNP
JS	|dist1000|	SF = 1	If sign is negative
JZ	|dist0100|	ZF = 1	If signed/unsigned data is zero

JCXZ/JECXZ: Jump if CX/ECX Is Zero

Operation. Jumps to a specified address if the CX or the ECX (80386 and later) contains zero. This operation could be useful at the start of a loop, although limited to a short jump.

Flags. Affects none.

Source code. JCXZ/JECXZ label

Object code. `|11100011|--disp--|`

JMP: Unconditional Jump

Operation. Jumps to a designated address under any condition. A JMP address may be short (−128 to +127 bytes), near (within ±32K, the default), or far (to another code segment). A short or near JMP replaces the IP with a destination offset address. A far jump (such as JMP FAR PTR label) replaces the CS:IP with a new segment address.

Flags. Affects none.

Source code. JMP register/memory

Object code. Five formats:

Direct within seg short: `|11101011|--disp--|`
Direct within segment: `|11101001|disp-low |disp-high|`
Indirect within segment: `|11111111|mod100r/m|`
Indirect intersegment: `|11111111|mod101r/m|`
Direct intersegment: `|11101010|offset-low|offset-high|seg-low|seg-high|`

LAHF: Load AH from Flags

Operation. Loads the rightmost eight bits of the flags register into the AH. (See also SAHF.)

Flags. Affects none.

Source code. LAHF (no operand)

Object code. `10011111`

LDS/LES/LFS/LGS/LSS: Load Segment Register

Operation. Initializes a far address and offset of a data item so that succeeding instructions can access it. The first operand references any of the general, index, or pointer registers. The second operand references four bytes in memory containing an offset and a segment address. The operation loads the segment address in the segment register and the offset address in the first operand's register. For example, LDS means load data segment register. LFS, LGS, and LSS are supported by the 80386 and later.

Flags. Affects none.

Source code. LDS/LES/LFS/LGS/LSS register,memory

Object code.
LDS: `|11000101|mod reg r/m|`
LES: `|11000100|mod reg r/m|`
LFS: `|00001111|10110100|mod reg r/m|`
LGS: `|00001111|10110101|mod reg r/m|`
LSS: `|00001111|10110010|mod reg r/m|`

LEA: Load Effective Address

Operation. Loads a near (offset) address into a register.

Flags. Affects none.

Source code. LEA register,memory

Object code. `10001101`

LES/LFS/LGS: Load Extra Segment Register

Operation. See LDS.

LOCK: Lock Bus

Operation. Prevents 80x87 or other coprocessors from changing a data item at the same time as the processor. LOCK is a 1-byte prefix that you may code immediately before any instruction. The operation sends a signal to the coprocessor to prevent it from using the data until the next instruction is completed.

Flags. Affects none.

Source code. LOCK instruction

Object code. `11110000`

LODS/LODSB/LODSW/LODSD: Load Byte, Word, or Doubleword String

Operation. Loads the accumulator register with a value from memory. Although LODS is a string operation, it does not require a REP prefix. The DS:SI registers address a byte (if LODSB), word (if LODSW), or doubleword (if LODSD, 80386 and later) and load it from memory into the AL, AX, or EAX, respectively. If the DF is 0, the operation adds 1 (if byte), 2 (if word), or 4 (if doubleword) to the SI; otherwise it subtracts 1, 2, or 4.

Flags. Affects none.

Source code. LODSB/LODSW/LODSD (no operand)

Object code. `1010110w`

LOOP/LOOPW/LOOPD: Loop Until Complete

Operation. Controls the execution of a routine a specified number of times. The CX should contain a count before starting the loop. LOOP appears at the end of the loop and decrements the CX by 1. If the CX is nonzero, LOOP transfers to its operand address (a short jump), which points to the start of the loop (adds the offset in the IP); otherwise LOOP drops through to the next instruction.

For the 80386 and later, LOOP uses the CX in 16-bit mode and the ECX in 32-bit mode. You can use LOOPW to specify the 16-bit CX, and LOOPD to specify the 32-bit ECX.

Flags. Affects none.

Source code. LOOPnn label

Object code. `|11100010|--disp--|`

LOOPE/LOOPZ/LOOPEW/LOOPZW/LOOPED/LOOPZD: Loop While Equal or Loop While Zero

Operation. Controls the repetitive execution of a routine. LOOPE and LOOPZ are similar to LOOP, except that they transfer to the operand address (a short jump) if the CX is nonzero and the ZF is 1 (zero condition, set by another instruction); otherwise the operation drops through to the next instruction. (See also LOOPNE/LOOPNZ.)

For the 80386 and later, LOOPE and LOOPZ use the CX in 16-bit mode and the ECX in 32-bit mode. You can use LOOPEW and LOOPZW for the 16-bit CX, and LOOPED and LOOPZD for the 32-bit ECX.

Flags. Affects none.

Source code. LOOPnn label

Object code. `|11100001|--disp--|`

LOOPNE/LOOPNZ/LOOPNEW/LOOPNZW: Loop While Not Equal or Loop While Not Zero

Operation. Controls the repetitive execution of a routine. LOOPNE and LOOPNZ are similar to LOOP, except that they transfer to the operand address (a short jump) if the CX is nonzero and the ZF is 0 (nonzero condition, set by another instruction); otherwise the operation drops through to the next instruction. (See also LOOPE/LOOPZ.)

For the 80386 and later, LOOPNE and LOOPNZ use the CX in 16-bit mode and the ECX in 32-bit mode. You can use LOOPNEW and LOOPNZW to specify the 16-bit CX and LOOPNED/LOOPNZD to specify the 32-bit ECX.

Flags. Affects none.

Source code. LOOPNE/LOOPNZ label

Object code. `|11100000|--disp--|`

LSS: Load Stack Segment Register

Operation. See LDS.

MOV: Move Data

Operation. Transfers data between two registers or between a register and memory, and transfers immediate data to a register or memory. The referenced data defines the number of bytes (1, 2, or 4) moved; the operands must agree in size. MOV cannot transfer between two memory locations (use MOVS), from immediate data to a segment register, or from a segment register to a segment register. (See also MOVSX/MOVZX.)

Flags. Affects none.

Source code. MOV register/memory,register/memory/immediate

Object code. Seven formats:

Reg/mem to/from reg: `|100010dw|modregr/m|`
Immed to reg/mem: `|1100011w|mod000r/m|---data---|data if w=1|`
Immed to register: `|1011wreg|---data--|data if w=1|`
Mem to accumulator: `|1010000w| addr-low| addr-high |`

Accumulator to mem: `|1010001w| addr-low| addr-high |`
Reg/mem to seg reg: `|10001110|mod0sgr/m| (sg = seg reg)`
Seg reg to reg/mem: `|10001100|mod0sgr/m| (sg = seg reg)`

MOVS/MOVSB/MOVSW/MOVSD: Move String

Operation. Moves data between memory locations. Normally used with the REP prefix and a length in the CX, MOVSB moves bytes, MOVSW moves words, and MOVSD (80386 and later) moves doublewords. The first operand is addressed by the ES:DI and the second by the DS:SI. If the DF is 0, the operation moves data from left to right into the first operand's destination and increments the DI and SI by 1, 2, or 4. If the DF is 1, the operation moves data from right to left and decrements the DI and SI. REP decrements the CX by 1 for each repetition. The operation ends when the CX is decremented to 0; the DI and SI are advanced past the last byte moved.

Flags. Affects none.

Source code. [REP] MOVSB/MOVSW/MOVSD (no operand)

Object code. `1010010w`

MOVSX/MOVZX: Move with Sign Extend or Zero Extend (80386 and Later)

Operation. Copies an 8- or 16-bit source operand into a larger 16- or 32-bit destination operand. MOVSX fills the sign bit into leftmost bits, and MOVZX fills zero bits.

Flags. Affects none.

Source code. MOVSX/MOVZX register/memory,register/memory/ immediate

Object code. MOVSX: `|00001111|1011111w|modregr/m|`
MOVZX: `|00001111|1011011w|modregr/m|`

MUL: Unsigned Multiply

Operation. Multiplies an unsigned multiplicand by an unsigned multiplier. MUL treats a leftmost 1-bit as a data bit, not a negative sign. The operation assumes the multiplicand is in the AL, AX, or EAX, and takes its size from that of the multiplier. (See also IMUL.) Here are the multiply operations according to the size of the multiplier:

Size	Multiplicand (Operand 1)	Multiplier (Operand 2)	Product	Example
8-bit	AL	8-bit register/memory	AX	MUL BL
16-bit	AX	16-bit register/memory	DX:AX	MUL BX
32-bit	EAX	32-bit register/memory	EDX:EAX	MUL ECX

Flags. Affects CF and OF. (AF, PF, SF, and ZF are undefined.)

Source code. MUL register/memory

Object code. `|1111011w|mod100r/m|`

NEG: Negate

Operation. Reverses a binary value from positive to negative or from negative to positive. NEG provides the two's complement of the specified operand by subtracting the operand from zero and adding 1. Operands may be a byte, word, or doubleword (80386 and later) in a register or memory. (See also NOT.)

Flags. Affects AF, CF, OF, PF, SF, and ZF.

Source code. NEG register/memory

Object code. `|1111011w|mod011r/m|`

NOP: No Operation

Operation. Used to delete or insert machine code or to delay execution for purposes of timing. NOP simply performs a null operation by executing XCHG AX,AX.

Flags. Affects none.

Source code. NOP (no operand)

Object code. `10010000`

NOT: Logical NOT

Operation. Changes 0-bits to 1-bits and vice versa. The operand is a byte, word, or doubleword (80386 and later) in a register or memory. (See also NEG.)

Flags. Affects none.

Source code. NOT register/memory

Object code. `|1111011w|mod 010 r/m|`

OR: Logical OR

Operation. Performs a logical OR operation on bits of two operands. Both operands are bytes, words, or doublewords (80386 and later), which OR matches bit for bit. For each pair of matched bits, if either or both are 1, the bit in the first operand is set to 1; otherwise the bit is unchanged. (See also AND and XOR.)

Flags. Affects CF (0), OF (0), PF, SF, and ZF. (AF is undefined.)

Source code. OR register/memory,register/memory/immediate

Object code. Three formats:
Reg/mem with register: `|000010dw|modregr/m|`
Immed to accumulator: `|0000110w|---data--|data if w=1|`
Immed to reg/mem: `|100000sw|mod001r/m|---data----|data if w=1|`

OUT: Output Byte or Word

Operation. Transfers a byte from the AL or a word from the AX to an output port. The port is a fixed numeric operand or a variable in the DX. Use the DX if the port number is greater than 256. (See also IN and OUTS.)

Flags. Affects none.

Source code. Fixed port: OUT port#,AX
Variable port: OUT DX,AX

Object code. Fixed port: `|1110011w|--port--|`
Variable port: `|1110111w|`

OUTS/OUTSB/OUTSW/OUTSD: Output String (80286 and Later)

Operation. Sends a string (the source) to a port. The source is addressed by the DS:SI, and the DX contains the port number. The standard practice is to use OUTSn with the REP prefix, with the CX containing the number of items (as byte, word, or doubleword) to be sent. Depending on the DF (0/1) the operation increments/decrements the SI according to the item size. (See also IN and OUTS.)

Flags. Affects none.

Source code. [REP] OUTSB/OUTSW/OUTSD (no operand)

Object code. `|0110111w|`

POP: Pop Word off Stack

Operation. Pops a word or doubleword (80386 and later) previously pushed on the stack to a specified destination—a memory location, general register, or segment register. The SP points to the current word at the top of the stack; POP transfers it to the specified destination and increments the SP by 2. On the 80386 and later, a 32-bit operand denotes a doubleword value, and the ESP is incremented by 4. (See also PUSH.)

Flags. Affects none.

Source code. POP register/memory

Object code. Three formats:

Register: `|01011reg|`
Segment reg: `|000sg111|` (sg implies segment reg)
Reg/memory: `|10001111|mod 000 r/m|`

POPA (80286 and Later)/POPAD (80386 and Later): Pop All General Registers

Operation. POPA pops the top eight words from the stack into the DI, SI, BP, SP, BX, DX, CX, and AX, in that order. POPAD pops the top eight doublewords from the stack into the EDI, ESI, EBP, ESP, EBX, EDX, ECX, and EAX. The SP value is discarded rather than loaded. Normally, a PUSHA/PUSHAD has previously pushed the registers.

Flags. Affects none.

Source code. POPA/POPAD (no operand)

Object code. `01100001`

POPF/POPFD: Pop Flags off Stack

Operation. POPF pops the top word from the stack to the flags register and increments the SP by 2. POPFD (80386 and later) pops the top doubleword from the stack to the 32-bit flags register and increments the SP by 4. Normally a PUSHF has pushed the flags.

Flags. Affects all.

Source code. POPF/POPFD (no operand)

Object code. `10011101`

PUSH: Push onto Stack

Operation. Pushes a word or doubleword (80386 and later) onto the stack for later use. The SP register points to the current (double)word at the top of the stack. PUSH decrements the SP by 2 or ESP by 4 and transfers a (double)word from the specified operand to the new top of the stack. The source may be a general register, segment register, or memory. (See also POP and PUSHF.)

Flags. Affects none.

Source code. PUSH register/memory (all processors)
PUSH immediate (80286 and later)

Object code. Three formats:
Register: `|01010reg|`
Segment reg: `|000sg110|` (sg implies segment reg)
Reg/memory: `|11111111|mod110r/m|`

PUSHA (80286 and Later)/PUSHAD (80386 and Later): Push All General Registers

Operation. PUSHA pushes the AX, CX, DX, BX, SP, BP, SI, and DI, in that order, onto the stack and decrements the SP by 16. PUSHAD pushes the EAX, ECX, EDX, EBX, ESP, EBP, ESI, and EDI and decrements the SP by 32. Normally, a POPA/POPAD subsequently pops the registers.

Flags. Affects none.

Source code. PUSHA/PUSHAD (no operand)

Object code. `01100000`

PUSHF/PUSHFD: Push Flags onto Stack

Operation. Pushes the contents of the flags register onto the stack for later use. PUSHF decrements the SP by 2. PUSHFD (80386 and later) pushes the 32-bit flags register and decrements the SP by 4. (See also POPF and PUSH.)

Flags. Affects none.

Source code. PUSHF (no operand)

Object code. `10011100`

RCL/RCR: Rotate Left Through Carry and Rotate Right Through Carry

Operation. Rotates bits through the CF. The operation rotates bits left or right in a byte, word, or doubleword (80386 and later) in a register or memory. The operand may be an immediate constant or a reference to the CL. On the 8088/86, the constant may be only 1; a larger rotate must be in the CL. On later processors, the constant may be up to 31. For RCL, the leftmost bit enters the CF, and the CF bit enters bit 0 of the destination; all other bits rotate left. For RCR, bit 0 enters the CF, and the CF bit enters the leftmost bit of the destination; all other bits rotate right. (See also ROL and ROR.)

Flags. Affects CF and OF.

Source code. RCL/RCR register/memory,CL/immediate

Object code.
RCL: `|110100cw|mod010r/m|(if c = 0, shift is 1;`
RCR: `|110100cw|mod011r/m|if c = 1, shift is in CL)`

REP: Repeat String

Operation. Repeats a string operation a specified number of times. REP is an optional repeat prefix coded before the string instructions MOVS, STOS, INS, and OUTS).

Load the CX with a count prior to execution. For each execution of the string instruction, REP decrements the CX by 1 and repeats the operation until the CX is 0, at which point processing continues with the next instruction. (See also REPE/REPZ/REPNE/REPNZ.)

Flags. See the associated string instructions.

Source code. REP string-instruction

Object code. `11110010`

REPE/REPZ/REPNE/REPNZ: Repeat String Conditionally

Operation. Repeats a string operation a specified number of times or until a condition is met. REPE, REPZ, REPNE, and REPNZ are optional repeat prefixes coded before the string instructions SCAS and CMPS, which change the ZF. Load the CX with a count prior to execution. For REPE/REPZ (repeat while equal/zero), the operation repeats while the ZF is 1 (equal/zero condition) and the CX is not zero. For REPNE/REPNZ (repeat while not equal/zero), the operation repeats while the ZF is 0 (unequal/nonzero condition) and the CX is not zero. While the conditions are true, the operation decrements the CX by 1 and executes the string instruction.

Flags. See the associated string instruction.

Source code. REPE/REPZ/REPNE/REPNZ string-instruction

Object code. REPNE/REPNZ: `11110010`
REPE/REPZ: `11110011`

RET/RETN/RETF: Return from a Procedure

Operation. Returns from a procedure previously entered by a near or far CALL. The assembler generates a near RET if it is within a procedure labeled NEAR and a far RET if it is within a procedure labeled FAR. For near, RET moves the word at the top of the stack to the IP and increments the SP by 2. For far, RET moves the words at the top of the stack to the IP and CS and increments the SP by 4. Any numeric operand (a pop value coded as RET 4) is added to the SP.

RETN and RETF were introduced by MASM 5.0 so that you can code a near or far return explicitly.

Flags. Affects none.

Source code. RET/RETN/RETF [pop-value]

Object code. Four formats:

Within a segment:	`|11000011|`
Within a segment with pop value:	`|11000010|data-low|data-high|`
Intersegment:	`|11001011|`
Intersegment with pop value:	`|11001010|data-low|data-high|`

ROL/ROR: Rotate Left or Rotate Right

Operation. Rotates bits left or right in a byte, word, or doubleword (80386 and later) in a register or memory. The operand may be an immediate constant or a reference to the CL. On the 8088/86, the constant may be only 1; a larger rotate must be in the CL. On later processors, the constant may be up to 31. For ROL, the leftmost bit enters bit 0 of the destination; all other bits rotate left. For ROR, bit 0 enters the leftmost bit of the destination; all other bits rotate right. (See also RCL and RCR.) The rotated bit also enters the CF.

Flags. Affects CF and OF.

Source code. ROL/ROR register/memory,CL/immediate

Object code. ROL: `|110100cw|mod000r/m|(if c = 0 count = 1;`
ROR: `|110100cw|mod001r/m|if c = 1 count is in CL)`

SAHF: Store AH Contents in Flags

Operation. Stores bits from the AH in the rightmost bits of the flags register. (See also LAHF.)

Flags. Affects AF, CF, PF, SF, and ZF.

Source code. SAHF (no operand)

Object code. `10011110`

SAL/SAR: Shift Algebraic Left or Shift Algebraic Right

Operation. Shifts bits to the left or right in a byte, word, or doubleword in a register or memory. The operand may be an immediate constant or a reference to the CL. On the 8088/86, the constant may be only 1; a larger shift must be in the CL. On later processors, the constant may be up to 31.

SAL shifts bits to the left a specified number and fills 0 bits in vacated positions to the right. SAL acts exactly like SHL. SAR is an arithmetic shift that considers the sign of the referenced field. SAR shifts bits to the right a specified number and fills the sign bit (0 or 1) to the left. All bits shifted off are lost.

Flags. Affects CF, OF, PF, SF, and ZF. (AF is undefined.)

Source code. SAL/SAR register/memory,CL/immediate

Object code. SAL: `|110100cw|mod100r/m|(If c = 0 count = 1;`
SAR: `|110100cw|mod111r/m|if c = 1 count in CL)`

SBB: Subtract with Borrow

Operation. Typically used in multiword binary subtraction to carry an overflowed 1 bit into the next stage of arithmetic. SBB first subtracts the contents of the CF (0/1) from the first operand and then subtracts the second operand from the first, just like SUB. (See also ADC.)

Flags. Affects AF, CF, OF, PF, SF, and ZF.

Source code. SBB register/memory,register/memory/immediate

Object code. Three formats:

Reg/mem with register:	`|000110dw|modregr/m|`
Immed from accumulator:	`|0001110w|---data--|data if w=1|`
Immed from reg/mem:	`|100000sw|mod011r/m|---data----|data if sw=01|`

SCAS/SCASB/SCASW/SCASD: Scan String

Operation. Scans a string in memory for a specified value. For SCASB load the value in the AL, for SCASW load it in the AX, and for SCASD (80386 and later) load it in the EAX. The ES:DI pair references the string in memory that is to be scanned. The operations are normally used with a REPE/REPNE prefix, along with a count in the CX; use REPE to find the first nonmatch and REPNE to find the first match. If the DF is 0, the operation scans memory from left to right and increments the DI. If the DF is 1, the operation scans memory from right to left and decrements the DI. REPn decrements the CX for each repetition. The operation ends on an equal (REPNE) or an unequal (REPE) condition or when the CX is decremented to 0. The *last* compare clears/sets the flags. If the specified condition is not found, REP has decremented the CX to 0; otherwise, the DI and SI contain the address of the following item.

Flags. Affects AF, CF, OF, PF, SF, and ZF.

Source code. [REPnn] SCASB/SCASW/SCASD (no operand)

Object code. `1010111w`

SETnn: Set Byte Conditionally (80386 and later)

Operation. Sets a specified byte based on a condition. This is a group of 30 instructions, including SET(N)E, SET(N)L, SET(N)C, and SET(N)S, that exactly parallel the set of conditional jumps. If a tested condition is true, the operation sets the byte operand to 1, otherwise to 0. An example is

```
CMP   AX,BX     ;Compare contents of AX to BX
SETE  CL        ;If equal, set CL to 1, else to 0
```

Flags. Affects none.

Source code. SETnn register/memory

Object code. `|00001111|1001cond|mod000r/m|`
(cond varies according to condition tested)

SHL/SHR: Shift Logical Left or Shift Logical Right

Operation. Shifts bits left or right in a byte, word, or doubleword in a register or memory. The operand may be an immediate constant or a reference to the CL. On the 8088/86, the constant may be only 1; a larger shift must be in the CL. On later processors, the constant may be up to 31. SHL and SHR are logical shifts that treat the sign bit as a data bit.

SHL shifts bits to the left a specified number and fills 0 bits in vacated positions to the right. SHL acts exactly like SAL. SHR shifts bits to the right a specified number and fills 0 bits to the left. All bits shifted off are lost.

Flags. Affects CF, OF, PF, SF, and ZF. (AF is undefined.)

Source code. SHL/SHR register/memory,CL/immediate

Object code. SHL: `|110100cw|mod100r/m| (If c = 0, count = 1;`
SHR: `|110100cw|mod101r/m| (If c = 1, count in CL)`

SHLD/SHRD: Shift Double Precision (80386 and later)

Operation. Shifts multiple bits into an operand. The instructions require three operands. The first operand is a 16- or 32-bit register or memory location containing the value to be shifted. The second operand is a register (same size as the first operand) containing the bits to be shifted into the first operand. The third operand is the CL or an immediate constant containing the shift value.

Flags. Affects CF, OF, PF, SF, and ZF. (AF is undefined.)

Source code. SHLD/SHRD register/memory,register,CL/immediate

Object code. `|00001111|10100100|modregr/m|`

STC: Set Carry Flag

Operation. Sets the CF to 1. (See CLC for clear CF.)

Flags. Sets CF.

Source code. STC (no operand)

Object code. `11111001`

STD: Set Direction Flag

Operation. Sets the DF to 1 to cause string operations such as MOVS to process from right to left. (See CLD for clear DF.)

Flags. Sets DF.

Source code. STD (no operand)

Object code. `11111101`

STI: Set Interrupt Flag

Operation. Sets the IF to 1 to enable maskable external interrupts after execution of the next instruction. (See CLI for clear IF.)

Flags. Sets IF.

Source code. STI (no operand)

Object code. `11111011`

STOS/STOSB/STOSW/STOSD: Store String

Operation. Stores the contents of the accumulator in memory. When used with a REP prefix along with a count in the CX, the operation duplicates a string value a specified number of times; this is suitable for such actions as clearing an area of memory. For STOSB load the value in the AL, for STOSW load the value in the AX, and for STOSD load the value in the EAX. The ES:DI pair references a location in memory where the value is to be stored. If the DF is 0, the operation stores in memory from left to right and increments the DI. If the DF is 1, the operation stores from right to left and decrements the DI. REP decrements the CX for each repetition and ends when it becomes 0.

Flags. Affects none.

Source code. [REP] STOSB/STOSW/STOSD (no operand)

Object code. `1010101w`

SUB: Subtract Binary Values

Operation. Subtracts binary values in a register, memory, or immediate from a register, or subtracts values in a register or immediate from memory. Values may be byte, word, or doubleword (80386 and later). (See also SBB.)

Flags. Affects AF, CF, OF, PF, SF, and ZF.

Source code. SUB register/memory,register/memory/immediate

Object code. Three formats:

Reg/mem with register: `|001010dw|modregr/m|`
Immed from accumulator: `|0010110w|---data--|data if w=1|`
Immed from reg/mem: `|100000sw|mod101r/m|---data----|data if sw=01|`

TEST: Test Bits

Operation. Uses AND logic to test a field for a specific bit configuration, but does not change the destination operand. Both operands are bytes, words, or doublewords (80386 and later) in a register or memory; the second operand may be immediate. After its execution, you may use, for example, JE or JNE to test the flags.

Flags. Clears CF and OF and affects PF, SF, and ZF. (AF is undefined.)

Source code. TEST register/memory,register/memory/immediate

Object code. Three formats:
Reg/mem and register: `|1000010w|modregr/m|`
Immed to accumulator: `|1010100w|---data--|data if w=1|`
Immed to reg/mem: `|1111011w|mod000r/m|---data----|data if w=1|`

WAIT: Put Processor in Wait State

Operation. Allows the main processor to remain in a wait state until an external interrupt occurs, in order to synchronize it with a coprocessor. The main processor waits until the coprocessor finishes executing and resumes processing on receiving a signal in the TEST pin.

Flags. Affects none.

Source code. WAIT (no operand)

Object code. `10011011`

XADD: Exchange and Add (80486 and Later)

Operation. Adds the source and destination operands and stores the sum in the destination. It also moves the original value of the destination to the source.

Flags. Affects AF, CF, OF, PF, SF, and ZF.

Source code. XADD register/memory,register

Object code. `|00001111|1100000b|mod reg r/m|`

XCHG: Exchange

Operation. Exchanges data between two registers (as XCHG AH,BL) or between a register and memory (as XCHG CX,word).

Flags. Affects none.

Source code. XCHG register/memory,register/memory

Object code. Two formats:
Reg with accumulator: `|10010reg|`
Reg/mem with reg: `|1000011w|mod reg r/m|`

XLAT/XLATB: Translate

Operation. Translates bytes into a different format, such as ASCII to EBCDIC. You define a table, load its address in the BX or EBX for 32-bit size, and then load the AL with a value that is to be translated. The operation uses the AL value as an offset into the table, selects the byte from the table, and stores it in the AL. (XLATB is a synonym for XLAT.)

Flags. Affects none.

Source code. XLAT [AL] (AL operand is optional)

Object code. `11010111`

XOR: Exclusive OR

Operation. Performs a logical exclusive OR on bits of two operands. Both operands are bytes, words, or doublewords (80386 and later), which XOR matches bit for bit. For each pair matched bits, if both are the same, the bit in the first operand is cleared to 0; if the matched bits are different the bit in the first operand is set to 1. (See also AND and OR.)

Flags. Affects CF (0), OF (0), PF, SF, and ZF. (AF is undefined.)

Source code. XOR register/memory,register/memory/immediate

Object code. Three formats:
Reg/mem with register: `|001100dw|mod reg r/m|`
Immed to reg/mem: `|1000000w|mod 110 r/m|---data----|data if w=1|`
Immed to accumulator: `|0011010w|---data----|data if w=1|`

APPENDIX: CONVERSION BETWEEN HEXADECIMAL AND DECIMAL NUMBERS

This appendix provides the steps required to convert between numbers in hexadecimal and decimal formats. The first section shows how to convert hex A7B8 to decimal 42,936, and the second section shows how to convert 42,936 back to hex A7B8.

CONVERTING A HEXADECIMAL NUMBER TO DECIMAL

To convert a hex number to a decimal number, start with the leftmost hex digit, continuously multiply each hex digit by 16, and accumulate the results. Because multiplication is in decimal, convert hex digits A through F to decimal 10 through 15. The steps to convert A7B8H to decimal format are:

```
First digit: A (10)       10
Multiply by 16          x 16
                        ----
                         160
Add next digit, 7        + 7
                        ----
                         167
Multiply by 16          x 16
                        ----
                        2672
Add next digit, B (11)  + 11
                        ----
                        2683
```

```
Multiply by 16              x 16
                          42,928
Add next digit, 8         +    8
Decimal value             42,936
```

You can also use a conversion table. For A7B8H, think of the rightmost digit (8) as position 1, the next digit to the left (B) as position 2, the next digit (7) as position 3, and the leftmost digit (A) as position 4. Refer to Table A-1 and locate the value for each hex digit:

```
For digit 8 in position 1, column 1 =      8
For digit B in position 2, column 2 =    176
For digit 7 in position 3, column 3 =  1,792
For digit A in position 4, column 4 = 40,960
                         Decimal value 42,936
```

CONVERTING A DECIMAL NUMBER TO HEXADECIMAL

To convert decimal number 42,936 to hexadecimal, first divide 42,936 by 16; the remainder becomes the rightmost hex digit, 8. Next divide the new quotient, 2,683, by 16; the remainder, 11 or B, becomes the next hex digit to the left. Continue in this manner developing the hex number from the remainders of each step of the division until the quotient is zero. The steps proceed as follows:

OPERATION	QUOTIENT	REMAINDER	HEX
42,936/16	2683	8	8 (rightmost)
2,683/16	167	11	B
167/16	10	7	7
10/16	0	10	A (leftmost)

You can also use Table A-1 to convert decimal to hexadecimal. For decimal number 42,936, locate the number in the table that is equal to or next smaller than it. Note the equivalent hex number and its position in the table. Subtract the decimal value of that hex digit from 42,936, and locate the difference in the table. The procedure works as follows:

```
                              DECIMAL   HEX
Starting decimal value         42,936
Subtract next smaller number  -40,960   A000
Difference                      1,976
Subtract next smaller number   -1,792    700
Difference                        184
Subtract next smaller number     -176     B0
Difference                          8      8
Final hex value                         A7B8
```

TABLE A–1 HEXADECIMAL-DECIMAL CONVERSION TABLE

Hex	Dec	Hex	Dec	Hex	Dec	Hex	Dec	Hex	Dec	Hex	Dec	Hex	Dec	Hex	Dec
0	0	0	0	0	0	0	0	0	0	0	0	0	0	0	0
1	268,435,456	1	16,777,216	1	1,048,576	1	65,536	1	4,096	1	256	1	16	1	1
2	536,870,912	2	33,554,432	2	2,097,152	2	131,072	2	8,192	2	512	2	32	2	2
3	805,306,368	3	50,331,648	3	3,145,728	3	196,608	3	12,288	3	768	3	48	3	3
4	1,073,741,824	4	67,108,864	4	4,194,304	4	262,144	4	16,384	4	1,024	4	64	4	4
5	1,342,177,280	5	83,886,080	5	5,242,880	5	327,680	5	20,480	5	1,280	5	80	5	5
6	1,610,612,736	6	100,663,296	6	6,291,456	6	393,216	6	24,576	6	1,536	6	96	6	6
7	1,879,048,192	7	117,440,512	7	7,340,032	7	458,752	7	28,672	7	1,792	7	112	7	7
8	2,147,483,648	8	134,217,728	8	8,388,608	8	524,288	8	32,768	8	2,048	8	128	8	8
9	2,415,919,104	9	150,994,944	9	9,437,184	9	589,824	9	36,864	9	2,304	9	144	9	9
A	2,684,354,560	A	167,772,160	A	10,485,760	A	655,360	A	40,960	A	2,560	A	160	A	10
B	2,952,790,016	B	184,549,376	B	11,534,336	B	720,896	B	45,056	B	2,816	B	176	B	11
C	3,221,225,472	C	201,326,592	C	12,582,912	C	786,432	C	49,152	C	3,072	C	192	C	12
D	3,489,660,928	D	218,103,808	D	13,631,488	D	851,968	D	53,248	D	3,328	D	208	D	13
E	3,758,096,384	E	234,881,024	E	14,680,064	E	917,504	E	57,344	E	3,584	E	224	E	14
F	4,026,531,840	F	251,658,240	F	15,728,640	F	983,040	F	61,440	F	3,840	F	240	F	15
8		7		6		5		4		3		2		1	

B APPENDIX: ASCII CHARACTER CODES

The term ASCII stands for "American Standard Code for Information Interchange." Table B-1 lists the representation of the entire 256 ASCII character codes (00H through FFH), along with their hexadecimal representations. The categories of character codes are:

00-1FH	Control codes for screens, printers, and data transmission, that are intended to cause an action.
20-7FH	Character codes for numbers, letters, and punctuation. (20H is the standard space or blank.)
80-FFH	Extended ASCII codes, foreign characters, Greek and mathematics symbols, and graphic characters for drawing boxes.

Here are the control codes from 00H through 1FH; those in parentheses do not have a printable symbol:

HEX	CHARACTER	HEX	CHARACTER	HEX	CHARACTER
00	(Null)	01	Happy face	02	Happy face
03	Heart	04	Diamond	05	Club
06	Spade	07	(Beep)	08	(Back space)
09	(Tab)	0A	(Line feed)	0B	(Vertical tab)
0C	(Form Feed)	0D	(Return)	0E	(Shift out)

0F	(Shift in)	10	(Data line esc)	11	(Dev ctl 1)
12	(Dev ctl 2)	13	(Dev ctl 3)	14	(Dev ctl 4)
15	(Neg acknowledge)	16	(Synch idle)	17	(End tran block)
18	(Cancel)	19	(End of medium)	1A	(Substitute)
1B	(Escape)	1C	(File separator)	1D	(Group separator)
1E	(Record separator)	1F	(Unit separator)		

TABLE B-1 ASCII CHARACTER SET

00		20		40	@	60	`	80	Ç	A0	á	C0	└	E0	α
01	☺	21	!	41	A	61	a	81	ü	A1	í	C1	┴	E1	ß
02	☻	22	"	42	B	62	b	82	é	A2	ó	C2	┬	E2	Γ
03	♥	23	#	43	C	63	c	83	â	A3	ú	C3	├	E3	π
04	♦	24	$	44	D	64	d	84	ä	A4	ñ	C4	─	E4	Σ
05	♣	25	%	45	E	65	e	85	à	A5	Ñ	C5	┼	E5	σ
06	♠	26	&	46	F	66	f	86	å	A6	ª	C6	╞	E6	µ
07		27	'	47	G	67	g	87	ç	A7	º	C7	╟	E7	τ
08		28	(	48	H	68	h	88	ê	A8	¿	C8	╚	E8	Φ
09		29	)	49	I	69	i	89	ë	A9	⌐	C9	╔	E9	Θ
0A		2A	*	4A	J	6A	j	8A	è	AA	¬	CA	╩	EA	Ω
0B		2B	+	4B	K	6B	k	8B	ï	AB	½	CB	╦	EB	δ
0C		2C	,	4C	L	6C	l	8C	î	AC	¼	CC	╠	EC	∞
0D		2D	-	4D	M	6D	m	8D	ì	AD	¡	CD	═	ED	φ
0E		2E	.	4E	N	6E	n	8E	Ä	AE	«	CE	╬	EE	ε
0F		2F	/	4F	O	6F	o	8F	Å	AF	»	CF	╧	EF	∩
10	►	30	0	50	P	70	p	90	É	B0	░	D0	╨	F0	≡
11	◄	31	1	51	Q	71	q	91	æ	B1	▒	D1	╤	F1	±
12	↕	32	2	52	R	72	r	92	Æ	B2	▓	D2	╥	F2	≥
13	‼	33	3	53	S	73	s	93	ô	B3	│	D3	╙	F3	≤
14	¶	34	4	54	T	74	t	94	ö	B4	┤	D4	╘	F4	⌠
15	§	35	5	55	U	75	u	95	ò	B5	╡	D5	╒	F5	⌡
16	▬	36	6	56	V	76	v	96	û	B6	╢	D6	╓	F6	÷
17	↨	37	7	57	W	77	w	97	ù	B7	╖	D7	╫	F7	≈
18	↑	38	8	58	X	78	x	98	ÿ	B8	╕	D8	╪	F8	°
19	↓	39	9	59	Y	79	y	99	Ö	B9	╣	D9	┘	F9	·
1A		3A	:	5A	Z	7A	z	9A	Ü	BA	║	DA	┌	FA	·
1B		3B	;	5B	[	7B	{	9B	¢	BB	╗	DB	█	FB	√
1C	∟	3C	<	5C	\	7C	|	9C	£	BC	╝	DC	▄	FC	^{n}
1D	↔	3D	=	5D	]	7D	}	9D	¥	BD	╜	DD	▌	FD	^{2}
1E	▲	3E	>	5E	^	7E	~	9E	Pt	BE	╛	DE	▐	FE	■
1F		3F	?	5F	_	7F	⌂	9F	ƒ	BF	┐	DF	▀	FF	

C APPENDIX: RESERVED WORDS

The assembler recognizes some words as having a specific meaning; you may use these words only under prescribed conditions. Words that the assembler reserves may be classed into four categories:

- Register names, such as AX and AH
- Symbolic instructions, such as ADD and MOV
- Directives (commands to the assembler), such as PROC and END
- Operators, such as DUP and SEG.

If used to define a data item, many of the reserved words that follow may confuse the assembler or cause an assembly error. A particular assembler version may have reserved words in addition to those listed here.

Register Names

AH, AL, AX, BH, BL, BP, BX, CH, CL, CS, CX, DH, DI, DL, DS, DX, EAX, EBP, EBX, ECX, EDI, EDX, EIP, ES, ESI, FS, GS, IP, SI, SP, SS

Symbolic Instructions

AAA, AAD, AAM, AAS, ADC, ADD, AND, ARPL, BOUND, BSF, BSR, BTn, CALL, CBW, CDQ, CLC, CLD, CLI, CLTS, CMC, CMP, CMPSn, CMPXCHG, CMPXCHG8B, CWDn, DAA, DAS, DEC, DIV, ENTER, ESC, HLT, IDIV, IMUL, IN, INC, INSn, INT, INTO, IRET, JA, JAE, JB, JBE, JCXZ, JE, JECXZ, JG, JGE, JL, JLE, JMP, JNA, JNAE, JNB, JNBE, JNE, JNG, JNGE, JNL, JNLE, JNO, JNP, JNS, JNZ, JO, JP, JPE, JPO, JS, JZ, LAHF, LAR, LDS, LEA, LEAVE, LES, LFS, LGDT, LGS, LIDT, LLDT, LMSW, LOCK, LODSn, LOOP, LOOPE, LOOPNEn, LOOPNZn, LOOPZ, LSL, LSS, LSS, LTR, MOV, MOVSn, MOVSX, MOVZX, MUL, NEG, NOP, NOT, OR, OUTn, POP, POPA, POPAD, POPF, POPFD, PUSH, PUSHAD, PUSHF, PUSHFD, RCL, RCR, REN, REP, REPE, REPNE, REPNZ, REPZ, RET, RETF, ROL, ROR, SAHF, SAL, SAR, SBB, SCASn, SETnn, SGDT, SHL, SHLD, SHR, SHRD, SIDT, SLDT, SMSW, STC, STD, STI, STOSn, STR, SUB, TEST, VERR, VERRW, WAIT, XADD, XCHG, XLAT, XOR

Directives

ALIGN, .ALPHA, ASSUME, BYTE, .CODE, COMM, COMMENT, .CONST, .CREF, .DATA, .DATA?, DB, DD, DF, DOSSEG, DQ, DT, DW, DWORD, ELSE, END, ENDIF, ENDM, ENDP, ENDS, EQU, .ERRnn, EVEN, EXITM, EXTRN, EXTERN, .FARDATA, .FARDATA?, FWORD, GROUP, IF, IF1, IF2, IFB, IFDEF, IFDIF, IFE, IFIDN, IFNB, IFNDEF, INCLUDE, INCLUDELIB, IRP, IRPC, LABEL, .LALL, .LFCOND, .LIST, LOCAL, MACRO, .MODEL, NAME, ORG, &OUT, PAGE, PROC, PUBLIC, PURGE, QWORD, .RADIX, RECORD, REPT, .SALL, SEGMENT, .SEQ, .SFCOND, .STACK, STRUC, SUBTTL, .TFCOND, TITLE, TWORD, UNION, WORD, .XALL, .XCREF, .XLIST

Operators

AND, BYTE, COMMENT, CON, DUP, EQ, FAR, GE, GT, HIGH, LE, LENGTH, LINE, LOW, LT, MASK, MOD, NE, NEAR, NOT, NOTHING, OFFSET, OR, PTR, SEG, SHL, SHORT, SHR, SIZE, STACK, THIS, TYPE, WHILE, WIDTH, WORD, XOR

D APPENDIX: ASSEMBLER AND LINK OPTIONS

This appendix covers the rules for assembling, linking, generating cross-reference files, and converting .EXE programs to .COM format. The Microsoft assembler version is (or was) MASM and Borland's is TASM, both of which are similar. Since version 6.0, the Microsoft assembler uses the ML command, which can perform an assembly and link in one command. Examples in this appendix arbitrarily use disk drive D: as the path for all programs and files; users of other drives can substitute the appropriate letter and path, such as C: or C:\subdirectory.

The various assembler versions provide a seemingly endless array of options, not all of which can be covered here.

ASSEMBLING A PROGRAM

You can use a command line to request an assembly, although MASM also provides for prompts.

Assembling with a Command Line

The general format for using a command line to assemble is

```
MASM/TASM [options] source[,object][,listing][,crossref]
```

- *Options* are explained later.
- *Source* identifies the source program. The assembler assumes the extension .ASM, so you need not enter it. You may also key in the path, such as D: or D:\subdirectory\filename.
- *Object* provides for a generated OBJ file. The path and filename may be the same as or different from the source.
- *Listing* provides for a generated .LST file that contains the source and object code. The path and filename may be the same as or different from the source.
- *Crossref* provides for a generated file containing symbols for a cross-reference listing. The extension is .CRF for MASM and .XRF for TASM. The path and filename may be the same or different from the source.

This example spells out all the files:

```
MASM D:name.ASM,D:name.OBJ,D:name.LST,D:name.CRF
```

The following shortcut command allows for defaults for the object, listing, and cross-reference files, all with the same name:

```
MASM D:filename,D:,D:,D:
```

This next example requests a cross-reference file, but no listing file (note the double commas):

```
MASM D:filename,D:,,D:
```

Assembling with Prompts

You can also key in just the name of the assembler with no command line, although TASM and MASM (through version 5.1) respond differently. TASM displays the general format for the command line and an explanation of the options, whereas MASM displays a list of prompts to which you are to reply:

```
Source filename [.ASM]:
Object filename [source.OBJ]:
Source listing  [NUL.LST]:
Cross-reference [NUL.CRF]:
```

- *Source filename* identifies the name of the source file. Key in the path (if it's not the default) and the name of the source file, without the extension .ASM.
- *Object filename* provides for the object file. The prompt assumes the same filename, although you may change it. To get an object file on drive D:, type D: and <Enter>.
- *Source listing* provides for an assembled listing, although the prompt assumes that you do not want one. To get a listing on drive D, type D: and <Enter>.

- *Cross-reference* provides for a cross-reference listing, although the prompt assumes that you do not want one. To get one on drive D, type D: and <Enter>. The Microsoft extension is .CRF and Borland's is .XRF.

For the last three prompts, just press <Enter> to accept the defaults.

Assembler Options

Assembler options for MASM and TASM include the following:

/A	Arrange source segments in alphabetic sequence.
/C	Create a cross-reference table in the .LST file.
/D	MASM: Produce listing files on both pass 1 and pass 2 to locate phase errors. For TASM, /Dsymbol means define a symbol.
/E	Accept 80×87 coprocessor instructions and generate a linkage to BASIC, C, or FORTRAN for emulated floating-point instructions.
/H	Display assembler options with a brief explanation. Enter /H (for help) with no filenames or other options.
/L	Create a normal listing (.LST) file. The command line also provides a path for this option.
/LA	For TASM, create an expanded listing (.LST) file.
/M#	For TASM, allow # number of passes to resolve forward references.
/ML	Make all names case sensitive.
/MU	Convert all names to uppercase.
/MX	Make public and external names case sensitive.
/N	Suppress generation of the symbol table in the .LST file.
/R	Provide real math coprocessor support.
/S	Leave source segments in original sequence.
/T	(Terse) Display diagnostics at the end of the assembly only if an error is encountered.
/V	(Verbose) At the end of the assembly, display the number of lines and symbols processed.
/Wn	Set the level of warning messages: 0 = display only severe errors; 1 = display severe errors and serious warnings (the default); 2 = display severe errors, serious warnings, and advisory warnings.
/Z	Display source lines on the screen for errors.
/ZD	Include information on line numbers in the object file for CodeView or TurboDebugger.

/ZI Include line-number and symbolic information in the object file for CodeView or TurboDebugger.

You may request options in either prompt or command-line mode. For prompts, you could code MASM/A/V <Enter>, for example, and then key in the usual filename. Or you may key in options in any prompt line, for example, as

```
filename[.ASM]: /A/V filename or filename /A/V <Enter>
```

The /A/V options tell the assembler to arrange segments in alphabetic sequence and to display additional diagnostics at the end of the assembly. See your assembler manual for other options.

Microsoft Version 6.x

The command line for Microsoft assemblers since version 6.0 is

```
ML [options] filenames [[options] filenames] ... [/link options]
```

The assembler allows you to assemble and link any number of programs into one executable module. One useful option is ML -?, which displays the complete command-line syntax and options.

Additional Turbo Assembler Features

Turbo Assembler lets you assemble multiple files, each with its own options, in one command line. You can also use the wild cards (* and ?). To assemble all source programs in the current directory, key in TASM *. To assemble all source programs named PROG1.ASM, PROG2.ASM, and so on, key in TASM PROG?. You can key in groups (or sets) of filenames, with each group separated by a plus sign (+). The following command assembles PROGA and PROGB with the /C option and PROGC with the /A option:

```
TASM /C PROGA PROGB+ /A PROGC
```

Requesting the /W option causes TASM to generate warning messages for inefficient code. Ideal mode also has many additional features. Borland supplies two other assembler versions, TASMX and TASM32, for protected mode.

Tables

Following an assembler .LST listing are a Segments and Groups table and a Symbols table.

Segments and groups table. This table has a heading similar to the following:

```
Name   Length  Align Combine Class
```

- The *name* column gives the names of all segments and groups, in alphabetic sequence.
- The *length* column gives the size, in hex, of each segment.

- The *align* column gives the alignment type, such as BYTE, WORD, or PARA.
- The *combine* column lists the defined combine type, such as STACK for a stack, NONE where no type is coded, PUBLIC for external definitions, or a hex address for AT types.
- The *class* column lists the segment class names, as coded in the SEGMENT statement.

Symbol table. A symbol table has a heading similar to the following:

```
Name   Type  Value  Attribute
```

- The *name* column lists the names of all defined items, in alphabetic sequence.
- The *type* column gives the type, as follows:

  L NEAR or L FAR: A near or far label

  N PROC or F PROC: A near or far procedure

  BYTE, WORD, DWORD, FWORD, QWORD, TBYTE: A data item

  ALIAS: An alias (or nickname) for another symbol

  NUMBER: An absolute label

  OPCODE: An equate for an instruction operand

  TEXT: An equate for text
- The *value* column gives the hex offset from the beginning of a segment for names, labels, and procedures.
- The *attribute* column lists a symbol's attributes, including its segment and length.

CROSS-REFERENCE FILE

A .CRF or .XRF file is used to produce a cross-reference listing of a program's labels, symbols, and variables. However, you have to use CREF for Microsoft or TCREF for Borland to convert the listing to a sorted cross-reference file. You can key in CREF or TCREF with a command line or use prompts.

Using a Command Line

The general format for using a command line is

```
CREF/TCREF d:xreffile,d:reffile
```

- *Xreffile* identifies the cross-reference file generated by the assembler. The program assumes the extension, so you need not enter it.
- *Reffile* provides for generating a .REF file. The path and filename may be the same as or different from those of the source.

The following example writes a cross-reference file named ASMPROG.REF on drive D:

```
CREF/TCREF D:ASMPROG,D:
```

Using Prompts

You can key in just CREF or TCREF with no command line. TCREF simply displays the general format for the command and an explanation of its options, whereas CREF displays these prompts:

```
Cross-reference [.CRF]:
Listing [filename.REF]:
```

For the first prompt, key in the name of the file, without a .CRF extension. For the second prompt, you can key in the path only and accept the default file name. This choice causes CREF to write a cross-reference file named filename.REF.

LINKING A PROGRAM

Microsoft's linker is LINK and Borland's is TLINK. Both linkers accept a command line to request linking; LINK also provides for prompts.

Linking with a Command Line

The general format for using a command line to link is

```
LINK/TLINK [options] objfile,exefile[,mapfile][,libraryfile]
```

- Options are described later.
- *Objfile* identifies the object file generated by the assembler. The linker assumes the extension .OBJ, so you need not enter it. You can also key a path.
- *Exefile* provides for generating an .EXE file. The path and filename may be the same as or different from the source.
- *Mapfile* provides for generating a file with an extension .MAP that indicates the relative location and the size of each segment and any errors that the linker has found; a typical error is failure to define a stack segment. Keying in CON tells the linker to display the map on the screen (instead of writing it on disk) so that you can view it immediately for errors.
- *Libraryfile* provides for the libraries option.

To link more than one object file into an executable module, combine them in one line like this:

```
LINK/TLINK D:PROGA+D:PROGB+D:PROGC
```

Linking Using Prompts

You can key in just the name of the linker with no command line, although TLINK and LINK respond differently. TLINK displays the general format for the command and an explanation of options, whereas LINK displays a list of prompts. Here are the LINK prompts to which you are to reply:

```
Object Modules [.OBJ]:
Run File [EXASM1.EXE]:
List File [NUL.MAP]:
Libraries [.LIB]:
```

- *Object Modules* asks for the name(s) of the object module(s) to be linked; it defaults to .OBJ if you omit the extension.
- *Run File* requests the name of the file that is to execute and allows a default to the object module filename. You just need to key in the path.
- *List File* provides for the map file, although the default is NUL.MAP (that is, no map). The reply CON tells the linker to display the map on the screen, a convenient choice.
- *Libraries* asks for the library option, which is outside the scope of this text.

For the last three prompts, just press <Enter> to accept the default. The following example tells the linker to produce .EXE and .CON files:

```
Object Modules [.OBJ]: D:ASMPROG <Enter>
Run File [ASMPROG.EXE]: D: <Enter>
List File [NUL.MAP]: CON <Enter>
Libraries [.LIB]: <Enter>
```

Debugging Options

If you intend to use CodeView or TurboDebugger, use the assembler's /ZI option for assembling. For linking, use Microsoft's LINK /CO option in either command-line or prompt mode, or Turbo TLINK's /V option:

```
LINK /CO filename ... or TLINK /V filename ...
```

Converting Turbo Object Files to .COM Programs

Borland's TLINK allows you to convert an object program directly to .COM format, provided that the source program was originally coded according to .COM requirements. Use the /T option:

```
TLINK /T objfile,comfile,CON
```

EXE2BIN OPTIONS

The Microsoft EXE2BIN program converts .EXE modules generated by MASM into .COM modules, provided that the source program was originally coded according to .COM requirements. Type in the following command:

```
EXE2BIN D:filename,D:filename.COM
```

The first operand is the name of the .EXE file, which you key in without an extension. The second operand is the name of the .COM file; you may change the name, but be sure to code a .COM extension. Delete the .OBJ and .EXE files.

E APPENDIX: THE DEBUG PROGRAM

The DOS DEBUG program is useful for writing very small programs, for debugging assembly programs, and for examining the contents of a file or memory. You may key in one of two commands to start DEBUG:

1. To create a file or examine memory, key in DEBUG with no filespec; or
2. To modify or debug a program (.COM or .EXE) or to modify a file, key in DEBUG with a filespec, such as DEBUG D:PROGC.COM.

The program loader loads DEBUG into memory, and DEBUG displays a hyphen (-) as a prompt. The memory area for your program is known as a program segment. The CS, DS, ES, and SS registers are initialized with the address of the 256-byte (100H) program segment prefix (PSP), and your work area begins at PSP + 100H.

A reference to a memory address may be in terms of a segment and offset, such as DS:120, or an offset only, such as 120. You may also make direct references to memory addresses, such as 40:17, where 40[0]H is the segment and 17H is the offset. DEBUG assumes that all numbers entered are hexadecimal, so you do not key in the trailing H. The F1 and F3 keys work for DEBUG just as they do for DOS; that is, F1 duplicates the previous command one key at a time, whereas F3 duplicates the entire previous command. Also, DEBUG does not distinguish between uppercase and lowercase letters.

Following is a description of each DEBUG command, in alphabetic sequence.

A (Assemble). Translates assembly source statements into machine code. The operation is especially useful for writing and testing small assembly programs and for examining small segments of code. The default starting address for code is CS:0100H, and the general format for the A command is A [address].

The following example creates an assembly program consisting of five statements. You code the instructions (but not the comments) on the left; DEBUG generates the code segment (shown here as xxxx:) and an offset beginning at 0100H:

```
           A (or A 100) <Enter>    Explanation
xxxx:0100  MOV CX,[10D] <Enter>    ;Get contents at 10D
xxxx:0104  ADD CX,1A <Enter>       ;Add immediate value
xxxx:0107  MOV [10D],CX <Enter>    ;Store CX in 10D
xxxx:010B  JMP 100 <Enter>         ;Jump back to start
xxxx:010D  DW 2500 <Enter>         ;Define constant
           <Enter>                 ;End of command
```

Because of the size of the PSP, DEBUG sets the IP to 100H, so that the statements begin at 100H. The last <Enter> (that's two in a row) tells DEBUG to end the program. You can now optionally use the U (Unassemble) command to examine the machine code and T (Trace) to trace program execution. Note that you can use DB and DW to define data items that the program needs to reference.

You may change any of the preceding instructions or data items, provided that the length of the new instruction is the same as that of the old one. For example, to change the ADD at 104H to SUB, type

```
           A 104 <Enter>
xxxx:0104  SUB CX,1A <Enter> <Enter>
```

When you reexecute the program, the IP is still incremented. Use the register (R) command to reset it to 100H. Use Q to quit.

C (Compare). Compares the contents of two areas of memory. The default register is the DS, and the general format is

```
C [range] [address]
```

You may code the command one of two ways:

1. A starting address (compare from), a length, and a starting address (compare to). The following example compares 20H bytes beginning at DS:050 with bytes beginning at DS:200:
   ```
   C 050 L20 200    ;Compare using a length of 20H
   ```
2. A starting address and an ending address (compare from) and a starting address (compare to). This example compares bytes beginning at DS:050 to bytes beginning at DS:200:
   ```
   C 050 070 200    ;Compare using a range
   ```

The operation displays the addresses and contents of unequal bytes.

D (Display or Dump). Displays the contents of a portion of memory in hex and ASCII. The default register is the DS, and the general format is

```
D [address] or D [range]
```

You may specify a starting address or a starting address with a range. Omission of a range or length causes a default to 80H. Examples of the D command are:

```
D 200          ;Display 80H bytes beginning at DS:200H
D              ;Display 80H bytes beginning at end of last display
D CS:150       ;Display 80H bytes beginning at CS:150H
D DS:20 L5     ;Display 5 bytes beginning at DS:20H
D 300 32C      ;Display the bytes from 300H through 32CH
```

E (Enter). Enables keying in data or machine instructions. The default register is the DS, and the general format is

```
E address [list]
```

The operation allows two options:

1. Replace bytes with those in a list, as shown next:
   ```
   E 105 13 3A 21       ;Type three bytes beginning at DS:105H
   E CS:211 21 2A       ;Type two bytes beginning at CS:211H
   E 110 'anything'     ;Type a character string beginning at DS:110H
   ```
   Use either single or double quotes for character strings.
2. Provide sequential editing of bytes; key in the address that you want displayed:
   ```
   E 12C    ;Show contents of DS:12CH
   ```
   The operation waits for input from the keyboard. Key in one or more bytes of hex values, separated by a space, beginning at DS:12CH.

F (Fill). Fills a range of memory locations with values in a list. The default register is the DS. The general format is

```
F range list
```

The next examples fill locations in memory beginning at DS:210H with bytes containing repetitions of 'Help':

```
F 210 L19 'Help!'     ;Use a length of 19H (25)
F 210 229 'Help!'     ;Use a range, 210H through 229H
```

G (Go). Executes a machine language program that you are debugging through to a specified breakpoint. Be sure to examine the machine code listing for valid IP addresses, because an invalid address may cause unpredictable results. Also, set break points only in your own program, not in DOS or BIOS program modules. The operation executes through INT operations and pauses, if necessary, to wait for keyboard input. The default register is the CS. The general format is

```
G [=address] address [address ...]
```

The entry *=address* provides an optional starting address. The other entries provide up to 10 break-point addresses. The following example tells DEBUG to begin executing all instructions from the current location of the IP to location 11AH: G 11A.

H (Hexadecimal). Shows the sum and difference of two hex values, coded as H value value. The maximum length is four hex digits. For example, the command H 14F 22 displays the result 171 (sum) and 12D (difference).

I (Input). Inputs and displays one byte from a port, coded as `I portaddress`.

L (Load). Loads a file or disk sectors into memory. Note that a file may be "named" so that DEBUG recognizes it one of two ways: either by requesting execution of DEBUG with a filespec, or from within DEBUG by issuing the N (Name) command. There are two general formats for the L command:

1. Load a named file: L [address].
   Use the *address* parameter to cause L to load beginning at a specific location. Omission of the address causes L to load at CS:100. To load a file that is not named, it should first be named (see N):
   ```
   N filespec   ;Name the file
   L            ;Load the file at CS:100H
   ```
   To reload the file, simply issue L with no address; DEBUG reloads the file and initializes registers accordingly.
2. Load data from disk sectors: L [address [drive start number]].
   - *Address* provides the starting memory location for loading the data. (The default is CS:100.)
   - *Drive* identifies the disk drive, where 0 = A, 1 = B, etc.
   - *Start* specifies the hex number of the first sector to load. (This is a relative number, where cylinder 0, track 0, sector 1, is relative sector 0.)
   - *Number* gives the hex number of consecutive sectors to load.

The following example loads beginning at CS:100 from drive 0 (A), starting at sector 20H for 15H sectors:

```
L 100 0 20 15
```

The L operation returns to the BX:CX the number of bytes loaded. For an .EXE file, DEBUG ignores the address parameter (if any) and uses the load address in the .EXE header. It also strips off the header; to preserve it, rename the file with a different extension before executing DEBUG.

M (Move). Moves (or copies) the contents of memory locations. The default register is the DS, and the general format is

```
M range address
```

These examples copy the bytes beginning at DS:050H through 150H into the address beginning at DS:400H:

```
M DS:50 L100 DS:400     ;Use a length for the move
M DS:50 150 DS:400      ;Use a range for the move
```

N (Name). Names a program or a file that you intend to read from or write onto disk. Code the command as N filespec, such as

```
N D:SAM.COM
```

The operation stores the name at CS:80 in the PSP. The first byte at CS:80 contains the length (0AH), followed by a space and the filespec. You may then use L (Load) or W (Write) to read or write the file.

O (Output). Sends a byte to a port, coded as `O portaddress byte`.

P (Proceed). Executes a subroutine call (CALL), loop (LOOP), interrupt (INT), or repeat string instruction (REP) through to the next instruction. Its general format is

```
P [=address] [value]
```

where *=address* is an optional starting address and value is an optional number of instructions to proceed through. Omission of *=address* causes a default to the CS:IP register pair. For example, if your trace of execution is at an INT 21H operation, just key in P to execute through the entire operation. See also G and T.

Q (Quit). Exits DEBUG. The operation does not save files; use W for that purpose.

R (Register). Displays the contents of registers and the next instruction. Its general format is

```
R [registername]
```

The following examples illustrate the use of this command:

R	Displays all registers
R DX	Displays the DX; DEBUG gives you an option: 1. Press <Enter>, which leaves the DX unchanged; or 2. Key in one to four hex digits to change the contents of the DX.
R IP	Displays the IP. Key in another value to change its contents.
R F	Displays the current setting of each flag as a two-letter code. You can change any number of flags, in any sequence:

FLAG	SET	CLEAR
overflow	ov	nv
direction	dn	up
sign	ng (−)	pl (+)
zero	zr	nz
carry	cy	nc

S (Search). Searches memory for characters in a list. The default register is the DS, and the general format is

```
S range list
```

If the characters are found, the operation delivers their addresses; otherwise it does not respond. The following example searches for the word "VIRUS" beginning at DS:300 for 2000H bytes:

```
S 300 L 2000 "VIRUS"
```

This example searches from CS:100 through CS:400 for a byte containing 51H:

```
S CS:100 400 51
```

T (Trace). Executes a program in single-step mode. Note that you should normally use P (Proceed) to execute through INT instructions. The default register is the CS:IP pair, and the general format is

```
T [=address] [value]
```

The optional entry *=address* tells DEBUG where to begin the trace, and the optional *value* gives the number of instructions to trace. Omission of the operands causes DEBUG to execute the next instruction and to display the registers. Here are two examples:

```
T       ;Executes the next instruction
T 10    ;Executes the next 10H (16) instructions
```

U (Unassemble). Unassembles machine instructions. The default register is the CS:IP pair, and the general format is

```
U [address] or U [range]
```

The area specified should contain valid machine code, which the operation displays as symbolic instructions. Here are three examples:

```
U 100        ;Unassemble 32 bytes beginning at CS:100
U            ;Unassemble 32 bytes since last U, if any
U 100 140    ;Unassemble from 100H through 140H
```

Note that DEBUG does not properly translate some conditional jumps and instructions specific to the 80386 and later processors, although they still execute correctly.

W (Write). Writes a file from DEBUG. The file should first be named (see N) if it wasn't already loaded. The default register is the CS, and the general format is

```
W [address [drive start-sector number-of-sectors]]
```

Write program files only with a .COM extension, because W does not support the .EXE format. (To modify an .EXE program, you may change the extension temporarily.) The following example uses W with no operands and sets the file size in the BX:CX pair:

```
R BX          ;Request BX register
0             ;Set BX to zero
N filespec    ;Name the file
R CX          ;Request CX register
length        ;Insert file size as hex value in CX
W             ;Write the file
```

If you modify a file and make no change to its length or name, DEBUG can still correctly write the file back to its original disk location. You may also write a file directly to specific disk sectors, although this practice requires considerable care.

DEBUG commands not covered here are:

- XA: Allocate expanded memory.
- XD: Deallocate expanded memory.
- XM: Map logical pages onto physical pages.
- XS: Display expanded memory status.

F APPENDIX: KEYBOARD SCAN CODES AND ASCII CODES

In the following lists, keys are grouped rather arbitrarily into categories. For each category, the columns show the format for a normal key (not combined with another key) and formats when the key is combined with the Shift, Ctrl, and Alt keys. Under the columns headed "Normal," "Shift," "Ctrl," and "Alt" are two hex bytes as they appear when a keyboard operation delivers them to the AH and AL registers. For example, pressing the letter "a" delivers 1EH in the AH for the scan code and 61H in the AL for the ASCII character. When shifted to uppercase ("A"), the keyboard delivers 1EH and 41H, respectively. Scan codes 85H and higher are for the extended keyboard.

LETTERS	NORMAL		SHIFT		CTRL		ALT	
a and A	1E	61	1E	41	1E	01	1E	00
b and B	30	62	30	42	30	02	30	00
c and C	2E	63	2E	43	2E	03	2E	00
d and D	20	64	20	44	20	04	20	00
e and E	12	65	12	45	12	05	12	00
f and F	21	66	21	46	21	06	21	00
g and G	22	67	22	47	22	07	22	00
h and H	23	68	23	48	23	08	23	00
i and I	17	69	17	49	17	09	17	00

j and J	24	6A	24	4A	24	0A	24	00
k and K	25	6B	25	4B	25	0B	25	00
l and L	26	6C	26	4C	26	0C	26	00
m and M	32	6D	32	4D	32	0D	32	00
n and N	31	6E	31	4E	31	0E	31	00
o and O	18	6F	18	4F	18	0F	18	00
p and P	19	70	19	50	19	10	19	00
q and Q	10	71	10	51	10	11	10	00
r and R	13	72	13	52	13	12	13	00
s and S	1F	73	1F	53	1F	13	1F	00
t and T	14	74	14	54	14	14	14	00
u and U	16	75	16	55	16	15	16	00
v and V	2F	76	2F	56	2F	16	2F	00
w and W	11	77	11	57	11	17	11	00
x and X	2D	78	2D	58	2D	18	2D	00
y and Y	15	79	15	59	15	19	15	00
z and Z	2C	7A	2C	5C	2C	1A	2C	00
Spacebar	39	20	39	20	39	20	39	20

FUNCTION KEYS	**NORMAL**		**SHIFT**		**CTRL**		**ALT**	
F1	3B	00	54	00	5E	00	68	00
F2	3C	00	55	00	5F	00	69	00
F3	3D	00	56	00	60	00	6A	00
F4	3E	00	57	00	61	00	6B	00
F5	3F	00	58	00	62	00	6C	00
F6	40	00	59	00	63	00	6D	00
F7	41	00	5A	00	64	00	6E	00
F8	42	00	5B	00	65	00	6F	00
F9	43	00	5C	00	66	00	70	00
F10	44	00	5D	00	67	00	71	00
F11	85	00	87	00	89	00	8B	00
F12	86	00	88	00	8A	00	8C	00

NUMERIC KEYPAD	**NORMAL**		**SHIFT**		**CTRL**		**ALT**	
Ins and 0	52	00	52	30	92	00		
End and 1	4F	00	4F	31	75	00	00	01

DnArrow and 2	50	00	50	32	91	00	00	02
PgDn and 3	51	00	51	33	76	00	00	03
LtArrow and 4	4B	00	4B	34	73	00	00	04
5 (keypad)	4C	00	4C	35	8F	00	00	05
RtArrow and 6	4D	00	4D	36	74	00	00	06
Home and 7	47	00	47	37	77	00	00	07
UpArrow and 8	48	00	48	38	8D	00	00	08
PgUp and 9	49	00	49	39	84	00	00	09
+ (gray key)	4E	2B	4E	2B	90	00	4E	00
− (gray key)	4A	2D	4A	2D	8E	00	4A	00
Del and .	53	00	53	2E	93	00		
* (gray key)	37	2A	37	2A	96	00	37	00

TOP ROW	**NORMAL**		**SHIFT**		**CTRL**		**ALT**	
` and ~	29	60	29	7E			29	00
1 and !	02	31	02	21			78	00
2 and @	03	32	03	40	03	00	79	00
3 and #	04	33	04	23			7A	00
4 and $	05	34	05	24			7B	00
5 and %	06	35	06	25			7C	00
6 and ^	07	36	07	5E	07	1E	7D	00
7 and &	08	37	08	26			7E	00
8 and *	09	38	09	2A			7F	00
9 and (	0A	39	0A	38			80	00
0 and)	0B	30	0B	29			81	00
− and _	0C	2D	0C	5F	0C	1F	82	00
= and +	0D	3D	0D	2B			83	00

OPERATION KEYS	**NORMAL**		**SHIFT**		**CTRL**		**ALT**	
Esc	01	1B	01	1B	01	1B	01	00
Backspace	0E	08	0E	08	0E	7F	0E	00
Tab	0F	09	0F	00	94	00	A5	00
Enter	1C	0D	1C	0D	1C	0A	1C	00

PUNCTUATION	**NORMAL**		**SHIFT**		**CTRL**		**ALT**	
[and {	1A	5B	1A	7B	1A	1B	1A	00
] and }	1B	5D	1B	7D	1B	1D	1B	00

<table>
<tr><td>; and :</td><td>27</td><td>3B</td><td>27</td><td>3A</td><td></td><td></td><td>27</td><td>00</td></tr>
<tr><td>‘ and “</td><td>28</td><td>27</td><td>28</td><td>22</td><td></td><td></td><td>28</td><td>00</td></tr>
<tr><td>\ and |</td><td>2B</td><td>5C</td><td>2B</td><td>7C</td><td>2B</td><td>1C</td><td>2B</td><td>00</td></tr>
<tr><td>, and <</td><td>33</td><td>2C</td><td>33</td><td>3C</td><td></td><td></td><td>33</td><td>00</td></tr>
<tr><td>. and ></td><td>34</td><td>2E</td><td>34</td><td>3E</td><td></td><td></td><td>34</td><td>00</td></tr>
<tr><td>/ and ?</td><td>35</td><td>2F</td><td>35</td><td>3F</td><td></td><td></td><td>35</td><td>00</td></tr>
</table>

Following are the duplicate keys for the enhanced keyboard (the first two entries are ASCII characters, and the rest are cursor keys):

KEY	NORMAL		SHIFT		CTRL		ALT	
Slash (/)	E0	2F	E0	2F	95	00	A4	00
Enter	E0	0D	E0	0D	E0	0A	A6	00
Home	47	E0	47	E0	77	E0	97	00
End	4F	E0	4F	E0	75	E0	9F	00
PageUp	49	E0	49	E0	84	E0	99	00
PageDown	51	E0	51	E0	76	E0	A1	00
DownArrow	50	E0	50	E0	91	E0	A0	00
LeftArrow	4B	E0	4B	E0	73	E0	9B	00
RightArrow	4D	E0	4D	E0	74	E0	9D	00
UpArrow	48	E0	48	E0	8D	E0	98	00
Ins	52	E0	52	E0	92	E0	A2	00
Del	53	E0	53	E0	93	E0	A3	00

Control keys also have identifying scan codes, although BIOS doesn't deliver them to the keyboard buffer. Here are their scan codes:

CapsLock	3A	Shift (Right)	36
NumLock	45	Alt	38
ScrollLock	46	Ctrl	1D
Shift (Left)	2A	PrtScreen	37

ANSWERS TO SELECTED QUESTIONS

CHAPTER 1

1-1. (a) Bit.

1-2. (a) Byte.

1-3. (a) Two.

1-4. (a) 0101; (c) 10111.

1-5. (a) 00100010; (c) 00100000.

1-6. (a) 11011010; (c) 10001000.

1-7. (a) 00111100; (c) 00000100.

1-8. (a) 57; (c) 57.

1-9. (a) 24D8; (c) 8000.

1-10. (a) 12; (c) 57; (e) FFF.

1-11. (a) 01010001; (c) 00111111.

1-13. ROM (read-only memory) is permanent, performs startup procedures, and handles input/output. RAM (random-access memory) is temporary and is the area where programs and data reside when executing.

1-15. (a) A section of a program, up to 64K in size, containing code, data, or the stack.

1-16. (a) Stack, data, and code.

1-18. (a) CS, DS, SS; (c) AX, BX, CX, DX, DI, SI; (e) CX.

1-20. (a) MOV BX,36.

CHAPTER 2

2-4. (a) The program segment prefix (PSP).

2-5. (a) DS and ES = address of the PSP.

2-7. (a) The system defines the stack for a .COM program.

2-8. (a) At its highest location, the size of the stack (such as 64) as initialized by the system in the SP.

2-9. (a) 6C3E2H.

2-10. (a) 74AA4H.

2-11. (a) 4D766H.

CHAPTER 3

3-1. The commands are identified at the beginning of the chapter.

3-2. (a) D DS:1A5; (c) E DS:18A 44 4E 41.

3-3. (a) B84B32.

3-4. E CS:101 54.

3-5. (a)
```
MOV  AX,2006
ADD  AX,3000
NOP
```
(c) Use R IP to reset the IP to 100.

3-6. The product is 0568H.

3-8. Use the N command to name the program, set the length in the BX:CX, and use the W command to write the program.

3-11. Start with MOV AH,09 for the display.

CHAPTER 4

4-3. Name (of a data item) and label (of an instruction).

4-4. (a) Valid only if it refers to the CX register; (c) valid.

4-6. (a) PAGE.

4-8. (a) Causes alignment of a segment on a boundary, such as a paragraph.

4-9. (a) Provides a section of related code, such as a subroutine.

4-10. (a) ENDP.

4-11. The END directive tells the assembler that there are no more instructions to assemble; instructions to cause control to return to the operating system are MOV AX,4C00H and INT 21H.

4-12. `ASSUME SS:STKSEG,DS:DATSEG,CS:CDSEG.`

4-15. (a) 1; (c) 10.

4-16. `CONAME DB 'Computer Services'`

4-17. (a) `AREA1 DB 00100011B`

(c) `AREA3 DW ?`

4-18. (a) `Hex 22.`

4-19. (a) `B2254A00; (c) 35.`

CHAPTER 5

5-1. `MASM/TASM E:SQUEEZE E:, E:, E:.`

5-3. (a) `E:SQUEEZE.`

5-4. (a) Executable file (module); (c) link map; (e) cross-reference file.

5-5.
```
MOV AX,DATSEGM
MOV DS,AX
```

5-6. Partial coding:
```
MOV AL,50H     ;Load immed. value
SHL AL,1       ;Shift left (double)
MOV CL,18H     ;Multiply AL
MUL CL         ;  by CL
```

5-8. The data segment should contain these data items:
```
FIELDX DB 50H
FIELDY DB 18H
FIELDZ DW ?
```

5-10. Note the effect of the EVEN directive on the location counter.

CHAPTER 6

6-2. (a) The first ADD adds immediate value 2548H to the CX; the second ADD adds the contents of locations 2548H and 2549H to the CX.

6-4. Add the contents to the DX of the memory location pointed to by the sum of the offset addresses in the BX plus the SI plus 8 (technically by DS:[BX+SI+8]).

6-5. (a) The processor cannot process data directly between memory locations.

6-6. (a) A memory-to-memory operation is invalid; instead, use two instructions:
```
MOV AL,BYTEY
ADD BYTEX,AL
```

6-7. (a) `ADD CX,48H`

(c) `SHR DH,1`

(e) `MOV CX,248`

6-8. Use XCHNG.

6-9. Use LEA (or MOV with OFFSET).

6-11. (a) Pushes the flags, IP, and CS onto the stack, replaces the IF and TF flags, and stores the interrupt address in the CS:IP.

CHAPTER 7

7-1. 64K.

7-4. It uses the high area of the .COM program or, if insufficient space, uses the end of memory.

7-5. (a) `EXE2BIN PRESSURE,PRESSURE.COM.`

CHAPTER 8

8-1. (a) Within −128 and +127 bytes.

8-2. (a) Within −128 and +127 bytes. (b) The operand is a one-byte value allowing for 00H through 7FH (0 through +128) and 80H through FFH (−128 through −1).

8-3. (a) 05DCH; (c) note the sign in FA34H.

8-4. Here is one of many possible solutions:

```
     MOV  AX,00
     MOV  BX,01
     MOV  CX,12
     MOV  DX,00
B20: ADD  AX,BX ;Number is in the AX
     MOV  BX,DX
     MOV  DX,AX
     LOOP B20
```

8-5. (a) `CMP AX,BX` `JBE address` (c) `CMP CX,DX` `JG address` (e) `CMP DX,0` `JE or JZ`

8-6. (a) TF (1); (c) SF (1).

8-8. The first (main) PROC must be FAR because the operating system links to its address for execution. A NEAR attribute means that the address is within this particular segment.

8-10. Three (one for each CALL).

8-11. (a) 11111011; (c) 10011010.

8-12. Lowercase letters a–z are 61H–7AH.

8-13. (a) B972H; (c) 1737H; (e) 72B9H.

CHAPTER 9

9-1. (a) Row = 18H and column = 4FH.

9-3.

```
MOV AX,0613H        ;Request
MOV BH,attribute    ;  clear
MOV CX,0600H        ;  window
MOV DX,184FH
INT 10H             ;Call interrupt service
```

9-4.
```
MSSGE      DB    'What is the date (mm/dd/yy)?',07H,'$'
           MOV   AH,09H        ;Request display
           LEA   DX,MSSGE      ;  of date
           INT   21H           ;Call interrupt service
```

9-5.
```
DATEPAR    LABEL BYTE
MAXLEN     DB    9                 ;Space for slashes and Enter
ACTLEN     DB
DATEFLD    DB    9 DUP(' ')
           ...
           MOV   AH,0AH            ;Request input
           LEA   DX,DATEPAR        ;  of date
           INT   21H               ;Call interrupt service
```

9-8. (a) 04.

CHAPTER 10

10-1. (a) 0110 1110.

10-2. (a) 0000 0001.

10-3. (a)
```
MOV AH,00H          ;Request set mode
MOV AL,02           ;80-column monochrome
INT 10H             ;Call interrupt service
```
(c)
```
MOV AH,060EH        ;Request scroll 14 lines
MOV BH,07           ;Normal video
MOV CX,0000         ;Entire screen
MOV DX,184FH
INT 10H             ;Call interrupt service
```

10-4. Eight colors for background and 16 for foreground.

10-5.
```
MOV AH,09H           ;Request display
MOV AL,05            ;Club
MOV BH,00            ;Page number 0
MOV BL,00011110B     ;Yellow on blue
MOV CX,06            ;Six times
INT 10H              ;Call interrupt service
```

10-8. Note that INT 16H does not advance the cursor or echo the entered characters on the screen. Similarly, INT 10H function 09H does not advance the cursor; also it displays only one unique character at a time.

10-10. (a)
```
MOV AH,00H     ;Request mode
MOV AL,04      ;Resolution 320 x 200
INT 10H        ;Call interrupt service
```

10-11. First set graphics mode, then use INT 10H function 0BH to set the background color.

10-12. First set graphics mode, then use INT 10H function 0DH to read dot.

CHAPTER 11

11-1. (a) Location 40:17H (417H).

11-2. (a) Keyboard input with echo; requires two INT operations if an extended keyboard function.

11-4. (a) 47H; (c) 50H.

11-6. Use INT 16H function 10H for keyboard input, CMP to test the scan code, and use INT 10H function 02H to set the cursor.

11-8. On any press or release of a key.

11-10. (a) Location 40:1EH (41EH).

11-12. (a) CapsLock and NumLock are bits 6 and 3.

CHAPTER 12

12-1. (a) DS:SI and ES:DI.

12-3. (a)

```
        JCXZ  label2     ;CX zero?
label1: MOV   AX,[SI]    ;Get character
        MOV   [DI],AX    ;Store character
        INC   DI         ;Increment
        INC   DI         ;  DI and
        INC   SI         ;  SI by 2
        INC   SI
        LOOP  label1
label2: ...
```

12-4. Set the DF for a right-to-left move. For MOVSB, initialize at HEADG1+9 and HEADG2+9. For MOVSW, initialize at HEADG1+8 and HEADG2+8.

12-6. (a)

```
CLD                   ;Left to right
MOV   CX,18           ;Initialize
LEA   DI,OUTAREA      ;  to move
LEA   SI,DESCRIP      ;  18 bytes
REP   MOVSB           ;Move string
```

(c)

```
CLD                   ;Left to right
LEA   SI,DESCRIP+4    ;Start at 5th byte
LODSW                 ;Load 2 bytes
```

(e)

```
CLD                   ;Left to right
MOV   CX,18           ;18 bytes
LEA   DI,OUTAREA      ;Initialize
LEA   SI,DESCRIP      ;  addresses
REPE  CMPSB           ;Compare strings
```

12-7. Here is one solution:

```
H10SCAS PROC NEAR
        CLD                ;Left to right
        MOV CX,10          ;10 bytes
        LEA DI,HEADG1      ;Initialize address
```

```
        MOV AL,'n'              ;  and scan character
H20:    REPNE SCASB             ;Scan
        JNE H30                 ;Found?
        CMP BYTE PTR[DI],'a'    ;Yes, next byte
        JNE H20                 ;  equals 'a'?
        MOV AL,03
H30:    RET
H10SCAS ENDP
```

12-8. Define PATTERN immediately before DISPLAY, initialize the CX, DI and SI, and use REP MOVSW. Then use INT 21H function 09H to display the data item DISPLAY.

CHAPTER 13

13-1. (a) 32,767 and 65,535.

13-3. (a) OF = 0, CF = 0.

13-5. (a)
```
MOV AX,VALUE2
ADD AX,VALUE1     ;Add VALUE1
MOV VALUE2,AX     ;  to VALUE2
```
(b) See Figure 13-2 for multiword addition.

13-6. STC sets the carry flag. The sum = 0153H plus 0328H plus 1.

13-7. (a)
```
MOV AX,VALUE1
MUL VALUE2     ;Product is in the DX:AX
```
(b) See Figure 13-4 for multiplying doubleword by word.

13-8. (a)
```
MOV AX,VALUE1
MOV BL,36     ;Divide VALUE1
DIV BL        ;  by 36
```

CHAPTER 14

14-1. (a) ADD generates 006DH and AAA generates 0103H.

(c) SUB generates 0002H and AAS has no effect.

14-2. (a) |33|37|39|36|.

14-3.
```
     LEA SI,BCDAMT       ;Initialize address
     MOV CX,04           ;  and 4 loops
B20: OR  [SI],30H        ;Insert ASCII 3
     INC SI              ;Increment for next byte
     LOOP B20            ;Loop 4 times
```

14-4. Use Figure 14-2 as a guide but initialize the CX to 03.

14-5. Use Figure 14-3 as a guide but initialize the CX to 03.

14-6. (a) See Appendix A for the procedure; the answer is 9BA6H.

14-7. Note that INT 12H returns to the AX the size of memory in terms of 1K bytes.

CHAPTER 15

15-2. (a) `TEMPTBL DW 365 DUP (0).`

15-3. (a) `ITEMNO  DB '05','09','12','19','23'`

(c) `ITPRICE DW 1250, 9375, 8745, 7935, 1595`

15-4.
```
ITEMTBL DB '05', 'Videotape'
        DW 1250
        ...
```

15-5. INT 16H function 10H is suggested for keyboard input; Figure 12-2 is a useful guide.

15-6. A possible organization is into the following procedures:

PROCEDURE	PURPOSE
A10MAIN	Initialize registers, call procedures.
B10READ	Display prompt, accept item number.
C10SRCH	Search table, display message if invalid item.
D10MOVE	Extract description and price from table.
E10CONV	Convert quantity from ASCII to binary.
F10CALC	Calculate value (quantity × price).
G10CONV	Convert value from binary to ASCII.
K10DISP	Display description and value on screen.

15-7. The following routine copies the table. Refer to Figure 15-7 for sorting table entries.
```
SORTABL DB  5 DUP(9 DUP(?))
        ...
        LEA SI,ITDESC      ;Initialize
        LEA DI,SORTABL     ;  table addresses and
        MOV CX,45          ;  number   of characters
        CLD                ;Left to right
        REP MOVSB          ;Move string
```

15-8. Define the ASCII values to be converted in the table:
```
ASCTABL DB 75 DUP(20H) ;
        ...
```

15-9. The intention is to use XLAT for translation.

CHAPTER 16

16-1. 512.

16-4. (a) A group of sectors (1, 2, 4, or 8) that the system treats as a unit of storage space on a disk.

16-5. (a) 80 cylinders × 18 sectors × 2 sides × 512 bytes = 1,474,560.

16-7. (a) Helps the system load its programs into memory.

16-8. In the directory, the first byte of filename is set to E5H.

16-9. (a) 00H.

16-11. (a) Positions 28–31 of the directory; (b) 0C5DH, stored as 5D0C.

16-12. (a) The first byte (media descriptor) contains F8H.

CHAPTER 17

17-1. (a) 06.

17-3. (a) `FHANDLE DW ?`

(b) Start the definition like this:

```
PATNTOUT LABEL BYTE
```

followed by a DB for each data item.

(c) Use INT 21H function 3CH to create the file, use JC to test for an error, and save the handle.

17-4. (a)

```
MOV AH,3DH          ;Request open
MOV AL,00           ;Read only
LEA DX,ASCPATH      ;ASCIIZ string
INT 21H             ;Call interrupt service
JC  error           ;Exit if error
MOV FHANDLE,AX      ;Save handle
```

17-5. Where a program opens many files.

17-7. Use Figure 17-2 as a guide for creating a disk file and Figure 14-5 for conversion from ASCII to binary.

17-8. Use Figure 17-3 as a guide for reading the file and Figure 14-6 for conversion from binary to ASCII.

17-10. See Figure 17-4 for the use of function 42H.

17-11. All the functions involve INT 21H: (a) 16H; (c) 15H.

17-12. (a) 128 bytes; (c) 144 (9 sectors × 4 tracks × 4 records/sector).

CHAPTER 18

All the questions for this chapter are exercises involving the use of DEBUG.

CHAPTER 19

19-2. Most likely as a developer of disk utility programs.

19-3. (a) In the AH.

19-5. Use INT 13H function 00H.

19-6. Use INT 13H function 01H.

19-8.

```
MOV AH,03H          ;Request write
MOV AL,01           ;1 sector
LEA BX,DATAOUT      ;Output area
MOV CH,07           ;Track 07
MOV CL,03           ;Sector 03
```

```
MOV DH,00             ;Head #0
MOV DL,00             ;Drive A
INT 13H               ;Call interrupt service
```

19-9. The status byte in the AH contains 00000011.

CHAPTER 20

20-1. (a) 0DH.

20-3. (a)
```
      MOV  AH,05H          ;Request print
      MOV  DL,0CH          ;Form feed
      INT  21H             ;Call interrupt service
```
(b)
```
      LEA  SI,NAMEFLD      ;Initialize name
      MOV  CX,length       ;  and length
B20:  MOV  AH,05H          ;Request print
      MOV  DL,[SI]         ;Character from name
      INT  21H             ;Call interrupt service
      INC  SI              ;Next character in name
      LOOP B20             ;Loop length times
```
(c) You could code a line feed (0AH) in front of the address. The solution is similar to part (b).

(e) Issue another form feed (0CH).

20-4. `HEADNG DB 13, 10, 15, 'Title', 12`

20-6. (a) Input/output error.

20-8. The CX is not available for looping because the loop that prints the name uses the CX. You could use the BX like this:
```
      MOV  BX,05     ;Set 5 loops
C20:  ...
      DEC  BX        ;Decrement loop count
      JNZ  C20       ;Loop if still nonzero
```

20-9. Figure 20-1 uses INT 21H function 40H. For function 05H, revise the solution according to the one in Question 20-3.

CHAPTER 21

21-1. (a) Unit of measure for mouse movement in increments of 1/200 of an inch.

21-2. All these functions are identified near the beginning of the chapter.

21-3. Controls display of the mouse pointer; displays when zero and conceals when nonzero.

21-4. (a)
```
MOV AX,00H
INT 33H
```

21-5. Run this program under DEBUG to view the returned values.

21-6. Note that the figure reverses the parallel ports, LPT1 and LPT2.

CHAPTER 22

22-1. The introduction to this chapter gives three reasons.

22-2. The statements include MACRO and ENDM.

22-5. (a) `.XALL`.

22-6. (a)
```
MULTBYTE MACRO  MULTPR,MULTCD
         MOV    AL,MULTCD
         MUL    MULTPR
         ENDM
```

22-7. To include the macro in pass 1, code the following:
```
IF1
     INCLUDE library-name
ENDIF
```

22-8. The macro definition could begin with
```
PRINT17 MACRO PRTLINE,PRLEN
```
`PRTLINE` and `PRLEN` are dummy arguments for the address and length, respectively, of the line to be printed. See Chapter 20 for using INT 17H to print.

22-9. Note that you cannot use a conditional IF to test for a zero divisor. A conditional IF works only during assembly, whereas the test must occur during program execution. Code assembly instructions such as these:
```
CMP DIVISOR,00     ;Zero divisor?
JNZ (bypass)       ;No, bypass
CALL (error message routine)
```

22-10. Parts (a) and (b) involve Question 22-6; part (c) involves Question 22-8 for printing and Chapter 14 on converting binary to ASCII format.

CHAPTER 23

23-1. The introduction to this chapter gives the reasons.

23-2. (a) PARA.

23-3. (a) NONE.

23-4. (a) 'code'.

23-6. (a) `EXTRN SCALC23:FAR`

23-7. (a) `PUBLIC QTY,VALUE,PRICE`

23-8. Use Figure 23-6 as a guide.

23-9. Use Figure 23-8 as a guide for passing parameters. However, this question involves pushing three variables onto the stack. The called program therefore has to access [BP+10] for the third entry (UNITCOST) in the stack. You can define your own standard for returning UNITCOST through the stack. Watch also for the pop-value in the RET operand.

23-10. This program involves material from Chapters 9 (screen I/0), 13 (binary multiplication), 14 (conversion between ASCII and binary), and 23 (linkage to subprograms). Be careful of using the stack.

CHAPTER 24

24-1. (a) In sector 1, track 0.

24-2. Acts as a low-level interface to the BIOS routines in ROM.

24-4. (a) Following MSDOS.SYS.

24-5. (a) The first 256 bytes of a program when loaded in memory for execution.

24-6.
```
5CH: 05 53 4C 49 4D 20 20 20 20 41 53 4D
80H: 0B 20 45 3A 53 4C 49 4D 2E 41 53 4D 0D
```

24-8. (a) 2CD4.

24-9. (a) 1B38[0] + 100H (PSP) + 0H = 1B48[0].

24-10. (a) The start of a memory block (not the last one).

24-11. INT 09H, in the interrupt vector table at 24H.

CHAPTER 25

25-1. The section on interrupts at the start of this chapter discusses these types.

25-2. The section on interrupts at the start of this chapter discusses these lines.

25-3. (a) FFFF[0]H.

25-5. At segment address 40[0]H.

25-6. (a) Equipment status; (c) second byte of shift status.

25-7. (a) The addresses (in reverse-byte sequence) of COM1 and COM2.

25-8. (a) INT 12H; (c) INT 11H.

25-9. INT 20H through 3FH.

25-10. (a) 31H; (c) 39H.

25-11. (a) Communications input; (c) reset disk drive.

INDEX

.286/.386/.486/.586 directives, 516
80x86 processors, 7, 8
80x87 coprocessor, 241
@CODE equate, 83
@CODESIZE equate, 83
@CPU equate, 80, 83
@DATASIZE equate, 83
@FILENAME equate, 83
@VERSION equate, 83

A (Assemble) DEBUG command, 30, 41, 573
A20 line, 446
AAA instruction, 246, 529
AAD instruction, 249, 530
AAM instruction, 249, 530
AAS instruction, 246, 530
ABS type, 424
Absolute disk I/O, 324
Accessing the PSP, 452
ADC instruction, 227, 530
ADD instruction, 37, 39, 222, 531
Adding
  ASCII data, 246
  binary data, 4, 222
  with carry. *See* ADC instruction
Address
  alignment, 104
  displacement, 97
  far, 115
  near, 115
  of memory location, 11
  of PSP, 493
  of segment, 501
  short, 115
Addressing, 25
  capacity, 13
  mode byte, 526
Adjusting ASCII data, 246, 530
AF flag, 17, 119
AH register, 15
AL register, 15
Align type operand, 55, 420, 519
ALIGN directive, 89, 104, 504
Aligning data, 89, 104, 504
Allocating memory, 461
.ALPHA directive, 505
Alphanumeric comparison, 211
Alt key, 186, 191, 199
Alternate disk reset, 366
AND instruction, 127, 531
AND logical operator, 500
Archive file, 295
Arena header, 452
Arithmetic
  carry, 4, 221
  operators, 498
  overflow, 221, 223
ASCII
  addition, 246
  adjust after addition. *See* AAA
  adjust after multiplication. *See* AAM
  adjust after subtraction. *See* AAS
  adjust before division. *See* AAD
  character set, 143, 167, 201, 560
  code, 7

ASCII (*cont.*)
  data, 7, 246, 253, 255, 529, 530
  division, 250
  file, 320, 374
  multiplication, 249
  subtraction, 247
ASCIIZ string, 305
.ASM file, 75
Assembler program, 50, 83
Assembly
  diagnostics, 87
  language, 41, 49
  of a program, 74, 564
  options, 566
  steps, 75
  with a command line, 564
  with prompts, 565
ASSUME directive, 56, 58, 59, 79, 505
AT combine type, 199, 520
Attribute byte (screen), 159, 161
Attribute of file. *See* File attribute
AUTOEXEC.BAT, 22
Auxiliary carry flag (AF), 17, 119
AX register, 15

Background (screen), 159
Backward jump, 116
Base memory, 43
Base pointer register. *See* BP register
Base register. *See* BX register
Basic Input/Output System. *See* BIOS
BCD (binary-coded decimal)
  addition, 251
  format, 67
  packed, 245, 251
  unpacked, 245, 249
Bell character, 147
Best fit strategy, 455
BH register, 16
Binary
  addition, 222, 531
  arithmetic, 4, 220
  data, 3, 64, 253, 255
  subtraction, 5, 222
Binary-coded decimal format. *See* BCD
BIOS, 10
  data area, 22, 32, 479
  disk operations, 357
  DOS interface, 487
  interrupts, 483
  status byte, 358
Bit, 1, 3
  rotating instructions, 132
  scan, 531
  shifting instructions, 130
  test, 532
BL register, 16
Blinking (screen), 159
Boolean operations, 127
Boot program, 21, 478
Boot record, 293, 294, 300, 301, 445
Bootstrap loader, 22, 486
BP (base pointer) register, 15, 435
Break point, 484
BSF/BSR instructions, 531
BT/BTn instructions, 532
Buffer for keyboard, 187, 189, 197
Bus interface unit (BIU), 8
Button (mouse), 386–388
BX register, 16, 97, 499
Byte, 1, 2, 65
BYTE
  attribute, 144
  boundary, 420, 519
  directive. *See* DB directive

C (Compare) DEBUG command, 573
C program, 440
Calculation operator, 498
CALL
  instruction, 123, 126, 426, 427, 429, 435, 532
  intersegment, 422
  intrasegment, 422
Calling procedures, 123
Capacity of a disk, 292
CapsLock key, 186, 191
Carriage return character, 149, 370
Carry flag (CF), 17, 119
Carry into/out of sign bit, 5, 221
CBW instruction, 224, 532
CDQ instruction, 533
CF flag. *See* Carry flag
CH register, 16
Change
  current directory, 346
  diskette status, 367
  uppercase to lowercase, 129
Character generator, 167
Character string, 64
Checking
  copyright notice, 33
  input status, 337
  keyboard status, 189
  memory size, 32
  model ID, 33
  output status, 338
  ROM BIOS date, 33
  serial number, 33
  system equipment, 32
CL register, 16
Class type, 55, 421, 520
CLC instruction, 227, 533
CLD instruction, 205, 533
Clear
  carry flag. *See* CLC instruction
  direction flag. *See* CLD instruction
  keyboard buffer, 189
  input area, 148
  screen, 141
CLI instruction, 533
Clock, 487
Close file, 302, 308, 327
Cluster on disk, 291
CMC instruction, 533
CMP instruction, 120, 534
CMPCHG8B instruction, 535
CMPS instruction, 203, 205, 211, 534
CMPSB instruction, 211, 212, 534
CMPSD/CMPSW instruction, 534
CMPXCHG instruction, 534
.CODE directive, 506
Code segment, 11, 12, 59, 79
Code segment register. *See* CS register
Cold boot, 21
Colon (:) for label, 115
Color display, 159
Color palette, 178
.COM program, 22, 23, 108, 456, 570
  code segment, 109
  conversion, 109

data segment, 109
initialization, 109
segment, 109
stack, 109, 111
Combine type, 55, 421, 519
COMM directive, 506
COMMAND.COM, 21, 446
COMMENT directive, 506
Comments
in a macro, 403
in a program, 50, 506
COMMON combine type, 421, 520
Common data in subprograms, 430, 432
Communications
input, 488
input/output, 485
output, 489
port, 485
COMPACT memory model, 61, 513
Comparing
data, 120
instructions, 120, 534
strings, 211
Compiler, 50
Completion status, 305
CON reply (linking), 84, 570
Concatenation (&) in macros, 410
Conceal mouse pointer, 386
Condensed print mode, 379
Conditional directives, 412
Conditional jump, 121, 122, 540
CONFIG.SYS, 22
.CONST directive, 507
Contents of a memory location, 11
Control characters for printing, 370, 379
Control characters for screen, 149
Control keys (keyboard), 186
Control+Break address, 488
Controller diagnostics, 366
Conventional segment definition, 76
Converting
ASCII data to binary, 253
binary data to ASCII, 255
byte to word. *See* CBW
decimal to hexadecimal, 558
doubleword to quadword. *See* CDQ
.EXE to .COM format, 109
hexadecimal to decimal, 557
word to doubleword. *See* CWD
Coprocessor, 241
Copyright notice, 33
Correcting a DEBUG entry, 38
Country-dependent information, 492
Creating
disk file, 302, 306, 307, 308, 326
new file, 353
subdirectory, 345
temporary file, 353
CREF command, 86, 568
.CREF directive, 507
.CRF file, 76, 86, 568
Critical-error handler, 488
Cross-reference file, 76, 568
Cross-reference listing, 86, 568
CS register, 11, 12, 14, 23, 56
CS:IP pair, 14, 23, 25
Ctrl key, 186, 191, 199
Ctrl+Break
exit address, 448
interrupt, 487
request, 189
Ctrl+C state, 491
Cursor, 140, 162
CWD/CWDE instructions, 224, 535
CX register, 16
Cylinder, 290

D (Display) DEBUG command, 30, 31, 573
d-bit, 527, 528
DAA instruction, 251, 535
DAS instruction, 251, 536
Data, 10, 507
definition, 62
item, 2
Data segment, 11, 12, 59, 68, 78
.DATA directive, 507
_DATA segment name, 61, 82
Date
file created, 295
get/set, 352, 490
in BIOS, 43, 490
in directory/file, 295, 352
DB (define byte) directive, 46, 65
DD (define doubleword) directive, 67
DEBUG
commands, 573
display, 31
program, 30, 572
Debugging options, 570
DEC instruction, 101, 536
Decimal adjust after addition. *See* DAA
Decimal adjust after subtraction. *See* DAS
Decimal format, 64, 245
Decimal point, 257
Default DTA buffer, 449
Defining
byte, 46, 65
doubleword, 67
farword, 67
macros, 401
quadword, 68
table, 265
tenbytes, 68
word, 67
Delete file, 349, 353
Destination index register. *See* DI register
Destination operand, 94
Determine if removable media, 338
Determine type of video adapter, 182
Device parameter block (DPB), 339
DF (define farword), 67
DF flag. *See* Direction flag
DH register, 16
DI register, 16
Diagnostics (assembly), 87
DIR command, 464
Direct addressing of a table, 267
Direct memory address (DMA), 291
Direct memory operand, 95
Direct video display, 173
Direction flag (DF), 17, 120, 205
Directives, 51, 52, 53, 63, 504
for defining data, 65
for processor, 516
Directory, 294, 300, 301

Disk
capacity, 292
cluster, 291
controller, 290, 291
data area, 293
device information, 337
drive parameters, 364
error codes, 342
file, 302
record, 302
sectors, 290
storage organization, 289
system area, 292
tracks, 290
transfer area. *See* DTA
write verification, 335
Diskette drive data area, 480
Diskette/hard disk data area, 482
Display
ASCII characters, 142
attribute/character, 165, 178
character, 166, 178
character string, 167
hex and ASCII characters, 278
memory contents, 37
menu, 170
mouse pointer, 386
on the screen, 151
DIV instruction, 235, 536
Division
ASCII data, 250
binary, 235, 536, 537
by shifting, 239
by subtraction, 239
by zero, 484
overflow, 238
signed, 238
unsigned, 237
DL register, 16
Dollar sign ($) delimiter, 142
DOS busy flag, 474
DOS functions, 21
DOS interrupts, 487
DOS version flag, 491
.DOSSEG directive, 507
Dots-on characters, 170
Doubleword
boundary, 420
defined, 2, 67
multiplication, 231
values, 225
shift and rotate, 134
DPB. *See* Drive parameter block
DQ directive, 68
Drive diagnostics, 366
Drive parameter block (DPB), 335, 336, 340
Drop shadow, 170, 193
DS register, 11, 12, 14, 23, 56
DS:SI pair, 204
DT directive, 68
DTA (disk transfer area), 327, 328, 449, 450, 491
Duplicate a file handle, 350
Duplicate a pattern, 215
DW directive, 67
DWORD
directive. *See* DD directive
type specifier, 420, 519
DX register, 16
Dynamic execution, 9

E (Enter) DEBUG command, 30, 34, 39, 573
EAX register, 15
EBCDIC data, 277
EBX register, 16
ECHO directive, 514
ECX register, 16
EDX register, 16
Eflags register, 17
EIP register, 14
ELSE directive (macros), 412
Emphasized print mode, 379
END directive, 57, 507
End of
file, 312, 316
input data (keyboard), 148
page, 371
program execution, 58, 59
.ENDIF directive, 409
ENDM directive, 401
ENDP directive, 56, 123, 508
ENDS directive, 54, 508
Enhanced keyboard, 187
Enter character (keyboard), 145
Entry point to BIOS, 21
Environment, 449
EQU directive, 69, 508
Equipment
status, 32, 479
determination, 484
.ERR directives, 509
Error diagnostics, 87
Error return codes, 305
ES register, 14, 204, 451
ES:DI pair, 204
Esc character, 379
ESC instruction, 536
ESI register, 16
ESP register, 15
EVEN directive, 89, 104, 509
Even-numbered (word) address, 104
Even parity, 2
Event handler (mouse), 389
.EXE program, 22, 23, 25, 57, 456
EXE2BIN program, 110, 570
Executing
a program, 86
a program function, 463
program instructions, 29, 35, 40
Execution unit (EU), 8
.EXIT directive, 62
EXITM directive, 413
Expanded print mode, 379
Expression (in an operand), 63
Extended ASCII characters, 170
Extended error code, 342
Extended function keys, 186, 190, 191
Extended memory, 486
Extended move, 101
EXTERN directive. *See* EXTRN
External reference, 426
Extra segment register. *See* ES register
EXTRN directive, 423, 424, 425, 431, 510

F (Fill) DEBUG command, 573
Far address, 104, 115
Far call, 422, 427, 429
Far call and return, 124
Far return, 437
FAR operator, 56, 123, 124, 422
.FARDATA directive, 511
Farword constant, 67
FAT (file allocation table), 293, 296–301
FCB (file control block), 325
Field, 2
File
attribute, 295, 349, 452
date and time, 352
disk, 302
management, 21

pointer, 306, 316
size, 295
File allocation table. *See* FAT
File control block (FCB), 325
File handle, 150, 305, 350
File handle table, 448
Filename, 295
Filename extension, 295
Find matching file, 350, 351
Flags register, 16, 35, 119
Foreground (screen), 159
Form feed, 370, 378
Format tracks, 339, 364
Forward jump, 116
Forward reference in assembly, 83
Free allocated memory, 462
Frequency of note, 397
FS register, 14
Function keys, 186
FWORD directive, 67

G (Go) DEBUG command, 30, 573
General-purpose registers, 15
Generating sound, 397
Get
address of internal DOS list, 453
address of PSP, 451
button-press information, 387
button-release information, 388
button status, 386
current date, 43
current directory, 346
current video mode, 166
default disk drive, 334
default drive parameter block (DPB), 335
device information, 336
device parameters, 339
disk drive parameters, 364
disk type, 366
display page for pointer, 391
DOS version, 447, 491
drive parameter block (DPB), 336
extended error, 341
file attribute, 349
file date and time, 352
free disk space, 336
information for default drive, 334
information for specific drive, 334
media ID, 340
mouse information, 391
mouse sensitivity, 390
printer port status, 381
time, 487, 490
verify state, 341
Global reference, 426
Graphics mode, 140, 175
GROUP directive, 511
GS register, 14

H (Hexadecimal) DEBUG command, 575
Hard disk. *See* Disk
Hard disk data area, 481
Hardware, 1
Header record, 456, 459
Hexadecimal (Hex)
arithmetic, 7
decimal conversion table, 559
representation, 6, 64
Hidden file, 295
High-level language, 50
High-memory area, 446
HIGH operator, 499
HIGHWORD operator, 499
HLT instruction, 537
HMA (high memory area), 446
HUGE memory model, 513

I (Input) DEBUG command, 575
I/O control for devices, 336
IBMDOS.COM/IBMBIO.COM, 21
Identifier, 51, 52
IDIV instruction, 235, 238, 537
IF directive, 412, 414
IF flag. *See* Interrupt flag
IF1/IF2 directives, 409, 412
IFB/IFNB directives, 412, 413
IFDEF/IFNDEF directives, 412, 414
IFDIF/IFIDN directives, 412, 414
IFE directive, 412
Immediate data, 34, 95, 99
IMUL instruction, 228, 234, 537
IN instruction, 394, 538
INC instruction, 101, 538
INCLUDE directive, 407, 511
Index
operator, 26, 27, 96, 499
register, 16, 499
specifier, 96, 147
Indexing, 101, 499
Indirect addressing, 96
Indirect memory operand, 96
inDOS flag, 474
Initialize
.COM program, 109
data segment, 58, 79
disk drive, 365
.EXE program, 57
mouse, 385
program, 57
Initialized value, 63
Input/output, 21
Input/output interface, 22
Input string, 539
INS/INSn instruction, 395, 539
Instruction
format, 52
label, 115
operands, 27
queue, 8
set, 91, 525, 529
Instruction pointer register. *See* IP register
INT instruction, 42, 103, 539
INT 00H Divide by zero, 484
INT 01H Single step, 484
INT 02H Nonmaskable interrupt, 484
INT 03H Break point, 484
INT 04H Overflow, 484
INT 05H Print screen, 484
INT 08H Timer, 484
INT 09H Keyboard interrupt, 197, 198, 484
INT 0BH Control COM1 port, 484
INT 0CH Control COM2 port, 484
INT 0DH Parallel device control, 484
INT 0EH Diskette control, 484
INT 10H Video functions, 161, 177, 484
00H set video mode, 161, 175, 177
01H set cursor size, 162
02H set cursor position, 140, 162

INT 10H Video functions (*cont.*)
03H read cursor position, 162
04H read light pen position, 178
05H select active page, 163
06H scroll up screen, 141, 163
07H scroll down screen, 164
08H read attribute/character, 164, 178
09H display attribute/character, 165, 178
0AH display character, 166, 178
0BH set color palette, 178
0CH write pixel dot, 179
0DH read pixel dot, 179
0EH write teletype, 166
0FH get current video mode, 166
10H set palette registers, 179
11H character generator, 167
12H alternative screen routine, 167
13H display character string, 167
1AH read/write combination code, 180
1BH get functionality information, 180
1CH save/restore video state, 180
INT 11H Equipment determination, 242, 484
INT 12H Memory size determination, 43, 485
INT 13H Disk functions, 358, 485
00H reset disk system, 358
01H read disk status, 359
02H read disk sectors, 359
03H write disk sectors, 360
04H verify sectors, 363
05H format tracks, 364
08H get drive parameters, 364
09H initialize drive, 365
0AH read extended sector buffer, 365
0BH write extended sector buffer, 365
0CH seek disk cylinder, 365
0DH alternate disk reset, 366
0EH read sector buffer, 366
0FH write sector buffer, 366
10H test for drive ready, 366
11H recalibrate hard drive, 366
12H ROM diagnostics, 366
13H drive diagnostics, 366
14H controller diagnostics, 366
15H get disk type, 366
16H change of diskette status, 367
17H set diskette type, 367
18H set media type, 367
19H park disk heads, 367
INT 14H Communications I/O, 485
INT 15H System services, 486
INT 16H keyboard functions, 44, 189, 198, 486
00H read character, 189
01H check if character present, 190
02H get shift status, 190
05H keyboard write, 190
10H read character, 190
11H check if character present, 191
12H get shift status, 191
INT 17H BIOS print functions, 486
00H print character, 380
01H initialize printer port, 380
02H get port status, 381
INT 18H ROM BASIC entry, 486
INT 19H Bootstrap loader, 486
INT 1AH Read and set time, 486
INT 1BH Control on keyboard break, 487
INT 20H Terminate program, 487
INT 21H system functions, 44, 59
00H terminate program, 488
01H keyboard input with echo, 188
02H display character, 150
03H communications input, 488
04H communications output, 489
05H printer output, 378
06H direct keyboard/display, 188
07H direct keyboard input without echo, 189
08H keyboard input without echo, 189
09H display string, 142
0AH buffered keyboard input, 144, 189
0BH check keyboard status, 189
0CH clear buffer and invoke input, 189
0DH reset disk drive, 333
0EH select default disk drive, 333
0FH open FCB file, 328
10H close FCB file, 327
11H get first matching disk entry, 489
12H get next matching disk entry, 489
13H delete FCB file, 489
14H read FCB record, 328
15H write FCB record, 327
16H create FCB file, 326
17H rename FCB file, 489
19H determine default drive, 334
1BH get information for default drive, 334
1CH get information for specific drive, 334
1FH get default DPB, 335
21H read FCB record randomly, 328
22H write FCB record randomly, 329
23H get FCB file size, 490
25H set interrupt vector, 471, 490
26H create new PSP, 490
27H read block randomly, 329
28H write block randomly, 329
29H parse filename, 348
2AH get system date, 490
2BH set system date, 490
2CH get system time, 490
2DH set system time, 490
2EH set/reset disk verification, 335
2FH get address of DTA, 491
30H get DOS version, 491
31H terminate stay resident, 470
32H get DPB, 336

3300H get/check Ctrl+C state, 491
3305H get startup drive, 491
3306H get DOS version, 491
34H get address of DOS busy flag, 474
35H get interrupt vector, 471
36H get free disk space, 336
38H get/set country-dependent information, 492
39H create subdirectory, 345
3AH remove subdirectory, 345
3BH change current directory, 346
3CH create file with handle, 307
3DH open file with handle, 311
3EH close file with handle, 308
3FH read file/device, 152, 312
40H write file/device, 151, 307, 370
41H delete file from directory, 349
42H move file pointer, 316
43H check/change file attribute, 349
44H I/O control for devices, 336, 492
4400H get device information, 336
4401H set device information, 337
4404H read control data, 337
4405H write control data, 337
4406H check input status, 337
4407H check output status, 338
4408H determine if removable media, 338
440DH minor code 41H write sector, 338
440DH minor code 42H format track, 339
440DH minor code 46H set media ID, 339
440DH minor code 60H get device parameters, 339
440DH minor code 61H read sector, 340
440DH minor code 66H get media ID, 340
440DH minor code 68H sense media type, 341
45H duplicate a file handle, 350
46H force duplicate of handle, 350
47H get current directory, 346
48H allocate memory, 461
49H free allocated memory, 462
4AH modify allocated memory, 462
4BH load/execute program, 462
4CH terminate program, 59
4DH get subprogram return value, 464
4EH find first matching directory entry, 350
4FH find next matching directory entry, 351
50H set address of PSP, 493
51H get address of PSP, 451
52H get address of DOS list, 453
54H get verify state, 341
56H rename file, 346, 352
57H get/set file date/time, 352
5800H get memory allocation strategy, 455
5801H set memory allocation strategy, 455
5802H get upper memory link, 455
5803H set upper memory link, 455
59H get extended error code, 341
5AH create temporary file, 353
5BH create new file, 353
5CH lock/unlock file access, 494
5DH set extended error, 494
5EH local area network services, 494
5FH local area network services, 494
62H get address of PSP, 494
65H get extended country information, 494
66H get/set global code page, 494
67H set maximum handle count,
6CH extended open file, 494
INT 22H Terminate address, 488
INT 23H Ctrl+Break address, 488
INT 24H Critical error handler, 488
INT 25H Absolute disk read, 324, 488
INT 26H Absolute disk write, 324, 488
INT 27H Terminate but stay resident, 488
INT 2FH Multiplex interrupt, 488
INT 33H Mouse functions, 384
- 00H initialize mouse, 385
- 01H display mouse pointer, 386
- 02H conceal mouse pointer, 386
- 03H get button status and pointer location, 386
- 04H set pointer location, 387
- 05H get button-press information, 387
- 06H get button-release information, 388
- 07H set horizontal limits for pointer, 388
- 08H set vertical limits for pointer, 388
- 0BH read mouse-motion counters, 389
- 0CH install interrupt handler, 389
- 10H set pointer exclusion area, 390
- 13H set double-speed threshold, 390
- 1AH set mouse sensitivity, 390
- 1BH get mouse sensitivity, 390
- 1DH select display page, 391
- 1EH get display page, 391
- 24H get mouse information, 391

Integer multiplication, 228
Intensity (screen), 159
Internal memory. *See* Memory
Interrupt, 17, 21, 539
- executing, 483
- external, 483
- flag (IF), 17, 120
- handler (mouse), 389
- internal, 483
- services, 482

Interrupt vector, 490
table, 22, 103, 471, 483
Intersegment call, 422
INTO instruction, 539
Intrasegment call, 421
IO.SYS, 21, 446, 487
IOCTL (I/O control for devices), 336
IP register, 14, 23, 26, 37
IRET/IRETD instructions, 539
IRP/IRPC directives, 411

JA/JAE instructions, 540
JB/JBE instructions, 540
JC instruction, 541
JCXZ/JECXZ instructions, 123, 541
JE instruction, 540
JG/JGE instructions, 540
JL/JLE instructions, 540
JMP instruction, 115-117, 541
JNA/JNAE instructions, 540
JNB/JNBE instructions, 540
JNC instruction, 541
JNE instruction, 540
JNG/JNGE instructions, 540
JNL/JNLE instructions, 540
JNO/JNP/JNS instructions, 541
JNZ instruction, 121, 541
JO/JPO instructions, 541
JP/JPE instructions, 541
JS instruction, 541
Jump
backward, 116
forward, 116
near, 116
on condition, 540
operation, 115
short, 116
tables, 134
JZ instruction, 541

Keyboard
buffer, 187, 197, 198
data area-1, 480
data area-2, 482
data area-3, 482
input, 44, 144, 152, 186
INT 16H functions, 189, 190, 191
INT 21H functions, 188, 189
scan codes, 579
status, 186, 189, 190, 191, 198
Keying in data, 153
Kilobyte, 2

L (Load) DEBUG command, 575
Label, 51, 115
LABEL directive, 144, 512
LAHF instruction, 542
.LALL directive, 404
LARGE memory model, 61, 513
Last fit strategy, 455
LDS instruction, 542
LEA instruction, 101, 542
LENGTH operator, 286, 500, 503
LES/LFS/LGS instructions, 542
Library for macros, 407
Line feed, 149, 370, 378
Link
map, 84, 85, 426, 431-437, 458, 469
object program, 74, 83, 84, 569
program, 50
separate modules, 424
to subprograms, 419
with a command line, 569
with C, 440
with Pascal, 437
with prompts, 569
LINK command, 84, 569
Linked list, 281
.LIST directive, 512
Load
a program for execution, 23, 74
a program function, 462
and execute a .COM program, 456
and execute an .EXE program, 456, 458
module, 456
LOCAL directive, 407
Local area network services, 494
Location counter, 89, 514
LOCK instruction, 542
LODS instruction, 203, 205, 207, 209, 543
LODSB instruction, 208, 543
LODSD/LODSW instructions, 543
Logical operators, 500
LOOP instruction, 118, 543
LOOPD instruction, 543
LOOPE/LOOPZ instructions, 119, 543
LOOPED/LOOPEW instructions, 543
LOOPNE/LOOPNZ instructions, 119, 543, 544
LOOPNEW/LOOPNZW instructions, 544
LOOPW instruction, 543
LOOPZD/LOOPZW instructions, 543
LOW operator, 500
Low-level language, 50
LOWWORD operator, 500
LPT printer port, 380, 395
LSS instruction, 542
.LST file, 75, 566

M (Move) DEBUG command, 575
Machine code, 34, 525
Machine language example, 34, 38
Macro
comments, 403
concatenation, 410
conditional directives, 412
definition, 401
dummy argument, 402
expansion, 401
instruction, 403
parameters, 402
stored in library, 407
used within macro definition, 405
MACRO directive, 401
.MAP file, 84
MASK operator, 517
MASM command, 74, 565
Media ID, 339, 340
MEDIUM memory model, 61, 513
Megabyte, 2
Memory, 9, 10
Memory allocation, 454
Memory blocks, 452
Memory control record, 452
Memory management, 21, 445
Memory model, 61, 513
Memory size, 43
data area, 479
determination, 485
Menu, 193
Mickey, 384
Microsoft C, 440

ML assembler command, 567
mod bit reference, 526, 527, 528
Mode byte, 526
.MODEL directive, 61, 513
Monochrome display, 160
Mouse
  button, 387, 388
  event mask, 389
  features, 383
  functions, 384
  information, 391
  interrupt handler, 389
  pixel, 383, 386
  pointer, 384, 386, 387, 388
  pointer exclusion area, 390
  sensitivity, 390
MOV instruction, 79, 36, 39, 97, 544
Move-and-fill instruction, 98
Move data. *See* MOV
Move string. *See* MOVS
MOVS instruction, 203-205, 214, 545
MOVSB/MOVSW/MOVSD instructions, 205, 545
MOVSX instruction, 98, 545
MOVZX instruction, 98, 545
MSDOS.SYS, 21, 446, 487
MUL instruction, 228, 545
Multiplex interrupt, 488
Multiplication
  ASCII data, 249
  binary data, 227, 537, 545
  by shifting, 235
  doubleword, 231
  signed, 229
  unsigned, 229

N (Name) DEBUG command, 30, 45, 576
Name (of data item), 51, 63
Near address, 104, 115
Near call and return, 124
Near jump, 116
NEAR operator, 56, 124, 502
NEG instruction, 240, 546
Negative numbers, 4, 221
.NOCREF directive, 524
.NOLIST directive, 524
NONE combine type, 421, 519
Nonmaskable interrupt, 484
NOP instruction, 42, 546
NOT instruction, 128, 546
NOTHING operand (in ASSUME), 56, 505
Numeric constants, 64
Numeric data processor, 240

O (Output) DEBUG command, 576
.OBJ file, 75, 569
Object program, 73, 569
OF flag. *See* Overflow flag
Offset address, 12, 14, 25, 78, 101
OFFSET operator, 500
Open file, 302, 311
Operand, 34, 53, 63, 94, 95
Operating system, 20, 445
Operation, 53
Operators, 51, 498
  arithmetic, 498
  index, 499
  logical, 500
OR instruction, 127, 546
OR logical operator, 500
ORG directive, 513
Organizing a program, 136
OUT instruction, 394, 547
%OUT directive, 514
OUT/OUTSn instructions, 547
Output string, 547
OUTSn instruction, 396
Overflow flag (OF), 17, 120
Overflow in arithmetic, 221, 223
Overlay, 463
Override segment register, 105

P (Proceed) DEBUG command, 30, 576
Packed BCD data, 245, 251
Page
  heading, 371, 378
  numbering, 373
  on the screen, 161, 163
  overflow, 371
PAGE
  align type, 420, 519
  directive, 53, 57, 515
Palette color, 178
Palette registers, 180
PARA align type, 55, 420, 519
Paragraph, 2, 519
  boundary, 12, 85, 519
Parallel port data area, 479
Parameter
  in a macro, 402
  list (keyboard input), 144
  passing, 433
Parity bit, 2
Parity flag (PF), 17, 119
Park disk heads, 367
Parse filename, 348
Pascal, 437
Passing parameters, 433
Pentium processor, 8
PentiumPro processor, 8
PF flag. *See* Parity flag
Physical sector, 291
Pipeline, 9
Pixel dot, 176, 179
Pointer entry, 297
Pointer registers, 14
POP instruction, 24, 547
Pop-value, 437
POPA/POPAD instructions, 25, 548
POPF/POPFD instructions, 25, 548
Port, 394, 485, 547
  addresses, 394
Predefined symbol, 51
Print characters, 370, 378
Print screen, 484
Printer
  control characters, 370, 379
  line spacing, 379
  port, 380, 381, 395
  status, 380, 381
Printing, 369
PROC directive, 56, 515
Procedure, 56, 123, 515
Processing
  ASCII data, 244
  BCD data, 244
  binary data, 220
  file randomly, 313, 316
Processor, 7
Processor directives, 516
Program
  comments, 50, 506
  entry point, 85
  loader, 21, 22, 58, 126, 456
  logic, 114
  overlay, 463, 464
  segment prefix. *See* PSP, 23
Program examples
  accept and display names, 145

Program examples (*cont.*)
add ASCII numbers, 248
assembler diagnostics, 88
blinking, reverse video, and scrolling, 171
change uppercase to lowercase, 129
check the keyboard status, 200
code segment defined as PUBLIC, 428
.COM source program, 111, 112
convert and add BCD numbers, 254
convert ASCII data, 257
create a disk file, 308
delete files selectively, 353
direct table addressing, 268, 269
display ASCII characters, 167
display hex and ASCII characters, 278
display the directory, 346
divide ASCII numbers, 252
extended move operations, 102
link C to assembler, 443
link Pascal to assembler, 438
linked list, 285
list and suppress macro expansion, 406
multiply ASCII numbers, 250
passing parameters, 436
print an ASCII file, 374
print with page overflow and headings, 371
read a file randomly, 316
read a file sequentially, 313
read an ASCII file, 320
read data from sectors, 342
resident program, 472
right adjusting screen display, 215
select from a menu, 193
set/display graphics mode, 180
sort a table of names, 282
table search using CMP, 273
table search using CMPSB, 275
using a jump table, 135
using a structure, 523
using CMPS string operation, 212
using EXTRN and PUBLIC, 425
using IF and IFNDEF, 407
using immediate operands, 100
using INT 13H to read sectors, 360
using LOCAL in a macro, 408
using LODSB string operation, 208
using macro parameters, 404
using MOVS string operations, 207
using SCASB string operation, 213
using STOSW string operation, 209
using the IFIDN macro, 417
using the JMP instruction, 117
using the LOOP instruction, 118
using the mouse, 391
using the RECORD directive, 518
Program segment prefix. *See* PSP
Protected mode, 60
PSP (program segment prefix), 58, 447, 451, 452, 460, 493
PTR operator, 45, 149, 174, 501
PUBLIC
combine type, 55, 421, 519
directive, 423-433, 516
PURGE directive, 409
PUSH instruction, 24, 435, 548
PUSHA/PUSHAD instructions, 25, 549
PUSHF instruction, 25, 549

Q (Quit) DEBUG command, 30, 576
Quadword, 2, 68
QWORD directive, 68

R (Register) DEBUG command, 30, 35, 576
r/m bit reference, 526, 527, 528
Radix point, 244, 257
Radix specifier, 64
RAM (random access memory). *See* Memory
Random block processing, 329
Random processing, 313, 328
RCL/RCR instructions, 132, 133, 549
Read
and set time, 486
attribute/character, 164, 178
control data from drive, 337
cursor position, 162
disk sector, 340, 359
disk status, 359
extended sector buffer, 365
light pen position, 178
mouse-motion counters, 389
pixel dot, 179
record, 312
sector buffer, 366
Read-only memory (ROM), 10
Real mode, 8, 13, 446
Real value, 65
Real-time clock data area, 482
Recalibrate hard drive, 366
Record, 302, 516
RECORD directive, 516
Record operators, 498
.REF file, 87, 568
reg bit reference, 526, 527, 528
Register, 13
Register notation, 526
Relative byte, 298
Relative sector, 291
Relocation table, 458
Remainder, 236
Removable media, 338
Remove subdirectory, 345
Rename file/directory, 346, 352
REP prefix, 204, 549
REPE/REPZ prefixes, 205, 211, 550
Repetition directives, 410
REPNE/REPNZ prefixes, 205, 213, 550
REPT directive, 410
Reserved words, 51, 562
Resetting
disk drive, 333
disk system, 358
IP register, 37
Resident program, 470
RET instruction, 123, 127, 422, 423, 550
RETF instruction, 423, 437, 550
RETN instruction, 124, 422, 550
Return code, 59
Reverse sign, 240
Reverse video, 171
Reversed-byte storage, 10, 11, 26, 39, 67

Right-adjusting on the screen, 215
Right shifting bits, 130
Rightmost zero for segment address, 13
ROL instruction, 133, 551
ROM, 10
  BIOS date, 33
  diagnostics, 366
ROR instruction, 132, 551
Rotate bits left, 133
Rotate bits right, 132
Rounding a product, 257
Rules of DEBUG commands, 30

S (Search) DEBUG command, 577
SAHF instruction, 551
SAL instruction, 131, 551
.SALL directive, 405
SAR instruction, 130, 551
Save a program in DEBUG, 45
Save pointer data area, 482
SBB instruction, 227, 552
Scan and replace, 214
Scan code, 191, 579
Scan line (screen), 163
Scan string. *See* SCAS
SCAS instruction, 203, 205, 213, 552
SCASB instruction, 213, 552
SCASD/SCASW instructions, 552
Screen, 140
  background, 159
  blinking, 159
  display, 44, 142, 150, 151
  foreground, 159
  intensity, 159
  page, 161, 174
Scroll down screen, 141, 164, 171
Scroll up screen, 163
Search a table, 267, 271, 274
Sector, 290, 291
Sector buffer, 365
Seek disk cylinder, 365
SEG operator, 501
Segment, 11, 421, 519, 519
  address, 26
  boundary, 12
  directives, 504
  offset, 12
  override, 502
  override prefix, 105
  registers, 14
SEGMENT AT directive, 199, 520
SEGMENT directive, 54, 420
Segments and Groups table, 80, 567
Selecting
  active page, 163
  alternative screen routine, 167
  default disk drive, 333
  display page for pointer, 391
Sense media type, 341
.SEQ directive, 521
Serial port data area, 479
Setting
  address of PSP, 493
  color palette, 178
  cursor, 140, 162
  cursor size, 162
  date, 490
  device information, 337
  direction flag. *See* STD instruction
  diskette type, 367
  double-speed threshold, 390
  file attribute, 350
  file date and time, 352
  horizontal limits for pointer, 388
  media ID, 339
  media type, 367
  mouse sensitivity, 390
  palette registers, 179
  pointer exclusion area, 390
  pointer location for mouse, 387
  screen attribute, 161
  vertical limits for pointer, 388
  video mode, 157, 161, 175, 177
Set/reset disk write verification, 335
SETnn instructions, 552
SF flag. *See* Sign flag
Shift
  algebraic instructions, 551
  and round a product, 257
  bits left, 131
  bits right, 130
  count, 517
  key, 199
  logical instructions, 553
  status, 187, 480
SHL instruction, 131, 553
SHL operator, 502
SHLD instruction, 553
Short address, 115
Short integer data, 241
Short jump, 116
SHORT operator, 116, 502, 540
SHR instruction, 130, 553
SHR operator, 502
SHRD instruction, 553
SI register, 16
Sign bit, 4, 131, 221
Sign flag (SF), 17, 120
Signed
Signed binary data, 221
Signed data, 121, 122
Signed division, 238
Signed multiplication, 229
Simplified segment directives, 61, 81, 429
Single-step mode, 484
SIZE operator, 286, 502, 503
SMALL memory model, 61, 513
SORT command, 308
Sorting table entries, 280
Sound, 397
Source index register. *See* SI register
Source operand, 94
Source program, 59, 73
SP register, 15, 23, 24, 435
Speaker, 397
Square brackets. *See* Index operator
SS register, 11, 12, 14, 56
SS:BP pair, 96
SS:SP pair, 14
Stack, 23, 59, 78, 82, 433, 519
Stack frame, 433
Stack pointer register. *See* SP register
Stack segment, 11, 12
STACK combine type, 55, 519
.STACK directive, 61, 521
Starting cluster, 295
.STARTUP directive, 62, 521
Statement, 52
Status codes, 358
STC instruction, 553
STD instruction, 205, 554
Steps in assembly, link, and execute, 75
STI instruction, 554
Store string. *See* STOS

STOS instruction, 203, 205, 208, 215, 554
STOSB instruction, 209, 554
STOSD instruction, 554
STOSW instruction, 209, 554
String comparison, 211
String data, 64, 203
String input/output, 395
String operations, 204
STRUC/STRUCT directive, 521
SUB instruction, 222, 554
Subdirectory, 345, 346
Subprograms, 419
SUBTITLE directive, 522
Subtracting
  ASCII data, 247
  binary data, 222
  with borrow. *See* SBB
SUBTTL directive, 522
Symbolic code, 34
Symbolic instruction set, 91
Symbols table, 426, 568, 80
System data area, 481
System date, 490
System equipment data area, 479
System time, 484, 490
Systems services interrupt, 486

T (Trace) DEBUG command, 30, 35, 577
Tab, 149
  character, 370
  stops, 374
Table, 265
  on disk, 266
  searching, 271, 274
  sorting, 280
TASM command, 74, 564
TBYTE directive, 68
TCREF command, 86, 568
Terminate address, 488
Terminate but stay resident (TSR), 470
Terminate program execution, 59, 488
Test for drive ready, 366
Test if diskette ready, 360
TEST instruction, 127, 555
Text mode, 140, 158
_TEXT segment name, 82
TEXTEQU directive, 522
TF flag, 17, 120
THIS operator, 503
Threshold speed, 384
Time-out data area, 482
Timer, 487
TINY memory model, 61, 513
TITLE directive, 53, 57, 524
TLINK command, 84, 110, 569
Tracing
  execution, 35, 40
  memory blocks, 536
Tracks on disk, 290
Translate data. *See* XLAT
Trap flag (TF), 17, 120
TSR program, 470
Turbo assembler, 80, 567
Turbo C, 441
Two's complement notation, 4
Two-pass assembler, 83
.TYPE operator, 286, 503
Type specifiers, 497

U (Unassemble) DEBUG command, 30, 42, 577
Unconditional transfer instructions, 94
Underline attribute, 160
Uninitialized value, 63
Unpacked BCD data, 245, 249
Unsigned data
  binary, 121, 122, 221
  division, 237
  multiplication, 229
Upper memory area, 454, 455
USE32 operand, 60

Verify sectors, 363
VGA monitor, 157
Video
  adapters, 157
  BIOS, 157
  controller, 157
  data area-1, 481
  data area-2, 482
  display area, 140, 157, 173
  mode, 157, 166
  monitor. *See* Screen
Viewing memory locations, 31
Volume label, 295

W (Write) DEBUG command, 30, 45, 578
w-bit, 526, 528
WAIT instruction, 555
WIDTH operator, 517
Word, 2, 67
WORD
  directive. *See* DW directive
  operator, 46, 149, 420, 519
Write
  .COM program, 108
  control data to drive, 337
  disk sector, 338, 360
  extended sector buffer, 365
  pixel dot, 179
  record, 307, 327
  sector buffer, 366
  teletype operation, 166

XADD instruction, 555
.XALL directive, 405
XCHG instruction, 100, 555
XCREF directive, 524
XLAT instruction, 277, 556
XLATB instruction, 556
.XLIST directive, 524
XOR
  instruction, 127, 556
  logical operator, 500

Zero flag (ZF), 17, 119